BENEDICT XVI: A LIFE

BENEDICT XVI: A LIFE

Volume I
Youth in Nazi Germany
to the Second Vatican Council
1927–1965

Peter Seewald

Translated by Dinah Livingstone

BLOOMSBURY CONTINUUM
LONDON · OXFORD · NEW YORK · NEW DELHI · SYDNEY

BLOOMSBURY CONTINUUM
Bloomsbury Publishing Plc
50 Bedford Square, London, WC1B 3DP, UK

BLOOMSBURY, BLOOMSBURY CONTINUUM and the Diana logo are
trademarks of Bloomsbury Publishing Plc

First published in 2020 in Germany as *Benedikt XVI: Ein Leben* by Droemer Verlag,
an imprint of Verlagsgruppe Droemer Knaur GmbH & Co.KG, Munich

First published in Great Britain 2020
Copyright © Peter Seewald, 2020

A catalogue record for this book is available from the British Library

Library of Congress Cataloguing-in-Publication data has been applied for

ISBN: HB: 978-1-4729-7919-3; TPB: 978-1-4729-7918-6;
eBook: 978-1-4729-7920-9; ePDF: 978-1-4729-7916-2

2 4 6 8 10 9 7 5 3 1

Typeset by Deanta Global Publishing Services, Chennai, India
Printed and bound in Great Britain by CPI Group (UK) Ltd, Croydon CR0 4YY

MIX
Paper from
responsible sources
FSC® C020471

To find out more about our authors and books visit www.bloomsbury.com
and sign up for our newsletters

Contents

List of Illustrations   vii
Foreword   ix

PART ONE   THE BOY

1. Easter Saturday   3
2. The Impediment   10
3. The Dreamland   17
4. 1933: 'Holy Year'   28
5. The 'German Christians'   37
6. With Burning Concern   47
7. The Calm before the Storm   62
8. The Seminary   73
9. War   89
10. Resistance   100
11. The End   113

PART TWO   THE MASTER STUDENT

12. Zero Hour   129
13. The Scholars' Mountain   141
14. Guilt and Atonement   152
15. Upheaval in Thinking   161
16. The Glass Bead Game   176
17. Augustine   188
18. Storm and Stress   202
19. The Key Reading   222
20. The Major Orders   238

21. The Curate 248
22. The Examination 262
23. The Abyss 276
24. The New Heathens and the Church 291

PART THREE THE COUNCIL

25. A Star is Born 307
26. The Network 320
27. Council 332
28. The Battle Begins 343
29. The Genoa Speech 356
30. The Spin Doctor 370
31. The World on the Brink 382
32. Seven Days That Changed the Catholic
   Church For Ever 393
33. German Wave 408
34. Power Sources 424
35. In the School of the Holy Spirit 437
36. The Legacy 449

Notes 465
Index 491

List of Illustrations

1. Joseph Ratzinger as a schoolboy in 1933 at Aschau am Inn, his father's last family home. (© picture-alliance/dpa/dpaweb)
2. The Ratzinger family in the mid-1930s. (© KNA Copyright 1938, KNA)
3. The former police station and family home in Marktl am Inn, in which Benedict was born. (© picture-alliance/dpa/Sven Hoppe)
4. The family in 1932 with grandparents in the Bavarian Forest, at the parental home. (© Archiv Nussbaum)
5. The young Ratzingers in 1930. (© Archiv Walter)
6. The three Ratzinger children in 1937 in Traunstein. (© Archiv Walter)
7. The farm building in the village of Hufschlag near Traunstein, acquired by Ratzinger's father after Hitler seized power. (© picture-alliance/dpa/Peter Kneffel)
8. The future Pope in uniform, Munich, 1943. (© Getty Images/ AFP)
9. Joseph Ratzinger in 1958 as Assistant Professor of Philosophical Theology at the High School in Freisung. (© KNA-Bild/KNA)
10. Ratzinger is ordained priest on June 29th 1951 in Freisung Cathedral by Cardinal Michael von Faulhaber. (© picture-alliance/dpa/lby/Erzbistum München-Freising)
11. Ratzinger as a newly ordained priest with his brother Georg and friend Rupert Berger (© Stadtarchiv Traunstein/Oswald Kettenberger)

12. Family photo in July 1951 at Traunstein. (© ddp/SIPA USA)
13. Ratzinger as chaplain in 1951 outside the Munich presbytery of the Church of the Holy Blood. (© Archiv Pfarrei Heilig Blut, München)
14. Mass in the mountains of the Chiemgauer Alps, Autumn 1952. (© KNA-Bild/KNA)
15. Solemn Mass at St Peter's in Rome during the Second Vatican Council. (© epd-bild/ Agenzia Romano Siciliani)
16. Joseph Ratzinger as Professor at the University of Bonn. (© picture-alliance/Privat dpa/lby)
17. Ratzinger with Cardinal Josef Frings of Cologne, at the opening of the Second Vatican Council. (© picture-alliance/dpa/dpaweb)
18. Ratzinger with his sister Maria at the garden gate of Bergstrasse 6, Pentling. (© Horst Hanske)

Foreword

It was a cold, wet day in November 1992 when I had my first 'date' with Joseph Ratzinger. It was about a profile of him for the *Süddeutsche Zeitung* magazine. I was surprised by how openly the 'Grand Inquisitor' talked to me.

During the following years I have put at least two thousand questions to the cardinal, the pope, the pope emeritus, perhaps even more. He only hesitated to answer the very last ones. He said an answer would 'inevitably interfere with the present pope's matters. I ought and want to avoid anything in that direction.'

No, Pope Emeritus Benedict XVI has never become a parallel pope or even an antipope. On the contrary, he is scrupulously careful not to get in his successor's way. But he has never taken a vow of silence. His last words in Castel Gandolfo as a reigning pope stressed that: 'From 8 p.m. I will no longer be pope, no longer the supreme pastor of the Catholic Church … But with all my heart, my love, my prayers, my thoughts and all my intellectual powers I should like to go on working for the general good, the good of the church and humanity.'

What a journey! A boy from a Bavarian village on the edge of the Alps becomes the supreme head of the oldest, greatest and most mysterious institution in the world, the Catholic Church, with its 1.3 billion members. He was the first German for 500 years to sit on the chair of St Peter. He was a theologian whose ecclesiastical and academic work was already important. Joseph Ratzinger has written history. As the Vatican Council 'greenhorn', as a renewer of theology, as a prefect who, side by side with Karol Wojtyła, kept the ship of the church on course through the storm of that time. He is also the first reigning pope to resign from the office on grounds of age. There has never been a 'pope emeritus'. Never before has a single person changed the papacy from one day to the next so much as he has.

The world is deeply divided about how to understand Benedict XVI. He is regarded as one of the cleverest thinkers of our time. At the same time he has remained a controversial figure. An uncomfortable one who exasperates his opponents. The French philosopher Bernard-Henri Lévy remarked that, as soon as Ratzinger's name came up, 'prejudices, falseness and even plain disinformation' ruled any discussion. The Austrian media expert Dr Friederike Glavanovics reported in an academic research paper that, with Joseph Ratzinger, many journalists tended compulsively to embed negative news into an even more negative context. An image has been constructed 'that is shaped not by reality but only by viability'.[1] It was a fictional picture meant to serve a particular purpose.

Who really is this man? What is his message? Was there actually a '1968 trauma' that changed him from a progressive theologian into a reactionary? Was he the 'Panzer Cardinal' he was made out to be? Did he keep silent and hush up the abuse scandal? Was his papacy an unparalleled failure, as his opponents never tire of maintaining? *Benedict XVI: A Life* searches for clues about the provenance, personality and the dramatic ups and downs in the life of the German pope. By putting the pieces back together – for example, in the Williamson and the Vatileaks affairs – it comes to some surprising conclusions. It was important to maintain a critical distance – but also to look without prejudice. Otherwise, genuine understanding is not possible.

No book can be written without help, especially not a biography covering nearly a century, from the end of the Weimar Republic to the digital age. My thanks go to the approximately one hundred contemporary witnesses who were available for interview. I also want to thank all the colleagues and friends who have accompanied me in this work with advice and assistance and with their prayers, especially the pope's brother, Georg Ratzinger, for details about the family history and Dr Manuel Schlögl, who talked to people who knew Ratzinger and was willing to read through the manuscript. Tanja Pilger brilliantly made excerpts from mountains of books and other materials. I'd like to thank Martina Wendl and my son Jakob for transcribing the recordings. I thank my wife and my family for their comforting support, especially shown at those times when the author despaired over the volume of material and his own insufficiency.

I owe thanks to Archbishop Georg Gänswein for supporting the project from the beginning and for his impressive frankness. My special thanks, though, go to Pope Benedict. Over the years he himself has answered the most abstruse questions with angelic patience. He is surely the only reigning pope who left messages on an answering machine, as he did for my sons. I especially remember the summer of 2012. I was visiting the pope in Castel Gandolfo. He was in a terrible state. He seemed not only exhausted but also strangely depressed. I only realised afterwards that during those weeks he was struggling with the decision that would change the papacy for ever.

As pope of a new epoch, Benedict XVI was both the end of the old and also the beginning of something new, a bridge between two worlds. He showed that religion and reason were not contraries. That reason was in fact the guarantee needed to protect religion from sliding into wild fantasies and fanaticism. He charmed people with his generous nature, his great spirit, the honesty of his analysis and the depth and beauty of his words. With him everyone knew that what he proclaimed, however uncomfortable it might be, was dependably in accord with the teaching of the gospel, continuity with the church fathers and the reforms of the Second Vatican Council. It went with the advice not just to fiddle about with externals but to take a deep look at the nature of things, at what life and faith actually are. We may not agree with all his positions. But there is no doubt that Joseph Ratzinger can be called not only an important academic but perhaps the greatest theologian ever to sit on the chair of St Peter. He was also a spiritual master who convinced through his uprightness and genuineness. His direction was not outdated: quite the contrary. As his successor put it: 'A great pope, great for the power and penetration of his intelligence; great for his important contribution to theology; great for his love of the church and human beings.' And finally, 'great for his virtues and faith'.

Peter Seewald
Munich, February 2020

PART ONE

The Boy

I

Easter Saturday

The few figures scurrying along the pavement had their collars well turned up. The air was cold and damp. A thin fog lay over the dimly lit streets, but in the dark night sky between the rooftops a few stars could be seen twinkling.

It was Good Friday, 15 April 1927. In St Oswald's Church the final preparations were being made for the Easter festival. In accordance with the official order of service before the reform by Pius XII, Christ's resurrection was not celebrated on the night before Easter Sunday but on the morning of Easter Saturday. Jesus was dead. Crucified, dead and buried. Descended into the 'deepest depths', as the Greek text of the Apostles' Creed puts it, into the Underworld, that godforsakenness which had long also invaded the upper world.

On his round, police officer Joseph Ratzinger inspected the western area of his beat, with the Brühl family's steam saw mill, the lemonade factory and the 'children's institution' run by nuns. Ratzinger was an upright, capable man, precise to his very bones. His hair was cut short at the sides, the 'German haircut'. He stood for dignity and decency and aimed for the happy medium. Nothing too little, nothing too much. At 1.64 metres tall he did not even reach the required height, but he stood up straight as a candle. He abhorred hypocrisy, vanity and opportunism. That also meant having the courage to defend the truth. Benedict XVI said later that his father had only completed elementary school, 'but he was a man with common sense. He thought differently from how you were supposed to think then, and had a certain mastery that convinced people.'[1]

He had been overseeing the place for the last two years, as station commander and chief, with an assistant who was called 'Wet Sepp', for good reason. The church, the pub and the town hall were at the centre of the town, both geographically and culturally. There was also a shop. The shop window displayed tools, aprons for housewives and toys, including a small teddy bear, which would play a certain part later. Of course, as a policeman he couldn't be on familiar terms with everyone. On Sunday he sang in the church choir. At home he passionately played the zither, which he had inherited from his Bohemian mother. However, he was also inclined to lose his temper. A testimonial dated 29 October 1920, from the Regional Police Headquarters, reported: 'At work diligent, reliable, useful, competent, satisfactory', but also 'easily provoked'. Nevertheless, it was remarked that his leadership was 'without complaints'.[2] The local newspaper reported that 'in the comparatively short time he has been here, through his sense of fairness, as well as approachability and friendliness in his dealings,' the police chief had 'won the respect of the inhabitants of Marktl'.[3]

The wind had grown stronger; the cold froze your nose onto your face. Winter seemed to be intent on a final stand against the oncoming spring. But the Holy Week silence already gave the place an air of peace, as if after a lost battle. Ten days earlier Ratzinger senior had celebrated his 50th birthday. Had he become more like a grandfather than a father? And Maria? She was 43 years old and could hardly be called a young mother. Some of the neighbours were gossiping unkindly about 'such an old woman having another child'. Now, upstairs on the first floor of their flat in the Police House, Maria was in labour with her third child.

Nineteen twenty-seven was a restless year. The jump from being under the Kaiser to democracy, from a monarchical authoritarian state to emancipation and self-determination, had changed Germany. Women could vote. Workers had rights. The social changes not only caused a new *feeling* about life but also required a new *model* of life. 'We are in the strange state,' said the then 20-year-old Klaus Mann, 'of constantly believing everything is possible'.

There was something in the air. Something new was on the way in, a wave of changes pushing the course of things in another direction. In the big cities a modern mass culture was developing, with films, fashion magazines and sports events. The theatre wanted not just to stage plays but also to interpret them. Architects and designers developed a new formal language. Mies van der Rohe became famous for building spectacular houses. Freud's psychoanalysis promised far-reaching discoveries about the human psyche and changed the relationship to sexuality.

For a few years Berlin, in particular, was on a cultural high, trying to break free from all the taboos of the Kaiser's time. The unbridled capital wanted the world to feel it was living as crazily and intensely as London, Paris and New York put together. Every evening, 30 theatres put on plays to attract the public. In the Haus Vaterland pleasure palace on the Potsdamer Platz, up to 8,000 partygoers celebrated every night. There were more than a hundred cabarets, night clubs, fringe shows, revues and gay and lesbian meeting places. One of the most famous artists of her time was Anita Berber, with her red hair and garish make-up, who stepped out of her car onto the Kurfürstendamm wearing her sable fur and monocle. She was well known for her expressive nude performances, such as her 'vice, terror and ecstasy dances'. The French writer Jean Cassou was enthralled. Berlin, he wrote, was the 'youngest, most systematically crazy, and most guiltlessly perverse city in the world'.[4]

In the field of literature, the birth year of the future pope blossomed with a creative wealth seldom seen anywhere in the world. There was Hermann Hesse's exciting *Steppenwolf,* Franz Kafka's *Amerika* and the final volume of Marcel Proust's *À la recherche du temps perdu (In Search of Lost Time).* In 1927 Ernest Hemingway published *Men without Women,* Arthur Schnitzler his *Spiel im Morgengrauen,* Carl Zuckmayer his *Schinderhannes.* The young Bertolt Brecht, author of the *Dreigroschenoper (Threepenny Opera),* with its world-famous 'Ballad of Mack the Knife', published his *Hauspostille.* In philosophy, the German academic Martin Heidegger sought the solution to the riddle of the world with his *Sein und Zeit (Being and Time),* which was to become the foundation of existentialist philosophy. Cecil B. DeMille, co-founder of the film metropolis Hollywood, offered a counterpoint. In 1927 he released the first Jesus blockbuster in film history. It was called *The King of Kings.*[5]

Suddenly, it felt as if the whole world was in the midst of upheaval. The Soviet Union began the collectivization of farming (4 million people died in the ensuing famine). In October, Mustafa Kemal Pascha, who later called himself Kemal Atatürk, gave his programmatic speech on 'the new Turkey' to representatives and supporters of the Republican People's Party in Angora (today Ankara). In Italy, Benito Mussolini, *il Duce,* was making fascism acceptable. Germany increasingly suffered from inflation, mass unemployment and the quarrelling of countless political groups. On average the 19 cabinets of the Weimar Republic lasted only about eight months. On the other hand, the longing for a new humanity, hope for a better future and the expectation of change remained.

And somewhere on the sidelines, the most notorious of leaders was rubbing his hands, feeling that his time would soon come. A certain Adolf Hitler re-founded a party in February 1925, the National Socialist German Workers' Party (NSDAP). When it was banned in 1923, it looked as if it had run aground. After the march on the Munich Feldherrnhalle (Field Marshals' Hall) in 1923, Hitler had been sentenced to five years' imprisonment. Winifred Wagner, Richard Wagner's daughter-in-law, sent woollen blankets, a jacket, stockings, 'nosh' and books to him in prison. Helene Bechstein, wife of the piano manufacturer Edwin Bechstein, sent him a gramophone with marching music.[6] In 1927 *Mein Kampf,* Hitler's crazy ideological–political and anti-Semitic hate work, became the Nazi movement's official programme. At that time the NSDAP had 27,000 members. Over the next three years that figure grew to 400,000.

Marktl, on the River Inn, was the 12th posting in Ratzinger's not particularly rapid career path. On the political map, the small town, with 600 residents, belonged to Upper Bavaria, but spiritually it belonged to the Lower Bavarian diocese of Passau. Quite close by, in the village of Pildenau, 20 kilometres away, a pope had come into the world, Pope Damasus II.[7] As bishop of Poppo, he was taken to Rome by a Tuscan army on 16 July 1048. The very next day he overthrew the reigning Pope Benedict IX. In fact, Pope Damasus's pontificate only lasted 24 days before he died of malaria. Possibly also, as some historians maintain, from a poisoned pill.

Ratzinger senior's postings were spread all over Bavaria. At posting number 11, in Pleiskirchen near Altötting, his daughter Maria was born on 7 December 1921. Her second name was Theogona, meaning dedicated to God (after the name her aunt took as a nun).

Then Georg was born on 15 January 1924. He was called after his mother's favourite brother, who had emigrated to the USA.

How come Ratzinger never really felt at home? Because he was headstrong? Because he basically did not like this job he carried out so conscientiously? He confessed to a neighbour that if he could have been born again, he certainly would not have been a policeman but a farmer. He studied religious and political literature and sat for hours over the daily paper, smoking a Virginia. His political idol was the Austrian Chancellor, Ignaz Seipel of the Christian Social Party, a prelate and theologian, several of whose books were on Ratzinger's shelves. Seipel was controversial, but even the social democratic Vienna newspaper *Arbeiterzeitung* praised him, saying he was 'one of the statesmen of European stature the bourgeois parties had produced'.

The actual love of Ratzinger senior's life, his whole passion, was of course religion, the Catholic Christian faith. Even when he was at elementary school he had stood out as particularly devout, encouraged by a committed curate. Another teacher recognized the child's musical gift and put him in the church choir. Like his religious model, the monastery porter Brother Konrad of Altötting, as a young man Ratzinger also longed to enter the religious life. However, his reception into the Passau Maria-Hilf Capuchin monastery was refused because he did not have a declaration of consent from his parents. 'His fundamental concern was religion,' his son was to say, and indeed 'a very deep, intense and masculine piety'.[8]

Police Officer Ratzinger finished his round. The biting cold had relented and the snowfall was followed by lighter rain and wind. Since Maundy Thursday, Christ's Passion had been present in every house in Marktl. After the celebration of the Last Supper the bells were silenced. Hour by hour the *Triduum Sacrum* – the three holy days from Maundy Thursday to Easter Saturday – proceeded to a climax. On Good Friday the inhabitants of the surrounding villages came in to pray the 14 stations of the Cross with the priest. Alcohol and meat were banned. Good Friday was the Catholic Church's strictest fast day. Only one full meal was allowed all day. At three o'clock, the time Christ died, the faithful gathered to commemorate his suffering and death. In an alcove in the church, Christ's tomb had been set up, before which the faithful knelt in prayer.

In St Oswald's Church, the very young curate Joseph Strangl would soon begin the final preparations for the Resurrection. In the police building near by, the former seat of the Bavarian Prince–Elector, a light was still burning on the first floor. The midwife Emilie Wallinger had arrived. The baby took its time – and did not come a minute too soon.

In the early morning of Easter Saturday, at 4.15 a.m., the police officer's youngest offspring came into the world, safe and sound – Joseph Aloisius Ratzinger. His mother was too weak to get up, but his father did not hesitate long. Rather awkwardly, he carried the baby into the church. The liturgy had already begun; all the church windows were covered with blackout curtains; the whole space was dimly lit by a few candles. Into the silent darkness soon would come a cry. Muted at first, then ever more clearly: 'Lumen Christi! The Light of Christ.' A glorious ceremony was on its way. The bells pealed so forcefully that it was as if they had drawn new breath from the days they had been kept silent. The organ rose to the Gloria. 'Christ is risen,' the priest sang out. All at once the curtains fell, and a flood of light broke in, dazzling the congregation.

It was 8.30 in the morning, exactly four hours and 15 minutes after the birth, when Ratzinger the police officer laid his child in the arms of the nun Adelma Rohrhirsch. She was standing in for his sister Anna, the actual godmother, who could no longer travel. While the priest spoke the words of blessing and let the freshly consecrated holy water flow over the baby, the child was literally immersed, body and soul, in the Easter mystery. Perhaps that was the happiest moment of his father's life. His child was healthy. The child was called Joseph, like himself and also his own father. 'God will add' is the Hebrew meaning of the name. It had pleased the Lord God to give him this boy at his advanced age. In all the circumstances and signs accompanying this event it was impossible not to see a special blessing, perhaps a promise, which it would be up to the child to fulfil.

That child, the future cardinal, has always been reserved about personal matters. But he himself has interpreted the circumstances of his birth as a sign of a special light. His being 'the first in the new Easter water' was also always seen by his family as 'a kind of privilege – a privilege containing a special hope and also a special commission, to be revealed in the course of time'.[9] His parents saw the event 'as very significant and told me so from the beginning,' he said to me in our conversation. That 'awareness' always 'accompanied' him and 'penetrated me deeper and deeper'. He saw these things as 'a message' and kept on trying to understand it. So his writings about what happened to Christ on Holy Saturday were not just 'something thought out', he explained, 'but something bound up with the basis, the beginning of my existence, which I not only thought but also experienced'.[10]

The testimony of Holy Saturday related 'to human history as a whole, as well as our own century', but also, he added, 'to my own life'. We find in it 'on the one hand, the darkness, uncertainty, questioning, the risk, the threat, but also the certainty that there is light, that life is worth living, worth continuing'. That day, 'dominated by Christ – mysterious, hidden and also present – has become a programme for my life.'

For the people of Marktl the year 1927 remained memorable for a quite different reason. After a long time being built, finally the new bridge over the River Inn was finished. It was dedicated with a festival procession. At the front went the cross with servers, clergy and plenty of incense. The ceremony was followed by a party with beer and brass band music. Police Commander Ratzinger was on the spot watching out that everything was in order. He could have had no idea that his child, whom his Maria had given birth to that year, would also be a 'bridge-builder' – a *Pontifex*.

2

The Impediment

It was not his fault that he and Maria had only been able to marry so late. It was not until he had been promoted to sergeant (*Wachtmeister*) with a monthly salary of 150 marks that Ratzinger could risk planning a family. Although at first sight the couple may have seemed very different, they clearly had plenty in common.

Both were intelligent, capable and good-looking. Both came from respectable, prolific families. Both had lost a father early on (Maria at 28 and Joseph at 26). Both practised a decent Catholic piety. But above all, both were still available. This was also because the master baker Schwarzmeier, a widower from Munich with two children, who had been intended for Maria, chose her sister Sabine instead. She was nine years younger.

The starting point for their relationship was the *Altöttinger Liebfrauenbote,* a local weekly paper which reached nearly every Catholic household. In the edition of 11 July 1920, Maria was able to read the following text: 'Mid. civ. serv. sgl. Cath. 43 y, clean past, from the country, seeks gd Cath. pure girl, gd cook & all hswk, loc. exper., with furn., to marry asap.' The advertiser, who clearly wanted to save as much money as possible by using as many abbreviations as possible, asked for 'offers if poss. wth pic'.[1] This announcement was not the first attempt by the police officer. Four months earlier he had advertised in similar terms for a wife 'with dowry & some assets'. This time he asked for 'assets desired, but not requirement'. In the meanwhile, he had been promoted from 'lower civil servant' to the more attractive 'mid-ranking civil servant'.

After a daughter, the father of the future pope was the first-born son of a farming family with nine children. He was born on 6 March

1877 in Rickering in Lower Bavaria, a hamlet with six houses and about 40 inhabitants. After his time at school he had to work as a farmhand on other farms. When he was 20, he was called up to the army. From 14 October 1897 he spent his two years of military service with the Royal Bavarian 16th Infantry Regiment in Passau, the 2,000-year-old Roman city on the Danube. He served as a private and was even promoted to non-commissioned officer. He was an attractive, dashing lad with a fashionable moustache, distinguished by a Golden Weapons Proficiency Badge for his sureness of aim.

After his discharge from active service on 19 September 1899, he remained in the army for three more years. Meanwhile, his father had become old and ill. Not only his older sister but also his brother Anton had established themselves on the farm in Rickering, which he himself was actually due to inherit. On 22 August 1902 he moved to the Royal Bavarian Police Corps Reserve as a non-commissioned officer. In April 1919 the Revolutionary Workers' Council in Munich, led by the anarchist writers Erich Mühsam and Ernst Toller, set up the first Socialist Soviet Republic on German soil. Ratzinger senior resigned from his position: 'I swore an oath to the King', he insisted, 'I can't now serve the Republic.'[2] He only returned to his job when King Ludwig III explicitly released his employees from their oath of loyalty.

The Ratzingers were not like any other family. They could almost be called a clerical family. At any rate, they had been in the church's service from time immemorial. The first traces of the family name can be found in the fourteenth century, in the prince–bishopric of Passau, one of the dioceses founded by the English missionary monk Boniface, which at one time stretched as far as Hungary. In a document from the cathedral chapter dated 1304, we find a farm attached to the name Recing, resident in Freinberg. The name attached to the property changed from Recing to Ratzing, from Recingers to Räzingers, then Ratzingers. The earliest evidence of that name comes in 1600, with a Georg Räzinger, followed by a Jakob Räzinger, who, with his first wife, Maria, and after her death with his second wife, Katharina, produced the remarkable total of 17 children.[3]

The Ratzingers moved on, took over an estate in the Bavarian forest belonging to the Passau Cathedral chapter, and finally, in 1801, a farm on the Danube belonging to the Niederaltaich monastery. That was Rickering number 1, in the parish of Schwannenkirchen, where Joseph was born. The farm must have done something for the education of his gifted sons and daughters. Directly and indirectly, it produced no fewer than two nuns and five priests. One of them was the pugnacious Dr Georg Ratzinger, who became part of Bavarian history as an important Catholic social politician and member of Parliament. Another was his gifted brother Thomas, who broke off his theological studies to become a lawyer. There were also the brothers Joseph and Georg, who remained faithful to the family home and visited the farm every year, always on the last Sunday in August.

On her wedding day, Joseph's Maria was 36 years old. She loved life, and was spontaneous, warm-hearted and sociable. A woman with feeling, interested in the theatre. Before the First World War her parents had earned the family considerable prosperity by their skill and hard work. Her father, Isidor Rieger, was originally a journeyman from Swabia; her mother, Maria Peintner, served as a house servant. The couple leased a bakery in Hopfgarten in Austria. Then, with their two first-born children – Maria and Benno – in a handcart, they moved to Bavaria to run their own bakery and a smallholding by Lake Chiemsee. At first, their third child, Georg, had to stay with foster parents. Seven more children were to be born, two of whom did not survive. Their Aunt Rosl described the Rieger family's daily life. They were 'good hard-working people', who 'also had God's blessing'. And she added, 'They always prayed before and after meals, and also usually said the rosary in the evening.'[4] The father was in the bakery from midnight, usually until four o'clock in the afternoon. At four o'clock in the morning the mother saw to three cows, a pig and a horse in the stable.

The day began during the night for little Maria too. Before school began, bread, pretzels and rolls had to be delivered. As well as the work for the bakery, soon she also had to help take care of her seven younger brothers and sisters, while her mother delivered to the larger customers by horse and cart. As well as attending elementary school, every Sunday from 12.30 to 3 p.m. Maria attended religious instruction in the 'Sunday and Holiday School'. Two of her uncles had designed the altars of St Andreas in Salzburg and the convent church of Perpetual Adoration in Innsbruck. In Rimsting her father,

Isidor, had set up not only a 'Village Beautifying Society' but also a 'Pastoral Society'. He was responsible for the community being promoted to a proper parish, so that Mass could be celebrated there every Sunday.

When she was 15, the future pope's mother was 'transferred' (as the school report put it) to Kufstein to work for other families. According to a 'registration form' of the city of Salzburg, from 1 October 1900 to 19 April 1901 she was employed as a house maid by the 'concert master's wife', Maria Zinke. The address was 2nd Floor, Priesterhausgasse 20. After that she worked at a General Zech's, near Frankfurt. When her brothers were called up to serve in the army in the First World War, she ran the bakery in Rimsting, together with her mother and sister Ida. Shortly before she met Joseph Ratzinger, she ended up as pudding cook in the Neuwittelsbach Hotel in the upmarket Munich area of Nymphenburg.[5]

We know nothing about the first meeting of the pope's parents. However, they seem to have quickly come to an agreement. Time was pressing. Then, in 1920, wedding fever broke out in the Rieger household. Ida married on 6 January, Benno on 3 February and brother Isidor on 16 October. Joseph and Maria seized the opportunity and planned for 9 November. By then, the First World War, that 'great catastrophe' which marked the twentieth century, had been over for two years. More than 2 million German soldiers had lost their lives on the battlefields; 720,000 men had returned severely wounded from the front. 'The rotten old order has collapsed!', the SPD (Social Democratic Party) politician Philipp Scheidemann shouted from the balcony of the Berlin Reichstag on the afternoon of 9 November 1918 to an excited crowd: 'The Hohenzollerns have abdicated! Long live the German Republic.'[6]

That new Republic suffered some terrible years, filled with street battles, armed strikes, workers' uprisings, putsch attempts and political murders, in which about 5,000 people violently lost their lives. When, on 11 February 1919, the National Assembly met for the first time, it was not in Berlin but in Weimar, in order to avoid the feared 'street pressure' in the capital. The heaviest burden proved to be the Versailles Treaty of 28 June 1919, which put the blame for the First World War on Germany and its allies alone – thereby making them responsible for the cost of all the damages.

Alsace-Lorraine went to France, large parts of Posen went to Poland – in total 70,000 km² of land, an area the size of Bavaria. Or, to put it a different way, three-quarters of the iron ore and a quarter of the coal. At the end of January 1921 the Allies made further demands: 226 billion (i.e., thousand million) gold marks, payable in 42 annual instalments (later this sum was reduced to 132 billion), as well as paying the pensions for the Allied war disabled and their families. Economically, Germany was to be radically weakened. At the same time, the victors wanted to profit from the economic power of their former enemy. Which was impossible.

Soon the Reichsmark went into free fall. At the beginning of 1923 a postage stamp still cost 15 *pfennig*. But by June it cost 100 marks, by August 1,000 marks, by the beginning of October 2 million marks and in November 100 million marks. At the height of the inflation in November 1923 one dollar cost 4.2 trillion (4.2 million million) marks. According to the British historian Frederick Taylor, the country was like an out-of-control railway train rushing towards an unknown destination at increasing speed.[7]

Ten days before the planned wedding date, 'Sergeant Joseph Ratzinger I' – the 'I' was officially added to avoid confusion with someone else of the same name – requested 'the Altötting Police Headquarters' in a handwritten letter the 'requisite permission' to 'marry the cook Maria Peintner, spinster'. The letter was barely sent before Joseph and Maria marched into the parish office at Pleiskirchen, where Ratzinger was currently posted, to make an 'engagement agreement' in the presence of the parish priest and the witnesses, Franz Hingerl and Josef Mitternmeier.[8]

Everything was ready, but just before the wedding, a huge problem suddenly arose. An 'impediment to the marriage', as it was officially called. What had happened? The 'impediment' had five letters, and it came up as an addition to the engagement agreement. 'Maria Peintner, Cath. Cook, Rimsting am Chiemsee' were the details given for the bride. But then came that awkward additional abbreviation: 'illeg.' – illegitimate. In plain language, not only had Maria been born out of wedlock but neither had she been 'legitimized' – that is, later acknowledged as her father's biological child. So she did not have the necessary papers.

Maria's mother's name was on the parish baptismal record as 'Maria Peintner from Mühlbach near Brixen, maidservant in Kufstein', but a father was not named. So was Isidor Rieger the baker only her foster father? And where was she actually born? On the 'police registration form' deposited in Munich on 6 May 1920, on the occasion of her beginning work in the Neuwittelsbach Hotel, she gave her place of birth as 'Mühlbach, near Brixen, Austria'. But was that right? And why was Maria known in the Rimsting school as the 'Rieger daughter' but in her reports always called 'Maria Peintner'?

There has been uncertainty about the pope's mother's birth up until our own time. Even when they were grown up, Joseph, Georg and Maria still believed that their mother came into the world in South Tyrol. To put it plainly: Maria was an illegitimate child. And not only Maria, but both her own mother and father – the grandparents of the future pope – were born out of wedlock. However, what was commonly regarded as a disgrace was not actually so uncommon. According to the baptismal registers in the municipality of Mühlbach, South Tyrol – Rio di Pusteria today – during the nineteenth century about one third of the women who already had children were not married. They were not able to get married. You needed the necessary money to do so, and many of them simply did not have it.

Maria's father, Isidor Rieger, was the illegitimate son of Johann Reiss from Günzburg, a journeyman who earned his living by repairing mills. Isidor's mother was Maria Anna Rieger, daughter of a day labourer. He was born on 22 March 1860, at 8 a.m., in Welden near Augsburg, and at noon he was 'hurriedly' (as it says literally on the birth register) baptized in the parish church of the Annunciation. He was likewise never 'legitimized' by his father.[9]

The later confusion was explained by the fact that both the grandmother and the mother of the future pope not only had the same first name and surname but also the same birthplace: Mühlbach. But one Mühlbach, the grandmother's, was really in South Tyrol (the old mill of a village called Raas). The other Mühlbach, the daughter's, was near Kiefersfelden, in the district of Rosenheim. Without her mother ever telling her, Maria was born on 8 January at 4 p.m. in a house that specialized in helping unmarried pregnant women to give birth. (This fact was discovered by the local historian Johann

Nussbaum.) The reason why the daughter was never legitimized was her mother's parsimony. Her mother argued that, anyway, girls would get another name when they got married.

However, after all the excitement the wedding was still able to take place. As they had planned, on 9 November 1920 Maria and Joseph said 'yes' to each other in the Pleiskirchen Registry Office. At the church wedding in St Nikolaus's Church on the same day, farmer Anton Ratzinger and cashier Johann Ratzinger were the witnesses. The reredos image was of the Immaculate Conception. Over the tabernacle the Lamb of God was enthroned on the book with seven seals.

The mayor of Rimsting had removed the 'marriage impediment' by officially declaring that Maria Peinter was 'the legitimate daughter of the bakers Isidor and Maria Rieger, born Peintner'. Full stop. 'Rieger Maria bears the name Peinter,' the mayor wrote, 'because up until now the father's recognition was lacking and the necessary proofs could not be brought from the Tyrol because of the Italian occupation.' Benedict XVI was firmly convinced that Isidor Rieger was really his grandfather and his mother's father. His parents had promised to marry early on, but without a fixed home they simply had not yet got married.[10] Isidor loved his daughter Maria 'very much and she also loved him'.

3

The Dreamland

Fundamental things in Joseph Ratzinger's life were set in his birthplace. It was 'the place where my parents gave life to me; the place where I took my first steps on this Earth; the place where I learned to talk'. And above all, it was 'the place where I was baptized on Holy Saturday morning and became a member of Jesus Christ's church'.[1]

The symbolism of Holy Saturday never left him. That 'darkest mystery of the faith', which is also 'the clearest sign of hope'. He thought about it all through his life. On the night of Christ's descent the 'unthinkable' happened: 'Love penetrated the realm of death. Even in the deepest darkness we can hear a voice calling us, we can reach for a hand to grasp us and lift us out.'[2]

His actual memories of Marktl were only what his parents and siblings passed on to him: for example, the story of the dentist who arrived at her practice on a motor bike. He kept the teddy from the small shop opposite, which he had wanted so much. Ultimately, it came to Rome and sat on a chair in the papal apartments.

He also kept the worry about his health, for as a late-born child he was not only a particularly delicate but also a particularly weak child. He nearly died when he contracted diphtheria. The despairing mother was reminded of her husband's youngest brother, who was paralysed on one side after getting diphtheria. Little Joseph could eat nothing and cried day and night. Finally, Sister Adlema, his godmother, saved him by feeding him gruel. A few years later, a doctor diagnosed him with a heart defect and his mother nursed him like the apple of her eye. This surely contributed to the fact that the future professor and cardinal always felt that his health was poor.

The family only stayed in Marktl for another two years. On 11 July 1929 the police officer moved with his whole household to the Baroque city of Tittmoning, 20 kilometres away. He had been promoted to Security Commissioner and hoped that here his children would have better educational opportunities. For Joseph it was a bull's eye. If there was a time when he was completely happy, then it was during these childhood years spent in an environment he later would simply call 'Dreamland'.

Their arrival itself was intoxicating. In Marktl they had lived in an imposing house. But in Tittmoning the Ratzingers moved into the most beautiful building in the whole city, the so-called 'Stubenrauchhaus', number 39 in the City Square, with its grand porch and the splendid Baroque façade; it also had oriel windows! From the second floor there was a view of the picturesque square, with its mighty gates, the noble fountains, the high towers of the collegiate church. Here and there a horse-drawn cab could be seen, occasionally also a motor car. On cattle market day the farmers bargained for the best prices, and there were festive processions of splendidly arrayed horses. Only the night watchman scared the children at first, as he monotonously called out the time on each hour: 'Hear you people and take stock, now it has struck twelve o'clock!'

Further down the street to the left there was an ironmongery, and on the right there was a haberdashery. In the building behind was the police station. The staff consisted of a city and a state police officer (one in a blue and the other in a green uniform) as well as the Security Commissioner. The detection rate would soon reach nearly 100 per cent. Once, the Commissioner even had to proceed against his own landlord after the landlord's maid Rosa complained of brutal treatment.

The house next door was the publishing house Anton Pustet. Its shop window displayed the latest titles, perhaps Erich Maria Remarque's *Im Westen nichts Neues* (*All Quiet on the Western Front*) or Alexander Döblin's *Berlin Alexanderplatz*. Later, Lion Feuchtwanger's *Erfolg* appeared there, a *roman-à-clef* and a multifaceted social panorama of the early 1920s. In it, a character called Rupert Kutzner and his movement called the 'True Germans' Hitler and the NSDAP were unmistakably portrayed.[3]

For Joseph's mother it was drudgery having to lug her shopping, wood and coal upstairs in the Stubenrauchhaus. The paving was cracked, the stairs narrow and the rooms full of nooks and crannies. But for the children their home was an adventure playground. The building had once belonged to Catholic canons. After the turmoil of the Thirty Years War they came together as a residential community – the 'Institute for Secular Priests living in Community' – and reintroduced the Rule of St Augustine. This became a model which caused a stir throughout the whole of Europe. Bartholomäus Holzhauser, the founder, consulted princes and dukes and even got support from Pope Innocent X. The very room in which the Ratzinger children slept and played was the former chapter meeting room, in which the canons used to confer over community affairs and read aloud from Augustine's writings. Holzhauser died with a reputation for holiness. In the Stubenrauchhaus, he not only wrote some 'Secret Visions' but also left behind an exegesis of the *Secret Revelation of John*.[4] In his memoirs Ratzinger expressly refers to Holzhauser's 'apocalyptic aspects', which clearly interested him early on.

With its 4,500 inhabitants, Tittmoning was a trading and artistic city, once a centre for important architects, sculptors, painters and goldsmiths. Its streets and squares were picturesque, with fountains, sculptures and ornate house façades. Its monastery church of the Augustinian Hermits (Austin Friars) was a Baroque jewel in black, white and gold. An imposing fortress stood on a hill. During the 1920s it accommodated a group belonging to the Catholic youth movement Quickborn, supported by Romano Guardini. To complete the idyll, this beautiful city was blessed with a view of mountain tops and ridges, mixed woodland and lush green hills. It was as if the whole of the region in which Tittmoning was set, the Rupertiwinkel ('Rupert's Corner', named after St Rupert), had fallen directly from the blue-and-white heaven above.

Above all, Tittmoning was a religious city, whose inhabitants clearly could not get enough of churches, chapels and monasteries, Mary and St John Nepomuk columns, processions and church festivals. Religion filled the space with sacred buildings and wayside crosses, and filled the time with the liturgy of the church year.

The Ratzinger children walked with their mother to the customs post on the bridge and were amazed that by taking just a few steps they would be in Austria. They played in the 'Bienenheim', a small park in which the residents kept bees. Then there was Auer Maxl, who lived near the cemetery. His great advantage: Maxl had a harmonium and was happy for Georg to play it. Georg's 'inner affinity with music', Ratzinger wrote in an appreciation of his elder brother, was already recognizable in Marktl, where 'anything to do with music' aroused 'his innermost interest'.

For the future cardinal, among his most beautiful memories of Tittmoning were the walks up to the Maria Brunn pilgrim church. The Baroque sanctuary stands in the middle of a wood, beside a rushing mountain stream. One of the ceiling paintings shows Jesus as a boy teaching in the temple in Jerusalem. Highlights of their family life were the open-air theatre performances and trips to Oberdorf on the River Salzach, where in 1818 the most famous carol in the world originated, 'Silent Night, Holy Night'. In St Radegund, also in Austria, the family attended the Passion plays. In retrospect, Ratzinger mentioned that this was where Franz Jägerstätter lived. This peasant father of a family, who was a member of the Third Order of St Francis, was executed by the Nazis on 9 August 1943 as a conscientious objector to military service. Sixty-four years later, on 26 October 2007, his beatification was celebrated in Rome – by that same Joseph Ratinzinger, who may have heard about the brave peasant from his father.

What actually made Tittmoning a 'Dreamland' for the three-to five-year-old boy was the place's spiritual atmosphere. In particular, he was fascinated by the 'mysterious splendour of the monastery church with its Baroque liturgy'. There was 'the rising incense', the psychedelic sound of Gregorian chant, the solemn church music, the perpetual light in a red glass jar, which although it was supposed to be perpetual, seemed only to hang by a silk thread. There was also the 'astonishment that someone could climb up into the pulpit' without being seen.

In this historic jewel of a church the two boys often walked up and down before a picture of the suffering Christ, amazed that Jesus followed them with his eyes, as if he had really come back to life. Georg soon becomes a stave-bearer in a white robe when one of the Tittmoning fraternities held their monthly procession in the church. His younger brother stared in open-eyed wonder at the strange, mystical wall paintings, recited a litany together with his mother and entered with sleepwalking ease into the world of faith, which he found both fantastic and exciting – full of tenderness, beauty and mystery. As Ratzinger said in a sermon on 28 August 1983, it was in this place that he had his 'first personal experiences of a church'. And like 'every first experience', it made a long-lasting impression on him. It was not just 'superficial and naive images', which can easily impress a child; quite early on these had also led to 'deep thoughts'.[5]

The Ratzingers had only been living in their new home for three months and 13 days when the financial crash occurred on the New York Stock Exchange on 24 October 1929. Because of the time difference, the news only reached the Old World after trading had closed. So in Europe it was only on Friday 25 October that there was a panic in the stock markets – Black Friday. The greatest stock market crash of all time resulted in the Great Depression in the USA. Banks were broken, companies went bankrupt. It was the prelude to an economic crisis that threw millions of people into unemployment and poverty. At a stroke the dance on the volcano that gave the 1920s their glamour and brilliance became a dance of death.

The stock market wipe-out inflamed the political conflict in Germany. Both the NSDAP and the Communist parties increased their membership as never before, especially with young people who no longer felt they were represented by the bourgeois parties. Skilfully, the Nazi Party set itself up as the true 'People's Party'. To farmers they stressed the 'preservation of farmland', which had to be 'the basis of our existence'. To the debt-laden middle classes and impoverished white-collar workers they presented themselves as saviours from want. To manual workers they presented themselves as the socialist alternative. To the younger generation they sought to represent the 'emergence of youth' and a movement against the sclerotic and reactionary 'system' of the 'bosses'.

The NSDAP programme offered a 'people's right to self-determination' and a 'share in the profits of the big companies'. 'We have grasped the sinking flag of socialism,' NSDAP propaganda chief Josef Goebbels assured the disappointed supporters of the left. This party would 'build a socialist state in the heart of Europe'. Gregor Strasser, who as Reich Organization Leader was one of the most powerful men in the party, seconded that: 'The people are protesting against an economic order that thinks only about money, profit and dividends. This great anti-capitalist yearning is proof that we are on the brink of a huge, wonderful change in the times.'[6] Above all, the NSDAP positioned itself as a party that would roll back the Versailles Treaty. 'Ten years of shame' had dishonoured and disgraced Germany. It was time for things to change.

Mass marches of the Brown Shirts offered a foretaste of the shared experience of a future world of German heroes. Soon, nearly 455,000 new party members had joined the NSDAP Sturmabteilung (SA), or 'Storm Troopers'. Their hard core assembled in 'Storm premises' and set up soup kitchens for unemployed members. There was even an SA insurance 'in case of damage': meaning the aftermath of 'warriors' smashing up other people's property in street battles.

In the early evening of 10 September 1930, some 10,000 workers, employees, employers businessmen, students and unemployed workers gathered in front of the Berlin Sports Hall in Potsdamer Street in Berlin to listen to one of the most radical opponents of the political system: Adolf Hitler. And Hitler was in his element. As he had explained in *Mein Kampf,* propaganda should be adapted to the low intellectual capacity of the masses. It was not a question of 'satisfying a few scholars or aesthetic youths'. Instead, he wanted to appeal to the emotions: 'The simpler your intellectual ballast and the more you appeal exclusively to the feelings of the masses, the more compelling will be your success.'[7] In the Berlin Sports Hall speech he lambasted the 'political, economic and moral bankruptcy'. The 'will of the people' must be set against 'capitalism and high finance'. 'The public is rushing,' Goebbels noted in his diary.

Hitler's plan made progress. When the polling stations closed four days later, a political earthquake shook what was left of the foundations of the Republic. Two years earlier, as a splinter party, the NSDAP had only received 2.6 per cent of the votes cast. However, when it won 6.4 million votes (18.3 per cent of the vote) in the 14 September 1930 election, it became the second strongest political force in Germany, after the SPD with 8.6 million votes cast (24.5 per cent). The NSDAP sent 107 deputies to the Reichstag, the SPD 143. The Communists also made gains. About 4.6 million voters had voted for the KPD (Communist Party of Germany), who thus gained 77 parliamentary seats.

The Weimar Republic had been unable to improve people's economic distress. The reparation demands of the victors suffocated the young democracy like a noose drawn tighter and tighter round its neck. According to the findings of electoral researcher Jürgen Falter, independent farmers in the Protestant areas were particularly susceptible to Hitler's message. The NSDAP achieved its best results in Wiefelstede, in the constituency of Weser-Ems, with 67.8 per cent, and in Schwesing in Schleswig-Holstein, with 61.7 per cent of the votes.[8] In the cities, Protestants migrated in droves to Nazi-linked German Christian groups, whose aim was to set up a non-denominational national church.

At first, the Catholic Church distanced itself from the growing Hitler party. In October 1930 *L'Osservatore Romano,* the official papal newspaper, declared that membership of the NSDAP was 'not compatible with a Catholic conscience'. The archbishop of Munich, Cardinal Michael von Faulhaber, described National Socialist ideology as 'heresy'. It was 'strictly forbidden' to support the Nazis in any way. In August 1932 the German Bishops' Conference condemned the NSDAP party programmes as 'heretical' and 'against the faith'. Catholics were forbidden 'to belong to the Party', and those who disobeyed this ruling were excluded from the sacraments.[9]

The Ratzingers were also affected by the stock market crash and its dramatic consequences. The salaries of state officials were then often paid late, but what was even worse was that inflation had eaten up their savings. 'We were poor,' as Joseph later described their situation. You had to 'economize hard,' said his brother Georg. Their mother, Maria, did everything herself. She knitted. She cleaned the duty room. She kept a vegetable garden. She even made soap herself. Their father, Joseph, cut the sausage into thinner and thinner slices to share it out fairly. Frugality became their master – and a virtue that marked their daily life.

Still, their mother did not want to give up on a certain style. She was determined that her children should be beautifully dressed in public, as befitted her comfortable baker's family background, and according to the standards she had learned from the well-off households where she had been employed. But at home Maria, Georg and Joseph wore blue pinafores, their 'rags', to save their good clothes. His mother was 'warm-hearted, loving, emotional and not that rational,' Joseph reported. 'She liked to live for the moment, as the thought struck her.' That meant that each of his parents had a 'very different' way of living. His father's strictness demanded 'punctuality and precision and if we did things we shouldn't he scolded us firmly and sometimes might even give us a clip round the ear. That was quite normal then in bringing up children.'[10]

Georg saw things differently: 'He was very keen on precision and order. But he never hit us, except occasionally on the behind.'[11] However, when the kids got out of hand, their mother even had a go at them with the mattress-beater. 'We were a completely normal family,' said the future pope. 'Everything wasn't always harmonious.' Between the parents there were also 'occasional rows', but 'the feeling of being together and their happiness with each other was far stronger'. In the long run there was 'a deep inner union', which made this marriage a happy partnership.

Joseph preferred playing at home, near his mother, with a wooden horse or with one of his toy animals. 'He was not particularly good with his hands,' Georg said, 'but he liked building things with bricks.' Sometimes their favourite uncle, the jolly Benno, came to visit from Rimsting. Benno loved the theatre, and regularly drove with his wife to the opera in Munich in a luxurious, six-seater car with an open top. He had a sports car, a British MG, and also a racing boat. He collected old motor cycles, and his weapon collection filled his whole loft. He was known as a lady-killer and gambler, who spent money like water. But he also surprised his nephews with a small altar with a revolving tabernacle, which he had made. On another occasion, he brought scenery he had painted himself for the family's carefully tended Christmas crib.

Uncle Georg in Buffalo in America sometimes sent a food parcel. On their father's side it was the nun Aunt Theogona who kept in contact. Uncle Alois, their father's brother, was a priest who passionately supported a people's liturgy. He sent letters, gave unsolicited advice and urged the children to visit him more often in his parish in Lower Bavaria. The family regarded Alois with his peculiar ideas as an odd character. 'He was clever,' his nephew knew, 'but very headstrong.'

A new chapter began for Georg. Together with his sister Maria, he now went to school and was mightily proud of it. Something also changed for Joseph. He was three years old when his father enrolled him in the kindergarten run by the Englische Fräulein nuns (of the Institute of the Blessed Virgin Mary, founded by the English Catholic nun Mary Ward) in the former Austin Friars monastery in Sparz, high above Traunstein. His parents hoped he would enjoy contact with children of his own age, as well as a religious education, even though it also involved considerable expense. The 'children's institute', founded in 1855, looked after 90 girls and boys in separate rooms. 'At midday we had to sleep with our arms on the table,' a former kindergarden child recalled. 'Beppi', as the others called the new boy, was not particularly happy with the strict discipline, the general atmosphere and just so many people. He did not like the 'institute' and would have preferred to stay at home with his mother. Nevertheless, in the spring of 1931 he had a meeting that remained deep in his memory.

Marktl belonged to the diocese of Passau, but Tittmoning was in the diocese of Munich-Freising. And the archbishop of Munich, Cardinal von Faulhaber, announced he would visit on 19 June 1931. The visit was for a confirmation, but because he was in the city, he also visited the kindergarden. Security Commissioner Ratzinger wore his full dress uniform with a shining gold helmet, and his little son Joseph was also standing in line. Joseph was as quiet as a mouse as the cardinal's driver brought the powerful car to a halt. It was only when the car door opened and the cardinal solemnly descended that the stiffness began to relax. Impressed by such dignity and splendour, Joseph was suddenly quite sure: 'I'll be a cardinal one day.' He may have been copying his elder brother. When his brother had asked his father what the people who made the music in church were called, he immediately declared: 'I'll be a cathedral music director one day too.' However, Faulhaber seems not to have impressed young Joseph so much that he never altered his career goal again. 'I'm going to be a painter,' he declared a few days later, after a house painter had given the family home a new brilliance.[12]

Their troubles continued. Maria, the eldest, had problems with her tonsils. Georg contracted a lung inflammation, and 'Josepherl', as the baby of the family was called at home, was already a worry. In a picture dating from that time, their mother looked completely exhausted. The woman who had once been attractive, almost ladylike, had become worn out. Her husband also looked bent and weak. More and more often, his son Joseph related, his father 'had to deal with the brutality of the SA men in assemblies' and 'take action against their Nazi strong arm tactics'. 'Pray children,' their mother begged, 'that your father will get home all right.' In Ratzinger's memory everyone in the family 'felt the dreadful worry that burdened him, which day by day he was unable to shake off'.

The Commissioner had breathed a sigh of relief when Hitler failed to get himself elected as German president. For him the Austrian was a wicked criminal who ought to be under lock and key, and his movement was an evil monstrosity. Ratzinger was a subscriber to the *Münchener Tagblatt*. The newspaper was linked to the Bavarian People's Party (BVP), with whom he was in sympathy. Another subscription in the household was to *Gerade Weg*, an anti-fascist weekly that was printed in Schelling Street in Munich, by the same firm that brought out Hitler's *Völkischer Beobachter*. The 'Führer' fumed each time a compositor laid a copy of it fresh off the press on his table. The founder and editor-in-chief of *Gerade Weg* was Fritz Gerlich, the former editor of the *Münchener Neueste Nachrichten* (the forerunner of the *Süddeutsche Zeitung*). The paper was supported by Prince Erich von Waldburg-Zeil. With the headlines of the edition of 31 July 1932, Gerlich, a north German Protestant converted to Catholicism, wanted to light a beacon: 'National Socialism is a Plague,' it declared in large print.[13]

The article itself warned in terms that could not have been plainer:

National Socialism means: enmity with neighbouring nations, tyranny at home, civil war, international war. National Socialism means lies, hatred, fratricide and dire poverty. Adolf Hitler preaches the right to lie. You who have fallen prey to this fraud practised by one who loves tyranny, wake up! Germany, your own and your children's fate are at stake!

Your children's fate! As Ratzinger senior put down the newspaper, he must have been thinking about Maria, George and Joseph. The clashes with the SA and SS henchmen were becoming more and more violent each month. Friends and colleagues had long been advising him to withdraw from the line of fire. Especially with his quick temper, which he found so hard to curb.

He was sorry about his home in the Stubenrauchhaus. And also about Tittmoning in general, which he found so 'picturesque' for the children. But wasn't it now time to take the family to safety? Hadn't he regularly seen the columns in *Gerade Weg* reporting in every edition about 'Hitler's battle against the Catholic Church'? One of its brief reports stated: 'The National Socialist Dr v. Leers declared at an SA assembly in Dresden in July 1931: "The night after the seizure of power belongs to you, SA people, and we all know it will be a night of the long knives".'

4

1933: 'Holy Year'

The Hitler Youth had called 'National Youth Days' for 1 and 2 October 1932 in the traditional Prussian city of Potsdam. The watchword was: 'Against Reaction – for the Socialist Revolution'. Seventy thousand boys and girls from all over Germany poured into the city in trains and lorries, to parade through the streets with torches and red-white-red Hitler Youth flags in the largest political youth march in the world to date. Hitler took the salute in jackboots and peaked cap. The young people gazed up at him with shining eyes. As one of the marchers reported, 'with thrilling faith', they saw in him 'the helper, the rescuer, the saviour from enormous distress'.[1]

Unemployment increased. At the beginning of 1931, nearly 5 million people were registered as unemployed. One year later it was about 7 million. Membership applications to Hitler's party rose in parallel. In just seven months the number of members had almost doubled, to more than 1 million. In the July 1932 Reichstag elections the NSDAP got 37.4 per cent of the vote – their greatest popularity being with first-time voters – and became the largest block in the Reichstag. Hitler claimed the chancellorship. But Hindenburg, the German president, refused. Instead, he dissolved the Reichstag again and called another election. Simultaneously, Germany was slipping insidiously into civil war. From the middle of June until 20 July 1932, in Prussia alone, there were 99 killed and 1,125 wounded in street battles.

How the mood in the country had changed was shown by the membership of the evangelical Neulandbund (New Country League). This was how a young editor expressed the yearning of her generation:

We women have always stood by and looked around us to see whether the men acquiesced in this morass of infamy, baseness, greed, self-seeking and class hatred. And then we felt with a shiver that the divine miracle had happened and that a saviour had really come, who was able to awaken the soul of the people. Then we joyfully joined in with 'Germany awake!' and realized: Here God is striding through world history, here he himself is inspiring his instrument.[2]

For Ratzinger senior, the time had now come to take his family to safety. In the course of his life the police officer had moved 13 times from place to place, but this last move was in fact a flight. On 5 December 1932, the day of their arrival in Aschau am Inn, a Sunday, it was cloudy and windy, with cold rain and snow showers. A neighbour had made tea to welcome them. Soon the mayor arrived and then the parish priest, for the newcomer with his family was to be the new chief of the police station. He was preceded by a certain reputation, since in Tittmoning, only 35 kilometres away, he had clashed with the SA and broken up their meetings and thus become known as a determined anti-Nazi.

Maria was eleven, Georg eight and Joseph five years old – they all looked miserable. Only their mother, Maria, was happy when she saw their new home. 'An actual villa,' she reckoned, with a proper eat-in kitchen. The broad landscape with its flat meadows was cheering and the stream also gave the village a romantic note. But what a change it was from the magic of 'the little city we were so proud of'. In Joseph's memory, nothing could compare 'with what we were used to in Tittmoning'. And then there was the villagers' 'coarse dialect', 'so that at first we could hardly understand any of their words'.[3]

In the early 1930s, Aschau am Inn was a prime example of the unspoilt Bavaria seen in nostalgic calendars. The big farmhouses were grouped round the church; the other houses stood on the right and left sides of the long village street. There was neither a doctor nor a pharmacist, but the inhabitants had a choice of several grocers, two pubs – one with its own brewery – two bakers, a butcher, blacksmith, carpenter, a bicycle shop and the tireless Herr Brand, the barber's, which was also an electrical and photo shop. The tailor came from outside the village to visit the farmsteads and repair the owners' clothes and those of their servants.

If the Aschau church bells rang louder than usual, it was either Sunday or a feast day, Whitsun or Corpus Christi. Or a procession would come round the corner, with cross and banners in front, to bring a citizen of the community to eternal rest after a hard-working life. The village women took it in turns to visit the bedridden Fanny Kifinger and her sister Wally. Fanny suffered from bone tuberculosis and other diseases. The ulcers around her mouth were particularly painful. The young dressmaker had humbly accepted her sufferings, 'offered them up' for Jesus, as it was said. She never complained. She took on the concerns of the village and promised to try and help through her prayers. Georg and Joseph were soon also involved as servers when the priest went from the church every morning at dawn, with stole and ciborium containing the host, over the little bridge to bring Fanny Holy Communion.

The Ratzingers' 'villa' at number 29 in the main street was rented from a rich farmer. The police station was on the ground floor, with a flat for the assistant policeman. A dark room built on to the house served as a prison cell for short-term detainees. On the first floor the newcomers had an eat-in kitchen, a living room and two bedrooms. One was for mother and daughter (since there was no girl's bedroom), and the other was shared by the boys and their father. In comparison with the old-established big famers and shop people, as the family of a lowly official they were 'in a somewhat humbler category', Joseph recalled. And a buttoned-up character like their father did not make it any easier to come closer. 'He was always serious,' says a contemporary witness, 'a strict man, a person commanding respect.'[4]

His 'good-hearted' wife was all the more sociable. Her kindness and warmth made up for some of her husband's severity. Word got round that she gave poor schoolchildren lunch. 'We actually fitted in quickly,' Georg recalled. And even the youngest boy 'very soon grew fond of our village and learned to appreciate its own beauties'. Looking back as a cardinal, he said he was 'very happy that for part of my life I grew up in a village, and got to know the smell of the earth and farming and living with nature'.

For people living in the country, the winter months were very hard. A deep covering of snow brought public life to a complete halt. The farmers warmed their feet at their wood stoves, and only occasionally would a horse- or ox-drawn cart jolt along the village street, very slowly, as if someone had brought time to a halt. Christmas was coming. In the early twentieth century, children asked in the wish letters first of all for religious things and God's blessing, to which they added their thanks to their 'dear parents'. A letter to the Christ Child from 1934 is the earliest written document of the future pope, written in Old German script: 'Dear Christ Child!, you will soon float down to Earth. You want to bring joy to children. You also want to bring me joy. I wish for the *Volks-Schott* [missal], a green Mass vestment and a JESUS heart. I will always be good. Best wishes from Joseph Ratzinger.'[5] The boy drew a picture on the letter of a fir tree branch with a candle and ball on it. In order to save paper, his brother and sister used the other side of the paper for their own letters. Maria wished for *Das Wünderstündlein,* then a popular Christmas book; Georg wanted scores for church music and, parallel to his brother, a white Mass vestment, so that they could play at being priests together.

Only very few Christians in Germany guessed that on 24 December 1932 they would be celebrating the last Christmas Eve on which Christmas was not drowned out by the noise of propaganda. In retrospect, Ratzinger said, getting the things to go with the crib, 'the juniper, the fir cones and then the moss, was something quite special with its own feeling. We brought nature into our lives and into salvation history. Thus the past became present and real in our own lives.'

Afternoon coffee at four o'clock was followed by the rosary together – kneeling on the floor with elbows on the seat of a chair – until finally the Christ child brought the waiting to an end with a gentle ring on the bell: 'Then we went into the living room, where the little spruce tree was already standing on the table with lit wax candles,' Georg recalled. 'The tree was decorated with balls, angel's hair and tinsel, as well as with stars, hearts and comets our mother had carved out of quince jelly.' Before they unwrapped their presents – home-knitted socks and jumpers – there were Christmas carols. Then the children gave the evening entertainment with music, first with one of their own compositions. 'Our mother was moved to tears,' over his debut, Georg recalled, 'and although more soberly, our father was also impressed.'[6]

It had all worked out. Every member of the family felt safe and secure. Their father's job had become less stressful. There was no election campaigning, as in Tittmoning, or aggressive meetings in the back rooms of pubs. Georg stood out at school for his musical talent, his sister through her extraordinary intelligence and phenomenal memory, thanks to which she was able to remember the 30-minute text of a play on stage with no trouble at all. Little Joseph had made friends with 'Bräu-Bärbel', the brewer's daughter next door, who was the same age. He was waiting impatiently to be able to go to school soon, like his brother and sister.

Then it was the Holy Year, which Pope Pius XI had set for 1933. It was planned in humble remembrance of Christ's sufferings 1900 years earlier. Many Catholics had hoped it would be a year of grace, but in fact Christ's anniversary proved to be a year of severe trials. It was a catharsis, like the gospel story of the Capernaum crisis, when many of Christ's disciples left him, because they had a different idea of a Messiah and the way to salvation. 'Who do people say that I am?' Jesus had asked his disciples, and 'Who do you say that I am?' It was a choice between confessing Christ or opting for a movement that saw salvation in terms of worldly-political ideas.

The Ratzingers had moved into their new home at the beginning of December. Exactly eight weeks later, on Monday, 30 January 1933, the swastika flag was hoisted in Aschau. It was the day Hitler seized power, which would govern the fate of Germany, Europe and the whole world for the next 12 years. The year of Jesus' death became the death year for justice and freedom, for faith, hope and love. It was a descent into the Holy Saturday darkness of death and terror, into an apocalyptic fury that was without example in human history.

Hitler's appointment as German Chancellor came not by a vote but through a decision by Paul von Hindenburg. The German president had hoped that involving the National Socialist movement would bring contentment to the country. He soon realized how naïve that idea had been. 'We have come this far', wrote Nazi Propaganda Chief Joseph Goebbels in his diary on the evening of 30 January.

We are sitting in Wilhelmstrasse. Hitler is Chancellor. Like in a fairy tale. Yesterday afternoon Kaiserhof: we are all waiting. Finally he comes. Result: he is Chancellor. The old man [President Hindenburg] has given in. In the end he was very moved. So it's all right. Now we must win him over completely. We all have tears in our eyes. We press Hitler's hand. He has deserved it. Great rejoicing. Down below the people are running riot. Straight to work. Reichstag will be dissolved.[7]

And then it happened blow by blow, in accordance with long-prepared plans:

1 February: Dissolution of the Reichstag by President Hindenburg.
3 February: The 'Führer' announced, in the presence of the army generals, the reintroduction of conscription and the 'conquest of living space in the east and its relentless Germanization' as the aim of his politics.
4 February: Decree issued: 'Presidential Decree for the Protection of the German People' with attacks on press freedom and freedom of assembly. At the same time, local government organs (councils and mayors) throughout Germany were forcibly dissolved and political representatives imprisoned.
20 February: At the 'invitation' of the NSDAP, 25 industrialists put at its disposal a campaign fund of 3 million Reichsmarks. The *crème de la crème* of German industry complied: Allianz, Hoesch, Vereinigte Stahlwerke [United Steelworks], Siemens, IG Farben, Opel. Among those 'invited', only Robert Bosch rejected the appeal for funds. Hitler made it clear to the industrial magnates: 'We must first get hold of all the instruments of power, if we want to throw the other side to the ground.' Goebbels noted the importance of the 'donation': 'We have raised a very large amount for the election, which removes all our money worries at a stroke. I will alert the propaganda apparatus, and one hour later the presses will already be rolling.'
22 February: 50,000 SS and SA members appointed as armed 'auxiliary police'.

27 February: The SA and SS used the arson attack on the Reichstag building in Berlin by the Dutchman Marinus van der Lubbe as a pretext to overrun Germany with a wave of terror: political opponents were imprisoned, tortured or liquidated.

28 February: The 'Presidential Decree for the Protection of the German People and the State', the so-called Reichstag Fire Order, suspended essential basic rights. On the same day came the 'Presidential Decree against the Betrayal of the German People and Treasonable Intrigues', intended to nip any resistance in the bud.

In Aschau, Commissioner Ratzinger furiously followed the flood of news, which hit the country like a hail of bombs. The election on 5 March was meant to give legitimacy to the Nazi takeover of power, but the NSDAP, together with the German National People's Party (DNVP), only just won a majority. What came next was a relentless terrorist coup.

8 March: Three days after the election, all the Reichstag seats of the KPD were abolished, in order to give the NSDAP a two-thirds majority.

21 March: 'Presidential Decree to Defend against Treacherous Attacks upon the National Rising Government', the so-called treachery law, which made anything said against the regime liable to punishment.

22 March: Establishment of the Dachau concentration camp to imprison political prisoners and resistant priests.

23 March: Surrounded by armed SA and SS units, the remaining deputies in the Reichstag passed the 'Law to Remedy the Distress of the People and the Reich', the 'Enabling Law' that put legislative power into the hands of the regime. The KPD deputies were imprisoned or went underground, The SPD deputies who had not yet been imprisoned voted against the law; the deputies of all the other parties voted for it.

31 March: The 'Law to Synchronize the States with the Reich' dissolved the local parliaments and ordered their replacement.

Beginning of April: Occupation of trade union buildings and 'spontaneous' boycotts of Jewish-owned businesses.

7 April: Appointment of local state 'governors' responsible for the implementation of the 'correct lines of policy set by the Reich Chancellor'. Numerous arrests by the SA and SS ensued. The 'Law for the Restoration of the Professional Civil Service' on the same day ordered the dismissal of undesirable and 'non-Aryan' officials.

May 1933: Book burnings in Berlin, Bremen, Dresden, Frankfurt, Hanover, Munich, Nuremberg and other cities. Into the fire were thrown works by Bertolt Brecht, Alfred Döblin, Lion Feuchtwanger, Sigmund Freud, Erich Kästner, Heinrich Mann, Erich Maria Remarque, Kurt Tucholsky, Franz Werfel, Stefan Zweig and many other 'subversive elements'.

June 1933: Banning of the SPD for alleged treason and high treason and 'self-dissolution' of the German National People's Party (Deutschnationale Volkspartei, or DNVP) and centre parties.

July 1933: By order of the interior Reich Minister for the Safety of the National Government, all parties except the NSDAP were banned. The 'Law against the Establishment of New Parties' established the one-party state.

One piece of news in the dramatic weeks of the Nazi takeover of power must have hit Commissioner Ratzinger particularly hard. The weekly paper *Gerade Weg* had passionately opposed Hitler. 'Rabble rouser, Criminal, Madman' was one of its headlines. This uncompromising stand against fascism was honoured by its readers. Its print run had risen to 100,000 copies. On 30 January its editor-in-chief, Dr Fritz Gerlich, wrote about Hitler's speech in the Reichstag: 'The German people will again become a people with Christian morals and its whole cultural tradition. One day we will be ashamed, lastingly ashamed, by how it was possible that a German Reich Chancellor could call for a regime that does such violence to the objective truth as the present Chancellor does.'

Just over a month later, on 9 March 1933, SA men stormed the editorial offices of *Gerade Weg* in Färbergraben in Munich, shouting: 'Where is Gerlich the pig?' They punched and trampled on the journalists and transported Gerlich to the Dachau concentration camp. After 15 months' imprisonment, on 30 June 1934, shortly before midnight, he was hauled out of his cell and murdered. The Nazis sent Gerlich's only 'legacy' in a cardboard box to his wife: his blood-smeared glasses.[8]

Ratzinger senior did not have to be a prophet to be able to see the future. He only needed his clear understanding: 'Now war is coming,' he told his family. 'Now we need a house.'

5

The 'German Christians'

One morning the youngest Ratzinger child was seen walking along the village street hand in hand with his friend Bräu-Bärbel. He was proudly wearing a scarf that his mother had wrapped round his neck for this special day.

It was 2 May 1933, Joseph's first day at school. In the three-stage elementary school, the first and the second year groups (one of which had 17 pupils, the other 25) were taught together by a single teacher in the same classroom, the boys in front and the girls at the back. They worked with slate and slate pencil. Lessons were six days a week, including afternoons from one until three o'clock. Once a week there was a compulsory school Mass with the parish priest, Father Igl. The Nazis could not stop that. However, now a portrait hung on the wall of that man whom Joseph knew from home as a 'vagabond' and a 'criminal'. Fräulein Anna Fahmüller, the teacher, wrote in big letters on the blackboard. The first words that the future pope learned to write were: 'AU MEINE NASE' ['Oh my nose']. She would suffer for that in her later life.

Joseph had become a good-looking boy. His delicate features showed a sensitive character. In his report it said: 'Attentive, does not chatter, does not scuffle, punctual and obedient.' His brother Georg added: 'Joseph was by far the best pupil in the elementary school in Aschau.'¹ There is no record of him taking part in a scrap or a snowball fight. Nor did he join in the wrangling when the others ran to the stream at break time, to lie on the footbridge to watch the fish. But his fellow pupils were deeply impressed when one of them discovered an accessory they had never seen before. Beautifully embroidered in the cloth wrapped round his slate there was a cross. Quite small but large enough not to be forgotten.

Joseph was quiet, reserved and composed, a former schoolfellow George Haas reported, 'not one who shouted out: "I know, I know!"' 'But,' according to Barbara Ametsbichler, 'when he was asked something, he knew it all.' He was 'blindly trusted,' said Franziska Salzeder, 'because what Ratzinger says must be right.' Fellow pupil Alois Steinbeisser even had 'the impression that he was ahead of the teachers'.[2] However, they did not find their fellow pupil shy. He was often appointed by the teacher to supervise the class. 'He was quite confident', according to Barbara Ametsbichler. That teacher who regularly used his stick never once tried it on Joseph. Ratzinger himself said: 'I was not a particularly imaginative kid.' He did not remember any special pranks from those early days. However, at school he occasionally 'rather discouraged' teachers, 'through my audacity'. In Tittmoning and Aschau, according to the future pope, he was 'a cheerful and fun-loving child, but later that changed.'[3]

Two things particularly struck his fellow pupils. Joseph never ran about barefoot, like nearly all the other farm children in summer, but always wore high lace-up boots. From Class 3 on, when he was eight, he dropped the usual school satchel. 'Now,' a school record reported, 'he was the only pupil to come to school with a briefcase.' Perhaps this was due to an important decision he had reached. Until then his parents and siblings had usually called him 'Josepherl'. Now he declared to the whole family: 'That won't do any longer. Otherwise I will go on being a Josepherl for the whole of my life. From now on, I am called Joseph.' Eighty years later he marvelled: 'In fact, that instruction was then kept.'

His brother George began a hopeful music career. At first, a girl pupil from the convent school in Au taught him the harmonium at home. When his father felt that being a dilettante would not help his son get on, he received piano lessons, together with Maria. For Christmas Georg asked for a *Liber Usualis,* a 1,950-page Latin hymnbook with all the music to sing the oratorios and the proper of the Masses for Sundays and feast days. His younger brother gasped open-mouthed when he saw that 'not a single word in it was German'. On 20 December 1934 the Aschau parish record remarked: 'A Class 5 pupil splendidly accompanied the German sung Masses and the Latin choral Masses.'[4] Georg was proud. 'My mother was very pleased, but my father did not say anything, which was just like him.'

The Benjamin of the family was also introduced to music. For a whole year, from 1936 to 1937, he went every week to the Au am Inn convent to learn the harmonium for a whole hour from Sister Berchmana Fischbacher. Later he also had violin lessons. In contrast to his brother, to whom his music teacher 'soon had nothing more to say', the younger boy said he had 'got no further than Beethoven sonatas, but could never play them right'.[5]

For a long time the Nazis found it difficult to gain a significant number of followers in strongly Catholic rural areas, especially when voters like the Ratzingers supported a ruggedly Bavarian anti-Prussian patriotism, always opposed to jingoistic Germanness. 'Rural life was still bound up in a firm symbiosis with the church's faith,' Ratzinger wrote in his memoirs. 'Birth and death, wedding and sickness, seedtime and harvest – were all encompassed by the faith.' However, with the NSDAP takeover a new state of affairs arose in Aschau too.

On 30 January 1933 the elementary school was ordered to hold a march for the 'Führer', once up and down the village street, and in the pouring rain. 'We marched bravely through the puddles,' Georg reported, 'which was rather ridiculous.' But open and covert Nazis now saw that 'their hour had come' and 'suddenly frightened us' by getting 'many of their brown uniforms out of their trunks', as Joseph remembered. For example, now the assistant policeman on the ground floor of the police station marched out every morning with his wife to 'military training'. However, the church was still at the centre of the village, not just as a building but in 'the whole attitude to life'. It was 'not clever to go against it too strongly', Ratzinger remarked. When the traditional maypole was set up, one of the teachers brought a 'prayer to the maypole', from now on a symbol of the new cult of Germanness. Faced with down-to-earth farming folk, this actually ended rather pathetically, as Joseph observed: 'The lads were more interested in the sausages hanging on the maypole than in the schoolmaster's highfalutin speech.'[6]

For no one in the area was the situation so precarious as it was for the Commissioner. To him the Nazis were simply villains. When he spoke of Hitler to the children, he called him a good-for-nothing and the worst kind of criminal. Suddenly, as a law enforcer now, he was meant to serve a state whose leadership filled him with loathing. 'I was still quite small,' his son reported, 'but I can remember how much he suffered.' Whenever he had a newspaper in his hands and read about the measures taken by the new masters, he 'fell into a fury'. The policeman was a man of action. In the very year when Hitler seized power he bought an old farmhouse near the school town of Traunstein for 5,500 Reichmarks. A lot of money for a lowly official. Also a lot of money for a 200-year-old shack, in a small hamlet, that the previous owner had let go to ruin.

After the dissolution of the political parties in Germany, several independent youth groups were also banned, but the Hitler Youth and the League of German Girls (Bund Deutscher Mädel, or BDM) were the state youth groups. In the kindergarden the cross was replaced by the swastika, the convent sisters by Nazi sisters; priests were denounced, spied on and harassed as potential enemies of the Reich. Christmas gave way to the Nordic-Germanic 'Yule Festival', Easter becamse a 'Hare Festival'. Gradually, Christianity was replaced by a kind of Nazi faith, a 'religion for all'. Christ's salvation was replaced by the 'Führer's *Sieg-Heil*, the new and true 'saviour'. (The German word *Heil* means both 'salvation', 'hale', and a greeting: 'hail'.) 'No earthly ruler gave us the order,' Hitler's booming voice rattled out on the NSDAP Reich Party Day in 1934. 'The order was given to us by the God who created our people.'

The Nazis had not grown big overnight. In other European countries too, fascist movements were pressing for social and political change. In fact, it took a whole decade to bring about the shift that brought the NSDAP to power. Its ideological foundation had been laid much earlier, especially by theories that used *völkisch*, nationalist and racist ideas to transform Christianity into a 'specific' national folk religion.

Particularly important here was the concept of 'positive Christianity' which, for pseudo-religious motives, promised to develop a progressive religion appropriate to the time. The alternative to the traditional gospel was a self-made religious mix, whose aim was to create a new national church ruled by a worldly dictator. Hitler proclaimed 'positive Christianity' to be the foundation of his political activity. He made this clear in 1941, at the height of his power, when he proclaimed: 'The war will come to an end and I will see as my final life work the resolution of the church problem. Only then will the German nation be wholly secure.'[7]

A pioneer of the national religious movement was the evangelical minister Arthur Bonus, who was already promoting a 'Germanization of Christianity' in 1896. Another was the Flensburg pastor Friedrich Andersen, who, from 1904 on had called for the abolition of the Old Testament and 'all Jewish obfuscation of the pure teaching of Jesus'. In 1917, on the 400th anniversary of the beginning of the Reformation, Andersen together with Adolf Bartels, Ernst Katzer and Hans von Wolzogen published 95 theses 'based on purely evangelical principles', which they saw as a programme for the 'Germanization and de-Jewification of Christianity'. They wrote: 'The most recent racial research has finally opened our eyes to the pernicious effects of mixing blood between Germanic and non-German peoples and urges us, with all our force, to strive to keep our national ethnicity [*Volkstum*] as pure and closed as possible.'[8]

As an important forerunner of a 'purified religion', we should mention the 'German Christians' (Deutsche Christen, or DC). Founded in 1927, they reinterpreted the Christian doctrine of the Trinity in favour of a new threesome of God, 'Führer' and *Volk*. Alfred Rosenberg's book *Der Mythus des 20. Jahrhunderts* (*The Myth of the 20th Century*), which was put on the Index by the Catholic Church on 7 February 1934, found strong approval in these circles. In it, Hitler's chief ideologue fulminated against Marxist and Catholic internationalism, which he presented as two facets of the same Jewish spirit. On the other hand, a renewed national religion was simply the completion of the Reformation. The 'Guidelines' of the new faith movement stated: 'We see in race, *Volkstum* and nation a way of life given and entrusted to us by God [...] In particular, marriage between German and Jews is to be forbidden.'[9] The prohibitions also ordered the exclusion of 'Jewish Christians', the 'de-Jewification' of the church's message through rejection of the Old Testament, reinterpretation of the New Testament, as well as 'keeping the German race pure' by 'protecting it from those who were "unacceptable" or "inferior"'.

The German Christians' programme was hardly any different from that of the NSDAP. Here, too, there was talk of 'positive Christianity' and an 'affirmative, appropriate Christian faith'. The propagandists appealed to a famous precursor. The reformer Martin Luther had also preached a programme of 'de-Jewification'. One of his anti-Semitic pamphlets from 1543 began: 'First, let their synagogues and schools be set on fire, and let what won't burn be buried in earth to ensure that no one ever again sees a single stone or cinder of them.'[10] Further on it says: 'And this should be done in order to honour our Lord and Christianity, so that God sees that we are Christians [...] Furthermore, let their houses likewise be smashed and destroyed.'[11] According to Luther, the practice of 'baptizing Jews' was a horror: 'I'll baptize the next Jew in the Elbe but with a stone round his neck.'[12]

For a good while now, the German Christians had no longer been a splinter group. With a million members – including a third of the Protestant clergy – soon the movement dominated all the Protestant churches, split into Lutheran, United and Reformed. When Hitler was appointed Reich Chancellor, quite a few regional churches held festive services of thanks. Pastors connected with the German Christians allowed swastika flags to be hung in churches as a 'symbol of German hope'. At a meeting in the Berlin Sports Hall on 13 November 1933, District Chairman Reinhold Krause clearly expressed the German Christian message to an audience of 20,000 enthusiastic listeners: 'If we National Socialists are ashamed to buy a tie from a Jew, how much more should we be ashamed to accept from the Jew anything that speaks to our soul, what is most intimately religious?' The 'soul of the German people' belonged 'wholly to the new State'. Its total claim could not 'stand back' even from the church. The order of the day was unification of all religions and denominations into a 'People's [völkisch] National Church'.[13]

According to a study by the political researcher Jürgen W. Falter, in the Reichstag election of July 1932, in areas with an 80 per cent

Protestant population, the NSDAP won on average 42.1 per cent of the votes.[14] But in areas with a similar percentage of Catholics, they won only 24.1 per cent of the votes. In 1924 the Reichstag was 25 per cent Catholic. But in the Greater Germany Reichstag of 1943, Catholics amounted to just 7 per cent. The voting patterns of a large number of Protestants led the evangelical sociologist Gerhard Schmidtchen to ask 'whether in a Catholic Germany, National Socialism would have come to power at all'. The historian Winfried Becker, professor of modern and contemporary history at the University of Passau until 2007, noted: 'The nearly 1,500 evangelical newspapers, with a combined print run of 12 million copies, almost unanimously welcomed the "national emergence" of the Hitler movement. But despite initial concessions, the opposition of the Catholic press to the Nazi regime cannot be overlooked.'[15]

A counter-movement in the Protestant camp began when, in September 1933 in Berlin, the General Synod of the Evangelical Church of the Old Prussian Union introduced the so-called 'Aryan paragraph'. This was accompanied by the forced retirement of all ministers and church officials, any of whose parents or grandparents were of Jewish stock. The faithful reacted to this unheard-of procedure with protests and left the church in large numbers. In the same month, the Pastors' Emergency League (*Pfarrernotbund*) was set up, from which the Confessing Church emerged in May 1934.

Leading figures in the Protestant opposition movement included the theologian Martin Niemöller and Dietrich Bonhoeffer. Bonhoeffer was arrested on 5 April 1943 and executed on 9 April 1945, at Hitler's express orders, as one of his last Nazi opponents who had been linked with the assassination plot of 20 July 1944 (the 'July Plot'). A bedrock of the Confessing Church proved to be the theology of the Swiss Protestant Karl Barth, who was teaching in Bonn. His theology was fundamentally opposed to any kind of 'updating' of the Gospel and sought to renew Evangelical theology by returning to the biblical revelation. According to Barth, the best service to humanity was the true proclamation of God's Word, as he entrusted it to us. When he became a professor, Ratzinger kept in active contact with Barth. And in return, Barth had a high regard for the Catholics and recommended to his students: 'Read Ratzinger!'

Despite the initiative of the Confessing Church, soon three-quarters of all the Evangelical regional churches founded the 'Institute for Research and Removal of Jewish Influence on German Church Life', the so-called De-Jewification Institute, in Eisenach. There in Wartburg Castle, where Luther had once translated the Bible, about 200 bishops, regional bishops, upper church councils, professors and artist were involved in producing a 'De-Jewified New Testament' and a 'Jew-free' catechism (with the title *Germans with God*). In a Festschrift of the Institute, its academic director, Walter Grundmann, professor of the New Testament at the University of Jena, included the following policy statement: 'A healthy people must and will reject Judaism in any form [...] The Jew must be seen as a hostile and destructive alien and eliminated from exerting any influence.'[16]

Hitler had cleverly dressed up his words with religious accessories, to appease critics and ensure the loyalty of church leaders. The 4 February 1933 decree 'For the Protection of the German People' threatened prosecution for those who disparaged religious establishments and practices. In his Government Statement of 23 March 1933, Hitler not only assured the Christian churches of state protection and support but also guaranteed their legal inviolability. Before that, on 1 February 1933, in his 'Reich Government Appeal to the German People', he had promised that the Reich government would 'take under its firm protection Christianity as the basis of our morality, and the family as the nucleus of our nation and our state'. Hitler concluded with the liturgically formulated prayer: 'May Almighty God favour our work, shape our will in the right way, bless our vision and bless us with the trust of our people.'[17]

The deceitful manoeuvre worked. In March 1933 the weekly paper *Das evangelische Deutschland* carried the headline 'One Reich one People [*Volk*], one God'. The Catholic bishops also made a calamitous change. On 25 March 1928, in view of the growing nationalist movements in Europe, in the pope's name the Holy Office (later the Congregation for the Doctrine of the Faith) had denounced racism as an ungodly doctrine. As the Holy Father 'condemns all envy and jealousy between nations,' it said in the declaration, 'so he also sharply condemns hatred of the people once chosen by God, namely that hatred which today is usually called anti-Semitism.'[18] In 1931 the Catholic newspaper *Junges Zentrum* warned: 'If we Catholics seek salvation, then we can never make any pact with these powers.' In September 1930 the Mainz episcopal ordinariate had stated that a Catholic cannot be 'an enrolled member of the Hitler Party'. On 10 February 1931 the Bavarian Bishops' Conference asserted that National Socialism was to be rejected. Similar declarations followed on 5 March 1931 from the Bishops of the Cologne Province and in August 1931 from the Fulda Bishops' Conference. The statement said that Catholic clergy were 'strictly forbidden' to co-operate with the National Socialist movement. Catholic laity were also advised that membership of the Party or agreement with their programme was not allowed and that, should the occasion arise, voting for the Nazis would also be a sin.

But then came a dramatic about-turn. On 25 March 1933, five days after Hitler's Government Statement, the Fulda and Freising Bishops' Conferences issued a joint pastoral letter. The crucial statement in it read: 'Without rescinding the condemnation of particular religious-moral errors expressed in our previous communications, the Episcopate believes that the aforementioned general prohibitions and warnings no longer need to be regarded as necessary.' Two months later, on 8 June 1933, a pastoral letter from the German bishops went a step further. The bishops welcomed the 'national awakening'. From now on, simple membership of the NSDAP or one of its organizations did not go against the ruling of the church. When it came, the German Catholic bishops did not openly oppose Hitler's war or tell Catholics not to serve in his armed forces.

A terrible day and a resounding slap in the face for Ratzinger senior, who declared that many of the bishops had been lulled into acquiescence and deceived. 'On the one hand he was an incredibly pious man, who prayed often and was deeply rooted in the church's faith,' his son Joseph said, 'and at the same time he was a very austere, critical man, who could even be very critical of pope and bishops.' He added: 'It was just that sober piety with which he practised his faith and deeply imbued me, that was so important for me.'[19]

The Protestants also offered loyal addresses. The April 1933 Easter message of Germany's biggest regional church, the Old Prussian Union, was given to a people to whom God had spoken 'through a great change'. They were 'gratefully associated with the leadership of the new Germany'. It was a matter of joyful 'co-operation with the national and moral renewal of our people'.[20]

The previous day, the Nazis had called for the boycotting of Jewish shops.

6

With Burning Concern

The Ratzinger family pulled together, and faith was the bond that held them. They always woke up to morning prayers and said grace at meals. Going to church was a duty. Also the rosary. In rural Bavaria that was as much taken for granted as eating and drinking. Pilgrimages, confessions, novenas, offering up sufferings and fasting belonged to the common treasury, just as folk wisdom and country weather lore did.

'Sometimes,' Joseph said, on Saturdays their father brought out his old Gospel commentary, 'to introduce us to the Gospel for Sunday'. 'At home,' Georg reported, there was 'a normal, healthy, robust religiousness'. We simply tried to be devout Catholics'. And although their parents were so different in temperament, his brother added, 'on this point – each in their different way – they were united. Religion was absolutely central.'

Whether by accident or not, everywhere the family had lived so far had been near Altötting, the 'heart of Bavaria', as this place of pilgrimage was called. The Commissioner was a passionate devotee of Mary. He was a member of the Altötting Men's Marian Congregation, a 400-year-old fraternity, and had taken a vow of lifelong dedication. As a responsible Christian man loyal to the pope, he aimed to meet God's demands in family, professional, church and public life, and to educate his conscience. That was bound up with an old Bavarian heartfelt piety, a faith that was charismatic, emotional, vivid and healing.

Since the mid-fourteenth century, the Chapel of Grace at the centre of Altötting had had a decorated statue of Mary Mother of God and the Child Jesus. From 1489 there had been reports of miracles of healing, so it was regarded as a place of special blessing. Soon, thousands of votive tablets were hung in the area outside the chapel. 'Mary helped!' was written on each of them. More and more churches, convents, chapels, cloisters, shops selling devotional articles and candlesticks, as well as assembly rooms and a papal basilica for 8,000 visitors (from 1912) turned it into a kind of holy city, drawing millions of pilgrims. Among them came seekers of God like the 31-year-old peasant Johann Birndorfer, who, as Brother Konrad and porter of the Capuchin Monastery became a model for his piety ('the cross is my book'), his humility and his love of humanity.

Altötting, Ratzinger confessed, had always impressed him. It was 'lucky' to have been born near the Marian pilgrimage site. 'The Chapel of Grace, the mysterious darkness, the splendidly dressed black Madonna, surrounded by devotional offerings, all those people silently praying [...], all that still touches my heart today exactly as it did all those years ago. The presence of a holy and healing kindness, the kindness of a mother in whom God's own kindness is given to us.'[1] When he was pope, on 11 September 2006, he laid his ring with a phoenix, which his siblings had given him when he was ordained bishop, at the feet of the Madonna in the Chapel of Grace. It was later incorporated into her statue's sceptre.

Ratzinger senior was rather like a rabbi, brooding over holy books, explaining biblical stories and teaching the family fundamental religious truths. He distanced himself from bigotry, and did not go along with a craving for miracles. He was also sceptical about phenomena such as those reported by Resi von Konnersreuth, a stigmatic who displayed Christ's bleeding wounds on Good Fridays. He gave his children reading material suited to their age and ability. For Joseph, first it was a children's prayer book, then a children's missal with short texts and drawings, which explained the structure of the Mass; after that it was the *Schott* for children, then the *Sunday Schott* and finally a complete Mass book for all the days of the year. The Mass books dated back to the Benedictine Anselm Schott, who had produced a 'Mass book for the Laity' in 1884 – for the first time. This was to enable the faithful to participate better in the Catholic rite in their mother tongue.

Musical education was part of their upbringing. 'He thought it very important that we children should make music,' said Joseph.

Enjoying music together bonded the family and made family occasions festive. It went without saying that his daughter Maria also received a more than elementary school education. One day their father announced: 'All three of you children must get a driving licence.' He himself did not have one. 'We did not feel excessive pressure at home,' Georg explained. However, 'the whole atmosphere pointed the way to us'. The basic message was to do it properly. 'We knew,' his brother said, 'that we had to keep in order: religious order, family order and what was right in general.' Our father was 'a very upright and fair man,' who took care that we followed this course. And we certainly felt that it would not be taken lightly if we stepped out of line.' The fact that their father's attitude was not offputting or even destructive but attractive and life-enhancing was due to his loving heart. 'We always felt that he was strict out of kindness. That meant we could actually accept his strictness.' Joseph added: 'I have to say, he became gentler. He was not nearly so strict with me as with my older brother and sister.'[2]

The political situation was not spoken about at home. The parents did not want to burden the children. There was also the worry that they might let slip a fatal word somewhere. Joseph picked up that the assistant policeman had tried to document the preaching of a priest who was known for his anti-fascist stance. At least, his father managed to warn the priest in time so that, instead of a sermon in the church, there was the 'Stations of the Cross'. The local people winked at each other because the spy had to kneel down, together with the faithful, at each of the Stations that showed how Christ was abused by his persecutors.

The pressure on Ratzinger the police officer became stronger. It could not be tolerated much longer that he, as a public servant and chief of a police station, was not a member of the State Party. He still kept his stand, together with his siblings. At family get-togethers at the Ratzingers' house in Rickering, Theogona, the nun, displayed her passionate temperament by launching into torrents of fury at the Nazis. Joseph also remembered his father's sister Teresa as 'a particularly savage opponent of the Nazis'. His father's younger brother Alois was named later in the book *Priester unter Hitlers Terror* as one of those Catholic clergy who openly opposed the regime. Among others things, he was pinpointed because after Mass he asked his parishioners to swear an oath of loyalty to the church. In 1938, the bishop of Passau thought it advisable to send Alois Ratzinger into early retirement to protect him from being sent to a concentration camp.[3]

The faith world that Joseph had experienced in Tittmoning as dreamlike and without any oppression acquired a stark realism in Aschau. Now with increasing frequency, you would meet a neighbour wearing the brown uniform. Teachers who sided with the rhetoric of strife and hatred, revenge and destruction. Students who spoke enthusiastically about the Hitler Youth. As he saw from his father, resistance meant staying with the church, defending her and, in return, being protected by the church – protected in your innermost being, the seat of your soul. It wasn't an exile into which the sensitive boy withdrew; it merely meant that the Holy seemed even holier to him.

The people of Aschau still laughed when they asked the policeman's son in the street what he wanted to do later on: 'So, Joseph, what do you want to be when you grow up?', even the parish priest, Father Ilg, asked him. But Joseph's answer was so funny that they could not stop themselves, especially as the kid pronounced it with such a deep 'ah' sound, as if there was nothing nobler on this planet. And what did he want to be? 'I'll be a cardinal.'

His brother, whom the younger boy felt he was 'beneath in keenness and ability', went ahead, as an altar server, and soon also as a pupil at the gymnasium and, finally, in his choice of the priesthood. Even as a child, Georg said, he had 'prayed to God to give me a job where I could combine work as a priest with making music'. He never doubted for a second 'this was the way I should go'. The only question was where exactly he could find that way. 'My father wanted me to be a missionary, and my mother wanted me to join a religious order.'[4] His father favoured the Mariannhill missionaries in Bavarian Swabia, his mother wanted the Redemptorist house of studies in Gars am Inn, just ten kilometres away.

Both these suggestions were rejected. Georg had his own ideas and opted for the humanities gymnasium in Traunstein and for St Michael's Archiepiscopal Seminary, founded in 1929, whose director – Johann Evangelist Mair, known as 'Rex' – was a fanatical music lover. Accompanied by his mother and siblings, Georg went to the next railway station with a small handcart, carrying the little suitcase with the things he would need at boarding school. He would not see them again for many long weeks. His father shortened the time by regular letters with the latest news from home.

Maria was also thinking about a life in religion. 'I'll be a black nun,' she announced at home. She wanted to help the poor children in Africa. During the summer she cycled every day to the middle school for girls in the Au convent, which was run by Franciscan nuns. In winter she stayed in the school's boarding house.

The school education had its price. 'We could eat our fill,' Georg reported, 'but we also had to save for the house', the old farmhouse in Hufschlag, near Traunstein, which their father was buying. Because of the existential threat to the family, the Commissioner's wife now joined the local branch of the Nazi Women's League. Her husband hoped that this would reduce the pressure on him as a police officer to become a Nazi Party member. It succeeded. At least the Nazi Women's Group in Aschau was not a militant organization: at their meetings they exchanged cooking recipes and prayed the rosary. Ratzinger senior also reported sick with increasing frequency, in order to serve the regime as little as possible in his final year of work.

For Joseph a new situation arose when his brother and sister went away. As he was now alone, Joseph confessed, he 'developed my own personal kingdom' – even though he once nearly drowned in the carp pond that belonged to the police house. He had hardly any playmates. After school, most of the farm children were busy working in the farmyard or the fields. But Joseph enjoyed indulging his romantic vein undisturbed. He loved picking flowers, wrote poems about nature and Christmas, enjoyed animals and dreamed of being 'in beautiful churches or castles'. He read romantic authors as 'that romantic feeling for life touched him deeply'.

The two Josephs were also seen roaming all over the place together. On bike trips and walks over the mountains, they explored their local area. 'Once upon a time a man and a woman ...' was the beginning of the exciting stories his father told on the way. 'He was really a novelist,' the future pope recalled. 'Proper homely novels' in instalments were created on their excursions together 'and I think he was also excited by how the story would develop.'

Walking and storytelling brought them 'very close together'. It was also ideal that the parents with their opposite temperaments complemented each other so well. The young Joseph found his mother 'very warm-hearted and with great inner strength' and his father 'rational and deliberately emphatic, with a reflective conviction of faith'. His father always had 'astonishingly good judgement' and gave him love and recognition even as a boy. 'In the end,' he added, 'when I grew older I began to like my father better.'

The model of his father helped the boy to find himself, to form his character and develop his personality. His parents' dominance gradually lessened as he developed. In the end, their role was just to go along with him. Both sons stress that their parents did not have particular expectations of them. Even in the early stages, they left decisions about their professional future completely to the children. However, their father played an important part through his example. 'When in the coming years I came to know about the job of a priest,' the future pope explained,

> then – besides my mother's more emotional faith – our father's strong, decidedly religious personality was crucial. He thought differently from how you were supposed to think then, and had a certain mastery that convinced people. He had read a great deal and was very interested in politics, but religion was the basic principle of his life in a thoroughgoing, manly way.

Georg Ratzinger once spoke emotionally about it. For his brother, Aschau had been a kind of 'Nazareth'. In the four and a half years of his 'starting out and growing up' there, Joseph learned 'the symphony of life' and 'matured as a growing shoot on the Lord's vine'. In fact, the roots of Ratzinger's strongly church-centred theology lay in his childhood. 'It was a thrilling adventure, to penetrate slowly into the mysterious world of the liturgy, which was acted out at the altar before us and for us,' he recorded in his papers.

> It became ever clearer to me that there I encountered a reality which had not been constructed by anyone: neither by an authoritative body nor a single great individual. This mysterious web of text and actions had grown over centuries out of the faith of the church. It bore the freight of the whole story within it and was thus much more than a product of human authorship.

In Aschau, the schoolchildren were fascinated by the Advent Mass of the Angels in the cold and snowy winter, the Mount of Olives devotions and the Easter Resurrection celebration, with all the colour and gestures, the music, the special drama and sensuousness of Catholic services, which always relieved the faithful a little of their earthly burdens. In the rich educational context that the future pope experienced while he was growing up, delight in music and the discovery of poetry went hand in hand with progress in learning to read and write, reading and thinking going together. He was so entranced by the liturgy as celebration – 'with its music and all its colourful spectacle' – that it became essential 'to bring out what is actually happening there, what it means, what is being said there'.[5]

Sensuousness was one powerful strand. But 'from the beginning, everything that was said in religion also interested me rationally.' In this way he 'progressed step by step in his own thinking'. The intellectually precocious schoolboy discovered another side to his talent at this stage, namely 'teaching, passing knowledge on, and also writing'. This confirmed him in a direction that he was beginning to glimpse: 'Thank God, the wish went well together with the idea of the priesthood.'

However, something was still lacking. Reading and thinking meant intellectually grasping how the liturgy 'functioned' so to speak. The other side was that opening of the soul which Christ called the heart of the mysteries of the faith, the 'code' that unlocked the doors. Without that, contact with the reality beyond was impossible. Contact and participation were essential for service as a priest. In retrospect, Ratzinger saw he took that step when he became an altar server in Aschau and when, on 15 March 1936 in the parish church of the Assumption of Our Lady, he was allowed to make his first communion. 'That was inwardly very necessary for me,' he explained later. The word 'inwardly', together with terms such as 'mystery', 'adventure' and 'experience', was another way of expressing Ratzinger's understanding of the search for God. 'When he was not there himself,' he said, he had 'felt excluded from what was most important'.[6]

For Joseph, the moment that burned into his soul was the daily meeting with the presence of Christ which genuine liturgy made possible. He acted as altar server every morning before school.

These experiences were then deepened at home. It was popular in Christian families to play at being priests and hold church services. But with the Ratzingers, the game took on a semi-professional aspect. Uncle Benno had contributed the small altar with a revolving tabernacle. Kind aunts made albs, stoles and vestments. The Altötting shops for devotional objects sold miniature tin vessels to contain the wine and water for the offertory of the Mass. They even had a small censer. Maria, Georg and Joseph walked in procession to their candle-decked altar, which was set up in the door frame. And since a sermon should not be lacking, the older or the younger brother preached the homily in turn (with a clean copy written in his own notebook). After young Joseph's brother and sister had gone to boarding school, Bräu-Bärbel came to the service to assist him. 'We were very reverent,' Barbara Ametsbichler recalled. At the consecration, Joseph solemnly raised the cup up high; at the distribution of communion, the girl took care that no crumb of the imaginary host fell on the floor.

In a television interview 60 years later, Ratzinger explained what this first playing at being a priest had meant for him: 'Suddenly playing the part myself, which we only saw reverently from afar, gave me the feeling of taking a big step forward – a mysterious anticipation of the future.' It was taking part in advance in what would be his future life work. It so happened that when he did become a cardinal, just as in his childhood days, once the congregation consisted of only one person sitting on the church bench, as the television journalist Siegfried Rappl observed when he took part in this ceremony in the crypt of a church in Naples. Later on, though, Ratzinger never gave a sermon without preparing it carefully.

After he became pope, when he was asked about his motives for his vocation, Ratzinger opened his heart in St Peter's Square in front of 50,000 young people on 5 April 2006. He spoke as *nonno del mondo,* the world's grandfather, as the Italians had long been calling him. 'I grew up in a world that was quite different from the world of today,' Benedict began and then continued:

On the one hand, there was the situation of Christianity, where it was normal to go to church, accept the faith as God's revelation and to try to live by it. On the other hand, there was the Nazi regime which loudly declared: 'In the new Germany there will be no more priests, there will be no more consecrated life, we no longer need these people; let them look for another job.'

[...]

In that situation, my vocation to the priesthood grew with me, almost naturally, without any dramatic conversion. Two things also helped me on this way. With the help of my parents and the parish priest, even as a boy, I had discovered the beauty of the liturgy. I came to love it more and more, because I felt that divine beauty appeared in it and heaven was revealed. The second thing was discovering the beauty of knowledge, knowing God and Scripture, through which it was possible to enter into that great adventure of dialogue with God, which was theology.[7]

The romantically inclined, dreamy boy wanted to see, feel, wonder and be moved. He also thirsted for knowledge. He instinctively grasped that, as opposed to the cheap trumpery and empty promises of the Nazis, this offered true beauty, but also that in that beauty lay truth. And that the truth, as it was expressed in the liturgy, could also be checked; it only offered the fullness of its wealth when it was explored. The inner world was different from the outer. But when the two of them were properly related to each other, you could plunge right into that virtual universe. It was no less real than the apparent reality, which was becoming more and more unreal and mad.

One of Ratzinger's finest phrases is the 'heart's home'. It expresses better than any other the fundamental driving force of his early years, in this passage about his childhood experiences in Aschau: 'I have so many beautiful memories of that place, where I learned to read, write and count. It was also where I was able to settle into the faith, so that it became my heart's home.' In retrospect Ratzinger also realized that under those circumstances, it had been necessary not only to celebrate his faith in devout Masses, but to seek a rational foundation for it. 'The public knew: he's a Catholic, he goes to church and even wants to be a priest. So you were drawn into arguments and had to learn how to arm yourself for them.'[8]

When Ratzinger the policeman reached his 60th birthday on 6 March 1937, he was able to celebrate not only his retirement but also his release from serving a regime that he deeply abhorred. Moving into their own house, which they were all longing for, was now only a matter of days away. It seemed almost like a confirmation of the rightness of their decisions, when a week later Pope Pius XI signed his first and only encyclical written in German, published on 21 March 1937. Its title was *Mit brennender Sorge: Über die Lage der katholischen Kirche im Deutschen Reich (With Burning Concern – On the Situation of the Catholic Church in the German Reich)*.

As well as the German pastoral letter, the encyclical *Divini redemptoris* on 'Atheistic Communism' appeared, on 19 March. In 1935 the Soviet dictator Josef Stalin had begun a campaign against 'counter-revolutionary terror groups'. No one, neither peasants nor workers, neither party members nor officials, was safe from being deported or shot. Between August 1937 and November 1938, about one and a half million Soviet citizens were victims of oppression; about 700,000 lost their lives. From 1937 there had been no Catholic bishop in office. New estimates say that up until 1941 about 350,000 Orthodox Christians were persecuted for their faith, including 140,000 clergy. In 1937 alone, the year the encyclicals *Divini redemptoris* and *With Burning Concern* were published, 150,000 Christians were arrested, 80,000 of them murdered. In the central area of the Soviet Union, 95 per cent of the churches existing in the 1920s were closed down or destroyed by 1941.[9]

Hitler had promised again and again that the church would be protected, as long as it restricted itself to the spiritual and did not pursue any political goals. On 20 July 1933 a Concordat was signed with the German Reich in the Vatican. At the time of the Weimar Republic, the Holy See had already negotiated one with Germany but because the government kept changing it was never ratified. By the Concordat, the German Reich guaranteed to preserve the safety of church institutions and religious education in Catholic faith schools. Four days later Cardinal von Faulhaber praised Hitler in a personal letter: 'It has now been proved to the whole world that Chancellor Hitler not only can make great speeches like his peace speech, but that he can also do great deeds, of world-historical import, like the Concordat. And we say with deep-felt sincerity: God keep our Chancellor for our people.'[10]

Presumably the cardinal wanted to score a political coup. His ingratiating letter had a purpose: 'Grant me one request: crown this great moment with a magnanimous amnesty for those who, without committing any crime, are in captivity merely for their political opinions, suffering terrible mental stress, together with their families.' Of course, the cardinal's gambit was ineffective. That Hitler 'not only can make great speeches' did not stand proof. According to the investigation *Priester unter Hitlers Terror*, during the Third Reich 8,021 Catholic secular and regular clergy were tortured and murdered. In the Bavarian dioceses, about 50 per cent of the clergy were directly persecuted, through fines, arrest, concentration camps and execution. In Dachau alone, about 2,720 clergy were imprisoned.[11] Of those, 1,034 did not survive the concentration camp. And in the Hartheim death camp, near Linz, 136 were gassed.

At their plenary assembly in January 1937, the German Bishops' Conference discussed their future attitude to the Nazi regime. Two views were expressed. One was for further cautious interaction with the holders of power. The other was for definite resistance. In particular, the latter view was held by the bishop of Münster, Graf von Galen, and the bishop of Berlin, Graf von Preysing. As cousins, they knew each other well and were in agreement. In the same month, Cardinals Adolf Bertram, Karl Joseph Schulte, Michael Faulhaber, Konrad Graf von Preysing and Clemens Graf von Galen went to Rome and informed Pius XI and Cardinal Secretary Eugenio Pacelli (later Pope Pius XII) about the situation of the church in their home country. Their trip to Rome was under the guise of an *ad limina* visit (*ad limina* is short for *visitatio ad limina Apostolorum,* literally 'visit to threshold of the Apostles'). Thereupon, Pacelli commissioned Faulhaber to draft an encyclical. The result was not particularly successful. Faulhaber himself described his draft as 'imperfect and probably unusable'.[12] The text was then edited by Pacelli, who substantially sharpened it, so that it became the clearest protest document against the Nazis to go into history. Pius XI had written 'with *great* concern'. Pacelli corrected the text to 'with *burning* concern'.

An encyclical in German was a novelty and has remained so to this day. For the first time ever, an encyclical was published first in the local language of the people concerned. The publication date, Passion Sunday, was also symbolic. By publishing it, the Vatican made it clear: the German bishops' appeasement policy was a failure. The change of course the bishops had undertaken when Hitler came to power was a terrible mistake. And Pacelli's editorial treatment would certainly have been even plainer, had he not been pushed by his German fellow clerics into avoiding terms like 'National Socialism' or 'Führer'.

The document was smuggled into Germany in strict secrecy on 12 March 1937. It was the task of the nuncio Cesare Orsenigo to pass the text on to the bishops, who in their turn were responsible for its distribution in their own dioceses. At night in darkened premises selected printers produced a special edition with an estimated print run of 300,000 copies. The printer Höfling received an order for a print run of 45,300 from the archdiocese of Munich. Diocesan newsletters were also used. For example, the *Kirchliche Amtsanzeiger für die Diözese Trier* (*Official Church Newsletter for the Diocese of Trier*) of 25 March 1937 consisted exclusively of the papal encyclical.

When, on 21 March 1937, the essential parts of the encyclical were read out in about 11,5000 Catholic churches, the Ratzinger family in Aschau were also in church. 'With burning anxiety and growing surprise,' the priest began reading out the pope's pastoral message, 'we have long been observing the church's Way of the Cross, and the increasing affliction of those men and women who have remained faithful to her in mind and deed amid the country and people to whom St Boniface once brought the light and the gospel of Christ and the Kingdom of God.'[13]

The first part of the document addressed the use of the term 'believer in God', as the Nazis interpreted it. Whoever through pantheistic vagueness identified God with the universe, whoever substituted a dark and gloomy fate for the personal God or whoever exalted race, or the people, or the State, or a particular form of State, or the holders of power or other instrument of human community organization to the highest norm, was not a believer in God. On the other hand, the pope praised those who fulfilled their Christian duty against an aggressive neo-paganism.

The text clearly condemned the National Socialists' racial doctrine: God 'in sovereign mastery has given his commandments. They are independent of time and space, country and race. As God's sun shines on every human face, so his law knows neither preferences nor exceptions.' Moreover, whoever wished to see 'Biblical history and the wise teaching of the Old Testament' banished from church and school blasphemes the name of God. The proposition that 'what is useful to the people is right' must be rejected. It was not morally good because it was useful, but rather, positive law was useful when it corresponded to the moral law. Whoever misconceived the difference between God and creatures and ventured to put any mortal being beside or above Christ was nothing but a 'false prophet' – a clear reference to the cult of the 'Führer'.

The church was a home and a refuge for people of all times and all nations, the encyclical continued. However, it was not enough simply to belong to the church: the faithful must also be active members of it. Only a self-aware Christianity that rejected every compromise with the world and was active in the love of God and neighbour could and should be a model to a world that was fundamentally sick, 'if it is to avoid an unspeakable catastrophe and destruction that boggles the imagination'. If anyone thought they could combine publicly leaving the church with inwardly remaining faithful to it, then let Jesus' words be a warning: 'Anyone who disowns me before others, I will also disown before my Father.'

In the fourth part of the encyclical, the pope condemned the idea of a German national church. 'So know this: It is nothing but a denial of the one church of Christ.' The history of other national churches 'with their paralysis, their embrace or enslavement by worldly powers' showed the 'hopeless sterility that inescapably befalls any branch severing itself from the living vine of the church'. The warning was directed, in particular, to the younger generation wooed by the Hitler Youth: 'If anyone wants to preach another Gospel to you than the one you received at the knees of a devout mother or from the lips of a believing father or from a teacher faithful to his God and his church – ignore them.'

In conclusion, the pope confirmed that every word of the encyclical had been weighed 'in the balance of truth and also of love. We wished neither to be complicit with a lack of clarity through untimely silence, nor by excessive severity harden the hearts of those who come within our pastoral responsibility, whom we still love as a shepherd, even though, for the time being, they have wandered off into error and estrangement.' He called God to witness that he wished for nothing but the restoration of true peace between church and state in Germany. But if peace was not to be, then the church would defend her rights and liberties.

The Nazis reacted immediately. The interior minister, Wilhelm Frick, described the printing of the encyclical as an action hostile to the Reich and the people. Distribution of the text would be treated as high treason. The bishops were charged with grave disloyalty to their Fatherland. As they had so often done, they were making pacts with states that were enemies of Germany. The Nazis sent a protest note to the Holy See, as a partner in an agreement with the German Reich, saying that with their pastoral message they had committed a serious breach of trust. Likewise, the press was forbidden to report anything about the encyclical or the reading of it, even by allusion.

Even before Good Friday came the first house searches and arrests. A number of monasteries and faith schools were shut immediately. Twelve printing works that had been involved in the dissemination of the encyclical were expropriated without compensation. In addition, Reinhard Heydrich, chief of the Security Service (SD) and the Secret Police (Gestapo), put a three-month publication ban on all episcopal newsletters that had included the encyclical.

But that was only the beginning. Then came thousands of house searches, hundreds of arrests and expropriations. In April 1937, on Hitler's order, there was a new wave of 'moral procedures' against priests and religious. Goebbels personally directed a campaign against the 'sexual plague' of priests, who were to 'be eradicated root and branch'. As a result, the private Catholic schools were closed down or taken over by the state. Priests and religious were no longer allowed to give religious instruction in elementary or vocational schools. All Catholic organizations and youth groups were dissolved, their publications banned and their assets confiscated.

The Ratzingers spent Good Friday and Easter in Aschau. A week later the family was on the move. A watchtower had just been set up on the Winterberg mountain near the village, allegedly to sight enemy planes. However, no planes flew over Aschau, and certainly no enemy planes. So when the watchtower's searchlight 'passed over the night sky with its harsh glare, it seemed dangerous to us like sheet lightning, a danger for which there was as yet no name'. That image became a powerful metaphor for later theologians: 'It was vaguely apprehended that something deeply disturbing was being prepared here. But no one could believe the ominous thing looming in a world that still seemed quite peaceful.'[14]

7

The Calm before the Storm

The removal van had gone on ahead; the family came in the car belonging to Frau Pichlmeier, the owner of the brewery in Aschau. Full of expectation, they drove past woods and fields, up hill and down. When they arrived, the first thing young Joseph saw was 'the meadow full of cowslips'.

Their new home with the odd name of Hufschlag lay just 40 kilometres from Aschau. But at last Joseph senior could turn his back on the hated regime. At last they could live in their own house. At last they'd be in a proper town and at the same time they'd be on the sidelines, far from the goings-on of this murderous time. In the future pope's memory, when he spoke about this 'greatest and best part of my youth', he had a feeling of rescue. 'Unbelievably beautiful', everything was for him here, a 'real paradise'.

Benedict XVI once quoted a saying of Goethe that 'anyone who wants to understand a poet must go to the poet's home'. That is true not only for poets. Ratzinger himself attributed enormous importance to the influence on him of the place where he grew up. That involved the language, the temperament and the way of life of the people. Even the particular landscape also had its effect, especially in an area that was 'very Salzburgish'. For 'there Mozart, so to speak, permeated us right through; he has always moved me profoundly because he is so light and at the same time so deep'. Here in the 'father town', as he called this new refuge, 'after many wanderings' the family had finally reached their 'true home'.

Hufschlag, near the Upper Bavarian town of Kleinstadt, once consisted of just a dozen houses, mostly farmhouses. But there was also a shop, a post office with a public telephone and a railway station. The railway lay on the route of a former Roman road. And the 'paradise' of which Ratzinger speaks in his memoirs was in fact a 300-year-old house with less than 100 m² of living space, in which no one would have been brought up had they not been forced by circumstance.

The roof was leaky, and the walls were damp. Instead of a modern toilet there was an earth closet. The water came from the well in the front garden, which was no fun in winter and often useless in summer, when the spring dried up. The back of the building consisted of an abandoned stable and a ramshackle barn. Perhaps, worst of all, the new householder, the retired policeman, was not exactly a handyman. As a farmer's son, he could mow grass and milk cows. In summer he made hay, but plastering cracks or repairing tiles was not his thing. Nevertheless, none of his fellow residents here was a Nazi.

The house at 'Number 11 Hufschlag' stood just by an oak wood. On the ground floor to the right there was the kitchen with a wood-burning stove to cook on. To the left was the living room, in which a cheaply acquired piano would soon stand. Joseph and Georg shared a room on the first floor. It had a chest of drawers with a mirror and two washbasins on top. There were two beds with big quilts: 'When we opened our eyes, the first thing we saw was the mountains.' The view was 'unbelievably beautiful'.

Their mother knew how to make things cosy by the simplest means, creating a kind of 'good whole world in which we were happy and felt at home', Georg reported. Beside the old apple, pear, cherry and plum trees she made a garden for vegetables, herbs and her favourite: flowers. A wealth of flowers. The family became self-sufficient. Their mother even exchanged part of their harvest for food in the shop. She was quickly accepted by the neighbours and took on the cooking in several households, when a cow was calving or the corn had to be brought in.

Their mother, Maria, was completely unpolitical. She read the death notices on the back of the newspaper, and the books she read were mainly by Catholic popular writers with historical themes: *Ben Hur*, *Quo Vadis* and also the novel *Der Mann den die Welt Nicht Sah* (*The Man the World Did Not See*). This was not about Jesus of Nazareth but about an artist who could make himself invisible. For her husband's birthday she had ordered the *Small Herder,* a popular encyclopaedia which the three children proudly brought home from the post office. When she fetched fresh milk from the neighbour in the evening, she sometimes made jokes about Hitler. Otherwise, she was known to be motherly and deeply pious, but not sanctimonious. 'She was simply a good-hearted woman,' Xavier Zeiser from the neighbouring farm declared, 'no one was more unassuming'.

Young Joseph went exploring in the old barn, where he 'had the most glorious dreams and could play wonderful games'. He sometimes tussled with his brother, either when they played ball games or 'when it was about who was right'. The neighbour's cheeky farm cats, the previous owner's weaving room, the trips into the oak wood – this whole 'unexplored and unfathomable world' – was endlessly rich. They had 'not felt at all' the lack of comfort, but enjoyed this 'adventurous, free and beautiful old house with its inner warmth'.

Soon it was reported of the retired policeman's sons that they walked up and down in the oak wood, reading books, using Latin phrases and making solemn gestures. In the holidays Georg read his adventure stories. They were called *Sydia the Faithful Son from India* and *In the Tents of the Mahdi.* Their bookshelves had the small yellow books of classics: Schiller, Goethe, Theodor Storm, published by Reclam for 35 pfennigs each. Sometimes there was home music-making, with Georg on the piano, their father on the zither and Joseph on the violin. Or the three of them played cards, their favourite game being *Schafkopf* (a German card game meaning 'sheep's head'). 'We didn't play very well,' Georg recalled, 'it was more for fun.' His brother always won. He was 'better at memorizing what cards lay on the table and what was still in the pack'.[1]

With a piece of land measuring about 3,500 m^2, at last their father, Joseph, could be a farmer. He collected wood from the forest in a handcart and kept hens, a cockerel and even a ram, which liked to run off, so that the boys had to go and catch him in the wood. On Sundays, Joseph occasionally allowed himself a glass of wine in a neighbouring village. Above all he read the newspaper, every line. And soon there was a radio by his place in the kitchen. He could listen to foreign stations on it and not be force-fed by the German broadcasting. When he brought Georg's trunk to the boarding school on the handcart after a weekend, he impressed on the director that with Hitler everything would go '100 per cent wrong' and they should take a much firmer stand against the Nazi regime.

Since their move, the 16-year-old Maria had lived in the nuns' boarding house in Au am Inn, in order to get her middle school leaving certificate. The school was called the 'House of Divine Providence'. She learned shorthand, English, domestic economy and also typing. She did not guess that she would some day put all these skills to use for her brother. Maria was highly intelligent and introverted, but also selfless. 'Don't force things. That was her way,' a relative reported, even though she could also be very determined. 'Everything had to be in its place,' Georg related; 'she was always tidying up my chaos, so that I couldn't find anything again.'

Now at boarding school, Georg progressed in his natural gifts. As soon as the holidays came, he sat at home at the piano, even when, to save money, the living room was unheated. His younger brother would slip away quietly. 'When I was there,' said the elder brother, 'he didn't dare play,' although he had 'a good average talent'.[2]

On 12 April 1937, four days before his tenth birthday, 'a new seriousness' began for Joseph. It was his first day in the humanities gymnasium in Traunstein. The school year was divided into trimesters. The first term ran from Easter to summer, the second from September to Christmas, the third from the New Year till Easter. After their move, his parents did not want to send him to the elementary school just for one more year. So unlike the others pupils, who changed schools after their fifth year, he enrolled at the gymnasium after his fourth year. He was not only the youngest but also among the smallest of the new intake of 32 boys and three girls. Only the boy sitting next to him on the front bench was even smaller than him. Besides the three girls, that boy was the only Protestant in the class.

Joseph did not begin well. At the beginning of every term there was a roll-call to salute the flag in the schoolyard, which all the pupils had to attend. His brother Georg and the pupils from the episcopal seminary – the 'Semi-Christians' or 'black pigs', as they were now rudely dubbed by many of their their fellow students – also stood in line. The event began with the director's 'rousing Nazi speech' to 'our much loved, ardently loved, deeply loved Führer',

George remembered. When a boy raised the flag of the German Reich, the headmaster, baton in hand, stretched out his arm rigid in the 'German salute'. Then followed the German national anthem. The business seemed to affect young Joseph badly. He fell ill, so his father took him to Paul Keller, the episcopal seminary doctor, who diagnosed the boy as suffering from malnutrition. Then the doctor stared straight at the old policeman with the grizzled moustache, who looked as if he could have been the boy's grandfather. The doctor said coldly that the gymnasium was not the right place for a pupil from such humble circumstances. It would have been better for him to have stayed at the elementary school.

It took about half an hour to get from his parents' house in Hufschlag to the gymnasium in the middle of the town. The journey to school made up to Joseph for his problems at the start. On his way he could reflect, look around, dream. Before him stood the Chiemgau Alps, with Hausbergen, Hochfelln and Hochgern. Up to the right, on a deep green hill, bright with yellow dandelions, stood the little Ettendorf church, with its onion dome in all its graceful Bavarian Baroque glory. According to the records, the church had stood there for a thousand years. On Easter Monday it was the scene of the annual St George procession with hundreds of horses, ahead of the heavy cold-blooded dragons with their wild manes and monstrous hindquarters. Then, when Joseph looked towards the valley, he saw the picturesque town on the Traun with its idyllic squares and fountains, quaint church towers and elaborately painted town houses, from whose chimneys even in April plumes of transparent smoke went up into the blue and white sky.

In the 1930s, Traunstein had at least 10,000 inhabitants. The medieval commercial, administrative and school town became rich through salt, the 'white gold' that was pumped through a pipeline (the first in the world) from Bad Reichenhall and processed here. Joseph's way to school led through the historic town square. In the middle of it stood the Baroque parish church of St Oswald, named after the seventh-century Scottish king and saint. Then, at the end of the town park, Joseph reached the gymnasium itself, an imposing building constructed in 1901. Here an obelisk commemorated the victims of Napoleon's wars from 1799 to 1815, which restructured Europe.

The little 'Hufschlagler' as children from the poor, not particularly distinguished village on the edge of the town were called, did not attract attention among the rowdies in the first class. From his brother he took over the name 'Hacki' (derived from a gaunt art teacher called Hicke). Georg was 'big Hacki' and Joseph was 'little Hacki'. At first he was still teased, but that soon died down. 'He was very skinny,' his schoolfellow Ludwig Wihr reported, 'always very quiet, a very calm student.' 'Ratzinger was not shy,' Joseph Strehhuber remembered, 'but neither did he seek contact.'³ Pictures from that time show wide-awake eyes, a distant look and a mischievous smile, more inward- than outward-directed. His body was fragile, as if made of glass. His face was soft and finely drawn. Small and thin as he was, in group photos his head was often ducked, as if he felt squeezed in a crowd, as in a vice.

Joseph was not a typical top-of-the-class high-flyer who always distinguished himself. He was not a combative or sporty type but the little slip of a boy to be found in every class, so he did not opportunistically vie for attention. He let others copy from him without making anything of it. Indeed, he showed traits that might have seemed slightly autistic or at least made him seem like a loner. In fact, there was a lack of neighbouring children of the same age in Hufschlag, 'not much community', so he 'really created his own poetic dream world', Ratzinger declared.⁴ 'He was reserved with people he did not know,' Georg added. His brother was by nature 'something of a romantic, sensitive soul'. But in a good atmosphere he was 'more open but just did not show it very well. He kept many things to himself.'

However, he certainly was not servile. 'In his class he earned respect through his mental ability,' said his schoolfellow Wihr. 'He was clever and quick-witted.' Ratzinger himself related that he went through a phase when he showed 'a tendency to impudence'. His 'cheeky answers' had even made many teachers angry. 'Cocky' was one entry on his school report.

Joseph began to find his feet. The whole nineteenth-century humanistic German education ideal, which was maintained in Traunstein by old teachers, was still directed towards the Greek thinkers and classical languages, towards the True, Beautiful and Good, not megalomania and Aryanism. Latin and Greek were subjects that he 'loved' – as well as Hebrew, which was still offered in his early school years, before it was axed from the curriculum by the Nazis. 'Latin was taught with the old strictness and thoroughness as the basis of our whole education,' he remembered, 'for which I have been grateful all my life.'[5] Looking back, not without pride, he said: 'As a theologian I had no difficulty in studying the sources in Latin and Greek, and at the [Second Vatican] Council in Rome, although I had never heard Latin lectures, I was quickly able to get into Latin as it was then spoken by theologians.' For some time, he had seen 'ancient philology as a promising path' and dreamed of becoming a professor of language and literature.[6]

The child Joseph was growing up, and the pupil whom the doctor had wanted to send back to the elementary school was soon giving extra help to others: for example, to his classmate Anton Tradler, whose marks, as a result, increased dramatically. 'We others just accepted things,' said a contemporary, 'but he thought about them.' Joseph became one of the three best pupils in the school. Once he was even made class prefect. As the teacher put it: 'The littlest one gets to be king.' And he would have been by far the best of all, had not his marks in sport and drawing brought his average down.

His mother proudly told the family how gifted young Joseph was, but he did not become a spoilt child as a result. And there was no special pressure on him. 'Father was very keen for us to learn and be orderly. But he didn't want or push us to become 'great'. However, he was glad we wanted to 'become priests'.'[7] Of course, success did not just fall into Joseph's lap. 'I was someone who just went for these things in a big way,' he said in retrospect. 'Many things came easily to him,' said his brother, 'but he always also stuck to his work very conscientiously.'

Even when he was just 11, Joseph set himself a firm pattern for his daily workload. On the way home he would 'repeat what he had learned in school'. After lunch he rested for a short time on the sofa in the living room, then he carefully did his homework. 'He could work very intensively, everything very exact, also very systematically,' George recalled, 'with the motto: Duty first then Pleasure.' On the door to his room in Hufschlag there was a small notice: 'Please do not disturb.' 'At least it was clear,' he reminisced in a conversation when he was pope, 'that I divided up my time and really did work during the time set for work.'

The *Semper Idem*, 'always the same', as Cicero described the equanimity of the Greek philosopher Socrates, also applied to Ratzinger. His regulated daily timetable, his disciplined working habits, the care always to keep time, with a set rhythm (at a low, constant frequency), led to enormous efficiency. That was the pattern followed by the early Ratzinger as well as later on. It was strictly ritualized. When something was once set, that was kept to – even his kindergarden habit of writing with a pencil. Even when he was pope, Ratzinger wrote his books with a pencil. 'It has the advantage that you can rub out. If I write with ink, then it is written.'

His 'joy in teaching' also remained. Even in the elementary school, teaching and writing were 'something that excited me'. However introverted he might appear by nature, when he became a professor he became extrovert when it was a question of communicating to others what he knew to be true and important. As a boy he had enjoyed writing poems, but what he really felt called to do, Ratzinger said in his self-assessment, was to 'pass on knowledge'. That 'vocation' corresponded with Ratzinger's faith journey. As a child he had entered step by step into 'a mysterious world' and wanted 'to penetrate further into it'. He did so emotionally through spiritual experience and rationally by approaching the propositions of the faith as an intellectual challenge.

Baptism and first communion were one initiation in religion. The other was the sacrament of confirmation in order to become an adult and fully fledged member of the Catholic Church. The sacrament was administered to Joseph on 9 June 1937 in the Traunstein parish church of St Oswald – by that very Cardinal Faulhaber who had already so impressed him when he was in the kindergarden. Solemnly, the cardinal spread his hands over the boy and prayed for the Holy Spirit and his gifts to descend upon him. Then he laid his right hand on Joseph's head and made the sign of the cross on his forehead with the consecrated oil. 'Be confirmed by God's gift, the Holy Spirit.' The laying on of hands by the bishop was a sign of God's protection and the presence of his Spirit. According to Catholic teaching, the Holy Spirit was to further his growth in 'supernatural life', in order to come nearer to God's kingdom, which was independent of time and space but nevertheless existed in time.

While his brother and sister were away at boarding school, except in the holidays, Joseph enjoyed his time with his retired father. They went mountain walking on Kampenwand and on bike rides together. At the same time, his father was becoming a house husband. He had polished the family's shoes in the past. 'That was his job,' according to his son. But now he would stand at the stove in a kitchen apron to make pancakes and apfelstrudel. It was always 'homely like in the good old days,' said Franz Niegel, a childhood friend of Joseph's, when you went to visit them in Hufschlag.

Two children in senior school, the instalments on the house, always some repair or other – and all that to be paid out of a small pension of 242 Reichsmarks a month. The Ratzingers' housekeeping money was always very over-stretched. Joseph was also due to go to the episcopal seminary, but there was not enough money to pay for it. The boy did not take it amiss: 'So I was granted two years at home, which did me a lot of good.' Now their mother had to go out to work as a seasonal cook in the Glück im Winkel guesthouse in the spa town of Reit im Winkel, 40 kilometres away, and then later in Kufstein.

The fact that the father of the family could not keep them on his own may have cast a shadow over his household. On the other hand, living on the breadline through their permanent shortage of money brought the family members unusually close together. They acquired a habit of frugality and carefulness that marked them for life. Through 'this very modest, financially strained situation', Ratzinger maintained, there 'arose an inner solidarity, which bound us very close together'. Their parents made 'enormous sacrifices' for them, and the children had, of course, 'felt that and tried to respond'. Thus a life of great simplicity 'also led to great joy – and love for one another'. In the end the situation had the advantage 'that we could be happy over the smallest things'. And that was something that you 'could not have with wealth'.

The more the pressure of the dictatorship and their general hardship increased, the more intense the family's life of prayer became. Their parents knelt to pray the rosary together every day. And of course it went without saying that they kept the Sabbath commandment. But now their father went to Mass not only on Sundays but daily, and often several times a day. In an old prayer book, his vade-mecum and indispensable companion, he collected brochures, pictures and memorial cards, sent to him as a patron of various missionary orders. 'He was simply a man who really lived a devout church life,' Joseph remembered. And, Georg said, prayers after supper were now 'very long'. There were many Our Fathers. Also prayers to St Judas Thaddeus (for divine providence and a good hour of death) and to St Dismas (for protection from robbers and any crime). 'I must admit,' said Georg, 'for us children it was a bit too much.'

Go carefully with the resources. Make life harmonious with what is possible. And from the little that we have create spirit and joy. That was basically the *ora et labora* from the Rule of St Benedict. From it also sprang a particular attitude that had to do with dignity and decency. It was a happy medium, with nothing too little and nothing too much, nothing too tight and nothing too slack – a stylistic assurance whose origin was not aristocratic but from the nobility of a convinced faith that held fast to the biblical tradition. Later on, Ratzinger also lived with monastic simplicity, without any luxury, and in an atmosphere that ignored and was indifferent to the essentials of comfort. When he was Prefect of the Congregation for the Doctrine of the Faith, Lufthansa once offered him a new suitcase, as his shabby old one was bad for business. In his papal apartment he decisively rejected a new desk. 'He always gave away a lot of his salary,' Peter Kuhn, Ratzinger's academic assistant in Tübingen, reported. When he discovered a student or young priest in financial straits, his reaction was: 'Write your account number on this paper.' After that, according to Kuhn, 'a bank transfer was paid in every month'.[8]

After getting her middle school leaving certificate, Maria spent a 'year in the country' near Schyern with the parish priest, Father Weber. That presbytery household also had a farm. Thus she was able to avoid the Nazi national service, which young women had to do as 'work maids'. In his seminary studies Georg was allowed to attend harmony lessons, the foundation for understanding chord structure and tonal range. The course was actually meant for students at the upper level, but he was allowed to attend early. Joseph was a cheerful boy, who enjoyed learning quietly and had begun translating the Greek original of the Gospels into German, in order to take in the material in his own way. Soon, however, a radical upheaval catapulted him out of his idyll, in which he felt so safe.

Something else also marked the end of a stage in his development. In the same year as the family moved to Hufschlag, Hitler began to convert his holiday home at Berchtesgaden into a 'small Reich Chancellory'. Obersalzberg – just 40 kilometres, as the crow flies, from the Ratzingers' house – was to become a second seat of government, a centre of National Socialist power. So the name Hufschlag (meaning 'hoof beat') acquired a new sound for Ratzinger senior. It meant he could actually hear the hoof beats of the riders of the Apocalypse on the horizon. In the not so distant future they would turn the fruitful Earth into a burned-out wasteland.

8

The Seminary

When thick, pearl-grey clouds, which might burst within minutes, hung over the rooftops, the new way to school was a pain. For two whole years he had 'walked daily to school from home with great enjoyment'. Now he marched two by two under supervision, as if in the army.

Joseph felt like a bird thrown out of its nest which had difficulty finding its feet. Having started school early, he was the youngest boy of all in the seminary boarding school. And almost the smallest. When they marched from the seminary to the gymnasium in the mornings, being in the troop gave a sense of security and community. Perhaps also the awareness of belonging to an elite. But what prospects has an elite threatened with imminent annihilation?

Every day on the way to school the episcopal seminary pupils experienced what becoming a priest meant. Locks and entrance doors to the boarding school were constantly rendered unusable by being plastered up. The street sign 'Kardinal-Faulhaber-Strasse' was smeared over with graffiti like 'Warme Bruderstrasse' ('Warm Brother Street') or 'Kardinal Faulhaber ist ein Hochverräter' ('Cardinal Faulhaber is a traitor'). 'We'll get even in the end,' the Hitler Youth called out after the 'cub priests', whom they mocked for their uniform, the 'flood trousers' which only reached to their ankles and the rather shabby-looking dark jackets. As they trotted along, didn't they look rather like lambs to the slaughter?

The Nazi regime won victory after victory. No one seemed to stand in its way. In 1938, just a few kilometres from Traunstein, Hitler had marched into Austria. The cheering of the masses could almost be heard in Traunstein: *'Ein Reich, ein Volk, ein Führer!'* ('One Reich, one People, one Leader'). At seven o'clock in the morning, the square opposite the Festival Hall was full to overflowing. From eight o'clock the loudspeakers announced the breaking news: 'The Führer is leaving Obersalzberg [...] The Führer is approaching home [...] The Führer will arrive in a few minutes [...]' An enormous procession of vehicles had preceded him. Children were already being held up high to reach out towards the 'Führer'. 'The announcements signalled a Saviour from the holy German nation coming ever closer,' Joseph's fellow student at Freising (and later friend) Walter Brugger remembered, who was then ten years old. 'With his simple clothes, his outstretched arm, Hitler had a tremendous fascination. I wanted to shout "Heil!" but I couldn't, because I was too excited.'[1]

In the last few months, Hitler's Berghof in Obersalzberg had become the dictator's control centre. An extensive 'Führer's Prohibited Area' was fenced off round it. A regime airport was created in Bad Reichenhall and a 'Reich Chancellory office' in Berchtesgaden.[2] In the Berghof, the 'Berchtesgaden Agreement' was signed, which sealed the end of the Austrian state. Then on 15 September 1938, the British prime minister, Neville Chamberlain, was a guest there to deal with the Sudetenland crisis. Five days later the British, together with the French and Italian heads of government signed the 'Munich Agreement' in the 'Führer's Building' in Königsplatz, Munich. The Agreement provided for the incorporation of Sudetenland into the German state, and its actual aim was the dissolution of Czechoslovakia. In Hufschlag, his son recalled, Ratzinger the pensioner raged 'that the French, whom he esteemed highly, seemed to accept Hitler's criminal acts one after another as something almost normal'.

It was the parish priest, Stefan Blum, who urged that Joseph should be sent to the episcopal seminary. In times like these this was obligatory for a systematic introduction to a life in the church. Until then, the step had been impossible for financial reasons. But now Maria had found a job as a clerk in Kreiler's ironmongery business and was prepared to hand over a large part of her wages. She had given up her dream of becoming a teacher, since she had received no reply from the Education Department to her inquiry.

For their father it may have been a sign when the death of Pope Pius XI was announced on 10 February 1939. 'It was the first time in our life,' Georg reported, 'that one papacy ended and another began.' His brother added: 'We honoured and loved the pope – and at the same time looked upon him as infinitely distant, infinitely far above us.'[3] The successor to Paul XI was Cardinal Secretary of State Eugenio Pacelli, the former nuncio in Munich. Even in 1924, when many regarded Hitler's party as a 'bunch of guttersnipes', Pacelli had branded National Socialism as 'perhaps the most dangerous heresy of our time'.[4]

The encyclical *Mit brennender Sorge* (*With Burning Concern*) had been published by his predecessor, but Pacelli had substantially sharpened the text and the tone. Immediately after Pacelli's election, the Bavarian minister of culture, Adolf Wagner, had closed down the theological faculty of Munich University. Two years before that, he had closed the late vocation seminary in Munich and the minor seminary in Schyern. So now Ratzinger senior's mind was made up. Two days after Pius XII came to office, he wrote a letter to the Director, Johann Evangelist Mair, requesting him also to admit his younger son into the episcopal seminary.

He duly enclosed a testimonial from the gymnasium, which described the boy as well behaved, diligent and reliable. He also added a certificate from Dr Keller. The doctor certified that the boy's strength and state of nutrition had improved. Though moderately underweight, he was in good health. Of course, Joseph still had to do the entrance exam. It was no surprise that he did very well in it. His father also asked for a reduction in the fees of 40 Reichsmarks per month. With a pension of 242 Reichsmarks, he could not afford more than 700 marks per year for his two sons.

On Sunday, 16 April 1939, Joseph celebrated his 12th birthday. On the same day, a new stage in his life began. Their mother cried as her two boys set out on their way. 'Take care of Joseph,' she called after her eldest son. Georg, who was two classes above him, encouraged his brother. No, he did not like sport either, 'because you might get hurt and then not be able to play the piano'. But there were all kinds of musical instruments, games and good comrades. 'I had no problem with the boarding school,' Georg reported, 'but my brother found it harder. He is a bit more sensitive than me.' In fact, his arrival was a real shock to Joseph. 'I am one of those people,' he said drily in retrospect, 'who are not made for boarding school.'[5]

At the end of the 1930s the episcopal seminary in Traunstein was one of the most modern and progressive institutions of its time, and one of the Bavaria's most renowned educational establishments. Even the outdoor areas for sport and recreation, the greenhouses, vegetable plots and parklike green spaces were impressive. As well as three classrooms, three dormitories and the huge dining room with its 'General's Platform', on which 'Rex' Mair sat enthroned, there was a music room, theatre, library, chapel, conference room and infirmary. There was even a bowling alley. Baths, footbaths and showers were up to the most modern standards. Together with 20 nuns from the Bad Adelholzen Sisters of Mercy, three menservants and six housemaids looked after the washing, cooking and household management. They even had their own poultry house.

For the dormitories, Cardinal von Faulhaber had personally ordered the white iron bedsteads to be fitted exclusively with horse hair mattresses 'like the students will get later from the parish priest when they become curates'. And in order to toughen them up, there should only be cold water for the washbasins in the dormitory. At the ceremonial opening of the building, the cardinal wrote the following words in the house Visitors' Book with his fountain pen:

> Today on 1 September 1929, a summery Sunday, at its consecration I invoked the name of the Lord upon this seminary in Traunstein. A great blessing will lie upon this house, because in economically difficult times it has been built with offerings from the people and with widows' mites. May the new seminary become what its name means, a 'plant nursery', a planting of God.

However, for a free spirit like Joseph the daily routine, timetabled to the last minute, must have felt as if he had entered not a 'plant nursery' but a living nightmare. Getting-up time was 5.30 in the morning. This was followed exactly 25 minutes later by personal morning prayers, then Mass in the chapel. At 6.30 a.m. study time began with the revision of the previous day's exercises. Breakfast at 7.00. At 7.20 the approximately 170 pupils stood lined up ready for the march to the gymnasium. Lunch was from 12.05 until 12.45. After a short period of free time came afternoon lessons, then an hour of play, sport or free time. At 4.30 p.m. they were offered coffee or cocoa, and from 5 to 7 p.m. there was another study period. From 7 to 7.30 p.m. they all had supper, with 35 minutes' further free time after that, before a quarter of an hour's devotion, spiritual reading or a talk at 8.05 p.m. That was followed by evening prayers in the chapel at 8.20. From 8.30 p.m. there had to be complete silence in the dormitory.[6]

According to the seminary regulations, the students were bound to show mutual respect. Particular friendships between students were forbidden, and too great familiarity with the town students was to be avoided. The rules were reverence, obedience, politeness, punctuality, orderliness, a sense of duty and honesty. Within the house 'bad' or 'indecent' conversations were to be reported. Individual outings needed permission. In the corridors, particularly on the way to chapel, they all had to keep silent. Disobeying the rules could result in immediate dismissal. Under the rubric 'Duties to God', the seminarians were bound 'in all sincerity and with all their might to struggle for deep godliness and true piety and towards perfection in Christian life'.[7]

What a change! Joseph had enjoyed the untrammelled freedom of Hufschlag, where no one kept him on a lead – 'I was used to being my own master'. But now he was suddenly confined: in a study hall with 50 other boys, supervised by a strict prefect, in a dormitory with 40 beds, where *silentium sacratum,* holy silence, was the rule till morning. And a notoriously late sleeper like him did not enjoy getting up so early. Ratzinger confessed that the previously 'unknown restriction by which I suddenly had to fit in to a fixed system' was 'extremely difficult' for him.

Leaving home had been hard enough, and it did not make things any easier for Joseph that his entry into the seminary boarding school coincided with his gymnasium merging with another secondary school, the *Realschule.* At a stroke, the teaching staff changed. Instead of classicists, now there were younger teachers, loyal to the regime, who belonged to the National Socialist Teachers' Federation (NSLB). One even came to school in uniform, and as soon as they came into the classroom, some 'stuck out their arm almost the whole way from the door to the teacher's desk'. The class teacher, Dr Josef Kopp, read the *Völkischer Beobachter* during lessons. But there were also others. The music teacher, 'a proper Catholic', told the students to cross out the words *Judah den Tod'* ('To Judah be death') and replace them with *'Wende die Not'* ('Tend our distress').

Because of its close connection with the episcopal seminary, the gymnasium had long been a thorn in the side of the National Socialist authorities. Nazi mothers complained to the ministry in Munich that in Traunstein far too much consideration was still given to the seminarians, so that good 'Hitler boys' and their 'faithful National Socialist parents' had to suffer.

In a report to the culture ministry in 1937, Kreisleiter ('Circle Leader', a Nazi Party political rank) Anton Endros declared that the school was 'ideologically very unsound' because 'the archepiscopal seminary provides the majority of students'. And 'the education in this seminary is expressly hostile to the state. Among the pupils there are fanatical haters of the Führer and National Socialism.'[8]

The Director, Dr Maximilian Leitschuh, was the next victim of the political purge at the gymnasium. He had made no secret of his distance from the Nazis. Other unpopular teachers were pensioned off or targeted. For example, in his lessons senior teacher Dr Peter Parzinger had not given a Nazi interpretation to verses by the German poet and freedom fighter Ernst Moritz Arndt ('What is a German's Fatherland?'), so the Nazi-aligned *Chiemgau-Bote* hounded him: the 'traitor to his country' had forfeited the right to be a German public servant, 'and he is sure to find an SA man who has a powerful boot to kick him with'.

Traunstein was a telling example of how the Nazi terror functioned. The NSDAP had only won one seat in the town council in 1929. In the Reichstag election of 31 July 1932 the Nazis only won 23.3 per cent of the votes. Ninety per cent of the inhabitants were Catholics, and church establishments were ubiquitous. For example, the Englische Fräulein nuns, founded by Mary Ward, ran not only a kindergarten but also a girls' elementary school and a girls' secondary school. The Franciscan sisters ran a children's home as well as an itinerant healthcare service. The Sisters of Mercy provided the care in the town hospital and home for the elderly. The Sisters of the Most Holy Saviour (Bridgettines) provided the care in the town's sanatorium. In all, 23 Catholic bodies – including the Corpus Christi and All Souls Confraternities, the Marianische Jungfrauen (Marian Girls') Congregation and the Students' Congregation – contributed to the life of the town. The Catholic Parents' Union alone had 1,350 members. The Nazis acted all the more aggressively after their takeover of power. 'There's just one thing to be said to opponents,' roared the *Chiemgau-Bote* on 4 February 1933: 'the times are past when the National Socialist movement, its Führer and its regime can be abused, defamed and treated with suspicion.'[9]

In March 1933 the SA with 150 men occupied the town hall, the district office and the trade union headquarters. At first the SPD and KPD representatives were arrested. On 24 June the representatives of the Bavarian People's Party were also taken into 'protective custody'. The mayor, Rupert Berger, was replaced immediately after the 'takeover of power' and sent to Dachau concentration camp. SA henchmen smashed the family's grocery shop in the night.

The controversial Traunstein parish priest, Joseph Stelzle, was removed. The fact that in his parish church every Sunday all five Masses were still well attended could not remain unpunished. Stelzle's curate was arrested, because he prohibited the Hitler salute in the school. Two of his assistants were forbidden to teach and were harassed with house searches and Gestapo interrogations. This was followed by a bomb attack on the presbytery. An informer reported on Stelzle's sermon for Epiphany 1934:

> Among other things he said that the three Kings came from abroad into the country of the Jews to the newborn king of the Jews, to our Lord and Saviour etc. After further explanations he said: Christ was born and died for all, for white, yellow and black. But today, he said, there are movements which refuse to believe this, who want to falsify Christ and make him an Aryan. This racial movement, he continued, preaches so-called positive Christianity, a bogus Christianity, a Germanized Christianity, that promotes a master race, which has always brought disaster to the people. Beware of this false prophet!

The very next day SA Special Commissioner Otto Mantler ordered the cleric to be taken into custody: 15 days' imprisonment. After a second bomb attack destroyed part of the presbytery courtyard, Stelzle was told to leave town immediately. Cardinal Faulhaber promptly ordered not only that the expulsion should be cancelled but also that, until his priest returned, bells were not to be rung or the organ played. Solemn High Mass was dropped. When Stelzle returned, despite being banned from the town, he was welcomed by several hundred Traunsteiners. They prevented their parish priest from being detained again.

The regime's stated aim was to expel the Catholic Church completely from public life. In 1936 morality trials began against members of religious orders and priests, which sought to present clerics in general as corrupters of the youth. Between 1934 and 1939, the Catholic youth organizations were banned. In the years 1935 to 1937 there followed the exclusion of clergy from religious instruction, and between 1935 and 1941 the abolition of faith schools. 'Practically speaking, Catholic life was driven back to being a "sacristy Christianity"', according to the historian Klaus-Rüdiger Mai; 'it could go on inside churches themselves but no longer in public places.'[10] In 1937 all elementary school teachers who belonged to an order of nuns were dismissed. Another attack ordered the 'abolition of schools run by religious orders' because, as a culture ministry document put it, it was unacceptable 'that still today a large number of future housewives and mothers should receive their education and training in convents'.

All this was part of Joseph's schoolboy experience. Despite the intimidation, in Traunstein there was no decrease in the number of people coming for baptisms, communion or church weddings, or any decline in church membership. For many Catholics, the threat to their faith led to an intensification of their religious life. Demonstrations by women and petitions forced the Nazis to withdraw the order banning crucifixes from classrooms. When SA Special Commissioner Mantler banned all Catholic groups from holding meetings or being active, groups like the Catholic Women's Association reacted by calling their meetings tea afternoons, meeting in secret or re-grouping under a different name.

With the restructuring of Joseph's gymnasium, Latin, Greek and religion were dropped and replaced by extra lessons in German, history and geography. Luckily for Joseph his 'Helios' class, as the students called it, was the last one that was allowed to enjoy a classical education. In the annual report it was described as a 'humanistic gymnasium in the process of being dismantled'. In a message for the school's 125th anniversary in 1997, Ratzinger said: 'There was no active resistance to the dictatorship,' but 'in the Christian humanism of the older generation of teachers there was a spiritual resistance, which protected us from being poisoned.'

From the humanist educational ideal, with its combination of Greek philosophy and Christian revelation, Ratzinger developed his awareness of Europe's foundations. He expressed it later in countless speeches, essays and books. Christianity was the continent's heritage but also its soul and its conscience. If it was lost, as he continually warned as a professor and teacher, that would have a critical effect on Europe's values and culture. When he was pope, he gave an address in the German Bundestag on 22 September 2011 on the foundations of law that would surely have pleased his old gymnasium teachers:

> The culture of Europe arose from the encounter between Jerusalem, Athens and Rome – the encounter between Israel's faith in God, the philosophical reason of the Greeks and Roman law. This three-way encounter has shaped Europe's inner identity. Aware of human responsibility before God and acknowledging the inviolable dignity of every single human person, it has established criteria of law: it is these criteria that we are called upon to defend now in our own historical moment.[11]

It almost seemed as if Nazis and the church were not only two ideological opponents but two different religions.

The party's assemblies, with their 'light organs' projecting lights high up into the sky, were celebrated like liturgies. Party ideologist Alfred Rosenberg strove for the 'Religion of Blood' and the 'Coming Reich'. The 'Führer' himself concocted religious rites and symbols into fantasies of omnipotence. He spoke of the 'Almighty', invoked 'the resurrection of the German people' in a 'blood and soil' rhetoric, and endowed the movement's 'martyrs' with a halo of holiness: 'The blood they shed has become baptismal water for the Third Reich.'

Hitler's speeches quite often ended with the word 'Amen'. However, the concepts, symbols and metaphors were twisted and perverted: the cross became the swastika (in German, *Hakenkreuz*). 'Heil' ('Hail/Salvation') became 'Sieg Heil!' 'Chosen people' came to mean domination over other nations; salvation through Christ became salvation from the Jewish people. In his crude table talk in his headquarters, Hitler declared that for him Christ had been a national leader: 'The Galilean intended to liberate his Galilean land from the Jews; in his teaching he turned against Jewish capitalism, and that is why the Jews killed him.' At the 1926 Christmas celebration of the Munich NSDAP, he compared the party's situation with that of the early Christians. The *Volkische Beobachter* noted in its subsequent edition: 'The work that Christ began but could not finish, he [Hitler] will bring to completion.'[12]

Until then 'Rex' Mair, the Director, had managed to prevent any of his pupils having to join the Hitler Youth. The seminary protected them like a fortress. But every fortress is also a prison. And for Joseph, however pleasant and valuable good comradeship was, it also meant being with a whole crowd of comrades who prevented him from being alone. 'At home I had lived and studied as I liked, in great freedom and built my own childish world.' Now everything was different.

The problem was that Joseph had to exchange the freedom he had so greatly enjoyed for 'being incorporated'. This meant that 'learning, which I had previously found so easy, now seemed nearly impossible.' When he remained sitting at his place in the classroom during the breaks and read a book while the others ran about playing together, he did not draw attention to himself. 'But the greatest burden for me was that – following a progressive idea of education – every day two hours of sport were scheduled in the house's big grounds.'[13]

For the lower school classes, football was still forbidden. Too dangerous. But so was everything else too for the boy who regarded himself as 'worse at sports than any of the others'. He could not do gymnastics, or the javelin or the shot put, and stood forlornly aside when the teams were picked for ball games. It was 'real torture'. With charming sarcasm Ratzinger added in retrospect: 'I must say that my comrades were very tolerant, but it is no fun in the long run having to live with other people's tolerance and knowing that you are just a nuisance for the team you have been assigned to.'[14]

In summer the seminarians had to go and help with the potato harvest in the fields. They were also allowed to go to the town swimming pool in their free time. The older seminarians were even allowed to drink beer and to smoke in their half-hour break.

In winter there was ice-skating, tobogganing or they might go to Winklmoosalm to ski. Joseph was the only one not to go on the skiing trip: it was sport and therefore something impossible for him.

His marks went down, his tender childhood spirit began to harden. Until then he had been 'a decidedly merry boy', Ratzinger reflected, 'but somehow later I became more thoughtful and not so cheerful'.[15] Clearly, he could not do what was asked of him here. He just couldn't. But there was something else, for with his handicap in sport this self-confident boy was led to question himself. Although he mastered other situations so easily, it did not compensate for his weakness on the sports field. That was the point where something was taken out of his hands. He realized: 'At least I was healthily humbled by not being able to do anything at all about it.'[16]

The situation also had a healthy effect on his ability to relate to others and to adapt, so that even in difficult situations he could eventually say: 'I had to learn to fit in with the rest, to emerge from my solitary state, give and take, and be together in a community with others.'

His schoolfellows remembered 'Hacki' as a particularly silent and serious comrade. 'Ratzinger was reserved, extremely quiet, modest, highly intelligent. He attracted attention for being shy and different, but also for his brief and, when appropriate, humorous remarks,' said Peter Freiwang, who was one year older than him. 'He was always an extraordinary person, and nothing got past him.' Freiwang thought Joseph was 'a decidedly intellectual type, who was naturally predestined to be a professor, a scholar'. However, 'In no way did he give the impression that he would particularly stand out, even in religious matters.' 'He was always one of the first to finish the work that was given,' said his comrade Joseph Strehhuber. Franz Weiss added: 'He wrote quickly, put the paper down and folded his arms, then looked at it again.'[17]

His schoolfellows knew Joseph was not a wimp or someone who tried to be a teacher's pet. Quite the contrary. If a Greek squib appeared on the blackboard, you could be sure who had put it up there. The future pope acknowledged he would have 'a moment of rebelliousness', a 'desire to contradict'. As will be seen, this desire was far from being confined just to a 'moment'. According to what his comrades said, the 12-year-old Joseph was neither pushy nor one of those eternal victims who are always being got at by others. He was a thoroughly helpful individual, perhaps a bit private but not withdrawn, someone who knows what he is and what he can do. 'People took him as he was, and he was respected by everyone,' said Freiwang. 'He was bright and a good sort. So naturally he earned the respect of his schoolfellows.'[18]

Many of Ratzinger's behaviour patterns were formed in the seminary and persisted when he became a professor, bishop and pope. This applied to his conscientiousness and tireless hard work but also to his sceptical distance from his surroundings and an air of authority which seemed as if it could not been affected by the pressure of external circumstances. There was also his inconspicuousness. He was known as someone who never pressed ahead from in front but then, as it were, he made even more of an impression from the second row.

Ratzinger's schoolboy psychological profile was confirmed in detail by later companions: for instance, his modesty and humility or his unwillingness to dominate. 'He does not exercise power, even in situations where he probably should exercise it,' his university assistant Peter Kuhn said. 'He never told anyone off. He never ordered anyone: you must do this or that.' Peter Stephan Horn, one of Ratzinger's university students, said of him: 'You felt he was a brilliant theologian. But he never showed his distinction. He never played the "boss".'[19]

Ratzinger's reserve, his cordial but distant attitude, also persisted. According to Kuhn, his professor was 'always a loner. He always did everything by himself. Perhaps he had never learned otherwise. But it also suited his character. He was not secretive, but he tended to be a non-communicator. He spoke little.' In retrospect, Ratzinger himself plainly admitted that he had found it difficult in the seminary 'to acclimatize himself to the group mentality and the rhythm of seminary life'. Possibly his reserve derived from a concern to 'discover his own point of view' so that he could then give an independent, sober and therefore appropriate analysis. Seen like that, his aloofness was essential to protect his own integrity and not let it be tethered or browbeaten.

Ratzinger's shyness had nothing to do with being blasé or wanting to tantalize. It derived from a religious education that stressed a sense of purity, to protect body and soul against moral corruption and stultification. As God's temple, a human being should strive not for what was murky but for higher things, in order to reach true fulfilment. His shyness was also part of his inborn temperament – a natural embarrassment and a learned discretion, out of respect for the personality of others.

However, the highly gifted and sensitive boy soaked up knowledge like a sponge, in order to progress in the world of the mind. Joseph was not really ambitious, said his brother Georg. He just had 'a clear idea of what to do' and dedicated himself to that. A poem by one of his classmates put it neatly:

Hacki is a man who seems
To go to opposite extremes.
Quite unfit for any sport,
He is the intellectual sort.

He appears as 'Joseph the Omniscient' in the school magazine *Helios*, under the heading 'Anecdotes and Comic Reminiscences from our School Days': 'Joseph the Omniscient is asked something. He stands up slowly and says: "I can't express that in words." *Nota bene:* This time even he failed.'[20]

The regime's grip kept tightening. In the summer of 1938, culture minister Adolf Wagner ordered that a reduction in school fees for the Traunstein seminary should only be given to pupils who belonged to the 'State Youth'. The archbishop's office reacted promptly. Membership of the Hitler Youth was categorically ruled out. And the parents' contribution to the boarding costs was lowered to exactly the reduced rate.

The situation changed on 25 March 1939, when a decree concerning the 'Hitler Youth Law' ordered that all boys between 10 and 14 had to join the Deutsches Jungvolk ('German Youngsters') and all 14- to 18-year-old boys had to join the Hitler Youth. At the same time a distinction was introduced between the Compulsory Hitler Youth and the Regular Hitler Youth. The latter category was reserved for boys who had been members of the Hitler Youth before April 1938. Non-compliance would be punished by fines and imprisonment for the parents or legal guardians. As a result, the number of members of the Hitler Youth and the League of German

Girls shot up from 7 to 8.7 million young people. That did not alter the seminary's resistance. It was not until October 1939 that all the seminarians of 14 years old and over were enrolled in the Hitler Youth. Those under 14 were still not enrolled. Three years later, in December 1942, the Traunstein Director of Schools noted with resignation: 'It is symptomatic that even today all the educational costs (accommodation, fees etc.) are paid by the archbishop, a proof that the abolition of this black educational establishment is illusory.'[21]

The manipulation of the young had a central place in Hitler's vision of an Aryan National Socialist Reich. 'In our eyes, the German youth of the future must be lean and fit,' yelled Hitler to the excited youths on the party marches, 'fast as greyhounds, tough as leather and hard as nails.' Training and parades in Traunstein were scheduled in a way that upset the seminary's rhythm. Unlike the Regular Hitler Youth, the Compulsory Hitler Youth were not given a uniform and were treated as a living example of a 'hateful reactionary spirit'. 'In the end we seminarians had to join the Compulsory Hitler Youth,' according to the seminarian Hans Altinger; 'unofficially we had been told that we were not worthy to wear the Führer's uniform.' 'When there was any kind of festivity, of course we dropped out,' reported Peter Freiwang, 'so we were rather pitied and they said, my God, those poor little sausages.'[22]

Compulsory parades in the Nazi period were lengthy and exhausting. 'First lining up for the parade, then marching to the parade ground, then standing in line either to "Attention!" or "At Ease!",' said Altinger. 'Then the ritual: raising the flag, the national anthem, greeting speeches and finally celebratory or propaganda speeches. The fanatics loved all this, we seminarians looked on.'[23] When they had to march through the town in three lines and sing Nazi songs, Georg Ratzinger reported, the Hitler Youth leader deliberately gave a wrong note, 'so that our singing was out of tune. We had to lie down in the street, get up, lie down, get up, lie down again.'[24] Joseph was also was forced to join the Hitler Youth following his 14th birthday. However, he refused to appear on 'duty'.

The boarding school managers advised their pupils to avoid provocation and not to get involved in political arguments. The German Bishops' Conference also fostered a policy of restraint and was anxious to maintain the Concordat. 'The pastoral letter which our parish priest read out made a strong impression on me,' Ratzinger reported. 'Even then it dawned on me that they (the bishops) partly misjudged the situation in their battle for the institution. A mere institutional guarantee is useless when the people are not there who can carry it out with inner conviction.' Otherwise, 'insisting on the institutional protection of Christianity amounts to nothing.'

The more the pressure from outside increased, the more the seminary intensified its catechesis within the school walls. A solid school education and religious instruction were the only way to prepare priests for their task in an atheist society under a regime hostile to the church. For 'Rex' Mair, who in his time in Rome had been choir director at the 'German national church', Santa Maria dell'Anima, religious teaching began with an introduction to music. The school had a choir and also an orchestra for feast days and celebrations, and concerts in their own theatre.

The introduction to spirituality was led by three tutors, supported by a spiritual leader who gave lectures on ascesis. The training was strict enough to astonish a Zen master in a Tibetan monastery. Before morning prayers the boys were given the text for the day's prayer intentions and short prompts for an 'internal meditation'. In the seminary church they received guidance on the ascetic celebration of the church's year, for receiving the holy sacraments and the duties of priesthood. They were each entrusted with their own particular practices and messages for the lesser and greater feast days, and also with resources for First Friday Devotion to the Sacred Heart of Jesus, the Priests' First Saturdays (a devotion to pray for priests) or the nightly meditations before the Holy Eucharist, which was displayed in a splendid monstrance on the house church's altar.

Then there were the different rituals for honouring Mary, Advent, the manger and other celebrations. At the beginning of each school year, the pupils undertook exercises – the older boys for four days, the younger ones for two. Twice a year a pilgrimage was planned to Maria Eck church in Siegsdorf (Bavaria). After Hitler's rise to power they also engaged in the 'living rosary', in which each pupil was committed to pray one mystery of the rosary each day, as well as the usual rosary and the Stations of the Cross in Lent. As a rule, there was daily communion and weekly confession as well as the devotions, or spiritual talks, with which the day ended.[25]

'When we keep order,' the seminarians heard from the teaching of the Desert Father St Anthony, 'we shall not not be confounded.' This was about when it was right to be silent, right to speak and right to listen. It was about dealing with time, working with moderation and balance, and avoiding excess and self-indulgence, as well as restlessness and agitation. The pupils learned to play an instrument; they learned to sing a chorale together; they learned not to go beyond the limits. Attaining the virtues helped self-control and strengthened character. Before you speak, the advice was, first reflect on what you want to say. You should not seek to appeal through knowledge, but strive for calm and gentleness and keep getting rid of self-centredness. You need the right posture in bowing, standing, kneeling in order to approach the mystery with due respect – and then sense God and be touched by him.

In truth, wasn't the world of the Nazi power holders, with their mania for nation and race, completely unreal? Instead, wasn't the seemingly unreal world of faith what was actually real, because its principles corresponded with an order that was in harmony with the greater order on which the whole of creation rested? Even though the Nazis changed all the values and symbols and rewrote everything, however much they claimed the future was theirs, the seminarians could be sure of one thing. In the end, Christ would rise again victorious from every battle, even if that end was the end of the world.

9

War

That weekend the inhabitants of Berlin were enjoying the beautiful summer weather. The banks of the Wannsee lake were seething with bathers and young lovers holding hands in the sunshine. However, in the city there was a noticeably growing number of soldiers in brand-new army boots strolling along the Kurfürstendamm.

A few days later, in the early hours of 1 September 1939, the invasion of Poland began. Hitler had been preparing it for the previous five months. At 4.37 a.m. German Stuka planes dropped bombs over the West Polish district capital city of Wielun and razed its centre to the ground. Eight minutes later, at 4.45, the armoured ship *Schleswig-Holstein,* lying in harbour in the port of Danzig, fired on the Polish barracks near the mouth of the River Vistula.

Before the raid, the German army had been increased to almost 3 million soldiers, 400,000 horses and 200,00 vehicles. One and a half million soldiers had advanced to the Polish border, many with blank ammunition, according to the British military historian Antony Beevor, 'on the pretext that they were on manoeuvres'.[1] The Nazi media had been stirring things up for months beforehand, claiming that the approximately 800,000 Germans living in Poland were being harassed and threatened with severe persecution. Alarmed, 70,00 Germans actually fled into the German Reich area, which appeared to be a safe haven.

The invasion was justified by a 'false flag' attack on a German customs post and the radio station near the frontier town of Gleiwitz. The SS had dressed prisoners from the Sachsenhaus concentration camp in Polish uniforms and had them shot in order to leave behind their corpses as 'proofs' of Polish aggression – a cunning operation for which the SS Obergruppenführer (Senior Group Leader) Reinhard Heydrich was responsible. He went on to become leader of the Reichssicherheitshauptamt, or RSHA (Reich Security Main Office). The code word with which he gave the start signal for the attack on the afternoon of 31 August was 'Grandmother dead'.

In 1941 Heydrich was tasked with the 'Final Solution of the Jewish Problem' and became the main organizer of the Holocaust. At the very moment when the German bombs fell on Kraków, a student was high over the city in the cathedral of the Polish kings in order to go to confession and receive communion. 'We must say the Mass, come what may,' a priest called out. He invited the young man to be his server. *Kyrie eleison, Christe eleison*: 'Lord have mercy, Christ, have mercy', the future theatre scholar recited, as he knelt before the altar of the crucified Christ, while the cathedral's glass windows threatened to shatter under the pressure of the explosion, His name was Karol Józef Wojtyła.

No one could have had any idea that this student would one day have to carry the cross, before which he was kneeling, for the whole world. Or that someone would help him who actually belonged to the nation which at that very moment was about to set the whole world on fire.

It was war. The Ratzingers heard about it at home on the SABA radio. Georg and Joseph were also in the living room listening. Their school things had long been packed. These were the last days of the summer holidays, 'From 5.45 a.m. fire will be returned,' rattled the 'Führer's voice in his radio broadcast, 'and from now on bombs will be met with bombs!'

Hitler pursued a vacillating strategy. At first he had hoped to win Great Britain as an ally and then be able to begin his actual goal of a war against the Soviet Union. Later he planned a preventive strike against France. As the eastern flank had to be secured for this, he let the foreign minister, Joachim von Ribbentrop, offer an alliance with Poland. After Hitler's seizure of power, Marshal Józef Piłsudski, Poland's autocratic head of government, had several times urged the Western powers in vain to launch a preventive strike against the German Reich. In January 1934 his foreign minister, Józef Beck, had finally come to an understanding with Berlin on a mutual non-aggression pact. The agreement was meant to be for ten years.

Four years later, as Germany marched into the Sudetenland, Polish troops occupied the Czechoslovakian province of Teschen, which Poland had claimed for itself since the 1920s, thus pushing their frontier eastward in the direction of the Carpathians.

The Soviet Union's territorial appetite went in precisely the opposite direction. According to Stalin's plans, the Communist empire should spread out towards the West. The red dictator had in his sights Romanian Bessarabia, Finland, the Baltic States and East Poland as well as parts of White Russia and Ukraine, which Russia had been forced to cede to Poland after their defeat in the Polish–Soviet war of 1919–21. On 18 April 1939 Stalin offered both the British and French governments an alliance pact. The British declined with thanks. They suspected the *démarche* had 'underhand' designs. At the same time, Chamberlain's government was afraid of provoking Hitler's Reich, which was still seen as a bulwark against Bolshevism.

Obersalzberg was again involved – 40 kilometres as the crow flies from the Ratzingers'. It was here that the start of the Second World War had been planned in detail early on. The house was expanded to become a strong fortress. For nearly a quarter of his time in power, Hitler was to govern from his mountain home. On 23 May 1939 he laid out his plans for the conquest of Poland before the supreme commanders of the Wehrmacht. It was not just a matter of bringing the Free City of Danzig 'home to the Reich', the 'Führer' announced, but also of dominating the southern part of Central Europe. He did not take Great Britain's guarantee to Poland seriously. 'I am now 50,' Hitler had told the Romanian foreign minister in early 1939, 'I'd rather have the war now than when I am 55 or 60.'[2]

Exactly eight days before the beginning of the war, on 23 August 1939, the foreign ministers of Germany and the Soviet Union – von Ribbentrop and Vyacheslav Molotov – signed a non-aggression agreement, which was to pass into history as the 'Hitler–Stalin' pact. In a secret additional protocol, the broad territories of Eastern Europe were shared out between them. Albert Speer, minister of armaments and war production, recalled that when the news of Stalin's consent reached Obersalzberg, Hitler sprang up from the dining table and crowed with excitement: 'I've got it! I've got it!' The pact enabled Hitler to wage his war against Poland first, and then against France and Great Britain. On his side, Stalin hoped that Germany would be weakened by its campaign in the west and saw the chance to incorporate large areas of Eastern Europe into his empire.

Most foreign governments reacted helplessly to the German army's invasion of Poland. In Britain the Cabinet and the Foreign Office worked all day on 1 September at drafting an ultimatum to Hitler to withdraw his troops immediately. When the demands appeared in written form, 'it did not sound like a proper ultimatum,' remarked Antony Beevor, 'because it lacked the date when it would expire'. On 17 September the Polish state collapsed. On the same day, the Red Army occupied parts of East Poland without any resistance. The government fled to Romania, and 700,000 Polish soldiers were taken as German prisoners of war, 200,00 as Soviet prisoners of war. As for Poland, Hitler in his mountain fortress declared to his assembled army commanders that every 'man, woman and child of Polish stock and language is to be put to death without mercy or pity. Only thus can we win the living space that we need.'[3]

In fact, soon the SS were hunting down Polish aristocrats, teachers and professors, doctors and lawyers, engineers and priests. Tens of thousands were murdered or imprisoned in concentration camps, including the whole of the teaching staff of Kraków University. The 'Slavic sub-humans' (Untermenschen) were to be 'germanized' and used for labour. In the newly created 'Reich provinces' and in the 'General Government' between Lemberg and Warsaw, Kraków and Lublin, Poles were forbidden to visit restaurants, cinemas or theatres. They could not sit in the front coach of trams and could only go shopping at certain times. They had to give way on the pavement to those wearing German uniforms, and 'anti-German remarks' carried the death penalty.

Ratzinger senior was not surprised by the events. The attack on Poland had brought about what he had foreseen six years earlier. That was why he had bought the old house in hidden-away Hufschlag. In September 1939, as a former police officer, he was recalled to service. On nightly patrols he had to check the black-out was observed. In his precise way, neighbours remembered, he would tap on the window if a curtain was not fully drawn. After a few months he found a doctor who certified him unfit, so that he could be released from war service for Hitler.

The outbreak of the Second World War changed Joseph's life significantly. He was still at the gymnasium. The big problem worrying him was that the Nazis had made sport a compulsory subject for the *Abitur* (the school-leaving examination, comparable to the French baccalaureate). 'That was a terrible outlook for me.' The prospect of failing it could not be dismissed. However, soon heavy military vehicles drove up to the episcopal seminary, and the war made possible what the Nazis could not achieve in peace time: the episcopal seminary boarding-school with its 'poisonous international teaching' was closed down. 'Rex' Mair had fought off the closure to the last. He himself stubbornly remained in the house like the captain of a sinking ship. Two nuns and two housemaids remained with him, separated by a thick wall, by which the Nazis isolated them.

From September 1939, at first the Wehrmacht set up a hospital for wounded soldiers in the rooms of the seminary boarding-school. From now on, normal seminary life was impossible, as was normal teaching. This meant that Ratzinger's regular time at the seminary boarding school lasted no longer than two years. His whole education in senior schools amounted to six years, not counting the gymnasium lessons when he later served as a flak auxiliary. However, soon he hit the jackpot. After the requisition of his house, Mair had advised the pupils to stay at home for the time being. Then he let some of the seminarians board in the town sanatorium. Finally, the pupils were shared out between three establishments around Traunstein. Joseph was among the lucky ones who were sent to the Englische Fräulein convent. It was a kind of hermitage, surrounded by streams, trees and fields. But perhaps for one of the new guests what *was* there was not as important as what was *not* there. Looking back, he remarked almost triumphantly: 'There was no sports ground.'

The removal to the former girls' school run by the nuns, long since closed down by the Nazis, was a heavenly relief for Joseph. In the afternoons they went for walks or played in the woods that stretched out around them or by the mountain stream. Here he became 'reconciled with the seminary', Ratzinger confessed, 'and had a good time'. The fact that his brother Georg was also there increased his sense of well-being. In this situation, now he learned 'to join in as part of the whole, to come out of my shell, to give and take and create a community with others [...] I am grateful for that experience. It was important for my life.'⁴

In the gymnasium the 'apprentice priests' had a special position. The fact that they were scholastically ahead of their schoolfellows did not endear them to the 'Führer's' followers. Accordingly, a spirit of friendship arose between them, which was to bind them all through their lives. Even when he became pope, Ratzinger stayed in touch with his former comrades, took an interest in what happened to them and asked about their friends and relations. His fellow students formed a circle that was whole-heartedly sympathetic and devoted to him, without any scepticism – simply because they knew him.

Ratzinger's strong attachment to the seminary was shown by the fact that, even when he was a cardinal of the Roman Curia, he never let a year go by without spending a few days in his former house of studies. His last visit was in January 2005, a few months before he was elected as the 265th successor of Peter. He came to accompany his brother, who had by then gone blind. 'They had breakfast together in the staff room,' said the house Director, 'and the cardinal read out the newspaper to his brother.'⁵

The happy interval at Sparz did not last long. Soon the former convent was also requisitioned, and the seminarians were turned out. Director Mair was unable to find any further alternative accommodation. So once again Joseph was playing at 'boarding-school life' at home. Now in the mornings he went to school together with his brother, sometimes accompanied by their sister. She was working as a clerk in the office of the lawyer Pankratz Schnappinger and came home with funny stories about the bizarre lawsuits in which the chambers were involved.

Georg and Joseph were inseparable. 'We were close from the beginning,' explained the future pope, 'we simply belonged together.' During his papacy Benedict XVI usually telephoned the former Regensburg Cathedral director of music several times a week. When he became pope emeritus, for his now blind brother he organized a housekeeper, whom he wished to get to know personally in an interview in the Vatican garden.

The Ratzinger boys wanted as little to do with the war as with the wretched Hitler Youth roll-calls to salute the colours and the training exercises. Joseph never wore a Hitler Youth uniform. According to his schoolfellow Peter Freiwang, the Traunstein Hitler Youth 'Second Troop', which consisted almost exclusively of seminarians, was soon dissolved 'for lack of members'.

Together with their sister Maria, they went on a week's cycling tour. In Salzburg they once stayed in the Tiger Hotel. The inclusive cost of bed and breakfast was 3.50 Reichsmarks. That enabled them to get up as early as possible next morning to be in Salzburg Cathedral, famous for its music, and get good seats to enjoy Mozart's Mass in C Minor in all its glory.

For Georg and Joseph, ever since their earliest childhood Salzburg had stood for cheerfulness, beauty and a kind of heavenly peace. In 1941, on the occasion of the 150th anniversary of its greatest son's death, the city celebrated a Mozart year with great pomp. And while the international public turned its back on Salzburg, the local people were happy with the reduction in the concert ticket prices. Georg had seized the opportunity and got tickets. As well as Mozart, they heard Beethoven's Ninth Symphony, conducted by Hans Knappertsbusch. One thing above all else electrified Georg: the news of a guest performance by the Regensburger Domspatzen ('Regensburg Cathedral Sparrows') of an arrangement of *Der Schauspieldirektor* (*The Impressario*), by Mozart. 'I couldn't sleep all night.' His brother was convinced: 'Love of the Domspatzen was born then. We had already heard a lot about them.' Enthusiastically, Georg attended lectures with slides, listened to records and absorbed all the available information about the 'secret inner world of a music college' like the Salzburg Mozarteum (a type of *Hochschule*, or higher education college). Above all, his 'way of practising the piano became much more concentrated on a goal,' according to Joseph. He also 'spent much longer at it', which cannot have been an unmitigated pleasure for his younger brother.

At home every Sunday afternoon the two boys sat glued to the radio. With the concert broadcasts, Georg carefully kept notes of the orchestra, choir, soloists, conductors and the individual pieces with exact details of the numbers in the Köchel catalogue. He was particularly taken with the Coronation Mass and the three shorter Masses in F major, D major and B flat major with string orchestration. He would later say about Mozart's music: 'It brings bliss like the bliss of heaven. And it proclaims the union of creation with its Creator.'[6]

Joseph was also an enthusiastic Mozart fan. Two of his favourites pieces were the clarinet concerto and the clarinet quintet.

In 1939 there was nothing like the enthusiasm for the war in Germany that there had been at the outbreak of the First World War. The survivors still remembered the terrible consequences of that catastrophe only too clearly. However, the rapid success of the Polish campaign seemed to justify Hitler, even when Britain and France responded to the invasion with a declaration of war – but did not attack. Instead, the German troops marched through Europe as if they had seven-league boots. Norway, Denmark, Luxembourg, the Netherlands, Belgium – all these countries were overrun and occupied. The campaign against France was almost ridiculously quick. As if in passing, the Balkans, Greece and parts of North Africa were also conquered.

Hitler was at the height of his power – and prestige. The victory over France gained the regime enormous kudos. At last the Versailles Treaty, which had humiliated and looted Germany, had received a fitting response. In the eyes of his supporters the 'Führer' had kept his word. Ratzinger senior was in despair. When the war began, he had hoped for stronger resistance from the Allies. He was convinced that the power of France and Britain would soon put a stop to the 'greatest general of all time', as Hitler loved to be congratulated, and thereby bring Nazi rule to an end. Instead, their success seemed to give the Nazis legitimacy. According to his son Joseph, his father was clear that 'a victory for Hitler would not be a victory for Germany but a victory for the Antichrist. It would bring about apocalyptic times for all believers, and not only for them.'[7]

That year Joseph's Class IV had 36 pupils. Ten of them were from farming families. One of the fathers gave his job as 'foreman'. Others gave theirs as district judge, shoemaker, carpenter, doctor, blacksmith, senior post supervisor or naval doctor. There were two girls in the class. Among the boys, seven were called Joseph. The advancing war affected the school routine, and this showed in the timetable. In the record of home and school work for the school year 1940–41 such subjects appear as 'What entitles the Führer from the the year 1941 to expect "the greatest victory in German history"?' Or 'What is the importance of colonies for the Reich?' Another subject was: 'Why do we do race research?' Presumably Joseph turned to the few innocuous topics such as 'Thoughts for Mother's Day' or 'Why do I enjoy going into the mountains so much?' Possibly he also went for an essay on 'The nature of the Germans reflected in their gods'.[8]

It was a Sunday in the early summer of 1941. Joseph's class had planned a boat trip on the nearby Lake Waginger. Then the news spread like wildfire that, together with their Axis allies, the German Reich had begun an attack on the Soviet Union on a front stretching from the North Cape to the Black Sea. Just two years earlier, on 30 November 1939, Stalin's Red Army had attacked Finland with 1,500 tanks and 3,000 planes, and taken over a large part of its territory. The heavy Soviet losses, with 200,000 fallen soldiers, had enormously increased Hitler's appetite for attack. The news of the 'further expansion of the war' hovered over the little boat trip on the lake 'like a nightmare', said Ratzinger. 'We thought of Napoleon, we thought of Russia's enormous expanse, in which the German army was bound to get lost.' We were all agreed: 'This could not go well.' In fact, 'Operation Barbarossa', with which the new *Blitzkrieg* on the Soviet Union got under way on 22 June, was to be a turning point in the war.

As well as Joseph's compulsory enrolment in the Hitler Youth, the school authorities had also enrolled him as a full member in the Altötting Marian Men's Congregation. On 12 January 1941 his 19-year-old sister Maria had entered the Franciscan Third Order, a community of lay people who strove for the ideals of St Francis of Assisi outside the convent and tried to live the Order's spiritual life in the world. Her investiture took place in the Maria Eck Convent. Her name in religion became Klara, after St Francis's woman friend and founder of the Order of St Clare. A year later at her 'profession' she took her final vows. She solemnly promised lifelong fidelity to the Order, to undertake particular daily prayers, charitable work in the church and the world and to make the Eucharist the centre of her life.

In Hufschlag, Joseph now followed his taste for literature. He read quicker than other people and devoured the great German writers week by week: Eichendorff, Mörike, Adalbert Stifter. He particularly enjoyed studying Goethe, but also Theodor Storm, whose *Schimmelreiter* strongly impressed him. Kleist remained foreign to him. He did not like Schiller. He said he found him 'too moralistic'.

He found his writing 'somewhat designed'. It was 'so intentional, with a clear moral ending you could see in advance'.[9] Moreover, his German teacher had inflicted Schiller plays such as *William Tell, The Maid of Orleans* and *Maria Stuart* on the students 'so persistently that you really couldn't listen to them any more'.

In a world of horror, literature was a refuge. Books became Ratzinger's true friends. The boy was fascinated by the 'high time' he found there, 'full of hope for the great things that opened up in the boundless world of the mind'.[10] He loved the works of Hermann Hesse. A favourite of his was *Peter Camenzind,* a novel about a sad Swiss country boy from a poor background who is treated unkindly by his parents and comes to regard nature as his teacher and true companion. Ratzinger's absolute favourite, though, was *Steppenwolf,* Hesse's novel portraying the spiritual brokenness of the time and offering radical social criticism. Later, he tackled Hesse's *Glass Bead Game,* which, as was still to be shown, anticipated his own course as a student in an astonishing way.

'Of course, I eagerly began to write myself,' Ratzinger confessed. His early pieces have not survived. But his love of poetry, the fine wording that fascinated the boy, can be seen in all his theological work. In recent centuries hardly any scholar has understood the relation between poetry and religion better than him. The literary power of highly academic texts has become Ratzinger's trademark. Even when the content is not always understood at once, the experience remains of a sound and a feeling that can alter your awareness.

Of course, in the terrible years of the war there was as little space for poetic dreams as for puberty. Joseph was at an age when the relationship to self, parents and the whole outside world is usually difficult. But the usual adolescent conflicts, such as challenging the father's authority, did not take place. Whereas the next generation would raise anti-authoritarian rebellion to a culture form, Ratzinger's growing up was bound by duty. A fierce confrontation with his parents was out of the question because, as common victims of the regime, they were closely bound together, for better or worse.

In their planning, the Nazi leadership calculated pitilessly on millions of victims. In the so-called General East Plan, the accountants of terror for Eastern Europe reckoned on the elimination of 30 million people as the the enforced consequence of displacement, enslavement and murder. In May 1941, in discussions between secretaries of state and the head of the war industry and arms procurement department, General Georg Thomas, it was stated: 'The war can only be carried on, if in its third year the whole army is fed by Russia. Doubtless, that will mean umpteen million people will go hungry, if we take what we need for ourselves from the land.'" Of the total of 3 million Soviet prisoners of war held by the Germans, by the beginning of 1942 2 million had died of hunger, disease or exhaustion. By the end of 1941 the SS and police task forces had shot more than half a million Jews in the occupied Soviet areas: first the men of military age, then also women, children and old people, followed by the systematic mass murder of Roma, Poles, Ukrainians, White Russians, Lithuanians and the mentally ill.

In Traunstein the seminarians saw transporters 'with some hideously wounded soldiers', constantly flowing into the town. More hospitals were set up. Every day the local paper gave the names of young men who remained at the front. 'More and more schoolfellows from the gymnasium were named, whom not long before we had known as comrades full of the joy of life and confidence,' Joseph remembered. Ratzinger senior had to beg for potatoes, meat and other food from local farmers, whom he knew from going to church. No one was expecting the war to end soon. Quite the opposite.

The Nazis stepped up the military training of the young. On 8 June 1942 Georg was called up to the SS military training camp at Königsdorf, near Bad Tölz. That ended his school career. After that he was drafted to the paramilitary National Service (Reichsarbeitsdienst, or RAD) at Deutsch-Gabel in Sudetengau. In December he was ordered to report to an infantry division of the Wehrmacht, which was sent to France before Christmas. His next postings were to a machine gun company in the Netherlands and finally to the south of France, where he served as a radio and telephone operator.

10

Resistance

In their heavy grey woollen uniforms with the Luftwaffe eagle on their breasts, the seminarians looked like real soldiers. And they were. Child soldiers. Under the eagle there was a swastika. The letters 'LH' stood for 'Luftwaffe Helper'. The schoolboys translated it as 'Last Hope'.

The air attacks on Germany began in 1941. At first, only the coastal towns and the Ruhr area were hit. But from the summer of 1943 southern Germany was also bombed. The powerful drone of the Allied planes could be heard 15 to 20 minutes before they came into sight. Often there were raids by 500 or more planes, in which the Royal Air Force headed for Munich. The attacks were still only at night. Then powerful beams lit up the bombed silhouette of the city. Sirens wailed. Explosions and mountains of flame turned the city centre around the Frauenkirche and the Hofbräuhaus into an eerie spectacle. Further out of the city, 16-year-old schoolboys were working on measuring instruments and anti-aircraft cannon (flak) to prevent the bombing, a forlorn undertaking.

The flak battery in the suburb of Ludwigsfeld had 18 8.8 cm guns at its disposal. The anti-aircraft cannons were controlled by a Number 1 gunner and a loader. Three pupils served as flak auxiliaries with the elevating drive, the traversing drive and the ignition timing. The heavy shells were lugged by four Russian prisoners of war from the munitions store, regardless of the Geneva Convention. As soon as the code word *'Edelweiss'* sounded, that was the pre-alarm. 'Get up, get dressed, get ready,' yelled a lieutenant. The code word *'Alpenrose'* meant: 'Run to the guns!'

There was a hectic rush to crank and screw the cannons correctly and prime the shell detonators. They could hit targets up to ten kilometres away, as long as they exploded at the right time and height, taking into account the speed of the attacking British bombers. The nightly attacks usually lasted four to six hours. When there was an air raid warning, the camp was covered by a smoke screen, so that the flak soldiers could barely see their hands in front of their faces. On the command 'Battery, ready to fire!' there was an infernal noise from the barrage of 8.8 cm guns, firing from all barrels. 'Our nerves were all jittery,' Hans Uhl remembered, 'the steady roar, that noise was terrible. Each of us was afraid but no one wanted it to show.'[1]

Joseph was assigned to the measuring battery for target detection. His radar crew was about 500 metres distant from the firing crew. They had the German Wehrmacht's most up-to-date equipment, the 'Freya', an early form of radar. It had been developed by Konrad Zuse, the computer pioneer. Joseph's job was 'to locate the approaching planes and pass on the readings to the guns'.[2] When the bomber streams in their typical triangular formation were 90 kilometres away, the bearing was fixed on the front point of the stream and tracked. The readings were passed on electronically, via a cable, to the flak battery. Ratzinger delivered readings for three guns. Then the flak auxiliaries cranked hard to manually elevate and traverse the cannons correctly. It was a dreadful conflict. The more precisely Joseph measured, the higher the hit rate. As the war demanded. But if he measured wrong, the bombers could go ahead and reduce the city to rubble and ashes.

The flak auxiliaries were accustomed to their batteries being ignored by the British bomber pilots. Their attempts to hit one of the plans were too feeble. But on one occasion the 'Tommies' did not simply fly over and away. The bombs, which dropped with an infernal thunder and strident explosions directly beside their gun emplacement, destroyed equipment and left huge craters. One comrade did not survive the attack; many others were badly wounded. Joseph escaped with a terrible fright.

In December 1940 the personnel of the German air defence consisted of about 500,000 men, and the Luftwaffe had about 520,000 men in the air. With the decree of 26 January 1943 on active war service of German youth in the Luftwaffe, school pupils in upper and middle schools were called up from the age of 16 to serve as Luftwaffe auxiliaries in the flak batteries. First 60,000 young men – in all it was to be 200,000 – were called up, most of them from upper schools with birth dates between 1926 and 1928. On 2 August 1943 the seminarians from the Chiemgau gymnasium in Traunstein who had not yet already been called up were also enlisted. For the first time Joseph left his home region; for the first time he was confronted with horror right before his eyes.

He did not make much of it. In his memoirs his barely two years of war service are described as a fleeting episode. In an earlier biographical essay he called it the 'War Intermezzo', as if here was someone who, physically as well as psychologically, had not been present. And yet it did leave traces when 'smoke and the smell of burning filled the air', and he had to watch as Munich 'sank bit by bit in ruins'. Years later, he confessed in an aside that he had 'sometimes woken up at night' bathed in sweat. The reason: 'I thought I was back with the flak.'

The first posting of the 12 seminarians from Traunstein was to Untermenzing, near Munich. They spent the night on straw mats in a run-down building with rats for company. After a health check and swearing in to their duties to the Fatherland, they were ordered to the great flak batteries in Ludwigsfeld. These were intended to protect the nearby Bavarian Motor Works (BMW), which were necessary to the war effort. There were five barracks for the flak auxiliaries, each divided into 'rooms' for 15 young men. 'Absence without leave from the troop' could be punished by death. Twice a year they were given a fortnight's leave. Their pay was one Reichsmark per day. The training consisted of instructions in ballistics, practical exercises in the scheduled fire area, determination of target height, alignment of the searchlights at an alarm and aircraft recognition for one-, two- and three-engine planes with single and dual steering systems. Part of the job was also guard duty, weapon maintenance, projectile maintenance and trench work. The commandant was a Lieutenant Stolker, 'an unpleasant type', as Ratzinger recalled: 'He had a personal grudge against me and regarded me as mentally retarded.'

Unlike the regular soldiers, after reveille the flak auxiliaries travelled into town to the Maximilian gymnasium to study German, mathematics, physics and other subjects. When the journey was not possible, the teachers too old for active service came to the camp and taught them in the barracks. 'We Traunsteiners were better at Latin and Greek, but we also noticed that we had lived in the provinces,' reported Joseph. There were 'frictions'. The seminarians were ahead of the Munich schoolboys in their studies and also formed a close-knit community consisting exclusively of anti-Nazis.

Joseph was a completely un-military type. In exercises he marched left hand to left foot, right hand to right foot, instead of vice versa. 'Ratzinger, you are every sergeant's nightmare,' his comrades called to him, shaking their heads. Joseph withdrew and read his books. 'He already knew he was going to be a priest, and nothing else interested him,' according to flak auxiliary Wilhelm Geiselbrecht; 'he was accepted and left in peace.' But the classicist Anton Fingerle, who taught at the Maximilian gymnasium, noticed him. After the war Fingerle co-founded the first Society for Christian–Jewish Co-Operation and gained a legendary reputation as a municipal education officer. Fingerle had been 'enraptured by the knowledge of his pupil Ratzinger'. According to Geiselbrecht: 'He read and learned a great deal and so was naturally ahead of us.'[3]

However much the still very young-looking country boy withdrew when the others were making a racket, he was not a coward. When, on a frosty winter's night the sergeant noticed that some of the flak auxiliaries had pushed the cannons before their guard duty, he yelled: 'Who's on guard duty?' Deep silence. In the bitter night the flak auxiliaries were hustled out for a pseudo-exercise until they almost collapsed on the ground. The sergeant looked at the smallest boy, who he realized was more dead than alive from the strain. 'Who can last longer', he shouted at him, 'me or you?' Joseph was quite unimpressed and answered in a strong Bavarian accent, 'Me'. Dumbstruck, the oppressor turned away. 'After that,' Peter Freiwang reported, 'we had peace.'

The group of active Catholics in the camp insisted that they had religious instruction and were allowed to take part in the May devotions. On many Sundays they even managed to steal into the Frauenkirche in Munich. A Philips receiver was installed in Ratzinger's quarters to hear broadcasts from the BBC. In order to prevent discovery they pushed their lockers up against the door. Listening to 'enemy broadcasts' was punished as resistance. 'We suddenly grew up there and dared to do things which we never would have done before,' said Josef Strehhuber. The seminarians were not traitors to their country, but they were in a terrible quandary. 'We knew that Hitler was against the church, he was against us,' Strehhuber explained, 'and we wanted the war to be lost.'[4]

In Ludwigsfeld an electric fence separated the schoolboy soldiers from a branch concentration camp surrounded by watchtowers. They saw the prisoners being escorted every day by heavily armed SS men to work at a deep grave, banked up by a wall. 'We were forbidden and unable to make any contact with the forced labourers,' Strehhuber reported. 'We knew that Dachau was a concentration camp for Nazi opponents. For us, they were political prisoners. They were seen almost as allies.'[5]

Joseph had heard of Dachau. 'Don't play it so loud, you'll go to Dachau,' his mother had warned at home, when his father listened to the 'enemy broadcasts'. In an early essay, he wrote about the forced labourers in the concentration camp, forced to work beside the flak battery barracks: 'Although they were better treated here than their fellow sufferers in the main concentration camps, the abysmal nature of Hitlerism could not be denied.' 'These prisoners wore a red, green or blue triangle,' he said, according to whether they had been imprisoned on political, religious or criminal grounds. 'So we threw bread over the fence. The whole thing disgusted us. But we did not know about the Jews. I don't think there were any Jews there.'

What Ratzinger and the other flak auxiliaries did not even imagine was that the BMW Allach works was part of an extensive system of slave labour in concentration camps. During the war, the Munich region developed into the most important site of the German arms industry. The concentration camp prisoners produced missile engines in Allach. One of the prisoners was Max Mannheimer, a Jew from Nordmähren. Later he would tirelessly insist in schools and meetings that the memory of the hideous crime should be kept alive. Mannheimer categorically rejected the assigning of collective responsibility. When he was asked about Ratzinger in an interview, he replied that, like other 16- and 17-year-olds, the boy was taken from school and forcibly enlisted. How could he be held responsible for all that? He too had been 'forced into "Command and Obedience".'

The Nazis tried to conceal the terror and murder in the concentration camps. They even made a promotional film about the Theresienstadt concentration camp, with pictures of happy people in a beautiful environment, to show how considerately the prisoners were treated. Despite a ban on news, the SS could not keep secret the resistance of the members of the anti-fascist underground White Rose movement. The movement's first leaflets appeared between the end of June and the middle of July 1942. They were anonymously sent by post to intellectuals in and around Munich to denounce the general oppression and the treatment of the Jews and to call for passive resistance. The Traunstein seminarians had also got wind of them. 'We spoke about them,' Ratzinger reported, 'and our whole class was sympathetic. They all said, "They are so brave".'[6]

The key figures belonging to the White Rose were the brother and sister Hans and Sophie Scholl, the students Christoph Probst, Alexander Schmorell and Willi Graf, and the philosophy professor Kurt Huber. As the third of four children born of Swiss parents, Huber had grown up in Stuttgart and studied music, psychology and philosophy. From 1926 he was an extraordinary professor in Munich teaching experimental and applied psychology, and later audio and music psychology, folk song studies and methodology. Like other intellectuals, such as Martin Heidegger, at first he had sympathized with various National Socialist ideas. When he became aware of the regime's crimes, he changed his mind. From the summer of 1942 he met privately with the members of the resistance group and decided actively to support them.

A wider network around the White Rose included painters, architects, a film director and a bookshop owner, whose cellar was used to hide the leaflets, as well as the writer Werner Bergengruen and the paediatrician Hubert Furtwängler. In Berlin the protest writings of the 'Onkel Emil' resistance group were circulated on the Elbe by students who signed themselves as 'White Rose Hamburg'.

In Munich on 13 January 1943, at the university's 470th anniversary celebrations, NSPAD Gauleiter Paul Giesler's speech was followed by rioting. Giesler berated female students for gadding about. Instead, they should 'give the Führer a child'. And he would send his adjutant to do the job. On 8 and 15 February Hans Scholl, Graf and Schmorell daubed graffiti on walls in 70 places with black tar and green oil paint. They read: 'Hitler the Mass Murderer!', 'Down with Hitler!' and 'Freedom!' beside a crossed-out swastika. In the same month the White Rose published a 'Call to all Germans!' Between 27 and 29 January 1943 the leaflet was distributed throughout a number of southern German and Austrian cities in a print run of between 6,000 and 9,000 copies. They declared: 'Hitler can't win the war, only lengthen it.' Germans should reject 'the National Socialist creed of sub-humans' and Prussian militarism 'for all time'.

During the night of 15–16 February, Hans and Sophie and some fellow campaigners managed to distribute almost 1,200 leaflets in the 'capital of the movement' without being discovered. This was leaflet number 6, produced following the lost Battle of Stalingrad at the end of January, when 230,000 German soldiers and a million Russians had been killed:

> Fellow students! Do we want to sacrifice the rest of our German youth to the basest instincts of a party clique? Never again! The day of reckoning has come, the reckoning of German youth with the most detestable tyranny that our people have ever endured [...] We have grown up in a state which ruthlessly gags any free expression of ideas. The Hitler Youth, the SA and SS have tried to put us in uniform, transform and drug us during the most fruitful learning years of our lives. A Führer elite, as they cannot be more devilishly or more densely called, gathers its future party bosses in Ordensburgs to become godless, shameless, remorseless exploiters and cut-throats, in blind, stupid discipleship of the Führer. [The term *Ordensburg,* given to special schools for a Nazi elite, was borrowed by the Nazis from the historic Teutonic Order.] [...] There is only one watchword for us: Fight against the Party! [...] Get out from the lecture halls of the SS non-commissioned and commissioned officers and Party toadies! [...] The name of Germany will remain for ever in disgrace if the youth of Germany does not finally stand up, avenge and atone, smash their tormentors and establish a new spirit of Europe.[7]

There was no one to be seen at 10.45 a.m. on 18 February 1943, when Hans and Sophie also planted their leaflets in the corridors of Munich University. The pair had already reached the back exit into Amalienstrasse, as they turned round once more. Sophie threw down her last leaflets from the second floor into the light well. Like paper aeroplanes some landed on the head of the Medusa and the ring of stars surrounding her in the mosaic decorating the vestibule floor. Perhaps it was that single minute that decided her life. It was the dutiful porter Jakob Schmid who discovered them both and held them until the Gestapo men stormed the building.

Under the pressure of a different *Zeitgeist,* knowledge about the religious motivation of the White Rose faded out. Their resistance was portrayed as mainly politically inspired. However, immediately after the war the events were too close not to be seen as they were. In his speech on 4 November 1945 at the first memorial for the freedom fighters, Romano Guardini spoke of a sacrifice 'that the faithful made by sharing in the mind of Christ'. The members of the White Rose were concerned 'to overcome the boundless confusion of ideas, the terrible disfigurement and pollution of spiritual values happening everywhere'. They wanted 'to put things in their bare truth and set out the ordering of existence as it really is'. It was an order that 'is not based on the world and this life. Its origin lies in the heart of God.'[8]

The Catholic Church added the Orthodox Christian Alexander Schmorell, the Catholics Christoph Probst, Kurt Huber and Willi Graf and the Evangelical Christians Hans and Sophie Scholl to its 'German martyrology'. The twentieth-century martyrs were 'witnesses to Christ'. According to Pope John Paul II in his work *Tertio Millennio Adveniente,* they 'shed their blood for the common heritage of Catholics, Orthodox, Anglicans and Protestants'. After a 50-year investigation, Schmorell was recognized in February 2012 as 'St Michael of Munich' by the Russian Orthodox Church abroad.

Let us look at just some of the protagonists more closely. Christoph Probst was born in Murnau, Upper Bavaria, in 1919. He was a medicine student and young father of a family. Before he was baptized, he had approached the Catholic Church step by step. In the run-up to his baptism he wrote to his half-brother:

It is to be a joyful occasion, in which we gratefully thank the Creator for sending Christ to us. Through him we know that our suffering and our life has a meaning. Out of pure kindness

Christ suffered before us in his own life, which has made suffering comprehensible and healed it. He pointed us towards life after death, he preached love and true human fellowship. He brought us the bread of life and there can be no doubt about him.

In his final letter, which was given to his mother after his execution, he said: 'Dear Mum. Thank you for giving me life. When I look at it rightly, it was a journey to God [...] I know I only have an hour left. Now I will receive holy baptism and communion.'[9]

At first, Hans and Sophie Scholl were enthusiastic adherents of the Hitler Youth and the League of German Girls (BDM), in which they had leadership roles. Sophie first had a change of heart when her Jewish school mate Luise Nathan was forbidden to join the BDM. She was increasingly oppressed by the restrictions on freedom of thought. At the turn of the year 1937–8 she joined a group round Otl Aicher. This young Catholic, who later married Inge Scholl, Hans and Sophie's sister, was to become a designer with a worldwide reputation after the war. Aicher introduced Sophie to the *Confessions* of St Augustine. In a ski cabin in Lechtal they read Georges Bernanos's *Journal d'un curé de campagne* (*Diary of a Country Priest*) together. Sophie wrote to her friend the regular officer Fritz Hartnagel: 'When you have time, look for the place where the psalm comes: "Give light to my eyes or I will sleep the sleep of death."'

The girl's spiritual circle was existential, full of questions, longing and doubt: 'I am still so far from God that I don't even feel him when I pray.' In the style of a Teresa of Ávila, she noted: 'Sometimes when I say God's name I want to sink into a nothingness.' Then again: 'When so many devils are raging I want to cling to the rope that God has thrown me in Jesus Christ.' According to the theologian Jakob Kahn, possibly it was a deep experience on Good Friday 1941 that gave Sophie the necessary shove to become certain of her faith. She quoted Augustine in a letter: 'It is written there: you have made us for yourself, and our heart is restless until it rests in you.'

Sophie went to church: 'I knelt down and tried to pray.' It was like a cry: 'Sometimes I think I can force my way to God just by my own longing, by the total surrender of my soul in a single moment.' She was enthusiastic about two volumes of the English convert and cardinal John Henry Newman, which she discovered in a small bookshop.

After a Catholic service on Easter Sunday 1942 in the Maria Himmelfährt church (church of the Assumption) in Ulm-Söflingen, she had a kind of breakthrough, as she acknowledged: 'This drama becomes a deep inner experience when one has faith.' Carl Muth, founder of the Catholic monthly journal *Hochland,* described how during a visit to him Sophie fell into a deep meditation on the famous image of Christ on the Turin shroud. It was as if she had found the face of the God she was seeking: 'Never has a beholder gone so deep as Sophie Scholl did that day,' he wrote.[10] 'Oh, these lazy thinkers!' she mocked about her contemporaries. 'They know nothing about a world of the spirit, where the law of sin and death is overcome.'

By 1941 Hans and Sophie had got to know the culture critic, philosopher of religion and contributor to the newspaper *Hochland,* Theodor Haecker. T. S. Eliot wrote of him: 'Theodor Haecker was a really great man, scholar, thinker and poet.' Haecker was converted to the Catholic Church in April 1921 and regarded himself as a Catholic existentialist and Christian renewer. Sophie was enraptured by him. 'He has a very still face, and a gaze as if he were looking inward. No one's face has ever convinced me like his.' In 1940 Haecker had complained: 'The church's prophetic voice is silent.' The 62-year-old was forbidden to publish by the Nazis and supported himself and his family by translating, including some of Newman's writings. On their evenings together he read to the Scholl siblings from his work *Schöpfer und Schöpfung (Creator and Creation)* or the notes for his *Day and Night Books.* There he wrote: 'The nature of modern dictatorship is the combination of one-dimensional, shallow thinking with power and terror.' [11]

In his regular meetings with the young people Haecker spoke about Newman's idea of conscience as a safeguard against atheistic ideologies. This 'voice of God' was a light in the dark confusion of the mind. Jakob Knaub pointed out that many passages in the White Rose leaflets had Haecker's characteristic style: for example, phrases like 'jaws of the insatiable demon' or 'fight against the demon, against the messengers of Anti-Christ'. The very first leaflet, of 27 June 1942, showed the way ahead when it spoke of stopping 'the continuation of this atheistic war machine before it's too late'. The third leaflet said: Our "State" today is a dictatorship of evil [...] With every day that you still waver, and don't resist this monstrosity from Hell, your guilt climbs up and up like a parabolic curve.' The fourth leaflet declared: 'Anyone today who still doubts the real existence of demonic powers has not grasped the metaphysical background of this war.'[12]

At a meeting with Haecker they discussed the apostle Paul's Second Letter to the Thessalonians, which speaks of 'falling away from God'. After the meeting, his friend Eugen Thurnher reported, Hans Scholl said: 'The Anti-Christ does not have to come first, he is already here!' The 'Demon' Adolf Hitler was the Beast of Revelation.[13]

After they were discovered, the Scholl siblings were condemned to death by the 'Bloody Judge' Roland Freisler, on 22 February 1943, for 'subversion of the war effort', 'aiding the enemy' and 'preparation for high treason'. They were executed the same day. They were 24 and 21 years old. Karl Alt, their Protestant prison chaplain, later reported that Hans and Sophie had asked to receive Catholic baptism at the hour of their death. He persuaded them against it, for their mother's sake.

On the same day and at the same time, Christoph Probst, aged 24, was murdered in Innsbruck. His wife lay in bed with puerperal fever after the birth of their third child. She did not know about either his arrest or his execution. Kurt Huber, 49, and Alexander Schmorell, 25, were beheaded on 13 July 1943 in Munich's Stadelheim prison. Huber had written the leaflet that Sophie and Hans Scholl had dropped into the university light well. He concluded his defence speech before the People's Court (*Volksgerichthof*) with a quotation from the philosopher Johann Gottlieb Fichte: 'You should act as if the fate of what is German depended on you and your action alone, and the responsibility was yours.'

The execution of Willi Graf, aged 25, followed on 12 October 1943, also by guillotine. The Gestapo had tried in vain to beat out of him the names of those involved in the White Rose. A few days before his execution Graf wrote: 'Every experience in human life has its own particular meaning, whether it is now called happiness or suffering. We are grateful for both. All that matters is that we stand the test and understand how to use the time trusting in God's care.' Romano Guardini ended his speech, mentioned above, by saying that the White Rose members who died were people who 'lived their lives fully, enjoyed the beautiful things life gave them, and bore the difficult things it laid upon them. They looked forward to the future, they were prepared to do good work and hoped in the promises their youth offered. But they were convinced Christians. So they had faith and the roots of their souls reached down into those depths.' On 22 February 1945, two years to the day after the beheading of her brother and sister, Inge Scholl was baptized as a Catholic in the St Gallus Church in Ewattingen.

Augustine, Newman and the *Hochland* monthly were all reference points for Sophie Scholl on her way to a deeper faith. Newman's works would also be decisively important for Ratzinger. Ratzinger owed to Newman the idea of conscience as the essential basis of responsible decision-making. As pope, however, he did not take it on himself personally to lead Newman's beatification celebration in Britain. A previously unknown link between Ratzinger and the White Rose was Dora Huber, the sister of the Nazi victim and martyr Kurt Huber. When he was archbishop of Munich, and as Prefect of the Congregation for the Doctrine of the Faith, Ratzinger developed a close friendship with Dora, who was now a Doctor of Philology. He also became friendly with Kurt Huber's daughter Brigit Weiss, as wall as Huber's granddaughter Esther Sepp, on whom he conferred the sacrament of confirmation. In an extensive exchange of letters, he gave Dora Huber counselling, recommended reading and advised her on questions that were bothering her, about life and also theology. In a letter of 22 June 1977 he wrote about Dora's 'brother, greatly respected by me': 'Even as a schoolboy I followed his tragic story with enormous interest. The great admiration I felt for him then has remained till today.'[14]

Dora visited Ratzinger on his holidays in Bad Hofgastein. She collected his sermons and broadcasts. 'I welcome your research, your thoughts, your way of being a Christian as a gift of grace,' she said in one of her letters. Ratzinger's farewell as archbishop of Munich left her 'deeply sad'. On the first Sunday of Advent 1981 she wrote that, during the social unrest of the late 1970s, he had been 'an important academic, a priest with deep faith, a personality strong enough to weather the onslaught of the inner enemy'. 'It is impossible to express what people in this diocese are losing – believers and unbelievers, everybody who has ever felt your strength and what you are.'[15] When Professor Huber's sister died at an advanced age in July

1996, Ratzinger said in his letter of condolence to the family that they should know that Dora Huber, whose deep faith, culture and humility he had learned to appreciate so greatly, was now 'safe with God'. And he added: 'There, after the long separation, she will have met her brave brother again who was killed by the Nazis.'

During their tyrannical rule the Nazis interned 180,000 opponents in concentration camps and prisons, 130,000 of whom were killed, and over a million people were grilled by the Gestapo. In an acknowledgment of the White Rose, the British prime minister, Winston Churchill, said: 'The political history of all nations has hardly ever produced anything greater and nobler than the opposition which existed in Germany [...] Their deeds and their sacrifices are the indestructible foundation of the reconstruction.'

11

The End

After a short posting to Unterföhring, near Munich, the Traunstein flak auxiliaries were sent to Natters, near Innsbruck, to a 10.5 cm battery, the largest and most accurate of all the flak calibres.

Innsbruck was of strategic importance for the Wehrmacht as it was the hub of all its Italian traffic. The students carefully shovelled the snow off the cannons. They were quartered in boarding houses in Stubaital. There was no longer any question of combat missions. After Allied bombers destroyed the station, the telephone lines were rolled up, and the guns were dismantled and made ready for removal.

In February 1944 they received instructions to go to Gilching, north of the Ammersee, to safeguard the airspace over the Dornier works. Dornier manufactured the first jet aircraft, the Nazi regime's final 'secret weapon'. Rail traffic had almost ceased. Munich's main station and the area round it were destroyed in April 1944. Many of the Munich flak auxiliaries no longer had a home. Their families had been bombed out.

Joseph could hardly believe his luck that he was now employed as a telephonist and even had his own office. 'Outside my office hours I could do or not do whatever I wanted and pursue my own interests unhindered.' So he had 'read and written a lot'. His room-mate Wilhelm Volkert often saw Joseph poring over a breviary. 'Ratzinger, are you reading again in your holy books?', snorted the superior telephone officer, a convinced Nazi. Of course, said Volkert, that did not stop Joseph reading or answering sharply. Volkert was a Protestant who later became professor of Bavarian history. It did not escape him that Ratzinger's father, of whom his son spoke proudly, must have been 'a very important person' for him. At first, he did not venture to engage in discussions about religion with Joseph: 'I realized instinctively that I should not get into theological arguments with him, because I would be hopelessly defeated.'[1]

On 10 September 1944 Ratzinger was discharged from the flak auxiliary service. Some of his comrades were posted to the air force, some to the Panzers going to Italy; others were posted to Russia and never came home. At home in Hufschlag, his call-up to the Reichsarbeitsdienst, or RAD (Reich Labour Service), lay on the table. As he recalled, the posting was 'an oppressive memory for me'. That was not just because his superiors, former members of the Austrian Legion, had been Nazis early on and were 'fanatical ideologues who brutally tyrannized us'.

The 550-kilometre journey in the narrow, rattling Reich railway wagons seemed endless. The call-up instruction for the RAD on 20 September 1944 was to strengthen the 'south-east rampart' as a final bastion against the victoriously advancing Red Army. The destination was Deutsch Jahrndorf, a place with 1,400 inhabitants, situated at the meeting point of three countries: Austria, Hungary and Czechoslovakia.

When the troop transporter came to a final halt, after a night journey and an intermediate stop in Vienna, at the tiny station of Austria's easternmost community, they still had a seven-kilometre march on foot through dusty streets. From Deutsch Jahrndorf they could see the citadel of Pressburg in the distance. The land was flat, the houses low and the fauna sparse. Straw stacks were dotted over the Hungarian plains. Gaggles of geese cackled in the ponds. Otherwise, fields and steppes, as far as you could see. Borderland.

The schoolboys were split up into groups of 15 in primitive wooden barracks. The taller ones in Barrack 1 and the shorter in Barrack 5. Joseph, who was 1.70 m tall, was of medium height and assigned to Barrack 2. They slept on straw sacks. Then there were exercises. Three long weeks.

In the exercise yard, the bellowed-out orders harassed the lads even more as they lined up. Spades up! Spades down! Spades over the shoulder! The old Nazis of the Austrian Legion, often former prison inmates, were in their element. The Nazis had introduced this paramilitary cult with the spade in the 1930s. With its brightly polished blade it was ceremoniously set down, then ceremoniously picked up. In this 'Spade Cult' Ratzinger saw the whole absurdity of the regime. It was a 'pseudo liturgy', a 'world of illusion', which was bound to collapse because it was without any substance.

A new threat was the sudden appearance of an SS officer with escort. In the middle of the night, the Nazi henchman forced each of the exhausted lads to step forward to notify them in front of the assembled troop of their 'voluntary' entry into the Waffen-SS. 'A whole series of good-natured comrades were thus forced into that criminal group,' Ratzinger recalled. When it came to Joseph's turn, he openly confessed that he wanted to become a Catholic priest. The SS man was known to spit with utter contempt on each wayside cross he passed. He poured 'ridicule and abuse' on Joseph. But 'that abuse sounded wonderful, because it freed us from the threat of that false "voluntary choice" and all its consequences.'[2]

In the bitterly cold early morning, the schoolboys went to their workplaces on old bikes. 'Sometimes you had back luck and got a horrible job.' Then in the evening from somewhere in the morass you had to get back to the camp with no light. In the 'final battle', a huge number of forced labourers, the most wretched of the wretched, were driven to the rampart to dig kilometre-long trenches and anti-tank ditches 10 metres deep. Joseph was assigned to guarding a group of about 40 prisoners, who burrowed with shovels and spades into the clay soil of the Burgenland vineyards. He had a carbine rifle on his shoulder but no ammunition for it.

In a letter to his fellow students for the school magazine *Helios*, the 17-year-old gave a description of his situation. This is the future pope's first printed document:

Dear Comrades! Perhaps you have been wondering for a long while why you have had no letters from me. I am partly to blame for this but the blame also lies with circumstances that overtook me by surprise, so that I had to put other matters first. [...] At four o'clock in the morning we had to get up, get ready in double quick time and then cycle 14 kilometres, partly over land with no roads to our place of work. Unfortunately, we came rather too late to the famous Burgenland vineyards, which had already been harvested so that we hardly got a taste of their sweet fruit [...] Soon, outlandish tasks were given out to us; we had to be driven with threats because of our lack of enthusiasm. This was not a pleasant job.[3]

One day, the lads from Upper Bavaria saw close up an endless line of haggard men being driven along like cattle to the slaughter by SS men. 'The Hungarian Jews' way of the Cross', said Ratzinger, was a 'horrific experience'. In our conversation, he told me that at home in Traunstein there had not been any Jews except for a timber merchant. The merchant had left the city when his windows were smashed. Joseph's father had never again bought anything from a cloth business in Augsburg when he heard that the previous Jewish owner had been expropriated. 'We eagerly listened to the news from abroad,' Ratzinger said, 'but we heard nothing about the gas chambers. We did know that the Jews were badly treated, that they were transported away, that we had to fear the worst. But we only heard about the actual gas chambers after the war. That was a new inconceivable dimension, which revealed everything as even more terrible.'[4]

The train full of half-starved people that Joseph could see in the distance contained Hungarian Jews, whom the church had tried in vain to protect. Up until then, with the help of countless priests and religious, Angelo Rotta, the nuncio in Budapest, had succeeded in giving out 150,000 papal safe-conducts and 20,000 Vatican passports. In the Balkans, Rotta had already been able to help Bulgarian Jews flee to Palestine by giving them baptism certificates and travel permits. Under pressure from Pius XII, the Hungarian Reich administrator Miklós Horthy stopped the transportations until SS Obersturmbannführer Adolf Eichmann, who was responsible for the expulsion and deportation of the Jews, ordered the 'deliveries' to Auschwitz to be resumed immediately. On 20 October 1944, when 22,000 Jews were driven to the Austrian frontier, the nuncio organized a convoy of lorries to follow them with church safe-conduct passes. Thus he succeeded in saving at least 2,000 Jews from the crematorium.[5]

Literally overnight, work on the tank traps and trenches in Burgenland was stopped. The gymnasium students expected they would be drafted immediately into the Wehrmacht. Instead, on 16 November, they were given their cases with civilian clothes, together with a train ticket. On the way home the train kept stopping on open stretches of track. Air raid warning. On his outward journey Joseph had been astonished to see Vienna completely untouched by the war, now he saw the city largely destroyed. The boys stared aghast from the windows as the train approached Salzburg. Even from a distance they saw that the jewel of the city, the great Renaissance cathedral, was no longer there. The station lay in ruins. Parts of the unique Old Town had been burned out. In 15 air attacks by the US Air Force about half the houses had been destroyed by 9,300 bombs, and 547 people had lost their lives.

The train did not stop in Traunstein, because of an air raid warning. Joseph had to jump from the moving train. It was afternoon as he reached Hufschlag and could hardly believe his luck. He mentioned in the school magazine how happy he was 'to escape the pressure for a few days', a daring remark that could have had consequences. In his memoirs he said: 'I have seldom felt the beauty of home so strongly as on this homecoming from a world distorted by ideology and hatred.'[6]

No one knew what would happen next. 'The war was raging, but for three weeks it was as if we were forgotten.' The odd situation came to an end when, on 11 December, Joseph was ordered to report immediately to the Wehrmacht allocation point in Munich. The question was, where would his next posting be. 'But the officer who had to allocate us was very humane and openly tired of the war, or perhaps even against it and said: "What shall we do with you? Where is your home?" "In Traunstein," I said. Then he said: "We have a barracks there. Go to Traunstein and don't set out at once but enjoy a nice few days."'

Joseph was now a soldier, an infantryman. Identity number 759. His unit was the 1st Infantry Training Company of the 179 Replacement and Training Rifle Battalion. The final remnant of the German Wehrmacht were kitted out with fatigues and uniform. There was even a brand-new dress uniform. The swearing-in to the 'Führer' took place on St Sylvester's Day, New Year's Eve. The basic training for the troop, which also included 35- to 40-year-old Germans from abroad, from Bessarabia and Russia, took place in the Badenweiler Barracks in Traunstein. On 7 January the recruits were stationed in a 'country billet' five kilometres from the town centre. The sleeping place for each group of 12 men was a dug-out wooden bunker at the edge of the forest, which was covered with earth for camouflage. The nearby inn served as the 'field mess'. Mostly they got just bread and butter. They were woken at six in the morning for a 6.30 start. There followed the early morning sports, so disliked by Ratzinger: obstacle races and hurdles that were very hard to get over.

They all knew the war could no longer be won. 'But no one rebelled or said I'm going to skedaddle,' Ratzinger's comrade Martin Tradler remembered. 'Everyone was afraid of the SS. They knew they made short shrift and had often hanged men.'[7] Hitler's final contingent learned not only how to handle rifles, bazookas, machine guns and bayonets (for hand-to-hand fighting) but also the correct salutes and how to march in step. 'The brittle bones tremble,' they sang. It was particularly grotesque when Joseph marched through Traunstsein with his troop. To show their staying power they had to belt out an old soldier's song: 'We're going to Enge-land.'

'Ratzinger was not a particularly good shot,' said Tradler. On the other hand, he could remember the most abstruse orders and help the others that way. He was noticeable for his high voice. Otherwise he was 'a quiet fellow', also 'a good comrade and not a loner'. Despite his poor physique, he withstood 40 km night marches, with a gas mask over his face. That was followed by simulating attacks on a bridge with the machine gun he had hauled along with him. Tradler would soon be called up to action. The entry on his service card was 'ZBV' – 'for special duties' (*zur besonderen Verwendung*). He became a prisoner of war in France and only returned at the beginning of 1947, half starved and traumatized.

It was the beginning of the final days of a Reich that was meant to last for a thousand years. In the middle of January, at first Joseph was posted to various places around Traunstein. In February he got a whitlow, a thumb infection. Not a very serious matter. But the doctor, 'who was more of a cattle doctor', not only cut the infected part without anaesthetic but also did it particularly badly. Even 70 years later visitors to the Vatican might notice the damaged thumb on the pope's left hand. But the botched operation turned out to be lucky. He was signed off as unfit for service and allowed home to be looked after by his mother in Hufschlag.

He spent 16 April, his 18th birthday, back in the barracks. Germany lay in ruins. More than 400 million cubic metres of rubble covered the land. More than 3 million people had been bombed out and evacuated. Countless people survived in cellars, huts and under broken-down railway bridges. On 1 May at 10.56 p.m. the Grossdeutsche Rundfunk broadcast the death of Adolf Hitler and the takeover of the regime by Admiral of the Fleet Karl Dönitz, the commander-in-chief of the German Navy. Jews and slave workers from the closed-down concentration camps were driven into the not yet occupied interior of the country. A train with 66 half-starved figures, mostly Hungarian and Polish Jews, arrived in Traunstein on 2 May 1945. They were locked in a brewery's pigsty overnight, to be shot by SS men next day on the edge of a forest near Surberg. Meanwhile, five kilometres away to the west, the US troops were marching in.[8]

Joseph's company was quartered in the girls' school in the city centre of Traunstein. During those days, as his memoirs report succinctly, 'I decided to go home'. What was stated there so lightly was in fact a suicide mission. The penalty for desertion was death. SS men had already hanged quite a few deserters from trees. 'Looking back, I am surprised at myself,' Ratzinger said about his action, 'I knew that there were guards there – you would be shot at once, and such an attempt could only turn out badly. Why, despite this, I went home unconcerned shows how naïve I was. I can no longer explain it.'

The decisive moment was when two medical sergeants left the building. Without any further ado he joined them. Seldom can a sling, which he was wearing for his thumb infection, have been so useful. 'Otherwise I would not have got out.' But his escape was not yet achieved. As he sneaked through the station subway, 'two soldiers were standing there on guard duty, and at that moment the situation became critical for me'. The men saw the lad with his bandaged hand and let him pass: 'Thank God there were some who were fed up with the war and did not want to become murderers.'[9]

Joseph's desertion was not a flight or a retreat through fear, but a considered decision. Typical Ratzinger. He had, so to speak, done his bit, and could do no more. As he walked through the door in Hufschlag and was joyfully welcomed by his sister and parents, two nuns were sitting at the kitchen table, who were friends of Maria.

They were studying a map in readiness for the Americans to march in. What a grotesque situation: 'Thank God, a soldier is here, now we are protected!' the deserter heard, who was happy to have escaped his pursuers with his skin intact. Then to increase the drama of the situation, instead of the expected GIs, two SS men turned up. Ratzinger senior 'could not forbear to let loose all his fury against Hitler to their faces, which normally would have been the death of him. But a special angel seemed to be protecting us. The two men disappeared the next day without causing any harm.'[10]

At last the Americans arrived in Hufschlag. It was 7 May, one day before the official end of the war. There was a tank in front pointing its cannons towards the Ratzingers' house. Soldiers sprang from the jeeps behind it to search for hidden German army personnel. In the house they found a box with hidden SA uniforms. Neighbours had asked them to store it without telling them what was inside. Joseph's uniform also emerged, which the boy had to put on again, to go and stand with his hands up on the grass in front of the house, together with the other prisoners of war. He was just able to pocket an empty notebook and a pencil. Then he joined the long trek leading to captivity.

On 7 May General Alfred Jodl signed the unconditional surrender of the German Reich in the name of the the high command of the German Wehrmacht at the headquarters of General Dwight D. Eisenhower, commander-in-chief of the Allied forces in Europe. The surrender came into force on 8 May 1945 at 11 p.m. Stalin had made clear beforehand that he would only recognize the validity of the total surrender when it had been signed by the Red Army commander-in-chief, Marshal Georgi K. Schukow. That took place shortly after zero hours on 9 May in the Soviet headquarters in Karlshorst in Berlin (and was backdated to 8 May). The day of the war's end, 8 May, was a Tuesday. The sun shone over Germany, but in the spring sunshine its cities looked even sadder. Hamburg, Berlin, Dresden, Würzburg and Munich lay in burned-out ruins. Their inhabitants wandered around like ghosts. Corpses lay by the roadside, in parks and on the pavements. Ten million people took to the country roads seeking refuge somewhere. Refugees from the east, forced labourers from France or Italy, concentration camp prisoners in striped prison clothes.

However, on the Champs Elysées in Paris hundreds of thousands of people were celebrating the victory over Hitler's Germany. In New York half a million people danced and sang in the streets to celebrate VE Day – Victory in Europe. In London 200,000 gathered in front of Buckingham Palace. 'In all our long history,' said Winston Churchill, 'we have never seen a greater day than this.'[11]

The madness had come to an end; the raging of evil forces had been stopped. In Hitler's Reich, human beings were 'crushed, used and abused for the mania of a power that wanted to create a new world'. As Ratzinger said in 2004 at the celebrations for the 60th Anniversary of the Allied Normandy Landings, that Reich was a 'non-place' – a false utopia (*ou topos*: 'non-place') – from which 'God was completely absent' and which, like all such 'non-places', embraced the destruction of others and self-destruction.[12] One in three German men born between 1910 and 1925 did not survive the war. Well over 12 million Wehrmacht soldiers became prisoners of war or were reported missing and never found. About 3.6 million were held in British camps, 1 million in French and about 3.1 million in American camps.[13]

Between 3.2 and 3.6 million Germans became Soviet prisoners.[14] Countless numbers of survivors were only able to return home after ten years. According to the German Red Cross's missing persons service, the fate of 1.3 million family members of the German military remained unknown. On the other side, those in German captivity included French, British, Greek and Italian prisoners, plus prisoners from other countries and 5 million Red Army soldiers, 3.3 million of whom lost their lives.[15]

A stream of refugees such as had never been seen before poured over the whole continent. From East Germany alone, 9.5 million people came in great treks into the West zone. A total of 14 million Germans were displaced, more than 2 million of them remained missing. Between 1937 and 1945, 1.3 million people had already been brought to Germany. Some 4.3 million fled from the Russians. In the other direction 4.25 million people were relocated from Poland to Russia. In the end, in the whole of Europe more than 19.75 million people were homeless, the greatest migration of all time.

The misery was palpable in the fate of families, women, children and the mentally unwell. More than half of the 5.3 million fallen German Wehrmacht soldiers died in the last ten months of the war.

After the end of the war more than another million became Allied prisoners of war. At the end of an unprecedented slaughter the number of the dead was over 50 million, almost half of them civilians. Among them were 20 million Russians, 7.35 million Germans, 6 million Poles, 537,000 French, 390,000 British and 320,000 Americans. From 1933 on, about 10 million people were interned in National Socialist concentration camps. The Nazis murdered 6 million of Europe's 9.6 million Jews.

With umpteen thousand other survivors of an annihilated army, Joseph went to a collection camp for prisoners of war in Bad Aibling. The procession of men was so broad that they took up the whole width of the motorway. This was a favourite photograph subject for US soldiers, 'to take home as a memento of the beaten army and its desolate personnel', as Ratzinger observed. The end of the prisoners' journey was an area of open fields near Ulm. Until the end of their captivity, 50,000 men lived in the open air in wind and all weather. At first they slept without tents or covering. 'The first 14 days went all right because the weather was fine', but when the rain came 'it was terrible'.

Some of the prisoners of war had been smart enough to bring a tent with them when they were arrested and formed tent groups with two to six other men. Joseph found a sergeant with a one-man tent. 'He was kind enough to take me in. We dug a sort of bed for ourselves and made a place to put bread beside it.' We lived 'without a clock or calendar or newspaper,' Ratzinger recalled, 'only confused, distorted rumours about what was going on in the world penetrated our strange world fenced off by barbed wire.' The worst thing was the hunger. In Bad Aibling for the first two days there was nothing to eat or drink. In Ulm the provision was 'a ladleful of soup and a bit of bread per day'.[16]

It got better when clubs were formed who organized talks. Prisoners of war who were lecturers or higher-grade students soon arranged a complete lecture programme, and priests celebrated Mass every day in the open air. Ratzinger said the notebook he had brought with him was a comfort and 'wonderful companion' that became a 'mirror of my days'. He wrote 'meditations on myself, on history and my situation', as well as 'all kinds of reflections'.[17] He worked on *Abitur* subjects that he could remember, composed

Greek hexameters and even began 'to put together a sort of Greek Grammar'. There were no books available, which led to early 'philological efforts'.

It was a time of privation, fasting, an experience of the wilderness. As 'spiritual nourishment and help to withstand this hard time', his notebook, which unfortunately was lost, had been 'something wonderful'. 'Because I could give my mind work to do, and so that empty time was filled.' Amazingly, the notebook 'lasted exactly for the time up until 19 June, then it was full up'. That was the date Joseph was released. After 40 days of physical and psychological deprivation and maturing. 'Being in captivity was somehow symbolic for me,' Ratzinger reflected. 'We were unhoused and unfree. The nights were cold, but the days were clear and the year advancing. We were on our way to a better future.'[18]

Joseph's first destination after his release was Munich, where he was driven in an American military vehicle. He and a comrade set out for home on foot. He had a tent in his rucksack to sleep in for the 120 km journey. But scarcely had the two walking companions left the outskirts of the city when the driver of a milk lorry, fuelled by wood gas, stopped. 'We were both too shy to hail him.' The lorry was on its way to a Traunstein dairy. It was the feast day of the Heart of Jesus as Joseph reached the town square shortly before sunset. He heard praying and singing coming from the church. Rejoicing over his regained freedom, he said: 'At that moment the heavenly Jerusalem could not have appeared more beautiful.' At home his father 'could hardly believe it when I suddenly stood there alive in front of him'. There was not a lot of food, but his mother made a fresh salad, and there was an egg from their own hens and a piece of bread: 'No other meal in my whole life tasted as delicious as that simple meal my mother got for me from our own garden.'[19]

A few weeks later, on a hot day in July, his brother Georg also came home on the first train carrying released prisoners of war from Italy. Many families lost fathers and sons. From Georg's seminary class alone, ten classmates had fallen in the war. In all, 45 former seminary students died. 'We had heard nothing from him since March,' Joseph reported, 'and the worry that he might had fallen in the final weeks of the war lay heavily on our hearts.' But suddenly someone was standing there at the door, 'tanned by the Italian sun, with his head shaven, and PW (Prisoner of War) in large letters on his threadbare uniform.' A son and brother. Before any word was spoken, Georg sat down at the piano and played, 'Großer Gott, wir loben dich' ('Holy God, we praise thy name'). 'None of us was ashamed of our tears which now flowed.'

The sociologist Heinz Bude described the 16- and 17-year-old German flak auxiliaries as men who became not 'go-getters' but 'cautious, sensitive types, although also doers with a strong will.' They would not 'put themselves in the foreground' but 'seek cover'. Early on, his academic colleague Helmut Schelsky used the term 'sceptical generation' to describe this age group. It included not only Ratzinger but also writers of the post-war period such as Günter Grass, Martin Walser and Sieigfried Lenz, and also the social theorist Niklas Luhmann and Hans-Dietrich Genscher, who went on to become German foreign minister.

According to Schelsky, this generation had a far from 'normal' adolescence, unlike that enjoyed by those born after. The 'sceptical generation' were thrown as teenagers into the hellish destruction of the Third Reich. They returned traumatized from the war and had to come to terms with the fact that the greatest crime in human history had been committed in their name, the name of Germany. According to Schelsky's research, the 'sceptical generation' were more critical in their social and self-awareness, more sceptical, distrustful and lacking in illusions than any previous generations in their youth. They felt no need to form collective elites or follow such systems, let alone break out into flaming passion.[20] Born in 1912, Schelsky himself later harboured 'a profound aversion to all ideological upsurges'. As can be seen with Joseph Ratzinger himself, that included the student movement of 1968 and its impetus, driven by moral indignation.

Although his experiences as a flak auxiliary and soldier may have been decisive for Joseph Ratzinger, what really shaped him was the example of his parental home and being rooted in the simple piety of liberal Bavarian Catholicism. Backed by his literary and academic gifts, he developed into an uncommon mixture of having his feet on the ground and intellectual brilliance. He soared into the highest spheres but did not become elitist. The second key to understanding Ratzinger's biography is his personal confrontation, at the risk of his life, with a totalitarian regime whose system and world view drove it, by its own logic, to war and genocide. The Nazi Terror, Benedict confessed, had an enduring influence on his career decision. In short, he said, 'My parents' faith gave me a confirmation of Catholicism as the bulwark of truth and justice against that Reich of atheism and lies presented by National Socialism.'

His youth was nearly over, the first stage of his life at an end. After he had grown into the secret of the liturgy, his first involvement with the truth of faith, and after his close encounter with atheism, the 18-year-old was ready for the radical commitment to a life for God. His basic decision was made at the end of the war: 'Now there was no more doubt, I knew where I belonged.'

PART TWO

The Master Student

12

Zero Hour

It was bitterly cold that winter. The snow on the streets was hardly cleared at all. Horse-drawn vehicles found it difficult to keep to the road. Breathing heavily, the three young men who staggered with their trunks up the hill in Freising on 3 January 1946 looked shy and serious. Cautiously they pressed on, as if they hardly dared to tread the holy ground with their clumsy shoes.

By the statue of God's mother, the *Patrona Bavariae,* they had made the sign of the cross. Below them, they saw the wild River Isar and Erdinger Moos stretching out. On the opposite hill they saw the splendid Weihenstephan Abbey with the world's oldest brewery. The higher they climbed, the more clearly they saw the outline of Munich on the horizon, just 30 km away as the crow flies. Seventy-three air attacks by British and American bombers had destroyed more than 60 per cent of the buildings and cost 6,000 lives. The towers of the Frauenkirche, capped by its distinctive onion domes, seemed to be the only landmark left standing in the former 'Capital of the Nazi Movement'.

Because of the war, Georg and Joseph were at the same starting point. Both were beginning at Freising with the first semester. Most importantly, neither of them had passed their *Abitur*, at least not in the normal way. Joseph's final school report stated that if he was still serving in the Wehrmacht at the date of the *Abitur* in April 1945, 'the maturity certificate' (*Reifevermerk*) should be given to him, the admission requirement for further studies. At least that meant a bad mark in sport would not stand in the way of his future. 'In this respect,' Ratzinger remarked, 'the war lasted just long enough for me to reach that position.'[1]

He had come to know his companion, Rupert Berger, in Traunstein during the great Advent singing festival, the first to take place after the war. Georg and Joseph sang in the choir; Rupert played the violin. 'We noticed at once that we were on the same road,' said Berger. Berger's father had been dismissed as mayor by the Nazis and interned in Dachau. His schoolmates had teased Rupert, constantly saying: 'Your father is in Dach...' – and then pinched him so that he loudly shouted 'au!' His father's arrest had led him to decide to become a priest. 'I was seven years old. But I had seen and felt that the Catholic Church was definitely the only firm support to be had against the Nazis.'[2]

The war had changed Joseph. Georg remarked that his brother, who before 'had still been just a boy without a proper man's voice', now seemed to have 'really grown up'.[3] For a long time he and his comrades would still hear the echo of the flak cannons in their nightmares, see the sudden flash as the bombs hit, images of body parts dragged out of a hospital in wooden crates. 'The years we spent in the unfreedom of military service,' the two brothers wrote in a letter to 'Rex' Mair shortly before Christmas, 'gave us the opportunity to grasp the beauty and grandeur of our vocation more deeply than perhaps would have been possible under normal circumstances.'[4] Now they looked forward to discovering the mysteries of God. Freely and openly. By means of scholarship. They needed to make sure that 'the faith is true. That it opens the way to the right understanding of our own life, the world and humanity.'

Even the journey there was an adventure. Traunstein station was bombed out, the rails only roughly repaired. It was with difficulty that they could just squeeze onto one of the few trains to Munich and find somewhere to stand. They were surrounded by peasant women with fruit and poultry for market, home-comers from the war in torn uniform jackets, tired refugees. But didn't they themselves also look rather like displaced persons, with their shabby trunks and worn clothes? At home they had dragged furniture about and sorted through bookcases to organize their return to study. They had had to find food ration cards and personal identity cards. They had visited wounded war comrades.

Joseph saw how 'the old Nazis suddenly bowed to the church'. A former French teacher, 'who was a horrible Nazi and a fearful hater of Catholics', came to the parish priest Stefan Blum with a bunch of flowers to ask him for a *Persilschein* (a de-Nazification certificate) for a job in the civil service. The priest had refused in disgust. 'It may even come to it,' he said ironically in a sermon to laughter from the congregation, 'that they will say the only Nazis were the priests.'

Blum was the same priest who had advised the Ratzingers to send their highly gifted younger son to the episcopal seminary. Now he pressed a pile of theology and philosophy books on to Joseph to read. Short trousers were forbidden in the seminary, he told him as he set out on his way. And even though modern theologians now wore ties in universities, priests-to-be had to wear dog collars, Roman clerical collars.

The hardest thing was saying goodbye. His mother had packed their trunks. A spare suit, two shirts, underclothes. But there was a gleam of pride and joy in their father's eyes 'that we wanted to become priests'.[5] Maria was sad to lose her brothers, even though it was only for a while. It was money from her wages that made studying possible for them both. 'If this is not for you,' their mother plucked up the courage to say, 'then it is better that you leave.' St John Bosco's mother had also said the same to her son: 'If one day you should doubt your vocation, then take off your cassock. Better a poor peasant than a bad priest.'

Eight months after the end of the war Germany was still a wreck. In the big cities, salvage parties were still looking for corpses. There was the risk of an epidemic. Millions of bricks were removed with bare hands from the gigantic piles of rubble. Then they were passed on, cleaned up and stored – material for rebuilding. Whole walls were stripped for firewood. Clothes were made out of old uniforms or parachute silk. In parks, acorns were gathered to grind for flour. Salad was made from dandelions, and schnapps from potatoes.

On 20 September 1945 Erika Mann wrote from Munich to her parents, who were living in exile in the USA in Pacific Palisades, near Los Angeles. 'Don't consider for a minute coming back to this lost land. It is simply unrecognizable.'[6] People put up 'Missing Person' notices on walls and trees, looking for a husband or wife, parents or siblings. In the diocese of Bamberg 'services without light' were permitted because of the lack of candles. Church leaders exhorted priests to be extremely economical with the consecrated oil; there were no supplies to replenish it. A third of the 60,000 km railway network was unusable. Of the 22,400 engines and 578,000 goods wagons half were only fit for scrap. Ration coupons gave just 1,000 calories per person per day, provided the food was available at all. In the winter famine of 1946–7 the fat ration was cut to 75 g per month. On the black market 20 cigarettes cost 150 Reichsmarks, 1 kg of coffee cost 1100 Reichsmarks, and 1 egg cost 12 Reichsmarks. 'People are eating grass and the bark from trees,' reported Anastas Mikoyan, the Soviet commissar for export trade from Berlin. Konrad Adenauer, the mayor of Cologne, who had been dismissed by the Nazis and reinstated by the British, spoke of a 'crash into the abyss'. Unless a miracle happens, he said, 'the German people will slowly but surely go under'.

Zero hour. The Moloch, the Ogre, the terrible Serpent of the Nazi terror regime, which had claimed to be an unconquerable thousand-year Reich, was defeated. 'There has hardly ever been a more eventful year in the whole of history,' noted Thomas Mann. 'Shock after shock and bitter blows kept thronging in', without any historical precedent. But it was also a year of new possibilities and a new beginning out of the wreckage, resurrection from ruins. One of those incomparable moments history offers, to pause, no longer to go on as before – a chance to change things, to kindle a light of hope.

Those born later can barely fathom the emotions of that time. To feel on your skin what freedom means. To have a future again after being persecuted, or even condemned to death. In a free world. Not everyone felt ready for it. The defeated militia man, the brown-shirted party comrade, the fanatical Hitler devotee were secretly clenching their fists. 'Fundamentally,' the future German president Theodor Heuss said, the day the war ended was 'the most tragic and most questionable paradox of history for each of us' who remained – 'because we had been saved and annihilated both at once'. 'Annihilated' in the sense of a moral and political-military defeat and universal hardship, but also 'saved' from the tyranny of National Socialism. 'The curse has been lifted, the swindle exposed,' shouted the mayor of Passau, the city on the Danube, 'the future is open for free, faithful and loving people.'[7]

The upheavals of the war had left a ghostly, sullen silence over the land. Destroyed villages and landscapes, ruins left by devastating incendiary bombs, the whole hell of fear and destruction, hunger and death. The over-full hospitals, the women without husbands, children without fathers, the gigantic streams of refugees rolling westward – all this was not God's work. But it was all calling for God's help. Wasn't it also a sign of Providence that the young men looking forward to their studies in Freising belonged to the first-year group of a new generation of priests? New spiritual teachers, shepherds of a beaten people, indeed genuine *Führers* – leaders – who could bless the stricken land again? Wasn't *spiritual* renewal also the necessary condition for *worldly* renewal: in politics, the economy, culture and lifestyle?

On 3 June 1945 a Corpus Christi procession set out in Munich in brilliant sunshine – the first major church event in Germany after the war. Through metre-high piles of rubble, for more than four hours, 25,000 people followed the Holy Eucharist, the body of the Lord, as a sign of life against death, which the 76-year-old Cardinal von Faulhaber carried in a monstrance under a baldachin for the first time again through the streets. 'You could see their enjoyment of the sunny day in the faces of the people of Munich,' Faulhaber wrote in his diary. 'It came from their hearts to confess Christ, the Lord of the new time, to the whole world.'[8]

'At the beginning it was the churches – not the state,' wrote the church historian Martin Greschat, that were the first resort for survival of a nation that had to overcome material want, disorientation and a massive breakdown of civilization.[9] According to the historian Thomas Grossbölting, the Catholic Church in particular stood out as an institution. At least in the early years of the Federal Republic of Germany, both in its own self-awareness and also in the perception of outsiders, it was seen as 'uncorrupted by National Socialism'. As a non-Nazified institution, the Catholic Church was not only accorded 'special authority among the German population',[10] but its representatives were accepted as legitimate speakers and partners in dialogue and negotiation by the Allied occupation officers. The bishop of Münster, Clemens August Graf von Galen, was even invited to the civil government summit in the British occupation zone.

On 23 August 1945, when the German Catholic bishops published a joint pastoral letter for the first time since the end of the war, they stated their views on guilt and sin: 'Many Germans, including from among our ranks, let themselves be fooled by the false teaching of National Socialism and were indifferent towards the crimes against human freedom and dignity', the letter said. 'Many aided and abetted the crimes by their behaviour; many became criminals themselves.' The bishops called for a 'conversion by becoming Christian'. The new beginning also required comprehensive peacemaking in society in the spirit of reconciliation. 'Do not wreak vengeance yourself,' it exhorted, 'bear with one another.'[11]

Two months later, on 18–19 October 1945, the leading representatives of the Protestant churches also signed a declaration about their church's role in the recent past. The text read: 'We lament that we did not confess more bravely, pray more faithfully, believe more joyfully and love more strongly.' However, according to Grossbölting, the unqualified confession of guilt was not the predominant message of the Stuttgart Declaration. Rather, the draft document of the newly founded Evangelical Church in Germany (EKD) was 'marked through and through by compromise'. So a sentence inserted into the Declaration, before the one quoted above, put the Protestant churches among those who had stood against National Socialism: 'We fought for long years in the name of Jesus Christ against the mentality that found its terrible expression in the National Socialist regime of violence.'

The roles of the two national churches in Germany were different. Since the nineteenth-century *Kulturkampf,* the Catholics had been branded as 'enemies of the state' and persecuted. But the heirs of Luther had formed an alliance with the state, at least by the time of the Kaiser's Reich, expressed in the conjunction of 'Evangelical and German; Throne and Altar; Kaiser, German Reich and Protestantism'.[12] The election results of the National Socialists were paralleled by the rise in many regional churches of the 'German Christians', who were close to the NSDAP. In the synodal elections of the newly created Evangelical National Church on 23 July 1933, they won a two-thirds majority and thereby occupied the most important church positions. As a Protestant resistance movement, the 'Confessing Churches' remained without notable influence.

Theologically, the idea of the authoritarian state was founded on Luther's doctrine of 'two realms', which defined both church and state as governed by God. In his *On Worldly Authority* (1523) the reformer demanded unconditional obedience to the ruling secular powers. It was only in the conflict with National Socialism that Dietrich Bonhoeffer succeeded in breaking with that line of thought. Thomas Mann drew support from Luther when, in May 1945, he gave a lecture in Washington with the title 'Germany and the Germans':'I frankly confess that I do not love him,' the Protestant Mann said about Luther.

> This Germanism in its unalloyed state, the separatist, anti-Roman, anti-European, shocks me and frightens me, even when it appears in the guise of evangelical freedom and spiritual emancipation, and the specifically Lutheran, the choleric coarseness, the invective, the fuming and raging, the extravagant rudeness coupled with a tender depth of feeling and with the most clumsy superstition and belief in incubi, and changelings, arouses my instinctive antipathy.[13]

Thomas Mann delivered a harsh judgement on both 'Germany and the Germans': formed by wars, the unholy German Reich of the Prussian nation was determined to be a warring Reich. As such, it drove a stake into the flesh of the world, and as such it collapsed.[14]

With the 'Declaration regarding the Defeat of Germany' of 5 June 1945, signed by the four Allied commanders-in-chief, Germany was divided into four occupation zones. Accordingly, the victors also divided Berlin, the former capital of the Reich, into four zones. An 'Allied Control Council', set up by the four supreme commanders, took over the tasks of government. The official language in each zone was that of the occupying power. Anyone wanting to travel from one zone to another had to have a zone passport. Directive 1067 of the US government to the high command of the American occupation troops stated clearly that Germany had not been occupied 'for the purpose of liberation', but that it should be treated as a 'conquered enemy state'. Nothing should be done that could lead 'to the economic recovery of Germany' or was likely 'to strengthen the German economy'. As the soldiers' newspaper *Stars and Stripes* put it, it was not about 'paying compliments to child murderers or feeding SS villains with corned beef'.

Stalin saw it the same way. 'This war is not like in the past,' said the Soviet leader in April 1945, even before the end of the war; 'those who conquer a territory impose their own social system on it.' The occupied part of Europe was to be developed as a 'protective shield' for the Soviet Union. It would be a Central European belt from the Baltic Sea to Albania. For the eastern parts of the former German Reich – now the 'Soviet Occupation Zone' – the Russian nomenklatura had in mind a 'Revolutionary Dictatorship of the Proletariat and Peasantry'. 'It must look democratic,' declared Walter Ulbricht, who arrived from Moscow with his 'Ulbricht Group' in April 1945 to organize the reconstruction, 'but we must keep everything in hand.'

Those who were not prepared to submit to the new rulers would in fact soon be interned in 'special camps'. Among them were 'out-of-favour bourgeois democrats and social democrats, even dissident communists', as the historian Heinrich August Winkler records. These prisons were partly built on the site of former concentration camps and remained until 1950. Of the 120,000 inmates, about 40,000 lost their lives. In the Soviet Union, more than 600,000 Red Army soldiers had surrendered to the Germans. They were treated as traitors and incorporated into a 'labour army' or sent straight to the gulags.

The division of Germany and the spheres of influence in Europe had already been discussed at the Yalta Conference in Crimea from 4 to 11 February 1945. Franklin D. Roosevelt, Winston Churchill and Josef Stalin posed happily for a group photograph. Further discussions were held a month and a half later, from 17 July until 2 August 1945, at the Cecilienhof, Potsdam. Those taking part were again the 'Big Three', with the difference that after the death of Roosevelt, the US was represented by President Harry S. Truman. The shifting of Poland 200 kilometres to the west was already a fact at that point. In that way, Poland was compensated for the loss of its eastern area, which had been annexed by the Soviet Union as a result of the 1939 Hitler–Stalin Pact.

From Haus Erlenkamp, where the American delegation was lodged, while still at the conference, Truman gave the order to drop the atomic bombs on Hiroshima and Nagasaki. On 6 and 9 August 1945 the mega weapons, used for the first time, killed approximately 100,000 people immediately. They were almost exclusively civilians and forced labourers kidnapped by the Japanese army. By the end of the year, a further 130,000 people had died from the resulting damage. One day before the destruction of Nagaski, the London Four Powers Agreement of 8 August 1945 decided to set up an international military tribunal in Nuremberg, initially to deal with 22 top German war criminals who were accused, among other things, of breaking treaties, war crimes and mass murder.

At the Potsdam Conference, from 17 July to 2 August 1945, the Allies had laid down five principles for the reconstruction of Germany: demilitarization, de-Nazification, democratization, decentralization and decartelization. The measures countered the doctrines of an aggressive, militaristic, racist, dictatorial and conformist state. Reflection also began in the churches on the causes of this cataclysm unexampled in history. According to a broad consensus, the main cause of the totalitarian system was turning away from God. Many Evangelical and Catholic clergy in the overfilled churches and makeshift places of worship even spoke of a 'judgement' to punish a godless society. Terror and breakdown, declared the evangelical theologian Walter Künneth, who had been a committed member of the Confessing Church during the Nazi madness, could only be seen as 'an apocalyptic event and judgment of God'.

The wind had changed. After the cataclysm of the Second World War and the attempted elimination of the Jewish people, totalitarian ideologies were shown to have failed. The leading church representatives were convinced that a vision for the development of a human future depended on religious renewal. After the collapse of the nation and a cleansing catharsis, a universal new awareness was required. Among the German people, there was 'hopefully no one left who would deny the supreme and decisive importance of religion, Christian faith, for social life,' said Cardinal von Galen and the Jesuit father Gustav Gundlach in their February 1946 essay on 'Catholic Principles for Public Life'.[15] They felt they were winning. The overwhelming destructive power of the recent past had made clear that only Christianity had the strength to overcome the lies, power-craving, hatred, greed, violence and egoism, and to give people hope again.

Heinrich Krone, a co-founder of the CDU (Christian Democratic Union) and close associate of Konrad Adenauer, noted in his diary on 1 September 1945: 'History teaches us that all attempts to give the German people a political shape have failed, unless the church has been involved in creating it [...] As a people, the only choice we have is to confess Christianity.'[16] That reminder also found its way into the Bavarian constitution in 1949. In its preamble it said, and still says today, that the blessings of peace, humanity and justice must 'be lastingly assured' – remembering 'the devastation to which a state and society ordered without God' had led.

Even before the end of the war, critical Christians were warning that the de-Christianization of society would lead to barbarism. For example, at a men's retreat day in Fulda on 22 October 1941, the Jesuit Alfred Delp lamented that the binding power of Christianity had appallingly decreased, and religion and culture had drifted apart. According to Delp, the present era had become 'blind and unresponsive to the essential part of our message and our reality'. In an 'un-Christian time' in which more and more people knew less and less about the church, traditional values were rejected in pursuit of a purely secular economic-technical rationalism. However, we should also ask 'why the awkward people in the church were so seldom' Christians who contradicted such questionable new ideals.

From 1942 Delp had belonged to the 'Kreisau Circle' of resistance fighters, who co-operated in the July Plot to assassinate Hitler. On 28 July he was arrested after early Mass in the Munich district of Bogenhausen. He was executed in the Plötzensee prison in Berlin on 2 February 1945. Shortly before his execution he drafted a programme for the 'healing of life and people today', as well as 'drawing people to God'; the church's mission depended on 'the seriousness of its transcendent commitment and worship'. Delp as a curate was the immediate predecessor of Ratzinger, whose first clerical posting was in Bogenhausen. It almost sounded as if Ratzinger had taken on a legacy when he himself later referred to a church that would become small. In his final work, written at the turn of the year 1944–5, Delp urged that in the time after Hitler 'every attempt must be made to keep and develop educated

Christian people'. Church renewal was imperative 'even if it gives up on a large number' of members.[17]

When they reached their destination, the three new students from Traunstein saw that the final Allied air attack had also severely damaged the college building and Freising Cathedral. So services could only be held in the crypt. And here too, as in the upper church, the smashed windows had been roughly sealed with straw sacks. Joseph was stunned and also stirred. What a spiritual treasury! There stood the mighty cathedral. The Benedictine church. The church of St John. There was the former monastery of the Premonstratensians, the Gothic cloister, the cathedral courtyard, the college – they all seemed to go together; it all had a meaning in accord with a higher order.

The impression it all made on Joseph was overwhelming; he felt like a discoverer of new worlds. He found the cathedral especially 'magnificent' and 'dazzlingly beautiful'. In the vestibule he was greeted by the figures of the emperor Friedrich Barbarossa and his wife, Beatrix. The ceiling paintings showed a glimpse of heaven, where in colourful fresco Christ bestowed the crown of eternal life on St Corbinian, the first bishop of Freising. At the high altar a copy of an enormous painting by Peter Paul Rubens dramatically depicted the 'Woman of the Apocalypse'. The scene is taken from the book of Revelation (Rev. 12), in which a woman clothed with the sun and 12 stars gives birth to a child. And while a dragon threatens the mother, the child is taken to heaven by angels.

Dragons are also to be seen on a pillar in the crypt. Knights in chain mail, armed with sword and shield, fight against the snarling beasts. One knight's foot is in a dragon's jaws. *Ecclesia,* Mother Church, in the picture looks to the east. Sure of victory, she holds a lily in both hands. Indeed, hadn't *Ecclesia* just defied a great beast? The dragon who threatened to drag whole nations down into the abyss?

The die had been cast. As Ratzinger said, it stirred fresh energy 'to live in freedom again, an age in which the church can set out again, is in demand and sought after'. Everything up till then was the prologue. Now the task was to lay the foundation. Freising's Domberg (Cathedral Mountain), would become Joseph Aloysius Ratzinger's spiritual home and stamp his life work. Apart from Rome, there was nowhere else he stayed so long as here on the *Mons doctus,* the

'Scholars' Mountain'. Here in Freising he discovered and developed his theological gift and talent as a writer. His doctoral work was created in the Domberg's spiritual atmosphere. He wrote his habilitation thesis (the post-doctoral qualification for a full professorship at a German university) there. Here as a young professor, he stood at the lectern in a higher education college (*Hochschule*) for the first time. And finally, in Freising he was ordained as a priest and bishop.

But first he had to settle in, which was not particularly difficult. In those tough times after the war, said Ratzinger, 'hope was stronger than anxiety'. When he arrived on the holy mountain he felt 'total gratitude', and an awareness that 'now a new time for Christianity was possible'. Rapturously he says in his memoirs: 'That gratitude forged an over-mastering determination, now at last to make up for what had been lost and to serve Christ in his church for a new, better time, a better Germany, a better world.'[18]

13

The Scholars' Mountain

There was a little story, told on the Freising Domberg in 1946 – nothing dramatic, but it threw light on the poverty of the first years after the war and also on a certain charm they had, owing to the hardship of the time.

It was about the bishops Joseph Frings, Konrad Graf von Preysing and August Graf von Galen, the 'Lion of Münster' who had been prominent in the fight against the Nazis' euthanasia programme. Pope Pius XII had invited the dignitaries from Cologne, Berlin and Münster to Rome, so that, as well as making them cardinals, he could acknowledge their determined opposition to the Nazi regime. In Cologne, the British occupying power offered Frings and Galen an army vehicle. However, one of the future wearers of the purple did not fit into it. 'It's just big enough for a coffin for me,' the 2.04-metre-tall Lion of Münster, remarked.

As a bad weather front was forecast, a brigadier-general called Sedgwick was going to accompany the pair to Italy in rapidly commandeered cars. But in the heavy rain one of the vehicles soon conked out. Because of the freak weather, the train that had been scheduled did not turn up. Without a penny in his pocket, Frings lost his patience: 'Herr General,' he implored Sedgwick, 'please go home – I can live without being a cardinal.'

Eventually, after a nine-day odyssey through Paris and Milan, Frings and von Galen arrived at Termini Station in Rome. On the train the Cologne archbishop had been provided with tea and biscuits by his fellow travellers. Bishop Preysing had already arrived, but he had also had to travel from Berlin through Paris. They presented 'a picture of poverty', noted Frings in his diary. 'I arrived with one suitcase, which was tied together by a piece of string. Galen had a big hatbox for his red velvet hat.' When, on 18 February 1946, the 32 newly appointed cardinals assembled in St Peter's Basilica, von Galen received the loudest applause of all, as a valiant opponent of the Nazis. 'Nobody knew me,' Frings wrote laconically. Fortunately, there were no problems on the return journey. Cardinal Francis Spellman from New York took pity on his German colleagues and bought them tickets for the return flight.[1] In fact, von Galen's time as a cardinal was very short. A few days after his appointment, the 68-year-old contracted appendicitis. Two days later, on 22 March 1946, he gave his soul back to his Creator, as it said in his obituaries. Frings, however, would still play an important part in the worldwide church and also as the mentor of one of those young men who were about to start their theological careers on the Domberg with the study of philosophy.

The prince-bishopric of Freising was once the cultural centre of Bavaria and ranked higher even than Munich, the capital and Residenz. In the aftermath of the French Revolution, the Holy Roman Empire of the German nation collapsed in 1802–3. That also resulted in the end of the bishopric of Freising. The bishop's seat moved to Munich, and the new archdiocese of Munich and Freising succeeded the old Freising diocese. The diocese was considerably extended by adding nearly all the Bavarian area of the old archdiocese of Salzburg, the bishopric of Chiemsee and the former prince-provost domain of Berchtesgaden. But the *Mons doctus,* the Scholars' Mountain, remained the spiritual stronghold, the centre of classical Catholicism, where the heritage of antiquity combined with modern knowledge.

'The city lived from its clergy.' The local historian Benno Hubensteiner described the place's *genius loci:* 'It was all about its spirituality, its churches and monasteries.' Altötting was the devout heart of Bavaria; Freising was its spiritual and intellectual jewel. With its many churches, the cathedral, the college, the libraries and arcades, the settlement on the mountain where the spiritual elite of the diocese had been educated for the last thousand years, was practically a clerical republic, with its own rules, its own spirit of faith, learning and divine service. 'At long last it was all wide open,' Ratzinger rejoiced at his arrival. Everything in him, he declared in retrospect, felt 'hope and expectation'. It was a real 'fulfilment' for him 'to begin at last to enter the world of scholarship, theology and the community of future priests'.[2]

Now the courtyard of the former prince–bishop's residence, with its splashing fountains and airy arcades, had none of the elegance of previous centuries. In one corner shoes were being unpacked – aid from a committee in New Zealand. In another corner refugees were pulling along a handcart full of household goods. A large part of the quad was a hospital, where nuns looked after wounded soldiers and victims of bombing raids. The college was lucky to have its own farm, even though in those months it was nearly always only baked potatoes on the menu.

When the 120 men who had been accepted as students for the priesthood in Freising gathered for the first time, they looked more like a bunch of desperadoes than a new spiritual elite. Selection was rigorous. Some of the candidates were rejected on the grounds that they would not be able to endure the nervous strain of the priesthood. Among the beginners there were former Wehrmacht officers with the rank of major, 'old soldiers' in their forties, as Ratzinger recalled, 'who looked on us young ones as immature children, lacking the experience of suffering necessary for service as a priest. We had not been through those dark nights in which saying yes to the priesthood can discover its full meaning.'[3]

With its strict order and clerical atmosphere the Scholars' Mountain was a special, wholly Catholic world. 'There was a unity: cathedral, lecturers, professors, the liturgical life of the seminary,' said the then student Walter Brugger. 'Here a special awareness arose. And there was a determined ideal. It marked generations of priests.'[4] Being definitely Catholic did not mean being defined by yesterday. On the contrary, 'we felt we were all progressive,' Ratzinger said: 'We wanted to radically renew theology, and thereby reshape the church in a new and more dynamic way.'[5] We were lucky to live at a time 'when new horizons and new paths were opening'. Despite the anxiety because 'there was still a war atmosphere in the air', it was 'a joy that we were now together'. Gratitude and a determination to begin afresh characterized both students and teaching staff in this new 'pilgrim community'. Immediately a 'very lively atmosphere' developed and 'a great intellectual impetus which carried us all along'.[6]

Most of the students came from Catholic minor seminaries. They were used to strict regulations and found the Domberg regime almost liberal. They were woken at 5.30 a.m. At 6.00 they met in the study hall for morning prayers and meditation. That was followed at 6.30 by Mass in the house chapel, of course fasting, as was required to receive holy communion. After that there was black bread, coffee and jam for breakfast. In the early period the jam was made from boiled turnips.

For Joseph a new world was opening up. There were the lecture rooms, the seminary library, the chapter house, in which they made music. Then the faculty rooms, endless corridors, the floor paving, the high rooms and, of course, the special smell that clerical institutions have – all this created a monastic-like atmosphere, and also the aura of a time-honoured Catholic university with a community united in silence and prayer. The study hall was the former prince–bishop's state room, whose walls were hung with red silk. The 'Red Room' was furnished with standing desks shaped like pitched roofs. At each of them four students could work at once, two on each side. In the dining room the board table for the rector, sub-rector and the lecturers stood facing the students' tables. The family atmosphere in the house was taken care of by 'Papa Höck', the seminary rector, a particularly humorous, cultured and caring man, 'who was a father to all of us', as Ratzinger recalled. He also took care of refugees, dealing with administrative matters and arranging accommodation and apprenticeships for them.

Like the three Traunstein students, Höck came from the Bavarian mountains, from Inzell. 'My dear fellow countrymen,' he called out to the three of them as they approached from afar. Possibly, he was particularly close to Joseph and Georg because he also had a brother who was a priest. After his *Abitur* in Freising and study at the Pontificium Collegium Germanicum et Hungaricum in Rome, called the Germanicum for short, Höck returned to the Domberg with two doctorates – in philosophy and theology. He was famous for his 'postzoenale', as he called his short talks after supper, which gave solicitous advice such as: 'You must think carefully about wearing long underpants.'

On the floor above the dining room, there were the dormitories, each large enough for 40 students. No one expected them to be heated. Each bed was surrounded by a floor-length curtain, which made it seem like a Bedouin tent or a wigwam. Every morning there was a big crush to get at the washbasins. The showers were in the cellar. Shower day was once a fortnight. Whoever wanted a shower had to book a slot on a timetable put up on the noticeboard.

The subjects in Joseph's philosophy course were general philosophy, history of philosophy, secular history, biology, educational theory and psychology. In addition, there was church law, dogmatics, ethics, Old Testament and New Testament. For beginners like the Ratzingers, who only had a 'maturity certificate', there were also catch-up courses in Latin, Greek, history and biology. There was also a lecture in Hebrew. Going for a walk was compulsory, every day for half an hour or an hour, not in order to relax but to 'think through' the lectures they had just heard. The students preferred the garden on the sunny side of the seminary, a 'paradise', as many felt it to be, with the warm *föhn* wind and a glorious view of the Bavarian Alps. In the evening the spiritual director gave a so-called 'point', a stimulus for meditation. Bedtime was at 8.15 p.m. After a rebellion by the former army veterans, late study in the hall was allowed on two evenings a week. Till 10 p.m. at the latest.

There was great excitement when the cardinal came to visit and ate at the 'high table' in the dining room. He was an old man, but still dignified with his stately figure and imposing appearance. On liturgical occasions Faulhaber wore the so-called *cappa magna* with a seven-metre-long train. Chosen by the prefects, one of the students – including Joseph – was appointed each time for service *ad caudam,* to carry the heavy train. When the cardinal spoke to one of the aspiring priests 'very slowly, with strong emphasis', Georg Ratzinger recalled, 'for us it was as if we had met dear God personally'.

Once again Joseph was the youngest and among the slightest of the group. A country boy, thin as a rake, with a bit of a rural accent and neatly parted hair. Among the 120 new students, Joseph attracted the least attention. There were hardly any anecdotes from that time about Ratzinger, according to his fellow student Josef Finkenzeller, 'because he was an extremely reserved student. That was simply his modesty.'[7] The reading-room prefect, his later friend and mentor Alfred Läpple, felt at once that a special gift was maturing in the boy. Joseph came to him and said: 'I am Joseph, I have a couple of questions,' Läpple recalled. This young man approached him regularly 'like a dry sponge soaking up water. His intellectual curiosity was boundless. When he heard something new, or could correct or develop something, he was tremendously happy.'[8]

His brother, Georg, soon took possession of the organ in the house chapel and otherwise managed to settle in. 'My brother was a very keen student,' Joseph remarked. He had learned how to 'use his time to the limit of the possible. Men's choir, cathedral choir. Deepening his knowledge of harmony and counterpoint was as much part of his workload as assiduously practising the piano and organ.'[9]

To distinguish the two brothers, Georg was given the nickname 'Organ Ratz' and Joseph was 'Book Ratz' – with good reason. He pored for hours over his desk, with a pencil in his right hand and his writing pad and the open book on the left. 'Whenever you went into the library,' said his fellow student Willibald Glas, 'Ratzinger was already sitting there.'[10] 'All he did was study,' a companion remembered, 'books, books, books.' Even before the war Ratzinger had been an enthusiastic reader of great literature. Now came a long list of writers to be discovered: Dostoevsky, Thomas Mann, Kafka, Gertrud von le Fort, Elisabeth Langgässer. Ernst Wiechert and Annette Kolb. All the great French writers: Claudel, Bernanos, Mauriac.

However, in Joseph's luggage brought from home there was also science fiction literature, such as Aldous Huxley's *Brave New World*, published in 1932, which appeared first in German as *Welt wohin?* and was then re-translated and published in 1953 with the title *Schöne neue Welt*. The novel described an anonymized and dehumanized society in the year 2540. His parents had given Joseph *Der Herr der Welt* (*Lord of the World*), the apocalyptic novel by the English writer and priest Robert Hugh Benson. Between 1923 and 1939 the German translation, promoted as a 'Catholic novel of the future' and an 'end of the world novel', came out in an edition of 40,000 copies. It is the vision of a modern Antichrist, who becomes ruler of the world under the cover of progress and humanity. After the elimination of Christianity, forced conformity and the installation of a new religion of humanity, he is honoured as a new God. Seventy years later *Lord of the World* was also commended by Pope Francis. In one of his morning homilies, Bergoglio said that Benson had 'recognized the drama of ideological colonization' early on. 'I recommend you to read this book.'[11]

During lectures Joseph took diligent notes. Once, Höck the rector asked him: 'Do you happen to know what Thomas Aquinas said on this point?' Answer: 'Yes. In eight places. Which one do you want?' Wasting time was not an option for him. As the rules prescribed, the others spent the weekend relaxing, by going for a walk or on an excursion, or swimming, but Joseph declined. 'Joseph could also be jolly,' said his friend Rupert Berger; 'he was not a loner who kept to himself, but nor was he a windbag.' At parties he sometimes performed poems, which might be in Latin or Greek in the classical style, paying a small homage to the birthday boy. Or he made people laugh when he glanced at the menu and called out: 'Habemus Apfelmus!'

Soon people got to know the small figure from Hufschlag as someone who would saunter along the bank of the Isar, debating with his friends without even noticing the river. With his 'spiritual and literary hunger', as he himself saw, he burned with a 'hunger for knowledge'.[12] Fellow students like Georg Lohmeier were impressed by 'his sharp understanding and gift for wording. He was serious and quiet and a model of learning and keenness.' His brother, Georg, was also astonished: 'After the war I learned that my brother was more gifted in many things than I was.' However, it had never been 'like a competition'. Each of them had their own talents. Rupert Berger mentioned his friend's 'sharp intelligence and incredible linguistic gifts'. 'He speaks as if ready for publication. Sometimes he was almost affected but always fascinating, particularly for women.' Berger gave his impression thus: 'Appearance: full of energy, fresh, interested, enthusiastic, inexperienced, innocent. His nature: clever but also very sensitive. And friendly to everybody.'

Pavlo Kohut was a dormitory companion of Joseph's, one year his senior. He was a Greek Catholic Ukrainian, who had had fled from Russia to Germany and now wanted to become a priest. Pavlo said: 'I knew at once that this was someone you are not equal to, someone really special.' Kohut had problems with the German language. Ratzinger helped him to write letters, do homework and improve his studies. He was never pressing but always unobtrusive. 'In everything he did,' said the Ukrainian, 'he was very concentrated – whether he was learning, working or talking to me. He never allowed himself to be distracted.' Kohut also said: 'He learned persistently, he was persistently hungry for new knowledge. Whenever I saw him, he was reading, he used every minute. And he was also very tidy, very organized.'[13]

Ratzinger was a bit like the 'little prince' in the story by the French writer Antoine de Saint-Exupéry, published in German for the first time in 1950. Wasn't he also one of those little princes on a journey through it all, who wanted to discover the secrets of friendship, care, responsibility and love? Indeed, Joseph was very moved by Saint-Exupéry. Later he would often quote the core sentence of the parable from *The Little Prince*: 'You only see well with your heart. What is essential is invisible to the eye.'

Ratzinger's own memories of his start on the *Mons doctus* seem rather sober. Only Georg realized that his younger brother suffered from an almost continuous headache, as their mother also did. Pills were useless. Later on, physiotherapy mitigated the pain a little, but the affliction remained. In fact, his coming to Freising had not been very easy for the young man. The Domberg was 'a great' but also 'a difficult beginning' for him, he said later. For one thing, there was the huge effort of studying. Perhaps homesickness also played a part, which he tried to alleviate by working hard. Läpple recalled that Joseph always looked 'rather lonely': 'He was always thinking.' He also noticed in his protégé a trait that was not particularly beneficial to a career: 'He can't play a game, or put on a show. It hurts him when someone isn't honest, or is acting.'[14]

In the course of his life Joseph Ratzinger would keep meeting people, mostly fatherly friends, who recognized and fostered the extraordinary gifts of the highly motivated young man. In Freising that was Alfred Läpple. Läpple prepared him for his final examinations and ordination as a priest on the Domberg. His job as a tutor was to give support to the freshmen, when they were tormenting themselves at their desks over concepts such as 'existential crisis' or 'sacramental-ontic making present' ('*sakramental-ontische Gegenwärtigsetzung*').

Läpple, who came from Garmisch-Partenkirchen, had been a prisoner of war in Foucarville, south of Le Havre, one of the biggest American camps, with nearly half a million Wehrmacht soldiers. While there, he had gathered students of theology to set up a 'camp university' with a well-attended series of lectures and a small library. Läpple was strongly influenced by his teacher Theodor Steinbüchel, who had introduced him to the thought of Heidegger, Japsers, Nietsche, Bergson and Husserl's new phenomenology.

On the *Mons doctus*, a network spread from Läpple out to future colleagues and companions, upon whom Ratzinger could firmly rely. Among them were the faithful Rupert Berger and his friends Franz Niegel and Franz Mussner. Another of those 'original students' was Vinzenz Pfnür, who followed Ratzinger from Freising to Bonn and later, when he was a professor himself, became an important promoter of the ecumenical process. There was also Leo Scheffczyk, a seminarian from Breslau, born in 1920. During Ratzinger's time as a bishop in Munich, Scheffczyk was a professor at Munich University, 'a guarantee that dogmatics were being taught properly in my diocese'. When Ratzinger was Prefect of the Congregation for the Doctrine of the Faith, he occasionally asked his Freising companion for expert opinions, so-called *Vota*. 'We always knew when he was asked for something, that first, he would really do the work, and second, he would do it well.'

His Munich and Freising acquaintances Ludwig Hödl and Johann Baptist Auer would also later assist Ratzinger when they were professors in Bonn and Regensburg. Ratzinger said of the brewer's son Johann Auer, who was 17 years older than him: 'The wealth of perspectives on the history of ideas he offered, the deep piety that marked his lectures and the human warmth he emanated drew me to him from the first.' Auer was a conservative with the proverbial *liberalitas Bavariae* – a 'live and let live' approach. 'I must unfortunately admit,' he used to say, 'that our dear God also created the so-called progressives. And presumably he even thought about it when he did so.'[15]

As Joseph made the highest demands on himself, his first semester was not exactly a walk in the park. There was his burning curiosity about scholarly discoveries, and also a pressing ambition. 'You felt he wanted to become a professor,' said Rupert Berger. 'While I and most of the other students wanted to go into pastoral care, he pursued theology as a science.' But there was still something else.

'When I began to study theology,' Ratzinger once confessed, 'I also began to get interested in the intellectual problems.' That, he continued 'was because they revealed the drama of my life and above all the secret of the truth'. The future pope explained what was meant by that. He had debated with himself, 'What I can do with my life? Should I become a priest or not? Would I be suited to it or not? Why am I here? What is going on with me? Who am I?'

Ratzinger freely admitted that for a long time he had had a problem seeing himself as a priest in the community: 'because I was rather shy and unpractical'. He did not feel himself to 'be gifted in sport, organization or administration'. And as he was inclined to be shy and solitary, he doubted whether he would be able 'to get on with people'. These were questions, Ratzinger admitted, 'that it had not been easy to resolve'. And 'there were crises'.[16]

While he was a prisoner of war, he had taken a decision: 'I knew where I belonged.' He was sure that his place would be in the church. But where exactly? He was still unclear about that. The basic conflict was more dramatic than might be expected: 'I couldn't just study theology to become a professor,' he acknowledged in the interview book *Salz der Erde*. And he candidly admitted: 'Even though that was my secret wish.'[17]

Whether the now 19-year-old youth also had conflicts with authority must remain an open question: 'Of course these always arose,' he told me in our conversation.[18] He said no more about it. But, he stressed, he had always had 'a very close relationship with his father'. Indeed, his father's piety invited him to venture into something new, without having to worry what might happen. In close association with tradition, aiming for new horizons was not about rebellion but simply the challenge to move on from familiar ground, take that legacy forward and expand it into new times. To use a metaphor: the glacier might be old, but it had to proceed like that. If it broke away, it would become unstable and might cause a massive flood.

In fact, as Joseph grew up, father and son became more and more alike in their thinking, their character, their rationality – and also in a certain rigour and stubbornness. They instinctively understood each other. 'My father was a man of plain, sober piety,' said his son 'and I belong there too.' The Ratzingers were 'not that emotional'. However, he did not speak to his father about his enthusiasm in Freising for learning about what was new or pioneering. 'That was not his thing to discuss. But he knew we had good guidance there and were not losing the spiritual foundation of prayer and the sacraments. That was the most important thing for him.'[19]

Wasn't his own awareness also due to a very special teacher, his father, whose lessons from life carried more weight of conviction than the best professor could have asked for? How alike father and son became is shown by an entry of Ratzinger senior's in the visitors' book in the small pilgrim church of Handlab in Lower Bavaria, which he often visited. His post-war text showed a writing talent with a sobriety and gift for description that would also become typical of his son:

Today I was lucky enough to come here on pilgrimage. The interior of this little pilgrim church offered me a sight that was overwhelming [...] The artist's hands have been able to expose the surviving ancient ceiling paintings and renovate them in their original form. The numerous old votive panels have been rearranged in a meaningful and beautifully harmonious way and set in appropriate new places. That has made plenty of room for new artistic and devoutly maintained panels [...] which always draw our thoughts upward. It would take too long for me to describe this renovation in detail, but I must mention one thing: in all its multiplicity, the whole presents a unity in a deeply religious way, a 'Sursum corda'.[20]

14

Guilt and Atonement

At last plays were being put on again in theatres in Munich and other big cities. There were plays by foreign writers such as Jean Anouilh, T. S. Eliot and Thornton Wilder, which had been banned under the Nazis. The minister president of Bavaria was the Social Democrat Wilhelm Hoegner, a lawyer who had returned from exile in Switzerland in 1945. In his first speech in Munich, Hoegner declared: 'Our mind says Germany for all sorts of reasons, but our heart belongs to Bavaria, our little home country.'[1]

His predecessor, Fritz Schäffer, who headed the first Bavarian post-war cabinet, had been proposed by Cardinal Faulhaber but removed. He was accused by the American headquarters of failing to implement de-Nazification. Schäffer, the leader of the Bavarian People's Party, which had been dissolved by the Nazis, argued that he could not thoroughly check and immediately dismiss about 470,000 officials or the whole system would collapse.

Now the newspapers were reporting almost daily on the Nuremberg war trials. They printed photos of the piles of corpses from the concentration camps, which showed the abysmal depths of the atheistic system. 'Of course we knew that there were concentration camps, in which people were murdered,' said Georg Ratzinger. A cousin on their mother's side, a cheerful boy with learning difficuties, had one day been picked up by the Nazis and was later murdered as a 'worthless life'. However, 'what we learned after the war went far beyond our darkest apprehensions'.

The confrontation with the recent past began tentatively and cautiously, but it began. Eugen Kogon's standard work *Der SS-Staat: Das System der deutschen Konzentrationslager (The SS State:*

The System of German Concentration Camps) came out in 1946, the year Ratzinger began his studies. The psychoanalyst Erich Fromm published *Die Furcht vor der Freiheit: Über die Antriebe zur Aufgabe der Freiheit in totalitären Staaten (The Fear of Freedom: On the Impulse to Give up Freedom in Totalitarian States)*. The philosopher Karl Jaspers soon caused a furore with his book *Die Schuldfrage (The Question of Guilt)*, which addressed the question of German 'collective guilt'.

In Freising the horror of the Nazi regime and the war, and the question of personal responsibility for it, was not decisively treated. The German Catholic bishops had not openly opposed Hitler's war or told Catholics not to serve in his armed forces.

Läpple said there was a predominant feeling of being guilty for having escaped the battlefields and wanting somehow to 'make amends'. Many of the survivors found it impossible 'to speak about their fate'. 'There was nothing to discuss,' said Läpple. 'None of our answers could explain how it could have happened that Christians had built concentration camps.' Nevertheless, the seminarians in training for the priesthood felt their pastoral work had gained a new dimension. 'We knew that people would come to us to confession and tell us that they had been in concentration camps, had shot people in the war, that they had shot partisans.' But as well as the victims and the perpetrators, one person also came to confession because he could not get rid of the fact that, on the return from Russia, he had shot a severely wounded comrade who had begged him to put him out of his misery.

Looking back on the Nazi era, Ratzinger stressed that he and his family had thought of the church as 'oppressed and as a place of resistance'. 'It was quite clear that after the war the Nazis would eliminate the church first of all, and they were only letting it be because they needed all their forces for the war.' On the Domberg, the students for the priesthood had a living example of that experience in the person of Rector Michael Höck. He had worked on the *Münchener Katholische Kirchenzeitung*, which kept being impounded by the Gestapo and the Reich press court. Early on, the Nazis had issued proceedings against the priest. The charge was preaching a critical sermon. In 1940, Höck was condemned to eight months' imprisonment for making statements critical of the regime. After a further arrest on 23 May 1941 he was sent to the Sachsenhausen-Oranienburg concentration camp and ended up in Dachau on 11 July 1941.[2] On 29 April 1945, nine days before the official end of the war, prisoner number 266788 was released from the camp by US soldiers.[3] Clergy from all over Europe were martyred in Dachau. Most of the 1,034 murdered Catholic priests in the camp were from Poland. There were about 40,000 Poles in Dachau, the largest group of prisoners.[4]

Like many other concentration camp survivors, after his release the rector usually kept silent about it. Ratzinger remembered that Höck had spoken about the Nazi terror system on just one afternoon. 'He drew a sketch on the wall and then explained it in detail.' However, in March 1946 Höck's fellow prisoner in Dachau the future auxiliary bishop of Munich Johannes Neuhäusler, published an extensive documentation of the Nazis' attack on Catholicism and the church's resistance. The title was *Kreuz und Hakenkreuz* (*Cross and Swastika*). In it, he described the different measures adopted to dismantle the Catholic faith. He listed them as: 'Attack on the papacy, attack on the bishops, attack on all the clergy, attack on religious instruction, attack on prayers and the crucifix in schools, attack on all Catholic groups, constraints on church services, constraints on pastoral care, constraints on Catholic religious orders, tendentious portrayals and misrepresentations, diatribes against Christianity, goodbye to the old God.' He described other measures adopted against the church in the battle to destroy it as 'Antichrist's rage against the holy. Antichrist's rage against "worthless lives". Antichrist's rage against Judaism'.

In his introduction, Neuhäusler wrote that he had learned from conversations with lay people after the war 'that most of them had no idea of the savagery, scope and cunning, the thoroughness and determination of the battle from beginning to end. Terror and secrecy had hidden the truth about this, as about so much else, during the whole twelve years.' Cardinal Faulhaber wrote a foreword to the book, in which he said: 'It is extraordinary how short people's memories are [...] after barely three years they can "no longer remember". This book may remind them of what happened in recent years.'[5]

After the war Faulhaber fell into disgrace. People remembered how, on the German Catholic Day in Munich in 1922, he had exchanged sharp words about the Weimar Republic with the mayor of Cologne, Konrad Adenauer. Among the 100,000 people in the Königsplatz stood a particularly interested member of the audience: the police officer Joseph Ratzinger, who had taken a day off to come. 'The revolution was perjury and high treason, it remains condemned in history and bears the mark of Cain,' insisted the cardinal.[6] The critics were now arguing that, as an opponent of the Weimar Republic, Faulhaber's opposition to the Nazis was doubtful, as well as his democratic convictions.

In fact, Faulhaber – the son of a Lower Franconian farmer and baker ennobled by Prince Regent Ludwig III in 1913 – had condemned National Socialism early on as a heresy, which 'cannot be reconciled with Christian doctrine'. Initially, Faulhaber had clashed with the Nazis over the Munich 'Beer Hall Putsch' on 9 November 1923. 'The particular target of the attack was the learned and conscientious cardinal archbishop who had [...] denounced the persecution of the Jews in a sermon in the cathedral on the 4th of that month,' said a telegram sent to Rome by the then apostolic nuncio in Munich, Archbishop Eugenio Pacelli, who later became Pope Pius XII. 'So it happened that during the tumult last Saturday afternoon a large group of demonstrators marched up to the archbishop's palace and shouted: "Down with the cardinal!"'[7]

In 1923 Faulhaber joined the Amici Israel, a group of high-ranking Catholic clergy and theologians trying to bring about a Christian–Jewish reconciliation. Faulhaber threw himself into the breach. For the journalist Fritz Gerlich, editor of *Gerade Weg,* whose blunt tone against the Hitler Party was criticized by some church people as too hardline: 'The clergy today are elated that at last on the Catholic side a man has arisen who stands up to the opponents – so long as he is not silenced by assassination, as has been threatened.'[8] The Nazis would not forgive Faulhaber's support for Gerlich, any more than they would forgive his sermons, in which he stressed the roots of the Christian faith in Judaism. In 1934 they reacted with an attack on him. In 1938 the archbishop's palace was stormed, when it became known that, on the night of the November pogrom, Faulhaber had given refuge to the Munich chief rabbi and allowed him to hide the Torah scrolls from the synagogue in his residence.

On 5 April 1946, in a packed Freising Cathedral, when the cardinal celebrated the memorial Mass for the 108 priests, theology students and minor seminarians from the diocese who had died in the Second World War, the student Joseph Ratzinger was sitting in one of the pews. Joseph felt deeply moved by the 'great figure of the venerable cardinal' and the 'awe-inspiring greatness of his task, with which he wholly concurred'.[9] 'Ideas and principles have been thrown among our people,' Faulhaber cried from the pulpit, 'that are inhuman and that either come from the mad house or from Hell.' In his deep voice he spoke of 'devilish hatred which demanded the extermination first of non-Arians and then of Christianity'. The survivors ought to 'thank the Lord and the Lord's mother' again and again. Every communion should be a feast of the 'Eucharist': that is to say, thanksgiving. 'It is up to you future priests to help in re-educating our people.' 'Learn to rethink and change attitudes,' he cried. 'Tell the young people: militarism is not acceptable, a return to playing soldiers is forbidden. But it is not forbidden to be a good Christian. It is not forbidden to fight the Lord's battles and be a moral hero in the fight for purity.'[10]

Ratzinger seldom wrote about Germany's darkest period in his essays and books. Observers reproached him for failing to address the subjects of guilt and complicity. Ratzinger explained that he had experienced the darkest hour in German history as a time when the 'new Reich, the German myth and Germanism were the great thing and Christianity contemptible, especially Catholicism, because it was Roman and Jewish [...] We knew we were in danger every day. As long as we had to fear that the Third Reich might win, it was clear that everything, our whole life, would be ruined.'[11]

Self-critically, Ratzinger admitted that 'Christian anti-Semitism' had 'prepared the ground up to a point' for the success of the Nazis. However, none of the people around him in those days had been in any doubt that, despite all its weaknesses and failures, the church was the antithesis of the destructive ideology of the brown-shirted ruling powers'. In one of our interviews he added: 'Reflecting on it now historically or philosophically, I did not see it as my job. What was important for me was to form ideas for the future. How will the church go forward? How will society go forward?'[12]

The world of Ratzinger's personal experience dictated the tone with which he spoke about the horrors of the Nazi past. Concentration camp survivor Elie Wiesel also described it. On 27 January 2000, Wiesel said in a speech to the German Bundestag that, since his liberation in April 1945, he had 'read everything I could get my hands on about the Holocaust': historical papers, psychological analyses, witness statements and testimonies, poems, diaries of the murderers and reflections by the victims. But still he 'couldn't grasp' what had happened under Hitler. How 'are you supposed to comprehend the cult of hatred and death that reigned in your land?' the Holocaust survivor asked the Bundestag members.[13]

The Nobel Prize winner also blamed other nations. 'Naturally it was soon clear to us Jews in occupied Europe that the Free World knew what was happening to us, and was therefore to some extent responsible. The Allies did not seem to be particularly bothered. They did not open their borders to us, when there was still time.' Wiesel also said a distinction should be made: 'I know that all Germans did not co-operate and we should also think about them. And also about those who had the courage to stand up against the official race ideology. Those who resisted the totalitarian Nazi regime. Those who tried to overthrow it and paid with their lives for that.'

For the schoolboy Joseph there was no 'untroubled, immune world in the Catholic milieu', as the Frankfurt sociologist Tilmann Allert once said, but a childhood full of danger and fear − with the prospect that after the 'final victory' Catholics would suffer an all-out attack: 'We knew that in the long run the church was meant to disappear,' Ratzinger said in our interview. 'There would be no more priesthood. That was clear to us: I have no future in that society.' As an anti-fascist and faithful Catholic family, the Ratzingers felt they were not active participants but partial victims. As seminarians, Georg and Joseph must have realized they would have no future in the Nazi state. 'First the Jews,' the Nazis bawled at them, 'then the Jews' friend.'

Ratzinger's personal experience of the atheistic terror system and God's absence in the dark night was crucially significant in his development and his work. In his memoirs, he spoke of the 'years of scarcity, being exposed to the philistine Moloch of power'. For him,

National Socialism was the embodiment of the demon of a society separated from God and ideologically bent on power and violence. It was a plunge into evil, which in principle could happen again at any time.

Ratzinger saw history as an enduring battle between faith and faithlessness, a battle between love of God to the point of self-denial – and of self-love to the point of denying God. Ultimately, a battle between good and evil. With eschatological realism, he saw everything earthly as imperfect when seen from an apocalyptic viewpoint. Every human attempt to reach perfection must necessarily end in disaster. Even when he became supreme pastor of the church, he never tired of warning: 'When the standard of the true God is not there, then humans destroy themselves.'

The wariness – foresight – which later characterized Ratzinger, the keen eye for developments that might lead a society into a critical state, arose from his own experience. It marked Ratzinger's thinking, his theology, his work as cardinal and guardian of the faith. It was the root cause of his first admonitions on social change in the 1950s, as well as many of his contributions to the Second Vatican Council, his quarrel with the student uprisings of 1968 and also his reasoning in the debate over liberation theology. The committed Catholicism he called for went with a society able to defend itself against mass manipulation, mass thinking and any kind of hubris – hubris by which human beings self-importantly claimed to become the autonomous creators of an earthly paradise. 'The totalitarian ideologies of the twentieth century promised us they could build a free and fair world,' he declared in June 2004 in Normandy at the celebrations for the 60th anniversary of the Allied landing, 'and for its sake they demanded the massacre of hecatombs of victims'.[14] Hitler's Reich had been a Reich in which human beings were 'crushed, used and abused for the madness of a power that wanted to create a new world'.

Ratzinger once gave an indication of how decisive the experiences of those years were in a *Laudatio* for his brother, who 'thoroughly detested Nazism and war'. The terror of the Nazi regime and the need for a new beginning had strengthened Georg's and his own readiness to devote themselves to a life with and for God. They had experienced a philistine and anti-Christian ideology, with its brutality and spiritual emptiness. 'In the headwind of history, an inner firmness and decisiveness arose in them, which gave strength for the way to go.'[15]

When Ratzinger became pope, he also said at a youth gathering in the Vatican in 2005 that his decision to enter the service of the church had explicitly been a counter-reaction to the atrocities of the Nazi regime. In contrast to that cult of inhumanity, he had realized that God and the faith showed the right way. In his memoirs, he wrote about the importance of the Catholic Church with his typical intensity:

> In the Inferno that had swallowed up the powerful she stood firm with her strength coming from eternity. It had proved true: the gates of Hell will not prevail against her. Now we had seen for ourselves what is meant by 'the gates of Hell' and we could also see with our own eyes that the house built on the rock had stood fast.[16]

Not only that. The former Hitler youth conscript also knew what guiding principles he wanted to follow. Even as a schoolboy in Traunstein he had reacted with admiration to the actions of the White Rose movement. As a professor, he became friends with the political scientist and philosopher Eric Voegelin, the founder of the Scholl Siblings Institute for Political Science. 'The great figures persecuted by the Nazi regime,' Ratzinger confessed, 'for example, Dietrich Bonhoeffer, became great models for me.'[17] His personal circle of acquaintances, as well as the literature he eagerly read, pointed to countless Nazi opponents and Nazi victims. Besides Dietrich Bonhoeffer there were people like Edith Stein, Fathers Rupert Mayer and Alfred Depp, the philosopher and theologian Josef Pieper, Henri de Lubac and Heinrich Schlier.

His Jewish friends included Hubert Jedin, who was half Jewish and had lived in exile in the Vatican during the Third Reich, Teddy Kollek, the former mayor of Jerusalem, the Israeli president Shimon Peres and Rabbi Jacob Neusner, the American academic scholar of religion. Ratzinger said he had seen it as his specific task to work for the future, using his experiences of the Nazi dictatorship. This meant that as professor and cardinal he laid the foundations for a new understanding between Christianity and Judaism, which he intended to consolidate as pope.

15

Upheaval in Thinking

The days became longer, the strength of the sun increased. Gradually the winter sky that hung over the Domberg yielded to the warm air of spring. Even the bells in the cathedral tower now sounded clearer and more friendly.

It was the time when Karol Wojtyła also returned to the university in Kraków. From April until August 1945, he worked as an assistant lecturer at Kraków University. For the 26 exams he had sat he received 'Excellent' 19 times and 'Very Good' six times. He received a lower mark in psychology. In his case that meant a mark of just 'Good'.

'Karol Wojtyła future saint,' he was teased by his friends from the Rhapsodic Theatre, with whom he had put on plays.[1] He kept applying to be accepted into a Carmelite monastery, but his bishop kept refusing him. Adam Sapieha, prince metropolitan archbishop of Kraków, had greater things in mind for him. On 1 November 1946, the feast of All Saints, he personally ordained Wojtyła as priest in the chapel of the archiepiscopal palace, six months before the other seminarians. His former work colleagues from the quarry where the Nazis had sent him gave him a cassock. On Wojtyła's commemorative card for his ordination there was a verse from the *Magnificat,* the prayer of Jesus's mother: 'He that is mighty has done great things for me/ And holy is his name.'[2]

In Freising, Joseph approached his days with burning curiosity. As with Wojtyła, it was not so much the theology that attracted him. He was more taken with the new, exciting things; he wanted to 'get to grips with modern philosophy'. Like the Polish Wojtyła, he had a special predilection for the German philosopher and anthropologist

Max Scheler, the son of an orthodox Jewish mother, whose book, *Vom Ewigen im Menschen* (*Of the Eternal in Humanity*), had started an intellectual-religious renewal movement in the 1920s. Scheler was brilliantly gifted, highly eccentric, several times married and constantly involved in affairs, which even led to him being taken to court for lacking 'the dignity of a college lecturer'. He saw modern people's estrangement from God as coupled with depersonalization. According to the Catholic convert Scheler, people today fled from God because they fled from themselves. So being concerned with religion was not about self-sacrifice or any other loss. Quite the opposite: 'You gain yourself as a person by losing yourself in God.'

Scheler was convinced that only Christian Socialism was capable of finding a way between the capitalist West and the communist East. In his philosophical anthropology, he stressed the special nature of humankind as 'co-operator with God'. After the philosophical trends of the past, Scheler was excited by Edmund Husserl's ideas, finally to get back to the 'objective' and the 'essence' of things. Scheler developed his own value ethics. He argued that intuitively experienced values were objective intellectual objects, clearly perceptible phenomena. And it was not the rational will – as in Kant's formulation – but the inwardly felt evidence of value that decided whether the value was right. That is to say: values stood for themselves. In Scheler's view, humans were a microcosm, who illustrated the macrocosm in themselves, consisting of body, soul and spirit, forming a unity. Through education, humans could surpass themselves and realize their own inherent essence, their divine nature. However, this education should not be one-sided 'performance knowledge' (*Leistungswissen*) but should also include 'salvation knowledge' (*Erlösungswissen*), as was the case in Asian cultures.

Since the 1920s, in western Europe, new trends had developed in theology: ecumenism, the departure from rigid neo-scholasticism (in favour of an active approach to Scripture), the rediscovery of the church fathers. Above all, a strong impulse came from the liturgical movement. Joseph was initially sceptical: 'Students like me, who came from the minor seminary, were, so to speak, schooled in the forms of the nineteenth century,' he explained. Now a new way of thinking was catching on: all those rather kitschy statues of saints, the conventional piety and over-sentimentality – all that was to be got rid of. And it was to be replaced by a new kind of devotion arising out of the liturgy, with its plainness and its greatness. It went back to the beginning – and for that very reason it was new and modern again.[3] There was a search for 'new depths. There was an awareness: we must go forward. That began in Freising.'[4]

When Joseph Ratzinger spoke about personal matters, as the Italian journalist Gianni Valente remarked, he nearly always went back to his time as a student and professor. 'The university,' he said, 'was my spiritual home.' He was thinking of lecture rooms, rostrums, lectures. Of a world that spoke a single, clear language. Of accuracy and firm rules in research and doctrine. And where it was understood that you had to present supporting evidence to prove your own statements.

The subjects he studied during his time at university were also the ones he remained concerned with after the end of his academic career: the meaning of the liturgy, the teaching of the church fathers and, first and foremost, the relationship between faith and reason. Was it possible to speak of the truth at all, or were there really many truths, each in its own way? After Auschwitz was it possible for an intelligent, critical person still to believe in God? In his studies would he really encounter the *doxa theou,* the transcendent glory of God? According to Valente, all these things acted as 'underground rivers, which flowed up out of his past as a student and professor'.[5] This openness of philosophical thinking also gave Ratzinger's papacy the depth that made it sophisticated and intellectual.

After the spiritual wilderness years of the dictatorship and the experience of Hell, this new time vibrated with expectation. For the eager young man from Hufschlag it seemed as if an unknown light, though still shining from afar, was now within in reach. 'For me it was like a breakthrough, a new atmosphere, to hear those things,' Ratzinger confessed: 'I wanted to learn about what was new, not just deal with a stagnant, bottled philosophy, but philosophy as questioning – what are we really? I wanted to understand and get to grips with modern philosophy.'

It all began really well. 'First, we had exercises, which Professor Angermair, the college's moralist, gave us, and they were very good. He was a fresh new thinker, who particularly wanted to drag us out of repressed nineteenth-century piety into the open.' For Joseph, a new world was revealed. There were Heidegger and Jaspers, Edmund

Husserl's new phenomenology, as well as the writings of Jean Anouilh and Jean-Paul Sartre. 'Sartre was, of course, someone you had to read. He translated Heidegger's clever existentialism into concrete terms.'[6] Ratzinger found that because the Frenchman 'had written his philosophy mainly in a café', his thinking was 'less deep but more forceful and realistic'.

On the other hand, the young student was 'not enthusiastic' about Heidegger. After Hitler's seizure of power, Heidegger had joined the NSDAP for a year. In his 'rector's inaugural lecture' of 27 May 1933, Heidegger said to his students: 'The rules of your being are not propositions and "ideas". The Führer himself and he alone is the German reality of today and tomorrow and your law.' At the same time Heidegger also distanced himself from the Catholic Church: 'Especially here, this public victory of Catholicism absolutely must not continue.'[7]

Ratzinger found much food for thought in the philosopher Peter Wust, one of those writers 'whose voice touched us most directly'. Wust, who had taken part in the resistance to Hitler, formulated an existentialist philosophy, like Heidegger, but on a Christian basis. In 1920 he had produced his *Auferstehung der Metaphysik (Resurrection of Metaphysics)*, which readdressed the question of being and humanity's relationship to it. According to Wust, what was needed was a return to a far-sighted, humbly respectful reason. His aim was to reconnect human thinking with higher values, in order to restrain the destructive potential that was inherent in reason. He died in 1940. In his farewell words, the philosopher advised: 'If you were still to ask me now before I go, and finally go, whether I know of a magic key to open the final door to wisdom, I would answer you: "Yes, indeed!" And the magic key is not reflection, as you might expect to hear from a philosopher, but prayer [...] The great things of existence are only given to praying spirits.'[8]

It must have been in the early New Year of 1946 that one day Läpple took his protégé (12 years his junior) aside and surprised him by giving him a special task, a translation. It was Thomas Aquinas's essay *Quaestio disputata de caritate,* which until then was only available in the Latin original. St Thomas himself! The man with the 'crystal logic'. Joseph, however, regarded his thinking as 'too tightly closed in upon itself', 'too impersonal', somewhat lifeless, static – 'too ready-made' and lacking in dynamism.

The Latin original lay on a long table. The accompanying literature beside it piled up higher and higher. First, Ratzinger had to get to grips with Thomas Aquinas's Latin in order to understand the terminology he used. Then it was a matter of putting it into German word for word. Joseph translated; his teacher corrected. 'It was a bold pioneering work, at the highest level,' Läpple recalled. Besides the actual translating, the problem was locating the countless quotations in the original biblical text, as well as quotations from philosophers and theologians – Plato, Aristotle, Augustine – finding and checking and then giving chapter and verse for each of them. A Sisyphean task. And it had to be done in his strictly limited free time.

Only someone with the patience of a saint, the endurance of a long-distance runner and the Buddha's ability to sit still could do the job. The work also brought Joseph and Läpple into contact with Edith Stein, who until then had been completely unknown to both of them. She was a Jew, born in Breslau, and a pupil of the philosopher Edmund Husserl. She was a campaigner for women's rights and the first female German doctor of philosophy. After her conversion to the Catholic Church and reception into the Carmelite Order, she adopted the name Teresia Benedicta a Cruce – Teresia Benedicta (blessed) by the Cross – after St Teresa of Ávila. Being, as she said, 'a Jew and a Christian', during the period of National Socialism, she became a victim of the Holocaust and was murdered in August 1942, together with her sister Rosa, in the Auschwitz-Birkenau concentration camp.

Edith Stein had translated a different work by Thomas Aquinas into German for the first time, the *Quaestio disputata de veritate* ('On Truth'), which filled two volumes – two fat volumes – very philosophical, very demanding, about all the most difficult questions: the question of being, the question of the human capacity to know, the question of God as Trinity, grace, faith, providence. Of course, Joseph's work, which took him a whole year, was not 1,500 pages long, like Edith Stein's. His was just 100 pages, but through it he learned how Thomas constructed his writings, how he formulated ideas and argued. Five decades later, he wrote to Läpple: 'By giving me the job of translating St Thomas's *Quaestio disputata* on love, you

[…] led me into the sources and taught me to create from first hand and be schooled by the Masters themselves.'⁹

Love and truth were to become among the core themes throughout all Ratzinger's work. For him, there could be no love without truth and no truth without love. A remarkable coincidence: love was not only his first subject as a theologian in the making but also the subject of his first encyclical as pope. His *opus* no. 1 at college, with the title *Eröffnung über die Liebe* (*On Love*) appeared in an edition of two copies (the first handwritten and the second typed). His *opus* no. 1 as pope, *Deus Caritas Est* (*God is Love*) was published in an edition of more than 3 million copies. Edith Stein was canonized in Ratzinger's presence on 11 October 1998 by Pope John Paul II in St Peter's Square in Rome. At the same time, the Polish pope appointed the German woman martyr as co-patron saint of Europe. 'Whoever seeks the truth, seeks God,' the Carmelite saint knew, 'whether they know it or not.'¹⁰

As well as his studies, Joseph pursued linguistic research and began 'Meditations on Myself', on 'my situation at that point in time'. According to his own estimation, the new student was not among those of his contemporaries who had 'a complex'. He was not one of those scholars who were afraid to work on important subjects simply because 'great minds' had written about them. Brashly, he approached what remained to be done. 'When you are young, you hold back then you start thinking you can do something.' What should hold him back? 'I was not afraid of great things, because I was certain we could build the world anew.'¹¹ That serene conviction often worried Ratzinger's companions and observers, because they thought it meant a lack of empathy. For Ratzinger, it was the guarantee that he could get on with his work in peace, pounding away at it calmly and steadily like the pistons of a diesel engine.

In his early years he was inspired by the young lecturer Jakob Fellermeier's lectures on the history of philosophy. Without any modesty, Ratzinger claimed they gave him 'a comprehensive overview from Socrates' intellectual circle and the pre-Socratics up to the present'.¹² He was also excited by thinkers like Josef Pieper, who interpreted the catastrophe of the recent past as the result of human hubris and therefore called for a renewed and deeper commitment to God. The cultural critic Theodor Haecker also urged attention to the Western Christian tradition. For him human freedom and dignity lay in the fact that each individual human was an 'idea of God'. Joseph regarded Haecker as 'the great figure after the war, one of the great minds. I read his *Virgil* enthusiastically.'[13]

Two further sources of inspiration for Ratzinger were the Munich philosopher and physicist Aloys Wenzl and the moral theologian Theodor Steinbüchel. Both were the kind of scholar who particularly excited him with their provoking, stirring, lateral thinking. They were also existential spirits bravely looking into the depths of their own self. Their self-questioning drove their thinking. Wenzl had tried to show that the deterministic world view of classical physics, which left no more room for God, had been superseded. And, said Ratzinger, Steinbüchel 'gave a very comprehensive insight into modern philosophy, which I tried to understand, to follow'. Even the two writers' book titles had an electrifying effect on him. In his book Wenzl promised a *Philosophy of Freedom* (*Philosophie der Freiheit*). Steinbüchel an *Upheaval in Thinking* (*Umbruch des Denkens*). To Joseph, they sounded like places he longed to reach, whose coastlines mysteriously loomed out of the white mist ahead of his ship's prow.

The sense of a new awakening was in no way lessened by the fact that in Freising now 'the new developments in natural sciences' were also 'followed with interest', particularly by the college natural scientist, Professor Karl Andersen. Didn't the findings of leading researchers sound completely different from the Enlightenment mantras, which proclaimed that progress in the sciences meant the end of the old faith in God? Physicists like the German Pascual Jordan, the co-founder of quantum mechanics, were suddenly talking about a 'creator God'. According to Jordan, 'modern developments had removed the earlier obstacles to a harmony between natural science and a religious world view'. The British astrophysicist Sir Arthur Eddington declared: 'Modern physics leads us necessarily to God, rather than away from him.' The Nobel Prize winner Werner Heisenberg, one of the most important physicists of the twentieth century, formulated: 'A first drink from the glass of natural science makes you atheistic but at the bottom of the glass, God is waiting.' And John Ambrose Fleming, the British physicist and radio engineer, was convinced: 'The universe appears before our eyes today as thought. And thought presupposes the presence of a thinker.'

Albert Einstein also created a sensation. The German physicist wrote in the *New York Times* in 1930: 'Science without religion is lame, religion without science is blind.' According to the founder of the theory of relativity: 'The current idea that I am an atheist is based on a major error. Anyone reading that from my scientific theories has hardly understood them.' Einstein found that 'in the incomprehensible universe an infinite supreme reason reveals itself'. God is not relative, being is not relative, but human thinking is relative: 'God does not play dice. Rather, he created the world according to an orderly plan. It is the scientist's task to discover it.'[14]

Elementary particles, light waves, gravity, cosmic radiation – the universe – scientists concluded, could only have been called into being by a power 'that did not derive from atoms and molecules within this world' or which was subject to the phenomena of time and space. That interpretation corresponded with an original human insight, according to which creation possessed an immaterial component. 'Wherever and however far we look,' Max Planck concluded, 'we never find a contradiction between religion and science, but full agreement on the decisive points.' The founder of quantum theory and Nobel Prize winner added: 'Religion and science do not exclude one another, as many people believe and fear today. They complement and imply one another. For the believer, God is at the beginning and for the physicist, he is at the end of all thinking.' The French chemical scientist and Nobel Prize winner Paul Sabatier agreed: 'The idea that science and religion contradict one another is held by those who are badly educated in both subjects.'

Joseph was particularly taken with the scientist Aloys Wenzl. Born in Munich in 1887, Wenzl had first studied mathematics and physics, then philosophy and psychology. He taught in the Philosophical Institute of the Ludwig Maximilian University, where he was its dean and rector. Although he was a member of the SPD (Social Democratic Party of Germany), chairman of the Munich Peace Union and a member of the 'Zwanglose Gesellschaft München' (Informal Munich Society), he joined the National Socialist Teachers' Federation in 1936. When his background became known, he was forbidden to teach. The reason given was that he was suspected of standing 'in implacable opposition to the present-day state, which he quietly and unobtrusively but tenaciously battles against'.[15] Wenzl's

Philosophie der Freiheit showed that the classical world view of physics, in which God no longer has a role, had now been definitely superseded by the natural sciences – by a world view that had opened up again. The conviction in Freising, Ratzinger recalled, was that 'with the radical changes brought about by Planck, Heisenberg and Einstein', scientists 'were back on the road to God'. Now was the time, Wenzl claimed, that metaphysics – the doctrine about what lay behind the known and figured-out world – was finally seen again as the common foundation of *all* sciences.

Wenzl was an eccentric but also brilliant professor who thought universally. He specialized in boundary problems between science and religion, wrote works such as *Das Leib-Seele Problem* (*The Body– Soul Problem*), *Wissenschaft und Weltanschauung* (*Science and World View*) and also *Unsterblichkeit* (*Immortality*), in which he investigated the 'metaphysical and anthropological meaning' of eternal life. In the foreword to *Philosophie der Freiheit,* which he dedicated to his son, who was killed in the Second World War, he wrote: 'So much unspeakably great suffering has come upon us, our home and our children through hubris and perversion, demonic possession and madness.' They had 'really experienced existence down to the abyss of nothingness'. So the future could only be 'rebuilt on spiritual foundations', according to the 'idea of life' described in the liberal, forgiving Christian view of humanity.

While Wenzl's writing gave Joseph food for thought and inspiration, Theodor Steinbüchel's *Umbruch des Denkens* became his 'key reading', a force that hit home like a meteorite from another star.[16] 'The new' was what he wanted to learn, not just a 'stagnant' and 'bottled' philosophy. He regularly felt disappointed by teachers who had given up on questioning and were content in their narrow thinking to 'defend what had been determined beforehand against all questions', or merely to maintain it.[17] 'Waste of time,' he whispered to his neighbour at the end of such lectures. Suddenly, he felt he had found what he was looking for.

Steinbüchel, with whom Alfred Läpple had studied for his doctorate, originally taught at the Ludwig Maximilian University in Munich. When the Nazis closed the Catholic theology faculty in 1939, he moved to Tübingen and worked there as professor of moral theology until his early death in 1949. Among his works were *Europa als Idee und geistige Verwirklichung* (*Europe as Idea and Intellectual Achievement*) and *Christliche Lebenshaltungen in der Krisis der Zeit und des Menschen* (*Christian Lifestyles in the Crisis of the Time and Humanity*) – themes that were also to be found later with Ratzinger. In the volume *Wahrheit, Werte, Macht* (*Truth, Values, Power*) and in *Werte in Zeiten des Umbruchs* (*Values in Times of Upheaval*) Joseph read sentences that moved him deeply: 'There are humans only in the presence of God, and only in freedom. Only in both are they persons', Steinbüchel had formulated. 'Become what you are' now only made sense when it was really known what humans were: namely, 'being to God'. And becoming themselves, as Heidegger demanded, was only real self-becoming if it was taken up into relationship with God, which fulfils what 'human' and 'self' really are. Therefore God was not, as Nietzsche said, the death of humans and their destruction, but their life: 'The guarantee of their freedom is God, because he created them as "being transcending towards a You", and because this transcendence of their essence is only realized in a life of personal freedom.'

Steinbüchel's teaching was essentially based on Ferdinand Ebner's views of the world and humanity. But Steinbüchel was better at expressing them than their author. Ebner, an Austrian elementary school teacher and philosopher of language, had at first devoted himself to 'pneumatology', the 'doctrine of spirit': more precisely, the spirit of the word. His first work dating from 1913–14 remained unpublished. Perhaps this was because of its eccentric title: *Ethik und Leben: Fragmente einer Metaphysik der individuellen Existenz* (*Ethics and Life: Fragments of a Metaphysics of individual Existence*). His major work, *Das Wort und die geistigen Realitäten: Pneumatologische Fragmente* (*Word and the Spiritual Realities: Pneumatological Fragments*), was devastatingly pulled to pieces by the critics. However, Steinbüchel established that Ebner developed a religiously based philosophy of language and prepared the way for the Christian existentialism of Gabriel Marcel. Moreover, as one of the first to recognize a 'new reality' with his philosophy of the I–You relationship between creature and Creator, Ebner was also a co-founder of 'dialogical thinking'.

For the student from Traunstein, it was – to use an image from the writer Karl Karlow – as if someone had shone a light from a window. How could you not be enthusiastic about the new breakthroughs that were now possible? And didn't what Steinbüchel wrote about the precarious situation of Christian people also touch him personally? Wasn't he also torn over the question of the meaning of his existence? Not lost, but seeking the right way, which he had to justify. Faith does not destroy or condemn thinking, he read. On the contrary: in faith, that capacity to think appeared as actually the great gift of the divine Logos, through which everything, including thought itself, was made. The time cried out for new thinking. The old answers of traditional faith had to be re-examined. But if they were accepted, they could enrich life anew.

In *Umbruch des Denkens* Steinbüchel sketched the development of philosophy from antiquity to Hegel, Schelling and Feuerbach. Hegel had seen himself as the completer of philosophy and proclaimed his findings as 'fullness of truth'. His idealist philosophy proffered the self-understanding of the Idea as the all-shaping, all-sustaining, all-being mind-spirit. Two centuries before him, the philosopher and mathematician René Descartes had ousted the late medieval God-sustained order of being. Until then, reality had been understood in terms of the vital relationship between God and human. Now the Frenchman introduced the self-contained subject. Descartes's *cogito ergo sum* – 'I think therefore I am' – had no counterpart, no partner. It was the self-related lone human being, enclosed in the ego-prison of self-reflection. Finally, with Hegel, any transcendence reaching out beyond an immanent world-God reality was eliminated. His concept of reason, in which he saw the only reality, became the foundation of the Enlightenment and conquered the intellectual world. As Steinbüchel summed it up, now God was only 'the this-worldly mind-spirit advancing towards self-awareness in the one reality witnessed and sustained by itself'.

Now Ferdinand Ebner again recognized reality where idealist philosophy wanted neither to seek nor to find it. He criticized idealism for overlooking not only the reality of the human person but also the reality of the personal God. Idealism had foundered on the newly awakened passionate questions people were asking about the meaning of their personal lives. Ebner became clear that by the Word of revelation, thinking was no longer a construct. It was finding and receiving: grasping what thinking had not conceived of its own accord. And, said Steinbüchel, that acknowledged Being was 'no longer the Absolute as the totality of reason-reality [...] but the reality of the personal God, who addressed the listening human with his Word'. It was only in that vital and decisive dynamic that human existence attained its deepest, most mysterious and responsible selfhood.

Joseph had hoped for an answer, and he had got one. The Christian faith's effect on the world appeared everywhere, although many people mistook it for a mere belief. He was clear that the God of the Bible was not an ethical 'Idea', like the God of the philosophers, but a supernatural and personal God, who addressed the individual human person in real time, and each in their own personal situation. 'The reality of the personal God grasped by faith,' Steinbüchel stressed, 'is the deepest, religious reason for the upheaval of the thought system, the change in thinking about human existence.' About each human self, whom God addressed personally and expected an answer from, an inmost personal turning towards him, this God.

The reality of the personal God, experienced in faith, and the real human person related with that God, now gave rise to the idea of critical existential realism. With it, human reality could again be fully understood. That is, understood not only from the viewpoint of humans but also from the perspective of their origin, their potential, their Creator. Critical realism's starting point was that, parallel to our immediate awareness and sensory perception, a wider world really somehow existed, even if it was not immediately apparent and could not be 'seen'. Rather like particular sound frequencies that are beyond human hearing. That realism of existence created a relationship between Me and You. And according to Ebner's basic thesis, it was only in this relationship that humans were really human.

It was clear to Joseph the student that the human individual's personal relationship with God was quite different from an external profession of religion. In Ebner's realism this relationship was no longer to do with some 'outside world', but with the individual existence of each human self. A groundbreaking insight. Because God, who was often so far off – Creator of heaven and earth, Lord of all power and might, ruler of the universe – suddenly became close and accessible. Not as an awe-inspiring world judge, but as a personal partner. I and You. I and God. It was a relationship with each individual, which was not mainly punitive but with an intimate kindness, whose essence was love. Mysteriously, that love was also the core and energy of creation, in a sense its operating system.

Responding to that creative mystery of being and freely self-giving love was the deep-rooted human impulse to pray. Seen thus, according to Ebner, 'true prayer was a 'dialogue with God'. The nature of prayer could only be understood in terms of an I–You relationship between God and humans, humans and God. In prayer 'the word returns to where it came from'. In prayer, humans discovered what they are: not each a single self alone, but belonging in a living-conversing twosome of Me and You.

The discovery of the dual system was an early breakthrough in Ratzinger's thinking. The I–You principle gave his theology its direction. There were as many ways to God 'as there were people,' he postulated later.[18] The relationship of 'I' and 'You' also meant that God had a way for each human person. Or at least he offered one. How else could he enter sympathetically into a relationship with them? How could he strengthen a fallen person? How could Christ say: 'Whoever has seen me has seen the Father'? Joseph's breakthrough was in his mind, not as a figment of his imagination but from the *Logos,* the revealing reason. The 'Word' – the *Logos* – who appears in the Prologue to John's Gospel, perhaps the most beautiful and brilliant passage in the whole Bible:

In the beginning was the Word
and the Word was with God
and the Word was God [...]
All things became through him
and nothing that has become
became without him.
In him was life
and the life was the light of humans.

Ferdinand Ebner warned that the term 'Word' – *Logos* in the original Greek – should never be translated just as 'reason'. That would miss part of its deep meaning. The mysterious active force of the Word in the Bible had to do not with magic but with the real spiritual principle within which lay the innovative power of the Creator's thought. Ratzinger expressed this 20 years later in a somewhat complicated sentence in his classic *Einführung in das Christentum* (*Introduction to Christianity*). It shows how persistent were the fruits of his first semester in philosophy:

> If Christian belief in God is first of all an option for the primacy of the *Logos,* faith in the pre-existing, world-sustaining reality of creative meaning, as belief in the personal nature of that meaning, it is also the belief that the original thought, whose being-thought constitutes the world, is not an anonymous, neutral consciousness but rather freedom, creative love, a person.[19]

The works of Martin Buber also gave the young Ratzinger in Freising further important key words and ideas. Besides Ferdinand Ebner, the Jewish philosopher of religion was the foremost advocate of dialogical thinking. His *Tales of the Hasidim* belong to world literature. The philosopher's writings could only be published again after 1945. For Joseph, they were his first encounter with Judaism. He wrote in his memoirs that the Jewish philosopher-mystic's work 'became a formative spiritual experience' for him.[20] Furthermore, 'his whole character fascinated me,' he confessed in one of our conversations, particularly 'his way of believing in this world of today'. Ratzinger stressed Buber's 'personalist view' and 'a philosophy nourished by the Bible': 'that Jewish piety, in which faith is quite unabashed, yet still current today.'[21] For his friend Läpple and the young philosophy student, it had been a 'hallelujah' when 'Buber's words struck a chord in our lives'.

In a work published in 1958, the Swiss theologian Hans Urs von Balthasar accused Buber of not understanding the consistent progress of salvation history from the prophets to Christ. Whereas Balthasar was far from accepting the mutual recognition of Judaism and Christianity, Ratzinger confessed: 'I highly respected Martin Buber.' 'He taught us to see human life as dialogical,' explained Läpple. 'Through dialogical personalism, Buber empowered dialogue with other people as You, and also dialogue with God.' Ratzinger shared Buber's approach when he constantly stressed that God did not come to people as an abstract definition: God was a 'You'. God accepted people, communicated with them, either in prayer or in the liturgy. Ratzinger might also have liked the Jewish mystic's saying: 'The best language about God is praising God.'

On their long walks through the river meadows by the Isar in Freising, Ratzinger and Läpple struck up a friendship, 'which revolved wholly round the great problems of philosophy and theology'.²² They talked about 'the spiritual meaning of language', which Ferdinand Ebner had introduced; about Karl Jaspers's saying 'Peace is only possible through freedom, freedom only possible through truth.' Sometimes Läpple wagged his finger: 'Theology is not a flight into the security of rational and religious certainties,' he lectured his young colleague; 'on the contrary, theology is an adventure *in Christo*, an increase in stress and danger!'²³ His friend referred to existentialist philosophy. He recalled the words of the Danish philosopher Søren Kierkegaard: 'Christianity is not a doctrine, but a communication of existence.' Christ created not lecturers but disciples. Joseph and Alfred agreed: the realities of revelation could not be approached in an abstract scientific way, neutrally and without presuppositions. Those realities involved the whole of existence. And they demanded a decision.

Perhaps Läpple overrated his influence on Ratzinger a bit. However, their dialogue remained important to him. 'Dear Alfred!' Ratzinger wrote, as Prefect of the Congregation for the Doctrine of the Faith, to his former companion on 23 June 1995: 'You opened my eyes to philosophy, more than any of our academic lecturers managed to do. Through you, I learned to understand the great figures of Western thought in their lasting presence and thus was able to begin to enter into thinking with them.'²⁴

Ratzinger adopted one of his favourite sayings of Cardinal Newman: a theologian was not someone who disposed of exam-ready knowledge but someone who put theology into practice, so that revelation and dogma became an existentially effective way of life.

16

The Glass Bead Game

The winter semester in Freising lasted four months, the summer semester three. Joseph and Georg spent the lecture-free time in Hufschlag. Together with their student colleague Rupert Berger they served at the daily eight o'clock Mass in St Oswald's Church. The celebrant was the Revd Georg Elst, whom his servers called 'Rocket Schorsch' because he got through the Mass in record time ('Schorsch' is a familiar form for 'Georg' in Bavaria). When he gave communion, instead of the solemn *'Corpus Domini nostri Jesu Christi custodiat animam tuam in vitam aeternam'*, at most communicants heard: *'Corps tam, tam, Corps tam, tam …'*

As musical accompaniment, Rupert sang tenor and Georg sang bass or played the organ. Joseph served the Mass. Thus the students received from the parish priest the confirmation required by Freising that they diligently attended Mass in the holidays and did not carry on any friendships with girls. Ratzinger senior often sang with them in the church choir. As well as this, every Thursday at the 7 a.m. service they carried a baldachin in a small procession up the nave of the church. 'Rocket Schorsch' usually rushed hectically in front of them with his monstrance, so that the four 'heaven bearers' – carrying 'heaven' on four poles to spread above the monstrance – had considerable trouble keeping up with him.

In their parents' house, Georg constantly practised the piano, and his brother listened patiently. Occasionally, they met with former schoolmates for a beer or a trip to the mountains. Joseph still had the first-floor bedroom for studying. The room was tiny, but he loved the view of the Chiemgau Alps and felt sheltered and snug there. His interests were not confined to philosophical and theological subjects.

He was also a sensitive, romantic youth who wrote poetry and was interested in the conflicts of the human soul. His favourite characters in literature were often somewhat solitary figures grappling with life's existential questions.

He had already read the German classics as a schoolboy, but also Rilke's *Stundenbuch* (*Book of Hours*), which he had discussed with his Freising mentor. 'We were both romantic,' Läpple recalled; 'with Rilke it was also that softness, almost too soft, the emotional side, which attracted us.'[1] Goethe was, of course a must. But they always felt it deeply when in *Faust,* the most German of all themes, the question of religion arose. And the protagonist says:

> I've studied now Philosophy
> And Jurisprudence, Medicine,
> And even, alas! Theology,
> From end to end, with labour keen;
> And here, poor fool! with all my lore
> I stand, no wiser than before.

When he began his studies, Joseph turned to new literature. He discovered the contemporary French writers Paul Claudel, Georges Bernanos and the novelist François Mauriac, all representatives of the *Renouveau Catholique* reform movement, which promoted a culture renewed through Catholicism. Joseph also read the extraordinary Léon Bloy. Born in 1846 in Périgueux, in south-west France, Bloy lost his faith as a young man in Paris. He became a socialist but later returned to Catholicism. For five years he shared his life with Anne-Marie Roulé, a prostitute who became a devout Christian under his influence. They read the Bible together, following the symbolic method of Abbé Tardif de Moidrey.

Nevertheless, Bloy repeatedly felt he had been abandoned by God. It was only when he stayed with the Carthusians in the Grande Chartreuse that he acquired a new stability, enabling him to bear witness as a writer for God and the church. 'Bloy fulminates against the moderns who relativize and make light of the faith and indeed anything absolutely true,' the Dominican father Wolfgang Spindler said of him. Bloy battled 'against letting Christianity become bourgeois, turning dogmas into platitudes in order to live pleasantly and comfortably'. Bloy regarded Catholics as renegades if the faith was just a decoration for them, not food for living. But for him, the greatest traitors were the priests who distorted Scripture through exegesis, to the point where it lost anything shocking, and beauty and holiness were transformed into trite commonplaces.

Joseph had inherited his affinity with the *Grande Nation* from his father. He was enthusiastic about the French cultural world, which he found especially vibrant and intellectually attractive. He enjoyed the outspokenness of Georges Bernanos, who said in one of his aphorisms: 'The great misfortune of this world is not that there are godless people but that we are such mediocre Christians!' Paul Claudel particularly interested him. The French diplomat – former ambassador to the United States – had a stirring awakening during Christmas Vespers in Notre-Dame de Paris, which he was visiting by chance. Widely educated, as a journalist he could create a powerful stir. He fenced with salon socialists like Émile Zola and exposed the hollowness he believed lay behind the façade of the celebrated atheist writer. 'Before you change the world,' he remarked, 'perhaps it would be more important not to wreck it.'

Among the younger German writers, Joseph reached for books by the French-German Gertrud von le Fort, the pacifist Annette Kolb and also Elisabeth Langgässer, whom he rated highly. As the daughter of a Jew who had converted to Catholicism, she was forbidden to publish under Hitler. The Nazis kidnapped her daughter, whom they sent first to Theresienstadt and later to Auschwitz. Miraculously, the girl survived. Joseph was 'very moved' by Franz Werfel's novel *The Song of Bernadette,* about the events at Lourdes. With the book the author fulfilled a vow he had taken, were he to be saved from the Nazis.

Ratzinger's reading list is instructive. It gives an impression of the person he was, his mind as a student, his feelings and interests. Strikingly often, converts were to be found among his literary and theological favourites, both then and in his later years as well. Gertrud von le Fort, the daughter of a Protestant Prussian officer, described her conversion to Catholicism in her two-volume novel *Das Schweisstuch der Veronika* (*The Veil of Veronica*). Her book was a reckoning with the liberal intellectual world in the form of Protestant-Prussian optimism about progress, and faith in humanity as master of its own destiny.

Ernst Wiechert, another writer read by Ratzinger, was imprisoned in Buchenwald concentration camp for two months after he supported Pastor Martin Niemöller. Like many other concentration camps, Buchenwald was at first set up for political and religious opponents of National Socialism. Resistance to the regime did not subside. That is shown by the total of 42 assassination attempts on Hitler either planned or carried out during the Nazi dictatorship. Wiechert had been targeted ever since he made a speech to young Germans in Munich University's Auditorium Maximum ('Audimax') on 6 July 1933: 'Yes, it may well be that a nation stops distinguishing between right and wrong and that any battle is in the "right". But that nation is already standing on a steep slippery slope and its downfall is already determined.'

The relevant authorities – they were called the 'Department for the Promotion of German Writing on the Instructions of the Führer for the Intellectual and Political Education of the NSDAP' – passed sentence on Ernst Wiechert's work *Das einfache Leben* (*The Simple Life*), in a report written in 1939: 'The over-emphasis on certain Christian themes is a clear sign of the completely different world in which these people live [...] The novel cannot be recommended.' After the end of the war, the writer gave another speech to young Germans in the Munich Playhouse on 11 November 1945. He criticized the thesis of collective guilt: 'We were not an illiterate people [...] the history of our spirit was a proud history and it was honourably written in the books of humanity.' But then he relentlessly held a mirror up to his compatriots. For the devilish system could have been recognized much earlier, and yes, should have been: 'You saw a new cross and it was not the old message written on its arms, "Come to me all you who are troubled and heavy-laden", but the new message, "Drop dead, Jew!"'

Ratzinger's settling in with the seminary routine was not without friction. That may have been due to the group pressure, which he resisted, even though the orderly rhythm of the daily timetable suited him and he felt in total accord with the liturgical life on the *Mons doctus*. He loved the daily quiet prayer in the house chapel, whose 'altarpiece and intimate atmosphere had a power that moved you'.[2] There were the great feasts when 100 seminarians in their black cassocks descended the steps from the gallery, two by two, in solemn procession into the cathedral. Or the mystical prayer in the crypt with its shrines and statues of saints, where he realized in the candlelight that he was 'being allowed to take part in that great procession of all times and carry it forward into the future'.[3]

Just when Ratzinger began his studies, Hermann Hesse's *Glasperlenspiel (Glass Bead Game)* was published. At home in Hufschlag, Joseph had already devoured Hesse's *Peter Camenzind*. The new work by the pessimistic, wisdom-seeking writer was bound to electrify him. For one thing, the intellectual world portrayed in the *Glass Bead Game* had an atmosphere so like that of Ratzinger's Scholars' Mountain that it was as if the author had based it on Freising's *Mons doctus*.

Hesse had begun work on his *magnum opus* in 1930. Twelve years later, on 29 April 1942, he completed it. A few months after that, his publisher, S. Fischer, in Frankfurt, was banned from printing it by the German 'Reich Ministry for National Enlightenment and Propaganda'. That meant the first edition only appeared in November 1943 – in Zurich. In Germany the work reached the bookshops in December 1946, shortly after Hesse had been awarded the Nobel Prize for Literature.

Joseph read the book as if it presented him with a kind of double, even though he was always just sitting at the table 'as is proper for a Christian'. Although the similarities in the *Glass Bead Game* with the Domberg were astonishing, they were not accidental. That was because the inner logic of worlds with the same set-up would not only have the same pattern but would also produce similar characters. They expressed the basic yearning of sensitive, spiritually gifted people for whom Hesse, from a pietistic parental home, created a kind of monastic scholars' mountain in a fantasy land called Castalia.

In Castalia the protagonist was to be initiated step by step into the mystery of a doctrine, the practice of an almost holy art, which lay beyond the whole superficial material world. Like the boy from Eichenweg ('Oak Way') in Hufschlag, the book's hero, a youth called Josef Knecht, attracted attention early through his special gifts and was received into the 'Eschholz' ('Ash Wood') Order. 'He powerfully felt the magic of that atmosphere,' it said in the *Glass Bead Game,* 'everything here seemed old, venerable, sacred, laden with tradition.'[4] Josef Knecht's temperament and life story also anticipated that of Ratzinger himself, who would later often describe himself as the 'servant' (*Knecht*), and 'burden-bearer' of God: he could see himself in Knecht like looking in a mirror.

In the novel, Castalia originated from an order founded by a group of scholars, who saw themselves as an ascetic counter-movement to a lightweight 'feuilletonistic age', in which 'the mind enjoyed an unprecedented freedom that it could no longer bear'. Reinforced by the 'Band of Voyagers to the East', the community strives for spiritual regeneration and piety, to make the values of Western culture flourish again, as an alternative to a public life interested only in superficial entertainment and diversion.

It is a whole world apart, a world of universality and harmony, built on the cultivation of meditation and music. Venerable scholars of the strict order recognize Josef Knecht's talent and take their protégé under their wing. When he meets the 'older brother', an outsider schooled in Chinese wisdom, he becomes aware of his own special nature and the tasks accompanying it. Then he learns from a historian to see his own life as something shaping reality and therefore demanding respect and responsibility.

But one of his earlier friends, who criticizes the Order with increasing sharpness, becomes a long-standing opponent. 'Both were highly gifted and competent, which made them brothers, whereas in everything else they were opposites.' Doesn't that also bring to mind a particular opponent of the future cardinal, when Hesse says of his Josef and opposite number: 'With astonishment and apprehension, he had heard from this speaker sentences in which everything was destructively criticized – whatever was authoritative and holy in Castalia. Everything in which he himself believed was doubted, questioned or ridiculed.'

Josef Knecht sharpened Ratzinger's insight into the dangers that threatened the Catalic – one might almost say Catholic – order: elitist self-sufficiency, meaningless virtuosity and isolation from the trends of the time. Mastering science, music and meditation, the student Josef rises higher and higher in the hierarchy of the Order, until he is crowned with the highest office, that of Grandmaster, *Magister Ludi*. The title is a Latin pun: *ludus* means both 'school' and 'game'. As schoolmaster and master of the game, the *Magister Ludi* is the 'leader and model of the spiritually cultivated and intellectually striving', with the task of maintaining and increasing 'the traditional spiritual heritage'. Hesse says: 'He not only reached and occupied the province of a master; he strode through it, it became a dimension of him, which we could only guess at with awe.'

We may recall the enthusiasm with which Ratzinger spoke about the solemn Masses of his childhood:

> When a Mozart Mass was sung on feast days in our Traunstein parish church, then for me as a little country boy, it was as if the heavens opened. Ahead in the sanctuary, pillars of incense rose, which the sun broke into. On the altar, the sacred rites were performed which we knew opened heaven for us. And the choir sang music that could only have come from heaven. Music which conveyed to us the angels' rejoicing over God's beauty. It brought something of that beauty down into our midst.[5]

Parallel to that in *The Glass Bead Game* we read:

> The boy's heart surged with reverence, with love for the Master, and as his ear caught the fugue, it was as if today he was hearing music for the first time. Behind the sound composition playing out before him, he had an inkling of the spirit, the joyful harmony of law and freedom [...] During those minutes he saw himself and his life, and saw the whole world directed, ordered and given meaning by the spirit of music.[6]

As Pope Benedict, Ratzinger remarked about the above-quoted passage:

> I have to say that something similar happens to me when I hear Mozart's music. Mozart is pure inspiration – at least that's how he strikes me. Every note is right and could not be different [...] Existence is not trivialized, or falsely harmonized. Nothing of its difficulty and grandeur is omitted; everything becomes a whole, in which we also sense the solution to the darkness in our lives and glimpse the beauty of truth, which we may so often have despaired of.

Given its origin, Hesse's *Glass Bead Game* is a courageous vision. However, in retrospect, the book's plot is revealing because it portrays the world in which Joseph Ratzinger matured: 'He had experienced the process of vocation, which can rightly be called a sacrament,' wrote Hesse. 'That world did not exist somewhere in the distance, in the past or the future. No, it was present and active, it beamed out, it sent messengers, apostles, envoys.' Through the magic process of those dedicated hours, the 'dreams and inklings' changed into an actual assignment, a summons into the real world, and suddenly became a 'bit of reality'.

Similarities with living people are not always accidental. The Josef of the novel had the gift 'of reverence and service of the cult'. As Hesse portrays him, he was 'doubtless always a good comrade and never sycophantic to those above him'. He was 'very shy', but at the same time he did not let himself be intimidated by anybody. He had read 'a lot, particularly German philosophers'. The close similarity of Josef Knecht to the real Joseph was also shown in his lack of strong preferences or aversions. 'In great souls and superior spirits, these passions do not occur,' Hesse knew. For 'those who direct their strongest desire towards real Being, towards what is perfect, seem calmer than those who are passionate, because their glowing fire is not always seen.'

On the question of whether there 'is no truth' or 'truly valid teaching', Knecht learns: 'You should long not for perfect doctrine, friend, but to perfect yourself.' Josef realizes: 'The godhead is in you, not in ideas and books. The truth is lived not lectured', lived 'by the person, through the Master's example'.

As *Magister Ludi,* Knecht also has to see that, in the changed world, the existence of Castalia rests on feet of clay. A status quo has been established in which nothing new has been discovered or created; it only 'plays' with what is to hand. Isolation has to give way to opening out, in order to survive. But that is not it. 'The role that had now fallen to him' determined his life. The 'task given to him' was to defend Castalia against its critics and carry the debate to the highest level. In 'his role as apologist' he was 'compelled, through study, meditation and self-discipline, to become ever more clearly and deeply aware of what he was there to defend [...] Through the trust and responsibility laid upon him, he mastered the task, and it was proof of the strength and quality of his nature that he carried it out without visible disgrace.' But Hesse knew that his lonely hero also 'had much to suffer in silence'.

The rules and mysteries of the Glass Bead Game in Hesse's Castalia cannot be expressed in language. They only become clear to the initiated, in hints, circumlocutions and, above all, in playing the game. The rules are not altogether unlike those of Ratzinger's own 'game'. He had to expound his message over many decades in thousands of religious lessons, lectures, sermons and books, in constantly new and different ways, like a kaleidoscope, whose pieces fall into countless patterns, without thereby changing the contents. With Hesse, the 'game' was ultimately the attempt to bring science and art into a synthesis, uniting all areas into one great whole in a kind of universal language, in order to put the 'player' in touch with the single spirit of the universe.

Hesse drew quite consciously on Catholicism:

As they were classically formulated and therefore seemed to belong to the common cultural treasury, the expressions of Christian theology, were, of course, adopted into the sign language of the game. A key concept of the faith, or the wording of a Bible passage, or a sentence from the church fathers, or the Latin Mass could be just as easily and precisely expressed and adopted into the game as an axiom of geometry or a Mozart melody. It was hardly an exaggeration to say: for the narrow circle of the true Glass Bead Game players, the game was practically tantamount to divine service, during which each player developed their own theology.

According to Hesse's motto: 'The strength does not lie in the branches, but in the roots. Only what is deeply rooted will withstand storms and brave tempests.' For Ratzinger, his roots lay in his family and in the tradition of his Bavarian home and his faith. But something changed when he began his studies. As a child, he had apprehended the Catholic cult as a deep emotional experience. Now he was, as it were, conversing with the great figures of church history. The *Magnum Mysterium* was no longer just an event that could be sensually and spiritually apprehended. Now it could be rationally tested and thereby even deepened. Properly understood, that was not slipping into a kind of professorial religiosity, but rising into a 'wider space', as Ratzinger wrote later. Here the *Mysterium Christi* was not deconstructed and pulled apart but illuminated, in order to go beyond what lay on the surface, penetrate more deeply and gain insight into the essence of the message.

According to Hansjürgen Verweyen, professor emeritus of fundamental theology in Freiburg, with Ratzinger there was a 'continual process of growth' into a 'surpassingly great reality', namely the reality of the liturgy and the Eucharist. What began with daily Mass when he was a child gained a theoretical-theological basis when he started his studies. It was nourished on the *Mons doctus* with the elements of liturgy, doctrine and prayer. Ratzinger would later use terms similar to the terminology used in the *Glass Bead Game*. He spoke of spaces for 'hearing and remembering'. 'The act of faith is an opening into immensity, breaking open the door of my subjectivity,' he said. 'The "I" dissolves and rediscovers itself in a new greater "I".'[7] This new 'I' is 'with Jesus. All the church's experiences also belong to me, become my own.' He referred to the relation between liturgy and contemplation as one of his deepest concerns: 'The root of contemplation is the liturgy; but the liturgy also needs contemplation, if it is not to fossilize into ritualism.'[8]

'Inmost' became one of his favourite words. He constantly spoke about the 'way inward': 'The way inward is also the only way outward, into freedom.' The search was never over. Even when you were convinced you had 'found ultimate certainty', God must 'always be rediscovered'. And 'that discovery is a discovery reaching down into a bottomless abyss.'[9] It was within you that it was finally decided whether temptation and sin could become purification and grace. Joseph even spoke about this in his inaugural sermon after he was elected pope: 'The outer wildernesses are spreading in the world, because the inner wildernesses have become so wide.'

Right at the beginning of his studies in 1946, Joseph got hold of Romano Guardini's first book, *Vom Geist der Liturgie* (*The Spirit of the Liturgy*). This added theological depth to the liturgical world intimated in the *Glass Bead Game*. From Guardini, Joseph learned that what he had felt as a child was not mere fantasy but a reality that went far beyond the evidence of worldly critieria. At first, he had been rather sceptical of the 'Liturgical Movement'. Later he found it had 'contributed largely to the liturgy being rediscovered in its beauty, hidden richness and timeless magnificence, as the heart of the church and Christian life'. It began to be understood 'as the church's prayer, worked and led by the Holy Spirit himself, in which Christ continually becomes with us and enters into our life'.[10]

In the tradition of both the Greek and the Latin church everything in a liturgical and theological context that relates to the Mystery of the Altar is called 'mystical'. Grasping the 'mystical sense' of Scripture means understanding it in terms of the *Mysterium Christi*, the *Magnum Mysterium* that is Christ himself. Knowledge of the mystery means understanding the love of Christ, which surpasses all knowledge. So, according to Catholic teaching, the sacrament of the Altar is the pre-eminent setting for mystical experience, engaging the height of the spirit. The 'eucharistic presence' of Jesus surpasses human understanding, but in contemplation of its secrets, it draws the human spirit 'up out of itself'.

From Guardini, Joseph the student learned that the apparent contradiction between knowledge and reason is overcome in Christianity. The Eucharist was about a mysterious transformation, being changed by a self-giving God, through which the Christian could become incorporated into the life of Christ. An incomparable treasure of the Catholic faith, which had to be defended throughout all ages. 'When we celebrate Mass prayerfully,' Benedict XVI explained to priests in Freising Cathedral (during his visit to Bavaria in 2006),

> when we truly say the words 'This is my body' in communion with Jesus Christ, who has laid hands on us and empowered us to speak in his own person, when we faithfully and prayerfully celebrate the Eucharist from our inmost self then [...] the *ars celebrandi* is there of its own accord; we celebrate from and with the Lord, and thereby rightly for humanity. Then we ourselves are given a gift and enriched, and at the same time we give what is more than our own, namely the Lord's presence to humanity.

Let us return to the *Glass Bead Game*. Didn't it sound rather like a passage from Hesse's book when Ratzinger spoke poetically about his own yearning aspiration? The sentence came from an article about his brother, the Freising 'Organ Ratz'. He was clearly inspired by thinking of the early years on the Domberg:

> God lives where love is given to him. God lives where faith and love become song. Faithful singing and praying to him together, so to speak, build the throne that befits God. Anyone will grasp this who has experience of great liturgy, in which everything is in accord, heart and sense and mind, when the pleading and distress of our being can be heard and seen, at the same time as our joy in God. When the sounds luminously float in the air, intermingle and the very walls turn into prayer, a song of praise, then we feel: yes, in this web of spirit and senses, in this opening of hearts and everything – this is the place for God's dwelling. No, he does not dwell in the nowhere. He is here and that is how humans reach their highest potential: offering God a place to be with us, at home among us.[11]

Like a young plant that suddenly begins to grow sturdily, the young Josef Knecht in the *Glass Bead Game* becomes aware of his stature. He discovers new harmonies between himself and the world, accomplishes many tasks that are way beyond his age and his fellow students. Likewise, with his own peculiar abandonment he is able to dream, listen to the rain and wind, 'grasping nothing, divining everything, filled with sympathy, curiosity, wanting to understand, drawn out of his own self towards others, the world, to mystery and sacrament, to the painful-beautiful game of phenomena'.

So, beginning and growing within himself, 'Josef Knecht's vocation flowered in perfect purity'. The 'unbearably old and tight garment had to be laid aside. A new one lay ready for him.'

17

Augustine

In the winter of 1946–7 Germany faced a new humanitarian disaster. Like a curse on an evil deed, one of the heaviest frosts of the twentieth century lay over the land. Ice and arctic cold down to −20° C turned the already ghostlike ruined cities into frozen scenes of Hell.

The war had laid waste the fields. After the hot summer, the harvest was as poor as in the biblical lean years in ancient Egypt. Industries collapsed as they were dismantled by the victorious powers. More than half the housing had been bombed, and 40 per cent of the transport links had been destroyed. There was a lack of coal and raw materials; all the war supplies were exhausted. In addition, millions of refugees from the east pushed into the individual occupation zones, particularly Bavaria. Eating food waste, begging, dying, was how the survivors described their situation. Despite food imports by the occupying powers, school meals and CARE packages from the USA, the calorie allowance sank even further. 'The hunt for food dominated our whole life,' a contemporary witness recalled; 'we developed tunnel vision, were permanently tired and apathetic.'

The Cologne writer Heinrich Böll, who had just reached the age of 29, noted: 'Coal, wood, building materials. Everyone could rightly have accused anyone else of stealing. Anyone who did not freeze to death in a ruined city must have stolen their wood or coal, and anyone who did not starve must have got food or procured it in an illegal way.'[1] Something the Cologne cardinal Josef Frings said in his New Year's Eve sermon of 1946 spread like wildfire: 'We live in times when individuals will be permitted to take what they need to preserve their life and health, if they cannot do so in any other way by work or asking for help.' From now on the term 'to fring' (*fringsen*) became the household word for the illicit 'organizing' of coal or the pilfering of potatoes from fields you did not own.

With regard to food, heating and housing, the former US president Herbert C. Hoover found that 'the great mass of Germans are experiencing the lowest standard of living known for hundreds of years to Western Civilization'.[2] A report by the German medical profession stated in the summer of 1947 that regionally up to 80 per cent of the population was undernourished. Altogether, according to the historian Wolfgang Benz, more than 100,000 people fell victim to the winter famine.

Together with other seminarians, Joseph cut trees and dug up roots in the fields around the Domberg to drag away anything that could be burned for firewood. Fellow students from farming families could eke out their emergency rations with bacon from home. 'Whenever a "festive dinner" had to be given for a visitor,' Ratzinger reported, 'we went hungry on the most meagre rations for four long weeks in order to gather the ingredients.'[3] However, in every free hour he sat over his books. He had been particularly moved in the *Glass Bead Game*, he told me in our conversation, that the protagonist Josef Knecht 'in the end has to break out again and departs. He is the great Master of the Glass Bead Game, but nothing is final. He has to begin all over again.'

Another of the young Ratzinger's favourite books by Hesse was *Der Steppenwolf,* a novel criticizing civilization. The work had been published in 1927. Fifty years later it became a cult book for the Woodstock generation. Guardians of moral standards had it banned from libraries for promoting drug misuse and sexual perversion. But for the beatniks in California, 'Born to Be Wild' belted out from all channels, the timeless song of a rock group taking its name from the work by the poet from the town of Calw: Steppenwolf.

Der Steppenwolf contains the notes of an oversensitive, isolated young protagonist called Harry Haller, who wants to diagnose the 'sickness of our time'. Haller is a bookish man of ideas, familiar with Mozart and Goethe, brought up by 'loving but strict and very pious parents and teachers'. He lives as a melancholic in tension between a sinking old European culture and a proliferating modern technocracy.

In his *Weltschmerz*, he looks back nostalgically to the 'books by the German poets people have forgotten'. But who could still carry on 'their spirited, playful and yearning voices'? 'Who bore a heart full of their spirit and their magic in a different world estranged from them?' Harry Haller's sighs sounded like unfulfilled love: 'Oh, it is difficult, to find that trace of God within this life we lead, in such a smug, bourgeois, spiritless time as this, in sight of this architecture, these shops, this politics, these people! Why shouldn't I be a *Steppenwolf* and a rough hermit in the midst of a world, none of whose aims I share?'

When Joseph the student, literature lover and poet read it, wouldn't his heart have beaten faster when, in the midst of his gloom, Haller experienced a bright moment in the everyday ordinariness, 'to make room for the extraordinary, wonder and grace'? Didn't Joseph also ask like the *Steppenwolf:* 'Was what we called "culture", spirit, soul, what we called holy, was it just a long-dead phantom, that only a couple of fools like us still held to be real and alive?' Are 'those who know and revere what Europe once was, its erstwhile genuine music, and erstwhile genuine poetry' now just 'a small stupid minority of complex neurotics who will be forgotten and derided tomorrow'?

Haller suffered from a split personality, in which a well-adjusted bourgeois and a *steppenwolfish,* lonely, socially critical soul were at war with one another. He was boxed in between two times and two cultures: bourgeois culture with its boredom and corruption suffocated him as much as his 'Steppenwolf' loneliness and despair. As a *man* he was an educated bourgeois, interested in beautiful thoughts, music and philosophy. As a *wolf* he was a despised critic of society and culture.

Joseph Ratzinger was not the Harry Haller from *Der Steppenwolf,* that 'single great cry for meaning, love and salvation'.[4] But we must also take into account his foundation in order to understand his later attitude to uncivilizing developments. It is easy to imagine that Hermann Hesse would have said the same about the morals of a hyper-sexualized society after the 'sexual revolution' as emeritus Pope Benedict did (and was heavily criticized for). Hesse's Steppenwolf said: 'Humans have the capability to devote themselves wholly to the spiritual, the quest to approach the divine, the ideal of the holy.' And 'on the other hand, they also have the capability to surrender wholly to instinct, their sensual desires, and direct all their efforts towards momentary pleasure. One way leads to becoming holy, a martyr to the spirit, giving yourself up to God. The other way leads to becoming a libertine, a martyr to instincts, giving yourself up to corruption.' Even in old age, Ratzinger remembered what had particularly captivated him in Hesse's book: 'There is a ruthless analysis of degraded humanity in it. It is a manifestation of what is happening to humanity today.'[5]

In his hunger to read, Joseph studied Romano Guardini and Cardinal Newman. He read Sartre, Camus and Claudel. As we have already said, he was struck by Aldous Huxley's vision of the future in *Brave New World,* and George Orwell's dark prophecy of a standardized, soulless and conformist world in *1984.* He would often quote from these works later. Naturally, he devoured Georges Bernanos's incomparable *Journal d'un curé de campagne,* published in 1936. From criticism of church and civil relations, Bernanos's priest character develops a heroic piety that is crystalline in its simplicity.

However, the book that impressed Joseph more than any other was not a contemporary work. It was the *Confessions* of St Augustine, which fell into the 19-year-old's hands in the spring of 1946. In Christian Latin the term *confessiones* means both the acknowledgement of your own weaknesses, the distress of a sinner, and also praise of God. Seeing your own wretchedness in God's light becomes gratitude that God accepts you and raises you to himself by changing you. The writer of these *Confessions,* a prodigal, reckless womanizer and passionate fighter, was an intellectual and spiritual giant such as humanity only produces every thousand years. For quite a while, Joseph found it hard to understand things in the book. He found it hard to grasp what it meant when Augustine described conversion as a lifelong process. He had not been able really to get to grips with Thomas Aquinas in Freising. We may remember that he found the Dominican 'too impersonal and too ready-made'. On the other hand, with Augustine now he discovered 'the passionate, suffering, questioning person was always directly there'. He was someone 'with whom you can identify'.[6] The spark was struck: 'I feel him as a friend,' Ratzinger confessed, 'a contemporary, who speaks to me.'[7]

With Hesse's characters, Joseph shared a pessimism about contemporary culture and the courage to take a critical position towards the spirit of the time. But here, Ratzinger found, was a true biography, a real human person active in history, someone 'who battled' astonishingly openly and honestly: 'A man who was imbued with the tireless desire to find the truth, to seek out what life is, to know how we should live.' Someone who 'despite all his humility', was 'also aware of his intellectual power'. Someone who thought about faith and lived it – and still lived his life completely. Someone for whom humanity was 'a great enigma' (*magna quaestio*) and 'a deep abyss' (*grande profundum*). 'Many and grave are the weaknesses, many and grave,' Augustine declared in his *Confessions.*

He was also someone with huge linguistic talent, who wrote the most beautiful sentences: 'Late have I loved you, Oh Beauty, so old and so new, late have I loved you. And look, you were within me and I was outside and sought you outside … You were with me, and I was not with you.'

As soon as he spoke about Augustine, Ratzinger became enthusiastic: 'Because of his passion for humanity he had to seek God; only in God's light can the greatness of humanity, the beauty of the adventure of being human appear fully.' For him, Augustine was 'the greatest father of the Latin church, besides being one of the greatest figures in the history of thought'. Later, he wrote that Augustine's writings were 'of fundamental importance and not only for the history of Christianity but for the development of the whole of Western culture'. For 'Seldom could a civilization have produced someone of such greatness of mind, who understood how to grasp its values and increase its inner wealth.'[8]

The man from Hippo had everything that Ratzinger himself apparently lacked. Passion, empathy, emotion. And also the openness to reveal his own spiritual life. But that was not all it was about. As a prospective theologian, what attracted Ratzinger in particular was Augustine's 'passionate search for the truth'. 'I want to know God and the soul, nothing else,' Augustine had confessed. 'Really nothing? No, nothing else at all.'[9]

The future pope summed it up thus:

So faith in Christ did not put an end to his philosophy or his intellectual boldness. On the contrary, it pushed him to probe further into the depths of being human, to help others to live well and discover life, the art of living. That was philosophy for him: knowing how to live with our whole mind, with the whole depth of our thinking and willing, in order to be led on the way of truth, which is a way of courage, humility, constant clarification.

In that way, Augustine was able to find God 'as the basic reason, and also as love, which embraces and leads us, and gives meaning to history and our personal life'.[10]

If he could only take two books with him to an island, Ratzinger confessed, they would be the Bible and the *Confessions*. He felt grateful to someone 'to whom I feel closely bound, because of the part he has played in my life as a theologian, priest and pastor'. Ratzinger called Augustine a 'man full of passion and faith, of the highest intelligence'. But also his 'friend' and 'my great master Augustine'.

Indeed, into none of his many portraits of saints did Ratzinger pour so much 'contemplation' as into those discourses in which he wrote about his 'master'. It was as if he wanted to point out: 'I see myself in Augustine – and Augustine as myself – it is a self-portrait.' Of course, few of his listeners guessed that, when Pope Benedict spoke about the bishop of Hippo in his 'catecheses' in St Peter's Square, he was also always speaking, in retrospect, about the student Joseph:

Augustine was described as a man of today, with all a young man's habits and passions, all his questions and problems. He lived like anyone else and yet there was something else too. He always remained a seeker. He was never just content with life, just as it is and how other people live it. He was always driven by the quest for truth. He wanted to find the truth. To get at what humanity is, where the world comes from; where we ourselves come from, where we are going and how we can find real life. He wanted to find the right life, not simply exist ... And there was something else in particular. Anything that did not bear the name of Christ did not satisfy him. He tells us he had drunk love for that name with his mother's milk. And he always believed, sometimes more faintly, sometimes more strongly, that there is God, and that he accepts us. But his great struggle in his early years was really recognizing God and really getting to know Jesus Christ. And saying Yes to him with all its consequences.

No other figure in church history impressed and influenced Ratzinger so much as Augustine, 'the heart genius', as his biographers called him. Joseph's enthusiasm was neither hero worship nor a cult of celebrity. You had to feel the same in order to be able to identify in that way. It was his wrestling with the question of God that moved Joseph, his fullness of knowledge, which could not come from mere book learning but only through a deep commitment of the soul. Here was someone in whom he saw himself reflected as in no one else, an *alter ego*, a second self. The Augustine scholar Cornelius Mayer thought Joseph's identification with Augustine went so deep that perhaps Ratzinger ought to be called a second, reborn Augustine, *Augustinus redivivus*.

In 1998 Ratzinger said Augustine had never given him the impression that 'this was a man who died more or less 1,600 years ago'. As soon as he had read his first pages, 'I recognized him practically at once as my contemporary, as a person who was not speaking to us from a distance or from a context completely different from our own.'[11]

Aurelius Augustinus was born on 13 November 354 in Thagaste, in the Roman province of Numidia, in north Africa. He was brought up as a Christian. His mother, Monica, came from a Christian Berber family, but did not have her son baptized. His father, Patricius, was a small landowner, who only converted to Christianity shortly before his death. Augustine studied grammar locally. Then in Carthage he studied rhetoric, at which he became a master and was celebrated as a brilliant speaker.

At that time Carthage, with its 300,000 inhabitants, was the fourth largest city of the Roman Empire, after Rome itself, Alexandria and Antioch. Apart from Rome, it was the most important diocese in the western half of the empire. Augustine engaged in exciting love affairs, had an illegitimate child and dreamed of a lucrative career in public service. A text by Cicero (*Hortensius on Philosophy*) aroused his love for philosophy. 'That book really changed my mind,' he wrote in his *Confessions*, so much that 'suddenly that vain hope became worthless to me and I longed with a glowing heart for the immortality of wisdom.'[12]

On the other hand, he found the Bible linguistically unsatisfying and philosophically weak. In his yearning for a religion that combined rationality, the search for truth and love for Jesus Christ, in 373 he fell into the net of the Manichees, but later left them again. A move to Milan caused the change. With growing enthusiasm, he listened to the brilliant sermons of Bishop Ambrose. He grasped that the Old Testament can only be understood in its depth and beauty when it is seen as a way to Jesus, 'as the synthesis between philosophy, reason and faith in the "Logos", in Christ', as Benedict XVI put it, 'the eternal Word becomes flesh'.

In one of the most famous passages of the *Confessions*, Augustine tell us that he was in a friend's garden in Milan when he suddenly heard a child's voice repeatedly singing in a tune he had never heard before the words *'Tolle lege, Tolle lege – Take and read! Take and read!'* In the house, he found an edition of Paul's letters and opened a page at random:

> The night is far gone, the day is near. Let us lay aside the works of darkness and put on the armour of light; let us live honourably as in the day, not in revelling and drunkenness, not in debauchery and licentiousness, not in quarrelling and jealousy. Instead, put on the Lord Jesus Christ, and make no provision for the flesh, to gratify its desires. (Rom. 13: 12–15)

Augustine wanted to discover the driving forces and ideas whereby God's plan was carried out. His restless heart, said Pope Benedict, 'becomes an expression of the longing for knowledge, the search for truth, the yearning for perfection and perfect peace. But time and again he sensed he was being guided in some inexplicable way, which he had to follow, and he was finally embraced by God.'

Augustine's work covered the whole thought of antiquity. 'It seemed impossible', his biographer Possidius wrote, 'that one man could write so much in his lifetime.' His writings influenced every century. In all he wrote more than 100 works, including the 15-book *De Trinitate* (*On the Trinity*), written to combat heresies, and the 22-book *De civitate Dei* (*On the City of God*). They dealt with the relationship between politics, state and church, as well as Augustine's theory of peace, whereby not war but peace was the God-given law of nature. A war was 'just' only when it was in defence of legitimate rights and did not cause greater suffering than those which it alleviated. For his final word of wisdom he was content with a single sentence: 'Lord, you have made us for yourself,' it says at the beginning of the *Confessions*, 'and our heart is restless until it rests in you!'

But could Augustine really – as Ratzinger believed – give 'an answer to the problems that are also our problems, even though they are expressed in their own way'? In the first half of the twentieth century Europe had become a scene of war, migration and new powers. Wasn't it also forgetfulness of God that had led half of humanity to the brink of the abyss? It had become impossible to overlook the negative consequences that had sprung from atheism in the West. The Communist parts of the world, which promised a paradise on Earth, were dominated by poverty and oppression.

In fact, the context of the third and fourth centuries, of which Ratzinger spoke, had remarkable parallels with the twentieth-century situation after the world war. Augustine's epoch was also a turning point in history. The transformation from antiquity to the Middle Ages began with it. The external signs were the fall of the *Imperium Romanum*, the conquests by warring tribes from the east and huge migrations. In late antiquity, religion was half pagan and half Christian, half for the church and half against it, passionate for the good but also for evil.

From its modest beginnings in the original Jerusalem community, Christianity had spread throughout the whole Roman Empire. Ten per cent of the empire's population – people of all races, classes and ages – had joined the 'New Way'. The faithful had been persecuted by the state for more than 300 years. The biggest pogroms covering the whole empire only broke out in the middle of the third century, particularly in Egypt. Here, in the year 303, up to 100 people a day were executed for being Christ's disciples. But then the apparently hopeless situation suddenly changed in a flash.

It was an unexpected change that came as if from nowhere, seemingly impossible in human terms. Constantine's predecessor, Diocletian, had still been fiercely persecuting and martyring Christians. But Constantine, who had inherited the imperial throne, attributed his decisive victory over his opponents at the Battle of Milvian Bridge on 28 October 312 to a Christian apparition.

According to the legend, Constantine saw Christ in a dream ordering him to carry the cross as his standard, saying '*in hoc signo vinces*': 'with this sign you will conquer'. And in fact, instead of the usual imperial eagles, his troops bore the *Labarum,* the standard on which the Christogram symbol, the Greek characters **XP** (*chi-rho*: the first two letters of the Greek word 'Christ'), could be seen. A year later Constantine, now emperor, issued the Milan Edict of Toleration, which made faith in the Saviour permissible for all subjects of the Roman Empire. After a further decisive victory over a rival, in 330 Constantine made Byzantium the capital of the Christian empire and in the new metropolis, now renamed Constantinople, he built magnificent palaces and churches – including the glorious Hagia Sofia, dedicated to the divine Wisdom.

The liberation of the church from the catacombs led to a rapid upturn. Christians had access again to social and political life. Their confiscated property was returned to them. Constantine gave the pope his imperial palace in the Lateran, beside which a basilica would soon be built. Many new laws in the spirit of the gospel promoted family life, care for the poor and protected slaves. Crucifixion was abolished, since from now on the cross became the sign of Christ's redemption and a symbol of victory.

The emperor's protection brought Christian communities privileges and gifts, safeguarded their institutional status and resulted in an even faster spread of Christianity. The church took over established Roman structures and forms of organization, including titles such as Prefect and *Pontifex Maximus.* With the emperor Theodosius, Christianity became the single state religion. In return, the Emperor claimed full sovereignty over the church.

However, the church had to pay not only by the loss of its independence. The massive numbers of newly baptized also brought members into the communities who had very little idea of the actual meaning of the faith. Then there was also the battle with followers of heresies such as Arianism, Manicheism, Pelagianism and Nestorianism. The separation between Western Rome and Eastern Rome was also fateful, and eventually led to a split between a Latin and an Orthodox church. What weighed almost more heavily was the paradigm shift from an alternative, purely spiritual faith community, committed to neighbourly love, into a conformist state church. The church was now under regular pressure to become more worldly. The result was not only a change in the mentality of the faithful but also an inner split, a split in the nature of the faith itself.

The church's temptation to forget her origin, the challenges from heresies, the fight for her identity: all these were symptoms that concerned the Freising students on the Domberg. Augustine was another 'Steppenwolf', someone who had discovered and come to know. However, he was no Glass Bead Game player but a teacher of humanity, whose timeless knowledge decisively marked Western thought. Augustine saw the foundation of knowledge in the Christian faith as *crede ut intellligas:* believe in order to understand. The truth was only reachable by humans through enlightenment given to them by God, who directly 'in-lights' the divine spirit (*mundus intelligibilis*), the 'eternal ideas' and rules, into the human spirit.[13]

The parallels between Ratzinger and Hesse's characters, on the one hand, and Augustine on the other, were astonishing. But clearly, the Freising student was a type to be found among historical as well as literary characters, a kind of guardian of the grail and also a herald. Ratzinger's encounter with the African theologian was the beginning of a wonderful friendship, which had no parallel in church history. However different these two churchmen might appear at first sight, the parallels in their life stories were extraordinary. Joseph learned from the *Confessions* that Augustine was also baptized on Easter night. That he also had a brother and a sister (who, when she was widowed, became the superior of a convent of nuns); that as a young man he too had had radical questions about himself. For both of them, as Ratzinger put it: 'Someone who is far from God is also far from himself.'

Didn't he also hope, like Augustine, to be able intensively to 'enter into the arguments of the present day'?[14] Neither of them was content with philosophies that did not reach the truth, did not reach God. For Augustine it was clear: the presence of God in humanity was deep and at the same time mysterious, but it could be recognized and discovered within yourself. Don't go outside, but 'turn inwards into yourself; the truth lies within you and when you find that your nature is changeable, then go out beyond yourself.'[15] Ratzinger later expressed it similarly: 'In reality the Creator has inscribed the "natural law" within our very being, which is the reflection of his plan of creation in our heart, as the guide and inner standard of our life.'[16]

As a student, Ratzinger could not have dreamed that in the biography of the master there were milestones and break points which would also occur for him. It was only in retrospect that he must have seen that the life course of his master read like a script, which also contained his own story. Augustine longed to be a writer. He had gone to Hippo Regius (today Annaba in Algeria) in order to found a monastery, together with a group of 'servants of God'. But instead of being able to lead a life of meditation as a writer, against his will he was ordained as a priest. And the Freising student? Didn't he at first want to be just a teacher, a professor, without having to be ordained as a priest, which he did not think himself fit for?

Augustine was also made a bishop against his declared will. 'I feel like someone who can't row who has been made second navigator,' he wrote to Bishop Valerius straight after his appointment: 'That was also the reason why I wept silently at my ordination.' Didn't Ratzinger also complain later that he had not been able to continue his theological work, because he had been made bishop, even though they knew about his lack of organizational skill and weak health? 'The beautiful dream of a contemplative life was over, Augustine's life had been fundamentally changed,' he remarked on the great theologian's ordination as bishop. 'He had to translate his high thoughts and knowledge into the way the simple people of his city thought and spoke. The great philosophical lifework he had dreamed of remained unwritten.'[17]

Looking further into the future, we can see another likeness: the duty of to be a defender of the faith. Without really wanting to, Augustine had to battle against heresies, which rejected the Catholic belief in the one God. Ratzinger was also called upon, against his will, to become a custodian of the faith, to defend Rome against extraneous currents. He described his task with words written by Augustine: 'Reproving troublemakers, comforting the faint-hearted, administering to the weak, refuting opponents ... encouraging the good, bearing with the bad and – oh dear! – loving them all.'[18] Augustine even went a step further in his complaint: 'Always preaching, disputing, admonishing, edifying, being available to everyone. That is a great burden, a heavy pressure, an arduous work.'[19]

Like Augustine, Ratzinger wanted to renew the world through a deepening of faith, theology and holiness. As for Augustine, so for Ratzinger Christian faith did not exclude reason. Humans had the capacity to grasp connections by intellect alone, without apprehending them through the senses. They also needed metaphysics in order to see beyond what was visible and know more fully. Augustine said: 'Faith means touching base, reaching the real substance of everything.' According to Augustine, faith and reason were 'the two powers that bring us to knowledge'.[20]

Augustine had learned from ancient philosophy that the origin of all being derived from a creative mind. But what that Logos made palpable and understandable, brought home, was only to be found in the faith of the church: the Word – the Logos – became flesh in Jesus Christ.

Like Augustine, Ratzinger's main focus was on the core of the faith: love. It was right 'to entrust our activity to working with God, to believe that – even in the world today – love is a power, love can change the world and invites our love.'[21] And over and above it all, they had a common criterion: holding fast to the true, the beautiful, the good and the holy. Beauty was a mark of creation, the Spirit, the Word, which both theologians took from God's glory, and which they also tried to express in the language they used, without it being purely aesthetic or just a matter of style.

'For Ratzinger,' the Spanish theologian Pablo Blanco Sarto said, 'everything began with Augustine.' With the master from Hippo someone came into his life who became his model and his destiny. It may also be mentioned in passing that Augustine also had an opponent, a British monk called Pelagius, who gained a large public through his teaching. According to the Augustine expert Cornelius Mayer, the themes of the church father 'run through the publications of Joseph Ratzinger like a golden thread'. The personalism that Ratzinger had discovered in Steinbüchel and Martin Buber was interwoven into Augustine's thought 'as if of its own accord'. It was only later that Ratzinger realized that Augustine's confession had to continue 'humbly until the end of his life'. 'He learned to communicate his faith to simple folk and carry out a selfless and difficult job,' Ratzinger wrote about his spiritual mentor, 'but he took this burden upon himself, because he realized it was the very way by which he could come closer to Christ. Understanding that we can reach others with modesty and humility was his true and second confession.'

In the summer of 1947 on the Domberg there was the *admissio,* the ceremonial admission of candidates for the priesthood towards the end of their philosophy studies. Ratzinger was sorry 'to have got to theology so soon' and 'not to be able to go deeper into philosophy, as I would have liked'. Nevertheless, he had not simply acquired 'a ready-made system' but had learned to question, 'how is it really?' And 'Augustine was a helper and leader for that.'

'Book Ratz' and 'Organ Ratz' had passed their examinations in biology, philosophy, history of philosophy and secular history with brilliance. However, now the two brothers would go their separate ways. Georg went for music. Joseph, together with two other students from the group of 50 seminarians in his year, received permission from Cardinal Faulhaber to continue his theological studies at the University of Munich.

As for the writer of the *Glass Bead Game* and *Der Steppenwolf,* he was initially declared a dead duck. In 1958 *Der Spiegel* prophesied that, as a typically German product of unpolitical unworldliness, Hermann Hesse would never make it abroad.[22] But with an estimated 150 million book sales, Hesse became the most successful German-language writer of the twentieth century worldwide. On the morning of 9 August 1962, the great writer died in his sleep. On his bedside table lay the *Confessions* of St Augustine.

18

Storm and Stress

On 15 September 1947 Joseph Ratzinger began his theology studies in Munich. To put it more precisely: fundamental theology and dogmatics, the supreme theological disciplines. The date of the beginning of the semester was brought forward in order to save on heating. Then the vacation started on 15 December, which was to last until Easter. Everywhere there were still mountains of rubble and bombed-out houses. At the same time, there was an awakening of cultural life. Shakespeare's *King Lear* was put on in the Residenz Theatre in Munich. It was Joseph's first great experience of a play. He shared his passion for the theatre with his mother, who seldom missed an amateur dramatic performance in Chiemgau.

All that was left of the venerable Munich University in Ludwigstrasse was the Great Hall, one of the few usable large halls in the city. Here the Constituent Regional Assembly sat and formed the first post-war Bavarian parliament. A campus on the edge of the city was found as alternative accommodation for the theologians. It was in the empty seminary for late vocations in Fürstenried Palace, the former royal hunting lodge. A hospital for wounded foreign soldiers was also on the site. There was a delightful park, laid out half in the English and half in the French style. But what a horrible change it was from the Domberg!

The accommodation for the professors, the meeting rooms, the secretariat, libraries, studies and dormitories were all crowded together in the same building. They slept on straw mattresses on bunk beds. As there was no lecture hall available, the lectures took place in the greenhouse in the castle gardens. It was scorching hot in summer and ice-cold in winter. Ratzinger remarked caustically about this new place of study: 'The unfortunate King Otto spent the decades of his madness there.'

With room for about 100, Fürstenried drew students from all parts of Germany. Most of them had been involved in the war. In contrast to the familiar Domberg atmosphere, the mood was rather 'aloof', without the 'spontaneous warmth' they were accustomed to. Students who had been studying longer cut themselves off and worked on their dissertations. But on Saturdays for Joseph and the other greenhorns it was: let's go into town! Not to take a stroll but to dig through rubble in the ruins of the Georgianum, the actual seminary opposite the university. The most exciting novelty was the advent of female students, who always sat at the back.

The theological faculty in Munich had been closed down by the Nazis in February 1939 as a punishment for Cardinal Faulhaber's refusal to agree to the appointment of a Hitler disciple as a professor. Now the most important chairs (Old and New Testament, church history, moral theology, fundamental theology) could be occupied by experts from all over Germany. Together they offered enormous breadth, from which something new and special could develop. As Ratzinger noted, they could penetrate 'the great world of the history of the faith', open up wide horizons for thinking and learning and broach the 'fundamental questions about being human'.

In Joseph's main subjects, the aim of fundamental theology was to confirm Christ's revelation by the light of reason and communicate it accordingly. The task of dogmatics was systematically to gather and sift through the church's doctrinal statements, construe them correctly and expound them in an understandable way. For example, the doctrine of the triune God, the Creator of the universe, the visible and also invisible world; the doctrine of Christ the Saviour and his mother, Mary. It was about the church and the doctrine of the Last Things, which God would bring about, completing both the life of the individual and the whole creation, finally concluding with the return of Jesus.

Ratzinger spoke about a 'great time of breakthrough', felt by everyone: 'We believed we were leading the church into a new future.' He and his contemporaries 'really had the feeling that Christianity can be lived anew'.[1] 'The hope for a new beginning, the feeling of breakthrough – also in the theological area – filled us all and even had an impact on Vatican II.'² During those 'exciting years', there reigned an awareness of 'a newly daring and questioning theology [...] and a spirituality that did away with what was stuffy and outdated, in order to find new joy in salvation'. It was important that dogma was not seen as an external constraint 'but as the living source, that makes knowledge possible at all'.³

The mood in Fürstenried was fully in accord with the realization that after the Inferno of the Second World War a new social foundation had to be laid. It was to be created from new beginnings and rediscoveries, which would lead humanity into a new future. In Eastern Europe that was based on Marxism-Leninism, in the West on Christian Western values, which were championed after the war beyond any doubt. Some 70 years later, weary of religion, the West was barely able to carry that on. But in the the years of reconstruction there was a broad social consensus that only a religious renewal – a return to Christianity – could guarantee a united, peaceful, free Europe.

The impetus to found a new Christian party came from political Catholicism in Germany. A 'coming together of all Christians on a political level' aimed at overcoming the Christian split. In preparation, the 'Cologne Principles' were published in July 1945. Among other things, they called for a 'true Christian socialism'. The Jesuit Oswald von Nell-Breuning led the development of the idea. The main emphasis was on the principle that the flourishing of the individual should be given more weight, as well as the common good.⁴ 'Social partnership', 'federalism', 'Europe' and 'subsidiarity' – many of the political and social foundations were already there in the Catholic theory of natural law, society and the state. In this way, Catholic social teaching almost obtained the function of a semi-official state philosophy.⁵

According to the social scientist Manfred Spieker, 'Catholic social teaching's view of human beings as persons and its conception of human rights, founded on natural law, unquestionably had the strongest influence on the new German constitution. They were the basis of the new rule of law, which the positivist orientation of the Weimar Republic had overridden.'⁶ In addition, there were programme points, such as the guarantee of a federalist democracy under the rule of law, the creation of a differentiated educational system, the development of a free market economy with welfare state provision and, in foreign policy, the incorporation of the German Federal Republic into the European and Atlantic democracies' community of values.

The bottom line was to build the new state on a foundation of natural law and Christian values. Konrad Adenauer expressed this in a keynote speech in Cologne University on 26 March 1946: 'The human person has a unique dignity and the value of each single human being is irreplaceable. This statement leads to an idea of the state, the economy and culture which is new in comparison with what has long been the case in Germany [...] The state has no unlimited right; the limits of its power are set by the the dignity and the inalienable rights of the person.'[7] That principle came up in the first article of the constitution. It was drafted by Adolf Süsterhenn, and Catholic social teaching had considerable influence on it. 'The dignity of human beings is inviolable. It is the duty of all state power to respect and protect it (para. 1). Therefore the German nation professes inviolable and inalienable human rights to be the foundation of any human community, of peace and justice in the world.'

Besides Konrad Adenauer, the protagonists of this new beginning in Europe were the Italian Alcide De Gasperi and the Frenchman Robert Schuman, both of whom were practising Catholics. 'Reconciliation between nations and peace and a new trust were at the heart of their political thought,' said the political scientist and former minister-president of Saxony-Anhalt, Werner Münch. 'As believing Christians with common philosophical and religious convictions, all three of them had that vision.'[8] Just one day after the end of the war, on 9 May 1945, Pope Pius XII had insisted that a new Europe could only be built on the fear of God and faithfulness to his commandments, as well as respect for human dignity and for the equal rights of all nations. Adenauer, whom the young Joseph Ratzinger greatly admired, called on his party to take up the 'battle for the soul of the German people and the soul of Europe, the Christian soul of Europe'.

The former mayor of Cologne had taken refuge from the Nazis in 1933 in the Maria Laach Benedictine monastery as 'Brother Konrad'. When he became the first chancellor of the Second German Republic, regular attendance at Mass, prayer and reflection remained a matter of course for him. 'Without the right, essential mental attitude,' said Adenauer, 'nothing else will be right; and nothing is so suited to creating that attitude as properly understood attention to the liturgy.' Before he set out for Moscow in 1955 to fight for the release of the German prisoners of war still held in Soviet gulags, he spent a whole night at the tomb of St Nicholas of Flüe in Switzerland. When he left the tomb, he asked that continual prayers should be said there for the whole time he was in Russia. 'There had never been such a symbiosis between the state and the Catholic Church before in modern Germany,' said the political scientist Franz Walter as 'under Chancellor Konrad Adenauer, the German Catholics' hero and role model'.[9]

The mood of a new beginning was troubled by the sharpening confrontation between East and West. With the Marshall Plan, named after the American foreign minister George C. Marshall, in June 1947 the USA offered comprehensive support for the rebuilding of the devastated Western European countries. It was intended to stabilize the political and social situation, partly with a view to preventing expansion of the Soviet empire. From 1947 Britain and the USA had agreed to unite their zones to form a single economic area, the 'Bizone'. When the three Western powers decided to found a 'Western State', the Soviet Union ceased to co-operate with the Allied Control Council. The introduction of the 'Deutsche Mark' (DM) in the Western occupation areas on 20 June 1948 sealed the separation of the two land areas of Germany.

In the West, from one day to the next, the shop windows were again filled with goods. Four days later Soviet troops closed the access routes to Berlin. More than 2 million West Berliners were cut off from the outside world. When 250,000 Berliners protested against the blockade of their city in the Platz der Republik on 9 September 1948, the mayor, Ernst Reuter, made a dramatic appeal to the international public: 'You nations of the world, you people in America, in England, in France, look at this city! And realize that you must not surrender, cannot surrender this city and these people, for anyone who surrendered these Berlin people, would be surrendering a world, and yes, they would even be surrendering themselves.'

The USA reacted and started the 'raisin bombers', as the Berliners called the supply planes. They dropped tinned food and dried food, fuel and medicines. In just 90 days an extra airfield was built in Berlin-Tegel. Soon 90 planes a day were landing in Berlin. Altogether, 200,00 flights delivered 1.5 million tons of vital supplies.

The blockade confirmed the USA as the leading Western power. On 1 July, the West German minister presidents of the three Western allied military governments were given the task of convening a constituent assembly in Koblenz. On 9 May 1949 the 'Constitution of the Federal Republic of Germany' lay on the table. In the final vote in the Parliamentary Council it was passed with 53 Yes votes and 12 No. But there was still something lacking for the foundation of a German Federal Republic: a capital. Four cities stood for election: Bonn, Frankfurt am Main, Kassel and Stuttgart. Bonn won, with 33 votes for and 29 against, and became the provisional capital.

On the question of the future German flag, the Christian Democratic Union party (CDU) had proposed a black-gold cross on a red background, as a symbol of the Christian culture of the West. However, the SPD (Social Democratic Party) and FDP (Free Democratic Party) prevailed with the Weimar flag with its black-red-gold stripes – as a symbol of unity and freedom. On the evening of 12 September 1949 the newly elected Federal president, Theodor Heuss, was welcomed in the Bonn marketplace for the first time. For lack of a national anthem, the orchestra played a church hymn. Thirty thousand people sang lustily together with the strong-voiced new president: 'Grosser Gott, wir loben dich' ('Holy God, we praise thy name').

Unlike the classes in the Freising college, the lectures in the theological faculty in Fürstenried were public. Apart from these lectures, the priests and candidates to the priesthood kept to themselves. The centre of each day was the Holy Eucharist, which no one would have dared to miss. At the communal lunch the Director, Josef Pascher, served the soup personally. At the same time a lector read out loud from a book. In the evening Pascher read a chapter from the Bible.

The day was structured by communal student prayers. Pascher took care that no one came late. 'Anyone coming late sins against love', he had written in large letters on a notice. A short time afterwards, when a young roebuck had wandered into the park, a notice appeared on a gate: 'Anyone who locks in a roebuck sins against love.' The writer was purported to be a certain Joseph Ratzinger. Not without reason. Even as a boy, Joseph had been very fond of animals and had sometimes even looked after a neighbour's cows in a meadow.

Fellow students like Josef Finkenzeller found Ratzinger 'very modest and ready to help'. He was 'a good comrade, a keen, very gifted student and good conversation partner, from whom you could learn something'. Georg Schwaiger, the future church historian and specialist in papal history, said: 'We already knew that he was clever, but he was never very communicative. He had no nickname and was simply Joseph. Joseph with a "ph", please, the biblical spelling, he insisted.'

Another fellow student, the same age as Joseph, was Hubert Luthe from the Rhineland, who later became bishop of Essen. During the Nazi period, Luthe's father had supported a Jewish couple. In 1937 the pages of the secretly published encyclical *Mit brennender Sorge* had rolled off the presses in his print works. Shortly afterwards, the Gestapo stormed the building. Hubert Luthe was to play another important part for Ratzinger. As private secretary to the blind Cologne cardinal Joseph Frings, he was the only chaplain to take part in the deliberations of the Second Vatican Council. 'Ratzinger's ability was felt by all,' he recalled about those early meetings. Typical of Joseph was his reserved manner: 'He attracted attention by his modesty, actually a paradox.'[10]

Despite his shyness, the young theologian had a certain comic talent. 'He is a real one-man show,' said a contemporary, 'you kill yourself laughing.' As a student, Ratzinger enjoyed the Munich comedian Karl Valentin with his 'odd curmudgeonly hilarity'. He even made a pilgrimage to the comedian's grave in Planegg, a walk of at least 30 kilometres. The former mayor of Munich, Christian Ude, reported that on a visit to Rome the cardinal had spontaneously come up with one of Valentin's sketches, a two-person act, in which Ratzinger played both parts. Valentin died on Shrove Monday, 9 February 1948. His last words were: 'If only I had known that dying is so beautiful.'

The aspiration in Fürstenried, Ratzinger reported, was 'to renew theology from scratch' and 'thereby also reshape and enliven the church'. He and his fellow students were lucky that 'we were living at a time when new horizons and new ways forward were opening up, both from the youth movement and the liturgical movement. Of course, we wanted to lead the way for the church, convinced that this would make her young again.' So Ratzinger's sympathy lay with teachers who were unconventional. One of them was Wilhelm Maier, professor of New Testament studies, a declared enemy of Rome and a lateral thinker. In his foreword to Maier's *Schriftauslegung in Widerstreit* (The Interpretation of Scipture in Conflict), Ratzinger said of of the author, 'Throughout my years of study I never missed a single one of his lectures.' For him, Maier had 'the most impressive personality' in his years of study, with 'an energy in dealing with the subject' and an 'explosive dynamism' that 'deeply impressed' him.[11] The fact that the professor 'was constantly in trouble because of his independent progressive exegesis' did not bother the student. On the contrary: 'The impartial questions from the viewpoint of the liberal-historical method created a new directness towards Scripture and exposed aspects of the text which were no longer recognized in the entrenched dogmatic reading.' The result: 'The Bible spoke to us with a new immediacy and freshness.'

Maier, a brilliant young scholar, had realized early on that Mark's Gospel was the first of the four gospels to have been written, and the two next 'synoptic' gospels had used it as a source. That thesis is universally recognized today, but at the time it was condemned as Modernism. Meier's writings had to be ripped out of already published joint works. On Rome's instructions, their author was not to be offered any more teaching posts. His return to the academic world only took place in the changed post-war climate. He could not forget this humiliating treatment. 'The Antichrist sits in Rome,' was one of his sayings. When Ratzinger was prefect of the Congregation for the Doctrine of the Faith, he wrote in a letter to his friend Frank Mussner about Maier's 'exceptionally deep-seated resentment against Rome'. At the same time he wrote: 'Nevertheless, he loved God's church at heart and helped his students and listeners a great deal to read the New Testament rightly and thus learn about the faith of the apostles.'[12]

Whereas Maier's lectures were packed, for those of Franz Xaver Seppelt the benches were empty. The church historian had achieved great public success with his illustrated history of the papacy. The academic world hailed the priest as a 'sovereign master' of his subject. Rome honoured him with the title of 'papal house prelate'. However, the Fürstenried students were not impressed. 'Too boring' was the verdict of the theological younger generation. In addition, the papal expert from Breslau cultivated an almost military style. 'Damned slackers!', he boomed as soon as he entered the lecture room and noted the small turnout once again. Then he marched up to the lectern in his knee-high military boots. Nevertheless, Seppelt's lectures were an opportunity for Joseph to come into contact with the greatness, but also the drama, of the papacy. For the first time, he heard about the only pope up to that point to resign from his high office, Pope Celestine V, whose family name was Pietro del Murrone. The *Studien zum Pontifikat Coelestins V* was Seppelt's special subject. Seventy years later, in his resignation speech, Ratzinger quoted almost verbatim from the text of Celestine's resignation, which he had heard first in the Füstenried lectures.

The special strengths of the Munich school were its biblical exegesis and its focus on the church fathers, and also its ecumenical emphasis. With the theologian Friedrich Stummer, 'a quiet and reserved man whose forte was strictly historical and philological work', Joseph could plunge anew into the world of the Old Testament. He was clear that the Bible had to be read as a whole, since both parts revealed the mystery of Christ, prefigured in the Old Testament: 'I came to understand that the New Testament is not a different book of a different religion which, for some reason, had adopted the Jewish Scriptures as a kind of preface. The New Testament is nothing but an interpretation of the "Law, Prophets and Writings" [...] from the standpoint of the story of Jesus.'[13]

However makeshift the accommodation in Fürstenried Palace was, it did not seem to affect the fresh spirit in the newly opened university. On the contrary. The rough-and-ready set-up inspired a progressive feeling. Above all, there was the will to let different theological views live in peaceful coexistence. But that did not mean there were no rivalries or limits. They were often 'warned' against many theologians, such as the Jesuit Augustin Bea, the future cardinal and influential spin doctor of the Second Vatican Council, who taught biblical geography and archaeology. Some professors would not accept students for doctoral work or habilitation if they had been recommended by 'false' colleagues.

Important stimulation was provided by the writings of August Adam, one of the great twentieth-century Catholic theologians, almost forgotten today. Like his 12 years older brother and fellow Catholic priest Karl, August Adam was an energetic anti-fascist. He warned against the church becoming bourgeois and insisted on a radical personal vocation and quest for holiness. Without constant striving for inner conversion and reflection, church members could, of course, regard themselves as 'correct' Catholics, uprightly attending Sunday Mass. But then they would badmouth their neighbours without any pangs of conscience. Adam's appointment to a chair of moral philosophy at Passau College was blocked by circles who regarded his views on sexual morality as the depths of indecency. The hostilities were even sharper when Adam's *Primat der Liebe* (*The Primacy of Love*) was published in 1931. The future pope described that book as 'a key text of my youth'.

Adam never tired of repeating that the accusation Christianity was hostile to the senses was baseless. The theologian stuck fast to the church's sexual teaching, at the same time insisting that chastity should not be seen as the core of all the virtues. That was love. Sexuality should be valued openly and positively. The sexual instinct should not be regarded as 'impure' but as a 'gift', hallowed through charity and love of neighbour: 'In Eros, passion and love, the sensual and the spiritual meet and become close-linked, filled with pleasure and charged with energy. Charity is Christian Eros baptized, which heightens the the natural love instinct because its power comes from supernatural sources.'

Adam held that the virtue of love should not be separated from sensual love: 'Eros is not just that demonic power that annihilates and destroys and ensnares all life in its bonds.' Love between a man and a woman, which the Creator instilled in the human heart as one of the strongest drives for the preservation of the species, is also one of the strongest power sources for human culture. 'Love is the blazing fire,' said Adam, 'which kindles the force of all ideals in the young heart, the energy source in God which leaps over all walls.' That inspiration was clearly echoed exactly 75 years later in *Deus caritas est*, Benedict XVI's first encyclical.

Once again chance – or 'Providence', as Ratzinger would say – offered the young student a decisive teacher. But this time it was a living one, not a dead one like Augustine. It was the temperamental Rhinelander Gottfried Söhngen, a tall, sturdy man with a prominent head. An unconventional theologian, he became the most influential figure in the future pope's learning years. He was a cheerful, vigorous and original priest, who was the product of a mixed marriage and therefore concerned with the ecumenical question. In addition, he was an impressive artist and music lover. In short, said Ratzinger, 'my Master'!

'From the very first lecture I was enraptured,' said the student. With Söhngen 'a word that had often been on your lips and you thought you understood, became clear in its depth.' For example, the famous scholastic axiom *gratia supponit naturam* ('grace presupposes nature'). Ratzinger found that Söhngen opened up a 'wholly new potential for Christian awareness: being a Christian did not mean breaking away from nature, but an enhancement and completion of it. Hence the great fulfilling Yes.' That expressed the wholeness of Catholicism, which did not separate spirit and body, God and human, grace and nature, but bound them together. 'Indeed, the word "catholic" itself seemed to express that basic idea,' Ratzinger enthused, 'the idea of the all-embracing, the great universal Yes of the analogy of being.' From Söhngen he acquired 'a truly theo-logical way of thinking, that is, God's Word becoming human word'. It 'made the ordinary become meaningful and revealed it in its true depth'.[14]

This clearly expressed Ratzinger's theological approach: the striving for 'depth', a way of thinking that makes 'the ordinary become meaningful' and sees 'God's word in its true depths'. Ratzinger confessed it was important for him to 'think through again what was currently being said' in order to raise what was known beforehand to a new level. Of course, not only his favourite teacher but the whole Munich faculty 'really shaped him'. That included dogmatics, taught by Michael Schmaus. Or the lectures by the liturgy expert Josef Pascher. But 'the highlight and the one who influenced me most, and from whom I discovered and learned most about what theology is, was of course Söhngen.'[15]

Söhngen was well known for enjoying going against the grain. However, he never said something on impulse; what he said was always well considered, even his provocative remarks. As a theologian, he united his criticism of current practices with steadfast faithfulness to the church. For that church was not set only in the present but came from eternity and was going to eternity. 'He had a natural rhetoric and way of speaking, which drew you directly into the matter,' said Ratzinger. Above all, with Söhngen there was 'that direct confrontation with problems'. 'He did not just present a kind of academic structure, that stands by itself and is magnificent. But he asked: What is it really like? Does it concern me? And that was what got to me.'[16]

The professor impressed Ratzinger, both 'as a character and a thinker'. Söhngen radiated 'a Cologner's zest and cheerfulness'; he enthused, in retrospect, through his 'rhetoric, mirth and joy of life'. There was the undogmatic approach, the great intellectual curiosity, which was always combined with care not to go for tradition instead of the new, but to treat it as the source of the new. His master was someone who 'always started from the sources in his thinking – beginning with Aristotle and Plato, through Clement of Alexandria and Augustine to Anselm, Bonaventure and Thomas, on to Luther and finally to the Tübingen theologians of the previous century'.[17] The approach of working 'from the sources', and 'not at second hand' but getting to know 'all the great figures of intellectual history by engaging with them personally' became very important for Ratzinger. 'He also helped you to leap over the ditch of the past and learn how history was still present.'[18]

Söhngen was born on 21 May 1892 in Cologne and came to theology through philosophy. He got his doctorate in 1914 with a historical-critical study of Immanuel Kant's theory of judgement. Then he became famous for his research on the theology of Thomas Aquinas. With Thomas he inquired into the cause and purpose of all things. And to answer that question he brought in current philosophy. At the same time, he engaged with Evangelical theology and belonged to an inter-denominational discussion group. 'What was seen later as new theology, new exegesis and new liturgy,' Läpple proudly declared, had long been 'refined and matured' by the students in Fürstenried.

In his lectures, Söhngen spoke completely freely. His only reference point was a small slip of paper with three or four words on it – and a couple of question marks. As soon as inspiration struck him, observed

Rupert Berger, he left the lectern and came to stand among his audience, 'set his eyes on the Infinite – then out it came'. With his students he took up the dispute with the Reformed theologians Karl Barth and Emil Brunner in Zurich. He engaged with the Mystery Theology of the Benedictine Odo Casel. In his lectures, he broached Husserl, who had opened a crack in the door for metaphysics with his phenomenology. There was also Heidegger, who asked questions about being, and Scheler, who asked about values.

There was also Nicolai Hartmann, professor of theoretical philosophy, who sought to develop a metaphysics in a strongly Aristotelian spirit. As a proponent of critical realism, Hartmann had laid 'the foundations of a metaphysics of knowledge', a work that made him suddenly famous. In his book *Das Problem des geistigen Seins,* he maintained that human beings can never fully grasp the nature of reality existing independently from subjective perception. Knowledge was dependent on the relationship to what exists, which lies outside the narrow boundaries of awareness. From that, an ethics of values could be derived. In fact, there was a constantly changing awareness of values, but the nature of the values themselves was timeless. They originated 'from an ethically ideal sphere of a realm with its own structures, laws and order'.[19]

Based on the Bible and salvation history, Söhngen's thinking aimed to rediscover forgotten islands and at the same time press forward into new territory – without losing sight of the 'unity of theology'. His master student called it 'breaking through to the reality that lay behind the words'. It was about having 'the courage to embark on the adventure of finding the truth'.

'Thinking from the sources as a starting point' later became the 'trademark' of Ratzinger's theology. He 'always quoted the text and then stretched out towards problems and challenges of the present,' observed Läpple. 'For him there was no good exegesis of a scriptural text if you did not start from the interpretation that the church had given it through the fathers. That was *traditio vivens,* living tradition.' Ratzinger was also to take over another characteristic from his master. Söhngen refused to ignore an interesting thinker just because he had unorthodox views. 'He took care always to go for the best of what was to be found in any writer or theological view,' said Läpple. It was important to him whether new scientific ideas could be integrated or whether they were dealing with theological dynamite that had to be deactivated.

To sum up, Ratzinger took from his professor:

unhampered access to current topics;
new approaches informed by the liturgical movement;
historical-critical investigation of tradition;
sympathy for the philosophical-theological 'Nouvelle Théologie';
the ecumenical impulse;
a passion for clear formulation of your own thinking, even if it was deviant, as the precondition for genuine dialogue.

In Söhngen's discussion of controversial theology you could confront an uncomfortable argument without immediately falling into moral abuse of your opponent. However, in one thing the professor and the student strongly disagreed. Söhngen was no friend of Rome and made no secret of his distance from the Vatican. 'Ratzinger never joined in the grumbling about the pope, the Congregation for the Doctrine of the Faith, or about what "that lot in Rome" were doing now, as we other students did,' said a fellow student, Joseph Finkenzeller; 'he was not only a very faithful but also a very churchy person.'

Ratzinger was particularly impressed by Söhngen's 'passion for the truth and resolute questioning'. His professor was never content with any kind of theological positivism, 'but very seriously raised the question of the truth and so also the question of what to believe now'. Söhngen's performances reminded him of Socrates, 'who woke up Athens from its self-righteous, complacent and comfortable daily life, and asked awkward questions. So awkward that they executed him, but then they recognized that he had told the truth. For people often flee from the truth, hide from it, because it demands what they don't want.'[20]

Ratzinger stressed he had never thought of himself as a master student. That would have been silly, 'because I was still just a boy, so to speak, and just beginning to inquire about things'.[21] On the other hand, Söhngen recognized his student's extraordinary talent early on, without letting him know. Indeed, he once invited him to the opera. But there were hardly any private conversations and when they occurred, 'they were about things like the idea of the church'. However, the professor left others in no doubt about his high regard for his favourite student. 'That Joseph Ratzinger's well bright,' he would say in a Cologne accent. With this student, he once said, it was like it had been for Albertus Magnus (Albert of Cologne) when he announced: 'My student will roar even louder than me!' That student happened to be Thomas Aquinas.

When Gottlieb Söhngen was buried, on 19 November 1971, in Cologne, the city of his birth, his master student gave the address. Once again he summed up what distinguished the great teacher in his eyes:

> Söhngen was a radical and critical questioner. At the same time he was a radical believer. What constantly fascinated us, his students, about him was that these both went together: the fearlessness with which he put every question, while taking for granted that faith had nothing to fear from an honest search for knowledge. So he was not alarmed that the thinking of an individual or a whole period can be at a loss and helplessly in contradiction. He knew that it was not necessary to force solutions, where they honestly could not be found [...] It was also clear to him that a theologian does not speak in his own name, however much of himself he gives, but stands for the faith of the church, which he does not discover but receives.[22]

Events came thick and fast. In Fürstenried, a time of nagging questions began for Joseph – and the first great crisis for his vocation. First, at the beginning of May 1948, together with three other candidates, he received the tonsure – in cassock and surplice, with candle in hand – from Cardinal Faulhaber, in the archiepiscopal house chapel. The bishop gripped the scissors and cut five small tufts of hair from their heads, in the shape of a cross. 'May the Holy Spirit,' Faulhaber prayed, protect 'these servants of God' from the world and earthly lusts, promote the growth of virtues in them and 'bring them the light of eternal grace'. The tonsure is a symbol of the candidate's renunciation of the world and earthly vanity. It is only given when there are sufficient signs of a real vocation and aptitude for becoming a priest. According to the law of the church, anyone who undertakes to receive Holy Orders when he is unfit or unworthy risks excommunication. 'The Lord is my portion, my heritage and my chalice,' Joseph said in the ancient form of words, before the bishop's blessing. 'He is the one who gives me my inheritance.'

Faulhaber often visited Fürstenried, carrying a case to bring the students something to eat. He had specially got some black material from Rome for his young theologians, so that each of them could have a suit made from it. Newly ordained in the minor orders, from now on they belonged to the clergy and were authorized as lectors and to give communion. In addition, they could hold ritual objects, such as a particular chalice, which the altar servers were forbidden to touch and which a sacristan was only allowed to touch with special permission. The minor orders were an essential step towards becoming priests, but the final decision was only taken at the stage of ordination as sub-deacon and deacon.

At that time in Poland a curate named Karol Wojtyła was writing his treatise *Liebe und Verantwortung* (*Love and Responsibility*), in which, among other things, he dealt with sexual excitement and fake orgasms. The unusual priest had discussed questions about marriage on his hiking and canoe trips with young people. When talking about love and reproduction, he recommended engaged couples to strengthen their self-discipline by not continually meeting.

In his place of study, Joseph Ratzinger also heard a tone he had not yet heard. On the one hand, he was fascinated by knowledge: 'I found it wonderful to enter into the great world of the history of faith,' he noted. Wholly new 'horizons of thinking and believing' had opened up for him. He had learned not only to inquire into the 'fundamental questions about humanity' but also to 'ponder questions about my own life'. And these became very challenging for him. Gloomily, he mentioned in his autobiography a 'time of very painful decisions'. Fellow students remembered how they saw him pacing for hours through the Fürstenried park, with his hands behind his back.

The secret had a name. A female one. It was never revealed. However, even in our first interview book, *Salz der Erde* in 1996, Ratzinger indirectly referred to it. Yes, he said, there had indeed been doubt about his vocation: 'particularly in the six years of theological study, you run into so many human problems and questions. Is celibacy right for me? Is being a priest right for me?'[23] He had asked himself 'whether I am prepared for all that throughout my whole life and whether it really is my vocation'. In a conversation on Bavarian Radio he confessed that finding himself was very 'hard won'. 'I had to come to terms with myself, with whether I could do it, whether I should do it, whether I would stick it out.'

His brother, Georg, suffered less from such questions:'Celibacy was no problem. It was just how it was. You had decided on it. That was it.'[24] It was different for Joseph. In our conversation Ratzinger hinted at the background to his problem. In the two years in Fürstenried Palace on the edge of the city, they had 'lived very closely together': 'Our community life was not only between professors and students but also between men and women students, so that in our daily meetings the question of renunciation and what it meant came up in a very practical way.'[25] Actually, he had 'never felt a direct desire for a family'. But, as he put it, he 'had been affected by friendship'. Years later I put the question to him, whether, since love was one of his central themes as a theologian and pope, he had personally experienced deep love, or whether it had remained just a philosophical subject for him. The pope emeritus answered:'No, no, no. If you have not felt it, you can't talk about it. I first experienced it at home, with my father, mother, brother and sister. And, well, I don't want to go into private details, but I have felt it, in various shapes and sizes. I have always recognized that being loved and loving others is vital for being able to live.'[26]

The student was a good-looking young man. Cultured, shy but polite and charming. It is not difficult to imagine how attractive to women fellow students this highly intelligent, bright young man, brimming with knowledge and yet so modest, might have been. 'Ratzinger knew my wife better than I did,' the future professor Wilhelm Gössmann reported. 'He proofread her doctoral work on the Annunciation in the theology of the Middle Ages.' With his 'huge linguistic talent' Joseph occasionally spoke 'in an almost mannered way', his friend Berger remarked, but was 'always fascinating, especially for women'.

For example, for Uta Heinemann, the daughter of the future German federal president Gustav Heinemann. She had converted to Catholicism, and as a young theologian she wanted to work with special devotion. 'Ratzinger struck me then as very intelligent,' she recalled, 'he was the star student.' She had sought a partner 'who would not suddenly plant a kiss on my cheek, when we sat for hours all alone in a big empty lecture room'.[27] Later Heinemann became a furious opponent of her fellow student, whom she accused of hostility to sex and women. In Munich, they had translated their doctoral theses into Latin together.

There was also Esther Betz, the daughter of a Rhineland newspaper publisher. She studied in Munich from 1946 until 1953 and worked as the private secretary of Professor Schmaus. For her, Ratzinger had 'always had something seraphic and celestial about him'. She had felt 'his tenderness and intelligence as if he was not altogether from this world. You had the feeling he needed to be protected.'[28]

It is not clear exactly who the young Ratzinger had his eye on. In our final conversations I wanted to go into the question more precisely:

'You spoke of Fürstenried in your memoirs as a "time of very painful decisions". Exactly what kind of pain was it?'

The pope emeritus replied, with a smile, that that was too personal and he could not say anything about it.

'Were you in love with a girl?'

'Perhaps.'

'So, yes?'

'It could be interpreted like that.'

'How long did that passionate time last? A few weeks? A few months?'

'Longer.'

For the reserved Benedict XVI, this was like an admission. At any rate, the statement clarified Ratzinger's rather cryptic remark in his memoirs. He was in love, and he felt loved in return. So he was not the firmly set man of God who subordinated every feeling to a career in the church. Of course, no one knew about it. Not even his brother. But he did not just push the thing away. He considered whether or not he was more suited to a career as professor of linguistics or history.

It was a hard struggle for Ratzinger. He weighed things up. He did some soul-searching. Who was he? What was his job? Would someone like him, who considered himself to be 'shy and quite unpractical', really be able to lead young Catholics as a priest? Could he 'get close to people', relate to children, old people and sick people, comfort those who were dying? In Georges Bernanos's *Journal d'un curé de campagne* he had read about the distress of a young priest who nearly broke down from the demands placed on him by his job, because he felt so inadequate. 'The average priest is hideous,' he read in the book, 'or rather the bad priest is an average priest. The really bad one is a monster.'

Ratzinger had believed he had found his way and decided on his life course once and for all. Amid the pressures of seminary life in the Freising Domberg, there had been no room for doubt. However, in Fürstenried there was not a committed community. The professors were scholars, rather than priests, and radiated scientific freedom. And ... there were girls. They sat at the back – but it was impossible to overlook them.

The student was clear that 'there is more to the vocation of a priest than delight in theology'. Parish work made quite different demands. As already mentioned, he confessed: 'I couldn't study theology in order to become a professor. Even though that was my silent wish.'

Ratzinger's way to faith was existential. He saw himself as a 'quite normal Christian person'. He had never felt 'illumination in the classical sense, half mystical or whatever'. However, he did also speak about an encounter with God in the beauty and mysteriousness of the old Roman Catholic liturgy. He said: 'The aesthetic aspect was so overwhelming, that it was a real meeting between God and me.' In Fürstenried the call of his heart finally prevailed. He felt that the question that had been bothering him about whether 'he could get on with people, lead youth groups etc.' was not really so important. There was more to it. What exactly that would be, he did not dare imagine. But he was reassured by the thought that God's protective hand would guide him. A sacrifice was demanded of him. A renunciation. But he did not decide *against* the girlfriend, he decided *for* something: a mission.

His inner battle raged for many months, until his ordination as a deacon, when in the autumn of 1950 he 'could finally say a convinced "yes"'. 'God always wants us to go further,' he said in our conversation; you had to 'keep learning' what he wanted from you. Human beings were not thrown into the world by accident, as

Heidegger said, 'but I am preceded by an awareness, an idea and a love. It is there at the heart of my existence.' And further: 'For me that means quite practically, my life is not accidental, but someone foresees and, as it were, goes ahead of me and thinks ahead of me and directs my life. I can refuse that or I can accept it, and then I notice that I am really being led by a "guiding" light. That does not mean human beings are completely determined, but that this purpose challenges their freedom.' Everyone must just 'try to learn what my life calling is and how do I answer that call, what is best of all for me'.[29]

Joseph Ratzinger was called upon to make many more renunciations during the course of his life. But what he renounced at Fürstenried must have be one of the most difficult. In this light, the confession he made at the point when he decided reads like a quiet prophecy: 'I was convinced – I don't know how – that God wanted something from me, that could only be achieved by my becoming a priest.'

The 'mystery of a vocation,' Ratzinger said decades later,[30] 'is that Christ invites us to leave everything in order to follow him more closely'. It was 'a movement of the spirit that persists throughout life'. Anyone who goes along with it experiences 'the beauty of a vocation that we could describe as a time of "being in love". Your inner self is filled with amazement, so you prayerfully ask: "Lord, why me?"' That question may develop a breath-taking dynamism. For 'the better you know Jesus, the more his mystery draws you in; the deeper you encounter him, the more he presses you to seek him.'

19

The Key Reading

In the autumn of 1949, Munich University in the Ludwigstrasse was refurbished enough for the theologians to be able to return to its familiar walls. The candidates for the priesthood moved into their quarters in the Georgianum seminary in the Ludwigstrasse, immediately opposite the university. Part of the building still lacked a roof, and on Saturdays Joseph was still involved in removing bricks and refuse in heavy wheelbarrows.

He found it hard to leave Fürstenried. He missed the walks in the park and the drama of his youthful romantic life crisis, which was painful but also beautiful. He shared his room on the third floor with his friend Rupert and another student. In the evening, when he climbed up the wooden ladder into his room – the stairs had been destroyed – he had to be careful not to be grabbed by the housemaster's German shepherd dog in the yard. There was no kitchen, but there was a stove and running water in the bedroom.

After the Almo Collegio Capranica in Rome, the Georgianum is the second-oldest Catholic seminary for priests in the world. It was founded in 1494 by Duke Georg the Rich. In its turbulent history it had nurtured Sebastian Kneipp, who gave his name to Kneipp-Medizin, and also a Georg Ratzinger, Joseph's active great uncle. For a time Georg had been a student and a very close collaborator with the theologian Ignaz von Döllinger, the key figure in the founding of the 'Old Catholics', who split from Rome.

At the Georgianum, compulsory attendance was only for the seven o'clock early Mass and for lunch. But who could afford cafés or restaurants? For lunch you had to bring food stamps – a meat stamp for about 50 grams – or the corresponding cash. Among the approximately 120 'Georgianers', there were priests who were catching up on their doctoral work after the turmoil of the war and barely left their desks. Others used their time in Munich to visit the Grünwalder football stadium on Sundays. At weekends, Joseph and Rupert preferred to go and see works of art in the city centre, which was almost empty of people. Or, thanks to the free tickets given to them by Berger's father, they enjoyed the opera and evening concerts in the Residenz Brunnenhof. In the theatre, they were fascinated by performances of Paul Claudel's *Silk Shoes* and Shakespeare's *A Midsummer Night's Dream*. 'Joseph was enthusiastic about everything beautiful,' Berger reported. But given his friend's reserved style, it did not mean that 'he exploded with joy'.

The Georgianum organized a celebration evening during Fasching (carnival) with music and drama. When, in a Last Judgement scene, the judge held up a copy of a work by the dogmatic theologian Michael Schmaus in one hand and one by the canon lawyer Klaus Mörsdorf in the other, each of the hooting students knew what sort of law books they would soon be stumbling over. The women fans of the dogmatic theologian were divided into three categories: first, *Schmausinen* (women students who worshipped the professor or were worshipped by him); second, *Schmausetten* (women students who were worshipped by the male students but were not approachable); and third, *Schmausinetten* (women students they could have hopes of).

In his new home, Ratzinger was impressed by the Feldherrnhalle, the Siegestor and the state library and the neighbouring Ludwigskirche. At the turn of the century these buildings had represented the perfect backdrop for the 'Golden Age' of that part of the city, whose liberal, open atmosphere attracted artists and 'artists in life' from all over the world.

'At last we took advantage of the broad horizons of a famous university,' his friend Rupert rejoiced. But in June 1950 the 'Synodal' was approaching, a final church examination comparable with the diploma today. The subjects were dogmatics, moral theology, canon law and the New Testament. It was conducted in the Georgianum rooms by a professor and a cathedral canon, who acted as scrutineer for the bishop. Joseph knew that the unpopular canon law would be his Achilles' heel. Indeed, with his marks for that he came nearly at the bottom of the list of 46 candidates.

Ordination for subdeacon and deacon in Freising Cathedral was set for 28 and 29 October, the feast of Christ the King. It was performed by the auxiliary bishop Johannes Neuhäusler, a former concentration camp prisoner, who stood in for the already very sick Cardinal Faulhaber. As a deacon, Joseph had the right to assist at High Mass and give communion. From now on, there was also the duty to pray the church office from the breviary every day. His brother Georg, who preferred to spend all day at the piano, called it 'time-consuming compulsory prayer'.[1] At least there was no more worry about living expenses. According to canon law, Joseph and Georg were now entitled, as clergy, to maintenance from the bishop.

Five years after the end of the war, the development of the German Federal Republic was taking clear shape. Unemployment remained static, hunger had been overcome and people were taking an interest in American limos on the streets, rock 'n' roll and Coca-Cola. In the election for the first German federal parliament on 14 August 1949, the CDU (Christian Democratic Union) and CSU (Christian Social Union) came top with 31 per cent (combined) of the votes. The Social Democrats got 29.2 per cent, and the FDP (Free Democratic Party) 11.9 per cent. In the election campaign, the CDU had promoted attachment to the West as the foundation for a Germany reunited in freedom. The left warned that alignment with the Western powers would aggravate the division of Germany even further. As there was not yet a 5 per cent hurdle, a total of 11 parties entered the Parliament in the provisional federal capital in Bonn. The election winner, the 'Old Man of the Rhine', the 73-year-old Konrad Adenauer, presented himself as an 'interim chancellor', a period that in the end lasted for 14 years.

In June 1950 the attack by the Communist North Korea on South Korea introduced a new escalation into the East–West conflict. A third world war seemed to be in the offing. In divided Germany, the fear increased that they might also become victims of an attack by superior Communist forces. At the same time, in the former Western zones an unprecedented symbiosis had developed between the state and the Catholic Church. Soon there would even be talk of a 'Catholic decade', which led the Protestant church leader Martin Niemöller to warn that, under Catholic influence, the German

Federal Republic was threatening to become a creation that was 'conceived in Rome and born in Washington'.

The post-war era had changed the proportion of the Christian denominations. After the end of the war, 95.8 per cent of the German population were members of the two national churches. At 51.5 per cent, the majority of the population still belonged to the Protestant Church. But because of the influx of refugees, the Catholic percentage had risen from about 33 per cent before 1945 to 44.3 per cent.[2] Catholicism not only provided the leading political personnel – nine of the 15 members of the federal cabinet were Catholics – but also undertook the vital roles in the shaping of the new beginning. In fact, according to an oft-quoted formula of the sociologist Gerhard Schmidtchen, Catholics were the 'actual discoverers' of the Federal Republic, and its 'guarantors of order' as architects of a new democratic state.[3]

Church attendance, pilgrimages, processions, full churches also graphically reflected the new situation. In the Adenauer era, between 1949 and 1963, the number of regular churchgoers rose from 51 to 55 per cent among Catholics, and from 13 to 15 per cent among Protestants. In the year 1946 alone, 31,313 citizens entered the Catholic Church. On the Protestant side the increase was even greater, with 47,000 admissions in 1945. However, between 1933 and 1939, 1.3 million members had left. And by the year 1949, the 43,000 admissions were more than outweighed by 86,000 who left.[4]

'The Catholics felt more secure in the new Federal Republic, safer than ever before since the Reich's foundation,' said the researcher Franz Walter.[5] In order to understand their new exhilaration, we need to take a look at history. In the Protestant-oriented German Reich founded in 1871, the German Kaiser functioned not only as the political ruler but also also as the supreme head of the Evangelical churches. Bismarck's 'Kanzelparagraph' ('Pulpit paragraph') of November 1871 threatened all Catholic clergy with punishment if they spoke about matters of state 'in a way that endangers the public peace'. Then followed the ban on clergy teaching in state schools. Under the 'Jesuits Law' of 4 July 1872, hundreds of religious houses were abolished and thousands of Jesuits, Lazarists and Redemptorists were expelled. In 1875, Prussia ordered the abolition of all convents that were not engaged in care services. Little by little, seminaries for priests were closed down. In 1874–5 in Prussia nearly half the Catholic bishops were imprisoned; others were deposed. At the height of the *Kulturkampf* more than 1,000 Catholic parishes and nine dioceses were abandoned, because priests and bishops were in prison or in exile. Only 24 of the 4,000 priests and none of the bishops submitted to the coercive measures.[6]

The persecution was even more painful because, 70 years earlier, the Catholic Church had had to overcome powerful attacks in the course of secularization. On 23 February 1803, the *Reichsdeputation* ('Imperial Deputation') ordered the expropriation and secularization of 22 Catholic dioceses, 80 abbeys with *reichsunmittelbar* status (i.e., self-governing under the Empire) and 200 convents. The measures were a result of the Napoleonic occupation. In France the widespread campaign of de-Christianization had begun in 1793. After their bloody revolution the Jacobins had not only brought in a new calendar, in order to destroy the church's weekly and yearly rhythm. They had also, at the insistence of Robespierre, decreed in 1794 a kind of civil religion, officially called the 'Religion of Reason'. Instead of the former Christian Mass, now in Notre-Dame in Paris they celebrated the 'cult of Reason' and the deistic 'cult of the Supreme Being'. The demolition of the cathedral had been determined upon and was only stopped by the bold intervention of the citizens of Paris. In Germany, the last restrictions on Catholic lives were only lifted in the Weimar Republic's constitution of 1919. Because of the repressive measures, Catholicism developed an unprecedented inner cohesion and formed the famous 'Catholic milieu', which persisted until the 1970s.

The 'Catholic spring' also changed the theology student Joseph Ratzinger's world. Romano Guardini's slim first book, *Vom Geist der Liturgie* (*The Spirit of the Liturgy*) had stirred a totally unexpected interest in the church. The liturgical movement sought a return to the origins, in order to purge the essential elements of the liturgy from accretions that over the centuries had settled on it like a layer of dust and dirt. Ratzinger was at first sceptical about the movement. He thought he saw in it 'a one-sided rationalism and historicism', which 'concentrated too much on form and historical origin'.[7] His mentor Gottlieb Söhngen criticized it as an 'iconoclastic fuss'. What also bothered the student about the movement was 'the narrow-mindedness of many of its adherents, who only wanted one form to be valid'.[8]

However, gradually Ratzinger's scepticism began to give way. 'The church came alive for us above all in the liturgy and in the great wealth of its theological tradition,' he enthused in retrospect about the 'thrilling years of my theological studies'. He could 'only be astonished' at all that was later 'said about the pre-conciliar church'. In fact, as a modern theologian – as he thought of himself – he had had a 'feeling of breakthrough: a theology asking questions with new boldness, and a spirituality that was doing away with what was fusty and obsolete, to lead to new joy in salvation'.[9]

After the end of the war Guardini, who had been expelled from the city by the Nazis, was given his own professorship at the University Catholic Faculty immediately opposite the Georgianum. Ratzinger had Guardini's small Jesus book on his shelf. It was 'one of the first books I read after the war – after other Jesus books seemed boring and with nothing to say'.[10] When Guardini (who was born in Verona in 1885 and grew up in Mainz) lectured in the Audimax lecture hall, he was in danger of being crushed by the mass of students. His female admirers stood ready to storm the lectern with torches in case of a power cut, so that the master would not be interrupted in his brilliant lecture.

In contrast to many other theologians, there was a coherence of content and form in Guardini which valued linguistic aesthetics. Guardini's writing brought countless people to an inward view of the faith. Many of them went to Rothenfels Castle in Franconia, the spiritual centre of the liturgical movement, to be introduced by Guardini into life wisdom, faith and liturgy. The brothers Georg and Joseph also had a short meeting with the scholar there. There were no other meetings. But later on, Ratzinger dedicated his 'Advent Sermons' to the great theologian, having obtained the master's personal consent.

In liturgical questions Ratzinger had Guardini for theory, and for the practice he had Josef Pascher, the Director of the Georgianum, who was an energetic supporter of the liturgical movement. Instead of the *Puncta mediationis,* suggestions for meditation each evening, three times a week the pastoral theologian invited them into the chapel and gave them half-hour talks on liturgical life, the texts and forms of the liturgy and the spirituality of priestly pastoral care. 'Without any set pattern,' as Ratzinger reported. And if after Vespers the Director occasionally went into the cellar to bring up a few bottles of the finest Riesling, that did not cause any interruption in the general enjoyment.

Pascher's lectures and good offices strengthened Ratzinger's attraction to the liturgical movement. That would also appear in his later contributions to the Second Vatican Council. 'In the liturgical movement and theological renewal of the first half of this century, there arose a real reform which caused a positive change.' He was convinced that it 'was only possible because there were people who loved the church keenly but "critically", with the gift of discrimination, and were prepared to suffer for her'.[11] In a 1962 Festschrift in honour of Söhngen, Ratzinger praised the fact that 'the liturgical movement discovered the emptiness that lay behind the anxiously guarded formulas', so that wholly new possibilities of Christian awareness were revealed. It had been a recovery of true Catholicism from the ascetic narrowness of the nineteenth century: 'The earlier theologians were read with new eyes. We refocused on the teaching of the Greek fathers about the consecration of the world in the flesh of Christ, the world's homecoming in the body of the Lord.'[12]

In the foreword to his own book *Der Geist der Liturgie* (*The Spirit of the Liturgy*), published in 2000, Ratzinger, as Prefect of the Congregation for the Doctrine of the Faith, went even further in his praise for the liturgical movement: 'It contributed vitally to the rediscovery of the liturgy in all its beauty, its hidden riches and timeless greatness as the the living soul of the church and the core of Christian life. It led to the liturgy being celebrated in a "more essential" way.'[13]

Meanwhile, at the university Joseph was taking seminars for the dogmatic theologian Michael Schmaus when he was engaged elsewhere. However, in Schmaus's lectures he would leaf through books in a bored way; the talk didn't inspire him much. In fact, for a long while his thoughts had been on a much more important project. It had begun on a December day in 1949, when Joseph Ratzinger's whole 'theological fate' was decided, as he himself said.[14] It set his course and was one of the crucial moments of his life.

Gottlieb Söhngen had conducted his favourite student's first examination. Immediately afterwards he had called him into his study in Fürstenried, and at first he just leafed through the notes lying on his desk. Since the publication of the encyclical *Mystici corporis Christi* on 29 June 1943, in which Pius XII defined the church as the 'mystical body of Christ', the idea had remained in the fundamental theologian's head. The pope's 'faith encyclical' aimed at overcoming the intellectual narrowness in the exposition of the church's teaching. The key statement said: 'To define this true church of Jesus Christ, which is the one, holy, Catholic, apostolic Roman church, we shall find nothing more noble, more sublime, or more divine than the expression "the Mystical Body of Jesus Christ".' Söhngen had, of course, realized that although the term 'mystical body of Jesus' related to Scripture and the church fathers, it did not, in fact occur in the Bible at all.

The professor kept on leafing through his notes until he suddenly turned to Ratzinger. In a rather roundabout way, he asked his master student whether he could imagine himself wanting to do a doctorate under him. After the war, when pastors were needed for the communities, being able to write a doctorate was both an accolade and an exception. Cardinal Faulhaber hardly approved more than three doctorates per yearly intake of priests. The work, Söhngen continued, was on the term 'people of God' in the church fathers, in relation to *Mystici corporis Christi*. Joseph realized that that was a huge, almost insuperable challenge for a 20-year-old. The task was also not without risk. It would be questioning a papal doctrinal document, which could be seen as a provocation.

A scholar's career usually begins with a dissertation. It is said to be like a first love, and gives a preliminary indication of the direction a researcher's thinking is taking. Joseph did not need long to think about it. Yes, indeed! Of course he wanted to do a doctorate. How could he say no, when it was also to do with his great model, Augustine? Söhngen was happy because the course his protégé would take would be shaped by the church fathers, whose teaching *about* the church was also aimed at love *for* the church.

The subject covered the core of a debate that was currently raging in German theology. Some theologians did not approve of calling the church the 'body of Christ'. That would be equating the dynamism of the life of grace with mere membership of the community. Would the young doctoral student now discover what Augustine meant when he defined the church as the 'people of God'? Didn't that term relate only to the Jewish people, whom God had called from among the nations to reveal himself to them and to the world? And wasn't the term also contradicted by the sinfulness of Christians, which could hardly be reconciled with a 'mystical body'? Ratzinger's discoveries were powerful enough soon to be taken up by the Second Vatican Council and, in particular, by Pope Paul VI. But more of that later.

The study years were drawing to a close. Söhngen had carefully led his protégé towards the great subjects and tasks and and made him increasingly familiar with Augustine. However, the dissertation project was not carried any further until the synodal examination in June 1950. In that year it fell to Söhngen to be in charge of the so-called prize work. This was rewarded not only with a small cash prize. For the winner of the competition a doctorate *summa cum laude* also beckoned. Söhngen chose a topic that was tailor-made for Ratzinger: 'People and the House of God in Augustine's Teaching on the Church'. 'Söhngen had already allowed him to work on parts of that dissertation for all those years,' Rupert Berger believed, 'just him.'[15] At the same time, the professor made clear that other competitors should not raise their hopes. Basically, only one student was up to the task. Everyone knew who that was.

The theme had to be tackled within nine months. Then the text had to be submitted anonymously with a password. The deadline was April 1951, so immediately before ordination to the priesthood. Now Joseph's parental home became his headquarters. Books and notes lay everywhere. His brother and sister had to keep as quiet as possible. His parents went about on tiptoe. Joseph read. What a mountain of work! The whole of Augustine had to be read from that specific angle and different versions of the text compared. Church fathers contemporary with him had to be taken into consideration.

As if that were not enough, questions of the Eucharist, the liturgy and the ritual had to be looked at in their historical development. They also had to be confronted with current theological discussion. How could that be done within the short time? Eventually, Ratzinger got help from a book that his friend Alfred Läpple had pressed into his hands at the end of 1949, the German edition of *Catholicisme,* the much-discussed work by the French Jesuit Henri de Lubac, an exponent of the 'Nouvelle Théologie'. *Catholicisme,* de Lubac's first book, published in 1938, did not focus on what was specific to Catholicism as a denomination, but on catholicity as a dimension of the church overall. From the first moment of its existence, de Lubac had established, the church had been 'catholic', because it 'addresses the whole human being and includes the whole of human nature'. It was not about the number of members it had or how far its teaching had spread. The church 'was already catholic on the morning of Pentecost, when its members were gathered together in a small room,' said de Lubac, ' and it would remain so even if it declined drastically and lost most of its faithful.'

Catholicism meant equality, diversity, universality. 'Because she reaches what is fundamental to humanity,' the church was able 'to reach all people and enable their own "harmonies" to sound'. De Lubac adduced important witnesses for his argument. 'When Ambrose looks at the church, it seems to him to be as immeasurable as the world and the sky itself, with Christ as its sun. He envisages the whole *oribis terrarum* embraced by her, since he realizes that all people without regard to their origin, race or situation in life are called to unity in Christ, and that the church fundamentally already presents that unity.' He quoted Cardinal Newman, who said that, as the one ark of salvation, the church must shelter the whole of humanity in all its diversity in her big ship. From Augustine he took the sentence: 'As the only dining hall for the great banquet, the dishes of the whole of creation must be brought into her.'

De Lubac came from Cambrai, in the far north of France. He spent his novitiate as a Jesuit in St Leonards on Sea, a suburb of Hastings, because Jesuits were forbidden to teach in France. The French Revolution from 1789 to 1799 had fomented passionate hatred against the church and against the Jesuit order in particular. In 1880, 37 Catholic colleges were dissolved. Between 1903 and 1904 about 20,000 members of religious orders were expelled and diplomatic relations with the Holy See were broken off. During the First World War, an atheist fellow soldier stimulated de Lubac's first literary activity to open modern people's eyes to the true meaning and beauty of faith and life in the church.

As a professor in Lyon, the cradle of Christianity in France, de Lubac combated anti-Semitism, joined the underground to oppose the Nazis and was hunted by the Gestapo. He came into contact with the ecumenical movement and met the young Swiss pastor Roger Schutz, who, together with Max Thurian, had founded the Evangelical religious community of Taizé during the 1940s. Before the Second World War, de Lubac had published *Corpus mysticum,* a theological history of the Eucharist, in which he showed how, even within the church, awareness of the actual mystery of Holy Communion had gradually disappeared. A third book, *Le drame de l'humaisme athée* (*The Tragedy of Atheist Humanism*), came out in 1944 and, according to Lubac's biographer Rudolf Voderholzer, 'clearly described the features of spiritual resistance to totalitarianism'. The basic thesis of the work, said Voderholzer, was 'the tragic misunderstanding of modern humanism, which sets God and humanity in a competition, and concludes that dependence upon God debases humans and makes them unfree'. 'They reject God as a restriction of humanity,' declared de Lubac, 'and they do not see that by their relationship with God, humans have "something eternal" in them. They reject God as if he enslaved humanity – and do not see that, through their relationship with God, humans escape all slavery.'[16]

A third of the text of *Catholicisme* consisted of quotations from the sources. De Lubac wanted to gather 'from the neglected treasury of the church fathers' that 'great crowd of witnesses' who showed how 'all who are faithful to the one church and live by the same faith in the same spirit, belong together without exception'. The illustrious names included Gregory of Nyssa, Severus of Antioch, Fulgentius of Ruspe, Baldwin of Canterbury, Theodore of Mopsuestia, Julian of Norwich, Adelmann of Lüttich – and, not least, great masters such as Bernard of Clairvaux, Origen, Ambrose and Augustine.

In *Catholicisme,* de Lubac inveighed, above all, against a privatized, moralizing individual 'patchwork' faith: I seek what suits me for myself and believe for myself alone. 'The church is a mother. But unlike other mothers, she draws to her those who are to be her children and keeps them united together in her womb. Her children, says St Maximus, come to her from all sides: men, women, children. However different they may be in race, nation, language, life style, work, knowledge, dignity, fortune, she makes them all new in spirit.'

This was not just allegorical. According to the apostle Paul, Christian newness had given rise to a new nation, the people of the new covenant. A spiritual Israel had replaced the Israel of the flesh. 'The tribe of Christians,' as Eusebius said, 'the family of those who honour God' calls all people to divine life, to the eternal light to bring forth that mysterious organism, which will only be full grown at the end of time, in perfect unity. St Cyprian also understood it like that: now whoever has the church as a mother can have God for a Father.'

'When the work appeared in France,' wrote Hans Urs von Balthasar, who translated the book, under the title *Katholizismus als Gemeinschft* (*Catholicism as Community*) – it was later given the title *Glauben aus der Liebe* (*Faith from Love*) – it gave 'the key thinkers a terrible fright. Was it possible that this had been so long disregarded? Didn't it mean re-laying the foundations of what the nature and mission of the church was about?' Balthasar summed up: '*Catholicisme* caused a groundswell, whose effect was hidden at first but all the more lasting: it was a conversion.'[17]

Catholicisme broadened Ratzinger's reading for his doctorate in an ideal way: 'I not only got a new and deep understanding of the thought of the fathers, but also a new way of looking at both theology and faith. Faith was inner contemplation and by thinking with the fathers it became present again.' De Lubac had stood forth with matchless self-assurance: 'Seeing Catholicism as one religion among others, one doctrine among others, meant mistaking its nature.' Catholicism essentially meant the visible and invisible community of the faithful, an all-embracing community of all thought, faith, all epochs, races and nations, in short: the all-embracing.

Brimming with spiritual awareness and devotion, the book was like a revelation to the young theologian. He was moved by its radical and modern Christianity, which he had long sought. Ratzinger later spoke openly of his 'real breakthrough' and the 'key reading' of all his years of theological study, which introduced him to 'a new understanding of church and Eucharist'.[18] With de Lubac, whom he described as his most important and formative theologian (besides Hans Urs von Balthasar), he had experienced the joy 'of being able to see Christianity released from its rather stale formulations and newly embedded in modern life'.[19] He had 'never again found people with such a comprehensive theological and intellectual-historical breadth as Balthasar and de Lubac' and could hardly express 'how grateful I am for the encounter'.[20]

He also took his guideline directly from the French writer.'I never claimed to offer a philosophical system or a theological overview,' de Lubac declared, 'my aim was only to revive the memory of the church's great tradition, which I understand as the common experience of all Christian ages. That experience [...] protects her from aberrations, deepens her in the spirit of Christ and opens ways for her into the future.'[21] What harmony! Ratzinger also saw his task as thinking with the great masters of the faith and 'not to stop there in the ancient church', but to get beneath the incrustations to the real core of the faith, to restore its power and dynamism'. 'That impulse,' he repeatedly confirmed, 'is the constant of my life.'[22]

De Lubac's publications were enthusiastically received. But all at once the wind changed. Suddenly, a stiff breeze from Rome was blowing against the 'Nouvelle Théologie'. The first to come into the firing line was the Jesuit Pierre Teilhard de Chardin. The theologian and natural scientist was concerned with cosmology. He came to understand that the whole cosmos was directed towards the arrival of humanity. Then humanity's whole course ran up to the incarnation of Jesus Christ, which became the starting point of a new dynamic process. De Lubac championed his friend Teilhard de Chardin. Together with the poet Paul Claudel, they were instrumental in the rediscovery of Mary as the 'archetype of the church'. Teilhard wrote a hymn about her. The nature of the church was embodied in Mary, because the Catholic principle of the importance of human co-operation in salvation became visible in her.

Then suddenly de Lubac also came under suspicion of watering down the correct faith through a lot of 'novelties'. After his book Surnaturel (Supernatural) was published in early 1946, he was charged with relativizing divine grace. His Jesuit superiors reacted by forbidding him to teach or publish from 1950 until 1958, as well as banning him from the Lyon Catholic University. Pius XII also expressed his displeasure in the encyclical Humani generis, published on 12 August 1950. Even though the French theologian was not mentioned by name, insiders knew who was meant: 'Dear Friend,' Hans Urs von Balthasar wrote to his colleague,'I can hardly believe it. It is shocking, incomprehensible. However, that form of martyrdom is bound to confirm your work. You are already a winner; nothing will prevent your thoughts continuing to have their effect.'

When they heard in Munich about the measures taken against de Lubac, at first Söhngen described the process syllable by syllable in his lecture, Läpple recalled. After that, he went with Läpple and Ratzinger into his office, where he sat down at the piano without a word to thump out all the fury of his soul.'[23] De Lubac himself accepted the sanctions without protest. His relation to Christ, his love for the church, could not be diminished by it, he said. 'Although the shocks which have assailed me from outside may also shake me to the depths of soul,' he declared in 1950, 'they can do nothing against the great and essential things, which make up every moment of our life. The church is always there, as a mother, with her sacraments and her prayers; with the gospel she transmits intact; with her saints who surround us; in short, with Jesus Christ, whom she gives to us even more at the moment when she lets us suffer.'[24]

In 1953 de Lubac went back to Lyon. He suffered terrible pains from a head wound received when he was a soldier in the First World War. His students often found him sitting in an armchair or lying on the bed, motionless, hardly able to speak. In the same year, he published his description of the nature of the church, in which he deepened his confession. He began with a quotation from the church father Origen: 'As for me, my wish is truly to be a church person.' A genuine Catholic truly loved 'God's beautiful house', de Lubac continued. Come what may, the church was 'his spiritual home'. Nothing concerning her left him indifferent. 'He is rooted in her soil, he is shaped in her image, he nestles in her knowledge. With her riches he feels rich. He is aware, through her and through her alone, of sharing in God's immutability. From her he learns how to live and die. He does not direct her but is directed by her.'[25]

Joseph was most enthusiastic about the passages in *Catholicism* in which de Lubac described the church as Christ's incarnation extended into history. She was also wholly human, de Lubac stressed. Her renewal could only take place through a 'return to the sources', through study of the church fathers and a way of life that took the faith as seriously as the early Christians did. If Christianity was eternal, said de Lubac, it could never be finally grasped. Like God himself, it was always there; it was only people who were temporarily absent. When people thought they possessed it as an institution, then habits and self-concern became enormously powerful, and led to wasting and ruining the foundations of faith and the church.

We may mention in passing that in de Lubac the idea of paradox is closely bound up with his theology. For him the mysteries of faith, as an unfolding of the one original mystery, have a paradoxical structure. To give some examples: 'God creates the World for his own glory but also out of pure kindness; people are active and free but can do nothing without grace.' It was the same with the church: she was a visible community but also invisible. Or with Mary: she was both virgin and mother. Christ was both wholly God and wholly human. The human mind tried to resolve the polarity in the paradoxical statements by means of a one-sided simplification. That was the background to every heresy, namely a reduction of the complex form of the mystery into something easier for humans to grasp. Relating this to the concept of dogma led to the insight that dogma was keeping the Catholic truth open – and to the rejection of one-sided reductive interpretations. Contrary to the popular understanding of dogma as a narrowing of thought, dogma in the Christian sense was the freeing and broadening of the spirit towards that mystery which was astonishingly new and baffled human imagination.

De Lubac himself refused to accept the label 'Nouvelle Théologie', since 'he had never used the expression and he hated the idea. On the contrary, I have always tried to make known the church's tradition in what she offers that is the most universal and least subject to temporal change.' He quoted Augustine's phrase to speak of 'proving by reason to heathens how unreasonable it is not to believe'. Because 'insight *into* faith' is always followed by 'insight *through* faith'.

Before the beginning of the Vatican Council, de Lubac was rehabilitated. Pope John XXIII summoned him to Rome so that de Lubac could take part in the intensive preparation work for it. But he was only made a cardinal in 1983. In 1969 he had still refused the honour. One of de Lubac's main concerns was to reunite what belonged together and had been torn apart, thereby overcoming false alternatives. He never tired of of lamenting that history was no longer understood as the setting for God's revelation: 'God works in history, he reveals himself through history. And he goes even further: he himself enters history and so gives it a "deeper blessing", which compels us to take him seriously at last.' The church must again always 'reckon with the fact that where she proclaims the Word of God most powerfully, she will be understood very well and for that very reason rejected'.

As a theological student, Joseph had not dreamed that one day he would come into close personal contact with his great role model, and even establish a periodical together with him. De Lubac would also become a link for him to the Polish Karol Wojtyła. 'I bow before Father de Lubac,' said Wojtyła as pope on a visit to Paris. He had spotted the gaunt theologian in the audience at his lecture and immediately interrupted it. There was also a bow to the idol of his youth in 1998, when Ratzinger was in the French Embassy to the Holy See to receive the insignia of 'Commandeur de la Légion d'honneur'. He burst into praise of the great French theologians, de Lubac in particular, and shouted: 'Long live the friendship between France and Germany. Vive la France!'[26]

20

The Major Orders

Even during his work on his doctoral thesis Joseph must have realized that, with his approach to the 'Nouvelle Théologie', he had trodden on dangerous ground. A further excitement arose on All Saints' Day, 1 November 1950, with the publication of the dogma of the bodily Assumption of Mary into heaven.

Although Pope Pius XII received solid approval in the rest of Catholic Germany, the relationship of the Munich theology faculty to Rome was very cool. 'The response of our teachers was strongly negative,' Ratzinger reported. In a worldwide survey, initiated by the Curia in the run up to the proclamation, both Söhngen and Schmaus had expressed their disapproval. It was not so much the content of the new dogma; the bodily Assumption of Mary into heaven had long been mentioned in prayers, such as the rosary. But they objected to its being made a dogma.

An expert patristic scholar had established that the doctrine of the bodily Assumption of Mary was completely unknown before the fifth century. So it was impossible to say it belonged to the 'tradition of the apostles'. Ratzinger saw things differently from his professor, at least in later years. He thought that, when you understood tradition as a living process, in which the Holy Spirit continuously entrusted the church with the truth, tradition did not have to be restricted to what the apostles themselves had handed down. When Söhngen was urged by his Protestant friends that, should the Assumption become a dogma, he would have to leave the Catholic Church, he found an answer which his student classed as a prime example of critical but faithful theology: 'If the dogma comes,' his master's statement declared, 'I shall remember that the church is wiser than me, and trust her more than my own scholarship.'[1]

The prize work was forging ahead. At the same time, Ratzinger was struggling with preparations for his ordination as a priest. The seminarians were also subjected to a six-month practical part of the training. Its purpose was to train them to give religious instruction, prepare engaged couples for marriage, celebrate Mass correctly and administer sacraments such as baptism, confession and extreme unction. A cathedral music director taught them breathing techniques and Gregorian chant. A spiritual director (the Jesuit Franz von Tattenbach, later rector of the Germanicum in Rome and a missionary in Costa Rica) took care of the candidates' 'ascetic training' with talks, advice and by acting as a father confessor. The Augustinian father Gabriel Schlachter, a typical lay mission preacher, was responsible for homiletics. Alfred Läpple lectured on 'sacramental practice' – what had to be attended to liturgically, ritually and pastorally in the administration of the sacraments.

In singing instruction, an opera singer called Kelch tried to improve Joseph's voice, which was not easy because, as Ratzinger said, 'you can't change that much there'. He did better at baptism practice. Using a doll, you had to sprinkle the candidate for baptism with holy water without actually drowning him or her. 'I was not as clumsy as usual in that.'[2] The liturgical prefect took care of clothes and correct footwear. In the early mornings before Mass he paced along the line of students and checked them. The general inspection of the candidates' progress was carried out by the sub-rector. 'And slowly,' said Ratzinger, 'we got there!'

For homiletics – learning how to preach – three probationary sermons were arranged in Freising churches. They were limited to ten minutes. The text was to be typed and learned by heart. Reading a sermon from the page was absolutely taboo. Joseph was given the task of preaching at a children's service. As it fell on 23 April, St George's day, obviously the homily would be about the legendary dragon slayer. When Father Gabriel asked when they next met how Joseph's debut had gone, there was an embarrassed silence among the seminarians. The sermon had been great, he heard finally. The children had sat reverently on their benches but had looked very doubtful. Joseph had spoken about the 'proud knight's armour' and explained that there had never been a dragon like the one in the St George legend. Only very few of them could have understood what he was saying. It was too demanding for children.

'The dragon is humanity's horrible nightmare,' Ratzinger preached, 'and the monster we tremble at is the terrible power of evil, which is called the Devil.' Still: 'Anyone who has the armour and a sword need not fear him. For God's weapons are stronger than the dragon.' And one more thing to be going home with: 'St George is not there for us to admire. He stands there for us to see what we have to do. He tells us that there is a dragon and he tells us that we are all called to be dragon slayers.'[3]

Ratzinger's first sermons are significant because they show the great continuity from the very beginning in the future pope's theology. Even in these contributions we find the social criticism, together with the apocalyptic hope-inspiring tone of his message. After his start in the children's Mass, his first sermon for adults was set for 3 December 1950, at the 7.30 a.m. Mass in Freising Cathedral. According to the liturgical calendar, it was to be about Advent, specifically the return of Christ, one of Ratzinger's favourite subjects. The prospective priest began with a question: 'So are we really saved?' he asked his congregation. 'Is this world saved when we can clearly see its unsaved state on every street?' It was necessary to determine whether all the talk about salvation through Christ was not just a pipe dream, a false self-deception, a pretence by a church interested in hanging on to power.

Ratzinger continued:

Anyone who knows nothing but this present world must see a terrifying message in the signs of its destruction. Anyone who hopes for nothing but the salvation of the West, must be filled with hopeless dread at the possibility of its collapse. But it does not have to be like that for us. We know that the catastrophe of this world merely opens the door to the arrival of a new, more glorious world. We know that the horrors of the downfall of the old world are the birth pangs of the new. Early Christianity spoke of a second birth of Christ at the end of days from the labour pains of the dying world. But at that birth, Christ will appear as the Glorious One, who changes the world into its blessed future shape, which has been the dream of centuries. So is there still anything to hope for? Yes. Is there still an Advent? Yes. That full salvation, which will only come when Christ alone is king. We are praying for that world every time we say: May your kingdom come to us, your royal reign.[4]

In his public debut, he was bound to pay further homage to his great master:

So let us turn once more to St Augustine [...] Despite all his weakness, he dared the impossible, the psychologically nonsensical and absurd: to live henceforth as a Christian. Through faith in him who is Day and will become Day in us [...] Between the two births of Christ, the first in Bethlehem and the last at the end of time, Christ will continually be born in us and change this world's unholy night into the holy night of his birth.

In his second probationary sermon, given on 21 January 1951 at 7 a.m. in the Freising church of the Holy Spirit, once again we meet the 'whole' Ratzinger. He spoke about the workers in the Lord's vineyard. This story is about how the workers who arrived in the final hours of the day earned just as much as those whom the vineyard owner had hired in the first hour. Jesus told that parable 'on the way to the Holy City', so 'also on the way to his death'. In that hour, said Ratzinger the deacon, he spoke 'about the salvation of the whole world'. For:

The mystery of Christ is the fathomless kindness of God, the love with which God loves, simply because he is full of love, even when we don't love him, when we are sinners. That is something we should never forget: we did not become or remain Christians because we were good, but because God was good first [...] In baptism we did not just become righteous but Christians. Being a Christian means being a part of Christ himself, the continuation of Christ into our own time. In us Christ walks the streets of this world, in us he continues to live through the centuries [...] But of course we feel that we can't live up to all this. We can't show Christ to the world, as long we ourselves don't know him. So what does that mean? That we must keep asking him to stay close to us. We must keep struggling to become like him and behave accordingly.

Joseph's fellow students saw him poring over his books every free minute, 'secluded as a hermit', as one of them, Anton Mayer, reported. In Freising and Fürstenried, Ratzinger laid the foundation on which his theological thinking and activity would be based. His fundamental awareness was knowing that God existed. That this world was both material and spiritual. That earthly life was just a beginning in order to gain eternity. That this God not only helped but also required this world's order to be respected and would demand an account one day. But wasn't it also the moment to scrutinize the whole structure of Christian belief? Could an intelligent, critical person still believe in God after Auschwitz? Shouldn't we also consider whether God was actually a human invention, as atheists maintained? A metaphor to satisfy certain needs for explanation? What if Jesus was actually a figure that had acquired its own momentum by constantly being glorified?

This also related to the question of whether truth was an objective element of creation or whether it was negotiable according to the prevailing taste. In fact, for a long time the question of truth had not been a core concern for him, Ratzinger conceded. On the contrary, in the course of his spiritual journey he had constantly worried 'whether it wasn't actually a presumption to say we can know the truth – given all our limitations'.

It was only when he considered the question more closely that he had learned to 'observe and also grasp' that 'giving up on the truth solves nothing; it leads to the dictatorship of the arbitrary. Anything remaining would then actually be interchangeable. Humans debase themselves if they cannot know truth; if everything is actually only the product of an individual or collective decision.' It was disastrous to accept what is false, dishonest or wrong or to buy success and public prestige by sacrificing the truth or by approving the prevailing opinion, if it relied on untruth. Truth and reality belonged together. A truth that lacked reality would be a pure abstraction. And truth that was not processed 'in human wisdom' would not be a humanly accepted truth but a distorted truth.

At this stage, Ratzinger would say later, he found he had finally advanced enough to be able to 'enter into conversation with Augustine', which 'I had been trying to do in various ways for a long time'.⁵ Although there were already extensive monographs on Augustine's conception of the church, he kept finding new angles. He was clear that, for the apostolic fathers, the term 'God's house' referred not to the temple but to the community assembled at the Holy Eucharist, the people. That 'people of God' was the church. Following the apostle Paul, Augustine preferred to call it the 'body of Christ'. This was displayed in the celebration of the Eucharist as active *caritas* and realized *unitas,* as unity. Augustine spoke of the church as a body with Christ as its head. Head and body together formed *totus Christus*, the whole Christ.

However, Joseph also took dealing with the everyday tasks of clerical life seriously. The practical training in pastoral care had been 'an important inner struggle' for him. He had consciously resolved: 'I don't have to become a professor. It was very important for me that, if the bishop wanted, I was also prepared and willing to become a parish priest.'⁶

The day of his long and eagerly awaited ordination as a priest, 29 June 1951, was a bright summer's day. The bells of Freising Cathedral rang out for a feast day, including the mighty bell of St Corbinian. At the last minute, Joseph had managed to give in his prize work, thanks to his sister's help. Maria had typed a clean copy of the handwritten pages. Meanwhile, Georg was dealing with the preparations for ordination and first Mass. The most necessary items of clothing were bought: surplice, biretta, scapula, stole. According to the regulations, after ordination clerical dress had always to be worn. Joseph, however, still did not know whether his work would be accepted or rejected for a doctorate.

A week before the ordination service, the candidates had to undergo seven days of strenuous exercises in Fürstenried. For Joseph, the exercises went 'deep into my soul', because 'you retraced in your mind the whole path you had taken and gathered it all together – in the very place where I had studied.'⁷ Once again he asked himself: 'Am I worthy? Am I capable?' He might have thought of Maurice Blondel, one of his favourite writers. The Frenchman had felt called to become a priest, but after an intensive inner struggle and with the support of his confessor, he realized that his 'mission field' was the world of philosophy, which he had kept completely separate from faith and religion. And how right he was in his decision! His first work, *L'Action* (1893), became a manifesto for Catholic renewal. According to the philosopher Xavier Tilliette, for a whole generation of students *L'Action* was a 'release', because it debunked the smugness and self-sufficiency of secularism.

Freising Cathedral was packed. Those who had managed to get tickets could count themselves lucky. In the gallery sat the Ratzinger parents, now old and grey. Joseph's father had a moustache and homely metal-rimmed glasses. His mother wore proper Sunday best with hat and coat. Together with the 43 other candidates for ordination, Joseph had been getting ready since the small hours for the 'high point of my life'. Before breakfast there was a meditation, then they all lined up in the cathedral courtyard. The entry procession, kneeling before the bishop, had all been practised a hundred times. The ceremony would last from 8.00 until 12.45. Because of his frail health, the 82-year-old Cardinal Faulhaber had already arrived the previous evening.

Now Faulhaber swept into the cathedral with a five-metre-long train. The organ boomed, and the male choir struck up the motet *Exico caelibus magnus*. In alphabetical order Rupert Berger went first in the procession, Georg and Joseph followed, one behind the other. The people stood up. A murmur went through the crowd. Then came the moment when the cardinal called out loud and solemnly for the *Adsum*. And from 22 throats came the united thunderous reply: *Adsum*: 'Yes, I am here!' The question the bishop put next to his archdeacon sounded serious and severe: '*Scis illos dignos esse*. Do you know that they are worthy?' When the archdeacon had answered yes, the bishop turned to the people and asked the congregation, whether they agreed that these young men should be ordained as priests in the church. And only after no one had raised an objection could the service proceed.

The ordination candidates in their snow-white long albs with red cinctures were still lying stretched out like penitents on the floor. Their eyes were closed. Remaining there, together they called upon the Holy Spirit in the litany of the saints. It was a seventh-century liturgical prayer, alternating between the cantor and the

(*Above*) Joseph as a schoolboy in 1933 at entry level with a satchel at Aschau am Inn, his father's last family home.

(*Below*) The Ratzinger family in the mid-1930s. (*From left*) Joseph, born in 1927, Georg, born 1924 and Maria, born 1921. They are with their parents, Maria and Joseph.

The former police station and family home in Marktl am Inn, in which Benedict was born.

The family in 1932 with grandparents in the Bavarian Forest, at the parental home. The occasion was the grandmother's 80th birthday. Little Joseph is seated on the front right, his brother Georg on the front left and a little behind is their sister, Maria. In the back row are Ratzinger's parents. Also seated on the second row left is Uncle Alois, who was a priest.

The young Ratzingers in 1930 in Sunday clothes, taken in a studio. Joseph is holding his ball like an orb, as if to say, 'One day I will be a Cardinal.'

The three children in 1937 in Traunstein, straight from high school. Joseph (*right*) looks a little over-confident.

The farm building in the village of Hufschlag near Traunstein, acquired by Ratzinger's father after Hitler seized power. Joseph lived in this 200-year-old building from early 1937, through childhood and adolescence.

The future Pope in uniform, Munich, 1943. His job was to look out for enemy planes. This was after a spell in the Reich's Labour Service and being called up for the *Wehrmacht*.

Joseph Ratzinger in 1958 as Assistant Professor of Philosophical Theology at the High School in Freisung. He was considered by his pupils to be somewhat precocious, though a friend said his teaching was 'like an epiphany'.

Ordained priest on June 29th 1951 in Freisung Cathedral by Cardinal Michael von Faulhaber. On the left is brother Georg. Ratzinger said 'This was the high point of my life.'

Proudly holding his head up as a newly ordained priest, with Georg (*left*). In the middle is his friend Rupert Berger, whose father was interned in Dachau.

Family photo in July 1951 at Traunstein, after the ordination of the two brothers.

Ratzinger as chaplain in 1951 outside the Munich presbytery of the Church of the Holy Blood with another chaplain. Also in the photograph is Father Max Blumschein, under whom Ratzinger studied canon law, sacramental theology, Gregorian chant and youth work.

Mass in the mountains of the Chiemgauer Alps, Autumn 1952.

Solemn Mass at St Peter's in Rome during the Second Vatican Council. The 35-year-old professor was appointed a *peritus*.

A new star in the theological firmament. Joseph Ratzinger as professor at the University of Bonn.

As right-hand man to Cardinal Josef Frings of Cologne, at the opening of the Council.

Ratzinger with his sister Maria at the garden gate of Bergstrasse 6, Pentling, after his appointment to the University of Regensburg. Maria was a constant companion and support to him and helped to shape his life.

congregation, which invoked various classes of saints: *Kyrie, eleison. Christe, eleison. Kyrie, eleison.* Lord, have mercy. Christ, have mercy. The list went on for ever. There came St Andrew, St John and St James, all holy apostles, St Luke and St Mark, St Mary Magdalene and St Agnes, then St Boniface, St Augustine, all holy martyrs, all holy popes, bishops and teachers of the church, the holy superstars Benedict, Bernard, Francis und Dominic and so on. The litany ended with: 'Hear us, merciful Lord. /Amen. /And may the souls of the faithful departed through the mercy of God rest in peace. /Amen.'[8]

For his souvenir card for his first Mass, Joseph had chosen a motto quoting some words of the apostle Paul: 'Not that we are competent of ourselves to claim anything as coming from us; our competence comes from God' (2 Cor. 3.5). On a second card, he had printed another quotation from the second letter to the Corinthians: 'We are not lords of your faith but servants of your joy' (2 Cor. 1.24). He said later that as a student he had realized that 'the fixation of calling a priest "Reverend" was wrong, and the priest always strives not to be put on that high pedestal'. He had never ventured to imagine himself as 'Reverend' for anybody: 'Knowing that we are servants, that we are not lords, was not only comforting for me but vital for me to accept being ordained at all.'[9]

As he lay on the floor he felt how 'conscious of his own wretchedness' he was. He asked himself again: 'Am I really capable of it?'[10] But while the names of all the saints and the prayers of the congregation were intoned, he became clear: 'Yes, I am weak and inadequate, but I am not alone, others are with me, the whole communion of saints is with me.'

All at once silence fell in the cathedral. The essential element in the sacrament of ordination is the laying on of hands by the bishop, together with the ordination prayer, *oratio consecrationis,* as well as the anointing of hands with holy oil. According to church doctrine, this is the actual moment of ordination. 'When the bishop's hand is laid on the head, that hand then actually no longer belongs to a human being,' Ratzinger noted, 'but is a symbol and instrument for the fatherly hand of God, reaching out for us, and for God's finger, the Holy Spirit who is being sent upon a human being.'[11] In one of his books Ratzinger later recalled a small rite that had 'gone deep into his soul' at his ordination.[12] After the anointing, the candidates' hands were joined together and, holding hands, they took up the chalice – 'our hands with our very self in them seemed to be locked to the chalice'. At that point Jesus' words to the brothers James and John went through his mind: 'Can you drink the cup that I will drink?' But he had also heard the Lord's voice saying: 'You belong to me, you are not just your own, I want you, you are in my service.' That made him aware 'that laying on of hands is grace; it not only confers a duty but above all is a gift; that he is with me and his love protects and guides me'.[13]

After the thousand-year-old ritual, through which the power to forgive sins was conferred, the cardinal spoke the words of Jesus in his quiet but firm voice. Many of those present had tears in their eyes: '*Iam non dico vos servos sed amicos*' – 'I no longer call you servants but friends.' Joseph seemed deeply moved: 'I knew that that was not just a quotation from John 15, but it was something the Lord was saying to me there and then. He accepted me as a friend. We are friends. He has given me his trust. And in this friendship, I can act and make others become friends of Christ.'

Exactly 60 years later, on the diamond jubilee of his ordination, Ratzinger as Pope Benedict in St Peter's Square in Rome recalled that memorable moment:

I knew: at that moment the Lord himself spoke to me quite personally. He called me his friend. He accepted me into the circle of those whom he had addressed in the supper room. Into the circle of those whom he knows in a special way, so that they also get to know him in a special way. He gave me the almost frightening authority to do what he, God's Son, can do and has the right to do: I forgive you your sins. He wants me – authorized by him and saying 'I' on his behalf – to speak what is not just a word but a deed, that changes something at the deepest level of being.

[...]

The friendship that he gives me can only mean that I must also keep trying to know him better; that I seek to know him, in Scripture, in the sacraments, in the encounter in prayer, in the communion of saints, in the people who come to me and whom he sends to me.[14]

It was over. They got up and put on their clerical clothes for the first time. At the end of the ceremony each of them carried a lit candle, which each then handed to the bishop. That rite, which was abolished after the Second Vatican Council, was a symbol that the celibate priest gave up his own life, so that the light of the gospel might shine and give light to the world.

To the singing of many voices and the mighty sound of the organ the flock of new priests, together with the clergy and Cardinal Faulhaber, processed past a long line of excited people. 'Ordination was of course a spiritual climax,' Georg recalled, 'but above all we were taking care not to do anything wrong.'[15] 'With such a big step into such an unknown future,' Joseph remarked, the question always remained: 'Have you done the right thing? Will you be able to stay the course?'[16] He admitted later that at the critical moment an unexpected happening 'helped me a lot'. None of the other candidates saw it, nor did any of the congregation. We should not be superstitious, said Ratzinger, 'but at the moment when the old archbishop laid his hands on me, a bird, a lark perhaps, rose from the cathedral high altar and trilled a little song of joy. That was like an encouragement from above. It is good. You are doing the right thing.'

And as a final confirmation, directly after the ordination came the result of the prize competition. At last. He had won. The judges were in agreement: no one could write more illuminatingly on *Volk und Haus Gottes in Augustins Lehre von der Kirche* ('People and House of God in Augustine's Teaching on the Church') than the student from Hufschlag, who still looked like a boy.

Everything had been said; everything had been done. In the seminary dining room there was a festive meal of Vienna schnitzel with potato salad. At the end of this historic feast day of Saints Peter and Paul, Cardinal Faulhaber wrote in his diary: '*Deo gratias.* It went well.'[17]

21

The Curate

It was a special occasion in Traunstein. Garlands were woven, poems learned and on a banner hung over the high street someone had written: 'This is the day the Lord has made.' For a First Mass blessing, as the saying goes, it is worth wearing out a pair of shoe soles. And this was a First Mass of three young men together from the same place, a world sensation, so to speak. Rupert's father had laid his Mercedes 170 at their disposal, together with a chauffeur. Directly after the ordination in Freising and the schnitzel lunch that followed it, the Glorious Three sat proudly in the back of the car. The convoy consisted of three cars. On the front seat beside the driver the parish priest Georg Elst, 'Rocket-Schorsch', gave final instructions. He had summarily incorporated the village of Hufschlag into Traunstein, so that Georg and Joseph could celebrate their first High Mass in St Oswald's. Concelebration was not yet permitted, so there had to be three Masses. Joseph was set for the early Mass, not a good time for an attendance record. In addition, a big cycle race was set for that day.

The welcome in Maxplatz in Traunstein at 7 p.m. was overwhelming – with bellringing, civic dignitaries and the town clergy. Thousands of people had come to celebrate the arrival of the young priests in a procession to the church. Pressured by Rupert and Georg that someone should say something, Joseph gave a statement on the Eucharist. Then he spoke about the 'fivefold task' he had been given by his ordination, namely 'to sacrifice, to bless, to lead, to preach and to baptize'. Finally, the Blessed Sacrament was displayed to give the faithful the opportunity to worship.

Rupert Berger's First Mass celebration took place first, on 1 July 1951 at nine o'clock in the morning. Joseph and Georg served as acolytes. Loudspeakers broadcast the High Mass in the forecourt. A week later it was Joseph and Georg's turn. On the evening before, neighbours in Hufschlag had decorated their houses and set up a triumphal arch. The mild summer night smelt of flowers and leaves, summer chafers flashed in the evening sky. A gigantic cross made up of lights shone from the neighbouring roof. A torchlight procession was joined by more and more people and a singing Catholic youth group. When it reached the parental home, Father Elst could no longer contain himself. He sprang on the table in the living room and burst into speech: 'From hard stone sprang a spark,' he began, referring to poor, despised Hufschlag. The seemingly unimportant suburb had now produced not just one but two priests.

The future pope's First Mass day was 8 July 1951. It began at 7 a.m. Nobody served it. The Joseph Haas opus 88 Mass of Christ the King for people and organ was sung. Joseph had pleaded for simple hymns from the hymnbook familiar to the people, but Father Elst had remained obstinate. The Mass of Christ the King was festive and beautiful and exactly the right thing for this great occasion. So what happened was bound to happen. The congregation could not join in and even the youth choir faltered with the composition. Elst gesticulated wildly, grumbled at them between the individual pieces to sing better: 'Just a couple of sparrows from the church choir are twittering, that's not singing.' The service was not poorly attended but neither was it jam-packed. This was attributed to the fact that the new celebrant was little known, except by those fans who had come to see 'the fine young man Joseph', who was said to be frightfully clever.[1]

At the same time in Hufschlag gun salutes were fired. When Joseph returned from his First Mass celebration, it was Georg's turn. A big procession started, to lead the family's eldest son along the gloriously decorated road to the second First Mass of the day. Children in white communion clothes, flag-bearers, altar servers and a brass band. The cycle race was forgotten. Instead, people thronged into the town square in order to be able to follow the Mass in the packed parish church through loudspeakers. Georg had picked the 'Nelson Mass', Joseph Haydn's great Mass for orchestra. The fact that the preacher forgot a large part of the text he had memorized and spoke for 15 rather than 25 minutes did not bother anyone. Deeply moved, the parents watched as at the end of the celebration their sons stood before the altar and raised their arms to give their First Blessing together. Georg smiled and looked upward; Joseph seemed solemn and his eyes were fixed on the floor, but also somehow on the unknown, the infinite.

At Joseph's own Mass, a few hours earlier, the congregation had observed his behaviour attentively, as he spoke the words of Jesus at the consecration: 'This is my body [...] This is the cup of my blood, of the new and everlasting covenant – mystery of faith – that is shed for you and for many for the forgiveness of sins.' By that formula, in use before the liturgical reform, the priest expressed Jesus' unconditional self-sacrifice for his followers. At the same time, the words were to express the priest's own fusion into this 'body-for-you', his own self-consecration. Joseph had held the Host up as high as his arms could reach, and then the chalice. He would never do anything differently from that first time in the more than 25,000 Masses he was still to celebrate. 'In the space of nearly half a century,' said one of his students, the theology professor Hansjürgen Verweyen, 'he had seen that double consecration in every one of his teacher's Masses.'[2] The future bishop of Essen, Hubert Luthe, also reported: 'We served side by side at Mass during the [Vatican] Council. You could feel there how you ought to go about it.' Luthe was sure: 'In his great, almost childish reverence, there is nothing showy, no acting. He is being wholly himself. And you can only do that when you live by the Bible and prayer.'[3] 'That the Lord himself is there, and that this Host is now no longer bread, but the body of Christ,' said Ratzinger, is 'so extraordinary and thrilling that it always strikes you afresh and goes right through you.'[4]

The double First Mass concluded with a festive meal for about a hundred invited guests in the Sailer-Keller Gasthaus in Traunstein – with many speeches on the shadowy and sunny side of life as a priest. As stuffed roast veal was served, clouds gathered and a powerful clap of thunder heralded torrents of warm summer rain. However, the festivities continued for almost another four weeks. In the parish office, there were queues of the faithful making appointments for a house visit from the new priests. All day long 'we were given a snack and some money as a present,' Georg reported.[5] Joseph added that he had 'directly experienced how much people looked forward to the priest, and to the blessing that comes from the power of the sacrament.'[6] Anna Mayer, who was then a young girl in the neighbourhood, swears that her grandmother was immediately certain after a visit from the brothers: 'You'll see, that Joseph will become pope one day!'[7]

Ratzinger's theology of the priesthood can be summed up as wholeheartedly undertaking Christ's commission to bring him to the people. A priest must 'be a shepherd appointed by the Lord for the people – and also someone who gives himself, a man of silence who retreats from worldly activities in a prayerful relationship with the living God,' he said many years later. The most intimate act of friendship towards people is 'prayerfully to bring all their worries, their sorrows, their suffering, their hopes, their joys to the sight of the living God in prayer. A priest should gather and offer up everything that is unresolved in the hurly-burly of daily life and what oppresses and threatens people in the events of this world.' Were he to think that there are quite different problems to solve first, then he would lose his way: 'For even when we don't see it, and particularly when we don't see it, God is the one really necessary and most necessary for people and the world. When God disappears, people disappear too.'[8]

From 1 August 1951, Joseph had the opportunity to embark on practical service, which he had been so anxious about before. It began with a fiasco. After their First Mass, the brothers went their separate ways. Georg became a curate in Grainau, near Garmisch-Partenkirchen. After that he became a teacher at the minor seminary in Freising. Approval to study church music at the Munich College of Music was accompanied by service in the parish of St Ludwig in Munich. Joseph was appointed to the parish of the Holy Blood in Munich-Bogenhausen, a good middle-class neighbourhood on the right of the River Isar. On the recommendation of Rector Michael Höck, he owed this position to a Canon Irschl, the 'episcopal meat distributor', as the young priests disrespectfully called him. The Bogenhausen job was coveted. Joseph particularly looked forward to meeting his parish priest, the Revd Max Blumschein, who had the reputation of being saintly. But he was not there yet. Before going to the upmarket area, he went first to the 12,000-soul community of Moosach, an outlying village district to the north-west of Munich. 'Almost everything happened that could happen,' Joseph reported in retrospect. He added dryly, 'That's when I learned how to bury.'

The parish priest, Josef Knogler, was ill, the curate was on leave, the sacristan was away and the woman parish assistant could not be found. Because the neighbouring parishes were thinly staffed, the new priest had to hold services, visit the sick and comfort the bereaved elsewhere as well. His tiny room in the old presbytery in Pelkonven Street had no running water. He had to use a small bowl for his morning wash. However, for the first time he was earning his living. From his 210 marks per month, 110 went on board and lodging, 20 on laundry. There were also payments for health insurance and the subscription to the official journal, as well as the 'Seminaristikum', a special fund to support seminaries for priests.

Ratzinger is seen, first and foremost, as a theologian and guardian of the faith. His intensive experiences as a student chaplain, supply priest and curate show that he was also a committed pastor of souls. Although he was unhappy with the idea of becoming a community priest and was terrified that with his shy and awkward manner he would be unable to get on with people, he always managed to establish himself. Later, he even called that period 'the best time of my life'.[9] However, according to canon law, Ratzinger was not permitted to become a parish priest. Church regulations stipulated that following an examination – the so-called *Pfarrkonkurs* – there should be a proper application for a parish. However, Ratzinger never completed one. Apart from his friend Berger, no one realized that, and Berger knew how to keep a secret.

In Moosach, Joseph loved the serene flowering meadows, the friendly Baroque and Rococo interior of old St Martin's Church, the attractive simplicity of the people. On 1 September, what awaited him in Bogenhausen was a hectic presbytery and a bombed-out church with only its outside walls left standing; it had been rebuilt in 1950 as a single hall. But above all, he was faced with a great deal of work. His job as a curate involved hearing four hours of confessions on Saturdays, saying two Masses and preaching two to three sermons on Sundays. There were also weddings, baptisms, funerals and house visits. But those were only the extras. The main work was getting up at 6 a.m. on weekdays to sit in the confessional for an hour, then say Mass at seven o'clock. From eight o'clock on, he had 16 hours a week teaching religion in the Gebele elementary school with boys and girls in five different classes. Then the older students demanded the same. 'Once, as so often happened, I was hard pressed for time,' Ratzinger related, 'and a little rascal was hanging on to me and said if we both arrived late it would not look so bad. When he wanted to know which class I was going into, I had to explain that in the school I was on the other side, so to speak.'

In Munich-Bogenhausen they remember the curate as 'a very skinny figure'. He had a 'reserved, almost shy manner', according to Konrad Kruis, who was then an altar boy and later became a judge in the Federal Constitutional Court. At the same time he struck you as having 'a friendly humanity' with 'a really lovable person shining through'. Kruis said: 'Although he was so religious and devout, he fitted in well with his parish children. That is to say, he never stood on his dignity as a cleric or intellectual.' The young people were 'under his spell'. And this was not only at his children's Masses on Thursday mornings at 6. 05 a.m., which were soon to be widely known about, or his Bible evenings (with an interpretation of the book of Revelation) or the singing group (which practised motets and madrigals, such as the *Ave Maria* by Tomás Luis de Victoria).

His youth evenings in an old, bare-brick building were particularly in demand. Here, Ratzinger led discussions on Hölderlin and Kierkegaard or explained to his audience that humans can know God through the light of natural reason. 'Everyone there could feel,' said Kruis, 'that the young priest was richly endowed with spiritual and intellectual gifts and that something extraordinary emanated from him.'[10] It was only with football that the curate had a problem, for reasons already explained. He also kept away from the meetings of the Catholic women servants, mostly splendid, robust women in their thirties. When he looked in on one of their evenings, in order to give a Bible class, the leader decidedly rebuffed him: 'No, Mr Curate, you are still too young. You can't come in.'[11]

Because of his lack of experience, at the beginning Ratzinger got on 'with some difficulty'. But once again 'Providence' was with him. As before in Freising and Fürstenried with Läpple and Söhngen, in Bogenhausen he also found a fatherly friend in the parish priest Max Blumschein, who was also a true pastor of the old school: diligent, passionate and kind. Ratzinger found Blumschein to be a 'model of the good shepherd; a person 'who was steeped in his work' and who 'impressed the mainly intellectual members of his parish more through his simple faith than he could have done by clever talk'.

Black suit and clerical collar were compulsory. Blumschein also preferred the clerical knee-length frock coat, which had been customary before. Thin as a rake, the 67-year-old priest set the pace. On lengthy cycle tours through the 10,000-soul parish, uphill and downhill, he familiarized Ratzinger with his area. And 'as he did not spare himself, I couldn't and wouldn't do so either.' In the church services at first Blumschein only let him give the sermons for the children's Masses. The homilies in the High Masses, he explained, were reserved for his 'Good Ones', the experienced Jesuits Wulf and Hilig. But he quickly realized that his 'Good Ones' were not as good as his supposedly 'Bad One', so he also entrusted his curate with the 'big' sermons. Esther Betz, the Fürstenried student, also turned up here. She now lived in Bogenhausen and enthused about the 'slender young cleric', who 'astonished me with his clear-voiced preaching'.[12]

Joseph felt good. The place suited him. A priest must inwardly 'glow', Blumschein urged him. Georg occasionally came to visit. The brothers compared notes about their experiences and went on walks in Munich's Englischer Garten. In the parish, Joseph stepped in when a St Nicholas was needed. On outings, he pointed out to the schoolchildren flowers and wild plants that were familiar to him from his country upbringing. The children loved the 'really nice man who had a lot of charisma,' the schoolgirl Barbara Bechteler reported. 'And he also looked fantastic and had a sense of humour.'[13] Once he accepted an invitation to a carnival party in the American Youth Club in Possart Street. However, he had not bothered with a special costume. 'Wow, look at this!' one of the young people shouted in glee, 'he's dressed as a curate.' Joseph was upset and left.

On 17 June 1952 the funeral cortège for Cardinal Faulhaber, who had died five days earlier, passed through the town. Wearing a huge cloak, a dalmatic that was far too big for him and made him look like a dervish, Ratzinger had to accompany the German apostolic nuncio Aloisius Muench. Although the curate sometimes seemed so shy, after the cardinal's death he vividly described in his sermons how a good bishop should behave. He also asked the faithful to pray that a suitable successor would be found.

In church services, large gestures were not his thing, but he was a good singer, who hit every note. Unlike other curates, he did not try 'to make an impression', said the priest Hermann Theissing, who was then a gymnasium student. It could be seen 'how incredibly simply he lived even from his room. There was no big desk with lots of pictures and so forth that a young curate might have. There was just a simple table with a couple of notebooks on it, a bookshelf and a bed. That was all.'[14]

When the theologian later explained his idea of priestly service, he often referred back to Max Blumschein as a model. 'He gave me the model of selfless commitment to his pastoral work until his death, which overtook him as he was bringing the viaticum sacrament to a very sick person.'[15] Priesthood, Ratzinger stressed, meant getting out of a bourgeois lifestyle. It had to 'guide people towards becoming reconciled, forgiving and forgetting, being tolerant and generous'. It was to help them 'put up with other people in their otherness, and have patience with one another'. A priest must 'above all, be able to support people in pain – in bodily suffering, as well as in all the disappointments, humiliations and fears, which no one is spared.' For 'the ability to accept and stand suffering' is 'a fundamental condition for successful human living. If that is not learned, then failure is inevitable.'[16]

The 'right definition of what a priest should be and do' was still Paul's message in his letter to the Corinthians: 'We are ambassadors for Christ.' A priest is required 'to know Jesus intimately; he has met him and learned to love him'. It was only by being a man of prayer that he was also a truly 'spiritual' person – a priest. When priests were overworked and felt tired and frustrated, it was often caused by a tense straining for performance. Then faith became a heavy burden, 'when it should be wings to carry us'. Whoever works for Christ knows that 'it is always someone else who sows and someone else who reaps. He does not have to continually question himself; he leaves the outcome to the Lord and does what he can without worrying, freely and happily, secure as part of the whole.'[17]

The people of Bogenhausen were sceptical at first, but gradually the whole community became enthusiastic about a curate who put so much energy and idealism into the day and astonished them by his naturalness. Soon publishers living in that part of the city began to notice him. For example, Hugo Schnell, whose firm later published Ratzinger's post-doctoral thesis. Or Dr Christoph Wild, head of Kösel Verlag in Munich, who soon signed up this hopeful talent with a contract and published both Ratzinger's first book, *Über die christliche Brüderlichkeit* (*The Meaning of Christian Brotherhood*), and his internationally successful *Einführung in das Christentum* (*Introduction to Christianity*). According to Hermann Theissing, Ratzinger 'already had a powerful aura then, but was still reserved and modest. He didn't need to "whip things up". He was simply Joseph Ratzinger.'

Theissing recalled a little story that is typical of the pragmatism with which Ratzinger always did what was useful without ignoring the spiritual. It was about a delegation from a youth centre in Cologne, which had organized a light relay across Germany. As in previous years, they also set up burning candles on a side-altar in the Bogenhausen church. However, next morning, to the horror of the acolytes, the lights had gone out. The sacristan had simply blown them out. There was a huge fuss. What would the curate have to say about it? 'Fearful thoughts ran through our heads,' said one of those present. Ratzinger stuck his head through the door. 'The light has gone out,' they chorused in agitation. But the curate kept a straight face and knew at once what to do. 'Then just light it again!'

The wholeheartedness of priestly service in the Holy Blood church also had to do with the *genius loci* of the parish. In Bogenhausen, Ratzinger was impressed not only by a particularly well-educated community but also by members of the congregation and predecessors in office who had become martyrs as witnesses to Christ. Pastor Blumschein had not only seen an opponent of the Nazis, Ludwig Freiherr von Leonrod, and the former minister of state Franz Sperr go to their deaths. He had also seen the arrest and murder of two of his curates, Alfred Delp and Hermann Josef Wehrle.

Delp came from a mixed-denomination family in Mannheim. He was confirmed as an Evangelical but, influenced by his Catholic mother's devotion, immediately after his *Abitur* he entered the Jesuit order and was ordained as a priest by Cardinal Faulhaber in Munich on 24 June 1937. People who knew him were fascinated by Delp's analytical power, his visionary spirit and his combination of mysticism and resistance. Elisabeth Gross, who had Delp as her religion teacher and leader of the Heliand Society (Heliand-Bund) in Bogenhauen, remembered, in particular, his rescue efforts for those buried by bomb attacks.[18] Or when at night, together with mothers and schoolchildren, he replaced the school crucifixes that had been removed by the Nazis. According to Gross, he behaved 'as if his conscience ordered him to do this as a Christian and a priest'.[19]

The Jesuit came to the Holy Blood as a curate in 1939. Three years later he joined the 'Kreisau Circle', that group of Nazi opponents centred round Counts von Moltke and von Stauffenberg, who were involved in the July Plot to assassinate Hitler. In the 'Kreisau Circle' he developed an idea for a Christian socialist social order based on Catholic social teaching, for the time when Nazi rule was over. (In fact, it played a part in the post-war establishment of the German Federal Republic.) Modern humans are 'formidable experts in many areas of life,' Delp wrote. At the same time, they had become 'pathologically unable to cope with life'. Instead of spiritual awareness, personal determination, sound judgement and conscience, they had become 'coerced and seduced' and 'the eternal object of decisions and violations by others'.

When, as curate of the Holy Blood church, Ratzinger encountered the legacy of his predecessor, he was particularly impressed by Delp's reflections on 'the challenge of history' for a 'theonomic humanism' and for the 'future of the churches', which he wrote 'in the sight of death' in late 1944 in Berlin's Tegel prison. Delp saw the reason for humanity's immense self-destruction was that people had become incapable of God. From the experiences of his time, Delp saw true humanity as being possible only in a return to God. God was the protector against the 'despotic pressure of the masses', the final surrender to 'We', which also 'prostituted the innermost self, engulfed the conscience, overpowered the judgement and finally blinded and choked the spirit'. An atheistic humanism was just an illusion and would always end in new hubris and aberration, new madness.

Ratzinger willingly adopted Delp's approach. In a later essay he contrasted him with the atheist existentialism of Jean-Paul Sartre, who called for the 'reign of humanity', in which there was 'no other lawgiver but humanity itself'. How it must have shaken the young curate when he read the lines that his predecessor had written on a scrap of paper just a few weeks before his execution: 'Woe to a time in which the voices crying in the wilderness are silenced, overwhelmed by the tumult of the day, banned or wrecked in the frenzy of progress, or suppressed or quietened out of fear or cowardice.'

Delp's arrest on 28 July 1944 was followed by condemnation to death for high treason. Delp was 'a rat, who should be stamped out,' raged Roland Freisler, the president of the People's Court. By that time 300 opponents of the Nazi regime had been executed in the notorious Berlin prison alone. After his death sentence, the curate wrote in a letter to his friend: 'When there has been a little more love and kindness, a little more light and truth in the world through *one* person, then that person's life has had a meaning.' The Jesuit turned down the offer of a 'release in exchange for leaving his order'.

On 2 February, Candlemas, Gestapo prisoner no. 1442 was strangled on a meat hook in Berlin's Plötzensee prison. On Hitler's orders, his ashes were scattered on the Berlin sewage farm, where vegetables were grown. Nothing was to be left to remember the priest and anti-fascist. But there could be no more powerful symbolism than those ashes being scattered on a field that was used to grow new fruits. A few of his sentences have survived, which after months of torture, and in handcuffs, he had scratched on the wall of his prison cell:

'The birth moment of human freedom is the moment of meeting with God.'

'The bended knee and outstretched empty hands are the two basic gestures of the free person.'

'Let us trust life, because we don't live it alone; God lives it with us.'[20]

Hermann Josef Wehrle, Delp's fellow priest in the Holy Blood parish from 1942, was a mystic who knelt for hours at night before the Blessed Sacrament. Ratzinger read in his diary: 'I have realized that for me mysticism starts with praying before the Lord in the tabernacle.' And: 'You must let yourself be led by the Lord in his wholly personal school. He will shape you, but certainly in a different way from what you expected.' As an accessory to the attack on Hitler, Wehrle was executed straight after being sentenced in 1944. It was 14 September, the day dedicated by the Catholic Church to the finding of Christ's cross. 'What a beautiful day!' Wehrle scribbled on a scrap of paper, 'today is the elevation of the cross.'

As well as his own quick awareness, Delp's ideas may have helped Ratzinger in his pastoral work, to realize 'how far from the faith many children's life and thinking was'. In the closed circle of the seminary there had been a spirit of new beginnings from the zero hour and the determination never to let the terror of an atheistic dictatorship, such as they had recently experienced, happen again. Things were quite different in the daily reality of life in an area of the city that was bent on recovering its prosperity. Ratzinger had to recognize that a whole Hitler-indoctrinated generation had been almost lost to the faith, even though people behaved as if nothing had happened.

In Freising, he had known resisters like Rector Michael Höck and the Jesuit Franz von Tattenbach, his spiritual adviser. Tattenbach had heard Delp's final vows in the Berlin prison shortly before his death. Ratzinger's predecessors in the Holy Blood church were a further personal connection with anti-fascist resistance motivated by Christianity. In Delp, he also discovered a priest who carried what he had previously learned about conscience from Newman into political action. It became clear to him that resistance to a spirit of the time turning to godlessness (and therefore contempt for humanity) had not run its course with the end of the Nazi Reich. He loved his parish but he also experienced a reality shock.

I came across this situation, particularly in religious instruction. There you have 40 boys and girls, who sort of go along with it dutifully, but you know that they hear the opposite at home. So it might be: 'But Dad says, you don't need to take that so seriously.' You felt that somehow church and faith were still there institutionally, but that the real world had moved on far away from them.' [21]

Unlike what he was used to in his rural home, in urban pastoral care he realized 'how little religious instruction there still was in family life and thinking'.²² He found that the traditional form of youth work 'would not do in times that were changing; new forms needed to be developed'.

Ratzinger took notes. His observations would soon become an essay with the almost prophetic title: *The New Heathens and the Church*. In the essay he used for the first time the word 'de-secularization' (*'Entweltlichung'*), which he said was vitally necessary. He had touched on a sensitive spot. Without his knowledge, at the same time 500 kilometres to the west, in Cologne, a famous cardinal had drafted a sobering document for the Bishops' Conference: 'The substance of the faith is no longer matched by the actual influence of the Catholic Church,' wrote Josef Frings; 'the secularization of life will – in the long run – lead to the secularization of hearts. The façade on its own will not always remain standing.'²³

On 1 October 1952 his job as curate in the Holy Blood church came to an end. Ratzinger was appointed by his superiors as a lecturer in the Freising seminary. Unexpectedly, he was sad about the news. 'The feeling of being needed and doing important service,' said Ratzinger, had helped him personally and 'given him joy in the priesthood'.²⁴ He had even begun to wonder 'whether I should have stayed in pastoral care'. Long after he had left, he had 'suffered from the loss of a fullness of human relationships and the experiences provided by pastoral care'. He kept his connection with Bogenhausen over the years. Herman Theissing, then a schoolboy, remembered his moving farewell. Ratzinger had never spoken about his theological qualifications. Of course, from his intellectually demanding sermons, the community had 'quickly realized who they were dealing with'. But no one was prepared for the disclosure of his academic career. 'He said, "People, I'm going to Freising in September and will be a lecturer there." We asked, "what will you be doing there?" Then he said, 'I'll be doing a doctorate." So we said sympathetically: "Then you'll have to write a doctoral thesis first." He replied: "I've already done that. That was the faculty prize work."'²⁵

Ratzinger weighed things up. In Bogenhausen he had had to 'move out of the intellectual sphere' and make contact with different people, and he had also managed to learn the rudiments of 'how to talk to children'. In Father Blumschein's final report, the curate had 'proved to be a very conscientious and capable priest'. His 'theological knowledge' was 'extraordinarily great for his young age, his zeal was exemplary, his ability to preach and also [...] youth work was very good'.[26] To their 'great regret' the whole parish community, especially the children and young people, had to give back their beloved priest far too soon. There was only one thing left to remark. The young man still had to overcome a 'certain shyness'.

22

The Examination

Ratzinger's appointment as lecturer in the Freising seminary set him definitively on an academic course. His friend Alfred Läpple had played a part in this. He suggested to Cardinal Faulhaber that the young theologian was second to none as a teacher of pastoral and sacramental theology. Ratzinger knew nothing about the conversation. 'The beginning was not that easy,' he reported, 'particularly because I was younger at that time than many of the students.'[1]

Georg and Joseph continued to go their separate ways. As well as continuing his music studies, Georg was sent outside Munich to work in Maria Dorfen as a pilgrimage curator, religion teacher and deanery music director. As a lecturer, Joseph was promoted to the Domberg seminary board, family-run by 'Papa Höck' and his niece Wetti. In the college lecture hall, he had to familiarize 17 seminarians with the correct administration of the sacraments. A later colleague, Josef Finkenzeller, said: 'The problem was that he had only done pastoral work for a year and now he had to teach us. We all felt that, but no one said anything. He always incorporated theology. As he was a charming man, it went all right.'[2]

It was a full-time job, and he also had to prepare for the decisive exam as well, so that finally he could bear the title Doctor of Theology. He gave religious instruction in the elementary school. He celebrated Mass daily in the cathedral (or in one of the city churches). And on Saturdays and Sundays, he sat in the confessional to hear poor souls' sins and worries: 'It was mostly seminarians who came. I was especially popular with them because I was so broad-minded.'[3] For a short time he was even chief of the household fire watch. When he led a fire practice with the students, it was not long before the whole seminary courtyard was under water. Biblically, fire chief Ratzinger called it 'The Flood'.

He still had other work to do. As youth and student chaplain, he led the women's Heliand Society. He taught catechism to hundreds more students in the Agricultural and Brewing College in Weihenstephan. It was known as the 'Oxford of Brewing' because of its international reputation. Students on scholarships came from every continent. A young man from Cuba enthused about the revolution led by the bearded lawyer Fidel Castro, which Ratzinger found quite in order: 'You could still be enthusiastic about it then, or perhaps even had to be.'[4] The lessons often took place in the tap room, which gave the curate honorary membership of the 'Isaria' student fraternity. Last but not least, he managed a fund he had set up to support young people in financial need.

Germany began to recover, at least in the West; whereas in the Soviet-occupied zone the standard of living was falling back to the level of the famine years, beyond the frontier the *Wirtschaftswunder* ('Economic miracle') was beginning. Unemployment was falling; wages and salaries kept rising. More than 500,000 new homes were built for war victims and those who had been bombed out or displaced. From 1949 to 1955 the gross national product tripled from 49 billion (thousand million) to over 180 billion Deutschmarks (DM).

After the war German companies were not allowed to produce armaments, so they concentrated on consumer and capital goods, with increasing sales. Cameras, microscopes, radios, machine tools: there was also demand for 'Made in Germany' on the world market again. Whole steel mills and rolling mills were ordered. Volkswagen exported its models to more than 100 countries. Products of the chemical industry such as aspirin and penicillin proved unrivalled. From 1950 to 1957 the value of German exports climbed from 8.4bn to 30.9bn DM. By 1954 the balance of trade surplus amounted to 2.7bn DM.

The golden 1950s. Opulent and without war. The blockbusters in the cinemas were called *The Black Forest Girl* and *The Heath is Green*. They attracted people with their tranquil image of a world at peace, something they had believed had almost been lost. For the first time, following the American model, 'pocket books' appeared on bookshop shelves. The '*rororo*' series, or 'Rowohlts-Rotations-Romane' (Rowohlt's Rotation Novels), first published by Rowohlt Press in 1950, was advertised as 'Good literature for every wallet'. Illustrated magazines such as *Stern, Quick* and *Kristall* ran to editions of millions of copies. In June 1952 the unparalleled success story of *Bild* newspaper began, accompanied by a public discussion about 'smut and trash' and their effect on endangered youth.

At the political and economic level, Federal Chancellor Konrad Adenauer continued the course of Western integration, with opposition from the SPD (Social Democratic Party). With the formation of the European Coal and Steel Community on 18 April 1951, France, Italy, the Benelux countries and Germany founded a first supranational European institution. In the GDR in June 1952, party leader Walter Ulbricht announced the planned 'Building of Socialism'. The Ministry for State Security ('Stasi'), set up in 1950, not only kept opponents of the Socialist Unity Party (SED, often referred to in English as the East German Communist Party) under surveillance but increasingly monitored the whole population. As a result of the political pressure, in 1952 about 60,000 citizens were in prison. Hundreds of thousands decided to leave their country and make a new life for themselves in the West.

Apart from the burden of the upcoming examination, Joseph felt well on the Domberg. Even many years later he enthused about a Corpus Christi festival in Freising:

> I can still smell the scent from the carpet of flowers and the fresh birch trees; the decorations on all the houses, the flags, the singing. I can still hear the village brass band, which on that day sometimes tried to do more than it was capable of. I hear the crack of bangers, by which the boys expressed their baroque enjoyment. But then there was Christ too, being greeted in their streets and their village like a head of state, indeed the sovereign, the Lord of the World.[5]

According to the Japanese historian Hajime Konno in an in-depth analysis, it is impossible to understand Ratzinger without taking into account his attachment to Bavaria, his love for his home, with its religiosity and its inhabitants. Ratzinger himself described his love of Bavaria and its people.

> So this place has always remained with me and for that very reason has also enabled me to persist, because it was open, because it saw itself as open to a great cultural exchange. Perhaps Bavaria has been awkward in German history precisely because it never allowed itself to become a purely national culture; it always remained open to a wide-ranging intellectual exchange.[6]

Looking at the calendar gave him less joy. His dissertation was written, but it still had to be prepared for printing. The work 'remained almost unchanged from its first draft', Ratzinger apologized in a later foreword, due to 'the very limited time available'.

Indeed, as well as his work as curate, lecturer and prefect in the seminary, he still had to take written and oral examinations in no fewer than eight theological subjects. In each of these subjects three Latin theses had to be formulated, on which his examiners would then dispute publicly with him. For this *questio inauguralis* he had to specify three themes, from which the faculty would pick one. It was a race against time. Furthermore, Gottlieb Söhngen was said to be extremely demanding and strict in exams. 'Whoever gets Gottlieb, gets beaten,' those in the higher classes whispered.

It was Saturday, 11 July 1953. Sounding almost triumphant, the Freising seminary chronicle reported 'three important events' for that date. The first was the visit of a Magdeburg auxiliary bishop; the second was the visit of the new federal president, Theodor Heuss, who was solemnly welcomed by Rector Höck. However, the climax was 'today's third event', namely 'our lecturer Josef Ratzinger's obtaining his doctorate at Munich University'. His first name was spelt wrong, but then the writer continued accurately with the details: 'Dean Mörsdorf led the *actus publicus*. Prof Dr Schmaus examined 3 theses on dogmatics, Prof. Dr Söhngen examined 2 theses on fundamental theology. The doctoral candidate passed every part of the examination and the *actus publicus* with "summa cum laude"*. Result: 'Dean Mörsdorf told the new Doctor that were he to go for the habilitation, he would not need to undergo a *colloquium* (oral examination). His prize work *Volk und Haus Gottes in Augustins*

Lehre von der Kirche (*People and House of God in Augustine's Teaching on the Church*) represented a substantial contribution to Augustine research.'[7]

On 11 July 1953, Ratzinger's entry into the world of scholarship was sealed. Shortly beforehand, Karol Wojtyła in Poland had just successfully completed his habilitation, but no one in Münich could have known that. In a long corridor in the Ludwig Maximilian University, uniformed attendants carrying staves ceremoniously walked in procession. Dean and rector followed in black robes, before Joseph had to defend his thesis publicly in the university hall. And how could it be otherwise: 'Both dissertation and disputation were brilliant,' the future diocesan judge Hermann Theissing said. Even Joseph's parents were impressed, especially by the Latin, in which their son defended his thesis in a masterly way. Only Professor Schmaus stood a little aside, as Theissing noted: 'There, a star was born who did not have the "Michael Schmaus" signature but was a student of Gottlieb Söhngen's.' The consequences were catastrophic, as would be seen later on.

There is a grotesque story that arose from these weeks, which the Munich comic KarlValentin also enjoyed. It just has to be told. Twelve days before the public disputation, as the brothers were celebrating the second anniversary of their ordination in the Georgianum, a telephone call gave them a terrible shock. A comrade telephoned the seminary and told Georg in a hushed voice that he had just received an urgent telegram for him and Joseph. It contained only four words: 'Our father is dead'. Georg and Joseph took the next train to Traunstein. To their surprise when they were half-way there, their mother got into the train at Bad Endorf, on her way home from the theatre. She was appalled when she heard the news. How could that be? She had left home at about noon. 'Your father was still fine then.' When the three of them finally arrived in Hufschlag by taxi from the station, the reportedly dead man was sitting in front of the house calmly polishing shoes. It turned out that the telegram had come from Rickering and referred to their father's younger brother, Anton, who had died suddenly.

The *disputatio publica* concluded the process of gaining his doctorate. Joseph was 26 years old and a recognized Doctor of Theology. The family celebrated in Georg's lodgings in the Georgianum.

There were veal sausages, pretzels and beer. The mood was typically Ratzingerish, still rather subdued: 'Now we'll have to see,' said his sceptical father, 'what happens next.'

With his work on *People and House of God in Augustine's Teaching on the Church*, Ratzinger not only gained professional respect. His research permanently marked his view of the church, his understanding of the state and the political importance of Christianity. Furthermore, according to the Irish theologian Vincent Twomey, Augustine gave him the inspiration 'which he used later to fight various misunderstandings of the [Vatican] Council, in particular, the attempt to describe the church as people of God in more or less empirical or sociological, even political terms'.[8]

Ratzinger's task had consisted in showing how Augustine's definition of the nature of the church contributed to the clarification of unresolved questions in the current ecclesiological debate, and also how it acted as a corrective to a one-sided or even erroneous interpretation of the church as the 'mystical body of Christ'. Ratzinger's starting point was a sentence with which Augustine described the church as 'the people of God spread over the Earth'.

In fact, the master student had brought out a lot more than his teacher had thought possible. In his research, the 25-year-old came to the conclusion that it was methodologically false and inadmissible to set the Augustinian definition of the church as 'people of God' against the definition of it as the 'mystical body of Christ'. *Societas Spiritus,* the Society of the Spirit, was what Augustine called the church in one of his sermons. The church lived not of its own accord but through the power and grace of the Holy Spirit, which was given through the sacraments, particularly the sacrament of the Eucharist. It was this uninterrupted action of Christ's grace that gathered together one people from all over the Earth and gave that people life as a mystical body.

The church's sacramental nature as mystical body of Christ stood as a warning against the attempt to indulge in self-satisfied pride. The salvation promised to the faithful was not the noble possession of eternal truths, but meant a humble sharing in the Lord's acts of grace in world history. That dependence on the sovereign power of the Holy Spirit was the church's true essence, to which *both* definitions, 'people of God' and 'body of Christ', referred. *Ecclesia sancta*, holy church, was also always *corpus permixtum*, a mixed body, in which wheat and tares grew together. In his work *De civatate dei* (*The City of God*) Augustine pointed out that this church was sometimes so much a 'church of sinners' that it might be questioned whether there was a single just person in it. But that mixed structure also pertained to the mystery of salvation. The gates of the city of God were always open, even to those who had persecuted it the day before.

Ratzinger brought the two different approaches together by creating a new, groundbreaking formula: the church, he said, 'is the people of God as it is the body of Christ'. That view was based on a Christological reading of the Old Testament and on the sacramental life with the Eucharist as its heart. In it, Christ gave his body to the faithful and at the same time transformed them into his body. Christ was the only mediator between God and humanity, so he was 'the universal way to freedom and salvation'. Apart from that way, according to Augustine, 'no one has ever been freed, no one is ever freed and no one will ever be freed'.

Ratzinger recalled this in similar words in one of his catecheses, which he gave as pope in Rome in January 2008 before thousands of people: 'As the only mediator of salvation Christ is the head of the church and mystically united with it, so that Augustine can say: We have become Christ. For if he is the head, we are the members, so he is and we are the whole human being.'[9]

Even in his first work Ratzinger displayed two typical characteristics of his way of doing theology: first, his criticism of an artificial dialectic of apparent contraries; second, his methodological ability to harmonize different approaches. This accords with the Catholic principle of relying not on the exclusive Either-Or but on the inclusive Both-And.

After the hard work for his doctorate and its successful conclusion, the new doctor allowed himself a pause for recovery. First, he went to Switzerland to visit Franz Böckle, professor of moral theology in Chur, whom his brother Georg had met in Munich. The connection with Böckle was important for Ratzinger. Through him, he got a personal introduction to Hans Urs von Balthasar, with whom Böckle had a lively exchange of views. Another trip was planned, Joseph's first big trip abroad, which was 'the reminder', said Ratzinger, that he had entered 'the great world of international scholarship and in particular the French intellectual world'.[10]

His excellent doctoral work had not only brought him much praise but also an invitation to the international Augustine Congress, which took place from 21 to 24 November 1954 in Paris, a city he longed to visit. Together with three companions from Bavaria he explored the city and took part in guided tours through the old university quarter and of Notre-Dame. They joked and drank, 'so we had a lot of fun together'. And best of all: 'We stayed in a very beautiful hotel and were received by the mayor in the Hôtel de Ville.'

They also did some work. Ratzinger spoke on the subject of the 'Origin and Meaning of Augustine's Doctrine of the City. Encounter and Discussion with Wilhelm Kamlah'.[11] He had probably become aware of the German philosopher Kamlah through his work published in 1935. It had the exciting title: *Apokalypse und Geschichtstheologie: die mittelalterliche Auslegung der Apokalypse von Joachim von Fiore* (*Apocalyspe and Theology of History: The Medieval Interpretation of the Apocalypse by Joachim of Fiore*). Confidently, in his lecture Ratzinger agreed with the Augustine expert in the main, but criticized Kamlah for understanding the church's eschatological character in a way that was too isolated and de-historicized. However, he pointedly referred to Kamlah's work *Christentum und Geschichtlichkeit* (*Christianity and Historicity*) later in his thesis, saying that Christianity was 'the synthesis mediated in Jesus Christ between the faith of Israel and the Greek spirit'.[12] But Ratzinger had to forgo the last item on the programme, a flight to Algeria, St Augustine's home: 'That would have cost too much. I couldn't afford it.'

In the spring of 1954, Ratzinger had revised his doctoral work *People and House of God in Augustine's Teaching on the Church* so that it was ready for typesetting. The publisher, Hugo Schnell from Bogenhausen, undertook the printing costs for the work, which ran to 331 pages. The Freising Professorial Council had long wanted Ratzinger to take over the vacant chair of dogmatics and fundamental theology, but he had declined with thanks. He thought he would have 'more freedom' as a lecturer in the seminary. And he needed it. Dr Söhngen had been urging him to go for the habilitation. His dissertation had dealt with the ancient church and an ecclesiological theme; now he was to turn to the Middle Ages and the modern era and research the concept of revelation. A title had already been found. It was *Die Geschichtstheologie des heiligen Bonaventura* (*St Bonaventure's Theology of History*). At first sight the title may have seemed rather succinct. But within it lay the exciting question of how God gave messages to humanity, and it also engaged with the apocalyptic vison of the end of time. Attractive enough for Joseph to take on the task: 'I set to work with enthusiasm and joy.' In the summer he had already finished gathering the material and worked out the basic ideas for his interpretation.

On 1 November 1954 Ratzinger did take up the vacant post of professor of dogmatics and fundamental theology at Freising College that had long been offered him. He still declined the accommodation that went with the job, in the former cathedrals canons' residence behind St Benedict's Church (Domberg 26, left staircase, first floor, on the right), and stayed on in the seminary until September 1955 in his digs without shower or toilet.

The subject he chose for his first semester of 1954–5 was less modest. It was hardly possible to begin with a more demanding lecture than one on 'the doctrine of the triune God'. But what would the reactions be? He had done modern philosophy, studied his Augustine and de Lubac, produced a fabulous doctoral thesis and had been promoted step by step by his sponsors. He had also done practical work in pastoral care. But on the holy mountain where many still knew him as a youth, would he have the necessary authority? Would he be able to carry his audience with him? In fact, not only the young professor (actually not yet a full professor) but almost the whole college went into a fever of enthusiasm. 'Ratzinger was the greatest experience and event at this time on the Domberg,' said Elmar Gruber, then a student in the first semester. Even the usually sober seminary chronicler could not disguise his excitement. Under the date 3 November 1954 he reported the solemn moment, as if broadcasting it to the whole world: 'The former lecturer Dr Ratzinger has taken over the professorship of dogmatics. The first couple of lectures have been a pleasure.'

Gruber recalled how the 27-year-old Ratzinger, who was scarcely older than many of his students, stood at the lectern for the first time. The hall was completely full, and there was absolute silence. Ratzinger was a bit pale but seemed self-assured. Later some of his students were referred to as the 'RAV', the *Ratzinger Anbetungsverein* ('Ratzinger Worship Society'). When he began the lecture, a quality appeared that the former Bavarian culture minister Hans Maier described as 'a Danubian flow'. His speech was 'filled with a soft enthusiasm, that cast the reader and listener irresistibly under its spell', especially through 'a music you felt in his choice of words and sentences'.[13] Elmar Gruber, who himself later became a successful writer, called it 'a completely new language' and a previously unknown way of explaining the Bible. It was there even in Ratzinger's first presentations: 'He could speak extempore ready for printing. He never faltered and he never repeated himself. You could have taken it down in shorthand and at the end you would have had a well-structured script.'[14]

It was not just his youthful appearance but his whole stance, his movements, his language, even his voice, which made him seem different from the others. And when he somewhat phlegmatically leaned on the lectern and put his head in his hands, it was clear that here was someone who did not stick to conventions. Quite simply, because he could let himself go. For all his shyness, he displayed aplomb and self-assurance that gave him great freedom. When some students wanted to see the script he was reading from with such concentration in the lecture, they realized with amazement that the desk was empty.

With the young theologian, a new tone had come into the world, at least into the world of Freising: 'He introduced things that we had never heard of before,' said his student Franz Niegel. 'It was a very stuffy time, and then someone came along who could give you the message afresh. We listened carefully to the content. It opened a new door for us. Up until then, there was only the traditional way of seeing things, and he was able to throw new light on them.'[15] Even Rupert Berger, who had known his friend best from their beginning, was surprised: 'We had the feeling that the old scholastic theology would be filed away. Now at last someone had come bringing a new wind, a new style. Joseph Ratzinger was the voice of that new direction, no one else.'

Had anyone ever explained the Jewish Feast of Tabernacles (the Feast of Booths) as 'a kind of *Oktoberfest,* at which the apostles Peter, John and James wanted to build three booths'? 'And the three of them are there outside and have been drinking,' said the Hufschlag apologist. He liked to bring together difficult theological questions in a new synthesis. The biblical message was 'quite simple': what is written in 47 books of the Old and 27 of the New Testament is summed up in dogma in one sentence: 'God is the almighty father, creator of heaven and Earth.' Ratzinger enjoyed surprising. 'Mr Candidate,' he asked an examinee, 'imagine that human beings were discovered on some other planet. Are they saved by Jesus' death on the cross or not?'

When the French feature film *Le défroqué* (*The Defrocked One*) went on general release, Ratzinger was asked to give an expert opinion. In the film an old priest who has fallen away from the faith asks a curate to consecrate a tub of wine. The curate drinks the 'blood of Christ' in one go and becomes completely drunk. The question was how should that kind of transubstantiation be assessed theologically. Ratzinger found an answer that was typical of him: because the Eucharist was essentially directed towards meaningful consumption, he would 'argue' that the blessing of the tub of wine in the film was not a consecration.

The clarity of his language, the sharpness of his mind, the unprecedented brilliance of the way he expressed things, attracted notice. Discussions with Ratzinger carried some risks. 'When you had said something,' Gruber reported, 'a profound and extensive answer came straight back, which would have taken you a day and a half to work out.'

These beginnings earned Ratzinger the label of being – in contrast to his later stance – an expressly progressive theologian, which does not quite fit the usual picture of him. At any rate, on the Domberg Joseph was soon spoken of as a 'left-wing Catholic'. 'He was seen by the students as 'forward-looking', reported Berger, 'because he did things which, in comparison with what they had heard up till then, were like a revelation.'[16] Furthermore, there was a fearlessness about asking questions 'which no one had dared to ask hitherto'. For example, on subjects such as ecumenism, which were regarded as a minefield. 'Ratzinger really entered new territory there,' said the doctor and psychotherapist Brigitte Pfnür, a former student, 'he was groundbreaking.'[17] As a student in Freising, Pfnür's husband, Vincenz, was so impressed by the way his teacher dealt with the Lutheran

Confessio Augustana that he made the topic his lifelong subject. This 'original student', as Ratzinger called Vincenz, who was born in Berchtesgaden, became a pioneer of ecumenism and wrote works that received great acclaim in the Protestant world.

The lecture on the 'triune God' was followed in the summer of 1955 by 'the doctrine of creation' and a seminar on basic problems in Augustine's *Confessions*. The subjects addressed after that also showed Ratzinger's ambition and confidence in his own ability. For example the lecture on the 'doctrine of our salvation in Christ Jesus' in the winter semester 1955–6 or his first fundamental theology lecture on the 'outlines of phenomenology of religion and philosophy of religion (Essence and Truth of Religion)' – as well as a seminar on modern Christological and Mariological literature. The theme for dogmatics in the 1955 summer semester was the doctrine of grace. Fundamental Theology II offered 'Religion and Revelation'.[18] He was also reading about the doctrine of the Last Things, the Creator God and his work, basic problems in the theological doctrine of knowledge and the modern discussion on the relationship between nature and the supernatural.[19] His seminar on fundamental theology in the 1956–7 winter semester had the title 'The Concept of the Church with Special Reference to the Peter Problem' – that is to say, the papacy.

When the young lecturer sat on the benches reserved for dignitaries at festive events, he appeared lost and ill at ease. But the old hands sneaked through the side-entrances into the cathedral whenever Ratzinger was announced as the celebrant or preacher. Eavesdropping on such a young colleague was actually incompatible with the dignity of seasoned professors. However, nobody wanted to forgo the pleasure Ratzinger gave when he brought forth unsuspected riches from the treasury of the Bible. 'Ratzinger was a superb preacher,' said Hermann Theissing. 'The astonishing thing was that he stood there at first looking helpless; he didn't know what to do with his hands, just let his hands and arms drop down by his side.'

Ratzinger's interpretation of the Bavarian yodel was unforgettable. At the traditional Advent singing in 1953, when it fell to him to conduct a theological reflection, he compared the yodel to the *jubilus* mentioned by the church father Augustine. 'I'll leave it to the greatest theologian of the Western Church, St Augustine. For he knew the "yodel". He called it the *jubilus*, but there can be no doubt that he meant the same thing: that wordless pouring out of joy so great it breaks down all words.'[20] Now the Bavarians knew that their songs without words, their yodelling, was basically of biblical origin and as pleasing to God as the angelic choir of Cherubim and Seraphim.

Elmar Gruber, who later attracted a mainly liberal public as a priest and writer, learned whole sentences of Ratzinger's by heart in the holidays 'in order to acquire some of his brilliant language for myself'. Gruber analysed the grammar and syntax of Ratzinger's texts and came to realize:

What was special and completely new in his way of speaking was his fascinating use of images, signs and symbols, through which he entered much more deeply into God's mystery than by rational definitions. Meditative, reflective thinking (emotional intelligence) is his strength, by which he can enthuse his listeners, while his rational aptitude linked to his linguistic skill caused boundless amazement. Whether it was a sermon, reflection or lecture: you always went away moved, enthused and comforted and looking forward to the next meeting.[21]

Besides his language and way of lecturing, Ratzinger's effect on his listeners depended above all on a 'plausible theology', as Gruber called Ratzinger's teaching. It was fascinating 'because you always felt it was giving answers to particular questions'. The former student spoke of a 'healing faith', which his teacher communicated to him. As a therapist, Gruber had to support people in danger of committing suicide who had illnesses 'that could no longer be helped by drugs'. Here especially, the awareness that 'it is good that I am alive and also how I live' was, as Ratzinger proclaimed in his theology, 'essential for the healing of many psychosomatic illnesses'.[22] In an absolutely authentic way, Ratzinger conveyed 'a basic existential motivation' that 'was not purely academic but directed towards human fulfilment, and expressed realities in a way that made them begin to have an effect on people's lives'. Gruber also said that he personally was grateful to his then teacher for the course of his studies: 'As my bad memory for facts threatened to become a problem for me with the professors, Ratzinger's backing enabled me to stay on and become a priest.'[23]

Ratzinger remained friends for life with Franz Niegel. When he was a cardinal, he enjoyed relaxing in his presbytery in Chiemgau, Bavaria, eating steamed noodles with vanilla sauce. Niegel summed him up: Ratzinger was not someone who wanted to harmonize at all costs, but he 'never spread distress. He never complains. He is always kind, cheerful, a Mozart type, who also knew heaven and hell, but never let his personal problems into his music. Ratzinger is that sort of Mozart type in theology. He is simply a genius.'[24]

Shortly before the first Sunday of Advent 1955, a grey cloudy November day, a removal van arrived in Freising. 'As my habilitation seemed secured and the flat on the Domberg was still awaiting a new tenant, it seemed right to us all to bring Father and Mother to Freising.'[25] They would live beside the church, their son had persuaded them; the shops were near by, and in winter there were no icy streets and heavy snow, as in Hufschlag. Later Maria would also come. Their father was 78, their mother 71. When the removal day arrived, it was a sad farewell to the farmhouse, which had been an important part of their life history for the whole family. They all felt melancholy. But as soon as the removal men arrived in Freising, their mother put on her apron and stood at the stove to prepare their first meal. Their father told the students where to put the removal boxes. Very soon they were to be seen daily, just before 6 a.m., two bolt upright figures hurrying along the cloister to church for the early Mass.

Joseph was happy. He would have lacked any talent for arranging a home, and now his father had also offered to take over part of the household expenses. Of course, some students immediately tried to cajole the old police officer to put in a good word for them, especially just before exams. 'No, I won't do that,' the father answered, 'All I'll say is Bepperl, be fair'.

When Georg and Maria also came to join the celebrations in their new home on Christmas Eve, the family happiness seemed perfect. In his memoirs, Ratzinger added: 'At that time none of us yet knew anything about the storm clouds gathering over me.'

23

The Abyss

For his dissertation, Ratzinger had investigated Augustine as an example of the church fathers' thought on the church's DNA. Now he had to find out whether there was a similar idea of 'salvation history' in the work of the medieval church teacher Bonaventure. And if so, whether that idea really connected with revelation. To put it less academically: does God act in human history and if so, how does he communicate? What is the church's role in this? And are there documented traditions about what we can know about the future of creation?

Söhngen's second big assignment, with the working title *Revelation and Salvation History according to the Teaching of St Bonaventure* (published 1959 in its second version with the title *St Bonaventure's Theology of History*), did not lack appeal. In every world culture wasn't there the ancient longing and even the certainty of being able to see into the future? And didn't all people of all times (except for atheists and a few others) also dream of a new Garden of Eden, a return to a lost paradise? For the Greeks that place was Arcadia and Elysium. The Sumerians called their paradise Dilum, the Celts Avalon. For Muslims it was the Paradise Gardens that would make the dream come true.

In Judaism, treasured prophecies had foretold the coming of the Messiah, the saviour, who would proclaim the Kingdom of God. The Old Testament is full of exact computations about it. And the closer that moment came the more the signs increased. Two thousand years ago the Magi from the East could even calculate the date and place where the vision was to become reality. But when God himself entered history, the Logos, who became incarnate in Jesus of Nazareth – as his disciples believed and still believe today – from that point onwards wasn't it possible still to look into the future, to see how history would continue to its end point?

Christ himself had not left the world in the dark about what they could expect. 'I will not leave you orphaned: I am coming to you,' he had assured them.[1] In Matthew's Gospel we read:

> And you will hear of wars and rumours of wars: see that you are not alarmed; for this must take place, but the end is not yet. For nation will rise against nation, and kingdom against kingdom, and there will be famines and earthquakes in various places: all this is but the beginning of birth pangs [...] you will be hated by all nations because of my name. Then many will fall away and they will betray one another and hate one another. And many false prophets will arise and lead many astray [...]

> Immediately after the suffering of those days, the sun will be darkened, and the moon will not give its light: the stars will fall from heaven and the powers of heaven will rock. Then the sign of the Son of Man will appear in the heavens [...] And he will send out his angels with a loud trumpet call, and they will gather his elect from the four winds, from one end of heaven to the other.[2]

Jesus added: 'Think about it: I have foretold it to you. However, no one can know the day or the hour, only the Father in heaven'. But weren't there also signs, words and works – even 'revelations', communications – to prepare humanity for a great change to the world? And if so, what exactly was 'revelation'? Was it restricted to statements in the Bible, or were there also things on different levels that were to be seen as revealing the order of creation?

The new Doctor's work went quickly and the deeper he went into the material, the richer were the rewards. He was also helped by 'the enthusiastic accompaniment of the students', who shared in the progress of his research. Now it was no longer a 'Glass Bead Game', as it was for Josef Knecht in Hermann Hesse's dreamland of the beautiful and the good. For, said Ratzinger, Bonaventure's theology was not about 'a fictional world, a kind of mental arithmetic, but about a confrontation with reality. And indeed about its whole scope and all that it entailed.'[3]

In St Bonaventure, Ratzinger encountered a theologian, philosopher and powerful head of a religious order, the 'prince of all mystics', as Pope Leo XIII called him. Bonaventure managed to mediate between the strict and more relaxed tendencies within the Franciscans and would, therefore, be seen as the second founder of the Order after Francis of Assisi.

The holy monk was born in Viterbo in Italy in 1221 as Giovanni di Fidanza. His name in religion was given to him personally by St Francis, almost from his deathbed, when he saw the young man for the first time. The Latin *bona ventura* can mean 'good fortune' or also 'the good to come'. Until 1242 the Italian studied at the University of Paris and became a professor of theology there, together with Thomas Aquinas. After he was appointed General of the Franciscan Order in 1257, he led the community for 17 years from Paris. There he held seminars with titles like 'The Knowledge of Christ' (*De scientia Christi*), 'The Mystery of the Trinity' (*De mysterio Trinitatis*) or 'Gospel Perfection' (*De perfectione evangelica*). His treatises on spiritual education, such as the *Soliloquy on Four Spiritual Exercises,* made him one of the most successful writers of his time. Readers celebrated Bonaventure's major mystical work, *The Mind's Road to God* (*Itinerarium mentis ad deum*) as the climax of speculative thought and almost unprecedented knowledge of God. He was soon called *Doctor seraphicus,* the angelic teacher, a name that expressed the admiration with which the scholarly world regarded the medieval master.

The other main figure in Ratzinger's research was no less exciting: Joachim of Fiore (1130–1202), a mysterious abbot from Calabria who expected a time of salvation to come within history. He spoke about the 'Third Age' and a state of complete salvation.

As the son of an administrative official in Sicily, Joachim could look forward to a fine career at the king's court. An experience on Mount Tabor, the mountain in the Holy Land where Jesus was transfigured, set his life on a completely different course. The former official withdrew into solitude and founded the monastery of San Giovanni di Fiore in Calabria. The strict religious order he created was ratified by Pope Celestine III. Joachim explained that the revelation on

Tabor had enabled him to understand the meaning of Scripture and the correlation between the Old and New Testaments. In his vision, humanity developed in three phases: after the 'Age of the Father' and the 'Age of the Son', the 'Age of the Spirit' would dawn, a new period in which contemplative life would be the dominant form of existence for Christians. In its final phase, the church would enter a charismatic state of immediate access to grace.

The abbot's prophecies caused excitement because a growing group of radicalized Franciscans believed they recognized in Francis of Assisi (born 14 years after the Abbot's death) that *Alter Christus* – the other, second Christ – whom Joachim had foretold. Joachim believed that the Third Age of the Spirit would be heralded by a God-sent figure who would conquer the Antichrist.

The abbot's ideas spread like lightning. They even influenced Dante Alighieri, who immortalized Joachim in his *Divine Comedy*. After-effects could also be traced to the time of the Reformation – for example, with Thomas Müntzer – and continued up to Hegel, Marx and Ernst Bloch's *Principle of Hope*. The Calabrian seer was never completely rejected by the Catholic Church. It was, in fact, Joseph Ratzinger who wrote the article 'Joachim of Fiore' in the 1960 *Lexicon for Theology and Church*. In it, he stressed that Joachim had never been anti-hierarchical. Still today in the Catholic Church's liturgical calendar, the following prayer is set to be said at Mass on his feast day, 29 May: 'God, who revealed your glory to the three apostles on Mount Tabor, at the same place you opened up the truth of the Scriptures to the blessed Joachim.'

To anticipate: against all expectations, Ratzinger found that with Bonaventure, as with all thirteenth-century theologians, the concept of 'revelation' did not match the way in which it was later understood. In the course of time, the concept came to be used as an umbrella term for Scripture. However, in the language of the Middle Ages, Bonaventure spoke of revelation as the 'disclosure of what was hidden'. God's already given revelation was to be regarded as final, but however final it might be, it was also inexhaustible, because it kept on offering new depths of insight.

According to medieval theology, one the one hand, God's historical activity was deposited in Scripture; on the other hand, Ratzinger said, what was revealed was 'always greater than what was merely written down', just as every event was not identical with the telling of it, which tried to pin down what happened. Thus Ratzinger had made an important discovery. It also concerned relations with the Protestants, who insisted on Scripture alone. No, revelation was not only given in Scripture but also in things like tradition, the inspiration of the fathers and saints, and the living faith itself. Not to speak of acknowledged miracles, inexplicable signs or appearances of Christ or Mary. And that meant, Ratzinger concluded, 'that there cannot be pure *sola scriptura* [Scripture alone]'.

According to the medieval view, Scripture in itself did not yet count as revelation, but only the deeper spiritual meaning contained in it, which could only be wholly understood by an allegorical reading. It was about a *visio intellectualis*, seeing through everything on the surface to the spiritual core of the text. That was a reason why the Catholic Church had set up a magisterium to deliver the Gospel faithfully.

The last part of Ratzinger's habilitation research investigated how Bonaventure dealt with Joachim of Fiore's end-time theories in his *Collationes in Hexaëmeron (Talks on the Six Days)*. Apparently, Ratzinger realized 'what a unique chance was being offered to him here', said the theologian Hansjürgen Verweyen. It seemed possible to him, through a historically exact analysis, 'to subject the major evil of neo-scholastic narrowness in philosophical-theological thinking to radical criticism, which it will be hard for the church magisterium to object to'.[4]

By comparing the different theological approaches of Bonaventure and Thomas Aquinas, the young theologian believed he could locate the Archimedean point from which the narrowness in the neo-scholastic interpretation of revelation, Scripture, tradition and faith could be overcome. The 28-year-old habilitation candidate was not bothered that he would thus have to query theses that were regarded as sacrosanct by the magisterium. For him 'the idea was decisive', he wrote in a later introduction to his work, 'that the prospect of comprehensive historical knowledge is greater, the wider the systematic horizon, the more it extends beyond the customary narrowing of scholastic theology'. That was why he had particularly taken into account the suggestions 'coming from Evangelical theology on this matter'.[5]

Söhngen's master student established that the minister-general of the Franciscans, 'as guardian of the salvation history tradition', had not rejected Joachim's visions completely. Engaging with Joachim's teaching, Bonaventure elaborated his own theology of history. It included improving conditions, through human religious activity which to some extent brought God into the world. He divided human history into a structure of seven or eight days, analogical with the Genesis story. According to this scheme, the laborious sixth day was already accompanied hiddenly by the glory of the seventh day. These two linked days were followed by the eternal eighth day, the 'God-given Sabbath rest'.

With the appearance of Christ, a new era had already begun, a period of both trouble and salvation. Thanks to the church founded by God's Son, said Ratzinger in his work, from that time on, despite constant crises, 'the breath of a new time' was blowing, 'in which the longing for the glory of the other world was overlaid by a deep love for this Earth, on which we live'.[6]

Like Joachim, Bonaventure also assumed that a new age of salvation did not dawn only at the last day. Both theologians were convinced that immediately before Christ's return – in a final period of time before the end of the world – the church would undergo a historical change and become contemplative (*ecclesia contemplativa*), without ceasing to be a church of ministry and the sacraments. During this end time the people of God would be able to enjoy a unique disclosure of what had been hidden, a fullness of revelation. Through an attitude of humility, purely discursive thinking would give way to simple inner awareness of the mysteries of the faith, which would be granted to the ordinary people and not the wise and clever.

Bonaventure saw a time coming in which Christianity would draw its power to convince not primarily from reason but from its vision of the future. That process of awareness, which accompanied a return of creation to the creator, would produce a real movement of the spirit through meditation and contemplation. Seen thus, history was not a succession of arbitrary events but should be understood as the temporal connecting of its end with its divine origin: above all, through revelation.

The habilitation thesis was a massive work and, at 700 pages, the most extensive Ratzinger had ever written. A good 500 pages of it would disappear into a drawer for more than half a century. The work was finished by the end of the 1955 summer semester. A copy was neatly written out in pencil in small handwriting on paper. The countless footnotes and cross-references alone displayed his diligence, thoroughness and erudition. Of course, he was anxious to prove his own qualifications once and for all. With extraordinary professional assurance for his age, the theological beginner was undaunted by the experts in his field. He showed them where they went wrong or at least had worked sloppily: 'Anyone who knows Augustine knows that such thoughts have no place in his work.'[7] Pointed formulations displayed his enjoyment of writing and his power of judgement: 'For Bonaventure the New Testament reaches its true fulfilment in the coming, but for Joachim it is in the going away, in order to make room for something greater.'[8] A typical Ratzinger statement: 'Professorial protests [...] which we are accustomed to hearing since the onset of liberal research on Francis, have a damaging lack of seriousness in such serious matters. They generally derive not from the desire for real renewal in eschatology but just from the will to criticize.'[9]

Joseph did not want to burden his sister again with typing up his handwritten 'giant screed'. He had a small sum of money which enabled him to employ a professional typist. The drama ran its course.

It began with the secretary proving to be completely incapable. Pages kept getting lost, sometimes whole chapters, which had to be rewritten from memory. In addition, 'a surfeit of errors' strained the habilitation candidate's nerves 'to the utmost'. The presentation was not of the highest standards, when in the late autumn of 1955 Ratzinger submitted the required two copies of *Offenbarung und Heilsgeschichte nach der Lehre des Heiligen Bonaventura* (*Revelation and Salvation History according to the Teaching of St Bonaventure*) to the University of Munich faculty of theology.

At least his scholarly work had been thorough. Söhngen was enthusiastic. He could barely stop himself quoting in advance from the work in his lectures. It seemed that nothing stood in the way of Ratzinger's habilitation. However, now the second examiner of the work came into play, Professor Michael Schmaus. Schmaus had a reputation. Schmaus was cock of the walk, as vain as he was vulnerable. And Schmaus took his time.

The farmer's son from Bavarian Swabia was five years younger than Söhngen and a prelate of honour to the pope. He was the editor of *Beiträge zur Geschichte der Philosophie und Theologie des Mittelalters* (*Contributions to the History of Philosophy and Theology of the Middle Ages*), the author of an eight-volume *Katholische Dogmatik* (*Catholic Dogmatics*), a member of the Papal Theological Academy (one of only 39) and claimed to be the authority in Munich on medieval research – including Bonaventure. He also bore a blatant stigma.

In 1949 Schmaus, a full professor (*Ordinarius*), was forbidden to hold any more lectures, seminars or examinations. The reason was a report in the *Münchner Abendzeitung* accusing him of sympathies for the Third Reich. In fact, after Hitler's takeover of power, Schamus had demonstrated a dubious proximity to the Nazis in lectures in Cologne and Münster. These texts were also published as a book in 1933 with the title *Reich und Kirche – Begegnungen zwischen katholischem Christentum und nationalsozialistischer Weltanschauung* (*Reich and Church – Encounters between Catholic Christianity and National Socialist World View*).[10]

Meanwhile the dogmatic theologian had been rehabilitated by some means or other. In 1951 he was appointed rector of the Ludwig Maximilian University and was spoken of as a possible minister of culture for Bavaria. In 1962 his powerful portrait graced the front cover of *Der Spiegel,* who called him 'the Catholic Church's most important scholar'. The priest allowed the magazine to question him on the dispute about Evangelical–Catholic 'mixed marriages'. Schmaus said it was well known that his academic colleague Söhngen was a child of such a 'sinful relationship' and 'sacrilegious union'.

Weeks and months went by. In 1955, Georg took his exam at the music college and passed the master class. His model was the composer Karl Höller. Joseph noted that Höller's way 'of teaching counterpoint and explaining the rules of composition fascinated his brother'. But now compositions arose, he grumbled, 'which sounded rather strange to our ears, attuned to Mozart and romantic music'.[11]

In Freising, the business continued. Ratzinger had won admiration and shown a charisma that many of his students and former student colleagues found hard to resist. He often held examinations in his work room, where his mother offered the agitated candidates tea and biscuits. He was an uncommonly fair examiner, contemporary witnesses observed. For example, he only asked questions on what the particular candidate could have really mastered. Academic colleagues were already congratulating Ratzinger on his habilitation, which was being praised everywhere. The first invitation to take over a vacant chair came from the Johannes Gutenberg University in Mainz. The University of Bonn also showed great interest in the newcomer.

Meanwhile, Joseph had also fetched Maria, who was given her own room. The biggest and best room of the 110 m² staff accommodation with a view of the mountains was for his parents. The only thing that was odd was that Joseph had bought a property in the Lerchenfeld district of the city, probably from the proceeds of the sale of the Hufschlag house and on the advice of his parents, who had lost a large part of their savings in the inflation of the 1920s and the monetary reform of 1949.

The blow fell at Easter 1956. Actually, on a Good Friday, the day of God's blackout, on which Joseph had once seen the light of the world. It was bitterly cold in Germany. In many places, the temperatures fell to the lowest they had ever been in April. 'Whoever can afford it,' *Die Zeit* recommended, 'goes east to the southern Swiss lakes or to the Riviera on the Italian or French sides.' 'The climate and the seasons have changed,' said the weekly paper, 'and scientists are still seeking the right explanation.'

In the media, pundits discussed Nikita Khrushchev's recent speech, in which the Soviet leader distanced himself in strong words from Stalin, his predecessor. Another debate was on the reintroduction of the armed forces in Germany. In (West) Berlin IBM introduced its new computer. It was of human height and the most modern computer in the world. In the meantime, in his Munich study Michael Schmaus used up quantities of coloured pencils to indicate that for him the work of Söhngen's theological protégé went completely against the grain.

The drama began when Ratzinger, as a promising junior theologian, was invited to the annual meeting of the Association of German Dogmatic and Fundamental Theologians, which took place from 30 March to 1 April in Königstein im Taunus. Here, for the first time, he met the famous Karl Rahner, who was 23 years older than him and was regarded as a particularly progressive theologian. They became 'humanly very close', he said. Of course, the co-referee of his habilitation, Professor Schmaus was also present. What now occurred was a meltdown of young Ratzinger's hopes. 'It was like being struck by thunder,' he later said, describing the scene, 'my whole world threatened to fall apart.'

The abyss opened up exactly in that minute when Schmaus took his young colleague aside during the day. 'Matter-of-factly and without emotion,' Ratzinger recalled, he explained to his opponent's master student that he would have to reject the *habilitiation* thesis. It did not meet the required academic standards either in form or in content. He would be given details after the relevant faculty decision.

The meeting was like a stab in the heart. Joseph must have thought of the 'Beast Column' in the crypt of Freising Cathedral with its bright side – the woman and the flower – but also with its dark side, where monsters reared up to engulf people and creatures. Failed. He thought first of all about his parents 'who had come to me in Freising in good faith'. What would become of them 'if I now had to leave the college as a failure'?

Rupert Berger remembered how his friend 'suddenly became downcast and despondent. It was a real blow for him.'[12] Ratzinger 'had never been a slave to anyone. Now that hit him hard. He bottled it up,' added his colleague Josef Finkenzeller.[13] It was noted on the Domberg how the young theologian's hair turned grey almost overnight. Neither his parents nor his brother and sister knew what had happened to him. Perhaps he could get a simple curate's post, with accommodation attached, he wondered in silence. 'But that was not a particularly comforting solution.'

What had happened? There are two versions explaining Schmaus's fateful verdict. There was no doubt that Ratzinger's work was extremely clever. But its cleverness was not the point. Basically, the subject of the work lay within Schmaus's province. In the faculty there had long been whispering about why Söhngen had assumed responsibility for the habilitation and thus put his student in an awkward position. Was it about his rivalry with Schmaus? He had publicly attacked his colleague, saying that in his theological work he just lined up quotations, texts from Nietzsche, Kant and Wolfgang Borchert, which he had not understood at all. In the run-up to his habilitation, Ratzinger himself had repeatedly implied that Schmaus's medieval studies were stuck in the pre-war period. The theologian 'had not taken any account at all of the new discoveries'. Indeed, the theological beginner had dared to criticize the famous professor's positions sharply. 'Clearly that was too much for Schmaus,' was how Ratzinger explained his rejection. He presumed that his second examiner had personal motives: 'It was unacceptable to him that I had worked on a medieval subject without entrusting myself to his guidance.'[14]

Students of Schamus regarded Ratzinger's presentation as too subjective. Schmaus was 'a very friendly and student-friendly professor'. Finkenzeller confirmed that Schmaus usually behaved generously to his habilitation candidates. But 'it did not always go like that. For example, he did not read my work properly.' 'Of course, he could also clobber you,' said his doctoral student Gerhard Gruber.[15]

The related documents of the University of Munich are not accessible under archive regulations. What is certain is that Ratzinger's work was besprinkled with multicoloured marginal glosses, which left nothing to be desired in their ferocity. The famous dogmatic theologian not only criticized his analyses but also declared that the young theologian was a modernist. 'Schmaus almost felt him to be dangerous,' recalled Eugen Biser, the successor to Karl Rahner in the Romano Guardini chair. 'Ratzinger was seen as a progressive, who made firmly established bastions totter.'[16]

Publicly, Schmaus criticized him: 'Ratzinger knows how to weave things into flowery formulations, but where is the heart of the matter?' Alfred Läpple knew Schamus had told Ratzinger to his face: 'You talk round it and avoid precise definitions.' Läpple understood the criticism: 'Ratzinger goes for a theology of feeling. He avoids clear definitions – *sic et non* – it is so or it is not so – he never kept to that medieval motto. He does not like firm definitions, but prefers a reshaping and constructs it as an artist constructs a picture. In the end, you wonder: what has he actually said?' Läpple added: 'Schmaus was right, that he is too emotional. That he is always coming out with new words and enjoys jumping from one formulation to the next.'[17]

However, the dogmatic theologian's victory did not last long. Schamus suffered a first defeat at the faculty board. Some professors did speak about a dangerous modernism in Ratzinger, which flowed from making the concept of revelation too subjective. Nevertheless,

Söhngen managed to ensure that the work was not rejected but returned for corrections. Schmaus remarked sarcastically that the master student would need several years to consider his remarks and make the corresponding amendments. By then Ratzinger's appointment would be out of date.

Schamaus's second defeat was due to a brainwave. Ratzinger had seen that the latter part of his work contained hardly any comments. Either Schmaus had lost the will to go any further or he had, in fact, had no objections. Ratzinger's brilliant stratagem was to make an independent work out of the last part of his research. Because Schmaus had made hardly any objections on those pages, that part could not be rejected as academically unacceptable.

The putatively failed candidate sat over his books, thought and wrote, endlessly copied quotations out by hand and added footnotes. 'Joseph, how's Herr Schmaus?' his former fellow students teased him. Ratzinger's answer: 'Important'. But that was the furthest he let himself go with abuse, said Hubert Luthe. Ratzinger himself told the author that during these dramatic weeks he neither cursed God nor made any vows. 'But I prayed hard and begged God to help me. Especially for the sake of my parents. That would have been a catastrophe, if I had had to put them out on the streets.'[18]

Shortly afterwards, he presented his text again. A gamble. For a work of just 180 pages, instead of the former 700, was barely fit to be accepted for habilitation. But the calculation worked. In February 1957, a year and a half after he had first submitted his thesis, the University of Munich's faculty of theology accepted the work. 'A book never belongs to one author alone,' said Ratzinger in his foreword, thanking all the living and dead theologians whose studies he had used. 'It could not happen without all the many intellectual influences that have consciously or unconsciously shaped his thinking.' On the incriminated part of his work, he remarked briefly: 'On the wider problem the material has been gathered and sifted.' Decades later, the fundamental theologian and philosopher Hansjürgen Verweyen took a very different view from Schmaus. He declared: 'It was a work which had great historical thoroughness and theological foresight.'[19]

The future professor still had one more hurdle to clear. It was 21 February 1957, a Thursday. And one of those fateful moments which either become a shining hour and change the course of history or end in terrible failure. We are in the great lecture hall of Ludwig Maximilian University (today Lecture Room A 140). The room is full to bursting. Two hundred students, professors, curious onlookers. Black suits and ties are worn. 'In the run-up, it had been rumoured there was a certain problem here,' said the church historian and contemporary witness Georg Schwaiger.[20] The tension rose as the dean of the theological faculty entered the room, followed by Professors Söhngen and Schmaus, one tall and thin, the other short and fat, two gods in black, at least according to their own estimation. The habilitation thesis had, indeed, been accepted ten days earlier, but you could still fail over the disputation of the work, this time in full public view.

Contrary to custom, the subject of the lecture was chosen not by the candidate but by the faculty. 'I had proposed a historical subject. Normally, the faculty always accepted what was proposed. But I was told, that would not do, they wanted "systematic theology". I had a couple of days and also had to give lectures in Freising.' The strain on Joseph was enormous: 'I knew that certain parts of the faculty would listen to me suspiciously and had already decided against me, so that my failure seemed almost to have been programmed.'[21]

There was dead silence when, after a short outline of his career by the dean, the candidate began his half-hour lecture. But afterwards, a controversy broke out that was reminiscent of the great medieval disputations. Söhngen, as his supervisor, began by asking the candidate some simple questions, but then Schmaus pitched in. He wanted to know whether for the young man the truth of revelation was something unchangeable or whether it was historically dynamic. Even before Ratzinger opened his mouth, Schmaus himself gave the answer: 'Your subjectivist way of interpreting revelation,' he ranted furiously like a public prosecutor, 'is not truly Catholic.'[22] As Ratzinger's mentor, Söhngen sprang up, incensed. The public murmured and clapped, the habilitation candidate stood silently between them. Söhngen was speaking to Schmaus and Schmaus to Söhngen. Joseph did not get a word in. The time allowed for the examination had run out.

The sitting of the 15 members of the faculty board at an oval table in a room in the Catholic theological deanery on the first floor of the university building seemed endless. Pass or fail, that was the question. It was no longer about marks. Outside in the corridor, Ratzinger strode impatiently up and down: 'I feared the worst.' His friend Rupert Berger, his brother Georg and the preacher Pakusch from St Ludwig's were with him. 'We stood at the window and talked and trembled with each other,' said Georg. Joseph had never said a word to him before that about the possible sudden ending of his career. His parents had never heard about it either. The door opened, and out came the dean, Professor Adolf Zieger, a church historian. Tense faces, blessed response: Passed. 'At that moment I was hardly able to feel any joy,' Ratzinger recalled, 'the recent nightmare still hung so heavily on me.'

The bulk of the future pope's early work on the history of religion lay unseen in a drawer for 54 years. It was only published together with Ratzinger's collected works in September 2007. In fact, the importance of this study can hardly be overrated. It pointed to the way he would go:

- Its key message was that the church's task as the body of Christ on Earth was to understand God's action in history better and better, and thus bring a part of God's light into the world in preparation for salvation. The church should never become a force in the political battle, for example, to bring about a this-worldly utopia.
- The future of the world is directly bound up with the welfare or otherwise of the church of Christ. According to Joachim and also Bonaventure, in the course of salvation history there was an Age of the Spirit, in which the church as 'church of the poor' – that is simple and firm believers – would work pneumatologically-prophetically as well as christologically-sacramentally.
- *St Bonaventure's Theology of History*, as well as Ratzinger's dissertation on the term 'people of God', would be echoed strongly in the documents of the Second Vatican Council. 'The insights I got from reading Bonaventure,' its author confessed, 'were very useful to me later in the Council dispute about revelation, Scripture and tradition.'
- Above all, it was with the help of Bonaventure that the professor-to-be clarified the church's traditional position on

the relationship between faith and politics, which during the papacy of John Paul II became the basis of the Catholic Church's doctrine on the radical tendencies of liberation theology.

• The work not only gave him his lifelong theme – that reason and faith belong together, and that philosophy and theology belong together – but, doubtless, also his inclination towards apocalyptic ideas. All his work is marked by the concern for faith and the church, which he saw as endangered in the modern world, above all, by the false developments in his own household, and tried to protect by building spiritual and intellectual barricades.

• His habilitation work is hardly ever considered in discussions about Ratzinger. But, against the claim that he changed from being a progressive to a conservative theologian, it proves that the future pope discovered his theological position early on and followed it consistently. The 26-year-old theologian already believed there could be no division into conservative or progressive theology, but only true or false theology.

Despite massive further harassment by Schmaus, on 1 January 1958 Ratzinger was appointed as extraordinary professor of dogmatics and fundamental theology at the Freising College of Philosophy and Theology. Before that, however, Ratzinger, who by then had been thoroughly examined, was summoned to the Ministry of Education and the Arts. Clearly someone had blackened his name. The intention was to refuse him the title of professor, despite the fact that he had passed his habilitation. The reason given for it was his well-known incompetence, the official accused him out of the blue. He only wanted the job in order to get a secure income. Such people could not be employed. Ratzinger was not impressed. His title of professor could no longer be taken away from him. But the demons that had gathered round him did not disappear.

24

The New Heathens and the Church

After the turbulence of his habilitation, Ratzinger and his brother enjoyed a holiday in Normandy, at the invitation of a priest friend. In July 1958 he took part in the Conference of German-Speaking Dogmatic and Fundamental Theologians, which was in Innsbruck on this occasion. It was his first meeting with the priest and theologian Hans Küng, who was the son of a Swiss businessman. A more than complicated relationship was to develop between them. But here, Küng noted, they 'immediately liked' one another.

On the Domberg, Ratzinger was celebrated as 'the youngest professor of theology in the world'. But the next storm was approaching. The cause was a religious and social-political article, published in October 1958 in *Hochland,* a 'journal for all areas of learning and the fine arts'. Even the title of the article sounded provocative. It was 'The New Heathens and the Church'.

The 'Catholic spring' that occurred in Germany after the end of the war had not remained without problems. The Swiss theologian Walter Nigg criticized the Catholic Church for enjoying its new-found institutional strength while, behind the façade, the deposit of faith was beginning to crumble again.

Already before that, in November 1946, the *Frankfurter Hefte* had published a 'Brief über der Kirche' ('Letter about the Church') by the writer and theologian Ida Friederike Görres, in which the disputatious Catholic, daughter of the Austrian diplomat Heinrich von Coudenhove-Kalergi and the Japanese Mitsuko Aoyama, described the disillusioning daily life in 'Catholicism as it actually exists', with alarming conditions among the clergy, which had nothing to do with the tradition that was constantly being invoked.

The article caused vehement debates, including on the Domberg. Student priests demanded that the author should come out and respond to questioning, but Cardinal Faulhaber banned Görres from any public appearances in his diocese. Later, Ratzinger would exchange correspondence with both Nigg and Görres. In his sermon at Görres's requiem in Freiburg Cathedral on 19 May 1971 he said: 'Certainly, it was not easy for her to cope with a church, which she herself no longer seemed to know, which often appeared as her opposite [...] We thank God that she existed. That this perceptive, brave and faithful woman was given to the church in this century.'[1]

Ratzinger had heard of the Görres article in Freising, but, according to his own account, he had not read it himself. That was unnecessary. From his 'own experience of the church, as it actually was' in his work as a priest, he had felt a clear disillusionment. One of the proofs for that is the sermon he gave at the First Mass of his former student Franz Niegel, on 4 July 1954, in Niegel's home community of Berchtesgaden:

> How often when I was student I looked forward to being allowed to preach, being allowed to proclaim God's word to the people, who must have been waiting for it in the perplexity of an often godforsaken daily life. I looked forward especially to when a word from Scripture or a new insight into our doctrine had struck me and made me happy. But how disappointed I was! The reality was quite different; people clearly weren't waiting for the sermon but for the end of it. Today God's word is not one of the fashion items people talk about and queue up for. On the contrary: it's fashionable to know better.[2]

In his homily, the 27-year-old asked the faithful 'to disregard the way the wind is blowing the times and embrace an unsensational, perhaps apparently useless, faith in God's truth'. Soon it might be 'necessary at work, in the office or wherever, to confess that you believe and live as a Christian and offer a word of faith to a world of unbelief'.[3]

A year later, on 10 July 1955, he sharpened his tone even more. This was in another First Mass sermon, this time for his former fellow student and war comrade Franz Niedermayer. The service in Kirchanschöring-Traunstein had to take place in the open air, because the church could not hold the number of people attending. Ratzinger's analysis sounds like Augustinian pessimism. It reads like one of those predictions that do not fade, but which from decade to decade become etched deeper into the stone, in order to make their truth visible to all:

> If someone came to this world from another planet today, they could not describe humanity better than by saying: they are like sheep without a shepherd. Today humans don't know what is right and wrong, what they should do or not do, what is actually all right now and what is impossible. In villages perhaps things are better, but when a young person is let loose in the city today, they soon see that all the common convictions have broken down. They notice that now everyone makes their own rules and just does what they feel is right.[4]

When the young man from Hufschlag first thought about becoming a priest, 'the powerful, firmly religious personality of our father was decisive'. He was a man who 'thought differently from how you were supposed to think then and had a certain mastery'. As a curate in Bogenhausen and from his experiences of the Third Reich he had become aware of a reality that cried out for responsible pastors, but was suppressed by the church establishment.

The *Hochland* essay was Ratzinger's first important work as a journalist. The editor had kept the first page for him. As an inexperienced young priest and theologian, to write on a subject that would provoke opposition from the church leadership, as the Görres case had shown, was not without risk. But he felt obliged, even duty-bound, to point out the open wound.

He gave in his copy shortly before the deadline. Nervously, he waited with his friends for the delivery of the journal. News was coming from Rome that caused high tension beyond the Catholic world. At the end of September there had already been rumours that Pius XII's health had seriously deteriorated. They were triggered on a Sunday afternoon in Castel Gandolfo, when the pope lost his voice while he was giving the blessing after the Angelus. For several long minutes, the 82-year-old stood motionless on the balcony of the papal residence. Then he raised his eyes to heaven, murmured 'A Dio!' and left the balcony.

For a long time the pope's legendary housekeeper, Sister Pascalina Lehnert from Altötting, had complained about his 'overwork and exhaustion'. But the Holy Father had 'taken no care of himself, everything had to be looked through, checked, filed and corrected by himself'.[5] Doctors recommended live cell therapy, which the pope had undergone successfully four years earlier. But after the balcony incident, the pope's condition dramatically worsened. A serious stroke deprived him temporarily of consciousness, so that two news agencies were already reporting his death. The report was not true but, just in case, the flag on the Italian presidential palace was flown at half mast. Konrad Adenauer, Queen Elizabeth and US President Dwight D. Eisenhower sent telegrams of condolence. In the following days the pope suffered two further strokes. On 9 October 1958 at 3.52 a.m. Eugenio Pacelli, the 260th successor to St Peter, finally closed his eyes for ever. Four minutes later, Vatican Radio announced: 'Today Pius XII, one of the century's greatest popes, appreciated and honoured throughout the world, passed peacefully away.'

The pope was dead. Millions of people gathered in Rome, as Pius's hearse, decked with four angels and the papal tiara, passed through the streets of the Italian capital. Columns of priests, religious and Swiss guards followed the coffin. The procession lasted for hours. Television stations broadcast it live all over Europe. A certain Giuseppe Roncalli, cardinal of Venice, also took part in the parade, which reached the torch-lit St Peter's Square at dusk. 'Did a Roman emperor ever have such a triumph?' Roncalli wrote in his diary.[6]

Of course, the real question was quite different. It was clear to all observers that an era in church history had come to an end with Pius XII. Pacelli's integrity was great, beyond any doubt. Accusations, which became standard later on, were unthinkable then. As secretary of state, he had written in 1938 to the bishops of the world urging them to try to ensure that the Jews fleeing from Germany were liberally given visas. According to the historian Karl-Joseph Hummel, during Pius XII's papacy up to 150,000 Jews were saved from the Nazi death camps through the help of the Catholic Church. Golda Meir, the future Israeli prime minister, declared in 1958: 'When our people suffered a terrible martyrdom during the decade of National Socialist terror, the pope's voice was raised for the victims.'

It was now clear to all that henceforth a pope of this kind was just as unlikely as a papacy claiming absolute power. But how should a successor be found? Wasn't it time to take a step forward, to reconcile the church with modernity? In the completely changed post-war world the church could not carry on as before. It needed a new awareness of its function. So the coming conclave would give the cardinals the task of finding a representative of Christ from among their ranks who would make the Ship of Peter fit for waters that had never been navigated before.

The very fact that the death of Pius XII became the greatest media event in the post-war period, with unprecedented press interest, showed how much the world had changed. Even Radio Vatican took part in the hype. The radio station had set up a studio in the room directly next to the pope's sickbed, in order to be able to report live on the pulse, temperature and blood pressure of the dying man. In his final hours Vatican Radio broadcast a Mass from the room in which he lay dying, at which the pope's heavy breathing could be heard. The pope's doctor Riccardo Galeazzi-Lisi secretly took photographs of him, which he sold to illustrated magazines such as *Stern* and *Paris Match*.

When Pope Pius was laid to rest in the Vatican Grottoes on 13 October 1958, for the first time in the church's history at the death of a pope, high-ranking delegations from 53 countries and all the world's great religions gathered in St Peter's Cathedral. With the electrifying news from Rome, during the period between the death of Pius XII and the choice of his successor, the October edition of *Hochland* was published. It carried the article by the nameless young professor, a 31-year-old doctor of theology. That moment set the perfect stage for his first appearance to a wide public. For how could it be otherwise, when during those very days Ratzinger not only put church and faith in the witness box

but also sketched a programme for the future? His article began
with the the following words:

> According to religion statistics, old Europe is still an almost
> completely Christian part of the Earth. But there can be no better
> case than this to prove what everyone knows, that statistics lie.
> The appearance of the church in the modern era shows that in
> a completely new way it has become a church of heathens, and
> increasingly so: no longer, as it once was, a church made up of
> heathens who have become Christians, but a church of heathens,
> who still call themselves Christians, but have really become
> heathens.

It was an outrageous statement, and in the next lines he would add
to it:

> Heathenism is entrenched today in the church itself. That is
> the mark both of the church of our time and also of the new
> heathenism. This heathenism is actually in the church and a church
> in whose heart heathenism lives.[7]

The article had the character of a manifesto. It positively called for
a revolution: 'In the long run the church cannot escape having to
dismantle bit by bit its semblance of worldliness, to become again
what she is: a community of believers.'[8]

In Ratzinger's analysis a language can be heard that unmistakably
goes back to Bonaventure's teaching on the church and the end
time. Clearly, he was happy to be developing a vision of the church
becoming small and mystical, once again a community convinced
of its language, its world view and its deep mysteries. For only then
could it display its whole sacramental force: 'Only when it ceases
to be an easy matter of course, only when it begins to present itself
again as what it is, will it be able to get its message across to the
new heathens, who at present indulge the illusion that they are not
heathens at all.'[9]

For the first time, Ratzinger used the term 'de-secularization'.
He was echoing the warning of the apostle Paul, that Christian

communities should not conform too much to the world. Otherwise, they would no longer be 'the salt of the Earth', which Jesus had spoken of. Of course, the church was in the world and *for* the world, to show the way and show love. But it was not *of* this world. It was not self-made and self-determining, but always remained the Lord's foundation on solid ground That also meant 'firmly renouncing worldly positions, getting rid of specious possessions, which were increasingly proving to be dangerous, because they stood in the way of the truth'. Ratzinger spoke against the apparently humane practice of offering anyone, however distant from the church, baptism, a church wedding or funeral without inquiring at all about their belief. 'Thus the sacraments are not only given away but cheapened and deeply devalued.'

In order to track the course of Ratzinger's life, we need to examine his first appearance as a journalist for a bit longer. The article already displays not only the style and mark of the future pope but also the direction of his impact on church politics. To some extent, his essay can be seen as the preliminary sign of that earthquake which erupted at the Vatican Council and poured out its lava. (As we shall see, the Bavarian theologian was to write the overture for it.) But what exactly drove him to write his article? Was it courage? Was it ambition? Was it the stubbornness that he had shown since childhood? 'He has to force himself to fight,' his brother said, 'but when he is compelled to, he will.'

The truth is: Ratzinger could not do otherwise. He could not remain silent when he saw things that had gone wrong. The urge to analyse, to utter the prophetic word, to oppose what he saw as false when required, the duty to resist error, seemed to have been inborn in him, together with his love for the church. The young theologian realized that the part of Henri de Lubac's *Catholicism* on the evaporation of knowledge of the nature of Catholicism was no longer future but present. In his analysis, he said the church had changed from its beginning as a small flock to becoming a world church. Then its great 'story', its truth, its faith, its centuries-old culture, learning, jurisdiction, lifestyle, even its landscapes stamped Western societies. Church and world had to some extent become co-extensive. But that broad coverage had become merely apparent.

It concealed the church's true nature and prevented its necessary missionary activity.

De Lubac had stressed that it remained the church's mission to 'purify, enliven and deepen every nation and every person, through the revelation entrusted to it, and lead them to their true goal'. But was the church itself still aware of the divine gift whose custodian it was? Ratzinger lectured in his diatribe:

> It has become inconceivable for Christians today to hold that Christianity, more precisely the Catholic Church, is the only way to salvation. So the absolute nature of the church, all her claims have become open to question. For example, who could still point out to 'faithful Muslims', as did the great Spanish missionary Francis Xavier, that they 'would certainly go to Hell because they did not belong to the church, which alone could save'?

Ratzinger added: 'It is simply our humanity that prevents us from having such ideas today. We cannot believe that the person beside us, who is a splendid, helpful and kind person, will go to Hell because he is not a practising Catholic.'

Clearly, he was not plagued by spectres and misanthropic fantasies about bottomless pits. By looking at the developments that actually occurred, the aptness of his analysis can be seen. The problem was this. He knew (or at least suspected) that the process of decline of the Christian faith could hardly be stopped. Of course, that which was, which is and which is to come was not wholly determined and unchangeable, but in a sense must be so. According to Bonaventure's and his own view of 'salvation history', there could indeed be improvements. However, under divine Providence, the course of time had long been written in the book of life, the book of meaning and being. 'The master-minding Divine Will leads it unerringly to port,' de Lubac had said of the Ship of Peter. 'For there is a harbour, there is a goal. The universe is crying out for salvation and is also certain of reaching it.'

De Lubac was convinced that it would not do just to copy Christian antiquity or imitate the Middle Ages. Indeed, the church had firm foundations, but at the same time it remained an ongoing building site. It was a house that 'had often changed its style since the time of the fathers'. And 'without feeling superior to them, we have to give it our own style, that is, a style that meets the needs and the questions of our time.' Nothing would be gained by dreaming of an impossible return to the past. But we could also 'marvel at the impressive oneness of the great stream of tradition, which has carried the same imperishable faith along on its continuously renewed and never stagnant current.'[10]

In his *Hochland* article, Ratzinger went a step further. Indeed, there was only one way to salvation, 'namely, through Christ,' he said. But that rested on the co-ordination of two opposing weights, upon two pans which together made up a set of scales, 'so that each pan on its own would be completely useless'. For God could 'choose people in two different ways': either directly or 'through their apparent rejection'. He did not divide humanity into the 'few' and the 'many' (a distinction that occurs frequently in the Bible), in order to throw the many 'onto the rubbish heap and to save the others, but he used the few as the Archimedean point, from which to lift the many, as the lever by which to draw them to himself. Both have their function on the road to salvation.'[11]

Unlike the Frenchman, who imagined that the faith would once more win 'the victory', Ratzinger saw in 'God's way of salvation' the coming of a church of the little people, a church of the simple and the confessors: 'It is given to the few, who are the church, to represent the many in the carrying out of Christ's mission.' Today it sounds like a timely word for the twenty-first century when he writes: 'Individual Christians will strive more vigorously for a fellowship of all Christians and at the same time seek to show their common humanity with unbelievers in a truly human and deeply Christian way.' But we should not deceive ourselves: 'The seriousness remains. There is still the group of those who will be rejected.' And with a side-swipe at his own colleagues, he remarked: 'And who knows whether among those rejected Pharisees there aren't many who believed they could call themselves good Catholics, but were really Pharisees.'

His article in *Hochland* confirmed Ratzinger's reputation as a highly modern theologian. 'When I came to Freising in 1957,' said the church historian Georg May, 'Ratzinger was regarded as the Catholic left genius there.'[12] Franz Josef Schöning, the editor of *Hochland* and co-founder and publishing director of the *Süddeutsche Zeitung,* congratulated the author and praised his analysis as an important contribution. Michael Schmaus, on the other hand, felt himself confirmed in his warning about the dangerous modernist, and used the opportunity for what today is called 'mobbing' or bullying. So it was hardly surprising that in Bonn, where they were considering whether to invite the promising talent to the university, it was discussed with dismay whether it was right to offer a chair to someone of that ilk.

Even some of the staff on the Domberg reacted with outrage. The words 'unsound' and 'heresy' did the rounds. 'In particular, Cardinal Wendel was roused,' Ratzinger recalled. 'He said to me he had heard it was dubious, but he would never base an objection to me on just one article.'[13]

However, the cardinal, the successor to Michael von Faulhaber, who had died in 1952, followed up the idea that had been suggested to him of transferring the young theologian to lecture in the Munich-Pasing College of Education, a training college for teachers of religion. This was a shock for Ratzinger. 'How could they come up with the idea of sending me to such a "piffling little school" as that?' he raged to his friends. That was not his 'charisma'. It would mean the end of theological research for him.

Once again stones had been thrown in his path, which looked like big boulders. Meanwhile, despite the intrigues, an official invitation had been sent to him by Bonn University. But the bishop of Munich declared categorically that he would not let Ratzinger go (although it was usual in Germany to allow theologians, without quibbling, to accept when they received the offer of a chair). 'Then there was an exchange of letters between us, which was troublesome and difficult,' the future pope reported on the dispute with his superior. But 'one day he told me, that he was not happy about it, particularly because of the *Hochland* article, but he did not want to stand in my way and, rather against his will, he let me go.'[14]

In his memoirs, Ratzinger wrote that in retrospect he had 'realized that the trials of these difficult years had been humanly beneficial for me and, so to speak, followed a higher logic than the purely academic'. In one of our conversations he explained what he meant by that rather cryptic remark:

> Well, I had got my doctorate very quickly. If I had also got my habilitation so fast, my awareness of my ability would have been too strong, and my self-awareness would have been one-sided. So I was made to feel very small. That does you good, having to recognize your littleness, not to just stand there as a big hero but as a little candidate on the brink of the abyss, and having to come to terms with what you will do. The logic was that I needed a humiliation and that it had rightly – in that sense rightly – come upon me.

Does that mean you were inclined to pride?

> No, not that. But I believe that if you go from goal to goal and are always being praised, that is dangerous for a young person. It is good to know your own limitations. That you may be subjected to criticism. You have to to endure a negative phase. You have to recognize your own limitations. It doesn't just go from triumph to triumph; there are also set-backs. You need to learn that, in order to rate yourself rightly. You need to endure something and not always think with others. Then not simply judge others quickly from above, but accept them positively with their difficulties and weaknesses.[15]

A key to Ratzinger's character and to his theology, says his student Vincent Twomey, lay in his acceptance of the fact that everything that people did was imperfect. All knowledge was limited, however brilliant and well-read you might be. Ratzinger knew only God was perfect. And every human attempt to rise to perfection ended in disaster. The dialectic and dynamic of the imperfect meant that it remained open to the future.

After these dramatic events, the new professor made a vow: as a teacher, never lightly 'to agree to the rejection of dissertations and habilitation theses but, if at all possible, to take the side of the weaker one'.[16] However, he never wanted to see the copy of his habilitation with the coloured marginal glosses by Schmaus again. It landed in the stove at his home, where it was soon burned up.

It was not easy for him to say farewell to the *Mons doctus*. For almost four years he had shared the flat behind St Benedict's Church with his parents. As a seminarian, doctoral student, lecturer and professor, he had lived on the Scholars' Mountain with only small interruptions from 1945 until 1959, longer than in any other home in Germany. His work for his doctorate and habilitation had been done in the intellectual atmosphere round the college and cathedral. He had got his first academic job here. Above all, he was bound to the place by the most beautiful day of his life, his ordination as a priest. However, Georg also encouraged him to accept the invitation to Bonn: 'I advise you not to let this important chance pass you by,' he told him. A happy coincidence decided him. Georg was appointed as pastor, choir and orchestra master in Traunstein and could take their parents with him. His sister would go with Joseph to the Rhine as his personal assistant.

It is a peculiarity of Ratzinger's biography that he was always in the right place at the right time. Fate catapulted him into a city that was not only the political centre of the rising West German Republic. With its proximity to Cologne, the most important German diocese, it was also the hub and fulcrum of the German Church. That was not all. On 28 October 1959, the conclave had surprisingly elected Angelo Roncalli, who as Pope John XXIII called an ecumenical council only three months after his election, while Ratzinger was still in Freising. It was due to open in October 1962. *Papa Buono* dreamed of a prophetic, servant church. He spoke of *aggiornamento,* the 'updating' of doctrine and the institution. Didn't that also mean a change of mind about the 'new heathens', whether outside or inside the church? Wouldn't Ratzinger's sensational article now become a beacon, or at least an anticipation, of the new pope's great project?

On the morning of 11 April 1959, a Saturday, Joseph stood on one of the platforms of the Munich main station and said farewell to Bavaria – black suit, dark tie, tiny suitcase. Wasn't this not just a departure to a new city but also into a new age for the church? He had announced his arrival beforehand in a letter of 20 March to Dr Hans Daniels, the Director of the Collegium Albertinum in

Bonn, the residence for theologians. 'Dear Reverend Director!' his letter began, cleanly typed by Maria. In it, he requested 'permission to enjoy the hospitality of your house'. It continued: 'I presume I am not mistaken that the room or rooms are furnished and so I need only arrive with "light luggage", until I find permanent accommodation.'[17]

The traveller got into a first-class compartment in the through train to Bonn, sat down by the window and began to read his breviary. Before the train began to move, there was a knock on the compartment door. Outside stood Dr Esther Betz, the young woman from Bogenhausen.

PART THREE

The Council

25

A Star is Born

In the mid-1950s, the German Federal Republic's economic upswing was so well established that the minister of economic affairs, Ludwig Hedland, proclaimed 'prosperity for all'. When the ratified Paris Treaties came into force, West Germany became a sovereign state. The Occupation Statute terminated. The Allied High Commission was dissolved. On 5 May 1955 the Federal Republic flag officially flew for the first time over the seat of government in Bonn. With its accession to the North Atlantic Treaty Organization (NATO), West Germany re-joined the community of nations.

The post-war period was over. But the 'hot' war was now followed by the 'Cold War', in which two hostile blocs stood against each other ready to attack. In the West, the introduction of compulsory military service aroused protests from trade unions, intellectuals and young Christians. In East Germany on 17 June 1953 citizens in 700 places took to the streets to protest against repression, work pressure and an economy of scarcity. The East German Socialist Unity Party (SED) leadership spoke of an 'attempted fascist coup'. The Soviet Union sent in tanks and took over government power in large parts of the country. More than 50 people died in this people's uprising, countless 'ringleaders' were imprisoned and the courts imposed death sentences. A fortnight after the revolt, the West German Bundestag declared 17 June a national holiday. In 1956 the USSR also responded to the popular uprising in Hungary with tanks. The Hungarian government's declaration of independence and call for freedom cost thousands of lives.

The young Professor Joseph Ratzinger took up his job in Bonn on 15 April 1959, a day before his 32nd birthday. The university building still bore marks of damage from the war. But it had kept its noble atmosphere. The Rhineland Friedrich Wilhelm University, founded in 1818 and named after the Prussian King Friedrich Wilhelm III, was one of the largest and most formidable higher education establishments in Germany. Everything seemed well set. The dean of the Catholic Theological Faculty even 'respectfully recommended' and invited his 'Most Reverend Eminence' Cardinal Joseph Frings, the archbishop of Cologne, to Ratzinger's official inaugural lecture on 24 June.

It was noon. Four hundred students, professors and clerical dignitaries sat waiting expectantly. The high windows of the auditorium on the second floor looked out on the romantic Hofgarten, a park with lime tree walks. Then the rather diminutive figure entering Lecture Room VIII aroused astonishment. He was 1.70 metres tall, thin, even scrawny, size 42 shoes and with a boyish appearance – not exactly a vision of authority and maturity. At first, many of the guests thought the man from Bavaria looked like 'the second or third curate in a big city parish'. The traditional headgear, a strange dark velvet cap, which professors had to wear at their inauguration, even made him look grotesque. But when the supposed curate had ended his lecture, all who had heard it knew that a new star had risen in the theologians' firmament.

The threat during the Nazi period, the terror of the war, the hardship in captivity – the course of Ratzinger's life had been anything but carefree. Then came Professor Schmaus's attacks, which had brought him within a hair's breadth of failing to get his habilitation. His bishop's veto had delayed his appointment on the Rhine for months. A year beforehand, on 20 June 1958, he had given a guest lecture in Bonn. The subject he had chosen was *Der Weg der religiösen Erkenntnis nach dem heiligen Augustinus* ('The Way to Religious Knowledge according to St Augustine'), his specialist subject, with which he could score points. Directly after the lecture the famous Bonn patrologist Theodor Klauser, head of the Catholic theological faculty, enthused in a letter to the culture minister about 'Ratzinger's clever and clear line of thought, the precision of his formulations and the assurance of his lecturing'. 'Regardless of his youth', the faculty had decided to 'put him first on the lecture list'. His now retired master had also spoken out strongly for him: 'With his extraordinary talent and astonishing diligence,' Gottlieb Söhngen wrote in a letter of recommendation, 'Ratzinger has an important future to look forward to.'

Bonn at last. Fresh air. Air to breathe. The city on the Rhine was like a revelation to Ratzinger, with its 'pulsing academic life', with 'ideas coming from everywhere', its nearness to Belgium, the Netherlands and, of course, as 'the doorway to France'. Dominican, Franciscan, Redemptorist and Divine Word Missionary establishments formed a ring around the city. He thought of using them as retreats. He found his future colleagues to be 'brilliantly engaged'. In the evenings he watched the boats on the Rhine. He was flooded with 'a feeling of openness and breadth', he said in retrospect. Wasn't the great river, on whose waves he would now also be carried, a metaphor for his dreams of the future? Researching, teaching, writing. Giving himself up to the 'adventure of thinking and knowing' – and altogether doing 'what you most deeply want to do'.[1]

They were eventful years. The first Soviet satellite bleeped in space. Its signal introduced the era of space exploration and caused the 'sputnik crisis', as fear of Soviet technical superiority was soon called. With the foundation of the European Economic Community (EEC), signed by representatives of France, Germany, Italy, Belgium, the Netherlands and Luxembourg, which came into existence on 1 January 1958, Europe took a big step towards unity. On 1 January 1959 Fidel Castro announced the victory of the revolution in Cuba. An event in Warsaw took place without publicity. Nevertheless, it also cast a light on the future.

Karol Wojtyła, a professor of philosophy and social ethics, was invited to the residence of Cardinal Stefan Wyszyński, the primate of Poland. 'Here is an interesting letter from the Holy Father,' began the cardinal. Then he read out Pius XII's letter: 'At the request of Archbishop Baziak I appoint Karol Wojtyła auxiliary bishop of Kraków. Please give your consent to this appointment.'[2] The primate paused to observe Wojtyła's reaction. Anyone else would have tried to gain time. He would have to think about it, spend a night in prayer. That sort of thing. But Wojtyła just said: 'Where must I sign?' Half an hour after that conversation, he hurried to the convent chapel of the Grey Ursulines and knelt before the altar. Hours later the priest was still to be found there sunk in meditation. He prayed for eight hours.

For the last ten years Bonn, Beethoven's city, famed for its magnificent palaces and glorious churches, had been the provisional capital of the German Federal Republic, instead of Berlin. Soon people were talking about the 'Bonn Republic', which clearly wanted to distinguish itself from the first republic, the 'Weimar Republic'. The political and religious complex of the new republic, centred on Bonn and Cologne, was the base for Konrad Adenauer's success and strength. As a practising Catholic, the Chancellor's political activity relied not only on political calculation but also on his Christian world view. He found a congenial partner in Cardinal Frings, the president of the German Bishops' Conference, whose residence in Cologne was just 25 kilometres away, as the crow flies. Frings was a popular church leader, tolerant, diplomatic, but clear in word and deed when it was a matter of Christian values.

Frings smoked cigarettes and cigars. Cigar in his left hand and fountain pen in his right. 'You can foresee the quality of my sermon,' he said, 'from the number of cigars I have smoked.' With Frings's support the Chancellor and leader of the CDU (Christian Democratic Union), managed to build a very successful interdenominational Christian people's party to succeed the purely Catholic-oriented Centre Party. But what Frings wanted from his alliance with Adenauer was a politics that, at least in its main outlines, was directed towards the ethics of the New Testament.

At almost every later period Ratzinger had a job that he had not chosen or wanted. But in his first academic chair, he was most fully himself. 'I never saw him as mellow as he was in Bonn,' said his student Hansjürgen Verweyen. 'Here he definitely felt at his most free.' Ratzinger described his start in Bonn and the stimulating atmosphere of the city enthusiastically as like 'a celebration of first love'. He found it a 'bright and beautiful' feeling 'to be able to contribute to a new beginning for the church and for our country'. In the mood of those years, a spirit reigned 'of being able to live Christianity in a new way' and to 'lead the church into a new future'.[3] Above all, in 'those unforgettable years of breakthrough, of youth and hope before the Council', you were aware that, as a young theologian, 'we had something to say'.[4]

Even the train journey to his 'dream destination' had that new feeling of freedom and lightness. Thanks to his travelling companion, the journey flew by. Esther Betz had knocked shyly on his compartment door while he was deep in his breviary. 'I won't disturb you while you are praying!' she assured him. But she did. 'There wasn't much more praying,' she reported later, 'we had much, so much to tell each other.'[5]

Ratzinger connected Esther – who was three years older than him – with enjoyable student meetings, enthusiasm for music, firm conviction in faith and the enthusiasm of the zero hour. Meanwhile, Betz had been working as a journalist. For the last three years she had been the co-editor of the daily *Rheinische Post* in Düsseldorf. The publisher's daughter was a self-confident and courageous woman. Her father, Anton, the co-founder of the newspaper, was regarded as one of the most influential personalities in the German press. He had been imprisoned by the Nazis and forbidden to do his job. He was a lawyer and journalist from a deeply Catholic family. After the war, he set up the German Press Agency, as well as the Catholic News Agency, and had considerable success in his efforts to democratize the West German media scene.

Ratzinger had been fascinated by publishing ever since he had been a curate. In Bogenhausen he made a first contact with publishers, who would soon be bringing out his books. Esther Betz opened his way to the world of the press and convinced him to adopt a proactive approach to the media. They both made time for meetings, visited each other and went on trips together. They met at Catholic festival days and Salzburg college weeks. During the Vatican Council, Esther regularly met Ratzinger in Rome at discussions behind the scenes. Later, the two of them gave sensational interviews: for example in 1970, on the possibilities and limits for 'criticism of the church'. Ratzinger was godfather to her nephew Florian, and in the mid-1970s he used her holiday home in Sachrang in Chiemgau for a week, to work with his colleague Aloys Grillmeier on a project for a joint series on dogmatics. However, that did not materialize for lack of time, although Maria had already typed hundreds of pages.

Esther remained unmarried, and Ratzinger remained in contact with her into old age. Even when personal meetings became less frequent when he was pope and *Papa emeritus,* he never missed sending his loyal companion greetings on her birthday. Ratzinger was 'an aesthete, who always strives for harmony,' the journalist said. 'When he feels happy with someone, he sticks with them.' She added: 'Even when I did not quite understand him.'

The passages in his correspondence with Betz are some of the most intimate confessions Ratzinger ever made. They say a lot about the man who wrote them. In his greetings from Rome, he wrote poetically about 'the melancholy of the past' and described nature vividly: 'The mimosas have flowered, soon followed by the almond blossom, crocuses and many others.' Not forgetting: 'On my lemon tree on the terrace a ripe lemon is hanging for the second time, and many blossoms are promising a rich harvest.'

Over the decades, the greetings cards are not only an expression of close attachment but also document Ratzinger's constant shortage of time. Early on, the longing can be seen to be released from the enormous weight of an office that he had not sought. 'With the passage of years you feel the burden of such days more and more,' he said in a letter of 16 February 1998 about his great number of meetings and arduous journeys. 'In future,' he would 'have to cut back on those adventures and be more sparing than before.'

In February 2003 he told Betz about 'the great upheavals' that staff changes in his Congregation for the Doctrine of the Faith had caused, which gave him hope of his own retirement. 'No wonder there are rumours that my end is coming. However, the pope does not yet seem to be thinking that way. Thank God we have found good new people [...] even though I should be glad if more restful times were coming for me.' On 13 February 2005, he told his penfriend: 'Unfortunately the work is getting heavier and heavier and my powers are getting weaker.' The letter was signed 'Your Joseph Ratzinger'. Only two months later he was no longer Joseph Ratzinger but Benedict XVI.

Back to Bonn. Upon his arrival, Ratzinger lived for the first eight weeks in the Albertinum residence on the banks of the Rhine. The director, Hans Daniels, gave him a simple room with a view of the river. The familiar seminary world with its clerical timetable (daily Mass, weekly confession, jolly parties with wine and fat cigars) made his transfer from the steady pace of Freising to the pulsing capital city easier. In the mornings he celebrated Mass, attended by an altar server who stood in for the community. The newcomer preferred the altar in the sacristy, because he found the big space in the church too cold.

Dressed in his worn loden coat, with his leather briefcase under his arm containing his notes, in the morning he strolled along Koblenz Street (today called Adenauerallee), then through the Hofgarten to the splendid university building. At last, he had come back to his 'special subject area' – fundamental theology – he wrote in his schoolboy handwriting on the big white pages of the *Album professorum,* the Golden Book for new professors. 'With God's help, it will be my life's work.'

There had never been a start like it at the Friedrich Wilhelm University. Just a few weeks after Ratzinger's arrival, the management had to move the new professor from lecture room IX to the larger lecture room X. And that was still not big enough. The crush was so great that his lectures had to be broadcast through loudspeakers to the Audimax or the Aula. 'His colleague had soon become the most visited person in the whole faculty,' the Albertinum chronicler noted. 'And that throng was not a flash in the pan but continued for the whole semester.'[6]

Ratzinger's manuscripts for the lectures are written in his own tiny shorthand. They contain just the headings. In the lecture room he spoke freely, in illuminating sentences full of images, which had a matchless rhetorical quality. 'He did put his manuscript on the lectern,' the student Gerhard Mockenhaupt reported, 'but he seldom looked at it. His eyes were fixed on the back top corner of the room, as if he could read from there what he was explaining in a fascinating language that was already fit for publication.'[7] But as soon as the bell went, to the students' amazement, the lecturer might stop in the middle of a sentence and leave the room without saying goodbye.

According to his future assistant Siegfried Wiedenhofer, the reason for Ratzinger's convincing performance was his preparation: 'He had internalized everything, gone over it in his mind and thought it through thoroughly.' Wiedenhofer noticed 'an extraordinarily quick ability to grasp things, a mixture of rationality and aesthetics, an amazing intellectual power to sort out and distinguish between positions'.[8] During the lectures it was as quiet as a mouse, like in a concert hall. 'When I heard the first sentences of the lecture on the "Nature and Reality of Divine Revelation",' said the musician and lawyer Horst Ferdinand, attending as a guest, 'it was clear to me that the encounter with Ratzinger would have spiritual consequences.'

In comparison with Ratzinger's, other professors' lectures were old-fashioned and stiff. In fact, the new professor was not concerned with meeting standards but with putting new questions and bringing what was exciting in theology to life again. 'For us, these lectures were an inner liberation,' said the student Agnes Fischer. 'We had experienced the post-war period with all its deprivations and had a strict and gloomy view of the church. Then we met Ratzinger, who explained the church to us from the New Testament and revealed all its breadth and beauty.'[9]

Ratzinger himself spoke with some pride of 'a great crowd of listeners, who absorbed the new tone they believed they heard from me'.[10] He was not interested in just increasing knowledge. He was convinced that you could only learn the true import of Christianity when 'it warms your heart'. He was quite aware of his phenomenal effect: 'When you give a lecture,' he said to Alfred Läpple, 'the students should lay down their pencils and simply listen to you. As long as they keep writing it down, you have not really got to them. But when they put down their pencils and look at you while you are speaking, then perhaps you have touched their hearts.'[11]

The Albertinum, with its cheerful Rhineland celebrations, where Ratzinger felt secure and happy, would soon become history. 'Of course, we all wished him to find his own place soon,' the house chronicler noted. 'But when he finally found one, we realized we would have liked to keep him with us longer.'[12] His new home was in a plain building divided into flats with about 32 tenants in the Bonn suburb of Bad Godesberg. His flat was 95 m², with kitchen, bathroom, two bedrooms, living room (with a pull-out bed for brother Georg) and a study, which of course had a sofa. ('When I have to think through something thoroughly, I lie on the sofa. I always need a sofa.') The rent of 400 DM cost him a third of his professor's salary. The flat became listed in the address book as: 'Ratzinger, Joseph, Dr, Univ.-Professor, and Ratzinger Maria, clerk, Wurzerstrasse 11'. That year the area was known locally for the 'Godesberg Programme', by which the Social Democratic Party of Germany (SPD) departed from its socialist mass base. With its acceptance of a market economy and national defence, and claiming to be no longer just a workers' party but a people's party, the SPD wanted to move into the middle of society.

Joseph had brought his piano with him, and an old walnut desk, a parting gift from his friends in Freising. Both would accompany him all the way to his highest office, along with the teddy from his birthplace, Marktl. With his liking for the practical and his slight hypochondria, he found the new location ideal. There was a doctor in the house ('whom I did not need') and a pharmacy opposite ('which I did not need either'), and then also a branch of the city savings bank: 'You went in and the manager knew all his regular customers' account numbers from memory. That was ideal.' His sister would say later that her coming with him to Bonn 'had been taken for granted'. Others saw it differently. Their father had urged Joseph to take care of Maria. He was worried that the delicate young woman would not cope alone in the world. And she was a support for Joseph. 'He came out of the seminary where everything was regulated. He would have been helpless,' said his student Peter Kuhn. 'He would have had to keep asking someone for everything. That would not have suited him.' But there was also something else.

Maria had become a reserved, shy woman. She preferred to wear an apron. When she went out, she liked to wear a headscarf. In her spare time, she would write letters to her women friends and acquaintances at home. She had once received a proposal but ruled out the idea of marriage. She saw life as service, not self-fulfilment. That did not mean that she didn't occasionally miss her job with the law firm. The relationship between brother and sister was not always untroubled. Maria did not allow him to write on the wall. Students praised her intelligence. Soon they were asking her to take on their doctoral theses, which she gave back to them in perfect shape. When her brother brought guests, Maria cooked for them. She ironed his shirts, darned his socks and told him what to wear.

She did not see herself as a housekeeper (a woman called Hildegard was employed to do that job). Rather, she saw herself as an assistant, who managed Joseph's correspondence and also kept an eye on his official post. (But it was just a myth that her brother gave her his lectures to read in advance to test whether they could be understood.) Nevertheless, his life with Maria meant that theology had to prove itself with someone who was in touch with her neighbours' concerns and heard about them at the grocer's. Thus, his sister became a constant warning to protect the faith of simple people from the cold religion of academics, who dared neither to confess nor to love the church. With Maria there with him it was impossible to float off up into the spheres of pride. A look was enough, and you were back down again where you were supposed to be.

Even though with her provincial appearance she was quite plain, Joseph did not hide her. 'Ratzinger really loved her and took her with him everywhere,' reported his student Viktor Hahn.[13] In fact it was part of the tacit agreement between the three siblings that they did not criticize one another or get in each other's hair, but accepted one another as they were. Even their faults and flaws. 'He believed they each had to take the other's character seriously,' said his professor colleague Ludwig Hödl, 'and you should not try to change their lifestyle.'

In his loden coat the Bavarian in Bonn looked more like a tradesman than a theological genius with wonderful career prospects. He loved concerts, but found going to cafés as unappealing as dinner in expensive restaurants. He enjoyed spending his free time with his neighbour Hödl and other colleagues, playing *Mensch-ärgere-dich-nicht* (a board game similar to ludo), or listening to Karl Valentin records. Frequent guests were the Protestant professor of philology Arno Esch, from the flat opposite, together with his wife, Hertha, who enjoyed discussing Catholic liturgy and art. In the mornings Ratzinger celebrated Mass in the church of the Name of Jesus in Bonngasse or in St Augustine's in Bad Godesberg, where he also celebrated the early Mass on Sundays and the eleven o'clock high Mass.

Ratzinger's ritualized timetable included a walk every morning and evening. Once a week he wrote to his brother Georg and his parents in Traunstein. He did not write 'theoretical discourses' or about his feelings, but just facts, George reported, things from everyday life, 'everything very plain and brief'. For his weekly confession a colleague had recommended an old Jesuit to him, who was deaf and also clearly short-sighted. After giving absolution the old priest would insist to Ratzinger: 'And now we go faithfully to Mass every day like everyone else.'

In Bonn, the priests Ludwig Hödl and Johann Baptist Auer formed a theological trio with Ratzinger. Hödl was a blacksmith's son from Sonnen, deep in the Bavarian forest. He was appointed professor of dogmatics in Bonn almost at the same time as Ratzinger. They knew each other from Freising, where Hödl had studied with Schmaus for his doctorate and habilitation. He had also brought his sister Ida with him. She kept house for him and became friends with Maria.

Auer, who belonged to the generation born in the 1900s, was the son of a Regensburg brewer. His brother had also chosen the priesthood. Auer was regarded as a typical Bavarian. The fatherly friend gave unsought advice, such as what wallpaper was conducive to intellectual work ('contrast makes the room come alive'), and described what went on within the faculty. 'He was our governess. We obeyed him gratefully,' said Hödl. When he said Mass in the Münster church, Auer pulled the great bell rope with one hand to call people to prayer. Every Saturday he was in church to hear his students' confessions.

Konrad Adenauer also had to pass along Wurzerstrasse in the diplomatic quarter of Bad Godesberg. The Chancellor was on the way from his home in Rhöndorf to the Schaumburg Palace, the seat of government. His Mercedes 300, the young Republic's biggest and fastest car (125 hp, costing 19,000 DM), was unmissable. Adenauer had insisted on a lowerable glass partition and an extended wheelbase. For the cost of an extra 3,000 DM the limousine's length was increased to 5.17 metres, giving 14 centimetres more legroom. Because of his father's interest, Ratzinger had been strongly politicized since childhood: 'I was always very interested in politics – and in the philosophy behind it. Politics depends on a philosophy. It can't be just pragmatic, it must have a view of the whole.'[14] As professor and prefect of the Congregation of the Doctrine of the Faith he would be prominent in the analysis of Europe's development, the theology of politics and the social-political formation of the modern era. His books had titles like *Die Einheit der Nationen* (*The Unity of Nations*) or *Wahrheit, Werte, Macht: Prüfsteine der pluralistischen Gesellschaft* (*Truth, Values, Power: Touchstones of the Pluralistic Society*). In Bonn, he developed into a 'convinced Adenauerian': 'And I am still one now like I was before', he told me in our conversations.

The excitement over Ratzinger also did not escape the papal nuncio, Archbishop Corrado Bafile. What could be more obvious than to press his draft lecture on ecumenism, which was still very skimpy, into the wonder-boy's hand? 'My park is your park at any time,' the archbishop told him when Ratzinger gave back the edited lecture. From then on, Ratzinger was a regular guest at the Vatican Embassy's yearly reception on the feast of Saints Peter and Paul. 'That somehow created a feeling of connection with Rome,' Ratzinger said. Half a century later he performed a final service for Bafile, when he celebrated the requiem in Rome for his friend from Bonn days.

He formed another embassy contact with Zachary Hayes, chaplain to the US Embassy. After attending Ratzinger's lectures, the Franciscan enthused: 'He was the best teacher I ever had, and a friendly, quiet, highly cultivated man with a wonderful background knowledge in art and philosophy.' And 'For many of my generation he was a man who opened up a theological vision, and a man who really believed there is something which is the truth.'[15]

For his inaugural lecture on 24 June, Ratzinger wrestled with the subject of *Der Gott des Glaubens und der Gott der Philosophen* ('The God of Faith and the God of the Philosophers'): 'He didn't introduce himself with any fuss,' said his then student Raymund Kottje, 'but just began the lecture. With a high squeaky voice.' Astonishingly, he showed no signs of stage fright. 'I had a good text,' he said later, 'so I didn't need to get worked up.'[16] The question arose from the subject: 'What actually is my own faith? How does it figure in the whole of my life?' Here you had the God of Plato and Aristotle, the God who was reached by thinking. There you had the God of faith, communicated in history to his people through the prophets, and finally through the coming of Christ. And indeed the only God, felt in our hearts, whom human awareness could never wholly cast off, even when it denied him. But didn't the rational approach to the question of God have to exclude both the metaphysical and the emotional?

The Greek philosophers rejected the God of Isaac, Jacob and Abraham, said Ratzinger in his lecture. Likewise, the Old Testament did not know the God of the philosophers. Since Luther, there had been a dispute between theologians as to whether the permeation of Christian dogmas by Greek philosophy had falsified the original true Christianity. Ratzinger saw it differently. In fact, modern research into the history of the relationship between philosophy and theology could show 'that the two ways lead to each other'. In other words: 'Christian faith in God incorporates the philosophical doctrine of God and completes it.'[17] 'Of course we need the God who has spoken, who speaks, the living God. The God who touches the heart, who knows and loves me,' said Ratzinger. 'But he must also somehow be accessible to reason.' A human being was a unity. And something that had nothing to do with reason, but merely ran alongside it, would 'not be integrated into the whole of my existence; it would be an extra, whose justification remained unclear'.[18]

Ratzinger would later call his renewed reflections on the coherence of faith and reason in the search for knowledge of God the 'Guidelines of my Thinking'. Even as a student he had been 'simply fascinated by that existential subject'.[19]

However strongly Ratzinger stressed the importance of reason, he always made clear that personal experience of God in faith and the language of the heart – being addressed by a personal 'you' – went far beyond any philosophical knowledge of God. But the two approaches did not contradict one another; in symbiosis, both helped human knowledge of God and the world. 'With that brilliant speech,' said Heinz-Josef Fabry, professor of Old Testament studies in Bonn; 'he went to his listeners' hearts'.[20] Hubert Luthe, Ratzinger's fellow student from Munich-Freising days, summed up: 'It was undeniable how wholly new it was to hear that kind of lecture and point of view. We had never heard dogmatics like that. All the students were saying: "You've got to go to him." So it's understandable that they piled in in droves.'[21]

26

The Network

The year 1959 is not famous as a 'fateful year', but all the signs of the times were already pointing to that altered mentality which would change Western societies more than even the war had been able to. For a long while now, life had not been just about somehow surviving. The morsel of bread, which had been the epitome of happiness in the hunger years, still fed people, but it did not satisfy their lust for life.

The process of change in the social superstructure could no longer be halted. Everything got faster. You could get faster from A to B, you could do the washing faster and cook faster – thanks to convenience foods. Even books came faster. In the past, people had kept every rusty nail to use again. Now consumption became an expression of the way of life. Letting something rest or ripen was now regarded as deadlock or lethargy. The integrating power of political parties and church and the value of the family were still unchallenged as the basis of society, but a new generation was already drawing dividing lines.

A clear expression of the new spirit of the times was the magazine *Twen,* founded in 1959. It was a new type of magazine: fresh in tone, and attractively designed. The cover showed wild young women and the inside pages were also attractively illustrated. Its theme was youth and youth culture. The intellectual touch was added by writers like Bertolt Brecht, Albert Camus, Hans Magnus Enzensberger and J. D. Salinger. According to the sociologist Norbert Elias, 'the break between those who had grown up *before* and *after* the war' and the revolt against the authorities of the previous generation and their bourgeois narrow-mindedness had descended into an edgy stand-off, which increasingly poisoned relations between young people and those in middle age. Long before 1968, the tension between generations broke into a running battle about the way to live. A lifestyle of blue jeans, bikinis and long hair became a form of self-expression for an increasing number of young people, and a successful life was no longer about *surviving* but about *experiencing*, whatever that might cost.

The 32-year-old Joseph Ratzinger was also a protagonist of the generation change. His 'new tone' struck home through the freshness of his theology, his youthful style and his questioning of traditional doctrines. But it was also because his students were not content to stick with traditional forms and contents. 'Even in his first seminar,' said his future assistant Peter Kuhn, you could feel 'this man is extraordinary, quite different from the usual Catholic professors'. His listeners found him mellow and helpful, without arrogance and with a dry sense of humour. Someone who got involved. A hilarious guest at parties, who gave off-the-cuff imitations of the quirks of his older colleagues. Ratzinger willingly undertook the spiritual instruction of lay students, who had no support studies in the seminary for priests. He also called for the establishment of a chair of general history of religions, which was regarded as too revolutionary (and silently ignored). The student Agnes Fischer, the first woman to get a doctorate in theology, found her teacher 'caring' and 'cheerful'. He was 'a priestly companion who made us feel you are not forgotten'. Theo Schäfer, who was then the student chaplain, said you could see his modesty was genuine because 'while other speakers wanted a hotel room, Ratzinger was happy to stay overnight in my flat in the student community'.

In Ratzinger's lectures, what was exciting and relevant in dogma was then applied to the problems of the modern world. According to Fischer, until then the image of the church had been 'rather dismal'. But with Ratzinger, you felt 'an inner liberation'. Norbert Blum, the future minister for work and social affairs, who was then the spokesman for lay theologians among the students, summed it up: 'He opened up a world, which I knew nothing about [...] When he criticized a prevailing idea, his criticism was always very thoughtful. He was modern but not modernistic. The questioning Ratzinger. That was his strength.'[1]

The professor went on excursions with his students and invited them to supper. 'There was an old-fashioned sofa in his living room with a teddy bear,' Roman Angulanza recalled. 'Ratzinger went up to it and said: "May I introduce you: Teddy, this is Mr Angulanza. Mr Angulanza, this is my Teddy, who has been with me since my childhood days." Then all my nervousness was blown away.' It was important for the new theologian that his students should link theory and practice, study and practise the faith together. So a group was also formed who were committed to helping the poor. Another group got involved with the socially marginalized or organized extra tuition for the children of prostitutes.

However, for many people, the man from Bavaria remained a riddle. Esther Betz spoke of an 'invisible defensive wall' that he had built round himself. Some felt newly moved by faith through meeting him; in others, he brought out behaviour patterns that they usually tried to keep hidden. Ratzinger seemed to be happy in himself, impervious to attacks despite his great sensitivity. His behaviour was also an expression of the careful discretion that he tried to exercise in dealings with others. But he avoided too much closeness and even kept his distance in relating to his assistant of many years: 'Form was observed in the relationship,' Siegfried Wiedenhofer recalled; 'it was correct but there was no familiarity.'

Ratzinger's start was a great success; invitations to academic meetings and requests to give guest lectures, introductions or welcoming speeches piled up. At the beginning of the 1960s he spoke for the first time to a wide readership with his book *Der christliche Brüderlichkeit* (*The Meaning of Christian Brotherhood*). Despite his youth, in a very short time 'he was on all the important faculty committees', according to Heinz-Josef Fabry. 'His thorough knowledge of Latin and his facility with polished language meant that he was almost automatically invited onto such committees, which had to keep in contact with Rome.'[2]

The new generation of theologians were not only developing a new theology but also their own network. Ratzinger was shy but not shy of meeting people. He was not afraid of contact. Particularly not with marginal figures and original personalities, those who did not fit into the usual pattern. He recognized the voices of tomorrow in unconventional thinkers who were often mistrusted by the church leadership and sometimes even persecuted. 'At that time I was regarded as someone who opened new doors and followed new paths,' said Ratzinger in our conversation, 'so sceptical people came to me.' He added:

> Of course it was a different time then. We were all aware that theology had its own freedom and its own job to do – and therefore should not be completely subservient to the magisterium. But we also knew that theology *without* the church became just speaking for yourself and then actually lost its significance. Later those two sides drifted apart. Those who rejected the magisterium went their own way, and those who said theology can only be done within the church went another.

The ring of satellites that now began to gather round the new star in the theological sky included the already mentioned colleagues Johann Baptist Auer and Ludwig Hödl, his Bavarian community. A second ring consisted of friends from his student days, including Hubert Luthe and Klaus Dick. Dick was now the leader of the Catholic College community in Bonn. Luthe was private secretary to Cardinal Frings in Cologne. There was a good connection with the Franciscan priest Sophronius Clasen, professor of medieval studies, a Bonaventure specialist and the editor responsible for a journal with the beautiful name of *Wissenschaft und Weisheit* (*Knowledge and Wisdom*).

A third ring was formed by academics from whose experience and ideas Ratzinger profited. They included: Hubert Jedin, the great Council historian; Heinrich Schlier, a master student of Rudolf Bultmann, the pope of Protestant theology; and the Indologist Paul Hacker, a polymath, who, to the astonishment of his young colleague spent 'whole nights with one or more bottles of red wine in conversation with the fathers or with Luther'. Ratzinger turned to Hacker's research when he lectured on the 'history of religions'. 'Now all he talks about is Rama, Krishna and especially Bhakti,' his listeners groaned, 'we can't stand any more.'

In a fourth ring, Ratzinger worked purposefully on his writing. For example, he planned to write a commentary on a work by Bonaventure with Wilhelm Nyssen, a specialist in Byzantine studies.

Together with Hubert Jedin, he began a *Handbuch der Kirchengeschichte* (*Handbook of Church History*), which the historian finally completed on his own. With Karl Rahner, in 1961 he published *Episkopat und Primat: das neue Volk Gottes* (*Episcopacy and Primacy: The New People of God*). In the run-up to the Second Vatican Council, the book debated questions on the position of the pope and church unity. That was followed by a series of joint projects. At least until the moment when Ratzinger found that, 'despite agreement on many matters and aims, Rahner and I lived on different planets.' [3]

The fifth ring consisted of a circle of close students. When he became pope, Ratzinger would still consult this loose association of people (for example, for suggestions about ecumenism, dialogue with Islam or the doctrine of evolution). The circle consisted of students of different political, theological and personal persuasions, who behaved far from uncritically towards the master and certainly were not subservient. Most of them later became professors of theology and they all agreed on how much they esteemed their teacher; all felt grateful for the respectful and helpful way he behaved towards them.

Later periods in Ratzinger's life, for example his time as a bishop, had their own value. They were not marginal, but they remained just episodes. But the Bonn years were crucial. During this time, as he wrestled with the questions of the day, he created a new kind of theology, made crucial contacts and laid the foundations of a unique career. Let us look more closely to see who and what made a lasting impression on the future pope.

Let us begin with Hubert Jedin, 27 years older than Ratzinger, a historian, whose *Handbook of Church History* remained for a long time the ultimate presentation of the 2,000-year history of the church. He was a priest from Silesia and of Jewish origin on his mother's side. He was banned from doing his job by the Nazis. He found refuge in the Campo Santo Teutonico in the Vatican and used the time in exile between 1938 and 1949 for his four-volume work on the Council of Trent (1545–63), which was praised among academics as an example of modern history writing. He said: 'Nothing did more to promote the schism in the church than the illusion that it did not exist.' [4]

Since 1946 Jedin had held the chair of medieval and modern church history. He was considered a particularly original thinker.

He dictated his books impromptu, while walking up and down in his room. Ratzinger called him a 'personal friend', an honour given to few of his colleagues. What Ratzinger found compelling about Jedin's work was that he was 'an independent historian' who, from the moment 'he saw the attempt to get away from the church, became a strong defender of the ecclesiastical nature of theology'.[5]

Ratzinger also felt drawn to another Nazi victim, his friend and colleague Heinrich Schlier. The Evangelical-Lutheran pastor and theologian was born on 31 March 1900 in the Upper Bavarian town of Neuberg on the Danube. As a member of the Confessing Church, in 1942 he was forbidden to publish. After the war he took over the chair of New Testament and early church history in the Evangelical theological faculty in Bonn. When he converted to Catholicism in 1953, it was a big scandal. He was, nevertheless, the favourite student of the great Protestant theologian Rudolf Bultmann, with whom he did his doctorate and habilitation. Schlier defended his conversion in his book *Bekenntnis zur katholischen Kirche* (*Declaration of Belief in the Catholic Church*). As an exegete, he had discovered that in order to understand Scripture the church was also necessarily involved, and the ecclesiological paradigm of the New Testament was realized best in the Catholic Church. His 'desire for Catholicism' was also increased by anti-Nazi models of resistance, such as Father Rupert Mayer, and also pamphlets and the magazine *Hochland*, which he had secretly bought in the vestibule of a Catholic Church.[6] The conversion of Bultmann's student was particularly bitter for Protestantism because his predecessor in the Bonn academic chair, Erik Peterson, had also gone over to the Catholic Church. Peterson's writings, with their rediscovery of the doctrine of the end time, became so important for Ratzinger that observers later even spoke of a 'papacy under the aegis of Erik Peterson'.

Because of his conversion, Schlier was ostracized as a renegade by Evangelical theologians and not accepted by Catholic theologians either. The professor lost his academic chair. Neither was he permitted to lecture in the Catholic theological faculty, for reasons of canon law. From then on, he continued to read early Christian literature without a salary, which did not prevent 200 Evangelical and Catholic students streaming into his unpaid lectures on a Friday afternoon.

Together with Rahner, Schlier edited the series *Quaestiones Disputatae*. In 1982, together with Ratzinger, he published *Lob der Weihnacht* (*Praise of Christmas*). He wrote about *Das bleibend Katholische* (*The Abidingly Catholic*) and was extensively preoccupied with the Apocalypse, particularly with the period given to the world before Christ's final victory. The warnings in John's Revelation also indicated, according to Schlier, that as the end time drew nearer, 'there would no longer be talk of a Christian world, but only of scattered saints and witnesses'.[7] Humanity's self-deification should be seen as a characteristic sign of the end time. 'Depersonalization, dehumanization, formalization and levelling' were accompanied by 'the disposition and deeds of that peculiar antagonism of all against everyone and everything – basically against God'.[8] Salvation in this phase of history would come from patience, calm, unshakeable faith in God and level-headedness: 'Being level-headed means seeing and taking things as they are.'[9]

The student Peter Kuhn said Schlier and Ratzinger were 'almost yoked together'. The spirituality that found expression in Benedict XVI's Jesus books was strongly influenced by Schlier. The close relationship of the two theologians was shown by the fact that, for eight years after their time in Bonn, they jointly gave a week-long holiday course at the Gustav Siewerth Academy near Lake Constance. Ratzinger confirmed that Schlier had 'certainly had a real influence on me, though it was not just one-way. His synthesis of the spiritual and the historical-critical is unique. I also admired him very much as a human being.'[10] Schlier was 'one of the noble figures in the theology of this century, deeply indebted to the legacy of Heidegger and Bultmann, his teacher, but going far beyond them'.[11] In the foreword to the Italian edition of Schlier's book *On the Resurrection of Jesus Christ,* published in 2004, he called his colleague someone who was 'overwhelmed' by the appearance of the Risen Christ: 'That means a believer, but someone who believes with reason. His whole course was to let himself be overwhelmed by the Lord leading him.'[12]

Paul Hacker, another close companion in Bonn, was also a Protestant – and later convert. Hacker was regarded as one of the leading Indologists of his time. He was born in the small town with the beautiful name of Seelscheid ('soul sheath'), in Sieg-Kreis. He combined a comprehensive academic grasp of Slavonic, English and Romance studies with the knowledge of Indology, Indian languages and research into Vedanta philosophy. A visiting professorship took him to Darbhanga in India in 1954. From 1955 he had held the chair of Indology at Bonn University. Hacker's writings had mysterious titles, such as *Vivarta: Studien zur Geschichte der illusionistischen Kosmologie und Erkenntnistheorie der Inder* (*Vivarta: Studies on the History of the Indians' Illusionist Cosmology and Theory of Knowledge*). However, it wasn't just the fascination with Hinduism that attracted Ratzinger but the fascination with Christianity, which he found to be confirmed by insight into Asiatic religions and cults. He maintained that in the world religions, whether Buddhism, Hinduism, Judaisim or Islam, there was 'a dynamic of longing for God become flesh', which drew them towards one another. That dynamic was directed towards religions' hidden point of unity, where eventually they could and must find each other together. 'In Christ we have the point where East and West meet.'[13]

With his curiosity about Catholicism, Hacker found an ideal conversation partner in Ratzinger, and vice versa. Ratzinger was introduced by the learned Indologist ('a great mind, a powerful but explosive mind') to the source texts of Hinduism, such as the *Bhagavadgita* and the Vedas. Ratzinger then lectured on these without any polemics. So a breath of India blew through the lecture room as the Bavarian professor demonstrated connections between Hindu and Catholic folk piety. The spirit of God also reigned in India, he said. With a Christo-centric overall view, he anticipated important statements from *Nostra aetate,* the SecondVatican Council's document on world religions. 'Generally, only the philosophical aspect of Hinduism was presented,' Ratzinger said, 'whereas I was of the opinion that we should also look into the cultic and mythic aspects too. I am glad I did that then, because when inter-religious dialogue came about, I was already somewhat prepared for it.'[14]

While they were still both in Bonn, Hacker converted to the Catholic Church. Unlike Martin Luther, who assigned love to the worldly sphere, Hacker found that love, as a moment of selflessness, always belonged with faith. Faith without love and kindness would be egoistic; love without faith would be just sentiment.[15] On 12 July 1966 Hacker sent a two-page letter to Ratzinger, in which he gave some key points about the motives for his conversion:

Dear Ratzinger [...] Perhaps something in the following list will be interesting for your work:

1. I have realized that as a Christian you have to be in the church and the church is the Catholic Church. I want to be a Christian.
2. I have realized that the NT (New Testament) is Catholic and I can only take my bearings for my faith from Scripture.
[...]
5. I am Cath. because the church is the embodiment of Christ's love, or to put it differently: because Catholicism is the religion of love.[16]

Yet another relationship begun in Bonn was important for Ratzinger's development. It was his encounter with the exceptional theologian Hans Urs von Balthasar. At first sight the Swiss Jesuit look like the antithesis of Ratzinger. Balthasar, born into a patrician family in Lucerne, was tall, thin and aristocratically reserved. Basically, he was not a theologian but a Germanist and philosopher. Together with the Swiss doctor Adrienne von Speyr, whom he personally baptized after her conversion to the Catholic Church, he founded the secular institute called the Community of St John in 1944 and worked as a freelance writer. Adrienne was a mystic and seer. She received explanations of the gospels and also the Apocalypse in visions, which Balthasar put into writing. After a conflict, Balthasar turned his back on his Order in 1950. In 1960 the theological outsider refused a job at the University of Tübingen. Balthasar was regarded as one of the most learned theological writers of the twentieth century. Above all, he had what Ratzinger lacked or, to put it better, what he kept hidden: a sense of the mystical, up to the most daring heights. 'But we simply got on very well from the first moment,' said his friend.

Ratzinger had already read Balthasar's writings when he was a student. In 1949 he attended Balthasar's guest lecture at Munich University. In Bonn, he got to know him personally in 1960. The occasion was a small discussion meeting on the *Der weltoffene Christ*

(*The Christian Open to the World*), a book by Alfons Auer, the brother of Johann Baptist Auer. Balthasar had invited the young Munich theologian to join the meeting. 'I don't know why he invited me,' said Ratzinger. However, the meeting was 'the beginning of a lifelong friendship for which I can only be grateful'.[17]

Joseph Ratzinger is the sort of person who prefers to let things come to him. He does not often take things into his own hands. He recalled that in the 1950s he had taken to heart a letter by St Ignatius of Antioch: 'It is better to be silent than to speak and not be. It is good to teach if you do what you say.' The city on the Rhine seemed like a gift to him with 'friendships that became important for my own way forward'.

But the paradox of his career also becomes apparent: reserve and a sense of mission, both at once. He made no career plan and did not ingratiate himself with anyone. Rather, his behaviour and the independence he demonstrated could be damaging to his career. As an academic, he saw no contradiction between being both conservative and a reformer.

Of course, Ratzinger's most important meeting was still in the future. It was a close alliance with a man who became an important sponsor of the young talent. Truthfully, we should add that it was not wholly clear who promoted whom most: whether the older man promoted the young man, or the young man the old. For without the 32-year-old newcomer from Bavaria, the older man could not have managed the tasks and the strains he was faced with. *Pro hominibus constitutus* was his heraldic motto: 'appointed for people'. It was Cardinal Joseph Richard Frings, the second of eight children of a cloth manufacturer. As the *éminence grise* of the upcoming Vatican Council, with the help of his 'theological teenager' he would gain the wings of an eagle.

At the end of July 1959, after the final semester exams, Joseph and Maria were sitting on the train to Traunstein. At home Ratzinger wanted to meet school friends, go walking in the mountains, visit concerts in nearby Salzburg and write texts for his lectures and books. He helped out 'Rocket Schorsch', Georg Elst the parish priest, by sharing the pastoral work and holding services in the town prison. As in the old days, he stayed in a simple room in St Michael's seminary.

Everything seemed in good order. But just as when he completed his habilitation thesis, his promotion to Bonn was followed by one of those painful occurrences that make life so difficult. It was not a crash as in Freising, but a harsh blow, a bitter loss, nevertheless.

His father had not been well for some days. On the morning of 23 August, a hot summer's day, he attended Mass in the parish church. At eleven o'clock he took part in the service celebrated by his younger son, high above the town in the seminary. In the afternoon he went for a long walk with his wife. Later his wife reported that on the way home her husband wanted to go back into the church, where he prayed very intensely. Meanwhile, Georg, Maria and Joseph were in Tittmoning, visiting the city of their childhood. 'A wonderful trip,' Georg reported, 'we were very happy.' In the evening their father collapsed. He had had a stroke. There followed two days of fear and hope. 'He always wanted to be 86 and three-quarters,' said Georg, 'when he got past 80 he increased the age and wanted to reach 90.' On 25 August 1959 at about seven o'clock in the evening, the family patriarch fell peacefully asleep. His close family were with him. He was 82 years old. 'We each prayed in silence,' said Georg. 'We were grateful,' Joseph added, 'that we all stood around the bed and could show him our love once more, which he gratefully accepted, even though he could no longer speak.' [18]

His father's death was the greatest loss the future pope had yet suffered. He knew what he owed his father – the talents he had inherited from him and his upbringing. And, above all, the model his father had been for him. From his mother, he had inherited 'a very warm-hearted, poetic soul, which embodied what the faith taught – kindness, the persuasive power of a simple life'. He got his love of nature, flowers and animals from her, and her sensitivity. But from his father he had inherited a sharp mind, straight thinking and behaviour, the sense of truth, honour, a morality drawn from the Gospel. His father combined absolute faithfulness to the church of Christ with criticism of the church leaders. Unmistakably, he also displayed a certain hesitancy, a lack of decisiveness. Joseph had also inherited that characteristic and knew it.

His father, the son of a peasant from the Bavarian forest, had no more than elementary schooling, no great career. He was a simple but bright, cultivated, honourable and upright man. He was the teacher, spiritual master, and literary mentor of his son Joseph. They had shared hardship together, work at home, prayer and festivals. As a child, his father told him stories full of adventure and excitement, introduced him to the Christian faith and was his guide. His natural strictness mellowed in old age. Ratzinger said how important his father had been to him as an adviser in a later foreword to his Bonn inaugural lecture. His father, he said, 'had cared and shared with me in all my work'.

Young Joseph was a late child, a bonus, a gift. Now, at the age of 32, he was half orphaned. His father had done his work and could let go. His son was on his way; he would quickly learn how to cope alone. Ratzinger's report on his first year on the big stage ended on a sad note: 'When I went back to Bonn after that event, I felt as if the world had become a bit emptier for me and that part of my home had moved on to the other world.'[19]

27

Council

The procession went from the Apostolic Palace Courtyard of St Damasus down the *Scala Regia* and through the bronze gate into the middle of St Peter's Square. The paving was wet and shiny, but the rain had given way to gentle sunbeams shining through the clouds. At the front walked the heads of religious orders, the abbots-general and the prelates nullius. They were followed by the bishops, archbishops and patriarchs. Their flowing white rochets and white mitres gave the procession brightness and majesty. Then came the cardinals, in their blood-red vestments, the colour for martyrs. Finally came the bearded Eastern clerics, who looked like a delegation from another world in their dark clothes.

The parade took a whole hour to go past. It was four kilometres long and consisted of 2,500 men. Behind the scenes countless others were at work: the notaries and promoters, the vote tellers, secretaries, telephonists, archivists, editors, interpreters, shorthand writers, technical assistants, ushers, ambulance staff and toilet attendants. Over a thousand journalists had been accredited. They pulled out their pencils and cameras and discussed the secrecy decreed by the pope, because he regarded 'such caution more necessary than ever'. In Germany, children had a day off school. As it was being broadcast live by the Italian public broadcasting company RAI, not just the 200,00 pilgrims present but millions of people in all parts of the globe could follow the procession as it went up the steps and disappeared into the main door of St Peter's, as if it had been sucked in by an invisible force.

It was Thursday, 11 October 1962, the feast of the motherhood of the Blessed Virgin Mary and the opening of the Second

Vatican Council, the largest church gathering of all time. The bishops had travelled to Rome from 133 countries, three times as many as for the First Vatican Council, of 1869–70. At that First Vatican Council, 1,056 were invited (of whom about 800 attended, more than a third of them being Italians).[1] Now there were more than 2,908 (of whom 2,540 took part in the opening ceremony). For the first time, there were bishops from Japan, China and India, and the number of Africans rose from zero to more than a hundred.

At the end of the procession, the pope appeared, carried on the *sedia gestatoria,* the gold-trimmed papal chair. He was accompanied by bearers of the *flabella,* the ceremonial peacock feather fans. The roar of the crowd rose to an ovation. His face shone with joy, as he bowed to the people, accepted their greetings and gave them his blessing.

Councils are conferences of cardinals, bishops, heads of religious orders, representatives of the Roman Curia and the pope, to settle the contents of the Catholic faith, define heresies and clarify the church's relationship to a world that is constantly changing. According to canon law, councils have 'the highest power over the universal church' – with one small restriction: all decisions must be ratified by the pope.

Up to the twentieth century, there have been 20 councils officially recognized as *ecumenical* – 'universal'. The Jerusalem Council of AD 46 – 'the 'apostles' council' – is regarded as a kind of prelude and is not counted with the others. So the first ecumenical council was the Council of Nicaea, today called Iznik, near Istanbul. It was summoned by the Roman emperor Constantine I in the year 325 to resolve the dispute about the nature of Jesus Christ, which was threatening to split the church. The assembly ended with a victory over the initially far more numerous Arian bishops, who disputed the divine Trinity. The Council decreed that the Son was 'of one being' – *homoousios* – with the Father.

The Nicaea confession of Christ as *homoousios* with God the Father is still the creed of the Christian faith today. The church's first doctrinal decisions were also listed in the canons of the Council. For example, that eunuchs could become priests. That bishops, priests and deacons were not allowed to live with a woman (except one who was above all suspicion). That church members who fell away from the faith could be permitted to receive communion again after 12 years of penance. In Canon 20 it was established that, on Sundays and during the season of Pentecost, prayers should be said standing, rather than kneeling. And Easter was always to be celebrated on a Sunday after the Jewish Passover festival.

At first the term 'ecumenical', used by Pope John XXIII, caused confusion. Many thought that it meant a Catholic–Protestant reunification congress. The ecumenical movement had arisen in 1910 within world Protestantism. After the Second World War, 'Una-Sancta' groups were set up in German-speaking areas. These were ecumenical prayer and discussion circles calling for a new ecumenical awareness. However, when the pope used the term 'ecumenical', a 'universal' council just meant a council for the whole Catholic Church, as opposed to national or provincial councils. Pope John had merely kept to ecclesiastical usage, following Roman Catholic Church law, the *Codex Iuris Canonicus* (Code of Canon Law). In it, the section on a universal council bears the heading *De concilio ecumenico*. The papacy could only envisage a reunification of separated Christians as their return to the Catholic Church, which in his 1943 encyclical *Mystici corporis* Pius XII had equated with the mystical body of Christ.

It was two and a half years since the critically ill pope had initiated the project. John XXIII could still see the shock on the faces of the 18 assembled cardinals when he first mentioned the well-nigh forbidden word, on 25 January 1959 in the chapter room of the abbey of St Paul outside the Walls in Rome. Those present had agreed with his speech outlining the condition of the world. For example, when he spoke about the good and evil powers in conflict. Or about modern people who increasingly sought to deify scientific progress. Moral confusion was rampant everywhere on Earth, in villages, cities and nations … No one was prepared for the moment when he dropped the bombshell.

It began quite innocuously. For Christians to contribute better to the world's well-being, Roncalli began his announcement, their faith had to be given new power. Then it came: he had therefore decided to summon a council, an ecumenical council, a council of the world church.

The silence that greeted that historic moment seemed to last for ever. Pope John must have thought of his secretary of state, Cardinal Domenico Tardini, 'Pope Domenico' as the Romans called him because of his powerful presence. The pope had also deplored the state of the world to him. The restlessness and anxiety that were spreading everywhere. The threatening situation between the superpowers. 'What can be done to give the world an example of peace and harmony?' he asked Tardini. But wasn't he himself shocked when suddenly the two unspeakable words unwittingly broke from his lips? 'A council,' he heard himself say.

Tardini, urbane, conservative, sharp-witted, a master of subtle negotiating skills, was an experienced statesman. 'The minister-president of the Vatican must know everything,' was his motto, 'he must have read everything, understand everything, but never divulge anything.' The press wrote that Tardini's ancient Roman reserve came from his self-assurance as a regent who exercises power not for himself but on the instruction of a higher power. As chief of the oldest diplomatic body in the world and the actual leader of Catholic world politics, he had served four popes. The last two, Pius XI and Pius XII, had even considered a council but decided it was unfeasible and all the plans had been filed away. And now? Tardini had said no to being made a cardinal three times, but to Roncalli's suggestion he just answered: 'Si, si!' He nodded his head. 'Si, si!! Un Concilio!'

In the basilica of St Paul outside the Walls, the 18 cardinals still looked frozen with shock. 'I'd like to have your advice,' Pope John interrupted the silence. But there was still no echo. Indeed, they had thought of him as just a 'transitional pope'. He had expected at least a stir, an emotional reaction to his sensational news. On the same evening, he wrote in his diary: 'Humanly speaking, we might have expected that after they had heard our speech, the cardinals would have flocked round us to express their agreement and good wishes.'[2]

For the Second Vatican Council unprecedented alterations were needed. With raised seating for 3,200 participants occupying the whole nave, the inside of St Peter's now looked more like a giant sports arena than the famous masterpiece of Michelangelo, Bernini, Bramante and other great Renaissance artists. The steel construction on both sides of the central nave consisted of ten ascending rows of seats, 190 metres long and 22 metres wide, divided into 40 blocks each with 80 seats. The seats were allocated according to church office and rank. Microphones were set up on the lower rows, and speeches – which had to be exclusively in Latin – were limited to eight minutes. Votes were cast by means of nine Olivetti-Bull voting machines with a magnetic pencil on a modern punch card system. The manufacturer promised that none of the counts should take longer than one hour.

A separate area was provided for observers from other Christian denominations. Official delegates were sent, among others, by the Russian Orthodox, the Coptic, the Jacobite-Syrian, the Ethiopian and Armenian Churches, the Anglicans, the Lutheran World Federation, the Evangelical Church in Germany and the World Council of Churches. In addition, more than a hundred Catholic theologians attended as advisers, so-called *periti*. In the nearby rooms, toilet facilities and infirmaries were set up. But what became the most important place in the Council was the improvised snack bar in the cathedral, which was a meeting point for informal conversations and expressions of indignation. It was called 'Bar Jonah'. 'Bar Jonah' is Aramaic for 'son of Jonah', called Peter, the fisher of men.

When the opening Mass began, each of the bishops removed his white mitre. Pope John strode through the lane of bishops. The Council fathers clapped and cheered him. With 540 million Catholics they represented almost a fifth of the world population of about 3 billion people. Latin America provided about 20 per cent of the fathers (South America 18 per cent, Central America 3 per cent), North America 14 per cent, Asia 12 per cent, Africa 12 per cent and Oceania 2 per cent. The European bishops accounted for about 40 per cent. Most of the more than 500 fathers from Africa and Asia were also of European descent, with a third being Italian.

Originally, 146 bishops were supposed to come from the Communist countries, but only 50 arrived. The rest were prevented from taking part or were in prison. Of the 144 Chinese bishops invited, 44 got to Rome, but none from Korea or North Vietnam. The oldest participant, Monsignor Alfonso Carinci, had also been at the First Vatican Council as a choirboy. He was approaching his 100th birthday. The youngest, the Peruvian Alcides Mendoza Castro, was just 34. Somewhere in the crowd was a certain Karol Wojtyła. Since June 1962 he had been acting head of the diocese of Kraków but was completely unknown throughout the church. 'I am setting out on this journey with deep emotion,' the 42-year-old had said in his farewell to the faithful in his home city, 'and with great trembling in my heart.'³

John XXIII was the son of peasants from Sotto il Monte in the diocese of Bergamo, which even in Catholic Italy was regarded as *cattolicissima terra,* the most Catholic soil. He had initiated the Council but saw himself merely as its midwife. He regarded everything else as due to divine Providence. 'God knows I am here,' he consoled himself in dark hours, 'that is enough for me, even if no one else could care less about me.' At the opening ceremony in St Peter's, when he reached the altar he knelt down. Then began the first official prayer of the Second Vatican Council, the *Veni Creator Spiritus* ('Come, Creator Spirit'), in which pope and Council fathers together asked the Holy Spirit for light and leadership. They all stood up and went along with the singing to the mighty sound of the organ. That included the guests from 18 non-Catholic Christian churches and communities from 79 states, who were following the spectacle enthralled. Germany was represented by the CDU foreign minister, Gerhard Schröder, who led a special delegation from the federal government.

The opening ceremony lasted seven hours. At the pope's express wish, the Gospel was sung in Greek, and the intercessions were also sung in Slavonic and Arabic languages, as a Byzantine *Ektenia,* a litany from the Divine Liturgy of the Orthodox Church. Then, according to the form prescribed in canon law, the head of the church led the Creed, which the fathers joined in together. In the following obedience ceremony, the cardinals and patriarchs went up one by one to the throne and declared their unconditional obedience to the *pontifex maximus* by genuflecting, many even kissing his foot.

According to protocol, Cardinal Alfredo Ottaviani stood at the right-hand side of the pope. Outside, in front of the cathedral, someone was waiting who would one day succeed the redoubtable pro-prefect of the Holy Office. Joseph Ratzinger was still merely an unofficial adviser and, as such, was not permitted to take part in the ceremony inside the cathedral, or in the meetings. However, the meaning of worldwide church and universality had never been so clear to him. The mighty Vatican buildings, the endless stream of dignitaries, the elaborate ritual and the masses of people from all corners of the Earth symbolized a religious Imperium which not only incorporated a thousand-year-old tradition but also had institutional, cultural, legal, intellectual and mental power. It was the paradox of an institution that was supposed to be both strong and weak, well defended and defenceless, strict and merciful. It was meant to be both rich and poor, formidable and forgiving, lofty and humble, both in heaven and wholly on Earth – basically an impossibility.

Of course, the Papal States had shrunk to a tiny area around St Peter's. But did that mean that 'the pope's divisions', as Stalin once scoffed, had become weaker? With its strictly organized army of hundreds of thousands of priests, monks, nuns, deacons, missionaries, preachers – and more or less faithful bishops, who operated in districts in every country. With millions of people involved in mainly charitable undertakings. With its own universities and an enormous throng of scholars. With schools, nurseries, hospitals, hospices, orphanages, care homes. With its own publishers, journals, printing presses. Countless millions of people visited its holy sites around the world. Somewhere in the world, from the outer limits of Mongolia to Times Square in Manhattan, the mysterious Eucharistic meal in the form of the host was constantly being given in communion at Mass in a Catholic church. The number of its adherents grew from day to day, apparently unstoppably. And at its head stood a monarch who claimed not only earthly but also divine authority: his holiness the pope, Christ's representative on Earth.

'In fact,' *Der Spiegel* commented ten days before the Council's opening, 'currently the Roman Catholic Church – after a 2,000-year-long history – has achieved a unity and consistency in teaching and structure never before seen. Today it presents an unprecedented example of a spiritual community: It possesses "a single truth" and a single custodian of the truth.' In that respect, it outstrips 'its only opponent today with similar mass impact: world communism'.[4]

Above all, this church stood for a sovereign message – and for a Lord, to whom not only the world but the whole universe belonged. Yet weren't the signs of the times pointing to a coming storm? No one spoke of a crisis. It was more of a feeling. A feeling that this church, as it was, was no longer fit for the time.

Somewhere in the crowd, the 35-year-old Joseph Ratzinger felt the 'moment of extraordinary expectation'. His inner voice told him: 'great things were to happen'. In the past 500 years the mechanism of a Council had only been resorted to twice. The first time was with the Council of Trent, the so-called Tridentinum, from 1545 until 1563, summoned by Pope Paul III on 22 May 1542. The second time was with the First Vatican Council, summoned by Pius XI on 29 June 1868 on the 1,800 anniversary of the martyrdom of Peter and Paul. At the Council of Trent, in 25 sessions, about 100 participants dealt with how to respond to Luther's Reformation. The most important decisions included measures against the abuse of indulgences and against the accumulation of offices by bishops. The Council also decided to set up seminaries to improve the training of priests. The First Vatican Council, from 1869 until 1870, was interrupted by the French declaration of war on Germany. It ended with a new schism – the secession of a group calling themselves the 'Old Catholics' – and the break-up of the Papal States, which had spread all over Central Italy and even had its own ships.

Unlike with all the previous Councils, this time there was 'no particular problem to solve'. In a way, it was about the whole thing. 'Christianity, which had built and shaped the West, seemed increasingly to be losing its defining power', Joseph Ratzinger thought, as he witnessed the historic moment. 'It seemed to have grown tired, and the future seemed to be determined by other spiritual forces.'[5] It had to catch up with 'the world of today so that it can again have power to shape tomorrow'.[6]

Pope John's word *aggiornamento* – 'updating' – had mobilized a new energy. Everything should become fresher, newer, more vivid. But wasn't it also clear that the Roman Curia with all its power – and all its guile – would undermine any attempt at reform? Didn't the prepared schemata bear the stamp, in content, style and mentality, of precisely that Roman neo-scholastic theology which needed to be overcome? Yes, the entry into St Peter's was impressive. But, Ratzinger wondered outside in the Square, 'Is it normal that 2,500 bishops, not to mention the many other believers, should be condemned to remain silent, become mute spectators of a liturgy in which, apart from the officiating clergy, only the *Capella Sistina* had a voice?' Where was the updating? 'Wasn't it a symptom of the situation that needed to be overcome, that the active participation of those present was not allowed?'[7]

Certainly, the committees had worked hard in preparing for the Council. But their diligence also had something oppressive about it. Their preparation work had produced 70 schemata, which filled a volume of more than 2,000 pages. 'How could you find your way through that enormous forest of texts?' he worried. 'How could the Council distil a comprehensible driving force from them to move the people of today.'[8]

Some bishops from the USA had given to understand that they would remain, as a matter of form, for two or three weeks in the Eternal City and then go home. In Rome, everything had been so well prepared in advance that only the signatures were lacking. Indeed, three years earlier, on 30 October 1959, Cardinal Secretary of State Tardini had asserted: 'The Council is so well prepared that it won't need to last very long.'[9] On 8 November 1961 the Council secretary, Pericle Felici, announced, 'The Council should begin in October 1962 and if possible close before the end of the year.' John XXIII had even refused to buy the equipment and seating for the council chamber; for such a short period it was better to rent it. When Felici presented him with the revised and approved schemata for the Council, Roncalli exclaimed enthusiastically: 'The Council is a done deed, we can end it by Christmas!'[10]

It was only Roncalli's opening speech that Ratzinger could judge less harshly. Nobody guessed that – one year ago – he himself had given the inspiration for the pope's homily. 'Mother Church rejoices that, by the singular gift of Divine Providence, the longed-for day has finally dawned,' Pope John XXIII his address. At this moment, 'the Christian, Catholic and apostolic spirit of the whole world expects a leap forward'. A leap forward 'to go more deeply into the teaching and raise consciousness in faithful and full agreement with the authentic doctrine'. The Council's greatest concern was 'that the sacred deposit of Christian doctrine should be guarded and taught more efficaciously'. The church should never depart 'from the sacred patrimony of truth received from the fathers'. But at the same time she must 'always look to the present, to the new conditions and new ways of life in the modern world, which have opened new avenues to the Catholic apostolate'.

The pope regarded 'Gaudet Mater Ecclesia', the Latin opening words of his speech, as the key and the pointer for the Council. In his speech he warned against false prophets:

> In these modern times, they can see nothing but destruction and ruin. In comparison with past eras, our own era is constantly getting worse [...] We must disagree with those prophets of gloom, who are always forecasting disaster, as though the end of the world were at hand. In what is happening at present, when humanity appears to be entering a new world order, we must rather see a hidden plan of Divine Providence.

He went on: 'The church has always opposed these errors. Frequently she has condemned them with the greatest severity. Nowadays, however, the church prefers to make use of the medicine of mercy rather than that of severity. She considers that she meets the needs of the present day by demonstrating the validity of her teaching rather than by condemnations.' He trusted that the church would draw new energy and strength from the Council and 'look fearlessly to the future'. In conclusion, the Bishop of Rome reminded the Council fathers of their duty to follow the inspirations of the Holy Spirit, so that their work might fulfil the expectations of the moment and the needs of the peoples of the world. That 'requires from you serenity of mind, fraternal harmony, moderation in proposals, dignity in discussion and sound advice'. John XXIII ended his speech with an emotional appeal: 'Illuminated by the light of this Council, we confidently trust that the church will increase in spiritual riches, and given that new strength, she will look fearlessly to the future.'[11]

The crowd had dissolved. Ratzinger wandered around for a while. Then he went and stood on the terrace in front of the cathedral, turned round and looked at the city of Rome. With his professorship in Bonn he was at the political centre, and by his close contact with Cologne he was at the ecclesiastical centre of the blossoming Federal Republic. But with the Council, he had gone beyond national boundaries. Hubert Luthe, bishop of Essen, later said of his travelling companion, that in those days in Rome he seemed 'like a supernova', a man aged just 35 who had left the enclosed arena of a German university to perform a new play on the world stage.

The Council's opening ceremony ended for Ratzinger with an 'unforgettable' experience' when, after dark, half a million people bearing torches entered St Peter's Square. In the moonlight they formed a giant circle round the obelisk. Then the third-floor window of the Apostolic Palace opened. Visibly moved, Pope John waved to the people. 'When you get home,' he called to them with a shaking voice, 'give your children a goodnight kiss and say: That's a goodnight kiss from the pope. You must know that especially in sad and bitter moments the pope is with his children. He is a brother, speaking to you, who by God's will has become a father.'

Nobody guessed that the church would be changed more radically by the Second Vatican Council than for many centuries before it. And that the road to its ending would be a particularly hard and stony one. Neither did anyone guess that, through secret events on the island of Cuba, during those very days the world would be brought to the brink of an unprecedented catastrophe, which threatened to destroy a large part of the planet.

28

The Battle Begins

Councils influenced the weal and woe of the church but were also milestones for world history. According to the Harvard professor Stephen Greenblatt, it was not the discovery of America or the impact of Luther's Theses that rang in the new era, but the Council of Constance from 1414 to 1418, the biggest congress of the late Middle Ages.

Indeed, the Council of Constance anticipated the colour and zest of the Renaissance and marked a change of epoch. It was the beginning of the period of great conquests overseas. There were now weapons with gunpowder. For the first time, people had mechanical clocks to go by. At Constance, for the first time, they voted by 'nations'. That led to the ending of the Western Schism and to the restoration of unity, albeit for only a short time.

When had here been such opulence and internationalism? With the onslaught of 29 cardinals, about 250 patriarchs, archbishops and bishops, over 150 abbots, 1,700 acrobats and musicians and people from everywhere, Constance became a bubbling kettle. People were even housed in wine barrels. Danish and Spanish scholars met at fish stalls. Orthodox Byzantines borrowed money from 'money changers from Florence'. During the summit, which lasted three and a half years, in total there were about 150,000 participants, including the head of the Sorbonne, the queen of Bosnia, nearly 2,000 mainly Italian clerks and writers and 73 bankers as well as bakers from northern Italy with portable ovens, in which they baked a kind of pizza. There were also 700 *Hübschlerinnen* ('little pretties'), as the itinerant prostitutes were called, who during pauses in the meeting sprawled in the run-down German monastic libraries – and discovered unknown speeches by Cicero beside them.

With great pomp on 28 October 1414, the Pisan pope John XXIII arrived in Constance on a white horse, accompanied by nine cardinals and the Curia. A few months later he had to flee by night, disguised as a page. In fact, he had come to oust his two rival antipopes. In the end, all three popes were deposed and a new fourth one elected. The Pontifex from Pisa was not counted in the official list of popes. So for more than 500 years there was no John XXIII, until Giovanni Roncalli came on stage.

The Council of Constance had three aims: first to restore the unity of the church; second, to eliminate the heresies that had begun to creep in; and third, to reform moral life, especially of the clergy. A decree on a radical clean-up was directed at the reorganization of the Roman Curia. Eliminating confusion in questions of authority, faith, indiscipline and immorality had to begin with the most important act: the right service of God in the liturgy: 'In such a demanding and difficult undertaking as the reform of the church,' the first session on 5 November 1414 declared, 'we can in no way rely on our own power but must trust in God's help. That is why we must begin with divine service, and particularly the devout celebration of Holy Mass.'[1]

Because Catholicism 'was often attacked, even by those who should have looked after the faith, but also by heinous liars', in its 39th session on 9 October 1417 the Council of Constance prescribed the following oath to be taken by future popes:

> As long as I live, I will loyally keep and confess to the Catholic faith in accordance with the tradition of the apostles, the general councils and the other holy fathers. I will keep this faith unchanged to the letter and confirm, defend and preach it, even to the point of giving my life and my blood. Likewise, I will follow and maintain the traditional rite of the Catholic sacraments in full.[2]

With the First Vatican Council from 8 December 1869 until 20 October 1870, the Council fathers passed three dogmatic constitutions. As decrees with constitutional status, they were intended to enshrine the contents of the true Catholic faith and give a definition of Christ's church. They included the infallibility of the pope in questions of faith and morals. The German participants wanted neither to accept nor to reject the dogma of infallibility and preferred to depart quietly. The expansion of bishops' responsibility, which aimed to ensure that no suffocating centralism arose from the power given to the pope, did not materialize. France declared war on Germany. Piedmontese troops occupied the Eternal City. The Council was at an end.

When the precipitously interrupted Council was due to be resumed 50 years later, after first approving the plan Pius XI rejected it. 'We prefer to wait a bit longer,' he stated in his encyclical *Ubi arcano dei consilio* of 23 December 1922, 'and like the famous leader of the Israelites, pray that the kind and merciful God may make his will clearer to us.' One of his advisers, the French cardinal Louis Billot had urgently dissuaded him: 'The resumption of the Council is desired by the wickedest enemies of the church, namely the modernists, who are preparing [...] to bring about the revolution, the new 1789, which is the object of their hopes and dreams.'[3]

Pius XII also aborted the idea. In February 1949 he had set up a preparatory committee for a new council but then cancelled the project. Clearly, the conflicts in the committee presaged powerful clashes. So the surprise was even greater when, in January 1959, John XXIII announced the summoning of the Second Vatican Council, just 90 days after he had been elected. There had been no previous consultations or forewarnings. In his diaries, the pope twice spoke about his decision. On 15 January 1959 he noted:

In conversation with Secretary of State Tardini I wanted to know his attitude to the idea that I intended to put to the members of the College of Cardinals [...] the plan for an ecumenical council [...] I was fairly hesitant and uncertain. His immediate answer was the most delighted surprise I could ever have expected. 'Oh, but that's a brilliant and holy idea. It comes straight from heaven. Holy Father, we must attend to it, work it out in detail and circulate it. That will be a great blessing for the whole world.'[4]

In the entry for 20 January, five days before the announcement, the pope's diary says:

> In the audience with Secretary of State Tardini, the word 'council' occurred to me for the first time. I'd almost call it accidental. That the pope could offer this as an invitation to a widespread stirring of spirituality for the holy church and for the whole world. I was afraid I would get a smile and a discouraging grimace for an answer.[5]

At first, Cardinals Ottaviani and Ruffini indicated that in the conclave of October 1958 they had already advised the newly elected John XXIII to summon the 21st general council. In an interview with the weekly paper *Epoca*, Ottaviani said:

> To be precise, it was me who sought him out in his bedroom on the night before the conclave and said to him: 'Your Eminence, we must think about a council.' Cardinal Ruffini, who was present at the interview, was of the same opinion. Cardinal Roncalli made the idea his own and later said: 'I thought about a council from the moment I became pope.' That's right, he took our advice.[6]

Pope John stuck to his version. According to a written record of his general audience at the beginning of May 1962, he said he had reasoned that 'today's world is sinking deeper and deeper into fear and uncertainty [...] Of course, people keep chattering noisily about peace and understanding, but it always ends up in sharper antagonisms and stronger threats.' This had led him to think:

> Should the mysterious little ship of Christ let itself be tossed up and down by the waves? Don't people expect more from the church than just a warning? [...] All at once the great idea dawned on me. To see it – with complete trust in the divine master – was to seize it. The word pressed itself onto our lips, solemnly and forcibly, and for the first time our tongue uttered it: a council! To be honest, the fear arose in us immediately that we had said something startling and shocking.[7]

Since the middle of the nineteenth century, the Catholic Church had been on the defensive. In the battle against liberalism, socialism and communism it was anti-modernism that dominated its image. Reputedly harmful doctrines were forbidden; critical theologians were put on the Index; contacts with the non-Catholic environment were strictly regulated. Many, therefore, interpreted Roncalli's word *aggiornamento* as the long-overdue adaptation to modern life and not, as the term actually meant, adjusting what they were doing. But for John XXIII, the Council was also a peace initiative, which had become necessary in the Cold War situation. One of his predecessors, Benedict XV, had failed in his attempts to make peace during the First World War. The first 'modern war' was followed by the collapse of Russia, the Hapsburg Empire and the rise of the communist world empire. Pius XII had to look on while powerful dictatorships developed in Europe, which led to millions of dead on battlefields, in concentration camps and gulags. After 1945, frontiers changed even more radically than after the First World War. Spheres of influence moved, and no stable order followed the tectonic shift. Now the pope thought it necessary to create a new relationship with the nations, to deal with the dangers of the increased power of the communist system and offer solutions for the mission countries in the Third World. The church should check what it was doing in order to be able to make its contribution. But to do that, it needed not only to become aware of its strengths but also to refashion itself.

What exactly the pope aimed to achieve by the Council still remained unclear for many people. Pope John was 'an exceptionally likeable, honest personality who was able to laugh at himself,' said Karl Rahner. At the same time, he was 'dauntlessly innocent and, apart from quite general ideas, had no inkling about how the Council should go'.[8] For a long time Roncalli had only occupied second-rate positions, such as Apostolic Visitor in Bulgaria or Apostolic Delegate in Greece and Turkey. He would have preferred to be a country priest or church historian. He had saved thousands of Slovakian Jews by diligently signing and handing out transit visas to Palestine. He calmly accepted that he was not taken seriously by the Curia. 'I will always speak the truth, but gently and say nothing about any of the injustice and offence which I feel I have suffered,' he scribbled in his diary.[9]

He received his first more important job – as nuncio in France – in December 1944. After that, Pius XII appointed him as Patriarch of Venice in 1953. After the death of the ascetic, aristocratic Eugenio Pacelli, it was regarded as certain that Giovanni Battista Montini, Cardinal of Milan, who belonged to the progressive wing of the church, would ascend the throne of Peter. However, after 12 rounds of voting, the 76-year-old peasant's son Angelo Giuseppe Roncalli emerged victorious from the conclave. He was the oldest head of the church for 200 years. There were 51 cardinals present. Of the 18 cardinals who were Italian, 11 belonged to the Curia.

Roncalli was hard to classify. As priest, papal diplomat and bishop (motto:'obedience and peace') he was not exactly a newcomer. The new pope aroused no expectations in advance; no one expected surprises. Many of those who voted for him saw him as a 'stand-in for a greater pope to come', as Cardinal Frings put it. John XXIII explained immediately after the conclave that he had chosen the most common papal name 'to shield the insignificance of our own name by adopting that of the largest number of Roman popes'. Moreover, all 22 popes with the name John had had a short papacy, he added with a smile.

It was clear that the main theme of the Council was to be the church itself. The aim was to shield the content of the faith and also express it afresh for the present time, to *aggiornare* – update it – as the pope put it. The church's teaching authority in dogma was not to be given up but clarified. *Der Spiegel* noted in October 1962: 'The inner unity and consistency of the Roman Catholic Church is, therefore, the central theme, the central challenge and the central object of the coming Council.'[10] That summary matched the opening speech of 11 October 1962, in which Pope John made clear that the Council's task was 'to convey doctrine clearly and fully [...] without toning it down or distorting it'. The primary task was 'to deepen the irrevocable and unchangeable doctrine, which must be faithfully respected'. Deepening meant 'formulating it in such a way that it meets the needs of our time'.

Titular Bishop Pericle Felici, the General Secretary of the Council, was relaxed about it. He calculated that the assembly of churches from all over the world would last about two months. Sebastiaan Tromp, Cardinal Ottaviani's influential adviser, said in the early autumn of

1962: 'The gentlemen will not have to stay long in Rome. They will soon see that the documents submitted can't be improved on. They will sign quickly and go home.'[11]

In fact, a brief history of the Council preparations tells a quite different story. The Vatican itself suffered serious crises. There were ugly animosities, malicious intrigues, suspicions and crucial votes, but also brilliant word battles, genuine fellowship and pioneering documents, which for better or worse brought about a decisive turning point in the 2,000-year history of the Catholic Church.

To anticipate: instead of just one session, as originally planned, the Second Vatican Council was extended over four sessions, each lasting several months, from 1962 until 1965. There were 281 days in session, attended by nearly 3,000 Council fathers. Two-thirds of them were secular clergy, from all over the world; the rest belonged to religious orders. The average age was 60. Between the opening and closing of the Council 253 fathers died. Some 296 additional clergy attended.

They convened in 136 general congregations. There were 640 Council speakers and 544 ballots. The four sessions produced four constitutions, nine decrees and three declarations. The complete written record of the Council filled 200 volumes; the tape recording of all the General Congregations had a playback time of 542 hours. The total costs were comparatively small. They amounted to $7.25 million.[12] That was $9 per participant per day, with considerable expenses incurred by the Council fathers themselves having to be contested.[13]

The first stage of preparations began at Pentecost, 17 May 1959, with the summoning of the *commissio antepreparatoria,* the Council's pre-preparatory committee. For it, the pope selected a representative from each of the ten congregations of the Roman Curia. He appointed the exuberant 48-year-old Curia official Pericle Felici as general secretary of the committee and raised him to the rank of archbishop three months later. The chairman was his right-hand man, Cardinal Tardini. In June 1959 Tardini sent out an international questionnaire to 2,700 individuals (bishops, patriarchs, abbots and other authorities), as well as to the dicasteries of the Curia, theological faculties etc. It asked for 'opinions, advice and wishes' about 'subjects and themes that could be discussed at the forthcoming Council'. The deadline for replies was 1 September 1959. As the response was too meagre, in March 1960 a reminder was sent out to those who had not yet replied.

At Pentecost on 5 June 1960 Pope John signalled the beginning of the second phase. The newly set up Central Preparatory Committee, subdivided into ten working groups, consisted of 108 cardinals, bishops and heads of religious orders (plus 27 advisers) from 79 countries. The chairman was the pope himself. The task of the working groups was to evaluate the approximately 3,000 answers to the questionnaire. Taking these into account, together with their own suggestions, they were to draw up the schemata for the Council to discuss and decide on. In the end, these drafts filled eight enormous tomes. In addition, three volumes came from the theological faculties, for whom the Curia Congregation for Catholic Education was responsible. One volume contained all the pope's statements about the Council, two volumes had an analysis of the suggestions and there was a one-volume index. Altogether, the material amounted to about 10,000 pages.

In order to approach the non-Catholic Christian churches and communities, Pope John set up the Secretariat for Promoting Christian Unity. It was to be led by the German Jesuit Cardinal Augustin Bea, Pius XII's confessor. On 9 July 1960 the themes to be worked on, selected or approved by the pope, were sent out by Felici to the members of the preparatory committees and secretariats. The Eucharistic World Congress that met in Munich from 31 July until 7 August 1960 (the first big event in Germany since the war) was seen by Pope John as a dress rehearsal for the Council. There 80,000 faithful experienced new changes to the liturgy, which later became established as a set part of it. Ratzinger gave lectures and attended a meeting of the Una Santa group, which strongly advocated ecumenism. November 1960 was the official beginning for the work of the committees. Pope John welcomed the 871 participants into St Peter's. They included 67 cardinals, 5 patriarchs, 116 archbishops, 135 bishops, 220 secular priests, 282 priests in religious orders and 8 lay people.

It was still too early to tell where the Council would lead and what consequences it would have. There were no limits to what was imagined. All over the world individuals and groups made announcements in order to throw their ideas into the ring and make the mega-congress serve their own interests. In particular, theologians regarded as belonging to the progressive wing strove to become opinion leaders through lectures, contributions to newspapers and books. The *Kleine Konzilsgeschicte (Ecumenical Councils of the Catholic Church: A Historical Outline)*, by Hubert Jedin, Ratzinger's colleague and friend, was published in 1950 in an edition of 100,000 copies. Ratzinger also joined in the battle. In 1961 he added to the debate about 'possible themes for discussion' by the Council with his book *Episkopat und Primat (Episcopacy and Primacy)*, a joint work with Karl Rahner. Another joint publication, *Offenbarung und Überlieferung (Revelation and Tradition)*, appeared a bit later. Up to 1966 Ratzinger published four more works, evaluating the individual sessions. 'There is an absolute blizzard of publications, lectures and meetings,' the 72-year-old Cardinal Ernesto Ruffini complained in *L'Osservatore Romano* on 24 August 1961, 'in which reckless judgements and fairly shocking interpretations often prevail.'

Ratzinger was first confronted with the Council in December 1959. At its monthly meeting the theological faculty of Bonn University pondered over a request from Cardinal Frings, a member of the Central Preparatory Committee, for subjects that he could raise in Rome. On 6 September 1959, Frings himself had already presented two schemata but was not happy with them. They were about trivial things like 'the reduction in the number of reports to be sent to Rome' or the 'simplification of the transfer of priests'. Ratzinger rose to much greater heights. He suggested that the Council should examine and define more precisely the relation between Scripture and tradition within their joint source. That had been a burning issue for him since his Bonaventure studies. But his colleagues blocked it. Instead, according to the church historian Norbert Trippen, at a later faculty meeting on 17 February 1960 they agreed on 'a meagre list of random desiderata'. It included 'the doctrine of the church, especially on the office of bishops' or the rearrangement of the Scripture readings in the breviary. Ratzinger was given the task of editing the suggestions and translating them into Latin, the official language of the Council.

Meanwhile, all over the world theologians were working through the night on statements and expert opinions for the Council fathers. International contacts between bishops were newly formed or refreshed. The papal nuncios reported in confidential dossiers on the activities in different countries. Of course, the pressure groups were active with conspiratorial meetings, approach planning and agreements about particular issues.

For example, in June 1962 Cardinal Léon Joseph Suenens, the new archbishop of Brussels-Malines, gathered a group of cardinals in the Belgian College in Rome to discuss their own 'plan for the Council'.[14] Cardinals Döpfner, Liénart, Montini and Siri took part at the meeting. In the Netherlands a new 'theology of the episcopacy' had taken shape, which its advocates hoped would prevail at the Council. Cardinal Primate Bernard Jan Alfrink had adopted this line with the formula 'magisterium of the twelve', which amounted to relativizing the pope's doctrinal power. The Dutch bishops' chief theologian was Edward Schillebeeckx, a Belgian-born professor of dogmatics at the Catholic University of Nijmegen. Although the Dominican theologian was not officially appointed as a *peritus*, as Alfrink's adviser he had a strong influence. 'It could well be asked,' he threw into the debate, 'whether it wouldn't be better to redraft the first four schemata completely.'

The French group was equally well organized. It consisted of representatives of the 'Nouvelle Théologie', condemned by Pius XII, including the Dominican Yves Congar as well the Jesuit Jean Daniélou and Henri de Lubac. Congar and de Lubac were appointed by Pope John as advisers to the preparatory committee, which caused some surprise. 'How can these theologians with modernistic mind-sets be appointed?', the outraged traditionalist Marcel Lefebvre asked Ottaviani.

In Belgium, the power centres of the progressives were the University of Louvain and the Benedictine Chevetogne Abbey. There was also the Dominican monastery of Le Saulchoir, whose director of studies was Marie-Dominique Chenu. In 1937 he had criticized the Curia's anti-modernist theology. After that, his *Manifesto* was put on the Index by order of the Holy Office and he was removed from his post. However, his students, such as Yves Congar, ten years his junior, who became a professor of theology at Le Saulchoir, were to be important inspirers of the Second Vatican Council.

On 15 February 1959, three weeks after the announcement of the Council, Congar was already pressing ahead. In a contribution to

Informations Catholiques, he said that the restoration of unity with the separated Christian churches and dialogue with 'the world of today' were the two most important tasks for the Council. The Council was 'an opportunity which had to be used as well as possible'. 'Perhaps only 5 per cent of what we are asking for will happen. That is one more reason to raise our demands. It is necessary for the pressure of public opinion from Christians to compel the Council to take itself really seriously and produce some results.'[15]

In 1960 Hans Küng, the Swiss 32-year-old professor of dogmatic theology at the University of Tübingen, published a programme document along the same lines. The title was *Konzil und Wiedervereinigung: Erneuerung als Ruf in die Einheit (The Council and Reunion: Renewal as a Call to Unity)*. Küng saw the Council as an opportunity for a radical change in church structures. On 8 June 1962, *Time* published an article on the book with the title 'A Second Reformation for Catholics as well as Protestants'. The article was illustrated with pictures showing Küng between Luther and Pope John. Küng recalled, 'We were already planning then how we could thwart the Curia's Council strategy.'[16]

In Germany, in the first instance, the Bishops' Conference set up orderly committees. After a conference that took place on 8 and 9 March 1960 in Buhl, the minute-keeper Lorenz Jaeger, archbishop of Paderborn, said they must at least avoid anything 'that might feed the mistrustful anxieties of the congregations' in Rome.[17] What frightened the Curia most of all was that their powerful position might 'be diminished'. In the note, there was perhaps a small side-swipe at the bishop of Munich, Cardinal Julius Döpfner, who in March 1959 had already asked the theologian Otto Karrer to draft an outline document 'on ecumenical questions with regard to the Second Vatican Council'. Karrer had left the Jesuit Order in 1923 to join the Evangelical-Lutheran Church in Bavaria. He was soon disappointed with it and left again. Karrer sent copies of his paper to 'Koenig, Montini, Milan; Joseph Frings; J. G. M. Willebrands, Yves Congar, Hans Urs von Balthasar and Hans Küng'.[18] Meanwhile, Döpfner had identified 'two tendencies; among the members of the Roman committees: 'α. Curial – conservative – stressing unity, order, law, continuity – mainly inward-looking. β. Diocesan – regional – progressive – stressing adaptation, the current situation, the needs of the time – mainly outward-looking.'[19] Döpfner listed the following 'individual groups': 'Curia cardinals, Italians, Central European Group (Austria, Germany, France, Belgium, Netherlands), Anglo-Saxon group, local mission bishops, South America.'

It was no secret that part of the Roman Curia and quite a few Italian bishops opposed the Council or regarded it as superfluous. In order at least to be able to steer the assembly in their own direction, the Curia tried to pack the committees with their own people. On the other hand, the Vatican itself did not represent any particular opinion by its attitude, but did represent a considerable number of the world's bishops. The approximately 3,000 answers to the questionnaire received from bishops and institutions did not document a desire for radical change, much less a revolution. Most of the *vota* simply wanted new doctrinal definitions, particularly about the Virgin Mary, and a condemnation of harmful modern influences within and outside the church.

For example, Geraldo de Proença Sigaud, bishop of Diamantina in Brazil, expressed the concerns of many bishops. In his recommendation sent to Rome he said: 'In my humble opinion, if the Council wants to have a beneficial effect, it must take into account the situation of the church today, which, like Christ, is suffering a new Good Friday and is being delivered into the hands of its enemies without any defence.'

The Brazilian bishop, born in Belo Horizonte, was a Divine Word missionary. He painted the situation as very dark:

The implacable enemy of our church and Catholic society [...] has overthrown nearly the whole Catholic order, i.e., the city of God, with his death-dealing, dogged and systematic progress. In its place, he is intent on raising the city of humanity. His name is Revolution. What does he want? To erect the whole structure of human life – society and humanity – without God, without the church, without Christ, without revelation. He relies solely on human reason, sensuality, greed and pride. So for his purpose, it is necessary to topple the church to its very foundations, destroy and supplant it.[20]

Sigaud concluded his *votum* for the Council with the words: 'That enemy is very active in our days. Indeed, he is sure of his victory in the coming years.' However, 'many church leaders' would regard 'what I am saying as dreams or a sick fantasy'. 'They are behaving blindly like the inhabitants of Constantinople did in the years before its downfall – they didn't want to see the danger.'[21]

Such messages must have caused Cardinal Ottaviani, the head of the former Holy Inquisition, not to sleep at night. For a long time, he was like a cat on hot bricks. 'I pray to God that I may die before the end of the Council,' he groaned,' so that I can at least die a Catholic.'[22]

29

The Genoa Speech

Essentially, Joseph Ratzinger's road to Rome began on 25 February 1961. The Thomas More Academy in Bensberg, near Bonn, had invited him to give a lecture. The subject came right on cue. It was 'The Theology of the Council', and as he stepped up to the lectern he saw a very attentive cardinal from Cologne sitting in the front row.

Recently, the new star theologian had attracted attention by critical remarks about the church. It had 'standardized too much,' he complained, 'so many rules had driven the century to unbelief rather than saving it from it'. In Bensberg, the young professor wanted just to set out historically what a Council actually was.

He began by saying, with reference to the strongly disputed dogma of papal infallibility passed by the First Vatican Council, that the erroneous view had arisen that Councils had lost their function. This failed to recognize 'that papal infallibility is not an isolated doctrine standing on its own, but a salient factor in an integral system with which it is organically linked'.[1] The pope could not be an absolute monarch in the usual sense 'because of his total subordination to Christ, for whom he has to act as a trustee'. But also because of his relation to the episcopacy. 'Both together, primacy and episcopacy are not simply an aristocracy,' while the people 'only have a passive role of obeying and doing what they are told.' There was also something like an infallibility of the faith of the whole church. That was the 'laity's share in infallibility'. Both structural elements had to be brought into play by the Council. Of its nature, the church was not a council meeting – *concilium* – but a Eucharistic community – *communio*.[2]

356

Many people in the room knew whom he meant when he now spoke of 'questionable historical proofs' and a 'simplification', which 'cannot do justice to tradition'. The speaker stopped briefly. He looked round the auditorium. In all the seats he perceived a growing tension. At that time Hans Küng had caused a stir by saying that the terms *ecclesia* and *concilium* had the same etymological root. The conclusion he drew from that was: the structure and form of the Council should be governed by the structure of the church, as a kind of council meeting with laity and not just bishops. Ratzinger saw it differently. And he named names.

Indeed, Hans Küng had 'made repeated attempts to put forward a new theology of the Council'. But, in fact, the terms *ecclesia* and *concilium* had a different origin from the one Küng ascribed to them. The first name given to what was later called a 'council' had been the word 'collegium', which was what St Ignatius called the circle of priests who acted as advisers to the bishop. The same usage was to be found in the Acts of Thomas. So it had to be taken 'from usage and the way the word was understood by those' who had 'made the term an ecclesiastical word'. *Concilium* was not understood in Küng's sense 'either in the Latin Bible or by the church fathers'. The word *ecclesia* meant 'call out of', and the word *concilium* meant 'call together'. The two words did not, as Küng claimed, converge to emphasize the identity of 'church' and 'council', and therefore the identity of laity and bishops.

Certainly, the 'overcoming of the false separation between clergy and laity' was an important task. 'Of course, non-bishops and non-priests, "lay people", could be consulted. Of course, it was very important to take care that the whole church was "represented". Every possible means had to be used to do that. But the Council did not need to be, and could not be, a display of the whole church.'

In brief: 'A council is an assembly to lead the whole church. That also means it is essentially an assembly of those whose job such leadership is. In the actual way the church is organized, that is the bishops.'

Ratzinger and Küng had got to know each other in 1957 at a congress in Salzburg. They appreciated each other. They also liked each other. Each respected the other for engaging in the new exciting theology. But they were never a team. Even the dispute about the nature of a council showed the fundamental disagreement between them. To some extent, the two theologians personified the conflict in the church in general – on the one hand, faithfulness to tradition; on the other, adaptation to the present time – the split between authenticity and invention. Ratzinger answered the question of what a council was on the basis of historical evidence and the nature of the church. Küng answered it by clutching at artful rhetoric.

In his lecture, Ratzinger put Küng in his place. His colleague was just a year younger than him. He added:

All errors in this area are ultimately caused by applying a secular constitutional model to the church. That misses her uniqueness, which she derives from her divine origin. The Council is not a parliament, and the bishops are not members of parliament, who receive their authority and mandate solely from the people who voted for them. They do not represent the people, but Christ, from whom they have received their mission and ordination.[3]

Pointedly, he ended his speech with an allusion to the devout 'people', so often disparaged by arrogant professors. It was precisely 'the day-to-day faith of simple people' that created 'the warp and weft for the divine loom', without whom the church 'would just be a clattering empty frame'.

The cardinal sitting in the front row kept his customary restrained demeanour, but it could be seen from his face that he was enthused by the lecture. Even on the first occasion they met, when Ratzinger visited him as a new theology professor, it had been clear that the two could get on. It was recognition at first sight. Frings spoke with a clear voice, briefly and succinctly. Always to the point. He did not want to be held up by inconsequential matters. Ratzinger also appreciated Frings's affection for simple people. In Cologne, the bishop went for an hour's walk in the town centre every day, in order to stay in touch with people. The manufacturer's son from Neuss had never aimed for a higher position. He wanted to be a 'people's priest'. He served for seven years as parish priest in a village, 13 years in the city, where he gained a reputation as a 'brawler priest' since he had been hit on the head with a heavy ashtray by a Nazi gang in 1932.

As chairman of the German Bishops' Conference, he was the voice of the German church, both a religious and a moral voice. He was attractive because of his sharp mind, his good humour and the curiosity with which he confronted new developments. Internationally, as the founder of the aid organizations Adveniat and Misereor, he had gained a reputation for being an active Samaritan, particularly in the mission fields of Africa, Asia and Latin America. 'He was a real Cologner, with the slightly ironical, cheerful manner of a Rhinelander, that was both elegant and cordial,' said Ratzinger. When they met 'it was immediately clear that we understood one another'.[4]

The old cardinal had a good theological education, but ultimately he was a practical man, rather than being one for theory. 'I must learn to think differently,' he told his secretary, Hubert Luthe. He had once studied neo-scholasticism, but since then theology had developed. He had heard early on from his friend Gottlieb Söhngen about the impressive talent from Munich. Luthe, who had been a fellow student and friend of Ratzinger's during their days together by the Isar, also told the cardinal about Ratzinger's 'great and good reputation'. 'Frings recognized at once that Ratzinger's progressive drive and impressive theological knowledge would be very useful to him,' Luthe said. 'In addition, there was Ratzinger's brilliant intellect, his lightning-swift grasp of an idea, his clear-sightedness, his ability to set things in order and make clear the distinction between different positions. Then there was also his attachment to the church and his love and loyalty to *Una sancta*.'[5]

Immediately after the lecture, the cardinal took the young theologian aside. They 'went for a walk together through the Academy's wide corridors'. They had a stimulating discussion and 'came very close', Ratzinger recalled.[6] What he did not know was that Frings had a problem which was greatly worrying him. Shortly beforehand, he had promised the Jesuit Angelo d'Arpa in Genoa to give the fourth in a series of six lectures. He was due to speak on the contemporary context of the coming Council and make clear its difference from the First Vatican Council. 'The subject attracted me and I agreed,' said Frings. Shortly afterwards he panicked. 'I saw that I alone would not be able to do justice to this subject.'[7] Then suddenly his problem seemed to have been solved. 'This young man, who was unassuming but impressive, whom he trusted,' said Luthe, 'could unearth all the things he didn't know. And he knew he could leave it up to him.'[8]

The handshake took place a short time later at a Bach Verein concert playing Handel's *Messiah* in the Gürzenich in Cologne, to which the two music lovers had both been invited. The cardinal used the interval to speak to Ratzinger: 'Herr Professor, I have promised to give a lecture in Genoa. Can you do it?' Frings stressed that he would give him a completely free hand in writing it. However, he imposed the strictest secrecy on the ghostwriter. Ratzinger set to work, and after a few days, the cardinal had the manuscript in his hands. He found it so good that 'I only made a small correction in one place.'[9]

When the nearly blind cardinal stepped before the public with the lecture in the Teatro Duse in Genoa on 20 November 1961, he only spoke the introductory words. After that it was taken over by his diocesan priest, Prelate Bruno Wüstenberg of the pope's secretariat of state, who had translated the lecture into Italian. It lasted 45 minutes. The audience were breathless, spellbound – then thunderous applause. It was a triumph. At last a key had been found for a problem that was difficult to define, a plan for the house that was to be built. The lecture, Frings wrote in his diary, not without pride, made 'a considerable impression'. Even Cardinal Siri of Milan, who was regarded as an arch-conservative, was struck by it. Frings's fellow-bishop Cardinal Döpfner, to whom he presented the text, even spoke of 'a historic document'.

That same year the Genoa speech was published in the journal *Geist und Leben*. It was 12 pages long. The author's name was given as Josef, Cardinal Frings. However, shortly afterwards Frings revealed the real writer. In fact, the Genoa speech was the most significant and long-lasting that Ratzinger ever wrote. He was 34 years old, a young, unimportant teacher with no great name. But he managed, as it were, to slip into the astral body of a highly respected, world-famous, influential old cardinal, to address the world of the church. In his address, the historian's view was combined with theological insight, philosophical penetration and the brilliant use of a language that was as plain as it was emotional. The speech also acquired importance in church history as a briefing for the forthcoming Council. This was due to a sequel to it when, on 23 February 1962, Frings was surprised to be called out of a session of the Central Preparatory Committee to see Pope John XXIII. The cardinal was uneasy. Had he been too audacious in Genoa? Did the Holy Father feel unpleasantly affected by his interventions? 'I did not know why,' Frings wrote in his memoirs, 'I said jokingly to my secretary Luthe: "Put my red cape round my shoulders. It might be for the last time."'[10]

Luthe later described the event thus. The Holy Father hurried up to Frings in the audience chamber and embraced him with the words: 'Eminence, I must say thank you. Last night I read your speech. *Che bella coincidenza del pensiero!* What beautiful harmony of thought!' Pope John spoke to Frings but meant Ratzinger: 'You have said everything that I've thought and wanted to say, but was unable to say myself.'[11]

At first, Frings seemed rooted to the spot. What should he say? Then he pulled himself together. 'Holy Father, I did not actually write the lecture; a young professor wrote it.' And the pope? He knew that: 'Herr Cardinal, I did not write my last encyclical myself either. You just need the right adviser.' Four days after the meeting the Pontifex sent a thank-you note through Cardinal Secretary of State Cicognani: 'His Holiness remembers with thanks the conversation he recently had with you and prays for the fullness of heavenly grace upon you.'

In the Genoa speech, Ratzinger had not only succeeded in finding the right tone. He had analysed the current situation and specified the expectations of reform, which up till then no one among the European bishops had been able to formulate in that way. How strongly the speech had impressed the pope, and so made an essential contribution to the Council's line, could be seen in Roncalli's opening speech, in which he quoted some passages almost literally. They can be read together like a dialogue in which each confirms the other:

Ratzinger (in the Genoa speech): 'As a "Council for Renewal" the Council's task must be less to formulate doctrines …'

John XXIII (at the Council opening): 'It is not our business to deal first and foremost with some key points of the church's teaching.'

Ratzinger: 'But rather, to enable a new and deeper witness of Christian life in the world today.'

John XXIII: 'Rather, it is necessary that instruction in Christian doctrine in our day should be reviewed in all points.'

Ratzinger: 'so that it is fully realized that Christ is not just a "Christ yesterday" but a Christ "yesterday, today and forever".

John XXIII: 'and indeed a serene and tranquil awareness without leaving anything out.'

In his Genoa speech, Ratzinger set out what the Council needed to do in the light of the social changes since the end of the war. He saw the world as shaped by three great forces: globalization, technology and faith in science. By the new means of communication and economic co-operation, cultures and nations were moving ever closer together, so that a kind of single culture was appearing. Ratzinger did not see 'the relativity of all human cultural forms' as just negative. 'It also leads to the depiction of the core of faith, which is shown in all cultures and languages in the person of Jesus Christ and his body the church.'

The theologian saw one of the main causes of modern atheism as humanity's unthinking concentration on its own powers. What had once been the deification of nature had become a 'self-deification of humanity'. However, faith in science could not give answers to the 'need for ethical striving', because it did not take people seriously as moral beings with freedom and conscience. So, in dialogue with secular modernity, the Council's task had to be to formulate the Christian faith as a genuine, liveable and worthwhile alternative. The church as a people made up of many peoples had to take into account the diversity of human life. 'In an age of a truly global Catholicism, which has therefore become truly catholic, the church must increasingly adapt. For not all rules can be equally applicable to every country. Above all, the liturgy as a mirror of unity must also be an appropriate expression of particular cultural characteristics.'

The theologian ventured a look into the future:

> In many ways religion will acquire a different shape. It will become leaner in form and content, but perhaps also deeper. People of today can rightly expect the church to help them in this process of change. Perhaps the church should drop many old forms, which are not longer suitable [...] be willing to strip off the faith's time-bound clothing. By letting go of the transitory, it focuses more clearly on the permanent. People today must again be able to recognize that the church neither fears science nor needs to fear it, because she is secure in God's truth, which no genuine truth or genuine progress can contradict.

The exact date for the beginning of the Council still had not been set. In his papal bull of 25 December 1961 convening the Council, *Humanae salutis,* Pope John had again stressed the need to discern 'the signs of the times'. He listed three aims for the Council: first, inner renewal; second, Christian unity; third, the church's contribution to social problems and world peace. In the Central Committee's preparations in Rome, the differences came ever more clearly to light between the curial party and the faction round Frings and other central European bishops. Frings turned more and more often to Ratzinger for advice. Ratzinger was a sharper analyst than his other two advisers, the church historian Hubert Jedin and Frings's general vicar, Josef Teusch. His judgement on papers received so far from Rome was clear. For example: 'The vocabulary of this section sounds really antiquated,' he remarked in the margin of a schema on the church. 'We should seek for wording that is more easily understood by modern people.' He found the schema *On the True Preservation of the Deposit of Faith* 'so inadequate, that it cannot be laid before the Council. Fragments from different areas of dogmatics are strung together in no apparent order. As such, they have little use or none at all.' So it seemed 'better to drop this schema altogether'.

The Central Preparatory Committee, to which Frings belonged, should examine whether schemata completed so far were appropriate to present to the pope. In his memoirs the cardinal said: 'As the sessions began, it soon became clear to us that the schemata before us had been drawn up in a very conservative spirit.' There had been a hefty clash with the conservative group.[12] Besides that, 'it is to be feared the the definitions of the Second Vatican Council might become a kind of "universal encyclical", a thick volume that no one reads, let alone respects, and which repels many who are outside the church or wavering.'

In accordance with Ratzinger's critical expertise, the cardinal from Cologne also criticized the *Dogmatic Constitution on the True Preservation of the Deposit of Faith*, presented by Ottaviani, which he compared to the 'work of an inquisitor, who sits in his den like a lion and looks about seeking whom he may devour'. Frings likewise voted against its first chapter, 'On the Truth', with a *non placet*. The reason: 'The schema seems not to be fully developed. It speaks about all kinds of things more negatively than positively, with words that might offend opponents. Such words are unfit to attract unbelievers or edify the faithful.'[13]

The conflict became so sharp that on 6 May 1961 the German Cardinals Frings and Döpfner tried to ask Pope John for a postponement of the Council. In a small gathering at supper, Döpfner had said he had got the impression that Pope John would welcome it if the reform-friendly group of Council participants became more active. Otherwise, he would be letting the curial party claim he was their 'prisoner'.[14] In his memoirs Frings said of the confidential meeting:

> The pope obviously gathered what we wanted. And he had no intention of yielding on this point. He once told me in an audience that he did not think greatly of visions, but he was firmly convinced that the idea that he should summon a council had been given to him from above. Now at this meeting he himself spoke continuously, clearly on purpose, and hardly let us get a word in edgeways. He did not want any argument on the matter.[15]

Ratzinger's lecture in Bensberg had impressed Frings. The Genoa speech confirmed his conviction that he had backed the right horse, even though this carthorse from Hufschlag was still practically a foal. The Bavarian professor had ambition; he radiated youthful energy and represented a type in whom one could imagine the future of the church lay. In addition, he was well connected: for example, with the nuncio Bafile and scholars like Karl Rahner. His Bonn colleague and friend Hubert Jedin was an expert on Councils right by his side. Two months after Frings's summons by the pope and Roncalli's enthusiastic response to the Genoa speech, Frings – a member of the Council steering committee – handed on all the other draft texts, the 'schemata,' to his new chief adviser. All were marked *sub secreto:* strictly secret. Any disclosure, spoken or written, was forbidden by church law.

At first Ratzinger only scribbled remarks in the margins of the documents. For example, in the schema *De ecclesia* he criticized the timid and defensive style and the lack of a genuine traditional understanding of the faith. He felt the style was not pastoral enough, and the document lacked historical awareness of the problem. He recommended that the text should not be limited to the 'negative and defensive' but also give a 'word of encouragement for Christian initiative'. Lastly, the church – here Ratzinger quoted Karl Rahner – was 'not one of those totalitarian states where outward power and deathly silent obedience are everything, and freedom and love are nothing'.

In Rome the pointlessly mounting bundle of ill-adapted Council documents enraged some of the consultants. Frings became their spokesman and expressed their dissatisfaction: how can the bishops, coming from all over the world, who know nothing so far about the materials to be dealt with, 'give their own judgement in a few weeks or months on so many and such important questions'? It was to be feared that the Council would choke under the mass of stuff piling up and grind to a halt. After two years' work, 75 schemata had been prepared. They were regarded as only 'preliminary drafts, capable of further improvement', and 'would only be finished through discussion at the Council with the help of the Holy Spirit'.[16]

After Ratzinger had initially just entered marginal glosses on the documents, soon Frings was asking for expert summaries with suggestions for changes – but please, no longer handwritten. The answers were not long in coming. His sister Maria was also to be thanked for that. At home in Bad Godesberg, she hammered away at her typewriter for page after page in faultless Latin, which she had never learned. The documents began with sentences like *'Eminentissime ac Reverendissime Domine, De prima serie schematum, de quibus in Concilii sessionibus disceptabitur, imprimis sequentia videntur dicenda.'* In English: 'Your Eminence and Most Reverend Sir, on the first series of draft texts which are to be discussed in the Council sessions, first, in my opinion, the following should be said.'[17]

Occasionally, the theologian took his reports to the archbishop's house in Cologne himself and used the visit for a short chat. 'Of couse I had a lot to settle,' Ratzinger said in his memoirs. That seems to be a big understatement. To give some examples, in volume 1 of the schemata *Constitutionum et decretorum*, it says in his note of 3 October 1962:

On Chapter II: The changes in lines 25–29 and on page 14, line 18, are to delete an exaggerated concept of infallibility, which has also become questionable in the light of historical research today and is incompatible with Scripture, and to replace it with a more correct concept of infallibility.

On Chapter III: The change proposed for page 33, line 9, is to be careful to delimitate correctly between philosophical and theological ways of knowing and speaking. The pre-philosophical way of speaking about the temporal beginning of the world fails to recognize that before time there was no time. By acknowledging the world's temporality, we express its non-eternity appropriately and precisely.

On Chapter X: The whole dogmatic schema (pages 23–69) is highly unsatisfactory. It lacks inner order […] The narrow-minded, scholastic manner of many formulations will repel people rather than attract new believers to the church.

Despite all the criticism, the expert reports showed circumspection and balance. They came from Ratzinger's attachment to the church, and also from a position less concerned about changing structures than about the faithful's immediate personal experience of Jesus Christ. Ratzinger knew that the truth was not to be voted on and that whoever rushed ahead of God could not be following him. If faith was no longer truth but just tolerance, then *what* was tolerated would matter less and less, and what would matter most was simply the fact that it was tolerated.

He 'sent many corrections' to the cardinal, Ratzinger said in our interview.

> He had not touched the fabric as a whole, except in the case of the decree on revelation. That could be improved. We were agreed that one the one hand, the basic direction was there, but on the other hand there was a lot needing improvement. Above all, there should be more emphasis on Scripture and the fathers and the current magisterium should be less dominant.

He added an appreciative postscript to the schema *De ecclesia*, which had been drafted by Cardinal Bea: 'If the Council was persuaded to adopt this text [...] it would be doing itself a favour [...] Here we have the spoken language that our time needs and which can be understood by people of goodwill.'

The decree on revelation was the Council's Achilles' heel – and Ratzinger's special subject. It was the fork in the road where the direction of the Catholic Church would be decided. 'The problem already arises with the heading *De fontibus revelationis*,' he wrote in his report.

> Granted that all textbooks say so, also granted that Vatican I uses this title as a subheading in Chapter 2, *De revelatione,* where it re-emphasizes the Tridentine resolutions on Scripture and tradition. But the Council of Trent itself did not use these words and in the actual Vatican text the expression does not occur again [...] Really, Scripture and tradition are not the sources of revelation. God revealing himself – his speaking and self-disclosure – is the *unus fons* from which the two *rivuli,* Scripture and tradition, flow.[18]

Ratzinger did not leave it there.

> First I should like to summarize the problems that arise from the above:

> The title *De fontibus revelationis* should be changed to *De revelatione* or *De verbo Dei*

[...]

The whole should be preceded by a Chapter I, *De revelatione ipsa*, for which materials from the former Chapter I and from Schema 2, Chapter IV can be used.

Wherever the term *fontes* occurs in the text, it should be replaced when possible by other expressions.

As the author himself realized, for outsiders Ratzinger's objections might have seemed like a 'quarrel over words among pedants. But it should not be forgotten that the understanding of the matter depends on the word used and so the right use of words acquires great importance in matters of faith.' In fact, the subject concerned the weighty question of the inerrancy and historicity of Scripture. On 8 April 1546 the Council of Trent, in its Fourth Session on Scripture and Tradition, had decreed, 'The truth and rule [of the Gospel] are contained in written books and in unwritten traditions.' The decree produced an ongoing debate: 'I say again: There is no statement which, on the one hand, does not occur in Scripture or, on the other, could not be traced with historical probability back to the time of the Apostles. If that is so – and it is so – then tradition cannot be defined as material transmission of unwritten statements.' To Ratzinger the most important conclusion to which the proposed schema led was: 'The great majority of the fathers and the classical scholastic theologians, pre-eminently Thomas Aquinas and Bonaventure', were condemned. Typical Ratzinger: 'But that cannot be. You can't condemn the greatest and most venerable part of tradition as false in the name of tradition.' Then the 34-year-old ended with an appeal: 'The world does not await further refinements of the system from us; it awaits the answer of faith at a time of unbelief.'

The summer semester of 1962 ended in July. Joseph and Maria made their way back home to Traunstein. At the end of August, a thick packet lay on his table. It was the volume with the seven schemata for the first session of the Council. In his accompanying letter, the Cologne cardinal wrote: 'Dear Professor Ratzinger, I send you herewith the first volume of Council schemata, which will be delivered in the coming days to the Council members. I'd be grateful if you would examine these drafts on the following counts:

What has changed from the first version?
What is to be absolutely rejected?
What could be better?'

Over the next weeks Ratzinger buried himself in the Latin texts, so that by 14 September he could send a three-page critique in Latin, giving his 'general impression'. On 29 September there followed an eight-page text in German. It contained suggestions for corrections to all seven schemata. At the last minute, on 3 October, eight days before the Council opening, a third 15-page text was posted 'to give the reasons for the suggested changes'.

Almost incidentally, the cardinal sent a further note by express mail: 'It is arranged that on Tuesday 9 October I am flying to Rome. Are you flying with me?'

Did he want to fly with him? Literally by return of post, the very next day Ratzinger agreed. He also had the confirmation that he would give the desired presentation on the *Two Sources of Revelation* in Rome to a large group of Council participants. 'The Council is a done thing,' Pope John had exclaimed enthusiastically when in July 1962 Pericle Felici had given him the revised and approved Council schemata, 'We can end it by Christmas!' It was barely believable that it would be Ratzinger's lecture on revelation whose consequences would unhinge the procedure.

30

The Spin Doctor

During the short time that Roncalli reigned, Ratzinger became his admirer, 'a real fan', as he put it later. Roncalli's predecessor, Pius XII, had marked his youth. 'He was the pope, full stop.' But as he grew older, Pacelli's 'stately ceremonial, grand gestures and majesty in general' began to alienate him, whereas John XXIII 'fascinated me from the beginning, particularly by his unconventionality. He was so direct, so simple, so human.'[1]

On 9 October 1962, two days before the ceremonial opening of the Council, he was sitting in an aeroplane to Rome, thirty-five years young, full of hope and zest for action. We must show 'more courage and faith', he had urged shortly beforehand in a speech. Christianity should become 'much more charged with reality, be more dynamic and original'.[2] Now he wanted to help initiate 'that purified new self-presentation of the church, which the pope wanted the result of the Council to be'. In his heart, he bore a saying by Pope John which had particularly struck him: 'We are not utopians of an earthly paradise but realists of the cross.'[3]

Cardinal Frings and his entourage checked into the German college, Santa Maria dell'Anima, in the Piazza Navona, where Frings had lived as a doctoral student from 1913 until 1915. At first, there was no room for Ratzinger there. He had to make do with the Albergo Genio, a hostel at number 28 via Zanardelli, just round the corner.

He was looking forward to meeting theologians like Henri de Lubac, Jean Daniélou, Yves Congar and the Belgian theology professor Gérard Philips, whom he admired. As Hans Urs von Balthasar put it, they all had problems with the current 'bleakness of theology': that is, with 'what people had made out of the glory of revelation'.

And somewhere Esther Betz was also waiting. She had come to Rome as a special correspondent for the *Rheinisiche Post* and was hoping to get background information despite, or because of, the secrecy rules. For according to Article 27 of the Council standing orders, 'authorized Council *periti* [advisers] and anyone else who has anything to do with the Council's affairs' were bound 'to swear that they will keep it secret'. This related not only to documents but also to 'discussions, opinions of individual fathers and votes'.[4] Betz would say later about her top informers: 'We often met with other prominent *periti* in convivial gatherings, at which Joseph Ratzinger's Bavarian soul shuddered when I ordered "*frutti di mare*".'[5]

In the run-up to the Council Ratzinger had met secretly with Karl Rahner, the adviser to Cardinal Franz König, from Vienna. Rahner wanted to keep the group for strategic discussions 'as small as possible on practical grounds' and 'not to leak anything on the matter'.[6] It was about an alternative draft to the documents submitted by Rome. He had confided in a letter to his colleague, the dogmatics professor Otto Semmelroth, in a letter of 4 April 1962, that they were going to try 'in this very small group to come up with a unanimous first draft of the expert report'. It all required the 'utmost discretion'. Between 15 and 25 October 1962 they were engaged in intensive work on alternative texts. Together with Rahner, Bishop Volk, Otto Semmelroth and Joseph Ratzinger were part of the team. According to one participant, Ratzinger had 'already composed a schema in Latin, which we liked a lot'.[7]

Rahner thought most of the Roman texts were abysmal and not capable of being improved. 'The whole thing gives the impression of a tired, grey, Roman scholastic theology,' he moaned. 'It is completely fails to realize how unfit it is to be understood by people of today.' Ratzinger fully agreed with him. On the revelation schema he noted: 'A council must not propound such a bog-standard philosophy.'[8]

Rahner expected that Ratzinger, 23 years younger, would offer 'useful co-operation'. 'If only Yr Eminence had such a theologian,' he wrote to Cardinal Döpfner of Munich on 17 April 1962, then 'together with him, the three theologians could surely do a proper job.' He remarked in a postscript: 'Please will Yr Eminence excuse the bad writing in this letter. But I have just spent about eight hours dictating the report and am rather worn out.'[9]

Ratzinger's connection with Rahner was not without risk. In Rome the Jesuit was regarded as a 'progressive' theologian – in other words, as someone it was better to keep a distance from. His 'Mariology' had fallen victim to censorship by his Order and was not permitted to be printed. A few months before the beginning of the Council, he was told that for the future he would be subject to pre-censorship. This had been ordered by Alfredo Ottaviani's Holy Office, the former Inquisition. Rahner protested. On 8 June 1962 he wrote to Cardinal König saying he felt he had been 'condemned without having been accused or tried'. Of course, he could just 'swallow it in silence'. But he had to say:

> In such a situation I can't work. Nothing occurs to me. I am paralysed, I can't think, when such censorship sort of keeps peering into my idea. In short: I can't write like this and so I won't write like this. No one can order that anything should occur to my poor brain in such circumstances […] Finally, as a theologian who has been placed under suspicion by a special order, I can't go to Rome with your Eminence for the Council.[10]

A large solidarity campaign by theologians and politicians made the case go public. Cardinals Döpfner, Frings and König intervened with Pope John, who in the summer of 1962 indirectly distanced himself from Ottaviani's procedure. Rahner travelled to Rome, but the scandal was not forgotten.

The journey to Rome was not Joseph's first visit to the Eternal City. Was it by chance that on Easter Sunday, 22 April 1962, ten months before the beginning of the Council, he had met his brother at Rome's Termini station, where they were both welcomed by the Munich theology student Helmut Brandner? As the cardinal's adviser, he had sworn the oath of strict secrecy a good two weeks beforehand. It was not yet certain that he would accompany Frings to the Council, but it was already foreseeable. At least Karl Rahner already knew more about it: 'With warm Easter greetings,' he informed his colleague Fr Semmelroth on 17 April 1962: 'Since Ratzinger will be going to Rome with Frings (which of course must still remain confidential) and I am expected to go with the Vienna Cardinal [Franz König], a preliminary talk with Ratzinger and yourself would be doubly desirable.'[11]

In order not to spend too much money, the brothers lodged in a double room in a nuns' convent near the Piazza di Risorgimento. Georg felt 'like a little worm in the huge city. With the traffic, so many people speaking all sorts of languages and wearing all kinds of clothes. Especially when people come from such simple backgrounds as we do.' However, they were not overwhelmed by their impressions of the Roman Forum, Santa Prisca, San Clemente or the mighty Vatican. 'There we were Ratzingerish,' said the future pope, 'not very emotional.' There had also always been a slightly anti-Rome resentment, especially of the theology created in Rome, so that 'we had no special urge to come here'.

However, the early Christian sites fascinated Joseph. 'There within reach' were the origins of the faith and 'that great continuity'. In a general audience for the first time he experienced Pope John live, speaking about the meaning of prayer. Joseph was surprised to meet 'a man with a comprehensive theological education', and at the same time someone 'who was a human being, who spoke for the simple people and managed to be understood by them'.[12]

On their visit to Rome, Georg and Joseph were bound to think of their great-uncle Georg, that zealous farmer's son from the hamlet of Rickering, where their father had also been born. Georg Ratzinger was a doctor of theology, priest, politician and journalist all in one. A whirlwind. A loner. An oddball. In his youth he had served as court chaplain to Duke Carl Theodor in Tegernsee. As a delegate to the Reichstag in Berlin, he was both respected and controversial, and not just because of his commitment to social reform and his fight against Prussian militarism and the German-nationalist mania for greatness. His sense of justice was so strong that he put his ordination as a priest at risk in order to defend his cousin, the young priest Jakob David, against a corrupt mayor. As director of the *Münchener Wochenblatt,* he attacked the authorities (under the pseudonym 'Razone'), which resulted in the confiscation of his newspaper and detention for himself as its editor-in-chief.

Joseph's similarity to his great-uncle was striking. It was not so much in his appearance, where he took after his mother's side, as in his expression and temperament, spirit and unruliness. When he was a gymnasium student, wasn't Georg also regarded as particularly sensitive and at the same time extraordinarily diligent and disciplined?

He was 'a gifted student and steady worker', his report said, 'with excellent understanding'.[13] Like Joseph later, his great-uncle also got his doctorate in theology through a prize work. His doctoral supervisor, the priest and church historian Ignaz von Döllinger, had given him a subject, *Geschichte der kirchlichen Armenpflege* (*History of the Church's Care for the Poor*), that suited him perfectly.

As a journalist Georg tackled a wide range of topics, stretching from antiquity to problems of the present day. However, they included (under a pseudonym) contributions that fostered the common slurs against the Jews. Georg Ratzinger polarized and created opponents from all sides. As one of the idea generators of Catholic social teaching, he was received in a private audience by Pope Leo XIII. The English prime minister William Gladstone sent him a handwritten note, in which he appreciated Ratzinger's *History of the Church's Care for the Poor*. After the death of his brother Thomas, whom he cared for to the end, Georg swung between euphoric dreams of the future and bouts of hypochondria. 'Now I only drink red wine and Apollinaris [a German mineral water],' he grumbled. His improvement was noticeable, 'but how long it will take is is frankly doubtful'.

Wasn't it remarkable that the great-uncle was also closely involved with a Council? As secretary to his doctoral supervisor, Georg Ratzinger delivered material to Döllinger's polemical *Janus,* published in 1868. Together with a work by the French critic of the Council, Henri Louis Charles Maret, it unleashed a wave of protest against Rome. 'By the way, it is absolutely necessary,' Döllinger instructed a colleague, 'that Ratzinger should undertake the revision both of what is written and what is published.' The publisher's editor was heartily grateful: 'It was very good that Dr Ratzinger read the proof, for he improved it substantially.' Shortly before the beginning of the First Vatican Council, Ratzinger summoned 'the Catholic scholars of Germany to open resistance'. It was time to stand up 'against the Jesuitical-Roman syncrasies that they wanted to impose as dogmas'.

As Döllinger became increasingly radical in his opposition to Pius IX, his protégé became more moderate. 'It is not the language of a man opposing on scholarly grounds,' he declared about his former mentor, 'it is the language of a mocker of religion', the 'tone of a Voltaire'. Döllinger's agitation against the Council led to the founding of the 'Old Catholics', who split from Rome. Döllinger himself never joined the schismatic movement. However, at the beginning of the year 1883 Georg Ratzinger noted that his former professor was 'completely surrounded by enemies of the church'. All efforts 'to get the old gentleman back on the rails' had been 'unfortunately without success'.

Georg Ratzinger remained critical of the Council. He shared the view of a contemporary that 'the Roman Curia' possessed 'no spiritual power any more'. That was 'a sign of rapid decline'. The former member of the Reichstag and the regional parliament retired: 'I don't belong any more in this servility,' he declared gloomily.

After his great-uncle's Council where, Joseph wondered, would his own Council, the Second Vatican Council, lead? Would everything stay the same as it had been? Reactionary, neo-scholastic, closed and narrow? Or was there a chance to rediscover and experience the gospel message?

In the Albergo Genio, Joseph unpacked the small suitcase Maria had packed for him. He himself had added the dictionary. He knew all sorts of languages, but not Italian. However, there would hardly to be time for the beauties of the city. The meeting for all the German-speaking Council fathers called by Frings was set for 5 p.m. the very next day, Monday 10 October, the evening before the official opening ceremony. Ratzinger was due to report at the meeting, which was certain to be well attended. *Il cardinale Frings* had earned a prominent position through his principled, objective attitude during the preparation period. 'The name Frings was a seal of quality, so to speak,' Ratzinger said later.[14]

The strain of the pre-Council had exhausted the old cardinal. A short-term new sub-committee, set up at his suggestion, had had to deal with four more schemata on 16 July. On 17 July they had had to rush through the schema *De ecclesia*. On 18 July they had had to examine more than 20 chapters of the schema *De religiosis*, and on 20 July they had had to finish four schemata. Frings spent his brief holiday before the beginning of the Mega-Congress in the Glacier Hotel in Saas Fee in Switzerland and then at the Palazzo Doria in Genoa. 'I look like a chicken,' he laughed at himself, when Luthe read to him from a document. For some time now he had held a torch, in order at least to be able to read short texts himself. But the glaucoma could not be stopped. Now in the evenings, he dictated his talks in Latin, in order to be able to memorize them and deliver them freely. 'Shall I read it out?' Luthe would ask. 'No. Let me say what I wanted to say and have a look to see if everything is in.' No one ever heard him complain. 'How can I, an old blind man, still serve my diocese?' was the most he said about his suffering. 'Herr Cardinal,' Luthe would comfort him, 'you show us how to carry the cross with good grace.'[15]

Joseph's thoughts wandered back to their journey together. During the war he had recognized planes by their noise. Now he was sitting in one himself. For the first stage, from Cologne to Frankfurt, they went by an aircraft whose propeller jerked through the air. After that, they went by jet. From the tiny windows they looked out on green fields, red roofs and grey streets until a cloud wrapped plane and passengers in a cocoon.

The cardinal had celebrated his farewell in Cologne Cathedral, as though he would not be coming back. Before they went to the airport, at 10.30 a.m. he prayed with Luthe and Ratzinger at the shrine of the Three Kings, surrounded by the whole cathedral chapter. Then heavy bells tolled for them through the great Gothic space downstairs in the crypt. Gropingly, the blind bishop felt the gravestones of his predecessors. 'I'd like to be buried here too one day,' he whispered to Luthe, who was holding his arm. Looking back on the scene, Ratzinger said the small episode had shown 'how the Cologne archbishop viewed his work in Rome [...] At that moment he had looked into the future in order to perform his coming task in the light of that responsibility.'[16]

Between November 1961 and June 1962, Frings had attended 47 days of meetings in Rome. He had voted '*non placet*' – 'No' – when his adviser had objections and 'Yes' when Ratzinger gave his agreement. Nearly all his speeches contained arguments and formulations that his adviser had proposed: for example, when the question was 'whether it is necessary to decide everything at a council when it had nearly all already been said in constitutions, encyclicals, papal statements or in dogmatic compilations and therefore already possessed great authority'. Or 'whether it is good to express all that and only say little about God and his greatness, his kindness and riches, and little about Jesus Christ, our Saviour. They are, indeed, frequently mentioned in the prefaces but seldom in the actual schemata.'[17]

Many of the documents produced by the Committee seemed to Ratzinger 'somewhat stiff and narrow, too closely bound to scholastic theology, too much the thought of academics and too little that of pastors'.[18] He constantly advised that things should be shortened, altered or clarified. He was convinced that the Council could not possibly cover every area of public life. What was crucial for the church's future was her faithfulness to Scripture and her fellowship with people in the world of today.

Ratzinger's expert reports merit special appreciation because they document the extraordinary consistency of his basic theological line. The agenda he formulated for the assembly of churches from all over the world shows the structure of his doctrine. He no longer wished to change it, and because of its timeless relevance he no longer needed to change it. And he remained faithful to it until the end of his life. Without attention to his lasting contributions to the Council, a picture of the future pope is not only incomplete but false. About the Council, Ratzinger himself placed on record: '[I was] of the opinion that scholastic theology, as it had been set, is no longer a means fit to bring the faith into the language of the time.' The faith must 'get out of this armour, adopt a new language, and be more open to the present situation. So there must also be greater freedom in the church.'[19]

The 34-year-old professor gave the 74-year old archbishop the line in the very first statements. Here was not an inexperienced student but a teacher with authority:

1. As the fathers of the First Vatican Council already demanded, the submission texts should not give the impression of being taken from theological handbooks written in the scholastic style. But they should allow the language of Scripture and the church fathers to be heard.

A further point: Yes, it is the Holy Father's intention that this Council should give a gentle prompting to our separated brethren to seek unity. It wants to bear new witness to Jesus and his holy church addressing people who, in today's changed life conditions, to our sorrow have become estranged from the faith of their ancestors. So we must always keep in mind the feelings and thoughts of our separated brethren; even though the truth must be proclaimed, 'whether welcome or unwelcome' (2 Tim. 4.2). But let this truth be spoken 'in love' (cf. Eph. 4.15). For according to the apostle's words, we who are strong must 'put up with the weaknesses of the weak and not be complacent' (Rom. 15.1).

2. As was the practice at earlier councils, the Council should not make any decisions about questions that are being discussed as controversial by theologians within the church. It should only rule on the errors which really lie far from the Christian spirit.[20]

Ratzinger kept referring to the 'feelings of the separated brethren'. He wanted to avoid 'the suspicion that the Council wanted to sow discord between the various non-Catholic Christian communities'. Elsewhere he wrote:

Among non-Catholics there is now the fear of an unlimited despotism by the pope; the idea is rife that if you were to deliver yourself over to him, you could no longer be certain of anything. Indeed this traumatic fear is perhaps the strongest obstacle to union with Rome. Couldn't a short paragraph be inserted here that would reassure them that the pope will not use his right arbitrarily?[21]

The relevant texts should be 'thoroughly checked, shortened and improved once more'.

He also seems to have thought of his friend Esther Betz, the journalist. 'On particular questions, for example, those about social media, it seems useful and right to seek the advice of lay people, who have experience in these matters.'

Ratzinger's expert reports were not only critical. In a comment on 17 September 1962 he said:

These two draft texts meet the aims of this Council in the highest degree. They have been stated by the pope as: the renewal of Christian life and adapting church practice to the demands of the present time, so that the witness of faith may shine out more clearly amid the darkness of this century. It appears very important that the Council should not broach the most difficult problems in its first sessions. These are problems that occupy theologians but are inaccessible to the people of our day; indeed they bewilder them. Rather, it is essential to say something that, so to speak, makes renewal noticeable and which can bring a little light to people of good will.[22]

Frings had no problem with seamlessly adopting his spin doctor's suggestions, mostly verbatim. There was one exception. On a schema from Ottaviani's Faith Committee, which was addressed by the Preparatory Committee in Rome on 20 June 1962, there was no comment by the Cologne cardinal. This was a paper *On the Blessed Virgin Mary, Mother of God and Humans.*

Ratzinger had recommended the following decision to the strongly Mary-oriented cardinal:

I believe this Marian schema should be abandoned, for the sake of the Council's goal. If the Council as a whole is supposed to be a *suave incitamentum* to the separated brethren and *ad quaerendum unitatem,* then it must take a certain amount of pastoral care [...] No new wealth will be given to the Catholics which they did not already have. But a new obstacle will be set up for outsiders (especially the Orthodox). By the adoption of such a schema the Council would endanger its whole effect. I would advise total renunciation of this *doktrinelles caput* (the Romans must simply make that sacrifice) and instead just put a simple prayer for unity to God's mother at the end of the Ecclesiology schema. This should be without undogmatized terms such as *mediatrix* etc.[23]

Frings's voting paper lies unused in the files. Ratzinger was still not an official *peritus,* merely the personal theological adviser of a German cardinal.

Pope John used the days immediately before the Council began to go on a pilgrimage to Assisi and Loreto. (This was seen worldwide as a new departure, since no pope had left the Eternal City since 1870.) Meanwhile, in his hotel room, Ratzinger went once more over his report, which he had to present on Monday to the highest dignitaries. Frings had booked the meeting by letter with the rector of the college of Santa Maria dell' Anima, Prelate Alois Stöger: 'There will be at least 50 gentlemen. Could you have the room prepared? During the Council, the Anima is to be the centre for the German bishops.'[24]

And so it was. But people arrived at widely varying judgements of it. For while some saw this centre as the sheet anchor and source of salvation, others regarded it as the source of a conspiracy. The US Council observer Ralph Wiltgen, who belonged to the Divine Word Missionaries in Chicago, described the impact from the German headquarters in a saying that became famous: 'The Rhine flows into the Tiber.' It expressed an infiltration, a kind of power takeover, remembered from the wild Germanic tribes who had brought about the fall of the Roman Empire. In retrospect, Ratzinger himself disputed the revolutionary potential of the Santa Maria dell' Anima camp. It was 'completely mistaken to suggest it was as if a solid progressive bloc had come to Rome with a fixed idea and caught the whole world episcopacy napping'. As he said in self-defence in 1976, behind the new approach there had merely been 'elementary insight [...] without any mutinous intentions'.[25]

At first sight that might be seen as correct. Frings's camp was fairly negligible. It consisted of his private secretary Hubert Luthe and 'a practically unknown young professor from Bonn University', as Ratzinger described himself.[26] Later they were joined by the church historian Jedin and a St Vincent Sister of Charity, Sister Elisabeth, the cardinal's secretary. In the headquarters, Luthe could only circulate papers by means of a Geha duplicator, operated by turning a handle. He also had to deal with the telephone. However, the surmises about the rebel momentun of the so-called Rhine Alliance were not completely unintelligible.

In fact, Santa Maria dell'Anima was at the heart of a development that led to bitter quarrels, up to an 'October crisis', a 'November crisis' and the famous 'Black Thursday', when the whole Council stood on the brink. There was even talk of a 'blitz'. Soon it was rumoured that the Germans would secretly aim for a revision of the First Vatican Council. That conspiracy theory was also leaked to Pope John by interested parties. 'Certain people have succeeded in warning the pope against the German bishops and theologians,' the Jesuit Oskar Simmel informed Cardinal Döpfner. The Holy Father had 'become mistrustful and it was to be feared that this rumour would make him even more so'.[27] However, the various, legitimate means of influence are not to be discounted. Hubert Luthe reported: 'The Germans strongly influenced the Council. There was one towering figure in particular: Ratzinger.'[28]

31

The World on the Brink

At the beginning of October 1962 Rome was like a beehive. Tens of thousands of priests, bishops and members of religious orders swarmed in the streets and squares of the Eternal City. Crowds of journalists thronged into the press centres. Theologians hurried from meeting to meeting and debated strategies in back rooms. Seats were scarce in the trattorias; the Campari ran out in the bars.

Nothing could dim the mood of the German delegation. 'There was a certain euphoria at our arrival in Rome, that mysterious feeling of a beginning, which stimulates and inspires people like almost nothing else,' said Ratzinger. 'It was increased by the sense of being a witness to an event of great historical importance.'[1] Ratzinger had become part of the action, someone co-writing the book of history: 'The expectation was unbelievable. We hoped that everything would be renewed, that there would really be a new Pentecost, a new era.'[2]

It was the same for his friend Hubert Luthe. He was excited that in these days 'we belong to a great church that embraces the whole world. That welds us together.'[3] For the first time he encountered the cheerful African bishops but also the troubles and distress of the church in China. For example: 'Many of the delegates did not know if they would be able to return to their own country.'

In Rome, Luthe saw that many of the Council fathers 'bore scars of persecution, whether they were from Europe or Asia'. For example, there was the archbishop of Orléans. When the Frenchman shook hands with him, Luthe noticed his crippled fingers, which had resulted from his imprisonment in a concentration camp.

In retrospect, there would be much said about the domination of Germans at the Council. There was even talk of a hostile takeover.

And the talk always referred to the headquarters of the German delegation, the college of Santa Maria dell' Anima, called Anima for short, meaning 'soul'. Nevertheless, the small troop had enough self-confidence, drawn from the reputation of German theology and the new strength of the German church as the biggest net contributor to the Vatican. There was also the reputation of Cardinal Frings, who, despite (or because of) his almost scrupulous faithfulness to the Holy Father, enjoyed a high international standing. However, no one among the thousands of observers and participants in Rome guessed that during these days the Council would nearly come to an end even before it had begun.

In October 1962, a US marine routine reconnaissance flight went out with its cameras from Edwards Air Force Base in California to take pictures over Cuba. For a long time, there had been speculation that the Soviet Union wanted to deliver missiles to Fidel Castro's regime, the Communist outpost of the USSR at America's front door. But there was as yet no proof.

When the spy planed landed again at the Edwards base, the appraisal of the pictures went beyond the Americans' worst fears. The aerial photographs showed that Soviet technicians had installed launch pads for medium-range atomic missiles. There were missile transporters in the secret military camps. This meant that all the big cities on the US East Coast were threatened with a nuclear strike.

The beginning of a military confrontation was only a matter of time. 'Perhaps even tomorrow,' noted Robert Kennedy, the US president's brother. The US armed forces planned seven days of massive air attacks against Cuba, more than a thousand on the first day. After that, 120,000 soldiers would invade the island. Despite their intensive spying, at that point the CIA did not know that 42,000 Soviet soldiers had also been stationed on Cuba. In addition, eight Russian medium-range missiles were ready for action – complete with atom bombs each with an explosive force of a megaton of TNT. That was 66 times greater than the destructive power of a single Hiroshima bomb. There were also 36 tactical atomic cruise missiles, enough to flatten the big American East Coast cities. Four Soviet submarines were still on the way, each armed with a nuclear weapon.

The world public was still not informed about the horror scene that was brewing over the northern hemisphere of the globe. Later historians would say that the days of the Cuba crisis had been the most dangerous moment in the history of humanity. Never before had the world faced a worse inferno, which within a very short time could have caused an unimaginable doom, with millions of dead in East and West, cities flattened, gigantic contaminated areas of land that had become uninhabitable. The US strategic air force command triggered a worldwide alert Phase Three. Then Phase Two for the first and only time ever. Phase One meant nuclear war.

But it was not only in the Cuba conflict that there was a threatened escalation. At the largest Council of all time there was also an impending storm. Observers would soon be speaking of an 'attempted putsch'. Others spoke of an uprising. Certainly, the Second Vatican Council congress began with a coup which no one had thought possible.

The German Council fathers were lodging either in the Germanicum papal college – the Anima – or in religious houses. For Frings the Anima, in the via della Pace, was a second home. He had studied there, had been a curate and gained his excellent knowledge of Italian there. With its large conglomerate of separate buildings, halls, smaller rooms, corridors, the church and the cardinal's room, the Anima was rather like a city within a city. Frings had booked a table for meals for himself, Luthe, Ratzinger and different guests. The top table was too unfamiliar to him. The cardinal also had problems with the stairs, so the following year a lift was put in.

For Joseph everything was new. Schoolchildren who carried their books not in satchels but in hand-held, tied bundles. Barbers who soaped their clients and then put the blade to their neck. And above all, 'this jollity, and most of life takes place on the street, and everything is so noisy'. In the Anima, he served at the morning Mass together with Luthe. In the sacristy, he could admire the wall paintings of the seven popes up till then who officially counted as 'German'. They were German in the sense that they were born within the borders of the then Holy Roman Empire of the German nation. And pretty well all of them were regarded as somewhat anomalous.

There was Gregory V, designated as pope by Otto III in Ravenna at the turn of the millennium, when he was just 24 years old. Then there was Clement II, who was elected as pope not by a College but by the German King Henry III. Obviously, the electors were not happy. Clement was allegedly poisoned by his opponents, who would not put up with a pope from the north. Damasus II had one of the shortest papacies in history. Twenty-three days after he came into office he died of malaria – or possibly was also poisoned. St Leo IX battled against simony (the buying and selling of church offices) and the investiture of laity (church offices for laity). The final separation between Rome and Constantinople took place during his papacy in the year 1054, the first great schism in history.

Hadrian VI came from Utrecht. He was the son of a ship's carpenter, became a professor at the University of Louvain, bishop of Tortosa and later the Grand Inquisitor of Spain. The professor was not only the last German pope but also the last non-Italian pope until the election of the Polish Karol Wojtyła in 1978. 'You're all scoundrels,' Hadrian shouted when he arrived at the College of Cardinals, which had elected him in his absence. The Romans did not like his inauguration either. 'Oh betrayers of the blood of Christ, thieving College that has delivered the beautiful Vatican to German fury!', said a poster put up in the Piazza Navona.

The beginnings of the Reformation took place during Hadrian's pontificate. The pope tried to enforce a universal ban on Martin Luther and to prevent a split in the church by carrying out his own reforms. His motto: the evil began in Rome, so it must also be eradicated here. His agenda included the reorganization of the Curia, the restoration of unity and resisting the Turks. His success was as modest as the man who aimed for it. So what was the result of the reigns of the seven German popes? To a fair extent, they had striven for reform. But was it just by chance that the two great schisms in history – the split with the Orthodox Church and Protestantism – both occurred during the papacy of a German pope? And now in the course of the Council would the Romans have reason to be worried again about 'German fury'?

The special session arranged by Frings for the afternoon of 10 October in the Anima was urgent. Immediately after it, at 7.15 p.m. there was a reception for the foreign minister, Gerhard Schröder, in the Federal German Republic's embassy to the Vatican. About 50 bishops were invited to the big meeting hall in the Anima. There were Germans, Austrians, Swiss, Belgians, Dutch and Alsatians. A single speaker undertook the briefing of the Central European fathers: Professor Dr Joseph Ratzinger.

The importance of theologians at the Second Vatican Council is hard to overestimate. The *periti* strongly influenced their bishops' opinions, shaped the content of the committees' work and formulated the textual sources for the decrees. Many of the advisers who had come to Rome had recently still been under suspicion of heresy. Among them were the French priests and cardinals Yves Marie-Joseph Congar, Jean Guénolé Marie Daniélou and Henri de Lubac, as well as Ratzinger's counterpart Karl Rahner.

In the small circle Congar warned 'of the danger of giving the adverse impression of a para-council of theologians, wanting to influence the real council of bishops'. They had to avoid letting it look as though:

1. Theologians wanted to predefine the direction of the Council. That would be an unpleasant reminder of Döllinger.
2. They were hatching a plot.[4]

By 'Döllinger' they meant the major critic of the First Vatican Council, who had worked with a Georg Ratzinger, just as Cardinal Frings was now profiting from the services of Georg's great-nephew Joseph Ratzinger.

Traditional participants put up resistance when they realized the extent to which the progressives wanted to damage the church (in their view). In trends such as the biblical, the liturgical, the philosophical-theological 'Nouvelle Théologie' and, above all, the ecumenical movement they saw the return of modernism, which St Pius X had once vigorously condemned. All those errors would now come back to life, warned Cardinal Ernesto Ruffini. And what made modernism 'even more formidable' was the fact that 'it was accredited by people who deserved special respect for so many reasons'.[5]

The influence of the advisers could be inferred from the explosive increase in their numbers. At the beginning of the Council there were just 224 names on the official list of *periti*;

by the end there would be more than 500. Frings's right-hand man was not only one of the most distinguished but also one of the most effective among them, as the Italian historian later commented: 'In the active progressive wing a shock troop of German theologians stood out, which was led by Father Karl Rahner of the Society of Jesus and the younger theologians Hans Küng and Joseph Ratzinger.'[6] For various reasons Ratzinger himself afterwards downplayed his own importance. However, the truth was that hardly anyone had come to Rome so well prepared as the 35-year-old professor from Bonn. The most important church event of the twentieth century seemed tailor-made for him, because:

- Areas that proved to be key to the Council – such as Scripture, patristics, tradition, the people of God and the term 'revelation' – were Ratzinger's special subjects, through his doctoral work.
- His formula for the church – 'people of God as it is the body of Christ' – replaced the inadequate term for the church as the 'people of God', which could also be understood politically or purely sociologically.
- Through his education in the 'Munich School', he brought the vison of a dynamic and sacramental church playing its part in salvation history, which he set against the strongly institutional and defensive view of the church held by Roman scholastic theology.
- In his Bensberg lecture, Genoa speech, books on the Council and his comprehensive reports for Frings in the run-up to it, he had not only formulated the expectations of reform by the Council but also the outlines for a renewal of the church. He had done so more adequately than Pope John himself had been able to, as the pope admitted.
- In order to modify the relationship between the local and the world church, between the office of pope and bishop, he had developed the idea of *communio*, which would become crucial for the Council. The church's constitution should be 'collegial' and 'federative', at the same stressing the primacy of the pope and unity in teaching and leadership.

- As he was acquainted with Protestant theology and through his work with world religions, he was familiar not only with ecumenical questions but also with the relationship between Catholics and Judaism – precisely the subject of the schema *Gaudium et spes,* which together with the schema on revelation was to become one of the most important Council documents.

Familiar with current trends and new findings in theology, fully aware of tradition but modern in habit, language and focus, he could gain a hearing and recognition in both the conservative and the progressive camps.

When the dignitaries met on 10 October in the Anima hall to hear Ratzinger's report, the way Frings had sung his protégé's praises had raised expectations. Cardinal Döpfner of Munich would also have liked to rely on the young professor as an adviser. But Ratzinger was already booked, even though he could still only act unofficially. In his briefing, he spoke of the inadequacy of many of the schemata to be discussed, as shown in the documents *De deposito fidei pure custodiendo* and *De fontibus revelationis.* The crux of the matter was that, contrary to what had been said, there was actually no further opportunity being offered to untangle and change the texts again. Moreover, Ottaviani had put it about that canon law forbade the rejection of schemata that had already been approved by the pope, unless a way could be found of replacing an unusable text with an alternative. And if so, couldn't an unacceptable document like the schema on God's revelation act like a torpedo that broke through the armour of the Council planning so far and made a new beginning possible?

It cannot be verified whether Ratzinger was aware of the implications of his intervention, which in the end derailed the Council. But he must have known he was playing with fire. 'For a very young professor,' he confessed in May 2005 in an interview with the left-wing Italian daily paper *La Repubblica,* 'it was a really big deal and a somewhat difficult one. The responsibility for pointing the way the German bishops should go lay heavily on my shoulders.' He confessed he had felt 'a huge responsibility to God and to history'.[7]

In his search for a suitable introduction to his talk, Ratzinger hit on Eusebius of Caesarea, a participant at the Council of Nicaea in

325. He quoted the ancient bishop: 'From all the churches covering the whole of Europe, Libya and Asia, God's most select servants were gathered and a house of prayer, stretched wide by God, contained Syrians and Cilicians, Phoenicians, Arabs and Palestinians, and also Egyptians, Thebans, Libyans and inhabitants of Mesopotamia.'[8] Behind the enthusiastic words, Ratzinger pointed out, lay a description of Pentecost, as given by Luke in the Acts of the Apostles. 'The Council is a Pentecost.' That was also what Pope John meant when he harboured the hope of a 'new historical moment'.[9]

Ratzinger was a master of the art of speaking on a subject profoundly and incisively. He was helped by his phenomenal memory. It was usually enough for him to have read a book once to be able to recall it verbatim from memory, make the necessary connections and bring them into the discussion. He came to the point. The schema *De fontibus revelationis* submitted by Rome 'raised questions mainly in three directions: the question of the relationship between Scripture and tradition; the question of the inspiration and inerrancy of Scripture; the peripheral question of the relationship between the Old and New Testaments and the integration of both in the whole of salvation and world history.'

The bishops pricked up their ears. This forceful theologian was speaking about a paper that had already been blessed by the pope and the Holy Office. The problem already arose in the title *De fontibus revelationis*, Ratzinger continued. For, 'despite being in common use, the formula is not without danger. It contains an extraordinary narrowing of of the concept of revelation.' Really, 'Scripture and tradition are not the sources of revelation'; rather, God's own speaking and self-disclosure were the source, from which the two streams Scripture and tradition flowed out. The manner in which the schema put forward by Rome expressed it showed 'a clear failure to distinguish between the order of being and the order of knowing'. It was 'dangerous and one-sided' to use a formulation 'that does not describe the order of reality but only that of our access to reality'.

Frings's adviser did not mince his words in criticizing Ottaviani's presentation: if Scripture and tradition were called the sources of revelation, 'then you are practically identifying revelation with its material expressions'. In that case, the danger arose of sliding into Luther's *sola scriptura* or identifying Scripture with revelation: 'In fact, the writers of our schema have clearly fallen into that mistake from their outset.'

That was outrageous enough. But when Ratzinger spoke, he also wanted to demand consequences: 'As soon as it has been grasped that this positivism is false, as soon as it has been grasped that revelation precedes its material expressions, then the danger of Scripturism no longer occurs. For then it is clear that revelation itself is always more than its fixed expression in Scripture; it is the living Word, which Scripture encompasses and unfolds.' This required that:

- The title 'On the Sources of Revelation' should be changed to 'On Revelation' or 'On the Word of God'.
- A Chapter 1, 'On Revelation' itself, should be inserted at the beginning of the document [...]
- Wherever the term 'sources' (*fontes*) occurs in the text, it should, where possible, be replaced by other expressions.[10]

Cardinal Döpfner was impressed and noted:
Ratzinger on the schemata ... too long ... too clerical... Consequences:

Change the title!

Introduce a chap. 1.

Fons should be changed where possible (*transmission*) ... Aim for openness... Clearer: Christ's salvation open to all![11]

Although Ratzinger's analysis was critical, it also, unlike that of other critics, always showed a concern for the right balance and was rooted in the church's teaching. For example, he demanded that an improved text should 'wherever possible use formulations that indicate the interconnection between Scripture, tradition and the church's proclamation, and show the church's deep bond with the word of Scripture'.

The talk in the Anima that made Ratzinger 'instantly famous' in Rome, as Hubert Luthe said, was soon to play a powerful part. Not only would the final Council decree actually be entitled *Dei Verbum* – the Word of God – but nearly all Ratzinger's desiderata were included. The pressing question was: if the schema was so poor and well nigh theologically false, shouldn't it be blocked or at least altered? And if so, by whom? Shouldn't fellow campaigners be won over, who would then command the necessary majorities in the relevant committees?

The coup that took shape after Ratzinger's presentation was perhaps not planned at general staff level. However, it was far from being an impulse of the moment, as Frings wanted it to be interpreted afterwards. His adviser Hubert Jedin reported that on 19 May 1961 the cardinal had already called him in 'to speak to me about questions related to the future Council agenda'.[12] As an expert on the Council of Trent and the First Vatican Council, the church historian knew the importance of the Council committees. 'Whatever is decided is decided there and not in the plenary,' he insisted to the cardinal. Ultimately only the committees are 'crucial to what happens' at a Council.[13] Frings confirmed in his memoirs that Professor Jedin had 'given him the tip that the choice of committee members was extremely important for the further course of the Council'.[14] 'Our first aim,' the cardinal's secretary Hubert Luthe said, 'was let's hope that we can get a blocking minority.'[15]

The meeting in the Anima was not a gathering of conspirators. But all present were concerned with the question of the pre-planned approval of a pre-arranged membership list for the committees, which reinforced the Curia's influence on the Council. Could that be blocked? And thereby also block those documents which, not only in Ratzinger's eyes, had given the Council a wrong direction? On the evening of that memorable 10 October, Cardinal Giuseppe Siri, the chairman of the Italian Bishops' Conference, wrote ominously in his diary: 'The cross, if you can call it that, will come as usual from the French-German area and its underground, because there the Protestant pressure and pragmatic sanction have never been eliminated. They are clever people but they do not understand that they are protagonists of a history that went wrong.'[16]

While the cardinals and their advisers were fretting over the beginning of the Council, the US government made 204 intercontinental missiles ready for take-off in the west of the USA. Without the public realizing it, the Cuba crisis had intensified. On the US side, 220 missiles on 5 aircraft carriers, together with 12 submarines with 140 Polaris missiles on board, were also operational.

They were ordered to stand off the coasts of the Soviet Union. The airspace was occupied by a total of 62 constantly circling B-52 bombers, loaded with 196 hydrogen bombs. Around the world, a further 628 US bombers with more than 2,000 atom bombs were on stand-by. Not forgetting the 60 Thor missiles in Great Britain and 30 Jupiter missiles in Italy, also equipped with atom bombs. On the other side, the Warsaw Pact troops were ordered to be on increased combat readiness and the Soviet armed forces on full combat readiness, including the 500,000 Soviet soldiers stationed in the GDR.[17]

The Cold War was at an end. The world stood on the brink of a hot, atomic world war. Washington had first strike capacity. One press on the button and the Soviet Union would be wiped out.

32

Seven Days That Changed the Catholic Church For Ever

It was pouring with rain on 13 October 1962, a Saturday, when the Council took up its work at the first General Congregation. The plenary assembly in St Peter's began with the Mass of the Holy Spirit. After the solemn enthronement of the Gospel, followed by the Creed, there was a remarkable prayer, which almost had the character of an oath, even though not all those taking part would remember it:

> Here we are, Holy Spirit [...] Teach us what we should do, point us the way we should go, show us what we must work on [...] Don't let us disrupt what you have ordered. Let not ignorance lead us astray. Let not human approval mislead us. Let us not be corrupted by fear or favour. Amen.

The General Congregations took place in St Peter's from 9 a.m. until 12.30 p.m. every day except for Thursdays and Sundays. Speeches were limited to ten, later to eight, minutes. Each speaker had to sign up in writing. They were admitted in order of rank and age: first cardinals, then patriarchs, archbishops, bishops. If they overran the allotted time for speaking, the microphone was switched off if necessary.

All the participants had come to the Council with 'great expectations', Ratzinger reported. 'But not everyone knew how to go about it.' Frings and his advisers did know. They had thoroughly studied the schemata. They had spoken with specialists and bishops and brought specific proposals for improvements with them to Rome. 'The ones who were best prepared,' Ratzinger declared, 'were the French, German, Belgian and Dutch bishops: the so-called Rhine Alliance. In the first part of the Council they showed the way.'[1]

The meeting in the Anima with Ratzinger's report and the discussion about the 'pseudo-election', with which the Council was supposed to open, had not remained without effect. 'Holy rage' had filled him about this proceeding,' Frings wrote later in his memoirs. He might explode.

When General Secretary Archbishop Pericle Felici explained the election procedure in St Peter's, Cardinal Achille Liénart stood up slowly from his seat. The 78-year-old bishop of Lille, chairman of the French Bishops' Conference, was one of the presidents of the assembly. 'If you please, I beg to speak,' he began. 'That is impossible,' replied Cardinal Tisserant, who was chairing the General Congregation. 'The agenda does not provide for a debate. We have simply come together to vote.'[2] But Liénart, a former military chaplain, would not be stopped. Without further ado, he grabbed the microphone and read out a prepared text. It was 'really impossible to vote in this way,' he insisted. Because the fathers did not know the candidates for the committees, first, the national bishops' conferences had to be consulted. The battle had begun.

To the applause of about 2,000 Council members, Cardinal Frings also rose to his feet. 'I put my arm up,' he wrote in his memoirs, 'but according to the agenda it wasn't possible to sign up to speak.' He was also speaking in the names of Cardinals Döpfner and König, said the German Cardinal Frings. Then he gave reasons why such an important matter as the election of committee members ought not to be left to chance. He therefore proposed that the election should be postponed until the next General Congregation. The fathers should have time to consider carefully and settle among themselves those they thought were particularly suitable. The minutes recorded several times: '*Plausus*'. Applause.

The interruptions appeared spontaneous, but Liénart and Frings had not come unprepared to the meeting in the cathedral on that 13 October. The text delivered by Liénart in the chamber had been prepared by writers in the French seminary of Santa Chiara on the night of 12 October. It had been pressed into the cardinal's hand the next morning, as he entered St Peter's.[3] Likewise, on the afternoon of 12 October there had been a meeting of the German-speaking bishops in the Anima. Wolfgang Gross, secretary to Bishop Hengsbach of Essen, wrote in his diary: 'Afternoon meeting in the Anima. About 100 present. Bad mood. Election tomorrow and no one knows how it will go.'[4] Frings's secretary, Hubert Jedin, also contributed an interesting detail. His boss, he said in an interview, had only 'let the cardinal from Lille speak first so that he, as a German, did not grab the first word. That was his tact.'[5]

Ratzinger has always rejected the accusation that the intervention was a put-up job. 'No, Cardinal Frings did not come to Rome as a conspirator with a well-prepared strategy,' he said in a 1976 article about his Council boss.[6] Fifty years later, on 14 February 2013, he explained in a speech to the Rome clergy: 'It was not a revolutionary action, but an action impelled by conscience, responsibility, on the part of the church fathers.'[7] The action had been completely on the cardinal's 'own initiative':

> Everyone was surprised and astonished that Frings, who was known as very conservative and strict, now took on the role of leader. We spoke about it. He said: it's one thing when I govern the diocese and am responsible for the local church to the pope and to the Lord. It's quite another thing when I am called to co-govern with the pope in Council. Then I take on a new, separate responsibility.[8]

The derailing of the pro-forma election was the first uprising against the Vatican old guard. The pope would have the last word, but the fathers had taken command of the Council proceedings. The session was adjourned and the 3,000 or so participants had to go home in pouring rain. As Monsignor Luigi Borromeo put it, they were 'to see to it that they got to know each other a bit better'. Unlike Borromeo, the progressive Cardinal Suenens immediately grasped the revolutionary significance of the incident: 'Happy coup and daring violation of the rules!' he summed up the fateful day in his memoirs. 'The fate of the Council was decided to a large extent at that moment. John XXIII was glad about it.'[9] Ratzinger was also glad: 'The Council was determined to act independently and not to be downgraded to becoming merely the executive body for the preparatory committees.' It had been shown that 'the episcopacy is a reality with its own weight in the universal church. It brings its own spiritual experiences into the conversation and into the life of the worldwide church.'[10]

However, the price for it was high. Later Ratzinger realized the collateral damage that the cardinal's intervention had caused, namely, a 'fateful ambiguity of the Council whose effects in the world at large were not foreseen'. It boosted those who saw the church as political and knew how to use the media. A short time afterwards, he summed it up in his report on the first session of the Council:

> In Frings's and Liénart's eyes, it was the logical consequence of the summoning of the Council and a concrete expression of catholicity. But the world at large was interested in quite a different aspect – obstructiveness and rebellion against the Curia. This appealed both to the anti-Rome sentiment and to the basic human desire to kick against the pricks of 'authority'.[11]

On the same day there was feverish activity in the Anima. Secretary Luthe telephoned until his fingers were sore. Emissaries hurried through the city to sound out coalitions. For the afternoon of 13 October Frings invited Cardinals Alfrink, Suenens, Liénart, König, Döpfner and other dignitaries from Central Europe to work together on an election plan with suitable candidates. The names were listed on cards, scraps of paper and letter-headed paper. The entry for 13 October in Cardinal Döpfner's diary reads: '16 h: Anima: Draw up a Central European list (France, Belgium, Netherlands, Germany, Austria, Switzerland, Poland, Scandinavia). We'll aim to exchange with other groups.' Clearly a list had been circulated in the run-up to the Council. As a memo of Döpfner's indicates, it had become obsolete: 'List fr. Friday 12.10.62 out of date!'

In the German headquarters there was a constant coming and going of delegates from the individual bishops' conferences to lodge proposals for candidates. Frings was keen to fill the committees with representatives from all continents and areas – from among bishops, academics and members of religious orders. Only the widest possible list of proposals would have the prospect of commanding a majority. On 14 October Döpfner noted: 'Fr Hirschmann notes that everything must be done to contact open-minded Italians so that a united front does not arise there.' A day later, his diary noted: '11.30 h: Visit to Card. Montini [the future Paul VI] to make contact with the Italians. Very prepared, believes only a small group of Italians with us. 15.30 h: Bishop Abed from Tripoli-Lebanon. Seeks contacts & understanding.'

Ratzinger saw yet another aspect: 'That openness to neighbouring countries shows that it was definitely not a secret conspiracy. Frings wanted the Italian Bishops' Conference also to know what the Germans were doing and was anxious that German bishops should forge links with those speaking other languages.'[12] Hubert Jedin said in his memoirs: 'In order not to be suspected of conspiracy, Frings requested Cardinal Ottaviani to suggest their candidates, but the Italian cardinals, including Montini and Siri, refused.' So, according to Ratzinger, it was 'not about a bloc, a "Rhine alliance"' but 'a comprehensive representation of all parts of the church on the Council committees'.

The campaign was successful. On the night of 15–16 October, Hubert Luthe was able to duplicate a list of attractive candidates in the Anima. Two thousand copies of it were sent out to the Council fathers eligible to vote; another 1,000 remained to be collected. The coalition of Germany, Austria, France, the Netherlands, Belgium and Switzerland put forward 109 names, which became the 'international' list. It also included candidates from Italy, Spain, USA, Great Britain, Canada, India, China, Japan, Chile, Bolivia and various African countries. Everything seemed to be going to plan. However, no one had thought about the practical implementation of that plan.

In fact, the vote on 16 October turned out to be a fiasco. It had not occurred to anyone that the approximately 2,400 Council members eligible to vote with about 160 candidates on the lists amounted to about 24,000 voting papers – with nearly 380,000 handwritten entries. It was impossible to sort everything out in the Council chamber. So General Secretary Felici ordered the Council fathers to fill out their voting papers in their lodgings. They were to give in the lists themselves by hand (and not through a messenger) during the course of the afternoon. Meanwhile, the over-taxed Olivetti counting machines would be replaced by students from the

Pontificio Collegio Urbano de Propaganda Fide. Then it took days for all the voting papers to be counted and analysed – with the result that hardly a single candidate got the required absolute majority. In order not to exacerbate the fiasco, Pope John declared without further ado that, at the suggestion of the Council presidium, he had cancelled Article 39 of the Council procedure rules. Candidates with the highest number of votes would simply count as having been elected.

In the end the coup succeeded: 79 of the 109 candidates on the 'international list' were elected. They got 49 per cent of all the seats up for election. Ottaviani and Siri had hoped to gain the votes from the mission regions, but they had underestimated the trust that the German bishops and their chairman Cardinal Frings enjoyed in the Third World, through the aid work of *Miserior* and *Adveniat*. If the pseudo-election had not been rejected, the Italian historian Andrea Riccardi said, it would have come 'to a total reconfirmation of the pre-conciliar committees – who would then have carried on working in accordance with the criteria and viewpoints they already had'.

The new elections had 'crucially influenced the further course of the Council', Frings also said. With hindsight, he had realized that 'the pope was not at all unhappy that the original list of members of the preparatory committees had not been elected'.[13] The journalist and eyewitness Ralph Wiltgen summed up: 'After that election it was not difficult to foresee which group was well enough organized to take over the leadership of the Second Vatican Council. The Rhine began to flow into the Tiber.'

Their election success had given the progressive wing courage. If elections could be upset, then perhaps whole schemata could also be ditched: all those constitutions from the Ottaviani factory that were both badly constructed and that predetermined a line that blocked the pope's call for renewal like a boulder on the road.

However, public attention was suddenly focused on quite different news. On 22 October 1962, the day when the debate on the schema *De sacra liturgia* began in St Peter's, the world was facing its most dangerous flashpoint. In a television speech, President John F. Kennedy informed the world public for the first time of the Soviet threat from Cuba. Kennedy announced a sea blockade and demanded the immediate removal of the Russian missiles. If the Russians launched an attack with atomic weapons, the USA would respond with a retaliatory nuclear strike.

These were no empty threats. Two days later, US war ships took up positions around Cuba. Soviet ships could no longer pass. The crisis threatened to escalate when, on 25 October, Pope John implored the warring parties in a dramatic appeal to do everything they could to settle the quarrel without resort to weapons. On 27 October the conflict stood on a knife-edge. A US war ship fired depth charges at a Soviet submarine, forcing it to break surface. Today we know that the submarine had torpedoes with nuclear warheads on board and the crew was authorized to fire them. On Cuba, Fidel Castro's flak units fired at several US Air Force reconnaissance planes. A US spy plane was hit by a Soviet anti-aircraft missile. The pilot, Rudolf Anderson, was killed.

It was still not too late. After a secret meeting between Robert Kennedy, the president's brother, and the Soviet ambassador to the USA, Anatoly Dobrynin, the Soviet leader, Nikita Khrushchev, stated that he was prepared to dismantle the missiles on Cuba. In return, the USA was to lift the blockade. In fact, after an exchange of messages between Kennedy and Khrushchev, a compromise was reached, which ended the crisis: removal of the missiles by the Russians, lifting of the blockade by the USA. The agreement was announced on 29 October. In the two weeks between 14 and 28 October the world came very close to a nuclear war that would have destroyed half the globe and a large part of its population.

The conferences in the Anima – always on Mondays, punctually at 5 p.m. – gave the German-speaking bishops a tactical advantage and stronger influence than any of the other groups. With about 100 participants, the meetings gathered together all the bishops from Germany, Austria, Switzerland, Luxembourg, Scandinavia, Iceland and Finland, as well as many missionary bishops and general superiors. In the briefing on 10 October, Ratzinger had sharply criticized the schema on the sources of revelation. The schema presented was 'wholly determined by the anti-modernist spirit, which had developed around the turn of the century'. It was an 'anti-spirit of negation which would be sure to have a cold, even shocking effect'.[14] Theologians around the Belgian Dominican Edward Schillebeeckx had also found the schema inadequate. It was aggressive, intolerant and one-sided. But it was Ratzinger who, on 15 October, already had a first chapter for a new schema to lay on the table. He and Karl Rahner had produced a second, more adequate draft. Between 15 and 25 October the bishop of Mainz, Hermann Volk, and the Jesuit Otto Semmelroth, together with Rahner and Ratzinger, met to do further work on the text. Rahner, who had also written a chapter, would take care of having it typed up.

Thanks to Frings's diplomatic skill, the committees were now peopled with members who were not exclusively those favoured by the Curia. But how could they succeed in also pushing through texts that, as Ratzinger hoped, would make the Council one that would create 'a new awareness making it possible to speak to one another openly and in a friendly way without infringing obedience to the faith?'[15]

A reconstruction of the events of autumn 1962 reveals the dynamic of an extraordinary change. It began on 19 October 1962 with a meeting between the German and French bishops in the Mater Dei house in the viale delle Mura Aurelie. Among the 25 present were the theologians Congar, Chenu, Daniélou, de Lubac, Küng, Philips, Rahner, Schillebeeckx and Semmelroth. Joseph Ratzinger was also there. Congar remarked in his diary: 'Theme for the future is to discuss and agree upon a tactic against the theological schemata.'[16] Küng suggested setting up an international meeting of theologians to put the necessary pressure on the Council fathers. Congar advised against it. They should in no way give the impression that they were hatching a plot. 'When we act,' he argued, 'it is always necessary to think of the reaction which we might provoke.'[17] Instead of Küng's impatient 'revolutionary expectations' he believed deeply 'in the ability to wait, the necessity to move in stages'.[18]

On 25 October, Cardinal Frings made the case to an illustrious circle of clerics for a new draft – which became known as the Ratzinger–Rahner schema. As well as Cardinals König, Alfrink, Liénart, Suenens and Döpfner, the influential Italians Siri (head of the Italian Bishops' Conference) and Montini (the future Pope Paul VI) were also there. Ratzinger introduced the alternative draft paper. According to Cardinal Siri later, the reaction of those present was 'enthusiastic'. However, Montini dampened the general euphoria.

At that point in time, it would be better to do further work on what was to hand and already well prepared.[19] Frings was not happy with this. After further revision he had about 3,000 copies of the alternative revelation schema distributed to all the Council fathers.[20]

At supper in a small restaurant not far from Sant' Ignazio, Cardinal Döpfner and Hubert Jedin checked through the Council agenda to see whether it would be possible to oust the prepared texts. (Jedin: 'From our side there did seem to be a point for some leverage.') At a meeting on the following day, 6 November, the plan was developed. Other participants, besides Frings, Rahner and Ratzinger, were the Belgian theology professor Gérard Philips and the Dominican Yves Congar.[21] In the afternoon Döpfner gave the Council expert Jedin the text of a new submission to the Cardinal Secretary of State. The aim of the proposal was that every General Congregation debate should be allowed to vote on whether the schema then being up for discussion should be returned for improvement or wholly rejected. In the latter case, the way would be clear for the presentation of a completely new draft. The Ratzinger–Rahner schema could act as a precedent to break up Ottaviani's Holy Office cement-hard documents.

The attack began on 14 November 1962, during the 19th General Congregation. Looking back, Ratzinger reported that 'the unavoidable storm' broke, 'which had already been prepared for with a private counter-draft'.[22] He did not say that the 'private counter-draft' stemmed partly from his own pen. Cardinal Ottaviani grabbed the floor without notice. It was his first appearance in the Council chamber since he had been silenced by Cardinal Alfrink two weeks earlier. During a debate on the liturgy when the head of the Holy Office overran his speaking time, the Dutch cardinal had simply had the microphone turned off – and received thunderous applause for it. Now Ottaviani began to speak again, saying that it was the first duty of pastors of souls to teach the truth, which always and everywhere remained the same. Then Salvatore Garofalo, a member of the Curia who was presenting the official schema on the *Sources of Revelation* in detail, took the same line. Here it was not a question of renewal. The primary task of the Council was to defend and promote Catholic doctrine in its purest form. The schema being presented was mature and balanced. Many scholars from many countries and the most diverse universities had contributed to the text. He was followed by Cardinals Ruffini and Siri, who had tried to make Ratzinger's alternative paper look ridiculous in the Italian Bishops' Conference. They too were determined to defend the committee's draft.

That was it. According to observer Ralph Wiltgen, 'The reaction in the Council chamber was swift and deadly.' Now, one after another, Cardinals Liénart (France), Frings (Germany), Léger (Canada), König (Austria), Alfrink (Netherlands), Suenens (Belgium), Ritter (USA), Bea (Curia) and others gave their reasons forcefully for rejecting the text. Liénart declared the draft to be categorically inadequate, defective and too scholastic: *non placet*. Then Cardinal Frings spoke. His intervention, which he had memorized the night before, came word for word from Ratzinger's pen:

> If I am allowed to speak openly: *Schema non placet*. In the schema put before us today I think the voice that can be heard is not that of a mother or guide, not that of the Good Shepherd who calls his sheep by name, so that they hear his voice. Rather, it is the language of a schoolmaster or professor, which does not nourish or stimulate. That pastoral voice is so important that Pope John wishes dearly that it should be used for all the utterances of the Second Vatican Council. But the language we have here does not go to the depths. It operates on the level of our human knowledge. But on the level of being, there is only one single source, which is revelation itself, the Word of God. And it is very regrettable that there is nothing, almost nothing, said about it in this schema.[23]

Still nothing was decided. At the 21st General Congregation on 17 November, Cardinal Döpfner reminded the meeting that the schema on revelation had already been controversially discussed. But the objections had been 'simply dismissed'. Ottaviani protested: canon law forbade the rejection of schemata that had already been approved by the pope. Cardinal Norman Gilroy, from Sidney, corrected him: according to Article 33, Section 1, of the procedure rules for the Council, schemata could indeed be rejected.

On 20 November, when voting was due to take place, the decisive battle over the future course of the Council broke out. It began with a commotion. To the surprise of the Council fathers, Council

General Secretary Felici announced that anyone supporting the schema and a continuation of the discussion must vote *non placet*. Anyone for withdrawing it must vote *placet*. The reversal of the former procedure was a trick and caused total confusion. Hardly anyone was clear what he was voting for when he voted 'yes', or what he was voting for with a 'no'. 'It would have been normal to present the schema for acceptance (or further discussion),' Ratzinger wrote, explaining the reason for the trick. 'Then it would have needed two-thirds of the votes. Instead of that, the question put was: who is for the dismissal of the schema? Now the opponents of the text had to obtain two-thirds of the votes and just a third was enough to save the schema.'[24]

The trick succeeded at first. More than 80 Council fathers had spoken in the course of the debate. A total of 2,209 cast their votes. Of these, 1368 (62 per cent) voted to break off the discussion, and 822 (37 per cent) voted to continue it. Nineteen ballot papers were spoilt. Frings had foreseen correctly. By manipulating the question, the Curia managed to turn the principle of a two-thirds majority on its head. Frings's camp fell just 105 votes short of achieving the rejection of the totally inadequate schema. But suddenly the tide turned.

It was a sensation. According to the rules, on the outcome of the previous day's vote the schema had to be accepted. But as Archbishop Felici came to the microphone, there was silence in the Council chamber. Felici read out a notice from the secretary of state. The pope had had the impression that the discussion on the schema would be laborious and wearisome. So he had decided it was sensible to withdraw *De fontibus revelationis* and have it revised by a committee of his own. The new revision committee would have two chairmen, Cardinals Ottaviani and Bea. Six more cardinals would join it, including Frings, and Liénart. At first no one could quite believe it. 'The pope had exercised his authority over the Council,' said Ratzinger, who had criticized the schema as 'determined by the anti-modernist spirit' and 'cold, even shocking'.[25] Now not only was a schema put forward by the Roman committees off the table, but there was actually a chance to reject it. 'I am surprised how boldly I spoke out then,' Benedict XVI told me in our interview. 'But it is true that because a proposed text was rejected, there was a real change and a completely new start to the discussion became possible.'

The psychological effect of the change on 21 November was enormous. 'Although they were a minority,' said Wiltgen, the observer, 'for the first time they felt they were in a majority.' In retrospect, it became clear how important this development was. At the beginning it was recognized that the great majority of fathers supported Ottaviani's line. 'But everything that had happened changed the situation radically,' Ratzinger said in his report on the first session. 'The bishops were no longer the same as they had been before the Council opened.' The wheel had turned. Here, 'instead of the old negative "anti", a new positive hope emerged to abandon the defensive and to think and act in a positively Christian way. The spark had been lit.'

On 24 November Pope John received the German bishops in a private audience at 7 p.m. They had no idea that for weeks the pope had been haemorrhaging and had been under close medical supervision. The Holy Father was optimistic. The Council must become 'a *signum caritatis,* a worldwide sign of love'. He was confident and had grounds for hope. In future, they must not rush things but seek for thorough clarification.[26] Cardinal Suenens and Döpfner had asked him beforehand to abandon the celebration of Mass at the beginning of the sessions. But on this point the pope remained firm. He was convinced that the Council had 'perhaps more need of prayer than of thinking'.

In his speech the next day, his 81st birthday, he expressed his conviction that God was leading the Council: 'You have the proof of that in the events of the last few weeks. Those weeks can be seen as a kind of novitiate for the Second Vatican Council.' It was only natural that ideas and proposals should differ: 'That is a sacred freedom, for which the church, especially in these circumstances, has shown her respect.'[27]

That was the last appearance of the pope for a long while. He had been overdoing things. As well as his regular duties, during November he had received 37 bishops' conferences. Because of further haemorrhages he was compelled to cancel all audiences. On 8 December he said at the closure of the first session that the course of the Council had been a slow and ceremonious introduction.

The Council had shown that the freedom of the children of God reigned in the church. The terminally ill pope wished a blessing on the future course of the Council and announced that its sessions would resume the following, year on 9 September 1963.[28]

'It can be said without exaggeration,' said Giuseppe Ruggieri, professor of fundamental theology in Bologna,

> that particularly the week from 14 to 21 November 1962, which was devoted to the debate on the schema *De fontibus revelationis,* was the moment when a decisive change took place for the future of the Council and therefore for the Catholic Church itself: from the Pacelli church, which was essentially hostile to modernity [...] to the church which is a friend to all humanity, even when they are children of modern society, its culture and history.[29]

Ratzinger saw it the same way. He viewed the rejection of the schema he had criticized as the 'turning point' of the Council. By their stand 'against the one-sided continued promotion of anti-modernist spirituality', the fathers had 'decided in favour of a new way of positive thinking and speaking'.[30]

The windows were open, just as Pope John had hoped. The real Council could begin, with all the shadows it would cast but also the light it was capable of receiving. What a point in history! In Munich a Professor Schmaus could thwart the young theologian's work and make it most of it disappear into a drawer. Rome could no longer do that. His knowledge about revelation had to come to light, even against the power of the machine.

Now the church could turn over 'a new leaf,' said Ratzinger immediately after the end of the first session, 'in a new positive encounter with its origins, its fellow Christians and the world of today'. Because 'such a clear majority of the Council had opted for the second alternative,' he said with reference to the schema he had formulated, 'this Council has become a new beginning'.[31] He also explained in detail what the change of course meant in practical terms 43 years later in an interview with *La Repubblica:*

> 'Pastoral' should not mean: fuzzy, without substance, merely edifying, as it is sometimes misunderstood. It should mean: formulated

with positive concern for people today, who are not helped by condemnations. They have been hearing long enough about everything that is wrong, everything that they must not do. Now they want to hear at last [...] what positive message the faith can give for our time, what it positively has to teach and to tell them [...]

And 'ecumenical' should not mean: suppressing truths in order not to upset others. What is true must be said openly, without concealment. Full truth is part of full love. 'Ecumenical' should mean: ceasing to regard the others just as opponents to defend ourselves against. It means trying to recognize them as fellow believers, with whom we talk and from whom we can learn.[32]

In November 1962, Frings's adviser was appointed as an official *peritus*. His Council identity card was issued by 'Hamlet, Johannes Cicognani, Cardinal Bishop of the Holy Roman Church, Titular of the suburbicarian Church of Frascati, Secretary of State to His Holiness Pope John XXIII'. It allowed him to take part in the General Debates in St Peter's and secured him 'safe conduct and if necessary the requisite help and support'. Ratzinger found it a 'great experience to see all the experts, great personalities, Henri de Lubac, Jean Daniélou, Yves Congar, Marie-Dominique Chenu – people I admired – and then, of course, the pope himself'.[33] Not far from him sat Karol Wojtyła, making notes on the debates. He marked the top right-hand corner of each new page with a cross and the initials *AMDG* – *ad majorem Dei Gloria* – to the greater glory of God.

Unlike Ratzinger, the bishop of Kraków seemed anything but pleased about his colleagues' revolt. In Poland, Wojtyła had experienced attacks on his church by the atheist authorities – so from the church's *enemies*. In his opinion, the aim of the Council should be to make clear statements against the growing materialism of the modern age and on the meaning of the transcendence of the human spirit. The subjects *he* would have liked to discuss included the importance of celibacy, the pastoral uses of sport and theatre, and ecumenical dialogue, together with reform of the breviary and the liturgy.

Once again Cardinal Ottaviani showed dignity. He accepted the dismissal of his proposed text with composure. But he could not refrain from a side-swipe. 'I don't look forward to hearing the usual litanies from all of you,' he uttered with disappointment into one of the microphones in St Peter's. Litanies such as

> it's not ecumenical and it's too scholastic. It's not pastoral and too negative and suchlike complaints. This time I want to tell *you* something: Those who are long accustomed to saying 'Take it away and replace it it' are already equipped for battle. And I'll tell you something else: even before this schema was distributed, an alternative schema had been prepared. So all that remains is for me to be silent. For as the Scripture says: when no one is listening it is pointless to speak.

From now on Ratzinger had a dubious reputation. Suddenly he was being reproached: 'I had fooled the cardinal.' Karl Rahner confirmed in a letter to his brother Hugo that, because of their alternative draft for the revelation schema, he and Ratzinger were roundly abused in a 'pamphlet by French integralists' and accused of being 'heretics who denied Hell and were worse than Teilhard and the modernists'. [34] The charges against the two advisers went so far as to say that the Ratzinger–Rahner schema was 'a typically freemason text and suchlike'. In our interview Benedict XVI winked and added: 'Now I really should not be suspected of being a freemason.'

33

German Wave

After the Council shut its doors on 8 December 1962, Cardinal Frings took the next plane to Vienna. An operation in an eye clinic hoped to restore his sight, at least partially. Joseph went home to Bonn. He had things to catch up on. Texts to correct, seminars to prepare, faculty meetings to attend.

Frings and his adviser had turned the Council round. The minority of those wanting reform had become a majority. At least the former stronghold of the Curia had been breached, the spell of its figureheads broken. Jokes were doing the rounds in St Peter's, which went more or less like this: 'A ship sails from Naples to Capri. On board are the Cardinals Ottaviani, Siri and Ruffini. The ship sinks. Who is saved? The Catholic Church.'

The first session was by far the most significant because it determined the direction of the whole Council. 'If many people perhaps were or are unhappy that the Council did not adopt any text or achieve any tangible result,' Ratzinger noted immediately after his return to Germany, then they should not worry about it: For 'it was precisely in this apparently negative balance that the great, surprising and really positive result of the first period lay.' The refusal just to nod through decrees or constitutions showed 'the radical change from the spirit of the prepared work. That was what was truly epoch-making in this first session.'[1]

It could be seen like that. Others saw it differently: 'The Council has shown that a doubtful form of leadership is emerging, represented by the German-speaking group and their associates or neighbours,' wrote Cardinal Siri of Milan on 1 January 1963 in a letter to Monsignor Alberto Castell, the secretary of the

Italian Bishops' Conference. Siri was beside himself over what he considered to be the tendencies flaring up: 'antipathy to or even hatred of theology'; 'proposal for a new theology'; 'proposal for a new method for theology'; 'prevalence of rhetorical and literary performance'; and 'ecstatic infatuation with new words and new paradigms'. Suddenly everything had to be subordinated to the 'pastoral', 'the ecumenical goal' and the 'expectations of the world', he remarked sarcastically. It was an attempt 'to eliminate tradition, Ecclesia etc'. – supported by those who wanted to suit as much as possible to the Protestants, the Orthodox and so on. As a result: 'The divine tradition becomes nullified.'[2]

In Germany, in Catholic faculties, bishops' residences and newspapers it was not only the sensational change in Rome that was discussed. Another change was just as exciting: the change in Josef Frings. The cardinal of Cologne had up till then been regarded as strictly conservative. He was known as a church leader close to the people, who relaxed from the duties of his office with music by Mozart or Stravinsky, accompanied by Moselle wine and cigarettes. He enjoyed reading Shakespeare's plays at least as much as the writings of the church fathers. Now even the news magazine *Der Spiegel* began to take notice of the old man of Cologne. Front cover title: 'German Wave'. This was a reference to the wave that Frings had set in motion in Rome. The article carried a quote from Cardinal Newman: 'To live is to change, and to be perfect is to have changed often.'

The magazine reported that the Cologne cardinal, who until then had been regarded as particularly loyal to the pope, had perpetrated an attack that was 'unprecedented in recent church history, against the dictatorship of the authoritarian top guardians of the faith'. The tone he had struck must sound like 'sheer revolution to conservative as well as to simple Catholics'. *Der Spiegel* had discovered the inspiration behind 'the astonishing change in the Rhineland bishop' to be none other than his 'most important adviser', one of 'the most gifted German pro-reform theologians'. His name: 'Professor Joseph Ratzinger, 36'. The article summed up: 'From many conversations' with Ratzinger, 'the scholar half his age', the cardinal had arrived at 'the theological conviction which he stood for in the Council today'.[3]

The journalists had been successful in their search for clues. 'The first news of the progressive Frings,' the magazine said, 'came from Italy.' This was an allusion to Frings's speech of November 1961 in the Teatro Duse in Genoa. *Der Spiegel* wrote: 'For the first time in his life Frings demanded that the church review "obsolete church forms" like the "Index" and "its whole previous practice", because people were "exceptionally sensitive and critical of all signs of totalitarian behaviour".' For the first time he had also called for great weight to be given to the 'idea of tolerance and respect for other people's spiritual freedom'. And for the first time he had broached the subject 'which he focused on later at the Council: the church's need to "strengthen the power of bishops".' Of course, what the Hamburg journalists did not discover was that the whole text had come from Ratzinger.

Now he was home again, Frings's top adviser was confronted with developments that had been awaiting him for a good while. In April 1962 the dean of the University of Münster had communicated to Bonn University that they wanted to appoint Ratzinger to the chair of dogmatics and history of dogma for the coming winter semester *primo loco* (in first place). On 18 June 1962 the culture minister for North Rhine and Westphalia officially asked Ratzinger what he thought about it. 'Unfortunately, I am unable to make a decision about accepting the appointment at the moment,' he replied. 'First, I should like to explore the duties and possibilities of the Münster chair [...] In the meanwhile, I can only say that I am not wholly averse to the appointment.'[4]

Münster had an imposing history and the largest Catholic faculty in Europe. Under Hitler, Cardinal Clemens August von Galen, the 'Lion of Münster' had stopped the Nazi euthanasia programme by his brave denunciation. On 29 June, just a week after the inquiry, Ratzinger's student Werner Böckenförde drove him, together with his sister Maria, to Münster to have a look round. In Bonn, the attempts at headhunting were followed attentively. In a letter to his culture minister on 2 July the rector of the university wrote: 'The Catholic theological faculty has a pressing interest in keeping the acknowledged and very promising scholar for the faculty and the University of Bonn.' 'In just a few years,' Ratzinger had 'gained an international reputation through his publications and lectures'. The rector was specific: 'On the instructions of the Catholic theological faculty, I request that you authorize that the increase in salary offered by Münster to Professor Ratzinger should also be paid to him were he to remain in Bonn.'[5]

The fight over Ratzinger had become a public matter. The magazine of the Collegium Albertinum in Bonn said: 'The theologians were disturbed when they heard that Prof. Ratzinger had been offered an appointment in Münster.' Now the students entered the fray, with an unprecedented demonstration: a torchlight march calling for Ratzinger to stay in Bonn. A decision still had not been taken. An internal ministry note of 6 August said: 'Prof. Ratzinger is still very undecided whether to opt for Bonn or for Münster.' Time to offer Ratzinger all sorts of benefits: a raised salary, an academic assistant and a research assistant and also half a typist. That would have made Ratzinger's chair the one with the best personnel and financial provision in the faculty. Finally, on 27 August 1962, 15 days before the opening of the Council, the much sought-after professor announced that he had decided to stay in Bonn. The relieved under-secretary Wegner recorded in a handwritten note dated 30 August: 'set[tled]. Prof. Ratzinger remains in Bonn.'[6]

In fact, Ratzinger should long since have been occupying a very different professor's chair – in Tübingen, the Olympus of German theology. In our interview, Ratzinger told me: 'The Dean in Tübingen had even said I could choose between the two vacant chairs myself.' But he had to decline the offer then. 'At that time I had already been appointed to Bonn, which was my dream destination.' That had been lucky for Hans Küng, who took up the coveted positon instead of Ratzinger, even though, as the staff in Tübingen sneered, he had no habilitation and his doctorate from Rome was not highly regarded in Germany.

The Council had not only changed Frings. It had also changed his adviser. Ratzinger the whizz-kid had become a mature man who was aware of his responsibilities. In his reports from Rome he did not come across as a distant observer of the Council, with devout respect for the great things happening at it. He analysed it as someone who had helped to shape it and who wanted to show his readers what was actually happening, whether it was about divine service ('a matter of life and death for the church') or the question of Roman centralism, the dialogue with non-Catholic Christians or the relationship between church and state, faith and science, ethics and religion. With great reserve, he revealed himself in only one aspect: the part he himself played in the proceedings.

On his return flight to Bonn, Joseph went back over the weeks he had spent in the Eternal City once again. His explorations in the surroundings of the Anima, with the Pantheon; the French national church, San Luigi dei Francesci; La Sapienza, the oldest university in Rome; the Palazzo Madama, the seat of the Senate; and so on. He recalled the 'booze ups' in Trastevere with colleagues from the theological committee. On one of his walks with Frings he had suddenly lost his way. The blind cardinal had taken his arm. 'Just tell me what you see,' he said eventually. Joseph described a historical statue. 'He did not know that it was the memorial to an Italian freedom fighter. 'Ah, that is Minghetti,' said Frings reassuringly, 'so we must now turn right and then left.'

Another event, the trip to Naples on a Council day off, had in fact been a fiasco. Together with other theologians, he had dragged Frings up a mountain for a better view. It did not occur to any of them that the cardinal could not see at all. And the adventurous crossing to Capri? The scenery on the wildly rocking boat recalled the apocalyptic paintings of the wreck of the ship of the church. Nearly all the vanguard of the German Council team were sick, including Frings. Ratzinger himself had somehow managed not to throw up.

The meeting with de Lubac was unforgettable. The Frenchman was extraordinary, not only in his diligence but also in his humility, kindness and warmth. The visit to him was like meeting an old friend. And de Lubac, who was born in 1896, could have been his father. Joseph did not rate any theologian higher. Perhaps de Lubac's *Catholicism* had not thrown him into ecstasy as a student so much as into a kind of rush of recognition. *Oui*, they conversed in French. The ascetic scholar lay sick in bed. He had constant pains from a wound in the First World War. But despite his illness, de Lubac had had a book brought to him from the Rome city library. It was by some sixteenth-century writer he was working on.

When Rahner and Ratzinger worked together on their alternative text in a room in the Anima, Rahner took the lead but, unlike Ratzinger, he did not know shorthand and despaired of transcribing the eternally long Bible quotations. 'Oh it's so boring,' Rahner had groaned. In a letter to his brother Hugo, who had Parkinson's disease, Rahner gave intimate glimpses of the Roman scenario. The great theologian wrote: 'What a poor *peritus* does is boring work. You produce texts which the Council fathers improve (or at least think they do) and of their wisdom present in the chamber. You give lectures to bishops. You take part in little meetings of small groups with theologians and bishops.'[7] For a whole month he had to travel to the outskirts of the city every Wednesday evening to speak to Brazilian bishops. It was 'such arduous and time-consuming work, and the good people did not even pay my bus fare.'[8]

Rahner and Ratzinger got on well. Since their first meeting in Königstein in 1956, Rahner, 23 years older than Ratzinger, had taken a decided interest in him. Both had brothers who were also priests. That was a link. Both had written fundamental articles for important theological lexicons – Rahner for the Catholic version, Ratzinger for the Protestant. (He also co-operated in the second edition of the *Lexicon für Theologie und Kirche* (1957–65). In volume 1 he is named as 'Dr J. Ratzinger, lecturer, Freising', in volume 10 as 'univ. prof., Münster'. He also wrote a series of fundamental articles for the subsequent volumes 12–14 on the Second Vatican Council.) Shortly before the Council, their first joint book was published. But they did not work well as a team. It became increasingly clear to Ratzinger that, as he said, theologically they were on different planets. His partner pursued a speculative and philosophical theology, all very complicated. As a former student of Martin Heidegger, Rahner's bent was towards German idealism, towards Hegel and Fichte. But Ratzinger went for historical thinking and the writings of the fathers.

With the Council, Joseph had entered a new world. His work was no longer confined to a lecture room or the margins of a book. There was also another change that brought something new. In the biography of everyone there comes a point which is an encounter with fate. Ratzinger would speak of 'Providence', which lies beyond human power of disposal. Up till then 'Providence' had set fatherly figures at his side: Läpple in Freising, Söhngen in Munich, Frings in Bonn. However, with Hans Küng he met someone who was not only the same age but would also turn out to be an opponent who did not want to let go of him.

Since they first met at the dogmatics conference in Innsbruck in 1957, the links between the two young stars had never been broken. Although others may have called them 'theological teenagers', they saw themselves as highly intelligent, self-aware, advocates for renewal – the church fathers of tomorrow. Ratzinger said of Küng: 'I had read his doctoral thesis with pleasure and it won my respect for the writer. I liked his congenial openness and straightforwardness.' Küng recalled a 'very friendly' colleague and 'most agreeable contemporary, of my own age'. Ratzinger had seemed a bit shy, but was someone 'with invisible spiritual force'. In the run-up to the Council, Karl Rahner wrote to Küng, who was coming as the bishop of Rottenburg's adviser: 'As Ratzinger and Semmelroth also seem to be coming, we could form a good club with Congar, Schillebeeckx etc.'[9]

Henri de Lubac had advised caution. He knew the Swiss Küng from his time studying in Paris. 'He is a great worker with a clear understanding and I felt only sympathy for him,' de Lubac wrote in a letter to the theologian Heinrich Bacht. 'But for a while now there has been a pushiness about him, a kind of *arrivisime*', as we say in French, that has something unpleasant about it. I hope Küng will work seriously, as he began to do in Paris, that he will give us mature works without too much loud propaganda and arrogant show.'[10]

Küng came from the small town of Sursee, with 4,000 inhabitants, in the canton of Lucerne. He was born on 19 March 1928. He had five sisters and was the only son of a well-to-do family in the shoe trade. He was the darling of his proud mother, Emma. As a boy, he was a member of the patriotic Catholic 'Jugendwacht' ('Youth Watch'). Later he became an armed local defence soldier. He was spared being called up in the war. When he entered the Germanicum in Rome, he joined the promising elite of the Catholic world, educated by Jesuits and firmly guided. The students of the papal college, founded in 1552, wore a sixteenth-century uniform: black cap, biretta and belt and the *domestica*, a red Roman coat down to the ground. Morning prayers began at 6 a.m. and night rest from 9 p.m. The house rules filled 40 pages with regulations for daytime and night-time. The informal 'Du' was forbidden; conversations in the dormitory were deemed undesirable.

The young Küng was regarded as a model in the house but was also a convivial fellow student. In the student theatre he took the part of Robespierre, the controversial hero of the French Revolution. His fellow student Gerhard Gruber, who later became vicar-general in Munich, recalled: 'There was a prison scene. Küng stood at a barred window in the moonlight and all the people [Robespierre] had killed came into his head. The he said to me: "Gruber, now I know how to act in a play. I can do it." If you want to understand Küng, you have to know that he is simply acting his part.'[11]

As a student priest, Küng accused those who were sceptical about church institutions of 'rationalistic presumption'. For him, Pius XII was a shining light and an ideal pope. In his spiritual diary he wrote: 'Lord, let me always stand by the pope in all things.' When the dogma of Mary's Assumption was proclaimed in 1950, he took the vow of total dedication 'to Mary and through Mary to Jesus'. On 10 October 1954 he was ordained as a priest in the college church. He celebrated his first Mass on the next day in the crypt of St Peter's, before the tomb of the Prince of Apostles, wholly 'in loyalty to the office of St Peter'.[12]

Like Joseph Ratzinger, who was a year older, Hans Küng had wanted to be a priest from an early age. The similarities are striking. Both practised an unobtrusive piety. Both came from an Alpine landscape. Both grew up in decidedly Christian families and were very close to their siblings. Both had a humanistic education, a love of Mozart, a weakness for France, a keen intellect and the gift of being able to communicate. That they were both supporters of scholars like de Lubac, Congar, Hans Urs von Balthasar and the Swiss Reformed evangelical theologian Karl Barth went without saying for bright young people like them. Ratzinger, as well as Küng, felt progressive enough to strike a new tone in their mission, to overcome what was outdated and to reveal 'the liberating Jesuan' (Küng) or 'the whole depth of the figure of Christ' (Ratzinger).

The two young theologians were concerned whether Christian faith could survive if it was not better attested. In a lecture in Vienna, Ratzinger promoted 'Christian brotherhood', a subject to which he also devoted his first book with the same name. A year beforehand Küng had brought out *Rechtfertigung (Justification)*, his doctoral dissertation on the doctrine of justification in Karl Barth, published by Hans Urs von Balthasar. It was a plea for ecumenical community. He gratefully noted that his colleague Ratzinger recommended it in two reviews.

When John XXIII surprisingly summoned the Second Vatican Council in January 1959, Ratzinger came to the fore with his lecture in Bensberg and the Genoa speech to formulate guidelines for the coming church assembly. He saw the great challenge for the Council was to address modernity. Küng chose the same theme when, at Barth's invitation, on 19 January 1959 he spoke at the Basel Protestant theological faculty on the 'church always to be reformed'. He wanted to turn his Basel lecture into a 'small pocket book'. (Meanwhile he had become an assistant to Hermann Volk in Münster.) The book's title was *Konzil und Wiedervereinigung: Erneuerung als Ruf in die Einheit* (*Council and Reunion: Renewal as a Call to Unity*). His line was clear: if the Council committed itself to the unity of the Christian denominations, that would show an unlimited readiness for dialogue, reform and reconciliation. Therefore the Council should not decide on any new dogmas about Mary or make any other decisions that would emphasize what separated the churches. Küng formulated his theses as 'questions', which made him harder to attack. He also supported his pleas with nods to tradition and quotations from the pope.

Originally, the work was to be called *Konzil, Reform und Wiedervereinigung* ('Council, Reform and Reunion'), but Barth, Küng's adviser, advised against it. Formally and stylistically, a 'Protestant smell' should be avoided. Meanwhile, the Evangelical theologian began to doubt whether his young colleague had rendered the Roman doctrine correctly. Barth said to Küng: 'If what you describe in your second part as the doctrine of the Roman Catholic Church actually is its doctrine, then I must certainly admit that my doctrine of justification accords with yours.'[13] What was lacking was a foreword recommending it. Küng's publisher, Balthasar, would not do. Cardinal Döpfner declined. When Küng visited the archbishop of Vienna, Franz König, in hospital after he had had an accident, the cardinal, who was in plaster up to his head, dictated a few lines in which he spoke of the author's 'true religious feeling' and hoped the book 'would be received with understanding, and spread far and wide'.

Küng's book on the Council became a best-seller. Within a year the Freiburg publisher Herder had brought out four editions and sold rights abroad. It was published in English as *The Council and Reunion* (London, 1961). More than 150 newspapers and journals published substantial, sometimes glowing, reviews. In June 1962 the US news magazine *Time* gave him a full-page feature and celebrated him as 'the most important theological talent in Germany since the Second World War'. In its Christmas edition of December 1961 *Der Spiegel* observed: 'Professor Dr Hans Küng has dared to enter new theological territory. The prominent academic has demanded a pro-Protestant reform of the Catholic Church from the ecumenical council.' The magazine added: 'Possible faithful readers' doubts about whether the writer is true enough to the church are dispelled by forewords from church leaders and by what it says in the text: every Catholic always and everywhere owes the church leadership "genuine, loyal, sincere and free obedience".'[14]

Küng had a sure instinct for developments that were in the air and could electrify people. According to his biographer Freddy Derwahl, he had written sentences 'that got under the skin of us young people. Not just because they sounded honest but because they cleared away the pretentious trimmings with which the church presented itself, that were commonplace at the beginning of the 1960s.'[15] The Catholic Church needed an 'atmosphere of freedom,' said Küng, especially for its theologians. However, the little people played no part in the theology of the bourgeois academic. He prophesied: in future, the 'decisive Catholic elites will be more important than the sluggish Catholic masses'.[16] His colleague was quite different. He decidedly wanted to defend the faith of simple people against 'the cold religion of the professors'.

At the Council, Küng did not take part in the actual work on the texts. He neither wrote a speech for a bishop nor was a member of a committee. Ratzinger argued that the Church was essentially a Eucharistic community – *communio*. Küng saw it differently. For him, church was council – *concilium*. While in Rome others wrangled over secondary passages in incomprehensible texts, Kung realized that besides the council chamber in St Peter's there was a wider and more prominent stage where he could use his talents – the stage of the media. His unconventional style, his stance as a progressive critic, his knowledge of languages, his upper-middle-class brio and his gift of briskly and pointedly formulating an idea made him an ideal contact for press, radio and television. And as a kind of independent speaker for the Council, he had no problem with claiming the prerogative of interpretation from a commanding height. For, as well as the usual parties to the Council, another one had arrived that was not on the list: the 'publicity party'. It was represented by a group whom Ratzinger later called the 'journalists' council'. Most of the fathers still had not realized that, unlike at any previous Councils, now there was an independent powerful media industry. But Küng played the press like a virtuoso. Postmodern theology was born, and it was journalistic theology.

In Rome, Cardinal Ottaviani had asked Küng 'not to hold a press conference with cameras running in St Peter's Square immediately after each meeting'. But part of Küng's strategy, his biographer Freddy Derwahl wrote, 'was the use of the media, at which Küng is a master to this day'. An irony of fate: Ratzinger contributed to a great extent to formulating the Council statements and thus shaping the modern face of the church. He would fight for 50 years to defend and implement the 'true Council' – though for decades he was reproached with having betrayed the Council. Küng neither had any part in the adopted texts nor did he think of acknowledging declarations such as those on celibacy or the papacy. Instead, he operated with a vague 'spirit of the Council' and from then on was regarded as the one who set the seal for progress.

One of them drove an Alfa-Romeo and was always well dressed. The other rode a second-hand bike and wore his characteristic beret and shabby suit. One cultivated a radical critique of the church and became the darling of the press. The other challenged the *Zeitgeist* and became a target of the media, which celebrated Küng as a model Christian. For millions of supporters worldwide Küng became the leading figure in church reform.

In Rome during the Council they met in a café in the via della Conciliazione, the glorious approach road to St Peter's Square. 'He had good tendencies,' said Benedict XVI in our conversation. His own failure to recognize Küng's bent for so long was due to his inexperience: 'I had the naïve view that Küng was a great talker and said daring things, but that basically he wanted to be a Catholic theologian.'

There is a story from the Council years which Hans Küng liked to tell. During the Council, he said, Paul VI had voiced the church's need for young talent in leading positions, like himself and Ratzinger. Then he had invited him – Küng – in a private audience to enter the service of the church, but he should just adapt himself a little. Naturally, he had indignantly refused. Ambiguously, Küng added: 'I don't know what the pope said to Ratzinger, but from then on we went our separate ways.' Joseph Ratzinger knew nothing about it. He stated that during that time he had never met Paul VI in an audience.

The Council was already a marathon. However, after his return from Rome a real endurance test awaited Ratzinger. From 28 to 30 December in Munich, together with his colleagues Rahner, Schnackenburg and Semmelroth, he had to report on the Council to Bishops Döpfner, Schröffer and Volk. Even his old adversary Professor Schmaus had announced he was coming.[17] On 5 and 6 February he was invited to a meeting of all the German-speaking Council fathers. On 7 February, a report on the 'dogmatic and acetic meaning of Christian brotherhood' had been arranged in the international seminary for priests of the Jesuit Order in Innsbruck, the Canisianum. On 9 and 10 February, in Munich, he took part in the Bavarian Catholic Academy's conference on the subject of 'Nature and Limits of the Church'. During his time in Bonn he had published a total of three books, 33 articles, 20 reviews and 22 lexicon entries. Hundreds of pages of the first drafts of a dogmatics textbook lay in a drawer. He had discussed it with the publishing house Wewel Verlag in 1961, but it was never published.

The battle for the right interpretation of the Council had begun. Ratzinger wrote a popular series of articles in the *Bonner Rundschau* and articles for professional journals. His book on the first session was displayed in Bonn bookshop windows. 'The acclaim Ratzinger received then,' said the theologian Hansjürgen Verweyen, was also shown in his eagerly awaited lecture in the university on 18 January 1963. Fifteen hundred people thronged into the crammed auditorium and also into Lecture Hall X, where the speech was relayed by loudspeaker. 'The students banged on the tables and would not stop,' said audience member Doris Heitkötter. 'Ratzinger shifted awkwardly from one foot to the other.'

Theology student Norbert Blüm was also in the audience. 'Ratzinger's lecture was an almost revolutionary event,' said the future Federal employment minister. Indeed, at the very beginning of the Council, the lecturer stressed, something new had been created by the actions of the Cologne cardinal and the Central European bishops: horizontal catholicity, which took into account the authority of bishops and set up a vital relationship between the church's periphery and the centre. Through the dispute about the schema on the *Sources of Revelation,* the Council had been pushed from a defensive position towards a new spirit of openness and encounter. Of course, that was only an interim assessment. But with the first Council session an epoch-making change had been initiated, which justified optimism. The altered attitude towards modernity could be characterized as 'Yes instead of Anti'. The *Bonner Rundschau* concluded its article on Ratzinger's 'report of his experience' with the sentence: 'At the end, the audience stood up to pray with the speaker for a good outcome to the Council.'

On 19 March 1964 Ratzinger even found time to make a detour to an ecumenical conference in the abbey of St Hildegard in Eibingen. The convent chronicle observed: 'Everyone was spellbound by the lofty spiritual ideas, the clear trains of thought and the wise and modest personality of the priest.' He had been devoted to the 'prophetess of the Germans', Hildegard of Bingen, since his childhood. She was the clairvoyant eleventh-century polymath, doctor, poet, composer and mystic, whose visions embraced a comprehensive knowledge of natural medicine, nutrition therapy, cosmology and the world's relationship to the Creator. Fifty years after that visit to Hildegard's convent, Ratzinger as Benedict XVI canonized her as a saint of the Catholic Church on 10 May 2012. On 7 October of the same year he appointed her as a Doctor of the Church, an honour which up till then had been given to only three women. Benedict stressed that Hildegard was a woman who loved Christ in his church but was not at all unworldly or afraid.

At that time Ratzinger's rise seemed unstoppable. 'Career planning was never his aim,' reported one of his students, 'but then he didn't need to plan – everything fell into his lap.' Not everything. There was also a darker strand running through the theologian's life. There were stray bullets, obstacles, the envy of colleagues, rejections. Even in Bonn, his 'dream destination', dark clouds were gathering over him.

The acclaim he had received from everywhere had also aroused jealousy, and his opponents were waiting for their chance. First, the university establishment looked askance at his sympathy for people who were classed by the theological dignitaries as 'borderline cases': for example, the Lutheran exegete Heinrich Schlier, the evangelical Indologist Paul Hacker or the scholar Chajjim Horowitz, leader of the Jewish community in Bonn. 'Certainly most colleagues regarded him as too modern and progressive, even as sometimes reckless in his theological thrust,' said Heinz-Josef Fabry, professor of Old Testament studies in Bonn. Wasn't Ratzinger's 'original student' Vincenz Pfnür actually working on a dissertation on the Protestant *Confessio Augustana?* And wasn't the Council adviser also a writer for the Protestant standard work *Religion in Geschichte und Gegenwart* (*Religion in History and the Present*)? The picture was not improved by the fact that crowds of young people flocked to the unconventional professor while their own lecture rooms were empty.

In particular, Ratzinger was now having problems getting his doctoral students through. In May 1962 he had vociferously supported allowing Orthodox theologians also to work for doctorates at Catholic faculties. This now concerned two of his own students, who attended his lectures in black monks' habits. One was Stylianos Harkianakis from Crete; the other was Damaskino Papandréou, who worked with immigrants in Bonn and Cologne. The faculty refused to admit the two Greek priests for doctorates. The New Testament scholar Gerhard Schäfer queried pointedly at a faculty meeting how their colleague Ratzinger could fulfil his lecturing duties if he was going to spend half of the coming semester in Rome as a Council theologian. Ratzinger had to justify himself and promised to make his lectures more concise.

By the beginning of the winter semester 1962–3, the situation had got worse. At the 7 November 1962 meeting, the doctorate of his student Johannes Dörmann was on the agenda, despite the absence of his supervisor Ratzinger (who was away at the Council). In a letter to Rome on 9 November, the dean reported to Ratzinger that Schäfer had officially registered objections to the dissertation. The tension erupted in the last faculty meeting of the year, six days before Christmas, on 19 December 1962. Ratzinger supported the Swiss lecturer Franz Böckle, who was regarded as progressive, and had recommended him for the chair of moral theology, which was about to become vacant. Schäfer objected that Böckle had no habilitation and had odd views about birth control. The Old Testament scholar Gerhard Johannes Botterweck added his verbal weight against him, and Böckle was out of the running. (However, Böckle was appointed later. He taught for 23 years in Bonn and became an adviser to the German Federal government. He is regarded today as one of the most influential moral theologians of the post-conciliar period.) That was the first blow. The second followed immediately.

Once again it was about the dissertation of Ratzinger's student Dörmann, who had been rejected on formal grounds. 'They want to get rid of you,' his Council colleague Jedin had whispered to him. Ratzinger had had enough. On 17 December he wrote in a letter to Dean Kessler in Münster that he would not rule out a second offer of a professorship, if certain conditions could be fulfilled.

Cardinal Frings still tried to make him change his mind, but in the end agreed: 'You must go where you believe you will be able to work better. But you must not let yourself be led by negative considerations because you have vexations in Bonn.'[18] Ratzinger's conditions were good provision for the professorship and the ability to bring his Greek Orthodox students with him. For them, and for himself as their teacher, he saw more favourable conditions in Münster. The die was cast.

At the end of February 1963, the news was out: 'Prof. Ratzinger is leaving Bonn,' the *Generalanzeiger* reported in large print: 'For the Bonn University Catholic theological faculty and even more so for his students, Ratzinger's move to Münster is a heavy loss. Their departing lecturer was very well loved for his simple and humanly engaging manner.'

In his memoirs, Ratzinger states that the circumstances had 'become so pressing that I bowed to them'. Heinz-Josef Fabry summed up: 'For nearly all his fellow staff he was a respected colleague, who drew unforeseen numbers of students to the faculty. His lectures were brilliant and brave (perhaps even progressive). He was an excellent colleague.' Nevertheless, a climate had developed in Bonn 'in which a man of the greatness and sensitivity of a Ratzinger could no longer breathe, let along research and teach'.[19]

The future pope revealed the motives for his move in his biography. He remembered his vow: 'I thought of the drama of my own habilitation and saw in Münster the way Providence had pointed out for me to be able to help them both.'[20] Anyhow, there was also no question that he felt himself drawn to dogmatics, 'which offered me a much broader field of work than fundamental theology'. The two Greek students became metropolitans of the ecumenical patriarchate of Constantinople. 'I used just to know about the Eastern Church from books and pictures,' he later thanked his students. 'But it was only through personal encounters that I came in contact with its vital force, which worked its way into my own theological thinking, my faith and my life.'

34

Power Sources

Münster, with 270,00 inhabitants, is a city of offices, trade and education. Two-thirds of it was flattened by air attacks in the war. But by 1963 large parts of the university had long since been rebuilt, and to the newest technical standards. There was plenty of money around. It was the period of the Economic Miracle.

Ratzinger's assistant Böckenförde had found a perfectly situated little house for him and Maria. Ten minutes to his place of work (by bike). Ten minutes to the church (on foot). Ten minutes to the Gasthaus Zum Himmelreich. Joseph was still 'homesick for Bonn, the city on the river, with its cheerfulness and intellectual dynamism'.

The Ratzingers' new address was 18 Annette-Allee, named after the nineteenth-century poet Annette von Droste-Hulshoff. Four rooms, kitchen, bathroom, garden by the cemetery. When Georg came to visit – and he usually spent every holiday with his brother and sister – he slept on the couch in the living room. The first floor was sublet to students Vinzenz Pfnür, Helmut Brandner and Lorenz Mösenlechner. They celebrated 'Bavarian evenings' together and when during a snowstorm the tune 'Gently Flutters the Snow' could be heard playing on the violin, the master of the house on the ground floor joined in with spirit on the piano. During the summer vacation candidates for the priesthood from the Munich-Freising diocese lodged in the professor's house and took care of mowing the lawn.

In the winter semester of 1963–4 there were 13,751 students enrolled at the University of Münster. In theology, the largest Catholic faculty in Germany, 343 candidates for the priesthood and 321 lay theologians, 113 of whom were women, were enrolled. Church attendance in the diocese was about 50 per cent. About 50 new priests were ordained every year. The town council and administration all took part in processions. On 28 June 1963, a Friday afternoon, almost the whole of Münster seemed to be afoot. Countless people thronged in front of the number 1 lecture room in the Fürstenberghaus in the cathedral square. The 600 seats had long been taken. More students and town citizens had gathered in the next room, where a loudspeaker had been set up. Then an unassuming 36-year-old figure came to the microphone.

It was the inaugural lecture of the now famous Professor Ratzinger, who had taken up the chair of dogmatics and history of dogma on 1 April. For his debut his wore the traditional thick-lined gown of a full professor. The obligatory velvet biretta decked his small head. His lecture was on 'Revelation and Tradition'. The subtitle on the invitation was 'Attempt at an Analysis of the Concept of Tradition'. In Bonn the old professors had been jealous of the younger one. In Münster it was different. When he came to the end of his lecture there was thunderous applause.

Ratzinger knew he had arrived. He liked the city and saw a new chance to bring with him the Council's sense of a new era, to teach a new theology without having to fear attack. He wrote enthusiastically to Hans Küng: 'I'd be delighted if we could try together to tackle the dogmatic work at the University of Münster.' He recommended his colleague for the newly created chair of ecumenism. As Tübingen offered Küng the prospect of his own ecumenical institute, in September 1963 he declined. Instead, he sent his assistant Walter Kasper, who arrived in Münster on 1 August 1964 after completing his habilitation. Another lifelong associate of Ratzinger's who was not easy to deal with.

At 6.30 in the morning, the new professor usually celebrated Mass in the chapel of the nearby maternity clinic. Then he went to the university. He went past the massive walls of the thirteenth-century St Paul's Cathedral and the town properties of the noble families. Understatement was as much a part of the town as the frequent rain and the armada of Dutch bicycles. The saying goes that in Düsseldorf they wear their coats with the fur on the outside, in Münster they wear them with the fur on the inside. At the university he was greeted by his secretary, Ursula Berger. Soon she would be suffering from boredom because her boss did too much himself.

When he corrected his students' essays he wrote many remarks in the margins. He wanted his students to share in his thoughts, to hold a dialogue. At midday, he went back to Annette-Allee or into his professor's office, where he had a sofa installed. Ursula Berger reported his secret was that 'even when he was heavily burdened he would still do something for himself'. Her boss had learned early on either to be wholly in the world, among people, conversing – or completely by himself, in mediation, in prayer, in his own work.

The newcomer did not completely fit the picture, with his baggy clothes, his old bicycle and his casual appearance. Also untypical were his cheerfulness, his hearty laugh, his gentle self-effacement and his natural enthusiasm for the arts. Students were used to professors being authoritarian and distant, but Ratzinger was approachable, humorous and enjoyed contact with them. He was appreciated for his language, which gave theology a vivid flavour they had not previously tasted.

Many things about the man from Bavaria appeared at times a bit awkward. Some people were amused by his odd walk: the stiff upper body, then the short, regular steps. Ratzinger was aware of his intellectual greatness, but he consciously made little of himself, so as not to seem like a giant to others. He was conspicuous by his inconspicuousness. His nature seemed to be paradoxical. Intellectual but down-to-earth. A rational person with a childlike piety. A soft voice that could be very loud. Modest but decisive. 'What stood out about him,' said one of his audience at that time, 'was the contrast between his inconspicuous appearance and how he spoke: with an incredible presence and mastery.' And he also had a certain rigour. In professional arguments he did not compromise.

His Advent sermons from the pulpit in St Paul's Cathedral became an important event for the town. The cathedral had never been so full – to the rafters. At 7 p.m. 1,500 mainly young people went to listen to Ratzinger's meditations on the Bible. The preacher quoted Blaise Pascal and Kierkegaard. He drew from the natural sciences. One member of the audience recalled: 'That was the first time I understood properly what "Advent" meant: taking into account the unsaved part of the world and also in ourselves.'

Until then in Catholic faculties Bible study had been regarded as 'rather Evangelical'. Now the prospective theologians saw how their professor derived his teaching directly from the Bible and thereby made possible a new approach to Scripture. He explained that the aim of theological study was truth and love of God, to strive for both knowledge and devotion. A 'personal involvement' was necessary, really turning towards God, who called you to be his partner, friend and disciple. In the end, studying theology meant 'accepting the truth about yourself in the light of God'.

They were all enthusiastic about him, particularly Sister Mechtild from the convent of the Sisters of the Cross in Aachen, who never missed a lecture by Ratzinger. No other lecturer had such a large audience. About 350 students enrolled for Ratzinger's lectures. In fact, at least 600 attended them, even though they were inconveniently at 8 o'clock in the morning. 'He came in like a little curate, went to the front and immediately began the lecture,' said his student Franz-Josef Dömer. 'Then it was suddenly quiet as a mouse and everybody hung on his words. And when you thought he had said everything, then he began on his own theology and said things we had never heard or read before.'[1] Sister Emanuela said: 'It was clear to us that here it was not just a learned professor talking to us but a man of great spiritual depth.'

The texts transcribed in shorthand in the lecture room were so sought after that assistants Vinzenz Pfnür and Roman Angulanza set up a small printing press in the university cellar to print the 200-page transcripts in an edition of at least 800 copies to send throughout Germany. The income came in handy for a needy student. The organizer, Vinzenz Pfnür, regularly brought homeless people home with him. 'His bank account was always empty because he gave away everything,' said his fellow student Angulanza. 'That greatly impressed Ratzinger.'[2]

One of Ratzinger's two main subjects in Münster was the closer definition of the concept of revelation. He taught that revelation was 'knowing oneself to be spoken to by God', and thus a thoroughly personal process. Revelation was not knowledge. It was more a matter of the free divine reality appearing to humans and wanting to bring them into a relationship. About the Trinity, he said: 'God is person, in that he makes us become "you", a partner. God is not a neutral destiny, but someone who is and has Word and Love. God is what makes prayer make sense, because he can hear; and what makes love make sense, because he has loved first.'³

The second main subject of Ratzinger's teaching was how the church understood itself. He looked at the most important New Testament passages about it and went into the current Council discussion. His lecture on the Eucharist was also relevant. The Eucharist, he said, was the sacrament of the Risen One, the sacrament of transformation. The meaning of the Eucharist was 'self-abandonment in order to find yourself'. In other words: the Eucharist was the permeation of our 'I' with the 'You' of the Risen Lord, and the opening up of our 'I' into that 'You'.

For him, the Christian Creed was not a lesson but a law of freedom. 'God is Creator, the world is creation, I am created.' It was a statement making trust and serenity possible. 'Before we ever make sense of ourselves, the meaning is there. It surrounds us. The meaning is not a function of our creation but a prior enabling of it. That is: the question of our *wherefore* is answered by our *where from*.' His proof of God was Jesus Christ, in whom God assumed a human face, a face full of kindness and mercy. Because Jesus was fully and wholly human, in him was found 'what is truest of myself', and God as 'the inmost core of all beings'. Those honestly trying to give an account of the Christian faith to themselves and to others must always be aware of 'the insecurity of their own faith, the besetting power of unbelief within their own will to believe'. But perhaps 'doubt, which stops both me and the other person being shut off in ourselves, may become a space for communication'.

In Münster it seemed as if Ratzinger produced a meditative, hypnotic effect, which hardly anyone could resist. 'What I have noticed above all about Ratzinger is his feeling. He does not just think with his head, he thinks with his heart,' said his then student Maria-Gratia Köhler: 'He was particularly kind and gentle to those who were uncertain and stammered their questions. He rephrased their question in his own words, so that in the end they were proud they had asked such a clever question!' 'Other theologians sounded great and intellectual at first but they left you feeling empty inside,' said Erhard Bögerhausen: 'Ratzinger's theology always led me back to the mystery of God. The Other comes through him. He is the eye of the needle through which the Other is threaded into our history.' Another contemporary witness said: 'He made us keenly sense the biblical message, that we must align our activity with the activity of Jesus. It was through that biblical focus that he brought us something new, which was not avant-garde but plausible and in a sense devout.'[4]

A quite different perception came from the church critic, psychologist and ex-priest Eugen Drewermann:

> I remember a meeting in 1965 when I experienced Ratzinger in a lecture. I see before me a wax-pale face, thin as a rake, the shrill voice. I felt faint, as if the air was becoming thinner. It was about the reality of the world, the whole area of sensual experience. And although I am almost smell-blind, the sensation was as if a kind of perfume kept wafting out. Extraordinary. I have never experienced that phenomenon in a lecture. A completely artificial existence, held together by a will that moves every part of the body, the thoughts, like a puppet. With extreme discipline and ease, and completely dead.[5]

Drewermann's judgement matched the image of the Grand Inquisitor in Dostoevsky's *The Brothers Karamazov*, which the critic projected onto Ratzinger. It sounds interesting. But it was shared by none of the countless other contemporary witnesses questioned. That does not mean Ratzinger's personality did not present a riddle. The doctor and psychotherapist Brigitte Pfnür said: 'With him there is a kind of mixture. In a supervision, I would say he does not seem completely free and easy. But the looks he gives are always very intense, powerful, very affirmative.' At any rate, with Ratzinger one felt 'a breath of something tender, when he speaks. Other men, especially professors, take up a lot of space with their presence. When Ratzinger speaks, what he *says* takes up the space; he withdraws as a person.'

As a theology student in Münster, Brigitte Pfnür experienced her teacher as 'simply fascinating':'He was so not clerically triumphal, so convincing, even the most difficult things became clear. [...] With him as a person you had the feeling that he is what he says, he is completely genuine.' Ratzinger talking, said the psychologist, 'gave you a feeling that put you in contact with the supra-personal'. Pfnür compared it with experiences she had in Nepal with Buddhism: 'Even when you didn't understand most of it, something just happened. All the everyday frippery vanished. It was an encounter with something quite different. Ratzinger expresses his mind but also communicates something quite other.'[6]

Ratzinger's method of supervising doctoral students was a novelty in Münster. He saw aspiring students individually but mainly as a group. It was a previously unknown academic-spiritual colloquium, in which each of the participants presented their own research and ideas for discussion. They began with a prayer. The session was intense, the atmosphere relaxed. Among his doctoral students he had 'seen people who are with me on a journey, who belong together,' Ratzinger said, 'so that we can all learn with and from each other.'[7]

The students did not form a homogeneous or elite group. The basis of the method was that there was no method. Ratzinger abhorred selection. 'He took on whoever knocked at his door, as if sent by fate,' Siegfried Wiedenhofer reported. 'That was part of his trust in God, that he accepted everyone.' The temptation to create his own streamlined group had not arisen at first. His teacher had just 'let it happen'. That 'letting it happen' was almost Ratzinger's fundamental principle.

In Bonn, for example, it had been Heinz Schütte who had profited from that principle. In 1963 Der Spiegel picked up his case, without knowing the background. According to the magazine, 'the change in Cardinal Frings' could be seen 'in his attitude to the popular reform-friendly priest Heinz Schütte'. Schütte, a 38-year-old priest, had written a work with the title On Reunion in Faith, 'in which he advocated a pro-Protestant reform of the Catholic Church'.[8] Guardian of the faith Ottaviani's Holy Office had issued a Monitum, an official warning, which ordered the 'errors' to be removed from the work. As Schütte's superior, Cardinal Frings, who had at first criticized the book, suddenly changed his mind and expressly promoted a new edition.

What Der Spiegel had not uncovered was that Schütte was a Ratzinger student. When the priest came to him in 1960, he was 'dodgy'. After the condemnation of his book by Rome, he lost his job as a teacher of religion and was forbidden to write. However, Ratzinger took him on as a doctoral student and suggested he should work on German Protestantism and how it saw itself – just the subject on which he had come to grief. But, unlike Ottaviani, Ratzinger told his student that he regarded his venture as 'a true ecumenical signal, which spread light wide and awakened gospel hope. Especially among our Evangelical brothers'.[9] Schütte returned the favour later when, as specialist for ecumenism, he energetically supported Ratzinger, the then Prefect of the Congregation for the Doctrine of the Faith, in the preparation of the 'Declaration on Justification' agreed with the Evangelical Church in 1999.

The already mentioned Siegfried Wiedenhofer had followed his professor from Bonn to Münster. He was from Graz, 21 years old and wanting to become a priest, when he enrolled in Ratzinger's seminar for the winter semester 1962–3. There Wiedenhofer got 'access to reformed theology and the ecumenical question'. He confessed: 'It could even be said that theologically Ratzinger became my salvation.'[10] The Austrian even followed his master to Tübingen and Regensburg, and for 11 years was one of his closest associates. Ratzinger conducted his marriage to his wife, Elke, and baptized the couple's children. As professor of fundamental theology and dogmatics in Frankfurt, Wiedenhofer won the prestigious Protestant Melanchthon prize in 1988. He did not share all his teacher's positions – for example, he remained in critical sympathy with the 'political theology' of Johann Baptist Metz – but he remained closely linked to Ratzinger: 'Whether it was about the craft of academic theology, generous advice in difficult life questions, or recognition of the student's freedom and own theological journey – I could not have found a better teacher.'[11]

Another member of the student group was Hansjürgen Verweyen. Like Wiedenhofer, he had also originally wanted to become a priest, but then decided against it. His application for a job at a Münster gymnasium failed, because the church authorities refused to give him approval as a Catholic teacher of religion, the so-called *missio*. 'Ratzinger was furious about it,' said Verweyen, 'I have seldom seen him like it.' His doctoral supervisor got him and his wife academic assistance jobs, 'so that we could live'. He baptized the couple's daughter and helped Verweyen get a professorship at Notre Dame University in Indiana. Verweyen's wife, Ingrid, had already become aware of Ratzinger when she was an Evangelical theology student in

Bonn. She attended his Christology lecture – 'and a year later I was a Catholic'.

Vinzenz Pfnür, who had known Ratzinger since Freising days and had completed his studies under him in Bonn, worked as an academic assistant to his professor in Münster. Like Wiedenhofer, Pfnür also developed into an important ecumenist. In 1982 he was elected to the chair of church history in Münster, which he kept until his retirement in August 2002. He became an adviser of the German Bishops' Conference Ecumenical Committee and a member of the Working Group of Evangelical and Catholic Theologians.

Pfnür summarized his impression of his teacher's lectures thus:

> Ratzinger started from questions about the current situation in society and theology and took his students on a journey in search of the truth. Unlike others, who always swam along with the latest trend, or those who were fundamentally opposed to the prevalent novelty, he combined openness and critical independence. He thought through the questions in depth and in terms of their consequences.[12]

However, in Münster a characteristic also became clear that would later prove to be Ratzinger's Achilles' heel. He was not basically credulous, but he did not reject people whom the much-invoked Providence set in his path. The problem was that he was almost helplessly at the mercy of possessive companions around him, who exceeded their competence and exercised a kind of psychic power.

There was also his pronounced feeling of loyalty, which prevented him from seeing the consequences. 'He never defends himself when he would thereby embarrass someone else,' said one of his students. 'He prefers to let it lie. Even when it would be quite easy to clear things up.'

His assistant Werner Böckenförde had an easy time in Münster with the young professor. Böckenförde, the brother of Ernst-Wolfgang Böckenförde, an expert in constitutional law, was just one year younger than his doctoral supervisor and thoroughly devoted to him. He regarded Ratzinger as a provincial but also as 'the most modern theologian in Germany'. Besides theology and Christian social teaching, Böckenförde had also studied law. He was ordained as a priest in Paderborn in 1957. In 1967, Ratzinger got him as a job as academic assistant. Energetic, self-confident and worldly-wise, with his practical ability Böckenförde made himself indispensable. He organized Ratzinger's day, defended him from annoying intrusions and sorted out the teaching when his boss was in Rome as a Council adviser. 'So he thought he should dictate every conceivable thing to Ratzinger,' said a contemporary witness, 'and Ratzinger went along with it.'

Students witnessed how the assistant chided his professor: 'What sort of idiocy are you up to now!' As a rule Ratzinger just let the insolence wash over him. But once, when it was about a sloppily corrected seminar essay, Ratzinger took away the task of correcting it from him. When Böckenförde protested, 'But I've always done it!' the professor responded drily: 'Now I'll do it.' Ratzinger was not unhappy when Böckenförde was ordered back to Paderborn by his bishop. He had put up with the battles with his overbearing assistant long enough – 'with patient kindness,' as Heinz-Josef Fabry said.

Soon after he left Bonn, Ratzinger was also followed by the Indologist Paul Hacker. Formerly a Protestant, he had converted to the Catholic Church one year before. In September 1963 he was appointed to the newly founded chair of Indology at Münster. However, things began to grate in his relationship with his colleague. The two professors met in Annette-Allee or in Hacker's house in Besselweg. In the religion scholar's huge library they spoke about the real presence of Christ in the Eucharist, but mainly about the ongoing Council. The newly converted Hacker gave Ratzinger detailed 'thoughts on church reform'. In his paper he demanded, among other things, the dissolution of the 'Vatican authorities' in favour of bishops' synods, the reduction of dioceses, the election of bishops by 'representatives of the whole diocesan community'. Of course, Hacker wanted Latin in church services to be replaced by the local language spoken. In sum, he thought 'Christ's kingdom is not of this world, and according to St Augustine, the church is a tent on the way, a citadel.'

Then the dispute became more controversial. Soon Hacker was talking about pseudo-ecumenism, warning against the Protestantization of the Catholic Church and castigating his colleague for his Mariology being too hazy. 'My father thought he saw a tendency to Protestantism in Ratzinger,' said his daughter, the biologist Ursula Hacker-Klom. 'He accused him of behaving and arguing like a Protestant.' But it was not right to give up what was essential to Catholicism, 'for then Catholicism would be digging its own grave'.[13] Instead of being critical of Rome, the convert was becoming increasingly critical of the Council and, above all, of Rahner. Rahner confirmed: 'There was a time when I wrote to him rather sharply. That it would not do. But we also knew that we both wanted the same thing. And that both of us – he especially but also me a bit – had very powerful minds and could also sometimes hit out. But we made it up again.'[14]

Since his philosophy studies in Freising, Ratzinger had remained faithful to philosophy, which he regarded as an inspiration for his theology. His reading included the writings of the German-American political scientist and philosopher Eric Voegelin. After the Nazis came to power, Voegelin had emigrated to the USA. He returned to Germany after the war, and in 1958 he was appointed to the Munich University Max Weber Chair (which had been unoccupied since Weber's death in 1920). He also founded the Scholl Institute for Political Science. Voegelin's core subjects were 'political religions' and the development of totalitarian systems. A democratic state should not neglect the 'relationship to the area of the religious', so as not to descend into pseudo-religious ideologies with their secular promises of salvation, he warned.

Voegelin distinguished three different 'types of truth': the cosmological truth of the oriental states, the anthropological truth of classical Greece and the truth of Christianity about human salvation. In the combination between the latter two he saw the realization of an ideal order. On the occasion of Voegelin's 80th birthday in 1981, Ratzinger thanked him for his philosophical meditation, 'in which you have sought to revive the so necessary and so very damaged sense of the imperfect against the magic of the utopian'. He confessed to Voegelin: 'Ever since I got hold of your small book *Wissenschaft – Politik – Gnosis (Science – Politics – Gnosis)* in 1959, your thinking has fascinated and nourished me.'[15]

A special relationship linked Ratzinger in Münster with Josef Pieper, one of the great German philosophers of the twentieth century. Pieper's book *On Love* – including its chapter 'What Caritas and Erotic Love Have in Common' – had a lasting influence on him. Pieper's books on the cardinal virtues, Ratzinger said, 'were among the first philosophy books I read, when I began my studies in 1946. They awakened in me the desire for philosophical thinking, the joy in a rational search for answers to the great questions of our life.'[16]

Pieper thought the separation of modern thought from the realism of spiritual possibilities of knowing was the reason for the emergence of ideologies. It prevented a life fit for human beings, because only someone who knows rightly can behave right. Young and old, students and ordinary citizens, believers and doubters thronged to his lectures in Münster on the Christian view of humanity, death and immortality, faith, hope and love. Like Ratzinger, Pieper belonged to the Ecumenical Working Group and the North Rhine Westphalia Study Group. Most importantly, Ratzinger became a member of an interdisciplinary group of five academics, which the philosopher called his 'club'. They met weekly on Saturday afternoons at 3 p.m. in the philosopher's house at 10 Malmedyweg to discuss God and the world, after the obligatory walk round the room with the fireplace in it.

Ratzinger mentioned Pieper's importance for him in many of his works. For example, his book *Auf Christus schauen* (*To Look on Christ*), published in 1989, drew inspiration from the philosopher's doctrine of the virtues. 'At that time Pieper, like me, saw himself as a progressive,' he explained in our conversation, 'as someone who was on the track of something new. Later, the same thing happened to him as it did to me and to Lubac. We realized that something new which we wanted had been destroyed. He turned energetically against it.'

Münster was important for Ratzinger's development. He liked the town. He liked the people. During these years, his experience of the Council consolidated his knowledge from his studies and his own research into the theological base from which he would rise to the highest offices. Other theologians were embarrassed to kneel down in a church and glossed over their spiritual emptiness with self-expression. Unlike them, rooted in the simple piety of his background, Ratzinger kept his childhood faith and remained a priest who believed.

'He never spoke about his spiritual life,' said his student Viktor Hahn, 'but you can see that he is a deeply meditative person because he speaks from a deep core.' Without that power source neither his personality nor his theology can be understood. After his lectures his students stood around discussing for ages, but Ratzinger would hurry through the cathedral square into the ancient church of St Servatii, where the Blessed Sacrament was exposed throughout the day. That was also his power source. 'The professor knelt down in silence,' said Manuel Schlögl. He had just been standing in the lecture room as a celebrated speaker, but now 'he became small and stayed awhile in the dusky church before the one who was his Light'.

35

In the School of the Holy Spirit

On Easter Sunday, 14 April 1963, the *Osservatore Romano* displayed a close-up photograph of the pope's face, clearly full of pain. From then on the rumours were no longer hushed. Officially, Luciano Casimirri, the head of the Vatican press office, spoke only of his boss's 'fatigue'. But unofficially he was preparing for his death.

Ten days earlier, Pope John had signed off his final encyclical with the title *Pacem in Terris* – *Peace on Earth*. In May he put on the pressure because the 12 texts already approved for the continuation of the Council had still not been dispatched. He said to his doctor: 'They tell me I have a tumour. But that means nothing as long as God's will is done.' All the Council fathers should know that the great work begun was definitely going to be finished.

On Whit Monday, 3 June, down in St Peter's Square, thousands were praying for *il papa buono*. Upstairs in the Apostolic Palace the doctor, Professor Antonio Gasbarrini, was whispering to Cardinal Fernando Cento, a friend of Roncalli's. Up until then the pope's strong heart had withstood the blood loss and fever. The death agony had already lasted for 83 hours. At 7.49 p.m. the cardinal went up to Pope John's bed, stood there a while and then spoke the words which no one wanted to hear: '*Vere papa mortuus est:* the pope is really dead.'[1]

For Joseph Ratzinger, Roncalli's death was a shock. As the news was broadcast around the world, he interrupted his lecture in Münster and paid tribute to John XXIII in words that left a deep impression on his students. In the humble church leader he had lost a kindred spirit. Roncalli impressed him by his piety, his spiritual independence, his capacity to laugh at himself and his optimism in faith. Like Ratzinger,

Roncalli had also come to a deeper understanding of the modern age from reading the work of Cardinal Newman – that modern age which, with all its dangers, also offered the chance to reconnect faith and history, tradition and progress.

Pope John had only once intervened in the Council. But by that intervention to redraft the schema on divine revelation, which Ratzinger had criticized so heavily, he had brought about the change. 'He was convinced he would only reign for a few years,' wrote the Vatican expert Reinhard Raffalt, so he had been all the more anxious 'to move the church on so forcefully that a return to its almost Byzantine character under Pius XII was impossible'.[2]

Roncalli's peasant nature gave a human face to the previously almost unearthly figure of the *summus pontifex*. So many regarded the *papa buono* as a kindly but also somewhat simple pastor who had not been aware of the implications of his decisions. On the other hand, the Austrian writer-priest Franz Michel William suggested that Pope John's way to the Council began in September 1954 when, as Patriarch of Venice, he opened the first *corso di aggiornamento*, a provincial council on the spiritual renewal of his diocese. Roncalli had also spoken early on about the 'reunion of the separated churches' and a modernization of the 'Catholic thing', in accordance with his motto 'Ancient in doctrine, thoroughly modern in its verbal expression'. *Aggiornamento* was not the only buzzword for church renewal. So was 'New Pentecost'. 'He knows exactly what he wants,' said Roncalli's long-term associate Don Giuseppe de Luca; 'he does not say and he does not instruct anyone to say it. He smiles, he jokes, but he keeps his secrets.'[3] In this way too, Ratzinger felt himself to be like the pope.

According to canon law, with the death of the pope the Council was suspended. A new pope had complete freedom to continue it or break it off. The conclave began on 19 June 1963. Canon law stipulated that any 'male member of the church endowed with reason', whether cleric or layman, could be elected as Peter's successor. But for the last thousand years it had always been a priest, for the last 600 years always a cardinal, and for the last 400 years always an Italian.

Roncalli had made no secret of whom he wanted to be his successor, and Giovanni Battista Montini was regarded as definitely *papabile*. The cardinal represented a pro-reform position and was one of the few Italian church leaders engaged in the ecumenical movement. For the last nine years he had presided over the archdiocese of Milan. For the first four of them he had not been a cardinal. Before then, he had worked in the Curia for three decades, and from 1937 until 1954 he had been a close colleague of Eugenio Pacelli. Like his boss, Montini controlled, checked and supervised everything. He wanted to be just as perfect. However, his power was not that of a Pius XII, whose rule he had suffered.

Even though Ratzinger had not spoken with Cardinal Frings during the time immediately before the conclave, he knew his boss would not have failed to make use of the days since Pope John's death. The Italian historian Andrea Riccardi saw in Frings the first of the great Council leaders, the pope-makers. Giulio Andreotti, Montini's friend and later Italian minister-president, observed that during those days 'to the great surprise of the inhabitants of Grottaferrata', a small town near Rome, quite a few cardinals gathered, and it was 'by invitation of Frings, the archbishop of Cologne'. A participant said, 'half in earnest and half as a joke': 'The canonical majority for electing a pope is here.'[4]

Each member of the conclave was obliged to prepare a short speech in case he was elected. Montini composed an hour-long speech from the throne in polished Latin. He was elected on 21 June 1963, on the sixth vote. In his first speech to the city of Rome and the world, he made clear he intended to devote 'the outstanding part' of his pontificate to 'the continuation of the Second Vatican Council'. 'This will be our main task, to which we intend to devote all the energy our Lord has given us.'[5] A personal meditation from those days shows how much he trembled inwardly. 'The position is unique. It brings me extreme loneliness. It was great before, now it is absolute and terrifying. Nothing and nobody is near me. I must be on my own, act of my own accord and speak with myself alone, reflect and think in my inmost conscience.' He concluded: 'Jesus was also alone on the cross. I must not be afraid, I must not seek for any outer support, which might release me from my duty.'[6]

'It was no surprise when we heard that Archbishop Montini had been elected pope,' Ratzinger recalled in an interview with the daily newspaper *La Repubblica*. Montini had 'embodied for us the continuity of the Council in the spirit of Pope John'. Nevertheless, in contrast to his 'charismatic predecessor', who 'lived from the inspiration of the moment and close to the people', Montini was 'an intellectual who pondered everything with incredible seriousness'.[7]

At Montini's coronation, the tiara was placed for the last time on the head of a successor to St Peter. One year later Paul VI sold the crown for the benefit of the poor. The new pope took no time off and worked indefatigably. His staff appreciated his enthusiasm, his friendliness and his art of *reservatio mentalis*, an unarticulated inner reserve. That made him an interested listener without himself taking a position about what he heard. However, the atmosphere in the Vatican became cooler and the elegance hollower, the more Montini stepped up the work tempo. The Council itself would also change. Instead of the previous not particularly competent presidium of ten, Paul VI appointed four moderators – including Cardinal Döpfner from Munich – so that a stronger leadership would increase the assembly's pace. At the same time, he lifted the obligation of secrecy from the General Congregations, since in Rome sooner or later everything got into the newspapers.

The beginning of the Council had polarized the members. Some were full of hope, others full of fear. There were reasonable men like Frings, clever enough to recognize that a leap forward was needed. And there were the unreasonable who did not want to acknowledge that many branches of the church had become rotten. It had become plainer and plainer that, as well as a change in theology, there had been a generation change. 'We wanted to say and understand that the church is not an organization, not something structural, legal, institutional,' said Ratzinger about his work as *peritus*. Of course, it was that too, but even more, it was 'an organism, a living reality, which permeates my soul' to make it become 'a structural element of the church'.[8] Moreover, the Catholic Church did not have two doctrines, 'one for itself and one for the others', he wrote in a speech for Frings on the schema *De ecclesia*. Rather, 'The church's doctrine must be set out in a way that is both truly Catholic and truly ecumenical. The more deeply Catholic a doctrine is, the more deeply it is also ecumenical, and vice versa.'[9]

Those are typical Ratzinger formulations. They show that the younger Ratzinger did not differ from the older one in his emphatically ecclesiastical, tradition-based attitude. In his speech for

Frings, he criticized the schema *On the Church* for using a 'rather legal language, deriving more from theological textbooks than from Scripture or the church fathers. Second, and this is a greater defect, the way of thinking seems to adopt mainly legal viewpoints; true Catholicity is missing.' In short, he formulated as 'an urgent requirement' for Frings: 'The schema should be "more Catholic". It should pay more attention to the holy, venerable tradition of centuries and thereby become more ecumenical, more theological and more pastoral.'[10]

On 29 September 1963, the Council resumed its work in its second session. The original 70 schemata, which covered about 2,000 printed pages, had been condensed down to 16. A 17th text was planned. It was to be on the church in the modern world and would offer answers to the burning problems of the present. The new pope set out the aims in his opening speech: strengthening the moral powers of the church, rejuvenation of its forms in accordance with the needs of the time, promotion of Christian unity and dialogue with the world. 'No light should shine on this assembly that is not Christ, the Light of the world,' Paul VI summed up. 'No truth should interest our spirit except the words of the Lord, our only Master. No endeavour should be our aim except the desire to be unconditionally faithful to him.' He addressed Christians of other denominations: 'Wherever we are to blame for the separation, we humbly beg God's forgiveness and also forgiveness from our brothers, if they feel hurt by us.'[11]

Pope Paul thereby unambiguously followed his predecessor's line. Joseph Ratzinger, who now as an official *peritus* followed the speech in St Peter's, was particularly moved by his 'cordial dialogue with his dead predecessor, John XXIII, that fraternal, respectful conversation with his predecessor and a decisive "yes" to his great and binding legacy'.[12] For Paul VI, continuity meant not only renewal but also faithfulness to tradition: 'The renewal the Council is aiming for must not be seen as overthrowing the church life of today, nor must it break with the church's important and venerable traditions. Rather, it should honour these traditions.' Paul VI became even clearer: 'Anyone looking for a relaxation of the church's previously binding commitments to its faith [...] or any indulgent concession to the weak and unstable relativist mentality of a world without principles and without a transcendent goal, to a kind of more agreeable, less demanding Christianity would be in error.'[13]

The programme for the second period contained subjects like bishops and collegiality, deacons, renewal of canon law and a decree on the mass media. It began with the schema on the church. After a first revision, now the draft schema contained four chapters instead of the previous 11. Ratzinger's objections, put by Frings in the first session, had borne fruit. 'I believe that on the whole we can be very happy with De ecclesia,' he wrote to Frings's secretary Luthe on 13 September. 'The progress is clear when the old schema is compared with the new one. In the old schema 90 per cent of the references were to nineteenth- or twentieth-century works; now patristics dominate. The Middle Ages and the modern period are present to a reasonable extent.'[14]

A major point was the continuation of the debate on De sacra liturgia, with which the first session had begun. No one yet guessed that this supposedly easier part of the Council would lead to the most difficult changes in the church and trigger a mighty landslide. Ratzinger himself was not involved, but he had expressed support for the local language to be used in the Mass. He regarded the Council dealing first with the liturgy as 'a recognition of what the true core of the church is'.[15] Besides: 'Here constructive work could be done, which led the way forward, and carried the hesitant along with it, because the draft showed them that it was not about destruction and criticism but greater fullness.' A fairly starry-eyed assessment, as would be seen later.

The German team had again prepared intensively for the battle in the Roman arena. In February 1963 there had been a conference in Munich, and on 26 August there was a meeting in Fulda, attended by four cardinals and 70 bishops from ten regions. Parallel with the meetings, there were consultations between the Council theologians Grillmeier, Semmelroth, Ratzinger and Rahner. In a letter to Rahner, Ratzinger assured his older colleague 'that everything that had seemed important to me is contained in your drafts, which agree with my wishes'.[16] However, the Fulda meeting aroused fury in Rome. Italian newspapers wrote about a 'conspiracy' and an 'attack' on the Curia. Frings was forced to hold a press conference, at which he rejected the charge with 'deep dismay'. Pointedly, he added that 'the completely absurd' conspiracy theory showed that 'unfortunately in Italy a certain national defensiveness against anything "transalpine" has not yet been overcome'.[17] However, the French theologian Yves Congar had also complained that the Germans had taken decisions among themselves and then wanted to force them through. On 2 September, Cardinal Julius Döpfner made a special trip to the papal summer residence Castel Gandolfo, to make things all right with Paul VI. He reported back home with 'great relief" that 'His Holiness had not taken the reports in the Italian press about Fulda seriously.'[18]

In their headquarters in the Piazza Navona, the Frings–Luthe–Ratzinger trio went to work following their well-tried system. First, the upcoming subject was discussed and a line of argument established. After that, Ratzinger drafted the speech and read it out to the cardinal. It was discussed again and, if necessary, revised. Then the blind cardinal – his eye operation in Vienna had been unsuccessful – learned it by heart. However, Frings's 'European alliance' was no longer without competition. In the meantime, the conservative forces under the banner of a 'world alliance' had forged a powerful opposition, headed by Archbishop Marcel Lefebvre, the superior-general of the Holy Ghost Fathers. Reviewing the Council's second session, Ratzinger remarked that there were 'no factions, no common interest groups'. What happened at the Council was not like 'traffic control or price-fixing'.[19] However, that was less a description of the actual events than the wish of the one analysing them.

There was no doubt that *il cardinale Frings* had become an almost legendary figure. 'To win him over was almost indispensable for anyone trying to organize any action in common,' Ratzinger said in retrospect.[20] *Der Spiegel* reported: 'Encouraged by Frings, the progressives at the Council developed the programme for bishops wanting to have a future share in church government.'[21] Antoine Wenger, a distinguished French journalist, noted in his Council report:

Cardinal Frings opened the discussion. That fact seems indicative to us. During the whole course of the second session, the archbishop of Cologne remained one of the prominent personalities of the Council. He had his own clear opinion about things and also about people. He did not hesitate to speak openly. But he always maintained great courtesy and never lost his mastery of thoughts or words.[22]

He was also a saviour in need when there seemed to be no way out of a discussion in progress. 'When argument came to an end, then an *auctoritas* could help: a voice which everyone trusted. Cardinal Frings had it and was probably the only one who did. Some believed him for the warmth of his deep Catholic and Marian piety, others for the objectivity of his reliable theological judgement.'[23]

Frings made one of his groundbreaking speeches, composed by Ratzinger, in the debate on ecumenism on 28 October 1963: 'At the Council we are also in the school of the Holy Spirit, and we must be prepared to learn,' said the old man from Cologne. 'I at least confess that the ecumenical movement, which is pervading the whole of Christianity, is a work of the Holy Spirit that must be promoted in every way.' It was a clear change of course. For example, up until then the cardinal had been against mixed marriages which, according to canon law (can. 2319 of the CIC [*Codex Iuris Canonici,* or Code of Canon Law]), still carried the penalty of excommunication.

Frings also supported not having a separate schema for Mary, the Mother of God. For the sake of dialogue with the Protestants, that subject was to become part of the schema on the church. Nevertheless, there were strong objections. Bishop Giocondo Grotti from Brazil demanded that Mary must be treated separately, 'because of her unique mission and unique privileges'. The Brazilian flew into a great rage: 'Does ecumenism mean confessing the truth or hiding it? Should the Council declare Catholic doctrine or the doctrine of our separated brethren?' Grotti concluded: 'Keep the schemata separate! Let us openly confess our faith! Let us be the teachers we are in the church by clearly teaching and not hiding what is true.'[24] However, in the end, Frings's speech on the Mother of God, which Ratzinger had written, was so convincing that even those bishops who at first had pleaded for a separate Mary schema changed their minds.

There was a spectacular meeting at which the Holy Office suffered a lethal blow. It was 8 November 1963, a Friday. As usual, the Bar Jona, the small café in St Peter's, emptied in a hurry when the acetic-looking old man from Cologne came to the microphone.

His words were chosen deliberately: 'I know well how hard, how difficult and thorny the task is of those who have worked for many years in the Holy Office to guard the revealed truth.' Praise for the Roman Curia from a cardinal who was usually so quick to attack? No. For Frings was battling against an institution 'whose procedures still often do not accord with our time, and cause damage to the church and scandal for many'. Therefore it should be required, the cardinal continued in his firm way,

> that in this Congregation as well, no one who is charged on a matter of correct faith should be judged or condemned, without him and his bishop first being heard themselves; without him first knowing the arguments put forward against him or the book written by him; without him first being given the opportunity to correct himself or his book.[25]

At this point the Council minutes record *plausus in aula*.

No one had ever dared before to criticize Cardinal Ottaviani's machinery so fiercely. The Holy Office watched over the purity of doctrine, condemned deviations and heresies, defined what was properly Catholic and what was not. It put books on the Index and withdrew permission to teach from theologians. So the Officium was called *Suprema,* because it stood over all the other 'ministries' of the pope. Frings's 'courage showed in his delivery of Ratzinger's startling texts,' said the writer Freddy Derwahl. 'Everyone knew that they came from Ratzinger, apart from a few stylistic amendments.' Derwahl continued:

> Ratzinger was playing a dangerous game, possibly an even more dangerous game than Küng. Küng operated mostly at the Council gates with the 'extra-parliamentary' forces of the critical media, whereas Ratzinger operated at the very heart of the church. Ratzinger had much, if not everything, to lose from the Curia. Though it had been driven into a corner, it still remained mighty after that happened, just as it had been before.[26]

Ottaviani had to endure two more speeches before it was his turn. 'I must protest most strongly (*"altissime protestor"*) against what has just been said against the Holy Office, whose president is the pope,' he expostulated. 'Those words were spoken through lack of knowledge – I won't use any other expression in order not to be insulting – of the Holy Office procedure.' After all, in cases being examined by his institution, experts from Catholic universities were always consulted. Ottaviani talked himself into a rage. Witnesses even called it a tantrum. 'Both received applause,' Council observer Wolfgang Grösse noted in his diary, but 'the hero was Cardinal Frings'. On the same evening, auxiliary bishop Heinrich Tenhumberg also noted in his diary: 'The 8th.11. was, in fact, a high point of the Council. Cardinal Frings was the first to have the courage *inter alia* to call the practices of the H[oly] Off[ice] what they are, and insist on change. By that speech, many of the fathers feel they have been released from a kind of nightmare.'

Frings's files contain Ratzinger's handwritten draft, which the cardinal made even more pointed when he spoke in the chamber. Frings himself wrote about his performance: 'That speech had a quite unexpected and even uncanny resonance. I had clearly spoken from the hearts and feelings of countless others, who knew they had been treated unjustly or wrongly by the Holy Office. When I appeared in the bar at about 11 a.m., I was congratulated for it on all sides.' Next day Ottaviani met him at the entrance to the sacristy, embraced him and assured him, 'Indeed, we both only want the same thing!'[27]

But clearly the brave Council father was also a bit shocked by the effects of his speech. 'Shortly after supper Cardinal Frings called some of the theologians close to him in the Anima,' Hubert Jedin reported.

> I was still alone with him. Then he asked: 'What do you say now?' My answer was: 'You can be completely reassured, all the Catholic scholars in the world who deserve the name are on your side.' That answer visibly calmed him. On the same evening, the pope asked him to make suggestions for the reform of the highest authority on the faith.

It was a full-blown scandal. Frings's exchange with Ottaviani, 'the Battle of the Titans', as the *Deutsche Tagespost* called it, was reported in the press worldwide. According to the *Corriere della Sera*, members of the Curia circulated a saying by Pope Pius IX: 'A council is ruled first by the devil, then by humans, but finally by God.' Clearly, they meant that at the moment it was the devil's turn.

When Paul VI ended the second session on 4 December 1963, the Council fathers were exhausted, but also happy about the recently successful conclusion. 'It seems to me it was shown during this period, just as it was in the first session, that it was the wrestling with each other which was indispensable and crucial to the Council,' said Ratzinger in an optimistic summing up. 'Here spiritual encounter really occurred. Here people matured each other and with each other.'[28] However an anonymous *Pamphlet against German Cardinals and Theologians* left a bitter aftertaste when it appeared on the breakfast table in the Anima a day before the closure of the Council. As well as Frings, Ratzinger was mentioned. As Jedin said, the leaflet had 'doubtless come from the camp of the Holy Office'.

The second session was not shaken by the threat of a nuclear war, as the first one had been, but by a political death. On 22 November 1963 at 12.30 p.m. the former US marine and Marxist Lee Harvey Oswald took aim through the telescopic sight of his rifle across Dealey Plaza in Dallas, Texas, at the open limousine in which the US president was accepting the cheers of his supporters. On that sunny afternoon Oswald only had a few seconds. Two shots went wide, but the third one hit. John F. Kennedy, the first Catholic president of the USA, was dead. So many hopes had rested on him; his youthful charisma and political style had been symbols of a fresh start.[29]

Ratzinger's personal memories of those months were troubled by a loss of his own. Since January his mother, who kept house for his brother in Traunstein, had been barely able to eat. Since July she had been consuming only liquids. The doctor had diagnosed stomach cancer. Joseph used a break in the Council for the feast of All Saints to visit her sickbed. The Sundays before Christmas now became farewell stages. On the first Sunday of Advent their mother still sang all the songs at the family musical gathering. On the second Advent Sunday her voice was just a whisper. On the third Sunday, she was completely sunk in pain. She had 'only looked as if from a distance' at her children, her son recalled. 'It's a long way home,' she said to Joseph, and when he asked her whether it was really a long way, she answered: 'Yes, very long.'

On the day after Gaudete Sunday, 16 December 1963, Maria Ratzinger's earthly life came to an end, shortly before her 80th birthday. Her children had taken turns by her sickbed, night and day over the last two weeks. After their mother's death, said Ratzinger, the house felt 'her absence, which took the warmth out of things'. Yet 'we felt the same as we had felt with our father. Her kindness became even clearer and more radiant and shone through unaltered even during her weeks of increasing pain.'[30] For the theologian, saying farewell to people like his mother, who had been wholly shaped by Christianity, was a 'verification of the faith'. There was 'no more convincing proof of faith than the pure and simple humanity which the faith nurtured in my parents and so many other people I was privileged to meet.'

36

The Legacy

The third session of the Council began on 14 December 1964. Something new was that Pope Paul had invited a number of nuns and lay women as official auditors – literally hearers. 'We are delighted to be able to welcome our beloved daughters in Christ, the first women in history to take part in a council assembly,' he announced in his opening speech. All heads were turned right and left to catch a glimpse of the delightful addition. But none of these women could be seen. Someone had forgotten to post the invitations.

Also new were the directives issued by the pope to the 'honourable *periti*'. Clearly, this was aimed at people like Hans Küng, but possibly also Joseph Ratzinger. From now on, advisers were 'banned from organizing currents of opinions or ideas, giving interviews or publicly defending their personal thoughts on the Council'. Furthermore, they should 'not criticize or communicate news to outsiders about the activity of the committees, but always observe the Holy Father's decree on the confidentiality of the Council's business'.[1]

The fascination with the Council arose from its electric atmosphere caused by colourful performances, audiences with the pope, the palaver in the Bar Jona, the meetings with important churchmen from all over the world. And, of course, from the substantial debates on questions such as the diaconate and the lack of priests, the ideal of holiness for those in religious orders and the reform of the Roman Curia. For example, one of Frings's/Ratzinger's speeches declared that anyone 'ordained as bishop should be a bishop and nothing else'. So 'the number of bishops and priests in the Roman Curia should be reduced and laity should be admitted to it.'[2]

Sometimes the Council fathers behaved like operetta stars. But the world's biggest and oldest religious organization had also become a powerful global player. Nonetheless, its task was also to proclaim the Kingdom of Heaven – the gospel of a master who himself had indignantly rejected earthly power. That was the gulf, but also the strong tension between the institutionalized power and Scripture, which these men of God had under their noses every day.

When the bishops in the Council chamber put down their kneelers, the silence of prayer was like the sound of silence after thunder. Half an hour later the fathers fished their documents and notes out of their briefcases, studied the morning papers or exchanged views with their neighbours. Latecomers hurried up the nave to their places. After another five minutes, the book of the Gospels was ceremoniously enthroned. Then one of the presidents began: 'In the name of the Father, and of the Son and of the Holy Spirit.' All the Council fathers joined in and the day's business could start.

For example: a tree must be judged by its fruit, declared Ignatius Bedros XVI Batanian, the Armenian patriarch of Cilicia with headquarters in Beirut, throwing himself into the breach for the beleaguered Curia. 'And we must say that, despite the catastrophes plaguing the world, the church is experiencing a glorious age, if you think of the Christian life of clergy and people, the spread of the faith, the universal beneficial influence which the church has on the world today.'[3]

Frings trusted Ratzinger, whom he regarded as solidly Catholic through and through. In return, Ratzinger appreciated his boss because he acted 'not as a conservative or progressive but as a believer'.[4] The cardinal was 'certainly no liberal in the ideological sense'. 'He was not one of those who went home and announced that all previously written books could be burned and completely new ones had to be written.' An attitude of 'being blown hither and thither by every wind and making ideas dependent on the way the dice of opinion fell was deeply abhorrent to him'. His battle for diversity in unity, freedom in commitment, was about 'Catholic liberality', which was 'in radical contradiction to ideological liberalism. He wanted to go beyond all outward obedience to authority, to a faithfulness whose power source lay in the insight of the believing conscience.' Ratzinger summed up: 'Cardinal Frings was God-fearing and therefore wise. For him God was a real standard, the standard he had to keep to. That was the viewpoint from which he acted.'[5]

Ratzinger was living and working tirelessly between Münster and Rome. But the situation had changed. The professor, now 37, noted that as a result of the Council fathers' dispute and 'the often exciting news', interest in theology in Germany had increased once more. But another effect also did not escape him.

> From time to time, on my return from Rome, I found the mood in the church and among theologians was more turbulent. The impression kept on growing that actually nothing was firm in the church, that everything was up for revision. Increasingly, the Council seemed like a great church parliament, which could change everything and reform everything to its liking. There was a clear growth of resentment against Rome and the Curia, which appeared to be the enemy of everything new and forward-looking.[6]

The genie was out of the bottle, and almost no one was more alarmed about it than its driving force from Bavaria. According to the general climate of opinion, suddenly the faith seemed 'no longer beyond human decision-making, but apparently was determined by it'. And 'if the bishops in Rome (as it now appeared) could alter the faith, why just the bishops?' Ratzinger's contributions in Rome showed prudence and a happy medium, which sought to avoid any radicalization. Perhaps, as John XXIII remarked, there was too much talking at the Council and too little praying. Never before at a church congress had so much paper been produced and printed in a difficult language, which even the writer of the texts could hardly understand.

The event was later criticized as a 'council of book-keepers' by the psychoanalyst Alfred Lorenzer. And perhaps there were also many young bucks who understood how to use their bishops as mouthpieces – and bishops who let that happen. Maybe they had a complex about understanding too little of modern theology. John Heenan, archbishop of the English diocese of Westminster, mentioned the problem by name: 'I am afraid of the *periti*, when it is left to them to explain what the bishops meant.' It made no sense to speak of a College of Bishops, 'when *periti* contradict what a group of bishops teach and pour out scorn in articles, books and speeches'.[7]

In Rome and elsewhere, Ratzinger had become a man in demand. He kept in contact with observers from other denominations and was invited to give lectures by Evangelical theological faculties (in Heidelberg, Bonn and Zürich). He went into the Rome press centre to explain the increasingly complex work of the Council to journalists. Frings's adviser 'was a highly valued speaker in centres and at bishops' conferences, because of his clarity and modesty,' said the Swiss correspondent Mario von Galli. Yves Congar also thought the same. After a meeting to formulate the decree on missions, *Ad gentes,* the French star theologian noted in his diary: 'Fortunately, we have Ratzinger! He is reasonable, modest, unbiased and very helpful.'[8]

Frings was anxious not to let things come to further polarization and ugly clashes. His greater restraint may have contributed to the fact that in the third session the influence of the Germans decreased. This did not meet with enthusiasm everywhere. In a letter of 27 September 1964, Johannes Hoeck, abbot of the Scheyern Benedictine monastery in Bavaria, complained to the Cologne cardinal:

> Eminence, I am afraid that the German bishops are gradually losing their spirit. With all due respect for being prepared to compromise in debatable theological questions, I believe a stronger stand must be made against the other side's tactical intrigues – I deliberately use this word. Otherwise, there is the danger that the world's confidence in the Council will be shaken, if it has not been shaken already [...] The others are taking advantage of this courtesy and putting pressure on the pope.[9]

The Council had moved on from the stage of a tentative search and was frantically trying somehow to come to grips with all the problems of the faith. The third session was supposed to pass the decrees on divine revelation, bishops, ecumenism, the apostolate of the laity and the church in the world – altogether an overwhelming programme. To give a few examples: in the debate on religious freedom some Roman, Spanish, Italian and American cardinals argued for a *duty* of religion. Cardinal Ottaviani argued it was 'a very serious matter' to say that any kind of religion should have the freedom to spread. That would 'quite clearly lead to harm for the countries where the Catholic religion is the only one the people follow'. According to the proposed revised text, said Cardinal Ruffini of Palermo, it might seem as if a country was not entitled to treat any religion with special favour.

Opposition came from Joseph Ratzinger and Cardinal Frings but also from Karol Wojtyła, the archbishop of Kraków, who brought experience from his own country of fascist *and* communist regimes. Religion, which prevailed in the end, should not be either enforced or forbidden by the state. Cardinal Richard Cushing of Boston said the church should 'show itself to the whole world as the champion of freedom, especially in the area of religion'.

In the debate on Jews and Muslims, the German bishops published their own statement 'because we know the terrible injustice done to the Jews in the name of our people'. In his draft speech for Frings for the 89th General Congregation on 28 September 1964, Ratzinger stated: 'Something else is still left out in the new text: it is merely said that the Jews of our day cannot be held responsible for the guilt of Christ's sufferings. Even without the Council that is as clear as daylight. However, it is also necessary to say that the Jewish people as a whole living at the time did not perpetrate the execution of Christ.'[10] Thereafter the document *Nostra aetate* ('In Our Time' or, officially: *Declaratio de Ecclesiae habitudine ad Religiones non-christianas: Statement on the Church's Relationship with Non-Christian Religions*) was revised during the third session.

Ratzinger's text for the speech on the Jewish question is important because it shows the line that the theologian also followed later, as office holder and pope, in relation to the Jewish world and reconciliation between Christians and Jews. It was linked with his belief that the New Testament cannot be read without the Old. While the Council was still in session, Zechariah Shuster, the European leader of the American Jewish Committee, described the draft on Catholic–Jewish relations as 'certainly one of the greatest moments in Jewish history'. 'The church's historic step' contained 'a total rejection of the myth of Jewish guilt for the crucifixion'.

Celibacy, however, was not intended to be a subject for the Second Vatican Council. No one had meant even to mention priestly celibacy. The question came onto the agenda only because of a banner headline saying the Council wanted to allow priests to marry in future. After that, the Council not only stressed the necessity of celibacy but also advised the faithful to respect and defend 'that precious gift'.

A dramatic battle developed over the question of collegiality. It was about the relationship between the bishops and the pope, and caused the 'November crisis', the so-called *settimana nera* – black week – the severest test for the Council. Up for discussion were a standing senate of bishops, reform of the Curia to set it under both the pope *and* the College of Bishops, power-sharing between the papacy and the national episcopates. According to the interpretation favoured by the conservative side, the pope alone should exercise the 'highest authority', and that by divine right. According to the other interpretation, the 'highest authority' belonged only to the College of Bishops. Indeed, the pope could also exercise it, but only as the head of the College. What the reformers wanted was a panel of bishops to control the Curia and lead the church *together* with the pope. Council journalist Ralph Wiltgen believed he knew that a secret paper by a progressive group had reached the Palazzo Apostolico and frightened Paul VI so badly that he wept.

Up until then, the pope's suggestions for changes at the Council had been regarded merely as recommendations and were only partially considered. This time the pope stood by his authority to set policy. He ordered an 'explanatory note' to preface the decree *Lumen gentium*. This was to prevent anyone putting forward their own interpretations of the concept of collegiality in the period after the Council. The *Nota praevia explicativa* declared once and for all that the supreme power, not to be shared, rested with the pope as Peter's successor. It stressed that the assembly of bishops had no function if it acted without the pope. It was not so much the content of the *Nota* that was surprising as the way in which Paul VI inserted it as a preface, written by himself, to an already determined text. All the Council fathers had to accept it if they did not want to reject *Lumen gentium* as a whole.

The excitement had still not calmed down by 19 November, when the highest-ranking member of the presidium, Cardinal Tisserant, cancelled the vote on the Declaration on Religious Freedom, announced the previous day. 'Never before had the St Peter's council chamber seen such an uproar as at that moment,' reported Hubert Jedin.

Council fathers left their places and expostulated in groups about the authoritarian procedure. American bishops circulated a petition to the pope, which immediately collected 441 signatures, later rising to about 1,000. "With all due respect,' it read, 'but with the greatest urgency – *instanter, instantius, instantissime* – we beg that before the end of this Council session there should be a vote on the Declaration on Religious Freedom. Otherwise, we shall lose the trust of the Christian and non-Christian world.' The Holy Father refused to be put under pressure by the petition. However, he promised to put the Declaration first on the programme for the fourth session.

Yet another order by the pope aroused strong feelings. On 18 November Pope Paul had announced that, despite the decision against it by the Council majority, on 21 November he would give Mary the title *Mater Ecclesiae,* Mother of the Church. On the very next day Cardinals Frings and Döpfner and several other German bishops responded with a petition. According to the church historian Norbert Trippen, the letter to the Holy Father was 'theologically so polished that it could be assumed it had come from Professor Ratzinger'. Word for word it said: 'It is a great joy to us that at the end of this Council period the Blessed Virgin should be especially honoured by your Holiness [...] However the title *Maria Mater Ecclesiae* could also be understood of the church as an institution, and so it is hard to justify.' For 'as far as can be seen', no one calls the heavenly Father, Christ or the Holy Spirit *Pater Ecclesiae.* We are therefore asking that 'the title *Maria Mater Ecclesiae* should be combined with the title *Mater fidelium* and be interpreted in that sense'.

Later, Ratzinger defended himself, arguing that, of course, the Council's efforts could not have been intended 'slowly but surely to dismantle devotion to Mary as such, and thus gradually assimilate itself to Protestantism'. But 'in response to the call from our separated brethren,' the purpose had been 'plainly and firmly to base ourselves on the testimony of the Bible'.[11] However, the die had long been cast. On Saturday morning, 21 November 1964, the last day of the third session, the pope announced in his closing speech that he was proclaiming 'the Blessed Mary as Mother of the Church': 'We wish that from now on the Blessed Virgin should be even more honoured and invoked by all Christian people with this dearest title.' The pope's speech was interrupted seven times with ever louder applause. At the end there was a standing ovation. Cardinal Ruffini from Palermo shouted: 'The Madonna has won!'

The way Ratzinger coped with the events of the 'black week' and its results gives an important indication for understanding his theological position. His first written commentary on it still speaks of the 'great disappointment' that spread among the Council fathers. But in a further commentary before the beginning of the fourth session, emotional terms such as 'subjugation' and 'disillusioning' have disappeared. Instead, the pope's directive is justified. 'First, it should not be forgotten that as Bishop of Rome the pope is also a Council father,' he stated. 'So we should be careful about the Council's control over the speech.' The changes to the Council text made by the pope did not go 'beyond the extent of the changes which relatively small groups of fathers could achieve at the vote by so-called *modi*'.[12]

Ratzinger's distance from over-progressive endeavours was also shown in a speech he gave to students in Münster on 18 June 1965. A year earlier, he had still been saying that there was 'no reason for scepticism and resignation' about the Council. On the contrary, there was 'every reason for hope, confidence, patience'. Suddenly there was a note of scepticism. The *peritus* now said people were beginning to wonder 'whether things were better under the so-called conservatives than they might be under progressive rule'. His opponents later propounded the theory of 'a great change' in Ratzinger and tried to explain it as the result of a 'trauma' he suffered from the student unrest of 1968. But the theologian Hansjürgen Verweyen is right to call the idea of 'Ratzinger's great change' a myth. Ratzinger had never been progressive or conservative in the usual sense. Rather, he had always tried to unite tradition and and progress, history and the present, out of a 'mystical awareness of faith'. And if there had been a change in Ratzinger, Verweyen concluded, it was not in 1968 but between the third and fourth session of the Council.

The final session began on 14 September 1965 with a surprise. Pope Paul announced the setting up of a Council of Bishops, through which in future the episcopate would be more closely involved in the work for the good of the universal church. 'The news did not arouse enthusiasm,' Ratzinger said, 'but it was enough to revive the almost lost optimism.' With intensive work, the 12 Council texts still outstanding were now brought to their final form and successively passed. The *Declaratio de libertate religiosa* (Declaration on Religious Freedom) included a clear acknowledgement of 'the right to religious freedom'. Compulsion to believe and pressuring those of a different faith were to be rejected as contrary to the gospel. In the decree *Nostra aetate* the Council gave new directions for dialogue with non-Christian religions and stated that the Catholic Church rejected 'nothing of what is true and holy in those religions'.[13] In the constitution *Dei Verbum*, on divine revelation, the fathers accepted Ratzinger's definition that there is only one source of revelation, namely God's self-communication in history and above all in Jesus Christ. From that one source flowed the two streams of Scripture *and* tradition.

Gaudium et spes, the 'Pastoral Constitution on the Church in the World Today' – still called Schema XIII in its working title – pointed out the opportunities for working in partnership in society, culture, economics, the international community and for peace. Without denying the weaknesses and dangers of the modern age, it offered the principle of dialogue, as opposed to a defensive dissociation from the world. After the initial ostracism of this schema, 3,000 amendments were suggested, which had to be considered. The adviser Otto Semmelroth noted in his diary on 24 September 1965: 'Cardinal Frings's (intervention) had been written by Prof. Ratzinger. We had spoken about it recently. And the thoughts could be easily recognized.'[14]

Particularly in the debates on *Gaudium et spes* strong bonds had developed between the German and the Polish Council members. They were strengthened by a letter of November 1965, in which the Polish bishops called for mutual forgiveness and reconciliation between the two countries. The letter's final appeal – 'We forgive and beg for forgiveness' – aroused a strong reaction from the Communist government. It also met with a lack of understanding from a large part of the population. Finally, there was a reconciliation, symbolically expressed by the German Federal Chancellor Willy Brandt's genuflection in Warsaw on 7 December 1970.

When the General Secretary of the Council announced on 6 December that this 168th general congregation was to be the last, loud applause thundered through the halls of St Peter's On that morning of the 544th and final vote, the whole text was voted on. Of the 2,373 votes cast, 2,111 were for *Placet* and 251 for *Non placet*, with 11 invalid votes. A day later, in the ninth public sitting, the excommunication was lifted that had been mutually pronounced by the Eastern and Western churches when they separated in 1054. Of the 2,391 votes cast, 2,309 were for the end of the mutual schism, with 75 votes against and 7 invalid. As the statement was being read out in St Peter's to wild applause from the Council fathers, the first secretary of the Holy Synod went into St George's Church in the former Constantinople to announce the decision to the faithful. At the same time, news of the 'Act of Love' went out to the Orthodox patriarchs of Alexandria, Antioch, Jerusalem, Moscow, Belgrade, Bucharest and Sofia, as well as to the Orthodox churches of Greece, Poland, Czechoslovakia, Azerbaijan and Cyprus.

On the morning of 8 December, a windy and cloudy winter's day, all the Council fathers assembled once more in St Peter's Square, together with more than 500 advisers, the representatives of other denominations and 89 national delegations for the closing ceremony. Ratzinger found the ceremony 'rather overdone and superficial'. However, the 300,000 faithful who had gathered cheered with enthusiasm as the long procession of Council fathers, led by Paul VI on his *sedia gestatoria*, reached the wide steps of St Peter's to the loud ringing of all the bells of Rome. After the Mass, the pope saluted the various ranks. It became quiet again and Archbishop Felici read out the papal farewell: 'The Second Vatican Ecumenical Council, gathered in the Holy Spirit and under the protection of the Blessed Virgin Mary, whom we have proclaimed as Mother of the Church, is to be counted without any doubt as one of the greatest events of the church.' It is hereby ordained 'that everything that has been determined by the Council should be observed conscientiously by all the faithful for the honour of God and the dignity of the church and for the tranquillity and peace of all people'.[15]

The Council had done its work. The fathers were exhausted and could go home at last. The journalists packed away their notepads and jostled for taxis, which were standing ready for the journey to the airport. Council observer Wiltgen scribbled a final assessment in his notebook and highlighted, in particular, Joseph Ratzinger's boss: 'After the pope, hardly anyone in this great assembly was more influential for the passage of the Council legislation than Cardinal Frings [...] Without the organization he inspired and led, the Council would not have been able to work at all efficiently.'

In his first assessment Ratzinger was cautious. 'It would require a whole book to take stock of the Council,' he wrote about the final session, 'and it would still be a bit too early to attempt it.' The 'unwritten events of the Council' also had to be considered. He quoted in agreement the Evangelical theologian Oscar Cullmann, for whom the Second Vatican Council had 'on the whole fulfilled expectations, in so far as they were not illusions, apart from on a few individual points. On many it had even gone beyond the expectations.' Ratzinger added as a warning that renewal should not 'be confused with watering down and cheapening the whole'. He was especially concerned 'that here and there people enjoy flights of liturgical creativity that miss the depths of divine service and thereby belittle and discredit true reform; that here and there people do not seek the truth but modernity, and seem to take it as a sufficient standard for all activity'.[16]

Was the Council really a breakthrough, as most of the fathers believed? Or was it the beginning of a break-up, such as the Catholic Church had not experienced since the Reformation? And wasn't it clearly foreseeable that the unholy battle would break out over the interpretation of the Council, for and against it? When he opened the window on the church, had John XXIII sown a wind to reap a whirlwind? 'The bishops knew themselves to be learners in the school of the Holy Spirit,' said Ratzinger. 'They could not and did not want to create a new church or a different church. They had neither the authority nor the mandate to do so.'[17]

It was the Council's task at a time of of worldwide upheaval to determine a new relationship between the church and the modern age. For the first time, a Council spoke of 'churches' and 'church communities' outside the Roman Catholic Church. Because of the Holocaust and a long and difficult history with Judaism, the relationship to the faith of Israel urgently needed to be reappraised. Achievements within the church included clarifying the collegiality between bishops and the primacy, defining the term 'people of God' and rediscovering the central importance of Scripture for the life of the church and all the faithful. By and large, said the theologian Siegfried Wiedenhofer, the Council had 'managed the unbelievable' feat of connecting the medieval and modern development of the church and theology with its biblical and early church origin.

On the return flight to Germany, John XXIII's words came into Ratzinger's mind. In his opening speech, Roncalli had declared the task of the Council was 'to deliver the doctrine clearly and fully without dilution or disfigurement'. Of course, it was 'necessary to deepen the irrevocable and unchangeable doctrine, which must be faithfully respected and formulated in a way that matches the requirements of our time'. At one of the Council's last public sittings, on 18 November 1965, his successor warned that the term *aggiornamento* should not be reinterpreted 'to mean making everything in the church relative – dogmas, laws, structures, traditions – in accordance with the spirit of the world'. The right understanding could only be found in connection with the right sense of the doctrine and structure of the Catholic Church. It was necessary to awaken a missionary enthusiasm and passionate search for truth and holiness, and finally, 'a desire for authenticity through a vigorous instinct to defend it against the intrusion of the spirit of the time'.[18]

How strongly the Council fathers were concerned for continuity can be seen from the more than a thousand references to the teaching of Pius XII in both the spoken and written contributions. Apart from Scripture, this pope was the most quoted source in the Council texts. The Council had by no means legitimized a rhetoric leading to a secularization of the faith. Priestly celibacy was not abandoned; the priesthood of women was not considered; the 'supreme authority' of the pope was not shared. Latin was neither banned from the liturgy nor was it called for. In future, priests would no longer celebrate Mass, together with the people, facing *ad orientem,* the rising sun and the returning Saviour. And in addition to Latin, the classical language of Europe, the local vernacular language could be used.

Joseph Ratzinger had been the youngest student in the seminary. He was the youngest professor for systematic theology in Germany. At the Council, as the youngest theological adviser, he became the youthful *spiritus rector* of the greatest and most important church assembly of all time. Recent research shows that his contribution was much greater than he himself revealed. It began with the Genoa speech of November 1961 and his appeal that the church should drop whatever impeded witness to the faith. Then there were his expert assessments of the schemata, in which he criticized the lack of ecumenism and pastoral language. There were the 11 great speeches for Cardinal Frings, which brought the Council chamber to the boil. Then there was also his work on the texts, which he undertook as a member of the various Council committees.

Particularly striking was the significant role played by Ratzinger in the 'putsch meeting' in the Anima, when he laid his alternative draft of the revelation schema on the table. He wrote the proposal by which, on 14 November, Frings wrecked the Council procedures predetermined by the Curia. He was behind the turning point of the rejection of the schema on revelation on 21 November 1962, which he criticized as 'cold, even shocking' in tone. From then on, something new could happen and the real Council could begin. Thus Joseph Ratzinger had: (a) defined the Council; (b) made it become future-directed; and (c) significantly helped shape the events through his contributions.

The fact that Frings was able to become an important leader of the Council alongside the pope was primarily due to his adviser. As well as *Nostra aetate, Gaudium et spes* and *Lumen gentium, Dei Verbum,* the *Dogmatic Constitution on Divine Revelation* was one of the Council key texts. Ratzinger's contribution to it opened up a new perspective: it turned away from the over-theoretical to a personal, historical understanding of God's revelation, focused on reconciliation and salvation.

According to New Testament scholar Claus-Peter März from the University of Erfurt, Ratzinger's work on this Dogmatic Constitution gained particular theological weight, because it 'encompassed' the way the Council went from beginning to end.[19] Ratzinger himself agreed. The document had had a 'revolutionizing importance' for the study of Scripture as the 'soul of Catholic theology'. For, 'first, it is the most important statement by the Council on theology as a whole [...] Second, it links with the requirement that all subjects in Catholic theology should be developed from Scripture. That is a break with the system of neo-scholasticism.'[20]

Of course, this meant a break with an outdated system of thought, not with tradition. What John XXIII wanted, said Ratzinger, was not pressure to water down the faith but a drive to 'radicalize' it. Later, as Pope Benedict XVI, the former *peritus* added that, all in all, the Vatican Council should be seen as the beginning of a new evangelization of the world.

Ratzinger was never a theologian set on theology as just an academic pursuit. During the Council years his intellectual independence was linked with an awareness of responsibility for the whole church. It was a stroke of fate that he met the experienced, mellow and also courageous and forward-moving Cardinal Frings. But it would have been impossible for the young theologian not to be engaged as an adviser. If Frings had not recruited him, Cardinal Döpfner or another German bishop would have done so.

Ratzinger's strengths clearly came to the fore at the Vatican Council. However, his weaknesses also cannot be overlooked. One was the failure to realize the consequences that the desire for change might have for the deconstruction of the church, especially in the area of the liturgy. Second, there was a naïvety about a situation that not only represented an interesting theological approach, as Ratzinger long believed, but also strove to change the system. He definitely underrated the power of a developing mass-media society. Never before had a Council been so exposed to a dynamic whereby external forces sought to influence what happened. With wise foresight, John XXIII had already warned about it in October 1961. It would be 'indeed a misfortune if, for lack of adequate information or lack of discretion and objectivity, a religious event of such importance was given an inaccurate presentation distorting its character and true aims.' Everything must be done to 'make the Council known in its true light'.[21]

A new phenomenon also arose of a culture in which, as the American media expert Marshall McLuhan described it in the 1960s, 'the medium is the message'. In the case of the Council, this meant not actually reporting the contents but the event as an *event,* and interpreting the event in a way that increasingly overlaid its content and message with legends. This then created a reality which finally appeared more real than what had really happened at the Council and was passed in its texts.

The media nurtured their own ideas of church and reform and not only interpreted and reinterpreted the Council but also a good number of its members. Just as there were somehow two councils – the real Council of the fathers and the virtual council of the media – so one day there would also be two Ratzingers: the real Ratzinger, as he was known to those who worked with him, and a media Ratzinger. That Frings's adviser could later be presented as a 'betrayer of the Council' is surely one of the most bizarre aftermaths of the Vatican Council.

The facts do not support the theory of a 'change', from a formerly progressive theologian into a reactionary thinker. 'The true legacy of the Council lies in its texts,' Ratzinger would never tire of saying. 'If they are construed carefully and clearly, then extremism in either direction is avoided. Then a way really opens up which still has a lot of future before it.'[22] He still called upon it as a legacy in a speech at his last appearance as pope three days before he resigned: 'It is always worth going back to the Council itself, to its depth and its vital ideas.'

The doors had barely shut on the last session when a Herculean task began for Ratzinger, a 50-year battle for the Council's legacy. His watchword was 'To make clear what we really want and what we don't want. That is the task I have undertaken since 1965.'[23]

Notes

FOREWORD

1 Friederike Glavanovics, 'Papst Benedikt XVI. und die Macht der Medien: Wie Papst- und Kommunikationsexperten das Medienimage von Papst Benedikt XVI. erklären', dissertation, University of Vienna, 2012.

CHAPTER 1. EASTER SATURDAY

1 Joseph Ratzinger and Peter Seewald, *Salz der Erde* (Stuttgart, 1996).
2 Staff report, 'Ratzinger I in the State Capital Archive in Munich', in Johann Nußbaum, '*Ich werde mal Kardinal!*': *Wurzeln, Kindheit und Jugend von Papst Benedikt XVI* (Rimsting, 2010).
3 Nußbaum, '*Ich werde mal Kardinal!*'
4 Der Spiegel Geschichte, *Die Weimarer Republik: Deutschlands erste Demokratie* (Hamburg, 2014).
5 Werner Stein, *Der große Kulturfahrplan* (Munich, 1979).
6 Der Spiegel Geschichte, *Die Weimarer Republik*.
7 Benno Hubensteiner, *Bayerische Geschichte* (Munich, 1992).
8 Interview with the author.
9 Joseph Ratzinger, interview with Bayerische Rundfunk, 18 December 1998.
10 Interview with the author.

CHAPTER 2. THE IMPEDIMENT

1 Nußbaum, '*Ich werde mal Kardinal!*'
2 Georg Ratzinger, interview with the author.
3 Marktl am Inn (ed.), *Geburtshaus Papst Benedikts XVI* (Marktl am Inn, 2009).
4 Author's archive.

5 Nußbaum, 'Ich werde mal Kardinal!'
6 Der Spiegel Geschichte, Die Weimarer Republik.
7 Ibid.
8 Nußbaum, 'Ich werde mal Kardinal!'
9 Genealogy in the author's archive.
10 Interview with the author.

CHAPTER 3. THE DREAMLAND

1 Joseph Ratzinger, sermon preached in Marktl, Whit Monday, 19 May 1986.
2 Joseph Ratzinger, *Meditationen zur Karwoche* (*Meditations on Holy Week*) (Freising, 1969).
3 Lion Feuchtwanger, *Erfolg: Drei Jahre Geschichte einer Provinz* (Berlin 1930).
4 Bartholomäus Holzhauser, *Lebensgeschichte und Gesichte, nebst dessen Erklärung der Offenbarung des heiligen Johannes* (Berlin, 2011).
5 Interview with Martin Lohmann on Bayerischen Fernsehen, 18 November 1998.
6 Der Spiegel Geschichte, *Die Weimarer Republik*.
7 Adolf Hitler, *Mein Kampf* (Munich, 1938).
8 Der Spiegel Geschichte, *Die Weimarer Republik*.
9 Herbert W. Wurster, *Das Bistum Passau und seine Geschichte* (Strasbourg, 2010).
10 Interview with the author.
11 Ibid.
12 Georg Ratzinger, interview with the author.
13 *Der Gerade Weg* (31 July 1932).

CHAPTER 4. 1933: 'HOLY YEAR'

1 Der Spiegel Geschichte, *Die Weimarer Republik*.
2 Ibid.
3 Joseph Ratzinger, *Aus meinem Leben* (Stuttgart, 1998).
4 Elisabeth Heinrich, *Auf Dein Wort hin: Erstkommunion in Aschau am Inn* (Aschau, 2007).
5 Archive of the Pope Benedict XVI Institute, Regensburg.
6 Interview with the author.
7 Joseph Goebbels, *Tagebücher 1924–1945* (Munich, 1992).
8 Erwein Frhr. von Arentin, *Fritz Michael Gerlich: Lebensbild des Publizisten und christlichen Widerstandskämpfers* (Munich, 1983).

CHAPTER 5. THE 'GERMAN CHRISTIANS'

1 Interview with the author.
2 Interview for the ZDF television film *Joseph Ratzinger – Die Jugend des Papstes* (August 2005).

3 Interview with the author.
4 Kathi Stimmer-Salzeder, *Joseph Ratzinger – Papst Benedikt XVI.: Kinderjahre in Aschau am Inn* (Aschau, 2006.)
5 Karl Wagner and Hermann Ruf (eds), *Kardinal Ratzinger: Der Erzbischof von München und Freising in Wort und Bild* (Munich, 1977).
6 Joseph Ratzinger, *Aus meinem Leben*.
7 Christoph Strohm, *Die Kirchen im Dritten Reich* (Munich, 2011).
8 *Die Zeit* (31 October 2012).
9 Strohm, *Die Kirchen im Dritten Reich*.
10 http://www.denkwege-zu-luther.de/toleranz/detail/luther_juden_luegen.asp?bURL=de/materialien_zeitgenoessische_quellen.asp.
11 Martin Luther, *Von den Juden und ihren Lügen* (Munich, 1936).
12 Cited by the Wittenberg Superintendent and Luther researcher Maximilian Meichßner in 1936 in his sermon on the 390th anniversary of the Reformer's death, in Ronny Kabus (ed.), *Schriftenreihe der Staatlichen Lutherhalle Wittenberg* (April 1988).
13 *Die Zeit* (31 October 2012).
14 Jürgen W. Falter, *Hitlers Wähler* (Munich, 1991).
15 Winfried Becker, *Presse und Kommunikation der Katholiken im Kirchenkampf des 'Dritten Reiches'*;https://doi.org/10.7788/hpm.2004.11.1.97
16 Hans Prolingheuer, 'Das kirchliche "Entjudungsinstitut" 1939 bis 1945 in der Lutherstadt Eisenach', manuscript text revised by the Evangelical high school teacher and publicist after his last lecture at the Dachau concentration camp memorial on 12 November 1997.
17 Max Domarus, *Hitler: Reden und Proklamationen 1932–1945, kommentiert von einem deutschen Zeitgenossen* (Würzburg, 1963).
18 Walter Hannot, *Die Judenfrage in der katholischen Tagespresse Deutschlands und Österreichs* (Mainz, 1990).
19 Interview with the author.
20 Strohm, *Die Kirchen im Dritten Reich*.

CHAPTER 6. WITH BURNING CONCERN

1 Quoted from a brochure of the city of Altötting.
2 Interview with the author.
3 Ulrich von Hehl and Christoph Kösters (eds), *Priester unter Hitlers Terror: Eine biographische und statistische Erhebung* (Paderborn, 1997).
4 Interview with the author.
5 Joseph Ratzinger, *Aus meinem Leben*.
6 Interview with the author.
7 kath.net (6 April 2006).
8 Ratzinger and Seewald, *Salz der Erde*.

9 Karl-Joseph Hummel and Christoph Kösters (eds), *Kirche, Krieg und Katholiken: Geschichte und Gedächtnis im 20. Jahrhundert* (Freiburg im Breisgau, 2014).

10 Strohm, *Die Kirchen im Dritten Reich.*

11 *Die Tagespost* (23 April 2015).

12 Wikipedia, 'Mit brennender Sorge', https://de.wikipedia.org/wiki/Mit_brennender_Sorge

13 'Mit brennender Sorge: Das päpstliche Rundschreiben gegen den Nationalsozialismus und seine Folgen in Deutschland', *Katholische Reihe,* vol. 1 (Freiburg im Breisgau, 1946).

14 Joseph Ratzinger, *Aus meinem Leben.*

CHAPTER 7. THE CALM BEFORE THE STORM

1 Interview with the author.

2 Joseph, Kardinal Ratzinger, 'Mein Bruder, der Domkapellmeister', in Paul Winterer (ed.), *Der Domkapellmeister Georg Ratzinger: Ein Leben für die Regensburger Domspatzen* (Regensburg, 1994).

3 Interview with the author.

4 Ibid.

5 Joseph Ratzinger, *Aus meinem Leben.*

6 Interview with the author.

7 Ibid.

8 Ibid.

CHAPTER 8. THE SEMINARY

1 Interview with the author.

2 H. van Capelle and A. P. van de Bovenkamp, *Der Berghof: Hitlers verborgenes Machtzentrum* (Fränkisch-Crumbach, 2010).

3 Interview with the author.

4 'Pius XII. und die Deutschen', *Der Spiegel* (18 November 1964).

5 Joseph Ratzinger, *Aus meinem Leben.*

6 Volker Laube, *Das erzbischöfliche Studienseminar St. Michael in Traunstein und sein Archiv,* Schriften des Archivs des Erzbisstums München und Freising, vol. 11 (Regensburg, 2006).

7 Ibid.

8 Ibid.

9 Ibid.

10 Klaus Rüdiger Mai, *Benedikt XVI.: Joseph Ratzinger: sein Leben – sein Glaube – seine Ziele* (Cologne-Mülheim, 2010).

11 Benedikt XVI, *Die Ökologie des Menschen,* Die großen Reden des Papstes (Munich, 2012).

12   Benno Hubensteiner, *Bayerische Geschichte* (Munich, 1992).

13   Joseph Ratzinger, *Aus meinem Leben*.

14   Ibid.

15   Interview with the author.

16   Ibid.

17   Ibid.

18   Interview for the ZDF television film *Joseph Ratzinger*.

19   Interview with the author.

20   Archive of fellow student Franz Weiss.

21   Laube, *Das erzbischöfliche Studienseminar*.

22   Interview for the ZDF film *Joseph Ratzinger*.

23   Laube, *Das erzbischöfliche Studienseminar*.

24   Interview with the author.

25   Laube, *Das erzbischöfliche Studienseminar*.

CHAPTER 9. WAR

1   Antony Beevor, *The Second World War* (London, 2012).

2   Sebastian Haffner, *Anmerkungen zu Hitler* (Munich, 1978).

3   Felix Escher and Jürgen Vietig, *Deutsche und Polen: Eine Chronik* (Berlin, 2002).

4   Joseph Ratzinger, *Aus meinem Leben*.

5   Interview with the author.

6   *Die Tagespost* (3 January 2006).

7   Interview with the author.

8   From the records of Traunstein Gymnasium.

9   Interview with Bayerischer Rundfunk, 18 December 1998.

10   Joseph Ratzinger, *Aus meinem Leben*.

11   Adam Tooze, *The Wages of Destruction* (London, 2006).

CHAPTER 10. RESISTANCE

1   Interview for the ZDF film *Joseph Ratzinger*.

2   Joseph Ratzinger, *Aus meinem Leben*.

3   Interview for the ZDF film *Joseph Ratzinger*.

4   Interview with the author.

5   Ibid.

6   Benedikt XVI, with Peter Seewald, *Letzte Gespräche* (Munich, 2016).

7   Lenelotte Möller, *Widerstand gegen den Nationalsozialismus, von 1923 bis 1945* (Wiesbaden, 2017).

8   Romano Guardini, *Freiheit und Verantwortung: Die Weiße Rose – Zum Widerstand im 'Dritten Reich'* (Kevelaer, 2010).

9   *Die Tagespost* (18 February 2015).

10   *Die Tagespost* (24 November 2017).

11   *Die Tagespost* (7 April 2015).

12   Ibid.

13   Jakob Knab, *Ich schweige nicht: Hans Scholl und die Weiße Rose* (Darmstadt, 2018).

14   Letter in the author's archive.

15   Ibid.

CHAPTER 11. THE END

1   Interview for the ZDF film *Joseph Ratzinger*.

2   Joseph Ratzinger, *Aus meinem Leben*.

3   Archive of fellow student Franz Weiß.

4   Interview with the author.

5   Hummel and Klosters (eds), *Kirche, Krieg und Katholiken*.

6   Joseph Ratzinger, *Aus meinem Leben*.

7   Interview with the author.

8   *Heimatbuch der Gemeinde Surberg* (Tittmoning, 1990).

9   Interview with the author.

10   Joseph Ratzinger, *Aus meinem Leben*.

11   *Der Spiegel*, no. 18 (25 April 2015).

12   Alexander Kissler, *Der deutsche Papst: Benedikt XVI. und seine schwierige Heimat* (Freiburg im Breisgau, 2005).

13   Matthias Reiß, *Die Schwarzen waren unsere Freunde: Deutsche Kriegsgefangene in der amerikanischen Gesellschaft, 1942–1946* (Munich, 2002).

14   Klaus-Dieter Müller, *Sowjetische und deutsche Kriegsgefangene in den Jahren des Zweiten Weltkriegs: Stiftung Sächsische Gedenkstätten zur Erinnerung an die Opfer politischer Gewaltherrschaft* (Dresden, 2004).

15   Christian Streit, *Keine Kameraden: Die Wehrmacht und die sowjetischen Kriegsgefangenen, 1941–1945* (Bonn, 1997).

16   Interview with the author.

17   Ibid.

18   Ibid.

19   Joseph Ratzinger, *Aus meinem Leben*.

20   Helmut Schelsky, *Die skeptische Generation: Eine Soziologie der deutschen Jugend* (Munich, 1957).

CHAPTER 12. ZERO HOUR

1   Karl Wagner and Hermann Ruf (eds), *Kardinal Ratzinger: Der Erzbischof von München und Freising in Wort und Bild* (Munich, 1977).

2   Interview with the author.

3 Georg Ratzinger, *Mein Bruder der Papst: Aufgezeichnet von Michael Hesemann* (Munich, 2011).

4 Peter Pfister (ed.), *Geliebte Heimat: Papst Benedikt XVI. und das Erzbistum München und Freising* (Munich, 2011).

5 Benedikt XVI, *Letzte Gespräche*.

6 *Der Spiegel*, no. 18 (25 April 2015).

7 Peter Seewald, '1945: Absturz ins Bodenlose', *Der Spiegel* (29 April 1985).

8 Erzbischöfl. Archiv München, EAM, NL Faulhaber 6381.

9 Martin Greschat, *Protestanten in der Zeit: Kirche und Gesellschaft in Deutschland vom Kaiserreich bis zur Gegenwart* (Stuttgart, 1994).

10 Thomas Großbölting, *Der verlorene Himmel: Glaube in Deutschland seit 1945* (Göttingen, 2013).

11 Ibid.

12 Ibid.

13 *Thomas Mann, Das essayistische Werk*, vol. 3 of *Politische Reden und Schriften* (Frankfurt am Main, 1960).

14 *Die Tagespost* (5 November 2016).

15 Großbölting, *Der verlorene Himmel*.

16 Franz Walter, 'Katholizismus in der Bundesrepublik: Von der Staatskirche zur Säkularisation', in *Blätter für deutsche und internationale Politik*, vol. 41, no. 9 (1996).

17 Bernhard Boudgoust and Günther Saltin (eds), *Alfred-Delp-Jahrbuch 2016*, vol. 9 (Berlin, 2016).

18 Joseph Ratzinger, *Aus meinem Leben*.

CHAPTER 13. THE SCHOLARS' MOUNTAIN

1 Alexander Brüggemann, report in Katholische Nachrichten-Agentur (18 February 2016).

2 Interview with the author.

3 Joseph Ratzinger, *Aus meinem Leben*.

4 Interview with the author.

5 Benedikt XVI, *Letzte Gespräche*.

6 Interview with the author.

7 Ibid.

8 Gianni Valente and Pierluca Azzaro, interview with Alfred Läpple in *30 Tage*, no. 1 (2006).

9 Paul Winterer (ed.), *Der Domkapellmeister Georg Ratzinger: Ein Leben für die Regensburger Domspatzen* (Regensburg, 1994).

10 *Focus* (23 April 2005).

11 kath.net (22 February 2016).

12 Ratzinger and Seewald, *Salz der Erde*.

13 Georg Ratzinger, *Mein Bruder der Papst*.

14 Valente and Azzaro, interview with Alfred Läpple.
15 *Mittelbayerische Zeitung* (30 March 2016).
16 Ratzinger and Seewald, *Salz der Erde.*
17 Ibid.
18 Ibid.
19 Interview with the author.
20 *Sursum corda* ('Lift up your hearts') are the opening words of the Preface to the Eucharistic Prayer in the liturgy of the Latin Mass in general use before the Second Vatican Council.

CHAPTER 14. GUILT AND ATONEMENT

1   Benno Hubensteiner, *Bayerische Geschichte* (Munich, 1977).
2   Rudolf Goerge, 'Der "Vater des Dombergs" und energische Gegner des Nationalsozialismus: Das Wirken von DDr. Michael Höck', in *fink – das Magazin aus Freising* (March 2011).
3   Alfred Läpple, *Benedikt XVI. und seine Wurzeln: Was sein Leben und seinen Glauben prägte* (Augsburg, 2006).
4   *Die Tagespost* (23 April 2015).
5   Johann Neuhäusler, *Kreuz und Hakenkreuz: Der Kampf des Nationalsozialismus gegen die katholische Kirche und der kirchliche Widerstand* (Munich, 1946).
6   *Süddeutsche Zeitung* (7 May 2016).
7   Georg Ratzinger, *Mein Bruder der Papst.*
8   *Kirche heute,* no. 11 (2014).
9   Joseph Ratzinger, *Aus meinem Leben.*
10 Ibid.
11 Benedikt XVI, *Letzte Gespräche.*
12 Ibid.
13 https://www.bundestag.de/parlament/geschichte/.../wiesel/rede_deutsch-247424.
14 Alexander Kissler, *Der deutsche Papst – Benedikt XVI. und seine schwierige Heimat* (Freiburg im Breisgau, 2005).
15 Joseph, Kardinal Ratzinger, 'Mein Bruder, der Domkapellmeister'.
16 Joseph Ratzinger, *Aus meinem Leben..*
17 Ratzinger and Seewald, *Salz der Erde.*

CHAPTER 15. UPHEAVAL IN THINKING

1   Carl Bernstein and Marco Politi, *Seine Heiligkeit Johannes Paul II: Macht und Menschlichkeit des Papstes* (Munich, 1996).
2   Lk. 1.49.
3   Benedikt XVI, *Letzte Gespräche.*
4   Interview with the author.

5 Gianni Valente, *Student Professor Papst: Joseph Ratzinger an der Universität* (Augsburg, 2009).
6 Interview with the author.
7 'Die Philosophen im Krieg', in *Die Tagespost* (18 September 2014).
8 Paul Wolf, *Ein Abschiedswort: Christliche Philosophie in Deutschland, 1920–1945* (Regensburg, 1949).
9 Läpple, *Benedikt XVI. und seine Wurzeln.*
10 http://www.kakigem.de/index.php/41-zitate/95-stein-wer-die-wahrheit-sucht
11 Interview with the author.
12 Joseph Ratzinger, *Aus meinem Leben.*
13 Interview with the author.
14 Gott und die Welt in Zitaten: http://dreifaltigkeit-altdorf.de/zitate.htm (quotes from internet pages: 'Was führende Naturwissenschaftler über Gott und Religion dachten' and 'Was denken Naturwissenschaftler über Gott?!').
15 Claudia Schorcht, *Philosophie an den bayerischen Universitäten, 1933–1945* (Erlangen, 1990).
16 Theodor Steinbüchel, *Der Umbruch des Denkens: Die Frage nach der christlichen Existenz erläutert an Ferdinand Ebners Menschdeutung* (Regensburg, 1936).
17 Joseph Ratzinger, *Aus meinem Leben.*
18 Ratzinger and Seewald, *Salz der Erde.*
19 Joseph Ratzinger, *Einführung in das Christentum: Vorlesungen über das Apostolische Glaubensbekenntnis* (Munich, 1961).
20 Joseph Ratzinger, *Aus meinem Leben.*
21 Interview with the author.
22 'Aus der Predigt von Joseph Card. Ratzinger zum 100. Todestag von Kardinal John Henry Newman. Rom, 28. April 1990', in *30 Tage.*
23 Läpple, *Benedikt XVI. und seine Wurzeln.*
24 Ibid.

CHAPTER 16. THE GLASS BEAD GAME

1 Interview with the author.
2 Ibid.
3 Joachim Hamberger, 'Joseph Ratzinger und Freising', sermon given on 14 September 2006.
4 This and the following quotations are translated from Hermann Hesse, *Das Glasperlenspiel* (Frankfurt am Main, 1977).
5 Joseph Ratzinger, *Im Angesicht der Engel* (Freiburg im Breisgau, 2008).
6 Hesse, *Das Glasperlenspiel.*

7   Stephan Otto Horn, 'Zum existentiellen und sakramentalen Grund der Theologie bei Joseph Ratzinger – Papst Benedikt XVI.', in *Didaskalia*, vol. XXXVIII, no. 2 (2008), pp. 301–10.

8   Marianne Schlosser, 'Ein Versuch zum Verhältnis von Liturgie und Kontemplation im Werk Joseph Ratzingers', in Rudolf Voderholzer, Christian Schaller and Franz-Xaver Heibl (eds), *Mitteilungen des Institut Papst Benedikt XVI.* (Regensburg, 2009).

9   Conversation with Martin Lohmann, *Bayerisches Fernsehen* (28 November 1998).

10 Joseph Ratzinger, *Der Geist der Liturgie* (Freiburg im Breisgau, 2000).

11 Joseph, Kardinal Ratzinger, 'Mein Bruder, der Domkapellmeister'.

CHAPTER 17. AUGUSTINE

1   *Spiegel Online* (20 February 2017).

2   Ibid.

3   *Süddeutsche Zeitung* (18 May 1977).

4   Matthias Matussek, 'Ich mach mein Ding', *Der Spiegel* (6 August 2012).

5   Interview with the author.

6   Joseph Ratzinger, *Aus meinem Leben*.

7   Benedict XVI, General Audience, 16 January 2008.

8   Benedict XVI, General Audience, 9 January 2008.

9   Hugo Lang, *Augustinus: Das Genie des Herzens* (Munich, 1930).

10 Benedict XVI, 3rd Augustine Catechesis, General Audience, 30 January 2008.

11 Book launch for Cardinal Joseph Ratzinger, *Il potere e la grazia: l'attualità di sant'Agostino* (*Macht und Gnade: Die Aktualität des heiligen Augustinus*), 21 September 1998.

12 Augustine, *Confessions*.

13 Augustine, *De vera religione*, 39, 72f.

14 Joseph Ratzinger, *Aus meinem Leben*.

15 Augustine, *De vera religione*, 39, 72.

16 Address to the Papal Biblical Commission, 27 April 2006, in *Freiheit und Glaube* (Augsburg, 2008).

17 Article on http://kath.net/news/51821, Benedict XVI: 'Die drei Bekehrungen des Heiligen Augustinus', sermon from 2007.

18 Augustine, *Sermons*, 340, 3

19 Ibid., 339, 4.

20 Augustine, *Contra Academicos* III, 20,43.

21 Augustine, quoted by Ratzinger, General Audience, 9 January 2008.

22 *Der Spiegel* (9 July 1958).

CHAPTER 18. STORM AND STRESS

1 Interview with Bayerischer Rundfunk, 18 December 1998.
2 *Süddeutsche Zeitung* (18 May 1977).
3 Joseph Ratzinger, *Aus meinem Leben.*
4 Karl-Egon Lönne, *Politischer Katholizismus im 19. und 20. Jahrhundert* (Frankfurt am Main, 1986).
5 Karl Gabriel, 'Die Kirchen in Westdeutschland: Ein asymmetrischer religiöser Pluralismus', in Bertelsmann Stiftung (ed.), *Woran glaubt die Welt? Analysen und Kommentare zum Religionsmonitor 2008* (Gütersloh, 2009).
6 Manfred Spieker, 'Der Beitrag der katholischen Kirche zur Entwicklung der Bundesrepublik Deutschland', in Bayerische Landeszentrale für politische Bildung (ed.), *Normen – Stile – Institutionen: Zur Geschichte der Bundesrepublik* (Munich, 2000).
7 Konrad Adenauer, *Reden 1917–1967,* ed. Hans Peter Schwarz (Stuttgart, 1975).
8 Werner Münch in *Die Tagespost* (10 February 2015).
9 Franz Walter, 'Katholizismus in der Bundesrepublik'.
10 Interview with the author.
11 *Süddeutsche Zeitung* (18 May 1977).
12 Unpublished letter to Franz Mussner dated 16 May 2007, in the author's archive.
13 Joseph Ratzinger, *Aus meinem Leben.*
14 Joseph Ratzinger and Heinrich Fries (eds), *Einsicht und Glaube* [for Gottlieb Söhngen on his 70th birthday] (Freiburg im Breisgau, 1962).
15 Interview with the author.
16 Ibid.
17 Joseph Ratzinger, *Aus meinem Leben.*
18 Interview with Bayerischer Rundfunk, 18 December 1998.
19 Nicolai Hartmann, *Ethik* (Berlin and Leipzig, 1925).
20 Interview with Bayerischer Rundfunk, 18 December 1998.
21 Interview with the author, 6 August 2012.
22 *30 Giorni,* 01/02 (2006).
23 Ratzinger and Seewald, *Salz der Erde.*
24 Interview with the author.
25 Ratzinger and Seewald, *Salz der Erde.*
26 Benedikt XVI, *Letzte Gespräche.*
27 Uta Ranke-Heinemann, 'Mein Leben mit Benedikt', *Zeit-online* (13 February 2013).
28 Interview by Manuel Schlögl.
29 Joseph Ratzinger and Peter Seewald, *Gott und die Welt* (Munich, 2000).
30 At a meeting with seminarians preparing for the priesthood on World Youth Day 2005 in Cologne.

CHAPTER 19. THE KEY READING

1 Georg Ratzinger, *Mein Bruder, der Papst*.
2 Karl-Egon Lönne, *Politischer Katholizismus im 19. und 20. Jahrhundert* (Frankfurt am Main, 1986).
3 Gerhard Schmidtchen, *Protestanten und Katholiken: Soziologische Analyse konfessioneller Kultur* (Berne, 1973).
4 Thomas Großbölting, *Der verlorene Himmel: Glaube in Deutschland seit 1945* (Göttingen, 2013).
5 Walter, 'Katholizismus in der Bundesrepublik'.
6 Walter Brandmüller, *Licht und Schatten: Kirchengeschichte zwischen Glauben, Fakten und Legenden* (Augsburg, 2007).
7 Joseph Ratzinger, *Aus meinem Leben*.
8 Ibid.
9 Ibid.
10 Interview with the author.
11 Hans Urs von Balthasar and Joseph Ratzinger, *2 Plädoyers: Warum ich noch ein Christ bin. Warum ich noch in der Kirche bin* (Munich 1971).
12 Ratzinger and Fries (eds), *Einsicht und Glaube*.
13 Joseph Ratzinger, *Der Geist der Liturgie: Eine Einführung* (Freiburg im Breisgau, 2000).
14 Joseph Ratzinger, 'Erinnerungen', in Karl Wagner and Hermann Ruf (eds), *Kardinal Ratzinger: Der Erzbischof von München und Freising in Wort und Bild. Mit dem Beitrag Aus meinem Leben* (Munich, 1977).
15 Interview with the author.
16 Quoted from Rudolf Voderholzer, *Henri de Lubac begegnen* (Augsburg, 1999).
17 Henri de Lubac, *Glauben aus der Liebe* (Einsiedeln, 1992).
18 Joseph Ratzinger, *Aus meinem Leben*.
19 Interview with the author.
20 Joseph Ratzinger, *Aus meinem Leben*.
21 Voderholzer, *Henri de Lubac begegnen*.
22 Ratzinger and Seewald, *Salz der Erde*.
23 Valente and Azzaro, interview with Alfred Läpple.
24 Quoted from Voderholzer, *Henri de Lubac begegnen*.
25 Henri de Lubac, *Die Kirche: Eine Betrachtung* (Einsiedeln, 2011).
26 *30 Tage*, no. 10 (2005).

CHAPTER 20. THE MAJOR ORDERS

1 Joseph Ratzinger, *Aus meinem Leben*.
2 Interview with the author.

3   Voderholzer, Schaller and Heibl (eds), *Mitteilungen des Instituts Papst Benedikt XVI.*, vol. 2 (Regensburg 2009).

4   Ibid.

5   Joseph Ratzinger, *Aus meinem Leben*

6   Interview with the author.

7   Ibid.

8   Anselm Schott, *Das Messbuch der heiligen Kirche* (Freiburg im Breisgau, 1938).

9   Interview with the author.

10 Speech when he was awarded the freedom of the city of Freising, on 16 January 2010, in Pfister (ed.), *Geliebte Heimat.*

11 Joseph Ratzinger, 'Primizpredigt für Franz Niedermayer in Kirchanschöring', in Voderholzer, Schaller and Heibl (eds), *Mitteilungen des Instituts Papst Benedikt XVI.*, vol. 2 (Regensburg, 2009).

12 Joseph, Kardinal Ratzinger, *Diener eurer Freude: Meditationen über die priesterliche Spiritualität* (Freiburg im Breisgau, 1988).

13 Ibid.

14 Sermon by Benedict XVI in Rome on 29 June 2011 (feast of Saints Peter and Paul).

15 Interview with the author.

16 Interview with Bayerische Rundfunk, 18 December 1998.

17 Peter Pfister (ed.), *Joseph Ratzinger und das Erzbistum München und Freising: Dokumente und Bilder aus kirchlichen Archiven, Beiträge und Erinnerungen* (Regensburg, 2006).

CHAPTER 21. THE CURATE

1   Ferdinand Fischer, *Papst Benedikt XVI: Eine Reise zu den Orten seines Lebens* (Munich, 2006).

2   Hansjürgen Verweyen, *Joseph Ratzinger – Benedikt XVI.: Die Entwicklung seines Denkens* (Darmstadt, 2007).

3   Interview with the author.

4   Ibid.

5   Ibid.

6   Joseph Ratzinger, *Aus meinem Leben.*

7   *Surberger Heimatkalender* (2011).

8   Sermon at the ordination of Fr M. Robert Hirtz on 15 September 1991 in the Mariawald monastery, in Voderholzer, Schaller and Heibl (eds), *Mitteilungen des Instituts Papst Benedikt XVI.*, vol. 2 (Regensburg, 2009).

9   Benedikt XVI, *Letzte Gespräche.*

10 Konrad Kruis, 'Erinnerungen an Joseph Ratzinger in Bogenhausen', handwritten document, 11 December 2005.

11 Ibid.

12 Interview with Manuel Schlögl.
13 *Süddeutsche Zeitung* (27 February 2005).
14 Pfister (ed.), *Joseph Ratzinger und das Erzbistum München und Freising.*
15 Pfister (ed.), *Geliebte Heimat.*
16 Anton Štrukelj, *Vertrauen: Mut zum Christsein* (St Ottilien, 2012).
17 Ibid.
18 The Heliand-Bund was founded in 1926 as a Catholic girls' and women's movement. It began as a youth and liturgical organization but also as a movement inspired by the love of nature. Its object was to integrate Christianity into the life of the individual and to encourage her participation in the life of the Church and in society as a whole. The group took its name from Heliand, from an early medieval paraphrase of the Bible, written in Old Saxon.
19 Roland Hartung and Günther Saltin (eds), *Alfred-Delp-Jahrbuch,* vol. 7 (Berlin, 2013).
20 Ibid.
21 Interview with the author.
22 Joseph Ratzinger, *Aus meinem Leben.*
23 Großbölting, *Der verlorene Himmel.*
24 Joseph Ratzinger, *Aus meinem Leben.*
25 Interview with Manuel Schlögl.
26 Pfister (ed.), *Geliebte Heimat.*

CHAPTER 22. THE EXAMINATION

1   Interview with the author.
2   Ibid.
3   Ibid..
4   Ibid.
5   Joseph Ratzinger, *Das Fest des Glaubens: Versuche zur Theologie des Gottesdienstes* (Einsiedeln, 1981).
6   Speech as archbishop of Munich in the Antiquarium of the Munich Residenz on 12 February 1982, on the occasion of his departure.
7   Pfister (ed.), *Joseph Ratzinger und das Erzbistum München und Freising.*
8   D. Vincent Twomey, *Pope Benedict XVI: The Conscience of Our Age* (San Francisco, 2007).
9   Third Augustine Catechesis of Benedict XVI on 30 January 2008, St Peter's Square, Rome.
10 Interview with the author.
11 From *Augustinus magister: congrés international augustinien,* Paris, 21–4 September 1954, vol. II (Paris, 1954).
12 Joseph Ratzinger, *Kirche, Ökumene und Politik: Neue Versuche zur Ekklesiologie* (Einsiedeln, 1987).

13 Läpple, *Benedikt XVI. und seine Wurzeln.*
14 Pfister (ed.), *Geliebte Heimat.*
15 Interview with the author.
16 Ibid.
17 Ibid.
18 Ulrike Götz (ed.), *39. Sammelblatt des historischen Vereins Freising: Papst Benedikt und Freising* (Freising, 2006).
19 Pfister (ed.) *Geliebte Heimat.*
20 Ibid.
21 Peter Seewald (ed.), *Der deutsche Papst* (Augsburg and Hamburg, 2005).
22 Pfister (ed.), *Ratzinger und das Erzbistum.*
23 Ibid.
24 Interview with the author.
25 Joseph Ratzinger, *Aus meinem Leben.*

CHAPTER 23. THE ABYSS

1   Jn 14.18.
2   Matthew 24: 6-31.
3   Ratzinger and Seewald, *Salz der Erde.*
4   Hansjürgen Verweyen, *Ein unbekannter Ratzinger: Die Habilitationsschrift von 1955 als Schlüssel zu seiner Theologie* (Regensburg, 2010).
5   Joseph Ratzinger, *Gesammelte Schriften*, vol. 2, *Offenbarungsverständnis und Geschichtstheologie Bonaventuras* (Freiburg im Breisgau, 2009.
6   Joseph Ratzinger, *Die Geschichtstheologie des heiligen Bonaventura* (Munich, 1959).
7   Joseph Ratzinger, *Die Geschichtstheologie des heiligen Bonaventura*, new edn (St Ottilien, 1992).
8   Ibid.
9   Ibid.
10 *Münchner Abendzeitung* (2 June 1949).
11 Joseph, Kardinal Ratzinger, 'Mein Bruder, der Domkapellmeister'.
12 Interview with the author.
13 Ibid.
14 Joseph Ratzinger, *Aus meinem Leben.*
15 Interview with the author.
16 Ibid.
17 Ibid.
18 Ibid.
19 Verweyen, *Ein unbekannter Ratzinger.*
20 Interview with the author.
21 Ibid.
22 Alfred Läpple, in Pfister (ed.) Joseph *Ratzinger und das Erzbistum.*

CHAPTER 24. THE NEW HEATHENS AND THE CHURCH

1 Läpple, *Benedikt XVI. und seine Wurzeln.*
2 'Der Priester – ein segnender Mensch: Primizpredigt für Franz Niedermayer in Kirchanschöring', in Voderholzer, Schaller and (eds), *Mitteilungen des Instituts Papst Benedikt XVI.*, vol. 2 (Regensburg, 2009).
3 Ibid.
4 Ibid.
5 S. M. Pascalina Lehnert, *Ich durfte ihm dienen: Erinnerungen an Papst Pius XII.* (Würzburg, 1982).
6 *spiegel.de* (8 October 2008).
7 *Hochland* (October 1958).
8 Ibid.
9 Ibid.
10 Lubac, *Glauben aus der Liebe.*
11 Joseph Ratzinger, 'Die neuen Heiden und die Kirche', in *Hochland* (October 1958).
12 Interview with Manuel Schlögl.
13 Interview with the author.
14 Ibid.
15 Benedikt XVI, *Letzte Gespräche.*
16 Joseph Ratzinger, *Aus meinem Leben.*
17 Archiv Collegium Albertinum, Bonn.

CHAPTER 25. A STAR IS BORN

1 Interview with the author.
2 Carl Bernstein and Marco Politi, *Seine Heiligkeit Johannes Paul II: Macht und Menschlichkeit des Papstes* (Munich, 1996).
3 Interview with the author.
4 Ibid.
5 Matthias Kopp (ed.), *Und plötzlich Papst: Benedikt XVI. im Spiegel persönlicher Begegnungen* (Freiburg im Breisgau, 2007).
6 Archiv Albertinum, Bonn.
7 Author's archive.
8 Interview with the author.
9 Manuel Schlögl, *Am Anfang eines großen Weges: Joseph Ratzinger in Bonn und Köln* (Regensburg, 2014).
10 Joseph Ratzinger, *Aus meinem Leben.*
11 Läpple, *Benedikt XVI. und seine Wurzeln.*
12 Archiv Albertinum, Bonn.
13 Interview with the author.

14 Ibid.
15 Schlögl, *Am Anfang*.
16 Interview with the author.
17 Joseph Ratzinger, *Der Gott des Glaubens und der Gott der Philosophen* (Munich and Zürich, 1960).
18 Interview with the author.
19 Ibid.
20 Heinz-Josef Fabry, '"Es war für mich sozusagen das Traumziel …": Prof. Dr. Joseph Ratzinger in Bonn (1959–1963)', private document.
21 Interview with the author.

CHAPTER 26. THE NETWORK

1 Schlögl, *Am Anfang*.
2 Heinz-Josef Fabry, 'Es war für mich sozusagen das Traumziel …'.
3 Joseph Ratzinger, *Aus meinem Leben*.
4 Hubert Jedin, *Lebensbericht* (Mainz, 1984).
5 Ibid.
6 Karl Hardt (ed.), *Bekenntnis zur katholischen Kirche* (Würzburg, 1955).
7 Heinrich Schlier, *Exegetische Aufsätze und Vorträge II: Besinnung auf das Neue Testament* (Freiburg im Breisgau, 1964).
8 Heinrich Schlier, *Exegetische Aufsätze und Vorträge III: Das Ende der Zeit* (Freiburg im Breisgau, 1971).
9 Ibid.
10 Interview with the author.
11 Joseph Ratzinger, *Aus meinem Leben*.
12 Joseph Ratzinger, foreword to the Italian edition (2004) of Heinrich Schlier, *Über die Auferstehung Jesu Christi* (*On the Resurrection of Jesus Christ*).
13 Quoted from Schlögl, *Am Anfang*.
14 Interview with the author.
15 Letter to Hans Urs von Balthasar, 16 February 1966; quoted here from Ursula Hacker-Klom, *Hackers Werk wird eines Tages wieder entdeckt werden!* (Münster, 2013).
16 Schlögl, *Am Anfang*.
17 Interview with the author.
18 Joseph Ratzinger, *Aus meinem Leben*.
19 Ibid.

CHAPTER 27. COUNCIL

1 https://www.herder.de/theologie-pastoral/historische-theologie/erstes-vatikanisches-konzil/

2 Xavier Rynne, *Die zweite Reformation: Die erste Sitzungsperiode des Zweiten Vatikanischen Konzils* (Cologne, 1964); originally published as edition *Letters from Vatican City* (New York, 1963).

3 Bernstein and Politi, *Seine Heiligkeit Johannes Paul II.*

4 *Der Spiegel* (1 February 1962).

5 Document by Pope Benedict XVI on the 50th anniversary of the beginning of the Second Vatican Council, Castel Gandolfo, 2 August 2012.

6 Ibid.

7 Joseph Ratzinger, *Die erste Sitzungsperiode des Zweiten Vatikanischen Konzils: Ein Rückblick* (Cologne, 1963); Joseph Ratzinger, 'Die erste Sitzungsperiode des zweiten Vatikanischen Konzils', in *Gesammelte Schriften,* vol. 7/1 (Freiburg im Breisgau, 2012).

8 Ibid.

9 Norbert Trippen, *Josef Kardinal Frings* (Paderborn, 2005).

10 P. Ralph M. Wiltgen, *Der Rhein fließt in den Tiber: Eine Geschichte des Zweiten Vatikanischen Konzils* (Feldkirch, 1988).

11 *50 Jahre Zweites Vatikanisches Konzil* (Kisslegg, 2018).

CHAPTER 28. THE BATTLE BEGINS

1 summorum-pontificum-karlsruhe.de/pdf/Bischof_Schneider_Predigt_Konstanz.pdf

2 *Spiegel* online (2 March 2014).

3 Roberto de Mattei, *Das Zweite Vatikanische Konzil: Eine bislang ungeschriebene Geschichte* (Ruppichteroth, 2011).

4 Ibid.

5 Ibid.

6 Ibid.

7 kathpedia, Zweites Vatikanisches Konzil, www.kath.net

8 Freddy Derwahl, *Benedikt XVI. und Hans Küng: Geschichte einer Freundschaft* (Munich, 2008).

9 *Frankfurter Allgemeine Zeitung* (19 April 2014).

10 *Der Spiegel* (1 October 1962).

11 Andreas R. Barlogg SJ, Clemens Brodkorb and Peter Pfister (eds), *Erneuerung in Christus: Das Zweite Vatikanische Konzil im Spiegel Münchener Kirchenarchive* (Regensburg, 2012).

12 Wiltgen, *Der Rhein fließ in den Tiber.*

13 Ibid.

14 L. J. Cardinal Suenens, 'Aux Origines du Concile Vatican II', in *Nouvelle Revue Théologique*, 107 (1985), p. 4; L. J. Suenens, *Souvenirs et espérances* (Paris, 1991), pp. 65–80. Quoted from de Mattei, *Das Zweite Vatikanische Konzil.*

15 Yves Congar, *Mon journal du concile*, 2 vols (Paris, 2002), vol. 1, p. 4.

16 Hans Küng, *Erkämpfte Freiheit* (Munich, 2002).

17 Norbert Trippen, *Josef Kardinal Frings* (Paderborn, 2005).
18 Julius, Kardinal Döpfner, *Konzilstagebücher, Briefe und Notizen zum Zweiten Vatikanischen Konzil* (Regensburg, 2006).
19 Ibid.
20 de Mattei, *Das Zweite Vatikanische Konzil.*
21 Ibid.
22 Derwahl, *Benedikt XVI. und Hans Küng.*

CHAPTER 29. THE GENOA SPEECH

1 Joseph Ratzinger, *Zur Lehre des Zweiten Vatikanischen Konzils, Gesammelte Schriften,* vol. 7/1 (Freiburg im Breisgau, 2012).
2 Ibid.
3 Ibid.
4 Interview with the author.
5 Ibid.
6 Ibid.
7 Josef Kardinal Frings, *Für die Menschen bestellt: Erinnerungen des Alt-Erzbischofs von Köln Josef Kardinal Frings* (Cologne, 1973).
8 Interview with the author.
9 Frings, *Für die Menschen.*
10 Trippen, *Josef Kardinal Frings.*
11 Interview with the author.
12 Trippen, *Josef Kardinal Frings.*
13 Ibid.
14 Jedin, *Lebensbericht.*
15 Trippen, *Josef Kardinal Frings.*
16 Wiltgen, *Der Rhein fließt in den Tiber.*
17 Joseph Ratzinger, 'Stellungnahmen in Latein zu den von Kardinal Cicognani übersandten Konzils-Schemata [Latin comments on the Council schemata sent by Cardinal Cicognani]', in *Zur Lehre des Zweiten Vatikanischen Konzils, Gesammelte Schriften,* vol. 7/1.
18 Joseph Ratzinger, 'Bemerkungen zum Schema "De fontibus revelationis"', in Voderholzer, Schaller and Heibl (eds), *Mitteilungen des Instituts Papst Benedikt XVI.,* vol. 2 (Regensburg, 2009).

CHAPTER 30. THE SPIN DOCTOR

1 Interview with the author.
2 Joseph Ratzinger, 'Grundgedanken der eucharistischen Erneuerung des 20. Jahrhunderts' (1960), in *Zur Lehre des Zweiten Vatikanischen Konzils, Gesammelte Schriften,* vol. 7/1.

3 Joseph Ratzinger, 'Der Eucharistische Weltkongress im Spiegel der Kritik' (1961), in *Zur Lehre des Zweiten Vatikanischen Konzils, Gesammelte Schriften,* vol. 7/1.

4 Wiltgen, *Der Rhein fließt in den Tiber.*

5 Kopp (ed.), *Und plötzlich Papst.*

6 Andreas R. Batlogg, 'Karl Rahner auf dem Zweiten Vatikanischen Konzil', in Batlogg, Brodkorb and Pfister (eds), *Erneuerung in Christus.*

7 Trippen, *Josef Kardinal Frings.*

8 Batlogg, Brodkorb and Pfister (eds), *Erneuerung in Christus.*

9 Döpfner, *Konzilstagebücher.*

10 Batlogg, 'Karl Rahner auf dem Zweiten Vatikanischen Konzil', in Batlogg, Brodkorb and Pfister (eds), *Erneuerung in Christus.*

11 Batlogg, "Karl Rahner SJ', in Pfister (ed.). *Joseph Ratzinger und das Erzbistum.*

12 Interview with the author.

13 Georg Ratzinger, *Ein Leben zwischen Politik, Geschichte und Seelsorge* (Regensburg, 2008).

14 Joseph Ratzinger, 'Kardinal Frings – Zu seinem 80. Geburtstag', in *Gesammelte Schriften,* vol. 7/1 (first published in *CiG,* no. 19, 1967).

15 Interview with the author.

16 Joseph Ratzinger, 'Stimme des Vertrauens', in Norbert Trippen (ed.), *Kardinal Josef Frings auf dem Zweiten Vaticanum,* Festschrift (Cologne, 1976).

17 Trippen (ed.), *Kardinal Josef Frings auf dem Zweiten Vaticanum.*

18 Joseph Ratzinger, *Aus meinem Leben.*

19 Ratzinger and Seewald, *Salz der Erde.*

20 Joseph Ratzinger, *Gesammelte Schriften,* vol. 7/1.

21 Trippen (ed.), *Kardinal Josef Frings auf dem Zweiten Vaticanum.*

22 Joseph Ratzinger, *Gesammelte Schriften,* vol. 7/1.

23 Trippen (ed.), *Kardinal Josef Frings auf dem Zweiten Vaticanum.*

24 Ibid.

25 Joseph Ratzinger, 'Stimme des Vertrauens: Kardinal Josef Frings auf dem Zweiten Vatikanum', in Norbert Trippen und Wilhlm Mogge (eds), *Ortskirche im Dienst der Weltkirche: Das Erzbistum Köln seit seiner Wiedererrichtung im Jahre 1825. Festgabe für die Kölner Kardinäle Erzbischof Joseph Höffner und Alt-Erzbischof Josef Frings* (Cologne, 1976).

26 Ibid.

27 Trippen (ed.), *Kardinal Josef Frings auf dem Zweiten Vaticanum.*

28 Interview with the author.

CHAPTER 31. THE WORLD ON THE BRINK

1 Joseph Ratzinger, *Die erste Sitzungsperiode des Zweiten Vatikanischen Konzils: Ein Rückblick* (Cologne, 1963); repr. in *Gesammelte Schriften,* vol. 7/1.

2   Address by Pope Benedict XVI to the Roman clergy on the SecondVatican Council, 14 February 2013; http://w2.vatican.va/content/benedict-xvi/de/speeches/2013/february/documents/hf_ben-xvi_spe_20130214_clero-roma.html

3   Interview with the author.

4   de Mattei, *Das Zweite Vatikanische Konzil.*

5   *L'Osservatore Romano* (24 August 1961).

6   Ibid.

7   *La Repubblica* (13 May 2005);'Die Erinnerungen des amtierenden Papstes', part of a text by Joseph Ratzinger; transcript of the interview for the 'Archiv der Erinnerungen' by Raisat-Extra.

8   Joseph Ratzinger, *Theologische Prinzipienlehre: Bausteine zur Fundamentaltheologie* (Munich, 1982).

9   Ibid.

10   Voderholzer, Schaller and Heibl (eds), *Mitteilungen des Instituts Benedikt XVI.,* vol. 2.

11   Peter Pfister, 'Der Konzilstheologe Joseph Ratzinger im Spiegel der Konzilsakten des Münchener Julius Kardinal Döpfner', in Pfister (ed.), *Joseph Ratzinger und das Erzbistum.*

12   Jedin, *Lebensbericht.*

13   Ibid.

14   Trippen, *Josef Kardinal Frings.*

15   Interview with the author.

16   Giuseppe Siri, *Diario*, 356, quoted from de Mattei, *Das Zweite Vatikanische Konzil.*

17   *Die Zeit* (4 October 2012).

CHAPTER 32. SEVEN DAYS THAT CHANGED THE CATHOLIC CHURCH FOR EVER

1   Pope Benedict XVI, speech to the Roman clergy on the II Vatican Council, 14 February 2013; http://w2.vatican.va/content/benedict-xvi/de/speeches/2013/february/documents/hf_ben-xvi_spe_20130214_clero-roma.html

2   de Mattei, *Das Zweite Vatikanische Konzil.*

3   Ibid.

4   Trippen, *Josef Kardinal Frings.*

5   Interview with the author.

6   Joseph Ratzinger, 'Stimme des Vertrauens: Kardinal Josef Frings auf dem Zweiten Vatikanum', in Norbert Trippen and Wilhelm Mogge (eds), *Ortskirche im Dienst der Weltkirche: Das Erzbistum Köln seit seiner Wiedererrichtung im Jahre 1825. Festgabe für die Kölner Kardinäle Erzbischof Joseph Höffner und Alt-Erzbischof Josef Frings* (Cologne, 1976).

7   Benedict XVI, speech, 14 February 2013.
8   Interview with the author.
9   L. J., Cardinal Suenens, *Souvenirs et espérances* (Paris, 1991).
10 Ratzinger, 'Stimme des Vertrauens', in Trippen and Mogge (eds), *Ortskirche im Dienst der Weltkirche*.
11 Ibid.
12 Ibid.
13 Trippen, *Josef Kardinal Frings*.
14 Ratzinger, *Die erste Sitzungsperiode des Zweiten Vatikanischen Konzils*.
15 Ratzinger, 'Stimme des Vertrauens', in Trippen and Mogge (eds), *Ortskirche im Dienst der Weltkirche*.
16 Yves Congar, *Mon Journal du concile*, 2 vols (Paris, 2002), vol. 1.
17 Ratzinger, 'Stimme des Vertrauens', in Trippen and Mogge (eds), *Ortskirche im Dienst der Weltkirche*.
18 de Mattei, *Das Zweite Vatikanische Konzil*.
19 Trippen, *Josef Kardinal Frings*.
20 Wiltgen, *Der Rhein fließt in den Tiber*.
21 Ibid.
22 Joseph Ratzinger, in his introduction (1967) to the constitution on Divine Revelation, in Ratzinger, *Gesammelte Schriften*, vol. 7/1.
23 Trippen, *Josef Kardinal Frings*.
24 Ratzinger, *Die erste Sitzungsperiode des Zweiten Vatikanischen Konzils*.
25 Ibid.
26 Döpfner, *Konzilstagebücher*.
27 Wiltgen, *Der Rhein fließt in den Tiber*.
28 Trippen, *Josef Kardinal Frings*.
29 G. Ruggieri, in Giuseppe Alberigo and Klaus Wittstadt (eds), *Geschichte des Zweiten Vatikanischen Konzils (1959–1965)*, vol. II (Mainz, 2000).
30 Ratzinger, *Die erste Sitzungsperiode des Zweiten Vatikanischen Konzils*.
31 Ibid.
32 Ibid.
33 *La Repubblica* (13 May 2005); 'Die Erinnerungen des amtierenden Papstes', part of a text by Joseph Ratzinger; transcript of the interview for the 'Archiv der Erinnerungen' by Raisat-Extra.
34 Batlogg, Brodkorb and Pfister (eds), *Erneuerung in Christus*.

CHAPTER 33. GERMAN WAVE

1   Ratzinger, *Die erste Sitzungsperiode des Zweiten Vatikanischen Konzils*.
2   de Mattei, *Das Zweite Vatikanische Konzil*.
3   *Der Spiegel*, no. 50 (1963).
4   Schlögl, *Am Anfang eines großen Weges*.
5   Ibid.

6 Ibid.

7 'Erneuerung in Christus', letter from Karl Rahner to Hugo Rahner, 2 November 1963, in *Stimmen der Zeit* (September 2012).

8 Ibid.

9 Derwahl, *Benedikt XVI. und Hans Küng.*

10 Voderholzer, Schaller and Heibl (eds), *Mitteilungen des Instituts Benedikt XVI.*, vol. 1.

11 Interview with the author.

12 Derwahl, *Benedikt XVI. und Hans Küng.*

13 Ibid.

14 *Der Spiegel* (20 December 1961).

15 Derwahl, *Benedikt XVI. und Hans Küng.*

16 *Der Spiegel* (20 December 1961).

17 Döpfner, *Konzilstagebücher.*

18 Interview with the author.

19 Heinz-Josef Fabry, 'Es war für mich sozusagen das Traumziel …'; Prof. Dr. Joseph Ratzinger in Bonn (1959–1963), reconstruction based on the records of the faculty meetings of the Bonn Catholic Theology Faculty. Private document.

20 Joseph Ratzinger, *Aus meinem Leben.*

CHAPTER 34. POWER SOURCES

1 Interview with Manuel Schlögl.

2 Interview with the author.

3 Manuel Schlögl, *Joseph Ratzinger in Münster, 1963–1966* (Münster, 2012).

4 Interview with Manuel Schlögl.

5 Interview with the author for the *Magazin der Süddeutschen Zeitung* (June 1993).

6 Interview with the author.

7 Ibid.

8 *Der Spiegel* (11 December 1963).

9 Interview with Manuel Schlögl.

10 Interview with the author.

11 Siegfried Wiedenhofer, 'Der Anfang einer langen wunderbaren Begegnung', in Kopp (ed.), *Und plötzlich Papst.*

12 Schlögl, *Ratzinger in Münster.*

13 Interview with the author.

14 Ibid.

15 Twomey, *Pope Benedict XVI.*

16 Letter of 4 July 2009 to the archbishop of Paderborn, Hans-Josef Becker; cited from Schlögl, *Ratzinger in Münster.*

CHAPTER 35. IN THE SCHOOL OF THE HOLY SPIRIT

1 *Der Spiegel* (12 June 1963).
2 Reinhard Raffalt, *Wohin steuert der Vatikan?* (Munich, 1973).
3 Franz Michel Willam, from *Geist und Leben,* issue 2 (March/April 1979).
4 Trippen, *Josef Kardinal Frings.*
5 Wiltgen, *Der Rhein fließt in den Tiber.*
6 Alexandra von Teuffenbach, 'Weg vom Schauspiel, hin zur Diskussion', in *Vatican-Magazin,* 6 (2013).
7 *La Repubblica* (13 May 2005).
8 Pope Benedict XVI, speech to the Roman clergy on the Second Vatican Council, 14 February 2013.
9 Joseph Ratzinger, *Zur Lehre des Zweiten Vatikanischen Konzils,* vol. 7/1 of *Gesammelte Schriften.*
10 Ibid.
11 *50 Jahre Zweites Vatikanisches Konzil* (Kißlegg, 2018).
12 Joseph Ratzinger, *Das Konzil auf dem Weg: Rückblick auf die zweite Sitzungsperiode des Zweiten Vatikanischen Konzils* (Cologne, 1964).
13 'Zweites Vatikanisches Konzil', Kathpedia; http://www.kathpedia.com/index.php/Zweites_Vatikanisches_Konzil
14 Trippen, *Josef Kardinal Frings.*
15 Joseph Ratzinger, *Die erste Sitzungsperiode des Zweiten Vatikanischen Konzils.*
16 Andreas R. Barlogg SJ, 'Karl Rahner SJ auf dem Zweiten Vatikanischen Konzil', in Barlogg, Brodkorb and Pfister (eds), *Erneuerung in Christus.*
17 Trippen, *Josef Kardinal Frings.*
18 Wiltgen, *Der Rhein fließt in den Tiber.*
19 Ratzinger, *Konzil auf dem Weg.*
20 Joseph Ratzinger, 'Kardinal Frings – Zu seinem 80. Geburtstag'.
21 *Der Spiegel,* no. 50 (1963).
22 Joseph Ratzinger, 'Kardinal Frings – Zu seinem 80. Geburtstag'.
23 Joseph Ratzinger, 'Stimme des Vertrauens', in Trippen and Mogge (eds), *Ortskirche im Dienst der Weltkirche.*
24 Wiltgen, *Der Rhein fließt in den Tiber.*
25 Derwahl, *Benedikt XVI. und Hans Küng.*
26 Ibid.
27 Joseph Frings, 'Erinnerungen', in Trippen, *Josef Kardinal Frings.*
28 Ratzinger, *Konzil auf dem Weg.*
29 Bill O'Reilly and Martin Dugard, *Killing Kennedy: Das Ende eines amerikanischen Traums* (Munich, 2013).
30 Joseph Ratzinger, *Aus meinem Leben.*

CHAPTER 36. THE LEGACY

1   Wiltgen, *Der Rhein fließt in den Tiber.*

2   Norbert Trippen, *Josef Kardinal Frings.*

3   Wiltgen, *Der Rhein fließt in den Tiber.*

4   Joseph Ratzinger, 'Kardinal Frings – Zu seinem 80. Geburtstag'.

5   Joseph Ratzinger, 'Zum 100. Geburtstag von Kardinal Frings', in *Communio* (1987).

6   Joseph Ratzinger, *Aus meinem Leben.*

7   Wiltgen, *Der Rhein fließt in den Tiber.*

8   Jedin, *Lebensbericht.*

9   Trippen, *Josef Kardinal Frings.*

10   Joseph Ratzinger, *Zur Lehre des Zweiten Vatikanischen Konzils,* vol. 7/1 of *Gesammelte Schriften.*

11   Joseph Ratzinger, 'Ergebnisse und Probleme der dritten Sitzungsperiode', in Ratzinger, *Gesammelte Schriften,* vol. 7/1.

12   Ibid.

13   Barlogg, Brodkorb and Pfister, *Erneuerung in Christus.*

14   Trippen, *Josef Kardinal Frings.*

15   Wiltgen, *Der Rhein fließt in den Tiber.*

16   Joseph Ratzinger, 'Die letzte Sitzungsperiode des Konzils', in *Gesammelte Schriften,* vol. 7/1.

17   Ibid.

18   Audience of 29 December 1965. Quoted from Rudolf Voderholzer: 'Der Geist des Konzils. Ein Blick auf seine Deutungsgeschichte', *Tagespost* (8 March 2014).

19   Claus-Peter März, '50 Jahre Konzil: Die Dogmatische Konstitution über die göttliche Offenbarung *Dei Verbum*', in *Theologie der Gegenwart,* 1 (2015).

20   Joseph Ratzinger, 'Kommentar zu *Dei Verbum* im Lexikon für Theologie und Kirche', in *Zur Lehre des Zweiten Vatikanischen Konzils,* vol. 7/2 of *Gesammelte Schriften* (Freiburg im Breisgau, 2012).

21   Wiltgen, *Der Rhein fließt in den Tiber.*

22   Ratzinger and Seewald, *Salz der Erde.*

23   Interview with the author.

Index

Acts of the Apostles 389
Acts of Thomas 357
Adam, August 211
Adam, Karl 211
Adelmann of Lüttich 232
Adenauer, Konrad 132,
 138, 155, 205–6, 224–5,
 264, 294, 310, 317
Adlema, Sister 17
Aicher, Otl 108
Albertus Magnus 216
Alfrink, Cardinal Bernard
 Jan 352, 396, 400–2
Allert, Tilmann 157
Alt, Karl 110
Altinger, Hans 86
Altötting 47–8
Ambrose, Bishop 195,
 231–2
Ametsbichler, Barbara 38,
 54
Amici Israel 155
Andersen, Friedrich 41
Andersen, Karl 167
Anderson, Rudolf 399
Andreotti, Giulio 439
Angermaier, Professor
 163
Anglican Church 336
Angulanza, Roman 322,
 427
Anouilh, Jean 152, 164
Anschluss 73–4
anti-Semitism 41–2, 44–6,
 82, 116, 156–7
Aoyama, Mitsuko 291

Aquinas, Thomas 147,
 164–5, 191, 213, 216, 278,
 280, 368
Arianism 197, 333
Aristotle 165, 213, 318
Arndt, Ernst Moritz 78
Aschau am Inn 29–32,
 39–40, 50–5, 60–1
Atatürk, Kemal 5
Auer, Alfons 329
Auer, Ida 317
Auer, Johann Baptist 149,
 317, 323, 329
Augustine Congress 269
Auschwitz 116, 163, 165,
 178, 242
Austrian Legion 114

Bacht, Heinrich 414
Bafile, Archbishop Corrado 318, 365
Baldwin of Canterbury 232
Balthasar, Hans Urs
 von 174, 233–4, 268,
 328–9, 353, 370, 415–16
Bartels, Adolf 41
Barth, Karl 43–4, 214,
 415–16
Bavarian People's Party
 (BVP) 26, 79, 152
Baziak, Archbishop 309
BBC broadcasts 103
Bea, Cardinal Augustin
 210, 360, 367, 402–3
Beatrix, Empress 139

Bechstein, Helene 6
Bechteler, Barbara 254
Beck, Józef 90
Becker, Winfried 43
Beethoven, Ludwig
 van 39, 95, 310
Beevor, Antony 92
Benedict IX, Pope 6
Benedict XV, Pope 347
Benedict XVI, Pope (Joseph
 Aloisus Ratzinger)
 'Advent Sermons' 227
 Bensberg lecture 356–9,
 364, 387
 and canon law 223–4
 closeness to his
  brother 94–5
 conscripted into Hitler
  Youth 86, 94–5, 97, 159
 credulousness and loy-
  alty 432
 crisis of vocation 216–21
 diamond jubilee 246
 discovers vocation 53–5
 doctoral disserta-
  tion 229–30, 238–9,
  243, 247, 265–9
 early life 8, 15, 17–32
 education 37–9, 48–9,
  65–70, 73–88, 93–4, 96–7
 and father's death 330
 father's influence 45,
  51–2, 113, 150–1, 330–1
 first clerical appoint-
  ments 138, 251–61
 First Mass 245, 248–51

first sermons 239–42
first venture into journal-
ism 295–300
friendship with Dora
Huber 111–12
friendship with Esther
Betz 311–12
and generational
change 321
Genoa speech 360–2,
364–5, 387, 461
habilitation 269–70,
275–90, 301–2
and Hermann
Hesse 180–7, 189–91
interest in politics 317
and Jewish question 453
and John XXIII 370,
437–8
lectures at Freising 260,
262, 270–5
and liturgical move-
ment 226–8
love of animals 208
love of Bavaria 264–5
and mother's death 447–8
moves to Bonn 300–3,
307–31
moves to Münster 410–11,
421–36
and the Nazi past 152–60
ordination 224, 239,
243–7
and outbreak of war 90,
93–7
progressive reputa-
tion 272, 286, 359
progressive vs. conservative
tendencies 456, 462–3
and Ratzinger Anbe-
tungsverein 271
receives tonsure 216
resignation speech 210
and St Augustine 191–201
and Second Vatican
Council 337–42, 350–1,
361–91, 393–412, 417–19,
439–47, 449–63
shyness 84–5, 208, 255,
261, 322

studies at Freising 139–50,
161–201
studies in Munich 202–37
suffers headaches 148
taste for literature 97–8,
146, 177–8, 191
theological termino-
logy 185
and uncle's death 266
and the war 100–4,
113–24, 129–30
and women 218–20
yodelling 273–4
Benedict XVI, *writings*:
Auf Christus schauen 435
*Der christliche
Brüderlichkeit* 322
*Einführung in das
Christentum* 174, 256
*Die Einheit der
Nationen* 317
*Episkopat und Primat: das
neue Volk Gottes* 324, 351
Der Geist der Liturgie 228
*Die Geschichtstheologie
des heiligen Bonaven-
tura* 270, 276, 289
*Handbuch der
Kirchengeschichte* 324
Lob der Weihnacht 326
*The New Heathens and the
Church* 260, 291, 293,
295–300
*Offenbarung und
Heilsgeschichte nach
der Lehre des heiligen
Bonaventura* 276, 282
*Über die christliche
Brüderlichkeit* 256
*Volk und Haus in Au-
gustins Lehre von der
Kirche* 247, 265–9
*Wahrheit, Werte, Macht:
Prüfsteine der pluralisten
Gesellschaft* 317
Benson, Robert Hugh 146
Benz, Wolfgang 189
Berber, Anita 5
Berchtesgaden Agree-
ment 74

Bergengruen, Werner 105
Berger, Rupert 79, 130,
147, 149, 176, 214, 218,
222–3, 230, 244, 248–9,
252, 271–2, 285, 289
Berger, Ursula 426
Bergson, Henri 149
Berlin blockade 206–7
Bernanos, Georges 108,
146, 177–8, 191, 220
Bernard of Clairvaux 232
Bertram, Cardinal
Adolf 57
Betz, Anton 311
Betz, Esther 219, 254, 303,
311–12, 322, 371, 378
Billot, Louis 345
Birndorfer, Johann (Brother
Konrad) 48
Biser, Eugen 286
Bismarck, Prince Otto
von 225
Blanco Sarto, Pablo 200
Bloch, Ernst 279
Blondel, Maurice 243–4
Bloy, Léon 177–8
Blum, Norbert 331, 420
Blum, Stefan 74, 131
Blumschein, Max 251,
254–6, 260
BMW (Bavarian Motor
Works) 102, 104
Böckenförde, Ernst-
Wolfgang 432
Böckenförde, Werner 410,
424, 432–3
Böckle, Franz 268, 422
Bögerhausen, Erhard 428
Böll, Heinrich 188
Bonhoeffer, Dietrich 43,
135, 159
Bonus, Arthur 41
book burnings, Nazi 35
Book of Genesis 281
Book of Revelation 139,
326
Borchert, Wolfgang 285
Borromeo, Monsignor
Luigi 395
Bosch, Robert 33

Botterweck, Gerhard
    Johannes 422
Brandner, Helmut 372, 424
Brandt, Willy 458
'Bräu-Bärbel' 32, 37, 54
Brecht, Bertolt 5, 35, 320
Brugger, Walter 74, 143
Brunner, Emil 214
Buber, Martin 174, 200
Buchenwald concentration
    camp 179
Bude, Heinz 124
Bultmann, Rudolf 323,
    325–6

Camus, Albert 191, 320
Carinici, Monsignor Alf-
    onso 336
Carl Theodor, Duke 373
Casel, Odo 214
Casimirri, Luciano 437
Cassou, Jean 5
Castell, Monsignor
    Alberto 408
Castro, Fidel 263, 309,
    383, 399
Catholic Principles for Pub-
    lic Life 137
Catholic social teach-
    ing 204–5, 257, 374
'Catholic spring' 226, 291
CDU (Christian Demo-
    cratic Union) 138, 207,
    224, 310, 337
Celestine III, Pope 278
Celestine V, Pope 210
celibacy 218, 247, 406, 418,
    454, 460
Cento, Cardinal
    Fernando 437
Chamberlain, Neville 74
Chenu, Marie-Domin-
    ique 352, 400, 406
Chiemgau-Bote 78–9
Christian Socialism 162,
    204
church attendance 225
Churchill, Winston 112,
    121, 136
Cicero 69, 194, 344

Cicognani, Cardinal
    Johannes 361, 406
Clasen, Sophronius 323
Claudel, Paul 146, 177–8,
    191, 223, 234
Clement II, Pope 385
Clement of Alexandria
    213
Codex Iuris Canonicus 334,
    444
Community of St John
    328
Confessing Church 43–4,
    134, 325
Congar, Yves 352–3, 370,
    386, 400–1, 406, 414–15,
    443, 452
Congregation for the
    Doctrine of the Faith
    (Holy Office/Holy
    Inquisition) 44, 71, 111,
    149, 175, 209, 215, 228,
    312, 317, 355, 372, 430–1,
    444–7
Constantine I, Em-
    peror 196–7, 333
Coudenhove-Kalergi,
    Heinrich von 291
Council of Con-
    stance 343–4
Council of Nicaea 333, 388
Council of Trent 339,
    367–8, 391
Cuban Missile Crisis 383–4,
    391–2, 398–9
Cullmann, Oscar 459
Cushing, Cardinal
    Richard 453

Dachau concentration
    camp 34–5, 57, 79, 104,
    130, 154
Damasus II, Pope 6, 385
Daniélou, Jean 352, 370,
    386, 400, 406
Daniels, Hans 302, 312
Dante 179
d'Arpa, Angelo 359
David, Jakob 373
De Gasperi, Alcide 205

de Lubac, Henri 159, 231–7,
    270, 297–9, 352, 370, 386,
    400, 406, 412, 414–15, 435
de Luca, Don
    Guiseppe 438
de Victoria, Tomás
    Luis 253
De-Jewification Insti-
    tute 44
Delp, Alfred 138, 256–9
DeMille, Cecil B. 5
Depp, Alfred 159
Derwahl, Freddy 417–18,
    445
Descartes, René 171
'de-secularization' 260, 296
Deutschmark, introduction
    of 206
Dick, Klaus 323
Diocletian, Emperor 196
Döblin, Alfred 18, 35
Dobrynin, Anatoly 399
Döllinger, Ignaz von 222,
    374, 386
Dömer, Franz-Josef 427
Dönitz, Admiral of the
    Fleet, Karl 119
Döpfner, Cardinal
    Julius 352–4, 360, 364,
    371–2, 380, 388, 390, 394,
    396, 400–2, 404, 419, 440,
    443, 455, 462
Dörmann, Johannes 421–2
Dostoevsky, Fyodor 146,
    429
Drewermann, Eugen 429
Droste-Hulshoff, Annette
    von 424

Ebner, Ferdinand 170–5
ecumenism 149, 162, 210,
    212, 215, 232, 272–3, 302,
    318, 324, 333–4, 345, 350,
    353, 386, 388, 406–7, 409,
    416–17, 420, 423, 425,
    431–3, 435, 439–41, 444,
    452, 458, 461
Eddington, Sir Arthur 167
Eichendorff, Joseph Freiherr
    von 97

Eichmann, Adolf 116
Einstein, Albert 168–9
Eisenhower, General
    Dwight D. 120, 294
Elias, Norbert 320
Eliot, T. S. 109, 152
Elisabeth, Sister 380
Elizabeth II, Queen 294
Elst, Georg 176, 248–9, 329
Emanuela, Sister 427
encyclicals 56–60, 75, 166,
    208, 211, 229, 234, 334,
    345, 361, 364, 376, 437
Endros, Anton 78
Enlightenment 167, 171
Enzensberger, Hans Mag-
    nus 320
Esch, Arno 316
Eucharistic World Con-
    gress 350
European Coal and Steel
    Community 264
European Economic Com-
    munity 309
Eusebius of Caesarea 388
euthanasia, Nazi pro-
    gramme 141, 410
Evangelical Church in
    Germany (EKD) 134,
    336, 431

Fabry, Heinz-Josef 319,
    322, 421–2
Fahmüller, Anna 37
Falter, Jürgen W. 23, 42
Faulhaber, Cardinal Michael
    von 23, 25, 56–7, 69,
    73, 76, 79, 133, 145, 152,
    154–6, 201, 203, 216–17,
    224, 229, 244, 247, 254–6,
    262, 292, 300
Fäzinger, Georg 11
FDP (Free Democratic
    Party) 207, 224
Felici, Bishop Pericle 340,
    348–9, 369, 394, 397, 403,
    458
Fellermeier, Jakob 166
Ferdinand, Horst 314
Feuchtwanger, Lion 18, 35

Feuerbach, Ludwig 171
Fichte, Johann Gottlieb
    110, 413
Fingerle, Anton 103
Finkenzeller, Josef 145,
    208, 215, 262, 285–6
First Vatican Council 333,
    336, 339, 344–5, 356, 359,
    374–5, 380, 386, 391
Fischbacher, Sister Berch-
    mana 39
Fischer, Agnes 314, 321
flak auxiliaries 100–4,
    113–14, 124
Fleming, John Ambrose 167
Foulé, Anne-Marie 177
Francis, Pope (Jorge Mario
    Bergoglio) 146
Freising, prince-bishopric
    of 142
Freising Cathedral 139, 156,
    186, 224, 240, 243–5, 285
Freisler, Roland 110, 258
Freiwang, Peter 83–4, 86,
    95, 103
French Revolution 142,
    231, 415
Freud, Sigmund 5, 35
Frick, Wilhelm 60
Friedrich Barbarossa, Em-
    peror 139
Friedrich Wilhelm III,
    King 308
Frings, Cardinal Joseph 141,
    188, 208, 260, 308, 310,
    323, 329, 348, 351, 353,
    358–61, 363–5, 368–70,
    372, 375–80, 383–7, 389,
    393–6, 398, 400–3, 406,
    408–13, 420, 422, 430,
    439-47, 449–53, 455, 457,
    461–3
Fromm, Erich 153
Fulgentius of Ruspe 232
Furtwängler, Hubert 105

Galeazzi-Lisi, Riccardo 295
Galen, Cardinal Clemens
    Graf von 57, 133, 137,
    141–2, 410

Galli, Mario von 452
Garofalo, Salvatore 401
Gasbarrini, Professor
    Antonio 437
Geiselbrecht, Wilhelm 103
Geist und Leben 360
Geneva Convention 100
Genscher, Hans-Dietrich
    124
Georg the Rich, Duke 222
Georgianum semin-
    ary 222–3
Gerade Weg 26–7, 35, 155
Gerlich, Fritz 26, 35–6, 155
German Christians
    (DC) 41–2
German National People's
    Party (DNVP) 34–5
Gestapo 60, 79, 110, 112,
    153
Giesler, Paul 105
Gilroy, Cardinal
    Norman 402
Gladstone, William 374
Glas, Willibald 146
Goebbels, Josef 21–2, 32–3
Goethe, Johann Wolfgang
    von 62, 64, 97, 177, 189
Görres, Ida Frederike
    291–2
Gospel of John 173
Gospel of Mark 209
Gospel of Matthew 277
Gössmann, Wilhelm 218
Graf, Willi 105, 107, 110
Grass, Günter 124
Great Depression 21
Greenblatt, Stephen 343
Gregory V, Pope 384
Gregory of Nyssa 232
Greschat, Martin 133
Grillmeier, Aloys 311, 442
Gross, Elisabeth 257
Grossbölting, Thomas
    133–4
Grösse, Wolfgang 395, 446
Grotti, Bishop
    Giocondo 444
Gruber, Elmar 270–2, 274
Gruber, Gerhard 286

Grundmann, Walter 44
Guardini, Romano 19,
107, 110, 185–6, 191,
226–7, 286
Gundlach, Gustav 137

Haas, Georg 38
Haas, Joseph 249
Hacker, Paul 323, 326–8,
421, 433
Hacker-Klom, Ursula 434
Hadrian VI, Pope 385
Haecker, Theodor 109–10,
166–7
Hahn, Viktor 316, 435
Handel, George
Frideric 360
Harkianakis, Stylianos 421
Hartmann, Nicolai 214
Hartnagel, Fritz 108
Haydn, Joseph 249
Hayes, Zachary 318
Heenan, Archbishop
John 451
Hegel, G. W. F. 171, 279, 413
Heidegger, Martin 5, 105,
149, 163–4, 170, 214, 221,
326, 413
Heinemann, Gustav 218
Heinemann, Uta 218–19
Heisenberg, Werner 167,
169
Heitkötter, Doris 420
Hemingway, Ernest 5
Hengsbach, Bishop 395
Henry III, King 385
Hesse, Hermann 5, 98,
180–7, 189–91, 198, 201,
277
Heuss, Theodor 132, 207,
265
Heydrich, Reinhard 60, 90
Hildegard of Bingen 420
Hindenburg, Paul von 28,
32–3
Hingerl, Franz 14
Hiroshima 137, 383
Hirschmann, Fr 397
Hitler, Adolf
Austrian Anschluss 73–4

and the church 41–6,
56–8, 60, 81–2, 104
his death 119
invasion of Poland 89–92,
96
rise of 6, 18, 22–3, 26–8,
32–3, 35, 40
total assassination
attempts 179
Hitler–Stalin Pact 91, 136
Hitler Youth 28, 40, 50,
59, 73, 82, 85–6, 94–5, 97,
106, 108, 159
Hitler Youth Law 85
Hochland 109, 293, 295,
299, 325
Höck, Michael 'Papa' 144,
147, 153–4, 251, 259, 262,
265
Höck, Wetti 262
Hödl, Ludwig 149, 316–17,
323
Hoeck, Johannes 452
Hoegner, Wilhelm 152
Hölderlin, Friedrich 253
Höller, Karl 283
Holocaust 90, 137, 157,
165, 460
Holy Inquisition see
Congregation for the
Doctrine of the Faith
Holy Office see Congreg-
ation for the Doctrine
of the Faith
Holy Roman Empire 142,
384
Holzhauser, Bartho-
lomäus 19
Hoover, Herbert C. 189
Horn, Peter Stephan 84
Horowitz, Chajjim 421
Horthy, Miklós 116
Hubensteiner, Benno 142
Huber, Brigit 111
Huber, Dora 111–12
Huber, Kurt 105, 107,
110–11
Hübschlerinnen 343
Hufschlag 62–72, 119–20
Hummel, Karl-Joseph 295

Hungarian uprising 307
Husserl, Edmund 149,
162–5, 214
Huxley, Aldous 146, 191

Igl, Father 37, 50
Ignatius Bedros XVI
Batanian 450
Innocent X, Pope 19
Irschl, Canon 251

Jaeger, Lorenz 353
Jägerstätter, Franz 20
Jaspers, Karl 149, 153, 163,
175
Jedin, Hubert 159, 323–5,
351, 363, 365, 380, 391, 395,
397, 401, 422, 446–7, 455
Jerusalem Council (AD
46) 333
Jesuits Law 225
Joachim of Fiore 278–82,
289
Jodl, General Alfred 120
John XXIII, Pope (Angelo
Giuseppe Roncalli) 236,
294, 302, 334–6, 339–42,
344–8, 350, 352–3, 361–4,
369–70, 372–3, 379–80,
389, 395, 398, 402–6,
416, 451
his death 437–8, 441,
459–60, 462
John XXIII, Pisan
Pope 344
John Paul II, Pope (Karol
Józef Wojtyła) 90, 107,
161, 166, 217, 237, 266,
290, 309, 337, 385, 406, 453
Jordan, Pascual 167
Julian of Norwich 232
July Plot 43, 138, 257
Junges Zentrum 45

Kafka, Franz 5, 146
Kahn, Jakob 108
Kamlah, Wilhelm 269
Kant, Immanuel 162, 213,
285
Karlow, Karl 170

Karrer, Otto 353
Kasper, Walter 425
Kästner, Erich 35
Katzer, Ernst 41
Keller, Paul 66, 75
Kennedy, John F. 398–9, 447
Kennedy, Robert 383, 399
Kessler, Dean 422
Khrushchev, Nikita 284, 399
Kierkegaard, Søren 175, 253, 426
Kifinger, Fanny 30
Kifinger, Wally 30
Klauser, Theodor 308
Knappertsbusch, Hans 95
Knaub, Jakob 109
Kneipp, Sebastian 222
Knogler, Josef 252
Kogon, Eugen 152
Köhler, Maria-Gratia 428
Kohut, Pavlo 147–8
Kolb, Annette 146, 178
Kollek, Teddy 159
König, Cardinal Franz 371–2, 394, 396, 400, 402, 416
Konnersreuth, Resi von 48
Konno, Hajime 264
Konrad of Altötting, Brother 7
Kopp, Dr Josef 77
Korean war 224
Kottje, Raymund 318
KPD (Communist Party of Germany) 21–2, 34, 79
Krause, Reinhold 42
Kreisau Circle 138, 257
Krone, Heinrich 138
Kruis, Konrad 253
Kuhn, Peter 71, 84, 315, 320, 326
Kulturkampf 134, 226
Küng, Emma 414
Küng, Hans 291, 353, 357–8, 387, 400, 411, 413–19, 425, 445, 449
Künneth, Walter 137

Langgässer, Elisabeth 146, 178
Läpple, Alfred 145–6, 148–9, 153, 164–5, 169, 174–5, 177, 213, 214, 230, 235, 239, 253, 262, 286, 314, 413
Le défroqué 272
le Fort, Gertrud von 146, 178
League of German Girls (BDM) 40, 85–6, 108
Lefebvre, Archbishop Marcel 352, 443
Léfer, Cardinal 402
Lehnert, Sister Pascalina 294
Leitschuh, Dr Maximilian 78
Lenz, Siegfried 124
Leo IX, Pope 385
Leo XIII, Pope 278, 374
Leonrod, Ludwig Freiherr von 256
liberation theology 158, 290
Liénart, Cardinal Achille 352, 394–6, 400, 402–3
liturgical movement 162, 186, 209, 215, 226–8
Lohmeier, Georg 147
Lorenzer, Alfred 451
L'Osservatore Romano 23, 351, 437
Lourdes 178
Ludwig III, King 11, 155
Luhmann, Miklas 124
Luthe, Hubert 208, 250, 287, 319, 323, 341, 359–61, 376, 380–2, 384, 390–1, 396–7, 443
Luther, Martin 42, 44, 134–5, 213, 318, 327, 339, 343, 353, 385, 389
Lutheran World Federation 336

McLuhan, Marshall 462
Magnificat 161
Mai, Klaus-Rüdiger 80
Maier, Hans 271

Maier, Wilhelm 209
Mair, Johann Evangelist 'Rex' 50, 75–6, 82, 87, 93–4, 130
Manicheism 197
Mann, Erika 131
Mann, Heinrich 35
Mann, Klaus 4
Mann, Thomas 132, 135, 146
Mannheimer, Max 104
Mantler, Otto 79–80
Marcel, Gabriel 170
Maret, Henri Louis Charles 374
Mark, Karl 279
Marktl am Inn 4–9
marriages, mixed 283
Marshall Plan 206
Marxism-Leninism 204
März, Claus-Peter 461
Mauriac, François 146, 177
Maxl, Auer 20
May, Georg 300
Mayer, Anna 251
Mayer, Anton 242
Mayer, Cornelius 194
Mayer, Rupert 159, 325
Mechtild, Sister 427
Meir, Golda 295
Mendoza Castro, Alcides 336
Metz, Johann Baptist 431
Mikoyan, Anastas 132
Milan Edict of Toleration 197
Milvian Bridge, Battle of 196
Minghetti, Marco 412
miracles 48, 280
Mitternmeier, Josef 14
Mockenhaupt, Gerhard 313
Molotov, Vyacheslav 91
Moltke, Count von 257
Montini, Cardinal Giovanni Battista see Paul VI, Pope
Mörike, Eduard 97
Mörsdorf, Klaus 223, 265
Mösenlechner, Lorenz 424

Mozart, Wolfgang
  Amadeus 62, 95–6, 182,
  189, 275, 283, 409, 415
Muench, Aloisius 255
Mühsam, Erich 11
Münch, Werner 205
Müntzer, Thomas 279
Mussner, Franz 149, 209
Mussolini, Benito 6
Muth, Carl 109
'Mystery Theology' 214

Napoleonic wars 66, 97,
  226
Nathan, Luise 108
National Socialist Teachers'
  Federation (NSLB) 77,
  168
NATO 307
Nazi Women's League 51
Nell-Breuning, Oswald 204
Nestorianism 197
Neuhäusler, Bishop
  Johannes 154, 224
Neulandbund (New Coun-
  try League) 28
Neusner, Rabbi Jacob 159
Newman, John
  Henry 108–9, 111, 175,
  191, 231, 259, 409, 438
Niedermayer, Franz 293
Niegel, Franz 70, 149, 271,
  275, 292
Niemöller, Martin 43,
  179, 224
Nietzsche, Friedrich 149,
  170, 285
Nigg, Walter 291–2
Night of the Long
  Knives 27
Normandy Landings,
  anniversary celebra-
  tions 121, 158
Nouvelle Théologie 231,
  234, 236, 238, 352, 386
NSDAP (Nazis)
  and the church 42–6,
  81–2, 134–5
  and papal encyclic-
  als 58–60

rise of 6, 18, 21–3, 28,
  33–4, 39–40, 42–3
terror in Traunstein 78–80
Nuremberg trials 137, 152
Nussbaum, Johann 15–16
Nyssen, Wilhelm 323

Obersalzberg 72, 74, 91
'Old Catholics' 222, 339,
  374
Old Prussian Union 43, 46
Origen 232, 235
Orsenigo, Cesare 58
Orwell, George 191
Oswald, Lee Harvey 447
Ottaviani, Cardinal Alfredo
  337, 346, 348, 352, 355, 364,
  372, 379, 388–9, 397–8,
  401, 403–4, 406, 408, 418,
  430–1, 445–6, 453
Otto, King 203
Otto III, Pope 384

Pacelli, Cardinal Eugenio
  see Pius XII, Pope
papal infallibility 345, 356,
  366
Papal States, break-up
  of 338–9
Papndréou, Damaskino 421
Paris Treaties 307
Parzinger, Dr Peter 78
Pascal, Blaise 426
Pascher, Josef 207, 212,
  227–8
Paul III, Pope 339
Paul VI, Pope (Giovanni
  Battista Montini) 230,
  348, 352–3, 397, 400, 419,
  438–41, 443, 447, 449,
  455, 457–8
Pelagianism 197
Pelagius 200
Peres, Shimon 159
Peterson, Erik 325
Pfnür, Brigitte 272, 429–30
Pfnür, Vinzenz 149, 272–3,
  421, 424, 427
Philips, Gérard 370, 400–1
Pichlmeier, Frau 62

Pieper, Josef 159, 166, 434–5
Piłsudski, Marshal Józef 90
Pius IX, Pope 374, 447
Pius X, Pope 386
Pius XI, Pope 32, 56–7,
  74–5, 335, 339, 345
Pius XII, Pope (Eugenio
  Pacelli) 3, 57–8, 75, 116,
  141, 155, 205, 229, 234,
  238, 293–5, 309, 334–5,
  345, 347–8, 350, 352, 370,
  415, 438–9, 460
Planck, Max 168–9
Plato 165, 213, 318
Poland, Nazi invasion
  of 89–92, 96
Polish–Soviet war 91
Possidius 195
Potsdam Conference 137
pre-Socratic philosophers
  166
Preysing, Cardinal Konrad
  Graf von 57, 141
Priester unter Hitlers
  Terror 49, 57
Probst, Christoph 105,
  107–8, 110
Proust, Marcel 5
Prussia, suppression of sem-
  inaries in 225–6
Pustet, Anton 18

Quickborn youth move-
  ment 19

Raffalt, Reinhard 438
Rahner, Hugo 407, 413
Rahner, Karl 284, 286,
  324, 326, 347, 351, 365,
  371–2, 386–7, 400–1, 407,
  412–14, 419, 434, 442
Rappl, Siegfried 54
Ratzinger, Alois 24, 49–50
Ratzinger, Anton 16, 266
Ratzinger, Georg (brother)
  7, 15, 20, 23–6, 29–32,
  37–9, 47, 49–52, 54, 63–7,
  71, 74–5, 85–6
  and Benedict's career 268,
  275, 289, 291, 302, 316

and celibacy 218
clerical and musical career
254, 262, 283, 302
and father's death 330
First Mass 248–51
and liturgical move-
ment 227
and the Nazi past 152,
157–9
ordination 224, 244, 247
and Second Vatican Coun-
cil 372–4
studies at Freising 144–8,
176, 187, 201
and uncle's death 266
and war 90, 93–5, 99,
123, 129–30
Ratzinger, Dr Georg (great-
uncle) 12, 222, 373–5,
386
Ratzinger, Johann 16
Ratzinger, Commissioner
Joseph 3–12, 14, 16,
23–6, 29–30, 32, 35–6
and Benedict's ordina-
tion 244
and Cardinal Faul-
haber 155
comes to Freising 275
devotion to Mary 47–8
influence on Benedict
45, 51–2, 113, 150–1
retirement 56, 62, 64, 74–5
and rise of Nazis 40, 45,
49, 51
and war 92, 96, 99, 116,
120
Ratzinger, Joseph Aloisus
see Benedict XVI, Pope
Ratzinger, Maria
(mother) 4, 9–10,
12–16, 19, 25, 29–30, 32,
51, 63, 244, 275
her death 447–8
Ratzinger, Maria (sister) 6,
15, 23–6, 29, 31, 49, 51,
54, 65, 74, 94–5, 97, 119,
131, 243, 275, 284
and Bonn years 302–3,
311, 314–17, 329–30

and move to Münster
410, 424
and Second Vatican Coun-
cil 365, 368, 375
Ratzinger, Teresa 49
Ratzinger, Thomas 374
Räzinger, Georg 11
Räzinger, Jakob 11
Reichsarbeitsdienst
(RAD) 114
Reichsdeputation 226
Reichstag Fire 34
religious freedom 455, 457
Remarque, Erich Maria 18,
35
Renouveau Catholique move-
ment 177
Reuter, Ernst 206
Rheinische Post 311, 371
'Rhine Alliance' 380
Ribbentrop, Joachim
von 90–1
Riccardi, Andrea 398, 439
Rieger, Benno 12–13,
24, 54
Rieger, Georg 12, 24
Rieger, Ida 13
Rieger, Isidor 12–13, 15–16
Rieger (Peintner),
Maria 12, 16
Rieger, Maria Anna 15
Rilke, Rainer Maria 177
Ritter, Cardinal 402
Robespierre, Maximi-
lien 226, 415
Rohrhirsch, Adelma 8
Roman Empire, Christian-
ization of 196–7
Roncalli, Giuseppe see
John XXIII, Pope
Roosevelt, Franklin D. 126
Rosenberg, Alfred 41, 81
Rotta, Angelo 116
RSHA (Reichssicherheit-
shauptamt) 90
Rubens, Peter Paul 139
Ruffini, Cardinal Ernesto
351, 386, 402, 408, 453, 456
Ruggieri, Giuseppe 405
Rule of St Augustine 19, 71

Russian Orthodox
Church 336
Russo–Finnish war 97

SA (Sturmabteilung) 22,
26–7, 29, 33–5, 79, 106,
120
Sabatier, Paul 168
Sachsenhausen concentra-
tion camp 89, 154
St Anselm 213
St Anthony 88
St Augustine 108, 111, 165,
191–201, 212–13, 229–32,
236, 243, 245, 247, 265–70,
273–4, 276, 282, 433
St Bonaventure 213, 270,
277–83, 289, 298, 323,
351, 368
St Corbinian 139, 243
St Cyprian 233
St Dismas 71
Saint-Exupéry, Antoine
de 148
St Francis of Assisi 97,
278–9, 282
St Francis Xavier 298
St George 240
St Ignatius 357
St Ignatius of Antioch 329
St John Bosco 131
St John Nepomuk 19
St Judas Thaddeus 71
St Maximus 232
St Michael of Munich 107
St Nicholas of Flüe 206
St Paul 110, 233, 243, 245,
255, 296
St Peter 94, 336, 440
St Teresa of Ávila 108, 165
Salinger, J. D. 320
Salzburg Mozarteum 95
Salzeder, Franziska 38
San Giovanni di Fiore mon-
astery 278
Santa Maria dell'Anima
(Rome) 87
Sapieha, Adam 161
Sartre, Jean-Paul 164, 191,
257

'sceptical generation' 124
Schäfer, Gerhard 421–2
Schäfer, Theo 321
Schäffer, Fritz 152
Scheffczyk, Leo 149
Scheidemann, Philipp 13
Scheler, Max 162, 214
Schelling, Friedrich Wil-
 helm Joseph 171
Schelsky, Helmut 124
Schillebeeckx, Edward
 352, 399–400, 414
Schiller, Friedrich 64, 97–8
Schlachter, Gabriel 239
Schlier, Heinrich 159, 323,
 325–6, 421
Schlögl, Manuel 436
Schmaus, Michael 212,
 219, 223, 228, 238, 265–6,
 282–8, 290, 300, 302,
 308, 317, 405, 419
Schmid, Jakob 107
Schmidtchen, Gerhard 225
Schmorell, Alexander 105,
 107, 110
Schnappinger, Pankratz 94
Schnell, Hugo 256, 269
Schnitzler, Arthur 5
Scholl, Hans and
 Sophie 105–11
Scholl, Inge 108, 111
Scholl Siblings Institute for
 Political Science 159,
 434
Schöning, Franz Josef 300
Schott, Anselm 48
Schröder, Gerhard 337, 385
Schukow, Marshal
 Georgi K. 120
Schulte, Cardinal Karl
 Joseph 57
Schuman, Robert 205
Schütte, Heinz 430–1
Schutz, Roger 232
Schwaiger, Georg 208, 288
science, and religion 167–9
SD (Security Service) 60
Second Vatican Council
 158, 204, 208, 210, 228,
 230, 236, 247, 250, 267,

297, 311, 324, 327, 332–42,
 345–55, 359–91, 393–412,
 416–19, 428, 434, 438
 continuation under new
 papacy 439–47, 449–63
SED (East German Socialist
 Unity Party) 264, 307
Sedgwick, General 141
Seipel, Ignaz 7
Semmelroth, Otto 371–2,
 400, 414, 419, 442, 457
Sepp, Esther 111
Seppelt, Franz Xaver
 209–10
Severus of Antioch 232
Shakespeare, William 202,
 223, 409
Shuster, Zechariah 453
Sigaud, Bishop Geraldo de
 Proença 354–5
Simmel, Oskar 380
Siri, Cardinal Giuseppe
 352, 360, 391, 397–8, 400,
 402, 408–9
Society for Christian–Jew-
 ish Co-Operation 103
Socrates 69, 166, 215
Söhngen, Gottlieb 212–16,
 226, 228–30, 235, 238,
 253, 265–6, 269, 281–5,
 287–8, 309, 359, 413
Soviet Union, Nazi invasion
 of 97–9
'Spade Cult' 114–15
SPD (Social Democratic
 Party) 13, 22, 34–5, 79,
 207, 224, 264, 314–15
Speer, Albert 91
Spellman, Cardinal Francis
 142
Sperr, Franz 256
Speyr, Adrienne von 328
Spieker, Manfred 204
Spindler, Wolfgang 177
'sputnik crisis' 309
SS 33–5, 89–90, 92, 104,
 106, 115–16, 118–20, 136
Stalin, Josef 56, 91–2, 136,
 284, 338
Stalingrad, Battle of 106

Stasi 264
Stauffenberg, Count
 von 257
Stein, Edith 159, 165–6
Stein, Rosa 165
Steinbeisser, Alois 38
Steinbüchel, Theodor 149,
 167, 169–72, 200
Stelzle, Joseph 79–80
Stifter, Adalbert 97
Stöger, Alois 380
Stolker, Lieutenant 102
Storm, Theodor 64, 97
Strangl, Joseph 8
Strasser, Gregor 21
Stravinsky, Igor 409
Strehhuber, Joseph 67,
 83, 104
student movement of
 1968 124, 158
Stummer, Friedrich 210
Stuttgart Declaration 134
Sudetenland crisis 74, 91
Suenens, Cardinal Léon
 Joseph 352, 395–6, 400,
 402, 404
Süsterhenn, Adolf 205

Taizé community 232
Tardif de Moidrey,
 Abbé 177
Tardini, Cardinal Domen-
 ico 335, 340, 345–6, 349
Tattenbach, Franz von 239,
 269
Taylor, Frederick 14
Teilhard de Chardin,
 Pierre 234
Tenhumberg, Hein-
 rich 446
Teusch, Josef 363
Theissing, Hermann 256,
 260, 266, 273
Theodore of Mopsues-
 tia 232
Theodosius, Emperor 197
Theogona, Sister 6, 49
Thirty Years War 19
Thomas, General
 Georg 99

Thurian, Max 232
Thurnher, Eugen 110
Tilliette, Xavier 244
Tisserant, Cardinal 394,
455
Tittmoning 18–20
Toller, Ernst 11
Tradler, Anton 68
Tradler, Martin 118
Traunstein 78–80
Treaty of Versailles 13,
22, 96
Trippen, Norbert 351, 455
Tromp, Sebastiaan 348
Truman, Harry S. 136
Tucholskuy, Kurt 35
Turin shroud 109
Twen 320
Twomey, Vincent 267, 301

Ude, Christian 208
Uhl, Hans 101
Ulbricht, Walter 136, 264
Una Sancta groups 334, 350
unemployment, in
Germany 28, 224, 263

Valente, Gianni 163
Valentin, Karl 208, 266,
316
Valerius, Bishop 199
van der Lubbe, Marius 34
van der Rohe, Mies 5
Vatican Concordat 56–7,
86
VE Day 121
Verweyen, Hansjürgen
185, 250, 280, 287, 310,
419, 431, 456

Verweyen, Ingrid 431–2
Virgin Mary 19, 47–8, 234,
236, 280, 354, 379, 444,
455–6
doctrine of the Assump-
tion 238, 415
Voderholzer, Rudolf
232
Voegelin, Eric 159, 434
Volk, Hermann 371, 400,
416, 419
Volkert, Wilhelm 113
Völkischer Beobachter 26,
77, 82

Waffen-SS 115
Wagner, Adolf 75, 85
Wagner, Winifred 6
Waldburg-Zeil, Prince
Erich von 26
Wall Street Crash 21, 23
Wallinger, Emilie 8
Walser, Martin 124
Walter, Franz 206, 225
Ward, Mary 78
Weber, Fr 71
Wehrle, Hermann
Josef 256, 258–9
Weihenstephan Agricultural
and Brewing
College 263
Weiss, Franz 83
Wendel, Cardinal 300
Wenzl, Aloys 167–9
Werfel, Franz 35, 178
White Rose move-
ment 105–12, 159
Wiechert, Ernst 146, 179
Wiedenhofer, Elke 431

Wiedenhofer,
Siegfried 313, 322,
430–2, 460
Wiesel, Elie 157
Wihr, Ludwig 67
Wild, Dr Christoph 156
Wilder, Thornton 152
Wilhelm II, Kaiser 4–5,
134
Willebrands, J. G. M. 353
William, Franz
Michel 438
Wiltgen, Ralph 380, 398,
402, 404, 459
Winkler, Heinrich
August 136
Wirtschaftswunder (Eco-
nomic Miracle) 263,
424
Wojtyła, Karol Józef *see*
John Paul II, Pope
Wolzogen, Hans von 41
World Council of
Churches 336
Wust, Peter 164
Wüstenberg, Bruno 360
Wyszyński, Cardinal
Stefan 309

Yalta Conference 136

Zech, General 13
Zeiser, Xavier 64
Zieger, Adolf 289
Zinke, Maria 13
Zola, Émile 178
Zuckmayer, Carl 5
Zuse, Konrad 101
Zweig, Stefan 35